THE ANALYSIS OF CHANGE

THE ANALYSIS OF CHANGE

Edited by
JOHN MORDECHAI GOTTMAN
University of Washington

LEA
LAWRENCE ERLBAUM ASSOCIATES, PUBLISHERS
1995 **Mahwah, New Jersey** Hove, UK

Lawrence Erlbaum Associates, Inc., Publishers
10 Industrial Avenue
Mahwah, New Jersey 07430

Library of Congress Cataloging-in-Publication Data

The analysis of change / edited by John Mordechai Gottman.
      p.   cm.
   Includes bibliographical references and indexes.
   ISBN 0-8058-1356-X (cloth : acid-free paper). — ISBN
0-8058-1357-8 (paper : acid-free paper)
   1. Psychometrics.   2. Change (Psychology)   I. Gottman, John
Mordechai.
BF39.A476   1995
150'.15195—dc20   94-38516
                                    CIP

Printed in the United States of America

10 9 8 7 6 5 4 3 2 1

Contents

Preface

John Gottman

Aristotle emphasized the stability and harmony of the universe. In his law of inertia everything had a "natural place," and he suggested that any object would settle in this natural place under normal conditions, if unperturbed. Almost a thousand years later, a series of experiments by Galileo with objects on inclined planes, in which the table was made as smooth and frictionless as possible, led to the overthrow of Aristotle's law of inertia. The smoother the table, the farther an object continued to move, in uniform motion. So, Galileo proposed an alternative law of inertia, that moving objects continue in uniform motion unless a force is applied. Because of friction, this "law" of inertia is never really observed in our laboratories on Earth. However, Galileo's new "ideal" law overthrew the view that it is stability that is the natural order of things and replaced it with the view that in fact change is ordinary and stability extraordinary in Nature.

The imagination of science was forever altered by Galileo, and the study of change became the business of science. In the next generation after Galileo, Sir Isaac Newton in England and Gottfried Wilhelm Leibnitz in Germany created a language and a mathematics of change, the differential calculus. Change was the subject matter of the new calculus.

Change has also been a major concern of the social and behavioral sciences. In the study of human development and in the study of processes that unfold in various ways across time, the study of continuity and change has been a central concern. Various statistical techniques have been proposed for the study of change, and in 1962 a conference was organized by Chester Harris that resulted in an influential volume, *Problems in Measuring Change*. In the 1960s and early 1970s various cautions about studying change became prominent, and they have deeply affected the beliefs of our scientists.

Since that time there has been a veritable explosion of techniques for studying change over time. These new techniques have really fundamentally changed how we need to think of and study change. Unfortunately, many of the old precepts and beliefs are still with us. Most of these beliefs are really myths (as they are termed by Rogosa's chapter in this volume).

What is really new in this volume? To start an outline of the news, consider the chapter by Rogosa. Rogosa's (1988) chapter, called "Myths About Longitudinal Research," addressed a number of these crucial fallacies about the analysis of change. Unfortunately, Rogosa's chapter is not widely known. Rogosa's chapter in this volume is an update of the "Myths" chapter. His original chapter was concerned with methods for the analysis of longitudinal data. He contended that longitudinal research in the behavioral and social sciences has been dominated, for the past 50 years or more, by a collection of related damaging myths and fallacies. He argued that the development and application of useful methods for the analysis of longitudinal data have been impeded by these myths. Using a very simple model of linear change over time, he challenged a number of cherished beliefs about change and showed that they were fallacies. Let us consider some of these cherished beliefs.

Fallacy 1: In Change, Regression Toward the Mean Is an Unavoidable Law of Nature

On the contrary, Rogosa showed that regression toward the mean is not a law of nature, but a mathematical tautology that comes from using the standard deviation as a metric of change. However, if the nonstandardized metric is used, regression toward the mean need not occur. Regression toward the mean implies that pre-scores far from the mean on either side of the mean will move in toward the mean on post-measurement, so that pre-scores "squeeze in" toward the mean upon post-assessment. However, in many applications one obtains instead a "fanning-out" effect, which is the opposite of regression toward the mean.

Fallacy 2: The Difference Score Between Pre- and Post-Measurement is Unreliable

Contrary to Cronbach and Furby's (1970) paper, Rogosa showed that the difference score is not intrinsically unreliable. On the contrary, under a wide range of (surprisingly) moderate test-retest reliabilities, the change score itself is quite reliable. Rogosa's discussion supported Lord's earlier (1967) landmark paper, which had pointed out that the change score is the most natural metric of change and that the residual from an analysis of covariance is often confusing. Lord had written that "some people assert that deviation from the regression line is the real measure of change and that the ordinary difference between initial and final measurements is not a measure of change. This can hardly be correct. If certain individuals gained 300 ounces, this is a definite fact, not a result of an improper definition of growth" (p. 23).

This leads us to the second most common mistaken belief about the proper way to assess change, which is the analysis of covariance (and derivative methods such as path analysis) in which the pre-score is the covariate.

Fallacy 3: Analysis of Covariance (or related methods such as path analysis) Is the Way to Analyze Change

Rogosa showed that residual change curves do not solve problems in the description of change over time, nor are analysis of covariance matrices informative about change. Rogosa reviewed results by Goldstein (1979) from a path analysis examining longitudinal reading test scores on a nationwide British sample at three ages. Goldstein fit a regression equation between time-1 and time-2 scores, estimating a regression coefficient beta(1), and an equation estimating time-3 reading scores from the time-1 and time-2 data, estimating beta(2) (the regression weight of time-2 scores) and beta(3) (the regression weight of the time-1 scores). Goldstein found that beta(1) was 0.841, beta(2) was 1.11, and beta(3) was −0.147. Goldstein was concerned about the negative estimate for beta(3) and confused about how to interpret it. However, Rogosa showed that, if one assumes only simple straight-line change functions, beta(3) is actually a parameter completely independent of the data, and dependent only upon the times of measurement! This astounding and alarming mathematical result shows how analysis of covariance (or its derivative methods) can yield completely incorrect conclusions about change.

Fallacy 4: Two Points (pre and post) Are Adequate for the Study of Change

The next most common fallacy is that two times of measurement are really all one needs for a truly descriptive longitudinal study. It is true that the pre-test–post-test design is the most common design in the study of change, and two repeated observations do indeed constitute a longitudinal study. However, two observations are not adequate for studying the form of change. Two observations can only estimate the amount of change. While a straight line can be passed between two points, there is no way to assess the adequacy of the line, nor to compare the line with other functional forms of change. Rogosa also showed that the amount of change can be deceptive. If the rate of growth is not constant, but depends on time, the amount of change will depend crucially on the times of measurement, and observations of individuals at a different set of two time points may give contradictory results. Hence, it could be misleading to characterize growth by the amount of change. Rankings among individuals can change as a function of the times of measurement, and this will also be true of correlations of other variables with change scores. Thus, in may respects, the pre–post design may be limited for the study of individual change and individual differences in change.

Fallacy 5: The Correlation Between Change and Initial Level Is Always Negative

A negative correlation between true change and true initial level is best known as the Law of Initial Values (Lacey & Lacey, 1962; Wilder, 1957). It is also referred to as the "ceiling effect," because the idea is that change will be small if the initial level is high. The negative correlation is also related to regression toward the mean. Rogosa pointed out that other correlations have also been discussed. He wrote

> A zero correlation between change in initial status is known as the Overlap Hypothesis, which dates back to Anderson (1939) and was prominent in Bloom (1964). One interpretation of the Overlap Hypothesis is that growth occurs via independent increments (similar to the formulation of simplex models in Humphreys, 1960). A positive correlation between change and initial status corresponds to "fanspread" where variances increase over time. The positive correlation can be described as 'them that has, gets'. (p. 182)

It turns out that the correlation between true change and true initial level depends crucially on the choice of the time when the initial level was measured. If we assume a straight-line set of growth curves, the correlation between true change and true initial level will depend on when the initial level was taken. Both in psychophysiology and in studies of academic growth widely different estimates of the correlation between true change and true initial level are obtained (see Cacioppo & Petty, 1983; Cacioppo & Tassinary, 1990; Rogosa, 1988).

The field of methodology for the study of change is itself ready to change. Recently, there have been many analytic and conceptual developments, and a number of recently published volumes reflect some of these (e.g., Collins & Horn, 1991; von Eye, 1990a, 1990b; Rovine & von Eye, 1991). Given that these cherished beliefs about the study of change are actually fallacies, how are we to think about change, and how are we to correctly analyze change?

In addition to Rogosa's seminal contribution, now updated, the remaining chapters in this volume are addressed to this question. The book is divided into two sections. The first section deals with designs that analyze change in multiple subjects, and the second section deals with change in single subjects and an interacting system.

In the first section we have Sackett and Shortt's chapter on the analysis of repeated measures using regression, Patterson's paper on change within the context of stability (a theme we return to in Stoolmiller and Bank's chapter),

Stoolmiller's introduction to latent growth curve models, Anderson's paper on estimating convergence with cohort sequential designs (potentially a useful design in short-term longitudinal designs), Raudenbush's chapter on hierarchical linear models for estimating the effects of social context, and Willett and Singer's paper on discrete-time survival analysis.

While the second section of the book is directed toward single subjects or single interacting systems, the methods are not necessarily limited to single subjects. In this second section three techniques are introduced: sequential analysis, time-series analysis, and dynamic modeling.

The first technique deals with the analysis of "structure" or "temporal form" in observational data, a method that has come to be known as "sequential analysis." Bakeman's chapter on logs and lags is a general introduction to these methods. Griffin's chapter introduces the use of event-history analysis for studying entrances and exists from behavioral states. Gardner deals with the tricky problems of appropriate assessments of reliability for sequential analysis.

The second technique is time-series analysis. This method was largely unknown at the time Harris's (1963) book was published. Many of the methods have been developed since then. Perhaps the most useful of these methods for the study of change is the interrupted time-series experiment. Crosbie's chapter is a summary of how one might deal with the analysis of change in interrupted time-series experiments when there are short series. Priestley's chapter is a summary of time-series model-fitting methods that includes nonlinear as well as linear methods.

The third technique reflects what might be an addage that the major scientific contribution of the mathematics of the 17th to the 19th centuries was in showing what could be learned about the world by assuming that processes were linear, and that the major scientific contribution of the last two centuries was in showing what could be learned about the world by assuming that processes were nonlinear. The study of Nature with nonlinear equations, particularly nonlinear difference or differential equations was pioneered by Poincaré in the 19th century. In recent years there has been widespread popular as well as scientific interest in chaos theory. A bit of discussion is necessary to understand why are these methods included in this volume on the analysis of change. There are several great advantages these methods hold. First, the writing down of the equations represents a theoretical statement about causal connection; to write the equations we must have a theory about what creates change in our problem. Murray's chapter provides many examples of how one might do this. The amazing thing is that some very simple equations can represent some very complex systems by virtue of the nonlinearity. An exciting example of this is the budworm outbreak problem in Murray's chapter, which represents a true application of a catastrophe theory of change, in which a gradual change in a parameter can suddenly produce a major qualitative change (as in the straw that broke the camel's back). The process of writing down the equations can be a way of generating theory from the data (Cook et al., in press). Second, the equations have the potential for going beyond the data. By using simulations with the equations it is possible to imagine how our system would behave under different parameters and different initial conditions. Baker's chapter demonstrates many of the concepts of chaos theory with a very simple and potentially general case, the driven pendulum. The concept of chaos itself stretches our thinking about what order and change are and can be. Chaotic regimes are not predictable, yet they are constrained. Chaos is not random, yet it is not predictable, and yet it results from deterministic and not stoichastic equations (such as are employed in time-series analysis).

The general strategy in selecting papers for this volume was to have them be accessible to the scientist who is not a methodologist. The character of the papers is more like that of primers than basic treatises on methodology, written for other methodologists. The idea was that it is time that people stop thinking in rigid ways about how to study change. It is time that people be introduced to a range of many possibilities. Change, stability, order, and chaos are elusive concepts. The pursuit of the laws of change must be approached in as flexible and creative a fashion as possible. We are now at a point when it is possible to unlock our imaginations from cherished fallacies and myths, when it is possible to approach the analysis of change with new eyes.

REFERENCES

Anderson, J. E. (1939). The limitations of infant and preschool tests in the measurement of intelligence. *Journal of Psychology, 8,* 351–379.

Bloom, B. S. (1964). *Stability and change in human characteristics.* New York: Wiley.

Cacioppo, J. T., & Petty, R. E. (Eds.). (1983). *Social psychophysiology: A sourcebook.* New York: Guilford.

Cacioppo, J. T., & Tassinary, L. G. (Eds.). (1990). *Principles of psychophysiology: Physical, social, and inferential elements.* New York: Cambridge.

Campbell, D. T. (1967). From description to experimentation: Interpreting trends as quasi-experiments. In C. W. Harris (Ed.), *Problems in measuring change* (pp. 212–242). Madison: University of Wisconsin Press.

Coleman, J. S. D. (1968). The mathematical study of change. In H. M. Blalock & A. B. Blalock (Eds.), *Methodology in social research* (pp. 428–478). New York: McGraw-Hill.

Collins, L. M., & Horn, J. L. (1991). *Best methods for the analysis of change: Recent advances, unanswered questions, future directions.* Washington, DC: American Psychological Association.

Cronbach, L. J., & Furby, L. (1970). How should we measure "change"—or should we? *Psychological Bulletin, 74,* 68–80.

Goldstein, H. (1979). *The design and analysis of longitudinal studies.* London: Academic Press.

Harris, C. W. (Ed.). (1967). *Problems in measuring change.* Madison: University of Wisconsin Press.

Holtzman, W. H. (1967). Statistical models for the study of change in the single case. In C. W. Harris, (Ed.), *Problems in measuring change* (pp. 199–211). Madison: University of Wisconsin Press.

Humphreys, L. G. (1960). Investigations of the simplex. *Psychometrika, 25,* 313–323.

Lacey, J. I., & Lacey, B. C. (1962). The law of initial value in the longitudinal study of autonomic constitution: Reproducibility of autonomic responses and response patterns over a four year interval. In W. M. Wolf (Ed.), Rhythmic functions in the living system. *Annals of the New York Academy of Sciences, 98,* 1257–1290.

Lord, F. M. (1967). Elementary models for measuring change. In C. W. Harris, (Ed.), *Problems in measuring change* (pp. 199–211). Madison: University of Wisconsin Press.

Newman, F. L., & Howard, K. I. (1991). Introduction to the special section on seeking new clinical research methods. *Journal of Consulting and Clinical Psychology, 59,* 8–11.

Nielson, F., & Rosenfeld, R. A. (1981). Substantive interpretations of differential equation models. *American Sociological Review, 42,* 73–98.

Rogosa, D. (1988). Myths about longitudinal research. In K. W. Schaie, R. T. Campbell, W. Meredith, & S. C. Rawlings (Eds.), *Methodological issues in aging research* (pp. 171–210). New York: Springer.

Rovine, M. J., & von Eye, A. (1991). *Applied computational statistics in longitudinal research.* Boston: Academic Press.

Salemi, M. K., & Tauchen, G. E. (1982). Estimation of nonlinear learning models. *Journal of the American Statistical Association, 77,* 725–731.

Tuma, N. B., & Hannan, M. T. (1984). *Social dynamics: Models and methods.* New York: Academic Press.

von Eye, A. (Ed.). (1990a). *Statistical methods in longitudinal research: Vol. 1. Principles and structuring change.* Boston: Academic Press.

von Eye, A. (Ed.). (1990b). *Statistical methods in longitudinal research: Vol. 2. Time series and categorical longitudinal data.* Boston: Academic Press.

Wilder, J. (1957). The law of initial value in neurology and psychiatry. *Journal of Nervous and Mental Disease, 125,* 73–86.

ANALYZING CHANGE IN MULTIPLE SUBJECTS

1 Myths and Methods: "Myths About Longitudinal Research" plus Supplemental Questions

David Rogosa
Stanford University

Rogosa's 1988 chapter "Myths about longitudinal research" challenged many classic assumptions about the analysis of change. Unfortunately, Rogosa's work is not widely enough followed even today. Many scientists and reviewers just assume that change scores are unreliable, that the analysis of covariance with time-1 scores as the covariate is an appropriate way for studying change, that regression toward the mean is almost a law of nature, and so on. Rogosa's work shows that many of these assumptions are wrong. He also offers a viable alternative. In this chapter, the original "Myths about longitudinal research" chapter is reprinted, augmented by new material on data analysis and the measurement of change in the form of supplemental questions and answers.

—Editor

PREAMBLE

A little more than 10 years ago I prepared the first version of a colloquium presentation "Myths About Longitudinal Research" (given at University of California, Berkeley, May 1983). The written version of that presentation appeared as Rogosa (1988), and is reprinted as part of this chapter. The purpose of that presentation was to summarize my technical publications on longitudinal research and the measurement of change, the theme of the work being that statistical models for collections of individual trajectories are the proper way to approach research questions about growth and change. The underlying two-part approach is to construct models for the individual time trajectory and then to represent individual differences by differences over individuals in the values of the model parameters (or even the form of the individual time trajectory). And thus the individual history, rather than between-variable relations such as time-1, time-2 scatterplots, provides the basic information for addressing longitudinal research questions.

In the 10 years since I constructed this Myths talk, I have found that the message to focus on the individual unit model carries over to many other settings outside the nonexperimental longitudinal research setting of these Myths. Much of my own work uses individual unit models as the fundamental starting point in various areas of behavioral science research. A critical distinction is between models which start with the individual process versus models for relations among variables, of which path analysis, covariance structure analysis, and other causal modeling strategies are prominent examples. My work on statistical models and methods for behavioral observations (Rogosa, Floden, & Willett, 1984; Rogosa and Ghandour, 1991) is based on this approach, using a renewal process model for the behavioral observations on an individual unit and allowing the parameters of the model to vary over individuals (in contrast to the analysis of variance or generalizability theory models that have mainly been applied in this context). Also, in an examination of methods for aptitude-treatment interaction research in Rogosa (1991), the basic modeling approach is through a combination of models for individual maturation in the outcome variable and models for individual differences in response to an intervention. From this formulation, the performance of standard statistical approaches to ATI research (e.g., time-2, time-1 regression analysis) for assessing the effects of the treatment versus control comparisons is studied. A more important example is the analysis of the estimation of causal effects from an intervention in Holland (1988). In this examination of "encouragement designs," simple representations of the individual processes define causal effects of interest at the level of the individual unit, and effects averaged over individuals yield analytic results to show the failure of path analysis methods to obtain the relevant effects (even though the example fits perfectly the "direct and indirect effects" template for path analysis).

4

To provide a partial update to the Myths, this chapter adds a set of supplemental questions and answers to the original chapter. The topics for this additional material are failures of structural equation models, descriptive and inferential data analysis based on individual growth curve models, limitations of time-1, time-2 data (including residual change scores), regression toward the mean, and methods for constructing longitudinal data examples. These supplemental items follow the same notation as in the Myths chapter, and numbering of figures, tables, and equations continues the sequence of the Myths chapter (e.g., the first figure is Figure 1.8). Original references are left as part of the reprinted chapter; additional references from this preamble and from the supplemental material are listed at the end of this chapter.

The data analysis discussion is perhaps the most important addition. The original Myths presentation can be regarded as providing the first half of the story for longitudinal research, by explaining productive ways to think about longitudinal panel data and also to demonstrate approaches that should be avoided. A full treatment of methods for longitudinal data analysis would complete that exposition (and a small part is given here). The overall message is that the basis for analyzing longitudinal data is the individual history, and an individual unit model, such as an individual growth curve, simply serves to smooth and summarize the individual history data.

MYTHS ABOUT LONGITUDINAL RESEARCH

This chapter is concerned with methods for the analysis of longitudinal data. Longitudinal research in the behavioral and social sciences has been dominated, for the past 50 years or more, by a collection of damaging myths and misunderstandings. The development and application of useful methods for the analysis of longitudinal data have been impeded by these myths. In debunking these myths the chapter seeks to convey "right thinking" about longitudinal research; in particular, productive statistical analyses require the identification of sensible research questions, appropriate statistical models, and unambiguous quantities to be estimated. The heroes of this chapter are statistical models for collections of individual growth (learning) curves. The myths to be discussed are:

1. Two observations a longitudinal study make.
2. The difference score is intrinsically unreliable and unfair.
3. You can determine from the correlation matrix for the longitudinal data whether or not you are measuring the same thing over time.
4. The correlation between change and initial status is
   (a) negative
   (b) zero
   (c) positive
   (d) all of the above
5. You can't avoid regression toward the mean.
6. Residual change cures what ails the difference score.
7. Analyses of covariance matrices inform about change.
8. Stability coefficients estimate
   (a) the consistency over time of an individual
   (b) the consistency over time of an average individual
   (c) the consistency over time of individual differences
   (d) none of the above
   (e) some of the above
9. Casual analyses support causal inferences about reciprocal effects.

The most prevalent type of longitudinal data in the behavioral and social sciences is longitudinal panel data. Longitudinal panel data consist of observations on many individual cases (persons) on relatively few (two or more) occasions (waves) of observation. An observation on a variable X at time t_i for individual p is written as X_{ip} where $i = 1, \ldots, T$, and $p = 1, \ldots, n$. (For statistical methods based on individual growth curves, observations need not be made at the same times for all individuals. But as this is necessary for the standard methods that predominate in the behavioral and social sciences, in my examples all individuals have the same values of t_i, which means everyone is measured at the same times.)

The X_{ip} are presumed to be composed of a true score $\xi_p(t_i)$ and an error of measurement ε_{ip} according to the classical test theory model: $X_{ip} = \xi_p(t_i) + \varepsilon_{ip}$. Many of the examples are in terms of the $\xi_p(t_i)$ and thus assume good measurement. The justification is that perfect measurement serves as a baseline for the examination of analysis methods. A statistical procedure that works poorly even with perfect measurement is clearly not attractive. Estimation of individual growth curves is not jeopardized by the presence of measurement error within reasonable bounds, but measurement errors cause more severe problems for methods based on the covariance matrix of the X_i (e.g., regression-based procedures).

The individual growth curves are functions of true score over time, $\xi_p(t)$. Research questions about growth, development, learning, and the like center on the systematic change in an attribute over time, and thus the individual growth curves are the natural foundation for modeling the longitudinal data. The growth curve models are kept relatively simple because the basic ideas and approaches remain valid for more complex growth models. The simplest and most widely used example will be straight-line growth, which specifies a constant rate of change denoted by θ. A second growth curve example is exponential growth to an asymptote.

The straight-line growth curve for individual p is written

$$\xi_p(t) = \xi_p(0) + \theta_p t. \tag{1.1}$$

A collection of straight-line growth curves is shown in Figure 1.1; the individual growth curves have different values of rate of change θ_p and level $\xi_p(0)$. The

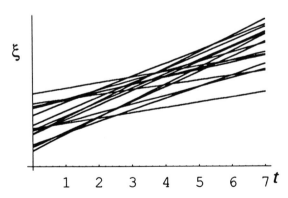

FIG. 1.1.   An illustrative collection of 15 straight-line growth curves in ξ (cf. Equation 1.1).

value of the growth curve at a discrete time t_i yields the $\xi_p(t_i)$, and the X_{ip} are formed by the addition of measurement error. (In particular, for the many examples based on the collection of growth curves in Figure 1.1, the numerical values are obtained for a population of growth curves illustrated by the 15 growth curves in Figure 1.1, not for a sample or population of size 15.)

In some variables, such as attitudinal measures, the volatility over time may be far more important in the data than a systematic trend. The myth about stability over occasions will address this, using measures of consistency over time based on growth curve models.

The discussion of each myth is based on simple numerical examples, using either the $\xi_p(t_i)$ or X_{ip}. Although these examples are constructed to illustrate a particular message, each message is supported by technical results from my papers on statistical methods for the analysis of longitudinal data. This chapter is intended to serve as a less formal, and more accessible, exposition of the key ideas in those publications. In fact, the exposition deliberately avoids the presentation of mathematical results; citations throughout the text and the "reference notes" section at the end of each myth locate the relevant technical presentations. A partial listing of the papers that serve as primary sources for this chapter are:

Rogosa, D. R. (1980). A critique of cross-lagged correlation. *Psychological Bulletin, 88,* 245–258.

Rogosa, D. R. (1985). Analysis of reciprocal effects. In T. Husen & N. Postlethwaite (Eds.), *International Encyclopedia of Education* (pp. 4221–4225). London: Pergamon Press.

Rogosa, D. R. (1987). Casual models do not support scientific conclusions. *Journal of Educational Statistics, 12,* 185–195.

Rogosa, D. R., Brandt, D., & Zimowski, M. (1982). A growth curve approach to the measurement of change. *Psychological Bulletin, 92,* 726–748.

Rogosa, D. R., Floden, R. E., & Willett, J. B. (1984). Assessing the stability of teacher behavior. *Journal of Educational Psychology, 76,* 1000–1027.

Rogosa, D. R., & Willett, J. B. (1983). Demonstrating the reliability of the difference score in the measurement of change. *Journal of Educational Measurement, 20,* 335–343.

Rogosa, D. R., & Willett, J. B. (1985a). Satisfying a simplex structure is simpler than it should be. *Journal of Educational Statistics, 10,* 99–107.

Rogosa, D. R., & Willett, J. B. (1985b). Understanding correlates of change by modeling individual differences in growth. *Psychometrika, 50,* 203–228.

MYTH 1: TWO OBSERVATIONS A LONGITUDINAL STUDY MAKE

Strictly speaking, two repeated observations do constitute a longitudinal study. A more exact statement of the myth would be that two observations are presumed to be adequate for studying change. This misunderstanding is inspired by the dominance of pre-test, post-test longitudinal designs in the methodological and empirical work of the behavioral and social sciences. Two observations do provide some information about change over time, but this design has many critical limitations. In Rogosa et al. (1982, p. 744), I expressed this by the motto: "Two waves of data are better than one, but maybe not much better." Longitudinal designs with only two observations may address some research questions marginally well—but many others rather poorly.

Two Observations Permit Estimation of the Amount of Change but Not of the Individual Growth Curve

Consider two observations on true score ξ for a single individual plotted against time; that is, time is on the horizontal axis and true score is on the vertical axis. With just two observations over time, what can be learned about an individual? Although it is statistically shaky, a growth curve can be fit to two points in time. A straight line passing through the two points is the most complex functional form that can be fit. Even then, the data contain no information on the adequacy of the straight-line functional form for growth or on the amount of scatter in the data. Furthermore, two points in time provide no basis for distinguishing among alternative growth curves; for example, a variety of exponential or logistic growth curves could pass perfectly through the two points. Even if the form of the growth curve were known (e.g., exponential), two observations are not sufficient to provide any estimates of the parameters of the growth curve. Although the investigation of the functional form of growth will often require far more than two points in time, two observations do allow estimation of the amount of change between t_1 and t_2. These remarks are obvious, and this discussion would be of little import if it were not for the preponderance of two-wave panel designs in methodological discussions and empirical studies of change and development.

The formulation of Coleman (1968) founded an alternative tradition for the study of change, mainly among sociologists. In this formulation the parameters of the growth function do not differ over individuals. This tradition assumes that "the process is identical for all persons" (p. 437) and allows the estimation of complex growth curves (e.g., exponential, logistic) where "the data may be two waves of a panel with two observations on many individuals or many observations on the same individual" (p. 432). Additional examples of this tradition are Nielson and Rosenfeld (1981), Salemi and Tauchen (1982), and Tuma and Hannan (1984, chap. 11). In order to estimate complex growth curves from only two observations on each individual, observations from many individuals must be "combined" into a single growth curve. Individual differences in growth preclude the validity of this approach unless some exogenous individual characteristics can be used to completely account for the individual differences. That is, violations of the assumption that the parameters of the growth function are the same for all individuals can be extremely consequential.

The Amount of Change Will Often Be Deceptive

The amount of change over a specified time interval is a natural quantity to estimate from longitudinal data. Define $\Delta_p(t, t + c) = \xi_p(t + c) - \xi_p(t)$ as the amount of true change for individual p over the time interval starting at time t and extending c units. For straight-line growth, $\Delta_p(t, t + c) = \theta_p c$. The amount of change between times t and time $t + c$ depends on t for growth curves having a nonconstant rate of change (i.e., growth curves other than straight-line) and will often be a complex function of t and c. Thus, in a two-wave study, choices of time-1, time-2 measurements are likely to be extremely consequential. In particular, the amount of change may be especially deceptive in comparing growth among individuals because observations over alternative time intervals may yield contradictory information. Below is an example showing that the amount of change is no guide to individual differences in growth.

Consider a collection of six individual growth curves, for individuals labeled A, B, C, D, E, F. Each growth curve has the form of exponential growth toward a ceiling or asymptote governed by the equation

$$\xi_p(t_i) = \lambda_p - (\lambda_p - \xi_p(0))e^{-\gamma_p t_i} \ . \tag{1.2}$$

Table 1.1 gives the parameter values for these six growth curves. The individuals differ on the asymptote λ, on the starting level $\xi(0)$, and on the curvature parameter γ. These growth curves also produce individual differences in the amount of change. Table 1.2 presents the amount of change $\Delta(t_I, t_I + 1)$ for individuals A, B, C, D, E, F for initial observation at time t_I and final observation at $t_I + 1$, with $t_I = 0, 4, 10$. For $t_I = 0$ the individual ranking on Δ is A, B, C, D, E, F (A improves the most in the interval $[0, 1]$, B the next most, C the next, and so on), with the largest Δ nearly double the smallest. If instead $t_I = 10$, the ranking for the amount of change is reversed, with the largest Δ nearly three times the smallest. So two different studies might obtain exactly the opposite results for individual differences in change depending on the choice of initial time of measurement. Furthermore, for $t_I = 4$, the Δ values are nearly equal (smaller individual differences in change) with yet a different ranking of individuals.

TABLE 1.1
Parameter Values for the Six Exponential
Growth Curves

Individual	$\xi(0)$	λ	γ
A	50	80	.25
B	40	70	.22
C	30	60	.19
D	20	50	.16
E	10	40	.13
F	0	30	.10

TABLE 1.2
Amount of True Change $\Delta(t_l, t_l + 1)$
for Exponential Growth Example

Individual	$t_l = 0$	$t_l = 4$	$t_l = 10$
A	6.64	2.44	.54
B	6.32	2.62	.70
C	5.88	2.75	.88
D	5.37	2.81	1.07
E	4.63	2.75	1.26
F	3.81	2.55	1.40

The reversals of individual standing on the amount of change may be most consequential for studies of the correlation of change with an exogenous background variable. Such a correlation might be found to be big, positive for a study using $t_l = 0$; big, negative for $t_l = 10$; and about zero for $t_l = 4$, even if all three studies had perfect measurement.

The example above illustrates the danger of characterizing the growth of individuals by the amount of change over a specific time interval. Even with perfect measurement, the pre-post longitudinal design provides meager information. Two-wave designs permit at best the study of individual differences in Δ or, equivalently, in some sort of average rate of change. Consequently, designs with only two observations are usually inadequate for the study of individual growth and individual differences in growth.

Reference Notes

The limitations of two-wave designs for the measurement of change are examined in Rogosa et al. (1982) and Rogosa and Willett (1985b). Mathematical results corresponding to the example in Table 1.1 are given in Section 1.4 of Rogosa and Willett (1985b). The advantages of multiwave data for the estimation of individual change are enumerated in Rogosa et al. (1982, p. 741–743).

MYTH 2: THE DIFFERENCE SCORE IS INTRINSICALLY UNRELIABLE AND UNFAIR

An impressive amount of psychometric literature over the last 50 years has sought to demonstrate deficiencies in the difference score. With only two observations, the difference score, $D = X_2 - X_1$, is a natural estimate of the amount of true change, $\Delta(t_1, t_2)$, regardless of the form of the growth curve. For a straight-line growth curve model the difference score estimates the (constant) rate of change times the time interval. In general, the difference score divided by the time elapsed estimates an average rate of change over the time interval.

Unreliability of the Difference Score

The traditional tabulation of the reliability of the difference score is shown by Table 1.3, which also appears in Linn and Slinde (1977) and in various forms in many other publications. The pre-test, post-test correlation of observed scores and the reliability of observed scores look reasonable, and for most combinations the difference score has little reliability. This type of numerical demonstration supports the assertions by Lord that "differences between scores tend to be much more unreliable than the scores themselves" (1956, p. 429) and that "the difference between two fallible measures is frequently much more fallible than either" (1963, p. 32).

The untold story is the limited and constrained nature of this table. The table employs the constraints of equal reliabilities $\rho(X_1) = \rho(X_2) = \rho(X)$ and equal variances $\sigma_{X_1}^2 = \sigma_{X_2}^2 = \sigma_X^2$ for the fallible observed scores, X_1 and X_2. Also, these constraints imply equal true-score variances at times 1 and 2 and also a negative value of $\rho_{\xi,\Delta}$, the correlation between true change and true initial status.

The most prominent feature of Table 1.3 is that the time-1, time-2 true-score correlation $\rho_{\xi_1\xi_2}$ is very large in almost all regions; this can be seen from the standard disattenuation formula $\rho_{\xi_1\xi_2} = \rho_{X_1X_2}/\rho(X)$. In particular, $\rho_{\xi_1\xi_2}$ is 1.0 along the diagonal of zero reliability for the difference score. What are the implications for individual growth of the table's restriction to this small portion of the parameter space? A collection of growth curves that exhibit high time-1, time-2 correlation and equal variances at times 1 and 2 will have all the growth curves nearly parallel. Thus all individuals are growing at nearly the same rate which translates into almost no individual differences in true change. (Figure 1 of Rogosa et al., 1982, shows such a collection of straight-line growth curves with time-1, time-2 correlation about .95.) If there are no individual differences in true change, the difference score cannot be expected to detect them. So after building into the traditional tabulations the constraints that there be almost no individual differences in growth, the low reliability of the difference score should be no surprise.

TABLE 1.3
Traditional Tabulation of the Reliability
of the Difference Score

$\rho_{X_1X_2}$	$\rho(X)$		
	.7	.8	.9
.5	.40	.60	.80
.6	.25	.50	.75
.7	.00	.33	.67
.8	—	.00	.50
.9	—	—	.00

TABLE 1.4
Values of $\rho(D)/\bar{\rho}(X)$ when $\rho_{\xi_1\Delta} = 0$
and $\rho(X_2) = .90$

	$\rho(X_1)$		
$\rho_{\xi_1\xi_2}$	.6	.7	.8
.4	1.06	1.03	1.00
.6	.86	.88	.90
.8	.53	.60	.67

If, instead, a moderate correlation, $\rho_{\xi_1\xi_2} = .4$, is used in conjunction with the other constraints in Table 1.3, the difference score appears much stronger. The quantity $\rho(D)/\rho(X)$ has values .83, .88, and .94 for $\rho(X)$ values .7, .8, and .9, respectively. Thus, even with the other constraints the difference score is nearly as reliable as the measure X. A moderate time-1, time-2 correlation corresponds to numerous crossings of the growth curves and considerable individual differences in change. (Rogosa et al. 1982, Figure 2, shows a time-1, time-2 correlation of about .5 for a collection of straight-line growth curves.)

Table 1.4 presents a slightly different tabulation of the reliability of the difference score in terms of the time-1, time-2 true-score correlation and the reliability of X. The reliability of X_2 is set to .9, and the reliability of X_1 is varied. (Setting $\rho(X_2) > \rho(X_1)$ maintains approximately equal error variances at times 1 and 2.) The correlation between true change and initial status is set to zero, which is a useful benchmark case, also known as the Overlap Hypothesis. For these parameter values, the difference score does extremely well; for a moderate true-score correlation the difference score is *more* reliable than the average reliability of the measures. Even for a high correlation, the difference score does rather well compared to reliability of X, and in absolute terms, $\rho(D)$ is also substantial. In sum, when there are individual differences in change, the difference score has decent reliability.

The message that debunks this myth is that the difference score is reliable when individual differences in true change exist. After all, the reliability of the difference score is the variance of true change divided by the sum of the variance of true change and the variance of the difference of the errors. For parameter configurations that require all individuals to grow at about the same rate, the low reliability of the difference score properly reveals that you can't detect individual differences that ain't there.

Unfairness of the Difference Score

The belief that the difference score is somehow not a "fair" measure of change is reflected in the statements that difference scores "give an advantage to persons with certain values of the pretest score" (Linn & Slinde, 1977, p. 125) and "the correlation between change and initial status made it inappropriate to use change [difference] scores to evaluate individuals with different initial scores" (O'Connor, 1972, p. 78). The difference score is an unbiased estimate of true change. How can an unbiased estimate be inequitable? That is a question to which I have no answer. The confusion is bound up with misunderstandings about the correlation between change and initial status and with misguided motivations for the use of residual change measures. These will be untangled in subsequent myths.

Reference Notes

A presentation of the reliability of the difference score in terms of individual differences in growth is given in Rogosa et al. (1982, pp. 731–734). The non-technical exposition of Rogosa and Willett (1983b) provides numerical examples demonstrating the reliability of the difference score when individual differences in growth exist. Statistical properties of D_p for estimating Δ_p are described in Rogosa et al. (1982); in particular, the construction and properties of "improved difference score" (Kelley-type, Lord-McNemar, and empirical Bayes) estimates, which use information from all n individuals in the estimation of Δ_p are examined in detail in Rogosa et al. (1982, pp. 735–738, 742–743, and the Appendix).

MYTH 3: YOU CAN DETERMINE FROM THE CORRELATION MATRIX FOR THE LONGITUDINAL DATA WHETHER OR NOT YOU ARE MEASURING THE SAME THING OVER TIME

A typical statement of the third myth is that with low correlations over time "it is questionable whether one is measuring the same thing on both occasions, and consequently the notion of change becomes questionable" (Bond, 1979). A very serious question in studies of development (whether it be in early child development or later in the aging process) is whether measures "change out from under you" in the sense of measuring something different on different occasions of observation. The important issue is whether asking about quantitative change in the measures over time is meaningful. The assumption that the psychological variable or dimension being studied retains the same meaning over the occasions of observation is a logical prerequisite for the measurement of quantitative change. This view is reflected by Lord (1958), who discussed an instructional setting in which "the test no longer measures the same thing when given after instruction as it did before instruction. If this is asserted, then the pretest and posttest are measuring different dimensions and no amount of statistical manipulation will produce a measure of gain or of growth" (p. 440). Similarly, Bereiter (1963) wrote: "Once it is allowed that the pretest and posttest measure different things it becomes embarrassing to talk about change. There seems no longer any way to answer the question, change on what?" (p. 11). (See also Cronbach & Furby, 1970, p. 76; Linn & Slinde, 1977, p. 24; Lord, 1963, p.21.)

In many situations these concerns may preclude the study of quantitative change. Nonetheless, valid and answerable questions about change should be pursued. Thus, the myth addresses a very important consideration; the misunderstanding is in thinking that this issue can be resolved by the between-wave correlation matrix. The truth is that much more and very different information may be required to resolve this issue.

Consider the picture of a collection of straight-line growth curves in Figure 1.1. Table 1.5 presents the corresponding correlation matrix, with entries of the correlation between ξ_i and $\xi_{i'}$ for t_i, $t_{i'} = 0, 1, \ldots, 8$. Now, between times 5 and 7 the correlation between true scores is very big, .94; even with some measurement error there would be a healthy correlation. Should we "conclude" that the same thing is being measured over this time interval? If, instead, the interval is from time 1 to 5, the correlation is .385. Should this correlation be taken to indicate that different things are being measured at times 1 and 5? Furthermore, for the interval with end points at times 1 and 7 (the concatenation of the two time intervals above) the correlation is .056. Are unrelated quantities being measured at times 1 and 7? According to the myth, the above three questions receive affirmative answers. Furthermore, the correlation between times 0 and 8 is $-.24$; should this correlation be taken to indicate that *opposite* attributes are being measured at times 0 and 8?

The correlations in Table 1.5 correspond to the collection of straight-line growth curves in Figure 1.1. As each individual has a constant rate of change on the attribute ξ, it is hard to imagine a configuration of individual growth that shows less discontinuity. Clearly, a way of thinking that indicates that different things are measured by ξ_i and $\xi_{i'}$ has deep flaws. In the same vein, large correlations cannot "prove" that the same thing is being measured at both ends of

TABLE 1.5
True-Score Correlation Matrix for Straight-Line Growth Example

	0	1	2	3	4	5	6	7	8
0	1.00								
1	.981	1.00							
2	.894	.965	1.00						
3	.707	.832	.949	1.00					
4	.448	.614	.800	.949	1.00				
5	.197	.385	.614	.832	.965	1.00			
6	.001	.197	.447	.707	.894	.981	1.00		
7	$-.140$	.056	.317	.600	.822	.943	.990	1.00	
8	$-.241$	$-.047$	.218	.515	.759	.904	.970	.995	1.00

the observation interval, only that the ordering of individuals in the initial measure is similar to the ordering of individuals in the final measure. Whether or not the same thing is being measured over time simply cannot be answered from the correlation matrix on a couple of occasions of measurement, and it is dangerous to do so. Even plotting the individual growth curves cannot completely resolve this question, although large discontinuities in individual growth would be cause for concern.

A side-note message to this myth is that large individual differences in growth lower the between-wave correlations. Myth 3 serves to discourage the study of change for variables that have sizable individual differences in growth on the grounds that these variables do not retain the same meaning over time. Thus, variables that are chosen for study have high time-1, time-2 correlations, which often result in low σ_Δ^2 (i.e., not much individual differences in change). In reference to Myth 2, if there are little individual differences in change, what will the difference score show? Low reliability.

Reference Notes

The results of Rogosa and Willett (1985b) can be used to obtain the between-wave covariance and correlation functions for different forms of individual growth; the results for straight-line growth were used in constructing the example in Table 1.5. Rogosa et al. (1982, pp. 731–733) discuss the consequences for the reliability of the difference score of limiting studies of change to variables with high between-wave correlations (stability).

MYTH 4: THE CORRELATION BETWEEN CHANGE AND INITIAL STATUS IS
  (a) negative
  (b) zero
  (c) positive
  (d) all of the above

Myth 4 is a multiple choice myth whose distractors have long-standing substantive interpretations. A negative correlation between change and initial status is best known as the Law of Initial Values (Lacey & Lacey, 1962; Wilder, 1957). The negative correlation is also bound up with regression toward the mean, as will be seen in Myth 5. A zero correlation between change and initial status is known as the Overlap Hypothesis, which dates back to Anderson (1939) and was prominent in Bloom (1964). One interpretation of the Overlap Hypothesis is that growth occurs via independent increments (similar to the formulation of simplex models in Humphreys, 1960). A positive correlation between change and initial status corresponds to "fanspread" where variances increase over time. The positive correlation can be described as "them that has, gets."

The correct answer is (d), "all of the above," because the correlation between change and initial status depends crucially on the choice of t_I, the time at which initial status is measured. For straight-line growth, the correlation between change and initial status is monotonically increasing, having a lower asymptote of -1.0 for $t_I = -\infty$, passing through 0 for a single t_I and increasing to an upper asymptote of 1.0 for $t_I = \infty$. For almost any collection of growth curves, a very different correlation between true change and true initial status will be obtained, depending on whether the time of initial status is chosen to be later, earlier, or in between—a likely reason that studies of academic growth obtain disparate estimates of the correlation between true change and true initial status.

One side note to the myth is that with fallible scores, the correlation between observed change and observed initial status is a poor estimate of the correlation between true change and true initial status. The estimate is negatively biased in addition to the attenuation (see, e.g., Rogosa et al., 1982, Eq. 11). Thus, because of the poor properties of this estimate, negative correlations between observed change and observed initial status are often obtained when the true-score correlation is zero or positive. The myth is stated and discussed in terms of true scores because these are of primary substantive interest; although of less interest, a similar dependence on time of initial status also holds for the observed score correlation.

Table 1.6 gives values of the correlation between the amount of true change $\Delta(t_I, t_I + c)$ and true initial status $\xi(t_I)$ for $t_I = 0, \ldots, 7$, using the collection of straight-line growth curves for true scores shown in Figure 1.1. The correlation does not depend on c. For each choice of t_I a different value for the correlation between change and initial status will be obtained. In this example, if initial status is chosen to be time 1, the correlation is big and negative. If initial status is time 3, the correlation is zero. And if initial status is time 5, the correlation is positive. Time 3 is the only time of initial status that would satisfy Anderson's

TABLE 1.6
Correlation Between Change
and Initial Status for Straight-Line
Growth Example in Figure 1.1

t_I	$\rho_{\xi(t_I)\Delta}$	$\rho_{X_I(X_{I+c}-X_I)}$	
		$c = 1$	$c = 3$
0	$-.71$	$-.50$	$-.69$
1	$-.55$	$-.48$	$-.59$
2	$-.32$	$-.44$	$-.47$
3	0.0	$-.36$	$-.29$
4	$.32$	$-.25$	$.00$
5	$.55$	$-.12$	$.17$
6	$.71$	$-.02$	$.30$
7	$.80$	$.02$	$.42$

Overlap Hypothesis. The Law of Initial Values would be satisfied for any $t_I < 3$.

Table 1.6 also gives values of the correlation between observed initial status X_i and observed change $X_{i+c} - X_i$ for $c = 1, 3$. The X_i are based on the $\xi(t_i)$ for this example, with the addition of measurement error (having equal error variance over the t_i), producing reliabilities of the X_i between .74 and .87. The difference between the $c = 1$ and $c = 3$ values is attributable to the larger reliability of the difference score for $c = 3$; except for $t_I = 2$, the $c = 3$ observed score correlation is closer to the true-score correlation. The difference between the observed-score and true-score correlations is somewhat complex. For $t_I > 2$ the observed-score correlation is always less than the true-score correlation, especially for nonnegative values of the true-score correlation ($t_I \geqslant 3$). For large negative values of the true-score correlation, the attenuation and negative bias in the observed-score correlation may offset each other.

Table 1.7 repeats the example for a different type of growth curve: exponential growth to an asymptote λ instead of straight-line growth. This collection of growth curves is illustrated in Figure 1.2. The exponential growth curves have the form of Equation 1.2 with $\gamma_p = \gamma$. This collection of growth curves was constructed to have a between-wave correlation structure similar to that for the straight-line growth example (with a translation of the time scale by 3 units). The correlation between change and initial status is monotone increasing in t_I, and like straight-line growth the correlation strongly depends on the choice of t_I. Unlike straight-line growth the correlation is no longer symmetric about the zero value, which for this example is $t° = 6$.

Reference Notes

Mathematical results for the form of $\rho_{\xi(t)\Delta}$ are obtained in Rogosa and Willett (1985b) for straight-line growth, exponential growth, and the simplex model (Eqs. 9, 16, and 13, respectively). In terms of the notation and parameters of Rogosa and Willett (1985b), for the straight-line growth example the parameter specifications are $t° = 3$, $\kappa = 3$. For the exponential growth example in Figure 1.2 and Table 1.7, the parameter specifications are $t° = 6$; $\gamma_p = \gamma = .23$; $\mu_\lambda = 30$; $\sigma_\lambda^2 = 1.4$, and $\sigma_{\xi(6)}^2 = .437$. Rogosa and Willett (1985b) also obtain the form of the regression of change on initial status. Rogosa et al. (1982, pp. 734–735) examine the bias of the correlation between observed change and observed initial status. Blomqvist (1977, Eq. 3.2) using straight-line growth and a linear repre-

TABLE 1.7
Correlation Between Change and Initial Status
for Exponential Growth Example in Figure 1.2

t_I	3	4	5	6	7	8	9	10
$\rho_{\xi(t_I)\Delta}$	−.84	−.67	−.37	0	.31	.50	.53	.68

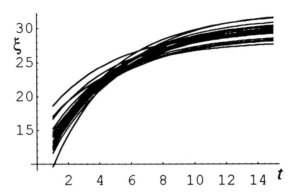

FIG. 1.2.   An illustrative collection of exponential growth curves in ξ following Equation 1.2, with $\gamma_p = \gamma$.

sentation of individual differences in growth as a function of initial status (Eq. 3.1), obtains maximum likelihood estimates of the elements of the covariance matrix of $\xi(0)$ and θ. The results of Rogosa and Willett (1985b, Section 2) for straight-line growth allow the construction of maximum-likelihood estimates of the correlation between change and initial status or the regression of change on initial status for t_I other than $t_I = 0$.

MYTH 5: YOU CAN'T AVOID REGRESSION TOWARD THE MEAN

Typical statements of this myth are Furby (1973, p. 172), "Regression toward the mean is ubiquitous in developmental psychological research" and Lord (1963, p. 24), "The regression effect is one of the two main reasons why studies of growth may become confusing or confused." What is nearly ubiquitous about regression toward the mean is the absence of explicit, defensible definitions of the phenomenon. That is, regression toward the mean is often talked about but rarely explicitly stated. Intuitively, regression toward the mean says that on the average you are going to be closer to the mean at time 2 than you were at time 1. The few formal statements of regression toward the mean in the literature define it in standard deviation units: for example, Furby (1973, p. 174) and Nesselroade, Stigler, and Baltes (1980, p. 623). Thus, in the population, regression toward the mean for true scores at times t_1 and t_2 is said to occur when

$$\frac{E[\xi(t_2) \mid \xi(t_1) = C] - \mu_{\xi(t_2)}}{\sigma_{\xi(t_2)}} < \frac{C - \mu_{\xi(t_1)}}{\sigma_{\xi(t_1)}}. \tag{1.3}$$

Because this inequality is satisfied whenever $\rho_{\xi(t_1)\xi(t_2)} < 1$, regression toward the mean is thought to be unavoidable. The formulation in Equation 1.3 is best thought of as a harmless mathematical tautology and one which provides little insight for the study of change.

A more realistic definition of regression toward the mean uses the actual metric of ξ to express closer to the mean at time 2 than at time 1. The alternative formulation of regression toward the mean is

$$E[\xi(t_2) \mid \xi(t_1) = C] - \mu_{\xi(t_2)} < C - \mu_{\xi(t_1)}. \tag{1.4}$$

Only if $\sigma_{\xi(t_1)}$ and $\sigma_{\xi(t_2)}$ are constrained to be equal, as is done in Lord (1963, p. 21) and in Furby (1973, p. 173), is Equation 1.4 equivalent to Equation 1.3. Most important, Equation 1.4 is satisfied only when $\rho_{\xi(t_1)\Delta} < 0$ (where $\Delta = \Delta(t_1, t_2)$). So, for the formulation in Equation 1.4, regression toward the mean is not ubiquitous; regression toward the mean pertains only when the correlation between change and initial status is negative. Myth 4 discusses conditions for this to hold.

The formulation in 1.4 corresponds to the original notion of Galton (1886) much more closely than does Equation 1.3. Specifically, Galton would indicate no regression toward the mean if the time 2 on time 1 regression coefficient $\beta_{\xi(t_2)\xi(t_1)}$ is greater than or equal to one. This is equivalent to $\rho_{\xi(t_1)\Delta} \geq 0$, for which the inequality in Equation 1.4 is not satisfied. By expressing the severity of the regression effect as the ratio

$$\frac{E[\xi(t_2) \mid \xi(t_1) = C] - \mu_{\xi(t_2)}}{C - \mu_{\xi(t_1)}} = \beta_{\xi(t_2)\xi(t_1)} \tag{1.5}$$

the correspondence of Equation 1.4 to Galton's formulation is seen.

The standard textbook representation of regression toward the mean employs a picture of the time 2 on time 1 plot with an ellipse representing the bivariate data (e.g., Nesselroade et al., 1980, Figure 1). For a choice of a time-1 value C, the time-2 on time-1 regression line gives the expected value at time 2. The peculiar aspect of this standard picture is that it is always drawn to show equal variances at time 1 and time 2, making Equation 1.4 equivalent to Equation 1.3. An alteration of the standard picture in Figure 1.3 allows variance to increase over time. Figure 1.3 shows that the expected value is farther away from the mean at time 2 than at time 1. Thus, regression toward the mean does not hold. Another example is seen in the collection of straight-line growth curves in Rogosa et al. (1982, Figure 3).

Reference Notes

Healy and Goldstein (1978), Rogosa et al. (1982, p. 735), and Rogosa and Willett (1985b, Section 2.5) provide similar discussions of regression toward the mean with reference to collections of individual growth curves. Rogosa and Willett (1985b) define explicitly the conditions for Equation 1.4 to hold. Nesselroade et al. (1980) examine the structure of regression toward the mean for

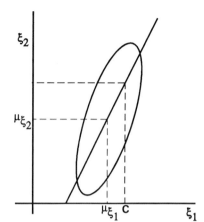

FIG. 1.3. An illustration based on the standard depiction of regression toward the mean, in which regression toward the mean does not hold.

multioccasion data. In the Nesselroade et al. paper, regression toward the mean is analyzed in terms of correlation structures. Consequently, some regression toward the mean will always pertain because of the standardization involved in the correlation matrix. Nesselroade et al. use the term "egression from the mean" to describe a regression toward the mean that is less severe between t_1 and t_3 than between t_1 and t_2 (even though there is regression toward the mean between t_1 and t_3). Perhaps a better use of this term would be egression from the mean as the opposite of regression toward the mean, which would exist over the time interval $[t_1, t_2]$ if and only if the correlation between $\xi(t_1)$ and $\Delta(t_1, t_2)$ is positive.

MYTH 6: RESIDUAL CHANGE CURES WHAT AILS THE DIFFERENCE SCORE

What ails the difference score, according to the psychometric literature, is low reliability and negative correlation with initial status. The discussion of previous myths has shown such deficiencies of the difference score to be more illusory than real. Nonetheless, these concerns have motivated the use of residual change scores. In terms of true scores, residual change is a deviation of true outcome at time 2 from the regression prediction using time 1 information; using $\xi(t_1)$ as the time 1 information yields a true residual change of the form $\xi_p(t_2) - \mu_{\xi(t_2)} - \beta_{\xi_2\xi_1}[\xi_p(t_1) - \mu_{\xi(t_1)}]$. With fallible measures, the usual sample estimate of residual change is the residual from the observed-score time-2 on time-1 regression which is denoted by $\hat{R}$.

A look at the properties of $\hat{R}$ is not pretty. Bias? Yes; $\hat{R}$ may be a badly biased estimate of true residual change. Precision? Not much; the sampling variability is rather large because $\hat{R}$ contains uncertainty both from measurement error and from finite sample size in the regression adjustment. Reliability? At best, not

TABLE 1.8
Reliability of Residual Change
for Straight-Line Growth Example

t_1	$t_2 - t_1$	
	1	3
0	.013	.557
2	.145	.683
4	.213	.487
6	.105	.347

much better than the reliability of the difference score. Various modifications of $\hat{R}$, mainly intended to ameliorate the effects of measurement error on the regression adjustment, do little to mend its severe deficiencies.

The demonstrations in the literature of superior reliability for residual change use time-1, time-2 true-score correlations near one and equal true-score and observed-score variances across time (Linn & Slinde, 1977, Table 2). Then, the reliability of the difference score is near zero, yet the reliability of residual change (even assuming an infinite sample size for making the regression adjustment) is only negligibly better. With $\rho_{\xi_1\xi_2} = 1$, the reliability for residual change is .09 for $\rho(X) = .8$ and .05 for $\rho(X) = .9$. Outside the extreme limitations of that comparison, not even the slight advantage for the residual change score holds up. Table 1.8 presents the reliability of the residual change score for different values of t_1 and $t_2 - t_1$ using the same X_i configuration as described for Table 1.6. The reliability of residual change increases with $t_2 - t_1$ and depends strongly on the choice of t_1. Compare these entries with the reliability of the difference score of .133 for $t_2 - t_1 = 1$ and .58 for $t_2 - t_1 = 3$; this reliability does not depend on t_1 as σ_Δ^2 does not change. Thus, for many t_1 values the difference score is *more* reliable than residual change. The values given in Table 1.8 are obtained from Rogosa et al. (1982, Eq. 20), which is the squared correlation between the true residual change and $\hat{R}$; this formula inflates the actual reliability of $\hat{R}$ as all available formulas for the reliability of residual change assume an infinite sample size for the regression adjustment (i.e., $\beta_{X_2 X_1}$ known).

The logical problems of the residual-change approach dwarf its technical shortcomings. Instead of addressing the relatively simple question—how much did individual p change on the attribute ξ?—residual change attempts to assess how much individual p would have changed on ξ if all individuals had started out "equal." The obvious question is, equal on what—true initial status, observed initial status, true initial status and other background characteristics? The correct answer is unknown, and it depends on the correct specification for the prediction of change. The difficulties with residual change are analogous to those with statistical comparisons of treatment effects in nonequivalent groups. Residual change is one example of attempts to statistically adjust for preexisting differences, which the literature on the analysis of quasi-experiments has shown to be doomed to failure.

A major use of residual change measures is to detect correlates of change. Questions about correlates of change are of the type, "What kind of people are improving or gaining the most"? When the potential correlate is a variable defining membership in an experimental group, the question is whether people getting care or treatment are improving more than people who are not. Questions about correlates of change can be expressed in terms of systematic individual differences in growth. Individual differences in growth exist when parameters of individual growth curves (e.g., the θ_p) differ across individuals, (i.e., some people grow faster than others). Individual differences in growth are systematic if individual differences in a growth parameter can be linked with one or more exogenous characteristics.

A common analysis consists of correlating the observed residual change with an exogenous, individual characteristic denoted by W. Tucker, Damarin, and Messick (1966) formed estimates of the correlation between the exogenous variable and the true residual-change score. Lord (1963) presented a slightly different measure, which is equivalent to a partial correlation instead of the part correlation in Tucker et al.

The failure of these measures to assess systematic individual differences in growth is demonstrated by an example using the collection of straight-line growth curves illustrated in Figure 1.1. The example includes two cases. Case 1 is no systematic individual differences in growth; that is, the correlation $\rho_{W\theta}$ between the exogenous variable and rate of change is zero. Case 2 is large systematic individual differences in growth; that is, $\rho_{W\theta} = .7$. The example assumes perfect measurement of ξ and W. Table 1.9 shows values of the correlation from Tucker et al. (1966), $\rho_{[\xi(t_2)\cdot\xi(t_1)]W}$ for $\rho_{W\theta} = 0, .7$. Table 1.10 repeats the display for the partial correlation from Lord (1963), $\rho_{\xi(t_2)W\cdot\xi(t_1)}$. When there are

TABLE 1.9
Values of $\rho_{[\xi(t_2)\cdot\xi(t_1)]W}$ for Straight-Line
Growth Example in Figure 1.1

t_1	$\rho_{W\theta} = 0$	$\rho_{W\theta} = .7$
0	.64	.92
1	.50	.92
2	.29	.85
3	0.0	.70
4	−.29	.47
5	−.50	.25
6	−.64	.07
7	−.73	−.06
8	−.78	−.15

TABLE 1.10
Values of $\rho_{\xi(t_2)W\cdot\xi(t_1)}$ for Straight-Line
Growth Example in Figure 1.1

t_1	$\rho_{W\theta} = 0$	$\rho_{W\theta} = .7$
0	.84	.92
1	.77	.92
2	.56	.91
3	0.0	.88
4	−.56	.77
5	−.77	.54
6	−.84	.18
7	−.89	−.15
8	−.90	−.37

no systematic individual differences in growth, the correlations may be large positive or large negative depending on the choice of t_1. Even large systematic individual differences in growth may result in near zero or even negative values of these correlations. Thus, neither of these correlations can be counted on to assess correlates of change.

Residual change correlations, whether partial or part correlations, are based on an adjustment for the effects of initial status. And this adjustment naturally depends on the choice of time at which initial status is measured. Thus, the attempt to purge initial status from the measure of change fails. The fatal flaw of the residual change procedures is the attempt to assess correlates of change by ignoring individual growth. Questions about systematic individual differences in growth cannot be answered without reference to individual growth. Yet these time-1, time-2 correlation procedures valiantly attempt to do so.

Reference Notes

Rogosa et al. (1982, pp. 738–741, p. 743, Appendix) enumerate the statistical, psychometric, and logical shortcomings of the residual-change score as a measure of individual change for both two-wave and multiwave longitudinal data. Rogosa and Willett (1985b, Section 3) obtain the mathematical forms for the Tucker et al. (1966) and Lord (1963) correlations and demonstrate the failure of these procedures for the assessment of correlates of change. The values in Tables 1.9 and 1.10 were obtained from Rogosa and Willett (1985b, Eqs. 23 & 24, respectively) for a collection of straight-line growth curves with parameter values $t^\circ = 3$, $\kappa = 3$; for case 1, $\rho_{W\xi(t^\circ)} = .91$, and for Case 2 $\rho_{\theta W} = .7$, $\rho_{W\xi(t^\circ)} = .6$, $t^u = 6.5$, and $t^l = .43$. With multiwave data, an estimate of $\rho_{\theta W}$ can be obtained by correcting the observed correlation between $\hat{\theta}$ and W for attenuation using a maximum-likelihood estimate of the reliability of $\hat{\theta}$ constructed by substituting estimates from Blomqvist (1977) into Equation 22 of Rogosa et al. (1982).

MYTH 7: ANALYSES OF COVARIANCE MATRICES INFORM ABOUT CHANGE

This myth serves as an umbrella for illustrations of the unattractiveness of three related approaches to the analysis of longitudinal data: path analysis, structural regressions, and simplex models. These three procedures all use the between-wave covariance matrix as the starting point for the statistical analysis. The main message of this myth is that the between-wave covariance matrix provides little information about change or growth. The examples illustrate this message.

Path Regressions Inform About Change?

Path analysis models for longitudinal data use the temporal ordering of the measurements to delimit the possible paths between the variables. Consider the example of a three-wave design with measures on X at times t_1, t_2, t_3. The path regressions for the unstandardized variables are

$$X_2 = \alpha_2 + \beta_1 X_1 + e_2,$$

$$X_3 = \alpha_3 + \beta_2 X_2 + \beta_3 X_1 + e_3. \tag{1.6}$$

Thus, the path analysis model includes direct paths from X_1 to X_2 and to X_3 (parameters β_1 and β_3, respectively) and from X_2 to X_3 (parameter β_2). The path coefficients are functions of the entries of the between-wave covariance matrix. An example of the use of this model is Goldstein (1979), in which X is a reading test score obtained on a nationwide British sample with measurements of ages 7, 11, and 16. Goldstein obtains the following estimates: $\hat{\beta}_1 = .841$, $\hat{\beta}_2 = 1.11$, $\hat{\beta}_3 = -.147$. The negative estimate for β_3 causes considerable discomfort, as summarized by Goldstein:

> This is difficult to interpret and may indicate that non-linear or interaction terms should be included in the model, or perhaps that the change in score between seven and 11 years is more important than the seven-year score itself. However, the addition of non-linear terms does not change this picture to any extent. (p. 139)

(Although not central to the present discussion, Goldstein's analysis employs complex transformations of the measures to straighten the X_i, $X_{i'}$ scatterplots and disattenuation of the sample regression coefficients.)

Compare those path analysis results with the following simple facts. Let the true scores $\xi(t_i)$ $(i = 1, 2, 3)$ be determined by a straight-line growth curve for each individual (cf. Figure 1.1). Then the partial regression coefficients are

$$\beta_{\xi(t_3)\xi(t_1)\cdot\xi(t_2)} = \frac{t_2 - t_3}{t_2 - t_1} < 0,$$

$$\beta_{\xi(t_3)\xi(t_2)\cdot\xi(t_1)} = \frac{t_3 - t_1}{t_2 - t_1} > 0. \tag{1.7}$$

Remarkably, the parameters depend only on the times at which the observations were taken, and thus neither regression coefficient contains any information about growth! Estimates of either parameter are totally independent of the information in the data. The implications of Equation 1.7 for the path analysis in Equation 1.6 are devastating. The first parameter in Equation 1.7 corresponds to β_3 in Equation 1.6 and agrees with Goldstein's negative value of $\hat{\beta}_3$, with the magnitude affected by the data transformations and the success of the disattenuation procedures. The second parameter corresponds to β_2 and is consistent with Goldstein's positive value for $\hat{\beta}_2$. Different results for the coefficients in Equation 1.7 will be obtained for different forms of the individual growth curve. The comparison of the path analysis with the mathematical results for straight-line growth attempts to illustrate some of the perils of summarizing the longitudinal data by the analysis of the between-wave covariance matrix of the X_i or even the $\xi(t_i)$, thereby ignoring the analysis of individual growth.

Structural Regression Models Inform about Change?

Structural regression models are a more sophisticated but equally flawed approach to the analysis of longitudinal data. These models incorporate regression relations among latent variables (i.e., $\xi(t_i)$), with measurement models relating the observed indicators (X_i) to the latent variables. Estimation of these models is based on fitting the covariance structure implied by the structural equation model to the between-wave covariance matrix of the observations. Consider the simple structural regression model shown in Figure 1.4 with one latent variable ξ observed at times t_1 and t_2 and a latent background measure, W. Each latent

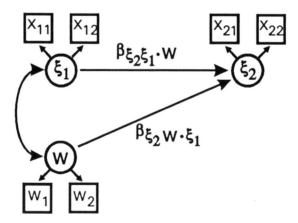

FIG. 1.4.   A depiction of the structural regression model for change in ξ with an exogenous variable W.

TABLE 1.11
Values of Structural Regression Parameter
for Straight-Line Growth Example

t_1	$\beta_{\xi(t_1+5)W \cdot \xi(t_1)}$	
	$\rho_{W\theta} = 0$	$\rho_{W\theta} = .7$
0	.85	.70
1	1.05	.85
2	1.15	1.0
3	0.0	1.2
4	−1.15	1.3
5	−1.05	1.1
6	−.85	.35
7	−.70	−.25
8	−.55	−.5

variable has two indicators. This model is equivalent to the model for change in alienation that appears frequently as an example in Jöreskog's papers (e.g., Jöreskog, 1979, Fig. 6). The path from W to ξ_2 represents the exogenous influence on change. The structural parameter for that path is the regression coefficient for the latent variable at time 2 on the exogenous variable, with the latent variable at time 1 partialed out. In Jöreskog's example, where ξ is alienation and W is socioeconomic status (SES), a negative estimate of this parameter is interpreted as indicating that high SES reduces alienation.

What does the structural parameter $\beta_{\xi(t_2)W \cdot \xi(t_1)}$ reveal about exogenous influences on growth? Not very much. For the simple case of a collection of straight-line growth curves, this structural parameter has a complicated functional form that depends strongly on the time chosen for the initial measurement. The time span that pertains to a particular study is unknown and depends on the particular substantive problem. For a specified relation between the exogenous variable and individual change, the structural parameter may be positive, negative, or zero, depending on the choice of time of initial status. Also, the structural parameter increases with the length of the interval between measurements. Consider two numerical examples based on the collection of growth curves in Figure 1.1: (a) large influences of the exogenous variable ($\rho_{W\theta} = .7$) and (b) no relation between the exogenous variable and rate of change. Table 1.11 shows values of the structural parameter for these two cases, with $t_2 - t_1$ of 5 units. The entries in the $\rho_{\theta W} = 0$ column should be compared with the zero value of the corresponding regression coefficient $\beta_{\Delta(t, t+5)W}$. For $\rho_{\theta W} = .7$, the entries should be compared with the regression coefficient $\beta_{\Delta(t, t+5)W} = 5\beta_{\theta W} = .77$. Thus, for both cases the structural regression coefficient may badly mislead about exogenous influences on growth.

Simplex Models Describe Most Longitudinal Data?

A third example of longitudinal analyses based on the between-wave covariance matrix is the simplex model, which specifies a first-order autoregressive process for true scores. The numerical example in this section seeks to caution against the propensity to base many analyses of longitudinal data on a simplex structure without careful consideration of the longitudinal data or of alternative growth models. Expositions of covariance structure analyses have encouraged such thinking. Moreover, Werts, Linn, and Jöreskog (1977) assert "The simplex model appears to be particularly appropriate for studies of academic growth" (p. 745). Well, maybe, maybe not.

Consider the 5 × 5 correlation matrix for observed scores X_{ip} over five occasions of observation in Table 1.12. To the eye, this correlation matrix corresponds extremely well to a simplex. Correlations decrease away from the diagonals, and on each subdiagonal the correlations are nearly equal. A covariance structure analysis of the corresponding covariance matrix, using LISREL with a quasi-simplex covariance structure, is exceptionally successful. The reproduced covariance and correlation matrices are almost perfect; the root mean square residuals are .003 and .006, respectively. The median discrepancy for the 10 fitted correlations is .003. The chi-square fit statistic, which has five degrees of freedom, is 2.13 (figured for 500 observations) with a p-value of .831. So it seems LISREL is very successful in fitting a simplex model to this example.

Guttman's (1954) condition for a simplex specifies that the partial correlation between earlier and later true scores with an intervening time partialed out is zero. This is the first-order Markov assumption. Straight-line growth turns out to be maximally "unsimplex" in that this partial correlation is −1 instead of 0. (For exponential growth the partial correlation is also −1.) The example in Table 1.12 actually was generated from straight-line growth in the true scores. Thus, the example shows that a simplex covariance structure marvelously fits a covariance matrix from growth curves that are maximally unsimplex. The consequences are far from benign because even when the simplex model fits wonderfully, the results of the covariance structure analysis can badly mislead. The covariance

TABLE 1.12
Observed-Score Correlation Matrix for Simplex Example

	X_1	X_2	X_3	X_4	X_5
X_1	1.000				
X_2	.746	1.000			
X_3	.727	.741	1.000		
X_4	.695	.723	.741	1.000	
X_5	.656	.695	.727	.746	1.000
Standard deviation	.787	.771	.766	.771	.787

structure analyses usually go on to compute growth statistics and reliability estimates based on the simplex model, and these growth statistics (such as the correlation between true change and true initial status), estimated from the LISREL analysis, can differ markedly from the actual values. Covariance structure analyses provide very limited information about growth, in the sense that covariance matrices arising from very different collections of growth curves can be indistinguishable. Therefore, analyses of covariance structures cannot support conclusions about growth. To reiterate my central message, analysis of the collection of growth curves cannot be ignored.

Reference Notes

Rogosa and Willett (1985b, Section 3.2.2) gives mathematical results for the form of the structural regression parameter examined in "Structural Regression Models Inform About Change"? (p. 193). In their notation the example in Table 1.11 used a collection of straight-line growth curves with parameter values $t^{\circ} = 3$, $\kappa = 3$. For Equation 27 of Rogosa and Willett with $\rho_{\theta W} = 0$, $\rho_{W\xi(t^{\circ})} = .91$: $\sigma_W^2 = 1$, $\tau = 5$, and $\sigma^2_{\xi(t^{\circ})} = .438$. For Equation 26, with $\rho_{\theta W} = .7$: $\rho_{W\xi(t^{\circ})} = .6$, $t^{u} = 6.5$, and $t^{1} = .43$. The simplex example is excerpted from the more extensive discussion in Rogosa and Willett (1985a).

MYTH 8: STABILITY COEFFICIENTS ESTIMATE
(a) the consistency over time of an individual
(b) the consistency over time of an average individual
(c) the consistency over time of individual differences
(d) none of the above
(e) some of the above

The absence or obscurity of definitions of stability, along with the proliferation of stability coefficients, results in considerable ambiguity as to what a particular stability coefficient is supposed to be estimating. Thus, it is fitting that this multiple choice myth possess a lack of clarity in the identification of the correct answer. For some stability coefficients (d) is most correct; for others (e) is more correct. Even when (e) is most appropriate, it is not always clear which of (a), (b), (c) would be identified. A coefficient corresponding to choice (a) would be based on an assessment of the heterogeneity (or lack thereof) in an individual's data over time. One procedure corresponding to choice (b) would be inferences about the average growth curve using repeated-measures analysis of variance; that is, is the average growth curve flat? Regarding choice (c), correlation coefficients are often used as measures of consistency of individual differences.

Rogosa et al. (1984) formulated two kinds of questions about stability, with application to the stability of behavior. The first question—is an individual consistent over time?—is rarely investigated. Unfortunately, substantive questions about the heterogeneity of an individual's data over time or about individual differences in heterogeneity rarely are addressed.

The second question—are individual differences consistent over time?—has been the focus of most empirical investigations and the major use for the menagerie of stability coefficients. Among the methods used for assessing stability of individual differences are time-1, time-2 correlations, intraclass correlations and generalizability coefficients, repeated-measures ANOVA, path analysis regression, and structural equation models with exogenous variables. The path analysis and structural regression coefficients are described in Wheaton, Muthen, Alwin, and Summers (1977, Figures 1, 2). The intraclass correlation approach fits a correlation matrix to multiwave data with all off-diagonal elements equal. Whenever individual time trends exist in the data, the intraclass correlation model will yield poor results. An example for science education question-asking is Rosenshine (1973), in which a zero intraclass coefficient is obtained because the between-wave correlation matrix contains both big positive and big negative entries.

The most attractive approach to assessing consistency of individual differences is the indices of tracking from the biometric literature, which assess maintenance of individual differences over time. Figure 1.5 depicts collections of growth curves displaying perfect maintenance of individual differences over time; in Figure 1.5 individual differences are consistent across time whether the criterion is maintenance of rank order or of absolute distance. The index of tracking, γ, presented by Foulkes and Davis (1981) assesses maintenance of rank order over time; this index is the probability of two growth curves not crossing in

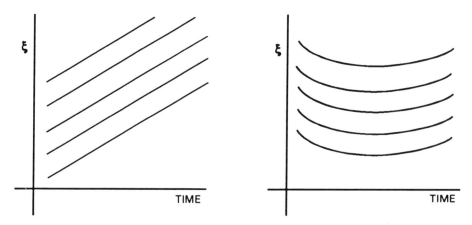

FIG. 1.5.   Two illustrations of perfect consistency of individual differences over time.

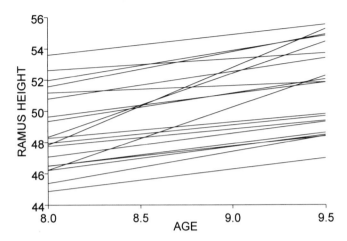

FIG. 1.6.   The fitted straight-line growth curves for the ramus data.

the specified time interval. Intersections of the individual growth curves are thus
evidence against tracking. No tracking is said to exist for $\gamma \leq .5$, the "chance
level" for the probability of no crossings. As the time interval is lengthened, γ
tends to decrease, as it is more difficult to maintain individual differences over a
longer interval.

Data on physical growth are used to illustrate the assessment of stability of
individual differences. Measurements of the height (in millimeters) of the mandibular ramus bone on a sample of 20 boys at four half-year intervals from 8.0 to
9.5 years of age are given in Goldstein (1979, Table 4.1) and have been used as
an illustrative example in many papers on the analysis of growth curves. Each
individual's data are very well described by a straight-line growth curve; the
median squared multiple correlation for the fit of a straight line to the four
observations is .95 for this sample, with upper and lower quartiles of .99 and
.91. Figure 1.6 plots the 20 fitted straight-line growth curves. The estimate of the
Foulkes-Davis γ index of tracking is .826, with an estimated standard error of
.032. Thus, these data show strong, but not perfect, maintenance of individual
differences over the 18-month interval.

Whereas the index of tracking provides a useful quantification of the consistency of individual differences, the stability coefficients widely used in the
behavioral and social sciences mainly provide confusion. Numerical examples
based on the collection of straight-line growth curves in Figure 1.1 are used to
illustrate the properties of some of the stability coefficients. The coefficients for
measurements over a time interval $[t_I, t_F]$ are:

$\hat{\gamma}(t_I, t_F)$ the estimated index of tracking from Foulkes and Davis (1981).

$\rho_{\xi(t_I)\xi(t_F)}$ the product-moment correlation.

TABLE 1.13
Stability Coefficients for Straight-Line Growth over the Interval $[t_I, 7]$

t_I	$\hat\gamma(t_I, 7)$	$\rho_{\xi(t_I)\xi(7)}$	$\beta_{\xi(7)\xi(t_I)}$	$\beta_{\xi(7)\xi(t_I)\cdot w}$	
				$\rho_{w\theta}=0$	$\rho_{w\theta}=.7$
0	.47	−.14	−.17	−.98	−.09
1	.53	.06	.08	−1.1	−.06
2	.58	.32	.50	−.93	−.007
3	.69	.60	1.00	1.0	−.12
4	.78	.82	1.30	2.16	.40
5	.88	.94	1.31	1.71	.83
6	.97	.99	1.17	1.28	1.10

$\beta_{\xi(t_F)\xi(t_I)}$ the regression coefficient for later on earlier consecutive waves of measurement proposed by Heise (1969).

$\beta_{\xi(t_F)\xi(t_I)\cdot w}$ the structural regression coefficient for later on earlier latent variables, with an exogenous variable partialed out, used by Wheaton et al. (1977).

Tables 1.13 and 1.14 are structured to show the effects of different $[t_I, t_F]$ intervals on the coefficients. The values of all coefficients except $\hat\gamma$ are determined by formulas using the population moments of the collection of growth curves; only $\hat\gamma$ is based on the $\xi(t_i)$ values for the 15 growth curves and has an estimated standard error less than .05 for all time intervals in the tables. All coefficients are computed in terms of true scores; only $\hat\gamma$ will be relatively unaffected by errors of measurement.

The coefficients differ among themselves for a given $[t_I, t_F]$ interval and differ, often in strange ways, over different intervals. Using the criterion $\hat\gamma\ -$

TABLE 1.14
Stability Coefficients for Straight-Line Growth over the Interval $[0, t_F]$

t_F	$\hat\gamma(0, t_F)$	$\rho_{\xi(0)\xi(t_F)}$	$\beta_{\xi(t_F)\xi(0)}$	$\beta_{\xi(t_F)\xi(0)\cdot w}$	
				$\rho_{w\theta}=0$	$\rho_{w\theta}=.7$
1	.93	.98	.83	.71	.85
2	.89	.89	.67	.42	.70
3	.86	.71	.50	.13	.55
4	.69	.45	.33	−.16	.40
5	.59	.12	.17	−.45	.25
6	.49	.001	0.0	−.75	.11
7	.47	−.14	−.16	−1.04	−.04

TABLE 1.15
Comparisons of Stability of Coefficients for Intervals
Having the Same Tracking Index

$[t_I, t_F]$	$\hat{\gamma}(t_I, t_F)$	$\rho_{\xi(t_I)\xi(t_F)}$	$\beta_{\xi(t_F)\xi(t_I)}$	$\beta_{\xi(t_F)\xi(t_I)\cdot W}$	
				$\rho_{W\theta} = 0$	$\rho_{W\theta} = .7$
[0, 4]	.69	.60	.33	−.16	.40
[3, 7]	.69	.45	1.0	1.0	.12
[5, 7]	.88	.94	1.3	1.71	.83
[0, 3]	.86	.71	.50	.13	.55

$2[\text{s.e.}(\hat{\gamma})] > .50$, tracking exists for $[t_I, 7]$ in Table 1.13 for $t_I \geqslant 3$, and for $[0, t_F]$ in Table 1.14, tracking exists for $t_F \leqslant 4$. None of the other stability coefficients has an easily interpretable scale. In fact, for the same degree of consistency of individual differences (as assessed by $\hat{\gamma}$) the other coefficients vary wildly. Table 1.15 displays two sets of $[t_I, t_F]$ intervals with matching on the values of $\hat{\gamma}$. For the intervals [0, 4] and [3, 7] individual differences track according to the Foulkes-Davis $\hat{\gamma}$, yet the regression coefficients are small, or negative for [0, 4] and much larger for [3, 7]. The second set of intervals [5, 7] and [0, 3] show stronger tracking and similar discordance in the regression coefficients.

Reference Notes

Wohlwill (1973, chap. 12) provides a lucid discussion and illustration of research questions about stability arising in developmental research. Foulkes and Davis (1981) and McMahan (1981) propose indices of tracking to assess consistency of individual differences. Rogosa and Willett (1983a) provide empirical comparisons of the two indices. Rogosa et al. (1984) formulate research questions about the stability of behavior; they also develop and illustrate statistical procedures for the assessment of stability. The parametric values displayed in the tables are obtained from results in Rogosa and Willett (1985b).

MYTH 9: CASUAL ANALYSES SUPPORT CAUSAL INFERENCES ABOUT RECIPROCAL EFFECTS

The best-known procedure associated with Myth 9 is cross-lagged correlation. A remarkable statement of the myth is provided by Crano and Mellon (1978): "With the introduction of the cross-lagged panel correlation method . . . , causal inferences based on correlational data obtained in longitudinal studies can be made and enjoy the same logical status as those derived in the more standard experimental settings" (p. 41). In other words, the use of cross-lagged correlation dispenses with the need for experiments, statistical models or careful data analysis; a quick comparison of a few correlation coefficients is all that is required to study reciprocal effects. Well, I suppose that would be wonderful if it were true.

The important thing to keep in mind is that questions about reciprocal effects are very, very complex and difficult. A hierarchy of research questions about longitudinal data might start with describing how a single attribute—say, aggression—changes over time. A next step would be questions about individual differences in change of aggression over time, especially correlates of change in aggression. Only after such questions are well understood does it seem reasonable to address a question about feedback or reciprocal effects, such as how change in aggression relates to change in exposure to TV violence or, does TV violence cause aggressive behavior? Despite the complexity of research questions about reciprocal effects, empirical research has attempted to answer the oversimplified question, does X cause Y or does Y cause X? by casually comparing a couple of correlations.

The mathematical and numerical demonstrations of the failures of cross-lagged correlation in Rogosa (1980) had the following simple, limited structure. Start with a basic path-analysis regression model for two variables, X and Y, measured at times 1 and 2 (the popular two-wave, two-variable panel design)

$$X_2 = \beta_0 + \beta_1 X_1 + \gamma_2 Y_1 + u,$$

$$Y_2 = \gamma_0 + \beta_2 X_1 + \gamma_1 Y_1 + v. \qquad (1.8)$$

In the context of the statistical model in Equation 1.8 the parameters β_1 and γ_1 represent the influence of a variable on itself over time. The parameters β_2 and γ_2 represent the lagged, reciprocal causal effects between X and Y; thus, the relative magnitudes of β_2 and γ_2 indicate the nature of the reciprocal causal effects. In Rogosa (1980) combinations of β_2 and γ_2 values are compared with the results of the method of cross-lagged correlation. Three examples from Rogosa (1980) are shown in Figure 1.7. In the first frame, the cross-lagged correlations are equal (.63), which indicates the conclusion of "spuriousness," no direct causal influences between X and Y, even though the model Equation 1.8 stipulated that the effect from X to Y ($\beta_2 = .42$) is twice the effect from Y to X ($\gamma_2 = .21$). In the second frame the model stipulates lagged influences of equal magnitude, yet cross-lagged correlation identifies X as the causal winner. In the third frame the model stipulates an effect from Y to X nearly double the effect from X to Y. Yet the attribution of causal predominance by cross-lagged correlation is the opposite—X would be chosen the causal winner. These examples are simplified by the assumption of equal variances for X and Y; when variances change over time, equations in Rogosa (1980) show that the comparison of the cross-lagged correlations is even more unsatisfactory.

The major (and perhaps only) virtue of the path analysis model Equation 1.8 is the identification of specific parameters believed to represent the reciprocal

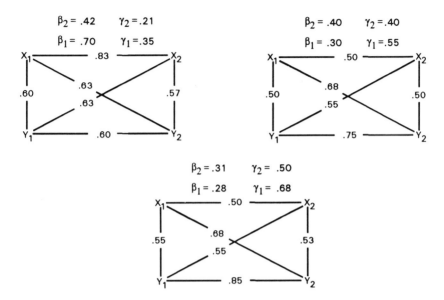

FIG. 1.7.   Numerical illustrations of misleading cross-lagged correlations in two-wave, two-variable panel data.

effects. If this model of the reciprocal influences between X and Y were valid, then estimation of β_2 and γ_2 would inform about reciprocal effects. Perhaps the best way to think about Equation 1.8 and the related structural regression models is that these comprise a simple statistical model for reciprocal effects which, however, may be a far from satisfactory scientific model of the psychological (etc.) process.

The real moral about the analysis of reciprocal effects is that you can't estimate something without first defining it, and statistical models are a good way of defining the key parameters. But this does not imply that all statistical models are sensible. The progress that has been made, especially in the use of structural equation modeling, is to move from no model at all to some statistical model. But having a statistical model does not mean it is an adequate scientific model. Regrettably, the seductive simplicity of cross-lagged correlation has inhibited serious work on the complex question of reciprocal effects.

Reference Notes

Rogosa (1980) was only one in a tradition of papers, starting with Goldberger (1971) and Heise (1970), sharply critical of cross-lagged correlation. Even Cook and Campbell (1979, chap. 7) are unenthusiastic about the usefulness of cross-lagged correlation, yet most advocates and users of this procedure rema. \ undaunted. Rogosa (1980) exposits a number of simple statistical models for reciprocal effects between two variables—structural regression models, continuous-time feedback models, and multiple-time series models. The mathematical results in Rogosa (1980) demonstrate the inability of the method of cross-lagged correlation to recover the structure of the reciprocal effects specified by these models. Results and numerical examples are presented for two-wave and multiwave data. Rogosa (1985) provides a nontechnical overview and extensive references on approaches to the analysis of reciprocal effects.

DISCUSSION

The message of the myths, which is carried through into my work on statistical methods for longitudinal data, is that models for collections of growth curves are the proper basis for the statistical analysis of longitudinal data. The nature of research questions about growth and development makes these models a natural, if not essential, starting point. What I tried to do with these myths was to indicate some of the beliefs that have impeded doing good longitudinal research. The myths have served either to make the analysis of change appear prohibitively difficult or to direct research in unproductive directions. Rather simple approaches work well with longitudinal data, and much progress can be made using straightforward descriptive analysis of individual trajectories followed by statistical estimation procedures for collections of growth curves. Although only a small number of observations often are available in empirical research, the resulting difficulties in statistical estimation arising from these limited longitudinal designs should not alter the research questions or the proper statistical models.

The nine myths discussed in this chapter are not exhaustive. Two additional candidates deserve some mention. The first could be stated as "The average growth curve informs about individual growth." This myth dominated practice in psychological learning experiments, although Estes (1956) demonstrated that the learning curve obtained from averaging individual responses at each trial was equivalent to the average of the individual learning curves only for special forms of the learning curve. This myth has also impeded studies of physical maturation (Bock, 1979). Another setting for this myth is the analysis of longitudinal data with a hierarchical or multilevel structure (Rogosa, 1979, pp. 168–174). A second candidate myth is that "standardizing longitudinal data can be useful." An inexplicable champion of this myth is Goldstein (1983). Standardization renders impossible useful analyses of longitudinal data by removing essential information about individual growth and individual differences in growth. A related, but complex, issue is the effects of different metric/transformations of X on the longitudinal analysis.

The myths speak against what I call the "Avoid Change at Any Cost Academy of Longitudinal Research," which recommends analyses that try to draw complex conclusions about change over time without any examination of individual growth. That doctrine appears counterproductive, as these myths and my technical papers so demonstrate. The doctrine of this Academy is sometimes justified by overinterpretations of the often-quoted last sentence of Cronbach and Furby (1970, p. 79): "Investigators who ask questions regarding gain [difference] scores would ordinarily be better advised to frame their questions another way." This statement could be regarded as a meta-myth. The factual basis for their conclusion is the shortcomings of the estimate of the amount of change from only two observations. But such facts do not support abandoning the framing of research questions about growth and change in a natural way. The suggested surrender to uninformative regression and residual-change analyses is to be much lamented; the proper lesson to draw from difficulties with the difference score is that richer longitudinal designs and the application of appropriate statistical models for the longitudinal data are needed.

An appropriate question to be raised at this point is, where do we go from here? The myths serve more to discredit popular analysis procedures than to prescribe replacements. This function is important in the sense of "first things first"; the groundwork for new approaches requires some appreciation of the flaws of past and current thinking.

Statistical methods respond to (well-formulated) research questions. Naturally, there is no *single* statistical procedure for the analysis of longitudinal data; different research questions dictate different data structures and thus different statistical models and methods. Although at present, the "toolkit" of dependable methods for the analysis of longitudinal data is not complete, I do believe that the natural approach of statistical modeling of individual time trajectories (promoted in this chapter and in my technical papers) serves well as the common basis for the development of statistical methods. To follow on this theme of the linking of research questions and useful statistical methods, I close this chapter with an organization of seven research topics (questions) commonly addressed with longitudinal data. The parenthetical listing of Myths under each topic indicates relevant portions of this chapter, but no attempt is made here to survey the available statistical procedures and literature.

1. *Individual and group growth (Myths 1, 2, 5, 6).* A basic type of question in longitudinal research concerns description of the form and amount of change. Such questions may be posed for an individual case or for the average of a group or subgroup of cases. Interest centers on the estimation of the individual (or group) growth curve, the heterogeneity (individual differences) in the individual growth curves, and the statistical and psychometric properties of these estimates.

2. *Correlates and predictors of change (Myths 6, 7).* Questions about systematic individual differences in growth are a natural sequel to the description of individual growth. A typical research question is given by "What kind of persons learn [grow] fastest?" (Cronbach & Furby, 1970, p. 77). The key quantities are the associations between parameters of the individual growth curves and the correlate(s) of change, which may be exogenous individual characteristics (e.g., gender, IQ) or the initial status on the attribute measured over time.

3. *Stability over time (Myth 8).* Questions about consistency over time are a natural complement to questions about change. In the behavioral sciences literature many different research questions fall under the heading of "stability." Two key topics are the consistency over time of an individual and the consistency of individual differences over time.

4. *Comparing experimental groups.* The comparison of change across experimental groups is a standard, well-developed area of statistical methodology employing some form of repeated measures analysis of variance. When the effects of each treatment can be assumed identical for all members within each group (no individual differences in response to treatment), comparison of the parameters of the group growth curves yields inferences about the "treatment effects."

5. *Comparing nonexperimental groups (Myths 1, 6).* The comparison of change among nonexperimental or nonequivalent groups has been a central topic in the methodology for the evaluation of social programs. The practical or political difficulties of random assignment of individuals to treatment are sometimes overwhelming in a field trial of a program. Yet the question of the relative efficacies of each program/treatment remains. The extensive literature on this topic is dominated by the application of statistical adjustment procedures (analysis of covariance and relatives) to very meager (pre-test, post-test) longitudinal data.

6. *Analysis of reciprocal effects (Myth 9).* As discussed in Myth 9, questions about reciprocal effects are common and complex. Clearly, considerable empirical research on simpler longitudinal questions should precede attempts to assess reciprocal effects. Despite the complexity of these questions, empirical research has attempted to answer the oversimplified question, "Does X cause Y or does Y cause X?" from meager longitudinal data by casually comparing a couple of correlations (or structural regression coefficients).

7. *Growth in multiple measures.* All questions about growth in a single attribute have extensions to multiple attributes. Natural questions include relative strengths and weaknesses in individual and group growth and associations of rates of growth across multiple attributes.

AUTHOR NOTES

This chapter is a revised version of a colloquium of the same title presented at National Institutes of Health, Stanford University, University of California–Berkeley, Center for Advanced Studies in the Behavioral Sciences, and Vanderbilt University.

Preparation of this chapter has been supported by a Seed Grant from the Spencer Foundation.

I would like to thank Ghassan Ghandour, John B. Willett, and Gary Williamson for computational assistance in preparing the examples.

REFERENCES

Anderson, J. E. (1939). The limitations of infant and preschool tests in the measurement of intelligence. *Journal of Psychology, 8,* 351–379.

Bereiter, C. (1963). Some persisting dilemmas in the measurement of change. In C. W. Harris (Ed.), *Problems in the measurement of change* (pp. 3–20). Madison, WI: University of Wisconsin Press.

Blomqvist, N. (1977). On the relation between change and initial value. *Journal of the American Statistical Association, 72,* 746–749.

Bloom, B. S. (1964). *Stability and change in human characteristics.* New York: Wiley.

Bock, R. D. (1979). Univariate and multivariate analysis of variance of time-structured data. In *Longitudinal methodology in the study of behavior and development,* J. R. Nesselroade and P. B. Baltes, Eds. New York: Academic Press, 199–232.

Bond, L. (1979). On the base-free measure of change proposed by Tucker, Damarin, and Messick. *Psychometrika, 44,* 351–355.

Coleman, J. S. (1968). The mathematical study of change. In H. M. Blalock & A. B. Blalock (Eds.), *Methodology in social research* (pp. 428–478). New York: McGraw-Hill.

Cook, T. D., & Campbell, D. T. (1979). *Quasi-experimentation: Design and analysis for field settings.* Boston: Houghton Mifflin.

Crano, W. D., & Mellon, P. M. (1978). Causal influence of teachers' expectations on children's academic performance: A cross-lagged panel analysis. *Journal of Educational Psychology, 70,* 39–49.

Cronbach, L. J., & Furby, L. (1970). How should we measure "change"—or should we? *Psychological Bulletin, 74,* 68–80.

Estes, W. K. (1956). The problem of inference from curves based on group data. *Psychological Bulletin, 53,* 134–140.

Foulkes, M. A., & Davis, C. E. (1981). An index of tracking for longitudinal data. *Biometrics, 37,* 439–446.

Furby, L. (1973). Interpreting regression toward the mean in development research. *Developmental Psychology, 8,* 172–179.

Galton, F. (1886). Regression towards mediocrity in hereditary stature. *Journal of the Anthropological Institute, 15,* 246–263.

Goldberger, A. S. (1971). Econometrics and psychometrics: A survey of communalities. *Psychometrika, 36,* 83–105.

Goldstein, H. (1979). *The design and analysis of longitudinal studies.* London: Academic Press.

Goldstein, H. (1983). Measuring changes in educational attainment over time: Problems and possibilities. *Journal of Educational Measurement, 20,* 369–378.

Guttman, L. A. (1954). A new approach to factor analysis: The radex. In P. F. Lazarsfeld (Ed.), *Mathematical thinking in the social sciences.* New York: Columbia University Press.

Healy, M. J. R., & Goldstein, H. (1978). Regression to the mean. *Annals of Human Biology, 5,* 277–280.

Heise, D. R. (1969). Separating reliability and stability in test-retest correlation. *American Sociological Review, 34,* 93–101.

Heise, D. R. (1970). Causal inference from panel data. In E. F. Borgatta & G. W. Bohrnstedt (Eds.), *Sociological methodology, 1970.* San Francisco: Jossey-Bass.

Humphreys, L. G. (1960). Investigations of the simplex. *Psychometrika, 25,* 313–323.

Jöreskog, K. G. (1979). Analyzing psychological data by structural analysis of covariance matrices. In K. G. Jöreskog & D. Sorböm (Eds.), *Advances in factor analysis and structural equation models.* Cambridge, MA: Abt Books.

Lacey, J. I., & Lacey, B. C. (1962). The law of initial value in the longitudinal study of autonomic constitution: Reproducibility of autonomic responses and response patterns over a four year interval. In W. M. Wolf (Ed.), Rhythmic functions in the living system. *Annals of the New York Academy of Science, 98,* 1257–1290.

Linn, R. L., & Slinde, J. A. (1977). The determination of the significance of change between pre- and post-testing periods. *Review of Educational Research, 47,* 121–150.

Lord, F. M. (1956). The measurement of growth. *Educational and Psychological Measurement, 16,* 421–437.

Lord, F. M. (1958). Further problems in the measurements of growth. *Educational and Psychological Measurement, 18,* 437–454.

Lord, F. M. (1963). Elementary models for measuring change. In C. W. Harris (Ed.), *Problems in measuring change* (pp. 21–38). Madison, WI: University of Wisconsin Press.

McMahan, C. A. (1981). An index of tracking. *Biometrics, 37,* 447–455.

Nesselroade, J. R., Stigler, S. M., & Baltes, P. B. (1980). Regression toward the mean and the study of change. *Psychological Bulletin, 88,* 622–637.

Nielson, F., & Rosenfeld, R. A. (1981). Substantive interpretations of differential equation models. *American Sociological Review, 46,* 159–174.

O'Connor, E. F. (1972). Extending classical test theory to the measurement of change. *Review of Educational Research, 42,* 73–98.

Rogosa, D. R. (1979). Time and time again: Some analysis problems in longitudinal research. In C. E. Bidwell & D. M. Windham (Eds.), *The analysis of educational productivity. Vol. II: Issues in microanalysis* (pp. 153–201). Boston, MA: Ballinger Press.

Rogosa, D. R. (1980). A critique of cross-lagged correlation. *Psychological Bulletin, 88,* 245–258.

Rogosa, D. R. (1985). Analysis of reciprocal effects. In T. Husen & N. Postlethwaite (Eds.), *International encyclopedia of education* (pp. 4221–4225). London: Pergamon Press.

Rogosa, D. R., Brandt, D., & Zimowski, M. (1982). A growth curve approach to the measurement of change. *Psychological Bulletin, 90,* 726–748.

Rogosa, D. R., Floden, R. E., & Willett, J. B. (1984). Assessing the stability of teacher behavior. *Journal of Educational Psychology, 76,* 1000–1027.

Rogosa, D. R., & Willett, J. B. (1983a). Comparing two indices of tracking. *Biometrics, 39,* 795–796.

Rogosa, D. R., & Willett, J. B. (1983b). Demonstrating the reliability of the difference score in the measurement of change. *Journal of Educational Measurement, 20,* 335–343.

Rogosa, D. R., & Willett, J. B. (1985a). Satisfying a simplex structure is simpler than it should be. *Journal of Educational Statistics, 10,* 99–107.

Rogosa, D. R., & Willett, J. B. (1985b). Understanding correlates of change by modeling individual differences in growth. *Psychometrika, 50,* 203–228.

Rosenshine, B. (1973). The smallest meaningful sample of classroom transactions. *Journal of Research in Science Teaching, 10,* 221–226.

Salemi, M. K., & Tauchen, G. E. (1982). Estimation of nonlinear learning models. *Journal of the American Statistical Association, 77,* 725–731.

Tucker, L. R., Damarin, F., & Messick, S. A. (1966). A base-free measure of change. *Psychometrika, 31,* 457–473.

Tuma, N. B., & Hannan, M. T. (1984). *Social dynamics: Models and methods.* New York: Academic Press.

Werts, C. E., Linn, R. L., & Jöreskog, K. G. (1977). A simplex model for analyzing academic growth. *Educational and Psychological Measurement, 37,* 745–756.

Wheaton, B., Muthen, B., Alwin, D., & Summers, G. (1977). Assessing reliability and stability in panel models with multiple indicators. In D. R. Heise (Ed.), *Sociological methodology, 1977* (pp. 84–136). San Francisco: Jossey-Bass.

Wilder, J. (1957). The law of initial value in neurology and psychiatry. *Journal of Nervous and Mental Disease, 125,* 73–86.

Wohlwill, J. F. (1973). *The study of behavioral development.* New York: Academic Press.

SUPPLEMENTAL QUESTIONS AND ANSWERS

1. SHOULD LISREL (STRUCTURAL EQUATION MODELING) ANALYSES ALWAYS BE AVOIDED?

In general, my answer is yes. Analyses of relationships among variables are fundamentally inadequate and askew, because such analyses do not address the individual level processes that generate the data. My analyses and results in making this argument are less ambitious than the heroic efforts of David Freedman (1987, 1991) who takes on these modeling issues in real-life research settings. In his critique of path analysis applications, Freedman (1987) makes an important appeal for more serious (rather than casual) attention to model building: "My opinion is that investigators need to think more about the underlying social processes . . .". and he argues that "as if by experiment" conclusions "must depend on a theory of how the data came to be generated." Continuing this theme, Freedman (1991) promotes the value of "shoe leather" science (close examination of the phenomena) as contrasted with the social science practice of (causal) inferences based on regression models for distant information (e.g., survey data, archival data).

For the longitudinal research setting, my answer is emphatically yes if the goal is to address longitudinal research questions like those listed previously. Longitudinal research examples have been prominent in expositions and illustrations of structural equation methods, and claims for the usefulness of structural equation methods are common—for example, according to Alwin (1988), structural equation methods "are perhaps most useful in longitudinal research designs where the research questions involve the descriptive analysis of change and its explanation" (p. 74). But the facts are that the parameters estimated in the standard structural equation model applications have little or no relevance to parameters of interest (i.e., those defined by useful longitudinal research questions). The main problems with the use of structural equation models is not in the details of those estimation procedures, but in the meaninglessness of the parameters being estimated. To supplement the brief exposition in Myth 7, here I give some detailed data examples of the inadequacies of the standard structural equation models approach, continuing the results and examples in Rogosa (1987, 1993). The expository strategy is to create an example of longitudinal data with simple and known structure and then see what results would be indicated by the standard structural equation modeling analyses.

The data example was chosen to be small and manageable. From a population of individuals, a data set of 40 cases, each observed at three time points, is drawn. For each individual the true observations fall on a straight-line growth curve (as in Figure 1.1). So for each case there is a longitudinal record with the times of observation having values {1, 3, 5}; in addition there is a background exogenous variable for each individual. Shown in Exhibit 1 are the values of the true scores, denoted by $\xi(t_i)$, and the exogenous variable W. The mean rate of change in the population is 5, with individual rates of change ranging between 0 and 9. The rate of change has zero correlation with the background variable, W.

EXHIBIT 1: STRAIGHT-LINE GROWTH DATA,
LISREL EXAMPLE

CASE	$\xi(1)$	$\xi(3)$	$\xi(5)$	W
1	37.56	49.29	61.02	15.97
2	45.65	51.58	57.51	15.38
3	40.94	52.88	64.82	11.48
4	47.36	55.45	63.54	16.89
5	52.71	62.70	72.70	19.18
6	30.45	46.34	62.23	11.82
7	43.65	58.37	73.09	15.33
8	41.16	49.26	57.37	13.21
9	44.15	52.00	59.84	13.09
10	38.16	46.59	55.03	10.32
11	37.68	39.87	42.06	10.26
12	45.30	54.38	63.47	15.60
13	39.37	48.15	56.94	13.90
14	36.66	43.75	50.84	13.53
15	53.40	62.32	71.23	14.45
16	59.35	62.80	66.25	20.16
17	53.14	64.35	75.56	16.11
18	44.90	58.82	72.75	15.06
19	41.79	59.44	77.09	18.33
20	38.25	48.98	59.71	13.77
21	47.24	60.79	74.34	15.88
22	53.57	67.71	81.84	18.25
23	35.54	43.51	51.48	10.15
24	37.54	50.25	62.95	9.46
25	37.07	49.71	62.35	15.81
26	32.40	44.69	56.98	11.60
27	45.22	62.08	78.94	14.08
28	35.67	47.42	59.17	12.19
29	38.30	51.13	63.97	14.07
30	52.61	55.52	58.42	16.68
31	38.36	48.49	58.62	15.07
32	45.14	51.44	57.73	13.94
33	53.82	64.27	74.73	20.40
34	49.46	61.42	73.39	16.00
35	56.29	59.04	61.80	17.47
36	49.59	57.58	65.57	17.30
37	41.45	59.43	77.41	15.86
38	47.42	57.42	67.43	18.95
39	57.00	65.73	74.47	18.90
40	41.06	43.54	46.03	13.79

Data Description.

	MEAN	MEDIAN	STDEV
$\xi(1)$	44.16	43.90	7.24
$\xi(3)$	54.21	53.63	7.24
$\xi(5)$	64.27	63.21	9.24
W	14.99	15.20	2.803

Correlations

	$\xi(1)$	$\xi(3)$	$\xi(5)$
$\xi(3)$	0.842		
$\xi(5)$	0.536	0.907	
W	0.766	0.765	0.598

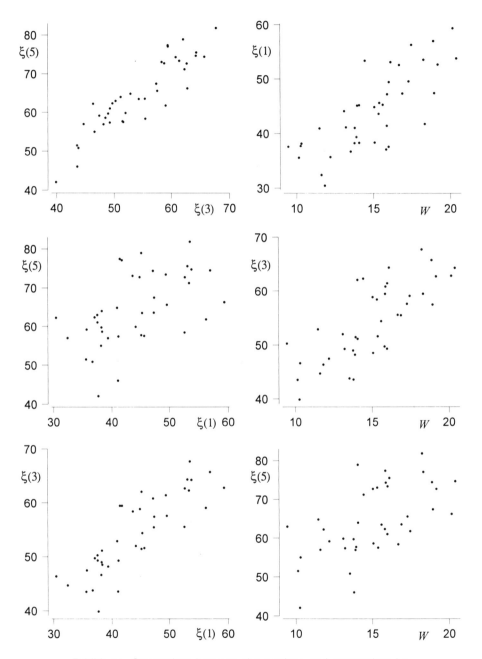

Exhibit 1: Scatterplots between the ξ-values and scatterplots between W and the ξ-values.

The scatterplots displayed in Exhibit 1 show that although the $\xi(t_i)$ are generated from straight-line individual growth curves, the between-variable scatterplots appear rather ordinary. That is, the standard view of between-variable relationships would not cause any concerns for a between-variable regression analysis.

Causal Influences on Change: Three-Waves, Single Variable

In this illustration we revisit the substantive setting of the first section of Myth 7 (relating to the discussion of the Goldstein example). With three observations on each individual, what can be learned about individual change, individual differences in change, and so forth? To supplement the argument in Myth 7 that the three-wave path analysis is uninformative, the data example in Exhibit 1 is used to illustrate the results in Equation 1.7. In terms of true scores, the pictorial form of the structural regression model is shown in Figure 1.8.

The regression for $\xi(t_3)$ matches exactly the theoretical results from Equation 1.7—$\beta_3 = (3 - 5)/(3 - 1)$ and $\beta_2 = (5 - 1)/(3 - 1)$—with squared multiple correlation of 1.0. The "structural coefficients" contain no information from the data, nonetheless about causal effects. So what can be learned about change from such an analysis? Annotated MINITAB output for the regression is

```
The regression equation is
ξ(5) = -0.000003 - 1.00 ξ(1) + 2.00 ξ(3)

Predictor            Coef      Stdev        t-ratio  p
Constant       -0.00000309   0.00000          *    *
ξ(1)              -1.00000      0.00           *    *
ξ(3)               2.00000      0.00           *    *

s = 0            R-sq = 100.0%      R-sq(adj) = 100.0%
```

Rogosa (1993, Equation 6 and Figure 4) gives the theoretical result for the corresponding path analysis regression on fallible observed scores. For this data example observed scores were generated by adding measurement error having variance 10; resulting reliabilities for the scores at times {1, 3, 5} are {.84, .84,

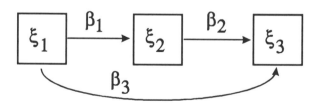

FIG. 1.8.   Representation of three-wave structural regression model.

.90}. The path analysis regression for $X(5)$ for these 40 cases produces the fit: $X(5) = 5.054 - .1212 X(1) + 1.19 X(3)$ with squared multiple correlation .552. Also in Rogosa (1993) are results and illustrations of similar failures for the structural regression model approach when the underlying individual growth curves are not simple straight line, but exponential growth to an asymptote (as in Equation 1.2).

Exogenous Variable and Change: Two Waves

To illustrate the second part of Myth 7, we use the data example from Exhibit 1 to illustrate the misleading consequences of basing an analysis of the standard structural model shown in Figure 1.4—two waves with an exogenous variable. In the population from which the example data are drawn there is *no* association between the background variable W and individual rate of change θ; $\rho_{W\theta} = 0$. Table 1.11 gives numerical theoretical results that the structural (causal) regression coefficients may be large positive or large negative even when $\rho_{W\theta} = 0$. The results of the structural regression using the example data set are shown below. When $\xi(3)$ is used as the initial value the structural coefficient for the influence of W on change is significant with a negative value and when $\xi(1)$ is used as the initial value the structural coefficient for the influence of W on change is significant with a positive value.

1. $\xi(3)$ as the Initial Value

```
The regression equation is
ξ(5) = 0.68 - 0.757 W + 1.38 ξ(3)

Predictor        Coef     Stdev     t-ratio        p
constant        0.683     4.555        0.15    0.882
W              -0.7570    0.3329       -2.27    0.029
ξ(3)            1.3822    0.1290       10.72    0.000

s = 3.752       R-sq = 84.4%      R-sq(adj) = 83.5%
```

2. $\xi(1)$ as the Initial Value

```
The regression equation is
ξ(5) = 31.2 + 1.50 W + 0.239 ξ(1)

Predictor        Coef     Stdev     t-ratio        p
Constant       31.213     7.546        4.14    0.000
W               1.5004    0.6678        2.25    0.031
ξ(1)            0.2392    0.2587        0.92    0.361
```

2. WHAT ARE USEFUL DATA ANALYSIS
APPROACHES?

Data analysis strategies and methods follow directly from the modeling approach that is the basis for the original Myths chapter. The unifying theme is that all questions can be addressed by models and methods that start with the individual unit trajectories. Thus, useful methods for the analysis of longitudinal data take as the starting point a model for the individual history.

The simplest instance of this type of model for a quantitative outcome is a straight-line growth curve for each individual. Fitting such a model to the individual's data points can be thought of as using the model to smooth the data in order to derive an attribute for the individual, such as the rate of improvement or decline in that measure. The power of this approach is the straightforward way in which such analyses can be built up for complex settings (e.g., comparing groups, assessments of stability, and so forth) without losing firm contact with the data. The examples given here illustrate analyses directed toward the first three questions described in the previous listing of research questions: (a) individual and group growth: description and estimation of the form and amount of change; (b) correlates and predictors of change: systematic individual differences in growth such as the question "What kind of persons learn (grow) fastest?"; (c) stability over time: consistency over time of individuals and individual differences. (Note that here we are limited to questions about quantitative outcomes, such as functional abilities or blood pressure.)

In this exposition, sketches of analyses are presented for two examples of actual longitudinal panel data: (1) the Ramus data (briefly treated as part of Myth 8), which consist of four longitudinal observations on each of 20 individuals with no exogenous measure and (2) the North Carolina data, which consist of eight longitudinal observations on each of 277 individuals and with an exogenous ability measure. These analyses methods typically work well for four or more longitudinal observations on each individual (although some missing data can be accommodated). Three longitudinal observations is an absolute minimum for the statistical procedures. In the subsequent question (Question 3: "What can be done with meager time-1, time-2 data?"), the situation of just two longitudinal observations is discussed; artificial time-1, time-2 data is used to illustrate the limited, but useful, descriptive analyses that can be supported when just two observations are available (the traditional measurement of change pre-test, post-test setting). In addition, these methods are contrasted with the (misleading) traditional measurement of change analysis procedures that are based on between-variable relations (see also Myth 6).

Data Structures

The simplest structure of the longitudinal panel data is illustrated by the display of the first four cases from the North Carolina achievement data (Williamson,

46

Applebaum, & Epanchin, 1991), shown below (total 277 females). Each individual has a row of data; the first column contains the verbal ability score, which is used as the exogenous background measure, W. The multiple longitudinal observations follow: eight waves of achievement test scores in math (grades 1–8).

W	T→	1.0	2.0	3.0	4.0	5.0	6.0	7.0	8.0
120		380	377	460	472	495	566	637	628
95		362	382	392	475	475	543	601	576
99		387	405	438	418	484	533	570	589
101		342	368	408	422	470	543	493	589

Model and Parameters of Interest

Form of the Individual Growth Curve

The simplest model, which serves as a basis for these data analysis examples, is the straight-line growth model,

$$\xi_p(t) = \xi_p(0) + \theta_p t,$$

where $\xi_p(t)$ is the true score of person p at time t and θ_p is the constant rate of change for person p. The straight-line growth model is useful for heuristic reasons because of its simplicity, as it yields a simple index for individual rate of progress. In addition, in applications, straight-line growth serves as a useful approximation to actual growth processes (see Hui & Berger 1983, p. 753; Rogosa & Willett 1985b, p. 205). Moreover, when observations at only a few time points are available (e.g., $T = 4$) the data may justify the estimation of nothing more complicated than a constant-rate-of-change model. Although many uses of straight-line growth curves can be justified, nonlinear growth functions may be crucially important in many applications, and methods for straight-line growth curves should be thought of as a first approximation toward the use of more complex growth models.

Individual Change

Thus, estimates of θ_p provide a simple index for individual rate of learning. The parameter θ_p is closely related to the amount of true change; for example, in two-wave (or pre-post) data, true change is equal to $\theta_p(t_2 - t_1)$. Growth curves for different individuals have different values of rate of change θ_p and level $\xi_p(0)$. When describing the learning of a group of individuals, the distribution, over individuals, of empirical rates of learning is informative. The first two moments of the rate of change are μ_θ and σ_θ^2. Similarly, we may want to describe the variability in level of performance at each time, $\xi_p(t)$. As it turns out, the variance of $\xi_p(t)$ has a functional dependence on time, and investigation of the form of this function leads naturally to the definition of a "centering" point and a scaling factor associated with the time scale. These have been denoted t°

and κ, respectively. (See Rogosa and Willett, 1985b.) Both t^o and κ are properties of the particular collection of straight-line growth curves.

Correlation Between Change and Initial Status

Another quantity of central importance is the correlation between change, θ, and initial status, $\xi(t_I)$, where t_I indicates initial time of measurement, and this was discussed in Myth 4. The correlation is used to investigate whether those with lowest initial status make the most progress (negative value) or those with the highest initial status make the most progress (positive value). As discussed in Rogosa and Willett (1985b), the choice of t_I is of critical importance because $\rho_{\xi(t_I)\theta}$ is functionally dependent on time. (The definitions of t^o and κ also arise naturally from an investigation of this dependence; see Rogosa and Willett, 1985b.)

Consistency of Individual Differences

As discussed in Myth 8, the index γ was proposed by Foulkes and Davis (1981) as an index of tracking, and is defined as the probability that two randomly chosen growth curves do not intersect. High values of γ indicate high consistency of individual differences over time. Another way of interpreting γ is to note that high values of γ denote "the maintenance over time of relative ranking within the response distribution" (Foulkes & Davis, 1981, p. 439). Thus γ indicates the stability of individual differences. If a collection of individual growth curves have a high estimated value of γ, that indicates that individuals that started out relatively high maintain that advantage and individuals starting out low retain that disadvantage (regardless of the overall growth rate).

Systematic Individual Differences

To address additional research questions about systematic individual differences in growth (i.e., correlates of change) longitudinal data sets often include measurements on one or more exogenous characteristic which are denoted here by W (e.g., home environment). This terminology derives from the structure of the inquiry that: "Individual differences in growth exist when different individuals have different values of θ_p. Systematic individual differences in growth exist when individual differences in a growth parameter such as θ_p can be linked with one or more W's" (Rogosa and Willett 1985b p. 205). A model for individual differences in growth is needed for investigating systematic individual differences in growth. For the purpose of this exposition, W is regarded as measured without error; in practice, with fallible measurement interest would normally be on relations between θ_p and the true score underlying W. The relation of W to the slope parameter, summarized by the conditional expectation $E(\theta \mid W)$, is stated here as the simplest possible straight-line regression.

$$E(\theta \mid W) = \mu_\theta + \beta_{\theta W}(W - \mu_W).$$

This equation for $E(\theta \mid W)$ is an example of a "between-unit" model. A similar relation can be stated for the intercept in the equation for $\xi_p(t)$. In the case where there is no measured exogenous variable, this between-unit model is $E(\theta) = \mu_\theta$.

A common procedure in the literature is to correlate the value of the background demographic variable or curricular variable with performance at a given time. That is, the cross-sectional correlation is computed, sometimes for every occasion in time. For example, with a background variable, W, correlations of the test score with W at various grades would be computed, and from these correlations conclusions about learning are attempted. Rogosa and Willett (1985b) have shown that such cross-sectional correlations are not useful for this purpose. To illustrate, consider a situation where the correlation between true rate of change and the background variable is zero. Then the correlation between the true test score, $\xi(t)$, and the demographic variable, W, at any one slice in time could be big or small. Consequently, this correlation really doesn't inform about systematic individual differences in learning. The reverse is true also. Consider a demographic variable for which this correlation is large. Regardless, the correlation between the background variable and a test score at a specific time can be positive, zero, or negative depending upon the time chosen for the cross-sectional correlation. Obviously, no useful conclusions about learning can be drawn from the cross-sectional correlations.

Data Analysis and Parameter Estimation

Since 1981, I have used various versions of a program we call TIMEPATH (originally developed with the assistance of John Willett and Gary Williamson, the current version written with Ghassan Ghandour) for the analysis of quantitative longitudinal panel data. In this program, ordinary least-squares regression is used to estimate the growth curve model from the longitudinal data for each individual. As the empirical rate of change can be treated as an attribute of an individual (just like a measurement on X or W), the obtained slopes for each individual regression can be profitably used for various descriptive analyses. Such descriptive analyses may, in many situations, be more important and informative than the formal parameter estimation.

To estimate many of the parameters discussed above, maximum likelihood estimates derived from the results in Blomqvist (1977) are used. In the current program (Rogosa & Ghandour, 1989), standard errors for these parameter estimates and confidence intervals for the parameters are obtained by bootstrap resampling methods in which rows (individual units) are resampled. In Tables 1.17 and 1.18, the reported standard errors are just the standard deviation over 4,000 bootstrap replications, and the endpoints of the reported 90% confidence intervals are just the 5% and 95% values of the empirical distributions from the resampling (i.e., the 200th values from the maximum and minimum values). More sophisticated and more accurate confidence intervals could be constructed using the methods in Efron and Tibshirani (1993), but these simpler intervals were chosen for the purposes of this exposition. In Rogosa and Saner (in press), equivalences obtained from the application of newer computational programs based on hierarchical linear model methodology (especially the HLM program of Bryk & Raudenbush; Bryk & Raudenbush, 1987) for these data are illustrated and some shortcomings discussed. More technical detail on estimation can be found in Rogosa and Saner (in press). When present, missing longitudinal observations are treated (deliberately) in a very simple manner—the individual growth curves are fit to the data that are present, and the overall SSE from the individual fits is just weighted according to the observations present.

Descriptive Analyses of Growth Rates

The most basic step in the analysis is the fitting of a straight-line growth curve (the regression of X on t for each p) by ordinary least squares. The estimates of slope, squared multiple correlation, and other properties of the straight-line fit including diagnostics can be displayed and summarized (see for example the output in Table 1.16). Estimation of the straight-line growth model allows comparisons of rates of change across individuals. Stem-and-leaf diagrams, boxplots, and the five-number summaries of the empirical rates are useful ways to describe both typical rates of learning and the heterogeneity across individuals (see, for example, Figure 1.9). Using the estimated $\hat{\theta}_p$ values for each individual, plots representing relations of change with initial status (see Figure 1.10) and relations with the exogenous measure W (see Figure 1.12) are especially useful for diagnostic examination of the corresponding correlation parameter estimates.

Parameter Estimates

Tables 1.17 and 1.18 present a collection of parameter estimates based on the growth curve model. As a first step, parameters of interest are "typical" rates of change μ_θ or median(θ), and a measure of heterogeneity σ_θ^2, the variance of the θ_p. Point and interval estimates are provided by the bootstrap resampling. The estimate of the reliability $\rho(\hat{\theta})$ is simply the estimate of σ_θ^2 divided by the observed variance of the $\hat{\theta}_p$. Our statistical procedures provide a maximum likelihood estimate of the correlation between true rate of change and true initial status $\rho_{\xi(t_i)\theta}$; the data examples show one negative value and one positive value for this correlation. A good estimate of this correlation is made possible by the availability of multiple (e.g., four or more) longitudinal observations; a pervasive problem in the pre-test, post-test dominated measurement of change literature was that when only two observations were available, the only estimate was the correlation between observed change and observed initial status which may have large, usually negative, bias (see Rogosa et al., 1982). Systematic individual differences in growth are indicated in these analyses by the quantity $\rho_{\theta W}$ or by $\beta_{\theta W}$; for example, nonzero values of $\beta_{\theta W}$ indicate that W is a predictor of growth. Maximum likelihood estimates of these parameters are simply obtained by disattentuating the observed relations by use of the estimate of $\rho(\hat{\theta})$; point estimates along with bootstrap standard error and confidence intervals are given for the North Carolina data in Table 1.18, which shows strong relations of θ with the verbal ability measure.

For the consistency of individual differences, as discussed in Myth 8, the index γ was proposed by Foulkes and Davis (1981) as an index of tracking, and is defined as the probability that two randomly chosen growth curves do not intersect. High values of γ indicate high consistency of individual differences over time. The probability of no intersection is estimated from a count of the number of intersections that each individual trajectory has with the other individuals; for each individual $\hat{\gamma}_p$ is one minus the number of intersections over $n - 1$. Individuals with a low value of $\hat{\gamma}_p$ are those whose relative standing changes considerably over the time period. The proportion of no intersections is accumulated over the n individuals to produce an overall $\hat{\gamma}$ estimate. The standard error can be obtained from a jackknife approximation given by Foulkes and Davis (1981) or by using bootstrap resampling. The value of $\hat{\gamma}$ in both Tables 1.17 and 1.18 indicate reasonably strong tracking.

Ramus Data

The first data example consists of four longitudinal observations on each of 20 cases. The measurement is the height of the mandibular ramus bone (in mm) for boys each measured at 8, 8.5, 9, 9.5 years of age. These data, which have been used by a number of authors, can be found in Table 4.1 of Goldstein (1979a). These data are small enough that it is convenient to present extended output. Fitting a straight line to each individual's observations yields output from the TIMEPATH program that is shown in part in Table 1.16. In Table 1.16, the columns are the ID number for the case, Rate the estimated rate of change (slope of the straight-line growth curve), R_sqr the squared multiple correlation for the straight-line fit, D_Rsq the increase in squared multiple correlation resulting from fitting a quadratic form (useful for detecting cases with large curvature), and the final columns contain the longitudinal observations.

This output provides the raw information and is a very first step in describing individual change. It can be seen that these individual histories correspond closely to the straight-line model by examining the individual R^2 (or the corresponding mean-square residuals) from each fit. For these data the median R^2 is .95, with only two of the 20 values below .91. For the individual rates of change both numerical summaries such as that below and graphical descriptive summaries as in Figure 1.9 are useful:

Rate of Change

	N	MEAN	MEDIAN	STDEV	MIN	MAX	Q1	Q3
$\hat{\theta}$	20	1.866	1.500	1.165	0.460	4.960	1.205	2.010

TABLE 1.16
TIMEPATH Individual Fit Output for Ramus Data

ID	Rate	R_sqr	D_Rsq	T→	8.00	8.50	9.00	9.50
1	1.180	94.2	1.2		47.80	48.80	49.00	49.70
2	1.280	97.9	.6		46.40	47.30	47.70	48.40
3	1.520	98.6	.3		46.30	46.80	47.80	48.50
4	1.420	92.4	7.4		45.10	45.30	46.10	47.20
5	1.100	95.3	3.9		47.60	48.50	48.90	49.30
6	.740	91.5	3.1		52.50	53.20	53.30	53.70
7	2.240	90.5	9.2		51.20	53.00	54.30	54.50
8	1.800	74.2	22.2		49.80	50.00	50.30	52.70
9	4.080	98.8	.4		48.10	50.80	52.30	54.40
10	2.040	90.6	4.3		45.00	47.00	47.30	48.30
11	.460	99.0	.8		51.20	51.40	51.60	51.90
12	4.960	94.5	2.5		48.50	49.20	53.00	55.50
13	1.920	98.0	1.9		52.10	52.80	53.70	55.00
14	1.040	98.8	.6		48.20	48.90	49.30	49.80
15	1.480	99.6	.4		49.60	50.40	51.20	51.80
16	1.760	98.8	1.0		50.70	51.70	52.70	53.30
17	1.520	96.9	3.0		47.20	47.70	48.40	49.50
18	1.300	87.1	12.4		53.30	54.60	55.10	55.30
19	1.440	90.9	8.8		46.20	47.50	48.10	48.40
20	4.040	92.2	.7		46.30	47.60	51.30	51.80

The display of the individual rates of change in Figure 1.9 shows three individuals "improving" considerably faster than the others. The most complete descriptive view is given by a plot of the fitted growth curves which is shown in Figure 1.6. That plot is used to illustrate the high stability of individual differences among these individuals (below estimate of γ is .826). The observed correlation between X_1 and $\hat{\theta}$ is -0.188; the corresponding scatterplot is given in Figure 1.10.

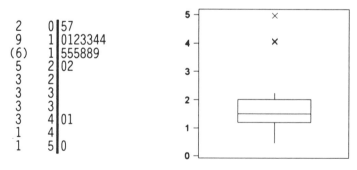

```
  2    0 | 57
  9    1 | 0123344
 (6)   1 | 555889
  5    2 | 02
  3    2 |
  3    3 |
  3    3 |
  3    4 | 01
  1    4 |
  1    5 | 0
```

FIG. 1.9. Graphical description of individual growth rates for ramus data: (a) stem-and-leaf display; (b) boxplot.

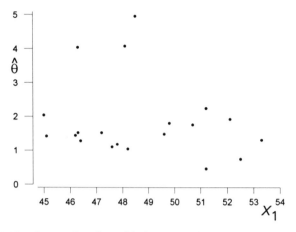

FIG. 1.10.   Scatterplot of empirical rate vs. observed initial status for ramus data.

Estimation and inferences for model parameters obtained from the maximum-likelihood estimation and bootstrap resampling procedures are shown in Table 1.17. Of note is the high estimated reliability of the rate of change; the standard error of measurement for an individual rate is .39. But even with considerable accuracy in assessing individual change, with only a small number of cases the between-person moments (variance components, correlations) have considerable uncertainty as can be seen from the rather wide confidence intervals.

Other quantities that can be estimated from the growth curve modeling include the reliabilities of the observed measures at each of the times of observation. For these ramus data the reliability estimates are: {.970, .969, .971, .975}. Bootstrap standard errors for these estimates are between .01 and .015.

TABLE 1.17
Parameter and Variance Component Estimation
for Ramus Data

Estimate of	Point	s.e.	90% CI
Median(θ)	1.48	.14	(1.30, 1.80)
μ_θ	1.85	.252	(1.474, 2.298)
σ_θ^2	1.203	.500	(.336, 1.971)
$\rho(\hat{\theta})$	.886	.086	(.725, 928)
$\rho_{\theta\xi(8)}$	−.196	.168	(−.439, .098)
γ	.826	.065	(.668, .879)

Path Analysis Controls

The analyses briefly described above do provide some information about change. Contrast those results with a standard path analysis of these 4-wave data using standard multiple regression methods shown in Figure 1.11. Using all plausible "causal paths", values of the path coefficients are shown; only the coefficients for the lag-1 paths are statistically significant. (Refitting using just the significant paths changes little.) The real question is, What in the world does this analysis reveal about change (or any conceivable longitudinal research question)?

North Carolina Data

The second data analysis example is real education data previously analyzed using the maximum-likelihood estimates in TIMEPATH in an excellent expository paper by Williamson et al. (1991). Descriptions of the individual trajectories and rates of change would use the same displays as in the Ramus data. Again, these data conform well to the straight-line growth model; the median value of R^2 for the 277 individual fits is .963. A brief numerical description of the individual rates of change is

Rate of Change

	N	MEAN	MEDIAN	STDEV	MIN	MAX	Q1	Q3
$\hat{\theta}$	277	36.45	36.39	7.472	9.71	64.24	31.46	41.02

One reason to examine this data example is the existence of the exogenous variable, the verbal ability measure, which allows questions about correlates of change to be addressed. The initial descriptive information would be the correlation between $\hat{\theta}$ and W, which is .624, and the corresponding scatterplot is shown in Figure 1.12.

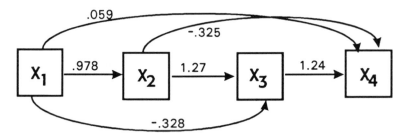

FIG. 1.11.   Four-wave path analysis results for ramus data.

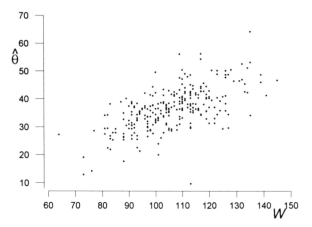

FIG. 1.12.   Scatterplot of observed rate of change vs. background ability measure for North Carolina data.

The parameter estimation summarized in Table 1.18 reveals that these data permit rather accurate assessment of rates of change; the reliability estimate is high, and the standard error of measurement of $\hat{\theta}$ is 3.1. Of considerable note in these data is the large positive value of .651 for the estimate of the correlation between true rate of change and true initial status. Also of note is that the estimates show a strong relation with W, the verbal ability measure. (Entries in Table 1.18 correspond to point estimates reported in Table 3 of Williamson et al., 1991). Note that with the larger sample of 277 cases, greater accuracy (smaller standard errors, narrower confidence intervals) for the estimation of the between-person moments is obtained.

TABLE 1.18
Parameter and Variance Component Estimation
for North Carolina Data

Estimate of	Point	s.e.	90% CI
μ_θ	36.45	.448	(35.72, 37.19)
Median(θ)	36.39	.327	(35.86, 36.95)
σ_θ^2	46.23	5.95	(36.67, 56.12)
$\rho(\hat{\theta})$	.828	.019	(.792, .854)
$\rho_{\theta\xi(1)}$	.651	.090	(.513, .809)
γ	.721	.0174	(.689, .746)
$\beta_{\theta W}$	.336	.028	(.291, .382)
$\rho_{\theta W}$	.686	.045	(.609, .754)

3. WHAT CAN BE DONE WITH (MEAGER) TIME-1, TIME-2 DATA?

The data used for illustration here consist of observations on 40 cases, and shown below are the values for observations at time 1, X_1, at time 2, X_2, and also values for an exogenous background variable W. For purposes of exposition the longitudinal observations might be reading achievement scores of elementary school children, and the background variable W might be some measure of home environment, leading to obvious substantive questions such as, Do students with "better" home environments (books in the home, etc.) make better progress or improvement in reading?

Some Descriptive Analyses of Individual Change with Two Observations

The estimate of the amount of change for each individual is simply the observed amount of improvement: $D = X_2 - X_1$. The display of the data given in Table 1.19 has this difference score appended in the first column. Descriptive analyses of D, such as those illustrated below have value, and are essentially the best one

TABLE 1.19
Data and Difference Scores for Two-Wave Example

Case	D	X_1	X_2	W	Case	D	X_1	X_2	W
1	21.93	37.52	59.45	15.97	21	30.90	45.57	76.47	15.88
2	16.52	45.13	61.65	15.38	22	31.35	50.79	82.14	18.25
3	31.00	35.15	66.15	11.48	23	4.96	36.56	41.52	10.15
4	20.44	44.13	64.57	16.89	24	18.02	39.48	57.50	9.46
5	17.75	52.74	70.49	19.18	25	26.36	38.34	64.69	15.81
6	33.86	30.43	64.29	11.82	26	21.72	32.57	54.29	11.60
7	22.18	45.86	68.04	15.33	27	39.74	44.18	83.92	14.08
8	14.95	41.09	56.04	13.21	28	24.97	32.79	57.76	12.19
9	10.80	45.60	56.39	13.09	29	24.91	38.61	63.52	14.07
10	11.79	41.64	53.43	10.32	30	4.46	54.90	59.36	16.68
11	2.12	40.55	42.67	10.26	31	16.79	37.42	54.22	15.07
12	17.71	43.60	61.30	15.60	32	11.51	43.19	54.71	13.94
13	16.49	40.33	56.82	13.90	33	18.79	57.07	75.86	20.40
14	19.51	36.47	55.98	13.53	34	24.57	52.40	76.97	16.00
15	22.33	50.94	73.27	14.45	35	6.74	53.35	60.09	17.47
16	10.08	56.39	66.47	20.16	36	16.56	47.21	63.77	17.30
17	24.16	54.82	78.98	16.11	37	42.52	37.53	80.05	15.86
18	22.97	46.23	69.21	15.06	38	21.08	47.89	68.97	18.95
19	39.50	40.34	79.84	18.33	39	23.16	58.79	81.95	18.90
20	21.81	39.78	61.59	13.77	40	2.69	39.98	42.67	13.79

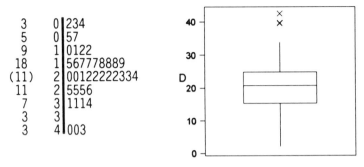

```
    3    0 | 234
    5    0 | 57
    9    1 | 0122
   18    1 | 567778889
  (11)   2 | 00122222334
   11    2 | 5556
    7    3 | 1114
    3    3 |
    3    4 | 003
```

FIG. 1.13. Graphical description of individual difference scores for two-wave example data: (a) stem-and-leaf display; (b) boxplot.

can do with these limited longitudinal data. If the individual history is merely two observations, the difference score is essentially (with unit time) the slope of the straight-line growth curve, and fitting a line to two points can yield disappointing statistical or psychometric properties. But the core problem is the meager data, not the summary. These limitations and statistical difficulties do preclude the estimation of variance components, etc., as was done in the two previous examples. Nonetheless, we can at least do simple descriptive summaries that address some of the longitudinal research questions. The data analysis setting is certainly not as hopeless as might be concluded from the (deliberate) overstatement in Motto 1 of Rogosa et al. (1982): "Two-waves are better than one, but not much."

Analyses of Individual Change

Below we have both a quantitative summary of the observed data and the amount of change; graphical summaries of the individual change are shown in Figure 1.13. For the "average" individual there was notable improvement of about 20 points. But clearly there also appear to be large individual differences in change, with some individuals gaining more than 40 points and others less than 5 points.

Observed Data

	N	MEAN	MEDIAN	STDEV	MIN	MAX	Q1	Q3
X_1	40	43.93	43.40	7.29	30.43	58.79	38.40	50.07
X_2	40	64.18	63.65	10.92	41.52	83.92	56.50	72.57
W	40	14.992	15.200	2.803	9.462	20.399	13.288	16.837

Change

	N	MEAN	MEDIAN	STDEV	MIN	MAX	Q1	Q3
D	40	20.25	20.76	9.71	2.12	42.52	15.34	24.82

One question that follows is whether these individual differences are linked to quantities such as initial status or the exogenous variable. The correlation between observed change and observed initial status (correlation between D and X_1) is $-.199$; this estimate is biased with a somewhat complicated form (as discussed in, for example, Rogosa, et al. 1982, Equation 11). The corresponding scatterplot is shown in Figure 1.14.

To describe relations between change and exogenous variables, start with the scatterplot shown in Figure 1.15. The sample correlation between W and D is 0.158, and the corresponding regression analysis for predicting individual change from W yields:

```
The regression equation is D = 12.0 + 0.549 W
Predictor      Coef     Stdev    t-ratio        p
Constant     12.015    8.460       1.42    0.164
W             0.5488   0.5549       0.99    0.329
s = 9.713      R-sq = 2.5%    R-sq(adj) = 0.0%
```

Apparently, there is little or no relation between individual change and the background variable W. Observed correlation is near zero, with test statistic of .99.

More generally, even with the meager two-wave data, valuable descriptions based on individual change can be built up to address more complex research questions and settings. For example, in two-group (or more) experimental studies, comparison of the difference scores across the experimental groups is equivalent to repeated measures analysis of variance. A thorough exposition of this equivalence to repeated measures ANOVA for the two-group, pre-test, post-test

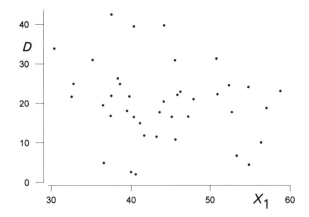

FIG. 1.14.   Scatterplot of observed change vs. observed initial status for two-wave example data.

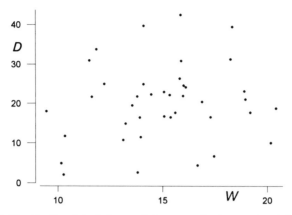

FIG. 1.15. Scatterplot of observed change vs. background variable for two-wave example data.

data structure is given in Brogan and Kutner (1980). Similar strategies are useful in nonexperimental, comparative settings. For quasiexperiments, a question that can and should be addressed in these nonexperimental studies is, Which group changed more (or declined less)? Of course, causal attribution (e.g., to the program or intervention) cannot be made, and, most important, attempts at statistical adjustments, explicit or implicit, to draw an "as if by experiment" conclusion are doomed. The difference score (or a measure of change obtained from richer data) is not the core problem. Approaches that start with assessments of individual change are far better than standard ANCOVA methods, or more esoteric adjustment procedures such as standardized change scores and the like.

Artificial Data with Known Structure

These exemplar time-1, time-2 data were produced from an underlying structure with known parameter values. The 40 individual cases were drawn from a population with specified characteristics (methods for constructing such artificial data are described in Question 5). True change, Δ, has a Uniform distribution with lower and upper values of 4 and 36; thus true change has mean 20 and variance 85.333. True status at time 1, ξ_1, has population mean 45 and variance 53.33 and for time 2 ξ_2 has population mean 65 and variance 96.0. Measurement error has mean 0 and variance 10 at each time point. Consequently, in the population the reliability of change, D, is .810, and the reliabilities of X_1 and of X_2 are .842 and .906, respectively. The correlation between true change and true initial status is $-.316$. The exogenous variable W was constructed to have no association with true change; $\rho_{\Delta W} = 0$.

Comparisons with Traditional Measurement of Change Analyses

The starting point for traditional analyses in the past measurement of change literature is not the description of individual change, but instead, the description of between-variable relations, most notably the time-2, time-1 scatterplot. The time-2 versus time-1 (X_2 versus X_1) scatterplot shown in Figure 1.16 has correlation .491. Also examined would be the between-variable relations with the exogenous variable in Figure 1.16, which show noticeable association between W and the longitudinal observations. However, Rogosa and Willett (1985b) have demonstrated that such cross-sectional associations do not provide useful information about correlates of change or progress. The correlation matrix provides the usual summary of these between-variable relations:

```
        X 1        X 2
X 1
X 2   0.491
W     0.716   0.619
```

It is unclear what is revealed about change from these between-variable relations.

To investigate the importance of the exogenous variable, it would be typical to carry out a regression analysis predicting X_2 from X_1 and W. The results from this regression, shown below, produce a highly significant coefficient for W (t-value 2.98) and thus would lead to exactly the wrong conclusion about W—even though in the structure of the data there is zero correlation between individual

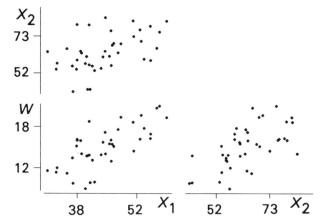

FIG. 1.16. Traditional scatterplots for two-wave example data arranged as time 2 vs. time 1 (top) and background variable vs. time 1 and time 2 (bottom).

change and W, the measurement of change analysis would flag W as an important predictor of change!

```
The regression equation is X₂ = 25.7 + 0.145 X₁ + 2.14 W
Predictor     Coef     Stdev      t-ratio        p
Constant     25.690    8.821        2.91      0.006
X₁            0.1447   0.2759       0.52      0.603
W             2.1431   0.7181       2.98      0.005
s = 8.770         R-sq = 38.8%   R-sq(adj) = 35.5%
```

Similarly, construction of the standard residual change score (see Myth 6) yields a correlation with W of .307 (double the sample correlation between W and D).

4. IS REGRESSION TOWARD THE MEAN REALLY AN IMPEDIMENT TO ASSESSING CHANGE?

The answer is no, but the material in Myth 5 would benefit from some augmentation. In that and other treatments of regression toward the mean, my focus has been on the importance of clear, explicit definition in the common references to "regression toward the mean" and then showing the consequences of that definition. My previous discussion has followed the literature in examining time-1, time-2 regression toward the mean, either in terms of perfectly measured $\xi(t_i)$ or in terms of the fallible X_i. And while those facts (reviewed below) are useful, the important additional message is that discussion of time-1, time-2 regression toward the mean, to some extent, misses the point—interest in assessing change should be on the estimate of change, such as the estimate of the amount of change Δ_p or of the rate of change θ_p.

The conventional definition of time-1, time-2 regression toward the mean in standard deviation units is uninteresting, whether it be in terms of X_1 and X_2 or in terms of $\xi(t_1)$ and $\xi(t_2)$, the latter in Equation 1.3. As is shown there, the condition for regression toward the mean to hold is for the time-1, time-2 correlation to be less than 1. This tautology (discussed following Equation 1.3) has the following derivation: starting with Equation 1.3, substitute $E[\xi(t_2) \mid \xi(t_1) = C] = \mu_{\xi(t_2)} + \rho_{\xi(t_1)\xi(t_2)} [\sigma_{\xi(t_2)}/\sigma_{\xi(t_1)}] (C - \mu_{\xi(t_1)})$ and then simplify to obtain the condition $\rho_{\xi(t_1)\xi(t_2)} < 1$.

One illustration that this statement of regression toward the mean is not important is provided by the sample collection of 15 growth curves depicted in Figure 1.17. This set of individual trajectories has values that satisfy the definition of time-1, time-2 regression toward the mean. Using, say, $t_1 = 3$, $t_2 = 7$, the population correlation $\rho_{\xi(3)\xi(7)} = .894$, and thus Equation 1.3 is satisfied—regression toward the mean "holds." Yet the correlation between $\xi(3)$ and the amount (or rate) of change is .707, which implies that rates of improvement for

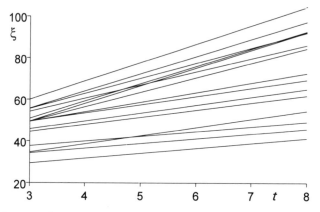

FIG. 1.17.   Collection of 15 straight-line growth trajectories for regression toward the mean illustration.

those high on $\xi(3)$ are larger than the rates of improvement for those low on $\xi(3)$. Intuitively, this is just the opposite of what is meant by the phrase regression toward the mean.

For illustration, values for $\xi(3)$, $\xi(7)$ and the corresponding fallible observations, the X-values are shown in Table 1.20. The population means at times 3 and 7 are 40 and 60, respectively. (The X-values are constructed by adding measure-

TABLE 1.20
True and Fallible Two-Wave Data for Regression
Toward the Mean Example

	ξ-values		X-values	
	$t = 3$	$t = 7$	$t = 3$	$t = 7$
1	41.93	57.27	40.11	54.88
2	27.02	36.49	29.05	40.23
3	42.37	70.52	41.15	73.72
4	47.82	73.36	52.09	72.19
5	41.02	54.89	41.97	62.37
6	51.06	86.68	50.67	82.19
7	44.81	63.33	47.36	69.74
8	47.38	80.69	48.70	83.13
9	30.68	46.52	35.04	51.35
10	31.93	41.15	31.24	49.51
11	42.53	76.04	51.05	69.02
12	45.50	61.40	51.97	53.52
13	35.43	44.59	29.40	31.12
14	40.91	75.20	40.05	78.89
15	48.28	77.50	56.36	77.66

ment error with variance 25 to the ξ-values yielding reliabilities of .631 for $t = 3$ and .895 for $t = 7$.) For the ξ-values, 13 of the 15 cases are further from the mean at $t = 7$ than at $t = 3$; only cases 7 and 12 are closer to the mean at $t = 7$ than at $t = 3$. For example, individual 3 is 2.4 units from the mean at $t = 3$ and 10.5 units away at $t = 7$.

The more appropriate statement of time-1, time-2 regression toward the mean in terms of the actual metric is given in Equation 1.4 and is equivalent to $\rho_{\xi(t_1)\theta} < 0$ or $\beta_{\xi(t_2)\xi(t_1)} < 1$. This condition is simply a statement about the collection of individual growth curves and has no relevance to the ability to assess change.

Regression in Terms of the Estimate of Change

Consideration of time-1, time-2 regression toward the mean had led me previously to believe that regression toward the mean was irrelevant to assessing change and was a concept/concern best ignored and forgotten. But that's not fully correct. The important point that is missed in presenting the facts above is that the quantity of interest is the estimate of change: of the amount of change Δ or the rate of change θ. This is where there is some constructive role for talking in terms of a regression toward the mean. The time-2 observation is not a replication of the time-1 observation whenever there is systematic individual change. Where regression toward the mean is a relevant concept is that an estimate of Δ or the rate of change θ from fallible data has more variability than if measurement were perfect; that is variance($\hat{\theta}$) > variance(θ). Thus an extreme value of $\hat{\theta}_p$ is likely to be larger than what would be obtained if measurement were perfect. This concern is a good justification for empirical Bayes estimates of individual growth rates (e.g., Fearn, 1975). For this concern about the error in $\hat{\theta}_p$, the traditional and sensible warning about selecting extremes based on fallible scores still pertains—i.e., selecting students with observed low rates of change for an intervention runs the risk of overstating the value of the intervention as their actual rates of improvement are likely greater than that observed.

5. HOW CAN LONGITUDINAL DATA EXAMPLES WITH KNOWN STRUCTURE BE CREATED?

To create examples of longitudinal panel data with known structure, we can use the basic relations and properties of collections of growth curves. The procedures illustrated here are for data based on underlying straight-line growth curves.

Simulation Procedure

Start by choosing the center for the time metric by specifying t° where $t^\circ = -\sigma_{\xi(0)\theta}/\sigma_\theta^2$. Then for the parameters of the straight-line growth model $\xi_p(t) = \xi_p(t^\circ) + \theta_p(t - t^\circ)$ specify the parameter distributions over individuals of the uncorrelated random variables $\xi(t^\circ)$ and θ (e.g., each distribution Gaussian or each distribution Uniform) to generate these parameter values for each p. By doing so, the scale for the time metric $\kappa = \sigma_{\xi(t^\circ)}/\sigma_\theta$ is specified. By then stating the discrete values of the times of observation $\{t_i\} = t_1, \ldots, t_T$, we then have values for the $\xi_p(t_i)$ for $p = 1, \ldots, n$. The exogenous characteristic W is generated with specified mean and variance, specifying the two correlations $\rho_{W\xi(t^\circ)}$ and $\rho_{W\theta}$ (under the constraint $(\rho_{W\xi(t^\circ)})^2 + (\rho_{W\theta})^2 \le 1$). The final step is to create the fallible observables by the addition of measurement error to the $\xi_p(t_i)$ according to the classical test theory model: $X_p(t_i) = \xi_p(t_i) + \varepsilon_i$ for $p = 1, \ldots, n$.

Consequences for Second Moments

The choices of the values above determine the population values of the familiar second moments of $\xi_p(t_i)$ or $X_p(t_i)$ for the artificial data. In practice, these values of these quantities—variances, correlations, etc.—are often chosen first (say to correspond to values familiar from empirical research or common sense), and then solutions (explicitly or by trial and error) for the corresponding values for the simulation procedure above are obtained. The relations that provide values of these second moments for the $\xi_p(t_i)$ are variance

$$\sigma^2_{\xi(t)} = \sigma^2_{\xi(t^\circ)} + ((t - t^\circ)/\kappa)^2 \sigma^2_{\xi(t^\circ)},$$

covariance (also yields correlation, using above)

$$\sigma_{\xi(t_1)\xi(t_2)} = (t_1 - t^\circ)(t_2 - t^\circ)\sigma^2_\theta + \sigma^2_{\xi(t^\circ)},$$

correlation between change and initial status

$$\rho_{\theta\xi(t)} = \frac{t - t^\circ}{[\kappa^2 + (t - t^\circ)^2]^{1/2}},$$

correlation with exogenous variable, W

$$\rho_{W\xi(t)} = \frac{(t - t^\circ)\rho_{W\theta} + \kappa\rho_{W\xi(t^\circ)}}{[\kappa^2 + (t + t^\circ)^2]^{1/2}}$$

Technical Specifications for Exhibit 1

In terms of the model parameters, the values for the artificial data in Exhibit 1 are $t^\circ = 2$; $\sigma^2_\theta = 5.333$; $\sigma^2_{\xi(t^\circ)} = 48$; for $\theta \sim U[1, 9]$, $\xi(t^\circ) \sim U[38, 62]$. Population mean rate of change is 5, and values of the population correlation coefficients among the $\xi(t_i)$ for observation times $t_1 = 1$, $t_2 = 3$, $t_3 = 5$ are $\rho_{\xi(1)\xi(3)} = .80$, $\rho_{\xi(1)\xi(5)} = .447$, $\rho_{\xi(3)\xi(5)} = .894$. Furthermore, for the fallible measure X with $\text{var}(\varepsilon) = 10$, the population correlations are $\rho_{X(1)X(3)} = .674$, $\rho_{X(1)X(5)} = .391$, $\rho_{X(3)X(5)} = .781$.

ACKNOWLEDGMENTS

I wish to thank Ghassan Ghandour and Haggai Kupermintz for computational and editorial assistance and Gary Williamson for providing the North Carolina data. Programs described in this chapter can be obtained by writing to David Rogosa at rag@leland.stanford.edu.

ADDITIONAL REFERENCES

Alwin, D. F. (1988). Structural equation models in research on human development and aging. In K. W. Schaie, R. T. Campbell, W. M. Meredith, & S. M. Rawlings (Eds.), *Methodological issues in aging research* (pp. 71–170). New York: Springer.

Brogan, D. R., & Kutner, M. H. (1980). Comparative analyses of pretest-postest research designs. *American Statistician, 34,* 229–232.

Bryk, A. S., & Raudenbush, S. W. (1987). Application of hierarchical linear models to assessing change. *Psychological Bulletin, 101,* 147–158.

Efron, B., & Tibshirani, R. J. (1993). *An introduction to the bootstrap.* New York: Chapman & Hall.

Fern, T. (1975). A Bayesian approach to growth curves. *Biometrika, 62,* 89–100.

Freedman, D. A. (1987). As others see us: A case study in path analysis. *Journal of Educational Statistics, 12,* 101–128.

Freedman, D. A. (1991). Statistical models and shoe leather. In P. Marsden (Ed.), *Sociological Methodology 1991* (pp. 291–313). Washington, DC: American Sociological Association.

Goldstein, H. (1979a). *The design and analysis of longitudinal studies.* London: Academic Press.

Goldstein, H. (1979b). Some models for analysing longitudinal data on educational attainment. *Journal of the Royal Statistical Society A, 142,* 407–442.

Holland, P. W. (1988). Causal inference, path analysis and recursive structural equation models. In C. Clogg (Ed.), *Sociological Methodology 1988* (pp. 449–484). Washington, DC: American Sociological Association.

Hui, S. L., & Berger, J. O. (1983). Empirical Bayes estimation of rates in longitudinal studies. *Journal of the American Statistical Association, 78,* 753–760.

Rogosa, D. R. (1987). Casual models do not support scientific conclusions: A comment in support of Freedman. *Journal of Educational Statistics, 12,* 185–195.

Rogosa, D. R. (1988). Myths about longitudinal research. In K. W. Schaie, R. T. Campbell, W. M. Meredith, and S. C. Rawlings (Eds.), *Methodological issues in aging research* (pp. 171–209). New York: Springer.

Rogosa, D. R. (1991). A longitudinal approach to ATI research: Models for individual growth and models for individual differences in response to intervention. In R. E. Snow and D. E. Wiley (Eds.), *Improving inquiry in social science: A volume in honor of Lee J. Cronbach* (pp. 221–248). Hillsdale, NJ: Lawrence Erlbaum.

Rogosa, D. R. (1993). Individual unit models versus structural equations: Growth curve examples. In K. Haagen, D. Bartholomew, and M. Diestler (Eds.), *Statistical modeling and latent variables* (pp. 259–281). Amsterdam: Elsevier North-Holland.

Rogosa, D. R., & Ghandour, G. A. (1989). TIMEPATH: Statistical analysis of individual trajectories. Stanford University.

Rogosa, D. R., & Ghandour, G. A. (1991). Statistical models for behavioral observations (with discussion). *Journal of Educational Statistics, 16,* 157–252.

Rogosa, D. R., & Saner, H. M. (in press). Longitudinal data analysis examples with random coefficient models. *Journal of Educational and Behavioral Statistics, 20.*

Williamson, G. L., Applebaum, M., & Epanchin, A. (1991). Longitudinal analyses of academic achievement. *Journal of Educational Measurement, 28*(1), 61–76.

2

Hierarchical Regression Analysis With Repeated-Measure Data

Gene P. Sackett and Joann Wu Shortt
University of Washington

The use of hierarchical regression analysis for repeated measures data, although straightforward, is not well known and by perusing the developmental journals, Sackett has found that it is not used very often by developmental researchers. In the following chapter Sackett and Shortt describe this method, which often has greater power than repeated measures analysis of variance, and also can have greater flexibility for dealing with practical problems such as missing data and correlated independent variables.

Studying change involves collecting repeated measurements on the same subjects. For example, developmental studies often involve collecting longitudinal data at two or more ages, learning studies involve data collected on at least two trials, and therapy research often involves a set of pre-treatment baseline measures followed by at least one post-treatment test. Some studies of change are straightforward. They involve groups with equal sample sizes, and factorial designs in which randomly assigned subjects actually receive every scheduled repeated measurement test. Under these conditions, the data are usually analyzed by means of an analysis of variance (ANOVA) with one or more uncorrelated factors and one or more nested repeated-measure factors.

Often, however, studies of change involve quasi-experiments. Levels of one or more independent variables (IVs) occur in the study population in nonrandom, unequal sample sizes. One or more covariates may be measured to control for possible confounding factors. Some of the repeated-measure data may be missing because subjects are not sampled at some of the scheduled measurement times. This latter situation almost always occurs for large-sample longitudinal studies: Some subjects are lost to follow-up, with sample sizes decreasing at each scheduled follow-up period. This type of study is often analyzed by regression techniques to determine the degree to which IVs predict change on the repeated measures. A number of regression models for studying developmental or other time-varying change functions are described by Nesselroade and Baltes (1979).

The purpose of this chapter is to describe a simple method for emulating repeated-measure ANOVA results using a hierarchical multiple-regression technique. Although this approach is fully described by Cohen and Cohen (1983, chapter 11), it is apparently not known by most behavioral researchers employing repeated measures in complex covariate or quasi-experimental studies. It is especially useful in studies involving two or more IVs that are naturally correlated or correlated due to unequal and disproportionate sample sizes among study groups. Although such conditions violate a basic assumption of the repeated-measures ANOVA, use of a hierarchical regression analysis can emulate an ANOVA and can correctly partition the variance among correlated IVs into shared and unshared portions. This chapter will proceed with a review of the basic features of a simple factorial repeated-measure ANOVA, then show how multiple regression can be used to make the same calculations, and finally suggest how the repeated-measure regression approach might be used to analyze a complex, quasi-experimental study.

FACTORIAL REPEATED-MEASURES ANOVA

The general features of repeated-measures ANOVA are illustrated by an example from Edwards (1985, pp. 397–401). As shown in Table 2.1, five subjects in each of three drug groups are tested on three trials. Thus, the Trial repeated-measure

TABLE 2.1
Edwards Drug * Trial Design and Data

Drug	Subject	Trial 1	Trial 2	Trial 3	$\Re Ss$
	1	2	4	7	13
	2	2	6	10	18
D1	3	3	7	10	20
	4	7	9	11	27
	5	6	9	12	27
	$\Re$D1	20	35	50	105
	1	5	6	10	21
	2	4	5	10	19
D2	3	7	8	11	26
	4	8	9	11	28
	5	11	12	13	36
	$\Re$D2	35	40	55	130
	1	3	4	7	14
	2	3	6	9	18
D3	3	4	7	9	20
	4	8	8	10	26
	5	7	10	10	27
	$\Re$D3	25	35	45	105
	$\Re T_i$	80	110	150	$\Re X = 340$

factor is nested within the independent group Drug variable. Table 2.2 shows the summary table for a repeated-measures ANOVA on these data.

In all factorial repeated-measures ANOVAs, the total variance is partitioned into a between-subjects (BS) and a within-subject (WS) component. The BS portion is based on a single score per subject, namely, the sum across the repeated-measure factor(s) ($\Re$Ss in Table 2.1). The BS variance includes all main effects and interactions that do not involve repeated-measure variables, as well as an error term based on the variance between the mean scores per subject ($\Re$Ss divided by the number of repeated-measure levels) within each independent group, summed across all groups.

The WS variance includes the repeated-measure main effect(s) and all interactions of the repeated-measure variable(s) with the BS variables. The WS error term(s) involves the subject by repeated measure(s) interaction within each independent group, summed across all groups. The only difference in calculations between repeated-measure and nonrepeated-measure factorial ANOVAs is this error partitioning. With uncorrelated data (one and only one score per subject)

TABLE 2.2
Repeated Measures ANOVA
on Edwards Drug * Trial Data

Source	SS	df	MS	F
Between Ss	*175.78*	*14*		
Drugs (D)	27.78	2	13.89	1.13
Error BS	148.00	12	12.33	
Within Ss	*193.33*	*30*		
Trials (T)	164.44	2	82.22	99.06
D × T	8.89	4	2.22	2.67
Error WS	20.00	24		
Total	369.11	44		

there is a single error term. With correlated data (one or more repeated-measure factors) there is an error term for each repeated-measure factor as well as the BS effects. Failure to partition the variance into these separate error terms will almost always produce an incorrect analysis and erroneous conclusions. The only exception is when the magnitudes of BS and WS error terms are the same. Using a regression approach with repeated measures will likewise give incorrect answers if the error variance is not appropriately partitioned into BS and WS components (see Cohen & Cohen, 1983, chapter 11).

EMULATING REPEATED-MEASURES ANOVA USING MULTIPLE REGRESSION

Ignoring the Repeated-Measure Factors

The qualitative IVs of ANOVA are represented in multiple regression (MR) analyses by vectors coding contrasts among the levels of the IVs. Those unfamiliar with these coding methods can consult Cohen and Cohen (1983) or Tabachnick and Fidell (1989) for details. Table 2.3 presents the Edwards data coded for MR analysis. Each subject has three lines of data, one for each of the three trials. The Drug and Trial factors have been "dummy coded" (Cohen & Cohen, 1983, chapter 5) into two vectors each, and the Drug * Trial interaction has been formed by multiplying the appropriate dummy coded scores. In addition, a vector of means across the three repeated-measure trials has been entered on each line for each subject. The value of the dependent variable (DV) completes each line of data. When using a computer system such as SPSS or SYSTAT to perform MR, the input data simply code the IV levels in a single numerical variable (i.e., Drug = 1, 2, or 3), and the program generates the MR code vectors.

TABLE 2.3
Edwards Drug Data Separated into Sections Representing
the Three Drug Groups and Dummy Coded for Regression Analysis,
Including the Mean per Subject across the Trials Repeated Measure

| | Drug | | Trial | | Drug * Trial | | | | Subject | |
Subj	D1	D2	T1	T2	D1T1	D1T2	D2T1	D2T2	Mean	DV
1	1	0	1	0	1	0	0	0	4.33	2
1	1	0	0	1	0	1	0	0	4.33	4
1	1	0	0	0	0	0	0	0	4.33	7
2	1	0	1	0	1	0	0	0	6.33	2
2	1	0	0	1	0	1	0	0	6.33	6
2	1	0	0	0	0	0	0	0	6.33	10
3	1	0	1	0	1	0	0	0	6.67	3
3	1	0	0	1	0	1	0	0	6.67	7
3	1	0	0	0	0	0	0	0	6.67	10
4	1	0	1	0	1	0	0	0	9.00	7
4	1	0	0	1	0	1	0	0	9.00	9
4	1	0	0	0	0	0	0	0	9.00	11
5	1	0	1	0	1	0	0	0	9.00	6
5	1	0	0	1	0	1	0	0	9.00	9
5	1	0	0	0	0	0	0	0	9.00	12
6	0	1	1	0	0	0	1	0	7.00	5
6	0	1	0	1	0	0	0	1	7.00	6
6	0	1	0	0	0	0	0	0	7.00	10
7	0	1	1	0	0	0	1	0	6.33	4
7	0	1	0	1	0	0	0	1	6.33	5
7	0	1	0	0	0	0	0	0	6.33	10
8	0	1	1	0	0	0	1	0	8.67	7
8	0	1	0	1	0	0	0	1	8.67	8
8	0	1	0	0	0	0	0	0	8.67	11
9	0	1	1	0	0	0	1	0	9.33	8
9	0	1	0	1	0	0	0	1	9.33	9
9	0	1	0	0	0	0	0	0	9.33	11
10	0	1	1	0	0	0	1	0	12.00	11
10	0	1	0	1	0	0	0	1	12.00	12
10	0	1	0	0	0	0	0	0	12.00	13
11	0	0	1	0	0	0	0	0	4.67	3
11	0	0	0	1	0	0	0	0	4.67	4
11	0	0	0	0	0	0	0	0	4.67	7
12	0	0	1	0	0	0	0	0	6.00	3
12	0	0	0	1	0	0	0	0	6.00	6
12	0	0	0	0	0	0	0	0	6.00	9
13	0	0	1	0	0	0	0	0	6.67	4
13	0	0	0	1	0	0	0	0	6.67	7
13	0	0	0	0	0	0	0	0	6.67	9
14	0	0	1	0	0	0	0	0	8.67	8

(continued)

TABLE 2.3 (Continued)

Subj	Drug		Trial		Drug * Trial				Subject Mean	DV
	D1	D2	T1	T2	D1T1	D1T2	D2T1	D2T2		
14	0	0	0	1	0	0	0	0	8.67	8
14	0	0	0	0	0	0	0	0	8.67	10
15	0	0	1	0	0	0	0	0	9.00	7
15	0	0	0	1	0	0	0	0	9.00	10
15	0	0	0	0	0	0	0	0	9.00	10

The data in Table 2.3 were submitted to the SPSS for Windows (Norusis, 1992) linear regression procedure, omitting the subject mean vector. This emulates an *uncorrelated data* ANOVA, generating a single residual error which would be the BS error variance if subjects contributed only a single score to the analysis. To emulate the factorial ANOVA, the main-effect vectors D1, D2, T1, and T2 are entered one at a time into the regression procedure; then the interaction vectors are entered. This is done using the ENTER method in the regression procedure. Entering main effects before interactions, and lower order before higher order interactions, must always be done when using MR to emulate ANOVA because the higher order effects contain the variance of all lower order components. Entering a higher order effect first would assign all of the variance to that effect, leaving none for its component parts (see Cohen & Cohen, 1983, chapter 8 for details). When group sample sizes are equal—and therefore IVs are not correlated—the order of entry within the main effects or interactions is unimportant. However, with unequal Ns, vectors entered first will account for their unique variance plus that shared with all other vectors in the analysis. Here entry order is crucial, and a rationale needs to be developed for determining entry order. This issue will be discussed below in the context of longitudinal studies.

Table 2.4 presents the MR results that will be provided by any MR program analyzing repeated-measure data without partitioning into the correct error terms. The left-hand section shows the SPSS output, which includes the cumulative R^2 (proportion of variance effect size estimate), sum of squares (SS), and degrees of freedom (df) as each vector is entered into the analysis. The center section shows the change in R^2, SS, and df after each vector enters the analysis. This is hand-calculated by subtracting the cumulative value for each vector from that of the previous vector. In addition, F tests based on the residual error are shown for each vector. D2, T1, and T2 are all significant ($p < .05$), indicating real differences between D2 and D3, and T1 and T2 versus T3.

The right portion of Table 2.4 shows the results of emulating an ANOVA by pooling the R^2, SS, and df values for the Drug, Trial, and interaction vectors. These effects could be calculated directly by entering D1 and D2, T1 and T2, and the four interaction vectors as three sets rather than eight individual vectors. How-

TABLE 2.4
Hierarchical Multiple Regression Using Residual Error Term

	SPSS Output			Change Values					Source	R^2	SS	df	MS	F
Source	$\Re R^2$	$\Re SS$	$\Re df$	R^2	SS	df	F							
D1	.019	6.944	1	.019	6.944	1	1.49		Drug	.075	27.778	2	13.889	2.98
D2	.075	27.778	2	.056	20.834	1	4.46							
T1	.376	138.889	3	.301	111.111	1	23.81		Trial	.446	164.444	2	82.222	17.62
T2	.521	192.222	4	.145	53.333	1	11.43							
D1T1	.539	199.028	5	.018	6.806	1	1.46		D * T	.024	8.889	4	2.222	0.48
D1T2	.540	199.444	6	.001	0.416	1	0.09							
D2T1	.541	199.861	7	.001	0.417	1	0.09							
D2T2	.545	201.111	8	.004	1.250	1	0.27							
Residual	.455	168.000	36	.455	168.000	36			Residual		168.000	36	4.667	
Total		369.111	44											

ever, this would not yield the potentially important information about single-vector comparisons—one of the main benefits of MR over ANOVA methods. The results should be compared with those in Table 2.2, the correct repeated-measures analysis. Note that the MR residual error is almost three times smaller than the correct BS error, but is over four times larger than the correct WS error. This has the effect in the MR analysis of more than doubling the F value for the Drug effect and greatly reducing the magnitude for the Trial effect. Clearly, analyzing repeated-measure data by MR using an overall residual error is not likely to yield correct significance tests or effect size estimates.

Accounting for Repeated-Measure Factors

Table 2.5 presents the correct MR analysis of the Edwards data. The rationale for this analysis is to partition the total variance into a BS and a WS component. Recall that in an ANOVA, the total BS variation is based on the variation about the subject means (see Tables 2.1 and 2.2). This can be represented in MR by the vector of subject means shown in Table 2.3. The variation about these means is *exactly* the BS variance containing all BS main effects and interactions as well as the BS error.

The complete data in Table 2.3 were submitted to the SPSS for Windows linear regression procedure using the ENTER method for each vector in the order shown in the left-hand portion of Table 2.5. This section also gives the SPSS cumulative outputs. The center section shows the change in each output value as each vector is entered. Comparing these results with those in Table 2.2, we can see that the R^2 and SS values are partitioned into BS and WS components, but the error df's are wrong. This occurs because MR procedures attribute only a single df to each vector in the analysis, and attribute the total df minus the sum of the analysis vectors as the residual error df. To calculate the correct df values we have to know how many total subjects are in the analysis and the total number of data values. The BS total df is simply one less than the total number of subjects. The WS total df is simply the grand total df minus the BS total df. The BS error df is then given by the BS total df minus the number of effect vectors in the BS part of the analysis. Likewise, the WS error df is given by the WS total df minus the number of effect vectors in the WS part of the analysis. The correct mean squares and df for each error term are shown in the right section of Table 2.5.

The center section of Table 2.5 presents correct F tests for each of the individual vectors in the analysis. These should be compared with the incorrect individual vector F tests in Table 2.4. When the correct error term is used, the D2 effect is not significant, the T1 and T2 effects are much larger than in the incorrect analysis, and the interaction effects are also larger, though still not significant. This pattern of reduced significance levels for the BS effects and increased significance for WS effects should be the general outcome when one correctly analyzes repeated-measure data that have positive correlations between the dependent variable across the levels of the repeated measure.

TABLE 2.5
Hierarchical Multiple Regression Partitioning Between-Subject (BS) and Within-Subject (WS) Error

Source	SPSS Output			Change Values				Source	R^2	SS	df	MS	F
	$\Re R^2$	$\Re SS$	$\Re df$	R^2	SS	df	F^a						
D1	.019	6.944	1	.019	6.944	1	0.56	BS	.476	175.517	14		
D2	.075	27.778	2	.056	20.834	1	1.69	Drug	.075	27.778	2	13.889	1.13
Mean	.476	175.517	3	.401	147.739	1		Error BS	.401	147.739	12	12.312	
T1	.776	286.635	4	.300	111.111	1	131.97	WS	.524	193.594	30		
T2	.921	339.960	5	.145	53.333	1	63.33	Trial	.445	164.443	2	82.222	97.65
D1T1	.939	346.768	6	.018	6.806	1	8.08						
D1T2	.941	347.183	7	.002	0.416	1	0.49	D * T	.024	8.890	4	2.222	2.64
D2T1	.942	347.600	8	.001	0.417	1	0.50						
D2T2	.945	348.850	9	.003	1.250	1	1.48						
Residual	.055	20.261	35	.055	168.000	35		Error WS	.055	20.261	24	0.842	
Total	.055	369.111	44										

^{a}Using correct BS and WS error terms with 12 and 24 df, respectively.

The right portion of Table 2.5 presents the complete repeated-measures AN-OVA emulation. With the exception of rounding error due to using only two significant digits for the subject means, the MR results are the same as those of the corresponding ANOVA in Table 2.2. Thus, we have seen that MR can accurately emulate a repeated-measure ANOVA. A more technical and complete discussion of coding MR with multiple repeated measures has been presented by Pedhazur (1977).

Regression Coefficients, Proportion of Variance, and Correlated Independent Variables

On the basis of the assumption that the reader has a working knowledge of both ANOVA and MR procedures, we have not addressed a number of details and caveats concerning assumptions of these analyses. In general, these are the same for ANOVA and MR, as discussed in detail by Cohen and Cohen (1983) and by Tabachnick and Fidell (1989). Nevertheless, MR analysis has several advantages over the equivalent ANOVA.

The regression approach can automatically generate regression coefficients for developing functional equations. Using appropriate coding schemes such as polynomial coefficients or vectors formed by raising quantitative IVs to appropriate powers, one can easily generate curvilinear functions (trend analyses) to describe phenomena such as developmental functions and learning curves. Effect size, as measured by proportion of variance, is a standard part of the MR output. Furthermore, when using MR with repeated measures, one can calculate proportions of variance relative to the total BS and total WS values. Effect size estimates relative to total WS variance may be more meaningful in estimating the magnitude of change and factors affecting this magnitude than effect size estimates relative to the total variance.

A major advantage of the MR approach concerns correlated IVs. These occur when there are unequal and disproportionate sample sizes, missing repeated-measure data, and/or natural correlation among the variables. The effect of correlated IVs is to produce shared variance in the dependent variable(s) under study. In such cases, the first among several correlated vectors to enter the MR analysis attains its unique variance as well as that shared with all vectors that have not yet entered the analysis. In ANOVA, this produces uninterpretable results. However, in MR the data analyst can alter the entry order to estimate both the unique and shared variance among a set of vectors (see Cohen & Cohen, 1983, chapter 5). When repeated-measure data are missing, ANOVA calculations can proceed only by dropping all subjects with any missing data or by "plugging" missing values with some type of estimate. If only a few among a large number of values are missing, the estimation approach is probably reasonable. However, when a large number of values are estimated the chance for a biased analysis is also large. In the MR approach, calculations can proceed even when some data are missing. However, this may produce bias due to the introduction of IV correlation involving the repeated-measure variable and any of its interactions. Plugging will remove this correlation. Defining a vector that identifies plugged data (perhaps real = 0 and plugged = 1) and its interactions with other factors can directly test the degree to which the estimated data have biased the analysis.

GROWTH DURING INFANCY IN PIGTAILED MACAQUES

The design of a complex repeated-measures regression analysis can be illustrated by an ongoing study in our laboratory concerning the effects of parental reproductive characteristics and prenatal stress on the growth of offspring during infancy (Sackett, 1984). Like many longitudinal studies, this research involves a mixture of historical, experimenter-manipulated, and naturally occurring IVs and covariates. The subjects are male and female pigtailed macaque (*Macaca nemestrina*) breeders with excellent or poor histories of reproductive success. Success is indexed by excessive (high risk) or minimal (low risk) rates of fetal loss, low-birth-weight infants, and/or infants that die of natural causes during the first 30 postnatal days. The monkeys are bred selectively both within and between risk groups. In about one-third of the pregnancies the dams experience a high-stress condition between days 30 and 130 of the 170-day gestation period; the stress consists of daily hand capture and brief confinement. Low-stress pregnancies involve a total of only three captures. Surviving offspring are weighed daily for 3 months, then twice weekly for the next 6 months. These data are being summarized as means per week, with about 5% of the weekly means missing due to clerical errors, computer malfunctions, and failure to take some weights. The current sample size is 235 offspring (BS *N*) and 8,030 weekly weights (total *N*).

Principle of Temporal Causation

Table 2.6 shows the independent variables and covariates involved in the study and how they could be coded for multiple regression. Because of unequal and disproportionate sample sizes, the maternal-risk, paternal-risk, prenatal-stress, and offspring-sex qualitative IVs are all correlated. Therefore, the order of entering these factors, as well as the quantitative covariates, determines which factors receive shared variance. If a theoretical or empirical rationale for determining regression entry order is unavailable, it is unlikely that replicable results can be obtained from the analysis. One rationale that would probably apply to most studies of growth or change concerns the idea of temporal causation. Variables that already exist can affect later variables, but later variables cannot have a causal effect on earlier ones. Therefore, earlier existing variables should receive

TABLE 2.6
Possible Design for a Regression Analysis to Study Effects
of Parental, Prenatal, and Perinatal Factors on Growth[a]
of Pigtailed Macaque Infants

Between-Subject Main Effects	
Source of Variation	*Variable Type or Coding*
Maternal Risk (MR)	1 = High 0 = Low
Paternal Risk (PR)	1 = High 0 = Low
Dam's Prepregnant Weight (PW)	Quantitative
PW^2	Quantitative
Offspring Sex (SX)	1 = Female 0 = Male
Prenatal Stress (ST)	1 = High 0 = Low
Birth Weight (BW)	Quantitative
BW^2	Quantitative
Gestation Length (GES)	Quantitative
Simian Apgar (APG)	Ordinal Rating
Neonatal Days on Medical Treatments (MT)	Quantitative
Mean of Weekly Weights	Quantitative

Some Between-Subject Interaction Sets	
Interaction	*Set Name*
MR*PR	Parental Risk
MR*SX PR*SX MR*PR*SX	Parental Risk * Sex
MR*ST PR*ST MR*PR*ST	Parental Risk * Stress
SX*ST	Sex * Stress
MR*SX*ST PR*SX*ST MR*PR*SX*ST	Parental Risk * Sex * Stress
BW*GES	Birth Weight * Gestation

Within-Subject Main Effects	
(Dependent Variable = 36 weekly mean weights for each subject)	
Source of Variation	*Variable Type or Coding*
Age (A)	Quantitative
A^2	Quantitative

Some Within-Subject Interaction Sets	
Interaction	*Set Name*
A*MR A^2 * MR	Age * Maternal Risk
A*PR A^2*PR	Age * Paternal Risk
A*SX A^2*SX	Age * Sex
A*ST A^2*ST	Age * Stress
A*MR*PR A^2*MR*PR	Age * Parental Risk
A*MR*SX A^2*MR*SX	Age * Maternal Risk * Sex

(*continued*)

TABLE 2.6   (Continued)

Some Between-Subject Interaction Sets

Interaction	Set Name
A*PR*SX A²*PR*SX	Age * Paternal Risk * Sex
A*MR*ST A²*MR*ST	Age * Maternal Risk * Stress
A*PR*ST A²*PR*ST	Age * Paternal Risk * Stress
A*MR*PR*SX A²*MR*PR*SX	Age * Parental Risk * Sex
A*MR*PR*ST A²*MR*PR*ST	Age * Parental Risk * Stress
A*BW A²*BW	Age * Birthweight
A*GES A²*GES	Age * Gestation Length
A*BW*GES A²*BW*GES	Age * Birth Weight * Gestation Length

ᵃWeekly body weight during year 1

any variance shared with later ones. The order of variable entry in Table 2.6 reflects this principle.

Maternal and paternal risk are entered first, as they are the earliest existing IVs in the study. The dam's prepregnant weight, a covariate, is entered next along with the weight squared because prior research suggests a quadratic relation between prepregnant weight and early growth of offspring. Sex is entered next, as this is determined at conception, followed by stress, which begins at 30 days of gestation. Birth weight and its square are entered next along with gestation length. The square is used because neonatal growth is not linear owing to weight loss followed by catch-up during weeks 1–2. Finally, a simian Apgar reflecting condition of the perinate at birth and a measure of illness during the 30-day neonatal period round out the covariates under study.

It should be noted that maternal and paternal risk cannot be temporally ordered, so their entry order is arbitrary. In fact, they will be studied as main effect and interaction sets described below. Birth weight and gestation are also highly correlated and not subject to temporal order. Thus, their analysis will also proceed as a set (Cohen and Cohen, 1983, chapter 4).

The second section of Table 2.6 shows how the risk, stress, and sex factors might be handled in the BS analysis. The maternal * paternal risk interaction studies the specific effects of parental risk combinations. The maternal * sex, paternal * sex, and maternal * paternal * sex interactions form a set studying effects of parental risk * sex. Similar sets are formed involving parental risk * stress, sex * stress, and the four-way interaction among these IVs. Given temporal priority, these IVs would be entered in the column-then-row order in Table 2.6. Also shown is the birth-weight * gestation-length interaction. Other sets involving the remaining covariates and IV-covariate interactions could also be defined, and their vectors entered together, with set order dictated by temporal priority.

The third section of Table 2.6 shows the repeated-measure IV, which consists of the quantitative variable age (week 1–36) and age squared. Age could be coded by 35 dummy vectors, but this would generate a prohibitively large number of interaction vectors involving age, and would ignore the large amount of past research showing that macaque infant growth can be well described using only linear and quadratic growth curve components. Thus, having a rationale for quantitatively coding a repeated-measure IV can save dozens and even hundreds of vectors and their corresponding degrees of freedom in studies such as this where a repeated measure has a large number of levels.

The fourth section of Table 2.6 presents the order in which the qualitative IVs would enter the WS analysis in interaction with age and age squared. Again, read the order across columns, then down rows. The table shows all interactions up to four-way effects involving parental risk, sex, and stress. Five-way effects could also be studied, but it is unlikely that they would be interpretable. Finally, any birth-weight and gestation effects over and above the degree to which they share variance with the qualitative IVs are assessed in interaction with the age variables. Sets involving the perinatal and neonatal covariates could also be entered after the birth-weight and gestation sets.

In sum, regardless of how the IVs and covariates are set up for an MR analysis of a study such as this, an appropriate analysis must split the predictors into BS and WS sets and generate separate error terms for the two parts. This is easily accomplished for designs involving only a single repeated-measure factor by using the mean of the repeated measure as presented here. If this is not done, the results of any MR analysis involving repeated measurement will almost certainly be incorrect.

ACKNOWLEDGMENTS

Preparation of this chapter was supported by NIH grants HD02274 from NICHHD to the Child Development and Mental Retardation Center and RR00166 from the DRR to the Regional Primate Research Center. We thank Kate Elias for editorial assistance.

REFERENCES

Cohen, J., & Cohen, P. (1983). *Applied multiple regression/correlation analysis for the behavioral sciences* (2nd ed.). Hillsdale, NJ: Lawrence Erlbaum Associates.

Edwards, A. L. (1985). *Experimental design in psychological research*. New York: Harper and Row.

Nesselroade, J. R., & Baltes, P. B. (1979). *Longitudinal research in the study of behavior and development*. New York: Academic Press.

Norusis, M. J. (1992). *SPSS for Windows: Advanced statistics* (Release 5). Chicago: SPSS Inc.

Pedhazur, E. J. (1977). Coding subjects in repeated measure designs. *Psychological Bulletin, 84,* 298–305.

Sackett, G. P. (1984). A nonhuman primate model of risk for deviant development. *American Journal of Mental Deficiency, 88,* 469–476.

Tabachnik, B. G., & Fidell, L. S. (1989). *Using multivariate statistics* (2nd ed.). New York: Harper Collins.

3 Orderly Change in a Stable World: The Antisocial Trait as a Chimera

Gerald R. Patterson
Oregon Social Learning Center

Let us turn to a real developmental application with an important phenomenon. Patterson raises the question of how one identifies developmental trajectories in a trait that has a reasonably high level of stability such as is the case with aggression. In previous research, by the way, Patterson has shown that the development of antisocial behavior in boys follows the type of fanning-out model that Rogosa discussed for achievement. In this chapter, Patterson approaches his question in a novel way by discussing the distinct trajectories of adolescent delinquents and the development of the strange and emergent beast of the Chimera.

—Editor

ORDERLY CHANGE IN A STABLE WORLD: THE
ANTISOCIAL TRAIT AS A CHIMERA

A developmental perspective implies that changes in social behavior are related to age in an orderly way. In the present report, the definition is expanded to include any changes in social behavior accompanied by explanatory variables that account for significant amounts of variance in the change score. The experiences that bring about change may or may not be related to the age of the child.

By definition, the availability of longitudinal data sets would be prerequisite to the study of change in social development. What gives the developmental perspective credibility is that highly sophisticated techniques for analyzing longitudinal data sets have been well understood for over a decade. For example, the lucid descriptions of time-series analysis and panel analysis for inter- and intraindividual longitudinal data sets were described by Nesselroade and Baltes (1979). Collins and Horn (1991) detailed further developments in the analysis of change, such as latent growth modeling (LGM), analysis of factor invariance, event-history analysis, and the Guttman longitudinal simplex. The analytic tools are there; in fact, they have been there for some time.

Given the long-standing commitment to a developmental perspective and 40 years worth of longitudinal data, one might expect that the construction of an empirically based theory for the development of children's social behaviors would be well under way. In fact, there is no such accumulative data base. In the area of delinquency, for example, Farrington (1986) identified 11 well-designed longitudinal projects. The most salient finding to emerge was that measures of children's antisocial behavior were significant predictors for adolescent delinquency (i.e., antisocial behavior is highly stable). Nevertheless, efforts to explain the stability or to predict change in antisocial behavior (desistors or late starters) have not been particularly successful (Farrington & Hawkins, 1991). With few notable exceptions, even the more recent studies assiduously avoid the study of change. This author's review of the empirical findings leads to the conclusion that the developmental emperor either has no clothes or, at the very least, is prone to indecent displays.

Beyond Stability Coefficients

The meager returns from longitudinal studies reflect the interactive contribution of three errors in research strategy. First, most investigators have been trained within a myopic conceptualization of the trait as a static or fixed unit that can be satisfactorily assessed by data from a single agent. In the discussion that follows, formulation of the trait concept is expanded to include changes over time. The measurement is based on multiagent, multimethod data. The second limiting factor is found in an overweening reliance upon the correlation coefficient as the analytic tool. Being wedded to both of these strategies leads unerringly to overproduction of stability coefficients as the main output for longitudinal studies. The major limitation in strategy, however, lies in failure to include a formulation about the nature of change in social behaviors. This failure may be due to the fact that developmental theories are exceedingly vague about what produces change and how to measure it. Most formulations consist of ambiguous metaphors about organismic variables, social learning, family systems, or attachment. Carrying out developmental research under the aegis of these three limitations is analogous to studying a dance through a tube. Not knowing where to look, we arbitrarily collect periodic data on the kind of shoes being worn. In so doing, we not only miss the point of the process, but produce yet another set of very high-order stability coefficients saying that people tend to wear the same shoes throughout the dance.

In the alternative perspective, the present report uses multiple indicators to define the trait concept. This strategy reflects the growing consensus that any single indicator measure would be systematically biased (Patterson, 1992; Patterson & Bank, 1987; Sullivan, 1974). The contemporary shift toward using multiple indicators and confirmatory factor analyses (Bentler, 1980) supposedly provides a basis for constructing models that are more generalizable. The utility of this strategy has been demonstrated by replicated models from a cross-sample (Forgatch, 1991) and across-site (Conger, Patterson, & Gé, 1995) studies. From this perspective, a trait such as antisocial behavior is embedded in a matrix of changing social behaviors (Patterson, Reid, & Dishion, 1992). Not only is the matrix changing, but some forms of the trait itself are changing. A study of this process requires having a theory about what produces the trait, how it will change, and when. Patterson, Reid, and Dishion (1992) detailed an empirically based theory about boys' aggression. The theory specifies what mechanisms produce changes and, to some extent, when these changes should occur. These considerations led to an expanded definition of the trait score requiring time of emergence as a necessary piece of information. For example, an early emergence for the trait increases the risk for qualitatively new problems directly caused by the problem child's coercive and antisocial behaviors. Literature that examines the covariation between the trait measures and these qualitative changes is reviewed in a section that follows.

A core problem for a developmental theory of aggression is the need to explain the systematic changes in form and in intensity of these behaviors. Changes in form occur at all stages of development, but particularly during adolescence. In this report, LGM is used to examine the increment in growth for two antisocial behaviors (truancy and drug use), and covariates that explain why these changes for new forms come about are examined (Stoolmiller & Bank, in press).

In this interpretation, the child's antisocial trait is viewed as a *chimera*. According to biologists, a chimera is an unusual hybrid produced by grafting tissue from different organisms. This metaphor is an apt descriptor for the antiso-cial trait. Each addition of a qualitatively new problem, and each change in the form of the coercive or antisocial behavior, might be thought of as a graft made onto the original trait score. If changes do occur, how can we say we are describing the "same thing"? Analyses are presented demonstrating that qualita-tive additions and changes in form define a second-order deviancy factor chang-ing in an orderly manner over time.

Before moving to a discussion of findings, one further problem in strategy needs to be raised. A frequent claim made for longitudinal design is that it can make an important contribution to evaluating causal status for developmental variables (Nesselroade & Baltes, 1979). Gollob and Reichardt (1987) extended this model to an autoregressive design where variable x measured at T1 is partialed out of the measure for x at T2. They asserted that a panel design could be used to test for the causal contribution of variable y measured at T1 by demonstrating that it covaried significantly with future changes in x. Cross-lag correlations could be used to test the hypothesis that x measured at T1 could demonstrate a causal effect on y measured at T2. Rogosa (1979) carefully delin-eated problems in measurement and specification that typically make this a very weak test for causal status. He also strongly endorsed multiple measures and the use of structural equation modeling (SEM) rather than traditional multiple-regression analyses. Testing the causal status of parenting practices was, in fact, one of the prime goals of the longitudinal Oregon Youth Study (OYS) (Patterson, 1988). The OYS was designed to fulfill the requirements Rogosa outlined. As we applied the autoregressive format suggested by Gollob and Reichardt (1987) to our longitudinal data, however, we were immediately confronted with a paradox. Using latent constructs to measure child traits and parenting practices routinely generated stability coefficients ranging from .70 to .85 for two- to four-year intervals (Patterson & Bank, 1989). Correlations with causal constructs were usually well above the .40 to .50 range. Paradoxically, our efforts to use auto-regressive panel models to test for causal status were doomed to failure because our measures were too good! Stoolmiller and Bank (in press) point out that the combination of high stabilities and high colinear relations make significant cross-lag effects extremely unlikely. They also point out that there are alternative analytic strategies which are more likely to be effective (e.g., LGM). The present author believes that, at best, SEM or LGM can provide only a weak test of causal status. A developmental theory must eventually be based on experimental evi-dence. For example, Dishion, Patterson, and Kavanagh (1992) and Forgatch (1991) have described longitudinal designs that included random assignment and experimental manipulations to test for causal status.

Longitudinal data from the OYS are used to address questions about quan-titative and qualitative change. The 206 families involved in the OYS live in high-risk (for crime) neighborhoods in a medium-sized metropolitan area. The recruitment procedures and sample characteristics were described by Capaldi and Patterson (1987). Each family participated in over 20 hours of assessment at each probe, when the boys were in grades 4, 6, 8, and 10.

STABLE BUT CHANGING

When studying changes in children's antisocial behavior, we must first establish a small island of stability. We begin by examining two very different facets of stability. First, the stability of the definition itself is considered; it may be that what is meant by stability changes as the individual moves from childhood through adolescence. The second question concerns the means for estimating the magnitude of stability coefficients. There is some reason to believe that the typical bivariate correlation of monoagent reports might overestimate stability.

Stability in Definition

It may be that both the form and the definition of antisocial behavior change as the child's age increases. Eddy, Heyman, and Weiss (1991) partialed out the effect of changes in form by constructing a pool of antisocial behaviors that could occur at any age. Maternal ratings of these 12 items were available for toddlers (age 27 months) and for five-year-olds. The items were rank-ordered at each age according to frequency of use. The correlation of .78 showed that items most frequently used to describe toddlers were also more likely to be used for preschool children. This same set of items, when scored for different samples of boys in grades 2 through 8, showed comparable stabilities in definition. For example, the rank ordering of items for toddlers correlated in the .71 to .75 range with the rank ordering of items used by mothers to describe their adolescent sons. In each case, the most frequently checked items tended to be "disobedience" and "temper tantrums," whereas the least frequently checked was "physical aggression." What mothers perceive to be "most" and "least" antisocial remains constant over child and adolescent development.

In the Eddy et al. (1991) article, mothers' stability in definitions for boys between grades 4 and 8 was .96. For that same sample, the individual difference stability for mothers' ratings of their sons was .65. By definition, however, the error terms for the two sets of ratings were intercorrelated. Not only does this violate a fundamental assumption for application of correlational analysis, but it also inflates the magnitude of the correlation. How does one partial out the joint contribution of shared method variance and stability? As Rogosa (1979) and others have pointed out, the use of trait indicators based on reports from multiple agents and methods would enable us to disentangle the contributions of shared method and stability variances. This possibility is examined in the following section.

Stable Individual Differences

The preceding analyses showed there is a core set of interpersonal reactions defining the antisocial trait that are stable over the period from age 10 through age 14. Adolescent boys, however, are involved in some antisocial acts that younger boys seldom engage in, so the definition was expanded to include all of the antisocial acts that are performed often by adolescents. SEM was used to estimate the stability of antisocial behavior for the 206 boys in the OYS. The trait was defined by parent reports, teacher reports, and child self-reports at grades 4 and 8. Details of the psychometric analyses from the grade 4 studies for each of the indicators and for the construct itself were presented by Capaldi and Patterson (1989).

In the model, when the same methods were used at the two assessment probes, the error terms were allowed to covary. In doing this, the contribution of shared method variance can be removed from the estimate of stability. As shown in Figure 3.1, all of the factor loadings were highly significant at both points in time; in fact, the loadings showed at least configural invariance. At both assessments, the highest loadings were for parent reports and the lowest were for child self-reports. The probability value of .63 for the chi-square test showed a solid fit between the data set and the a priori model.

The traditional equation for test-retest correlation $(1 - r^2)$ defines the error of measurement for a given trait score. Although the current stability path coefficient suggests that the error of measurement might be about 31% of the variance, it is plausible that a significant proportion of this error estimate might reflect changes in level for a subgroup. A portion of the unexplained variance could

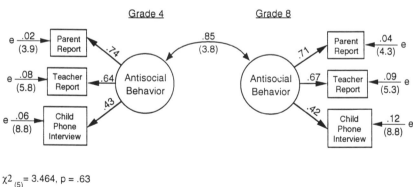

$\chi^2_{(5)} = 3.464$, p = .63

BBN = .990
BBNN = 1.014
CFI = 1.000

FIG. 3.1.   Stability of antisocial behavior from grade 4 to grade 8.

reflect systematic changes in individual growth over time. In the next section I examine the possibility of systematic changes under conditions of high stability.

TWO DEVELOPMENTAL MODELS

A formulation about late-starting delinquents (Patterson, DeBaryshe, & Ramsey, 1989) suggested that there would be substantial numbers who become antisocial for the first time during midadolescence. This would result in significant shifts in mean level for antisocial behaviors; presumably, the resulting shifts in ordinal rankings would in turn contribute to lowered stability coefficients. Intraindividual growth curve analyses will be used to (a) demonstrate that such systematic shifts do occur and (b) identify a set of variables thought to bring this about.

It was hypothesized that early- and late-onset antisocial boys represent two very different groups. Each group has different determinants and outcomes. A two-parameter latent growth model would seem useful in examining this general model. For example, one parameter (the intercept) would define where the process starts (i.e., the early onset boys). The other parameter would describe how intraindividual growth unfolds over time (i.e., the late-onset boys). In the present context, the intercept describes the individual differences in the antisocial trait at age 10. The second parameter constitutes an operational definition of late starter (i.e., nonproblem children who developed antisocial traits in early adolescence).

Part of the beauty of the latent growth model is that it operationally defines *early* and *late* starters. In addition, it introduces covariates that might account for the variance in the intercepts as well as the individual differences in growth (i.e., provides a correlation test for potential determinants). The covariates provide a direct test for the assumption that determinants for one developmental phase (early starters) may be different from the determinants for another phase (late starters). Initially, Patterson et al. (1989) hypothesized that determinants for early starters would be provided by contingencies embedded in family interaction; these in turn are controlled by the effectiveness of parenting practices. Latent constructs for parental effectiveness in discipline and monitoring practices assessed at age 10 serve as covariates accounting for individual differences in intercept scores for the OYS.

A second parameter in the LGM, the shape parameter, described the differences among the boys in intraindividual growth patterns for antisocial behavior assessed at grades 4, 6, 7, and 8. These late starters did not begin their antisocial careers until early adolescence; they showed few, if any, adjustment problems during childhood and possessed at least marginal social and survival skills (Patterson & Yoerger, 1993). The assumption is that some of the late starters will be arrested, but few will be chronic delinquents, and they will have a better prognosis than early starters for moderate levels of adult adjustment. The mechanisms that determine the delinquent behavior for late starters are an earlier than normal presence on the street (i.e., *wandering*) and a heavy commitment to the deviant peer group. This formulation was based on Stoolmiller's (1990) use of the OYS longitudinal data to demonstrate that, during the interval from childhood to midadolescence, changes in antisocial behavior covaried with changes in wandering and changes in involvement with deviant peers. The hypothesis about the involvement of deviant peers in direct training for delinquent acts is tested in a later section. Multiple indicators are used to define the constructs for wandering and involvement with deviant peers that would presumably covary with changes in individual growth for antisocial behavior (Rogosa & Willett, 1985).

Changes in Antisocial Behavior

For the entire OYS sample, teachers' ratings for antisocial behavior showed a significant increase in mean level from grade 4 to grade 5, but no significant change over the next four years (Patterson, 1992). Current studies using parent ratings and child self-report data showed the same general pattern (i.e., essentially a nonsignificant slope for measures from grade 4 through grade 8). The finding of no increase in antisocial behavior from early to midadolescence is consistent with the findings from teacher and adolescent ratings in the Chapel Hill longitudinal study (Cairns & Cairns, 1991).

In the OYS, the same assessment battery was used at grades 4, 6, 7, and 8. At each point in time, the raw scores from teacher, parent, and child telephone interviews were added to generate a single score. The same set of items was used at each point in time.

A Two-Factor Latent Growth Model

The results from the simultaneous test of the early- and late-starter models are summarized in Figure 3.2. Using a two-factor model requires that the correlation between the slope and intercept parameters be minimal or zero. In fact, the data showed that the initial level for the antisocial score was unrelated to slope changes. This is a crucial piece of information for a developmental model of antisocial behavior; where a child starts is not necessarily related to his or her future growth (in mean level).

The error terms for each wave of measurement for the antisocial construct were set equal. The intercept was defined by the antisocial scores obtained at grade 4; the factor loadings for the antisocial measures were set at 1.0 for each wave. Based on prior work by Stoolmiller (1990), the factor loadings for the shape parameter were set at zero for grade 4 and at 2 for grades 6, 7, and 8. All the error terms for the covariates were allowed to covary.

The data showed that measures collected at the four points in time defined the same latent construct for antisocial behavior. Evidence for this assertion lies in

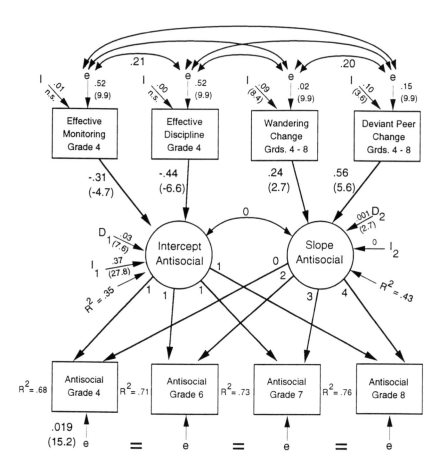

$\chi^2_{(22)} = 25.21$, $p = .29$

BBN = .960
BBNN = .993
CFI = .995
$N = 201$
Note: Only significant correlations shown

FIG. 3.2.   Developmental models for early and late starters.

the r^2 values (adjoining each measured variable), which ranged from .68 at grade 4 to .76 at grade 8. These values show that the latent construct loads at a very high level on the measures at each point in time.

It was hypothesized that there would be a significant contribution by the discipline and monitoring constructs in accounting for initial level of child antisocial behavior. The findings were consistent with the hypothesis. Ineffective parental discipline $(-.44)$ was associated with higher intercept scores for antisocial behavior even after the contribution of inept monitoring had been partialed out. The comparable path coefficient for monitoring was $-.37$. Together, the parenting practices accounted for 35% of the variance in the initial level of antisocial scores. Neither set of initial parenting skills covaried with late intraindividual changes in antisocial behavior. The results suggest that a single-minded focus on parenting skills is helpful in understanding initial levels of aggression, but it does not tell us very much about which boys will be at risk for an increase in antisocial behavior at midadolescence.

The next hypothesis examined in Figure 3.2 was that the boys who showed increases in wandering (i.e., unsupervised street time) and in involvement with deviant peers would also show increases in antisocial behavior. Changes in wandering and in involvement with deviant peers were expressed as a simple difference score (Stoolmiller & Patterson, 1995). The difference scores showed a mean increase in wandering of .09 from grade 4 to grade 8 and a mean increase in deviant peer involvement of .10. The increases in wandering contributed significantly (.24) to the slope index for increases in antisocial behavior. Increases in deviant peer involvement contributed heavily (.56) to changes in antisocial behavior even after the contribution of increased wandering had been partialed out. The combined contribution of the two variables accounted for 43% of the variance in the measures (shape parameter) of intraindividual growth in aggression.

The nonsignificant chi-square value demonstrated an acceptable fit of the data to the a priori early/late starter model presented in the original statement (Patterson et al., 1989). The implication is that there are two developmental paths for antisocial behavior. As hypothesized, each path is characterized by a different set of covariates. The path of the parenting skills model relates significantly to the start point, childhood aggression measured at age 10. The path of the deviant peer involvement model relates to antisocial behavior that begins in early adolescence.

Early and late starters seem to have different determinants. It was also hypothesized that the two groups would differ significantly in the timing for their first arrest and for their risk of chronic offending (Patterson et al., 1989). Presumably, antisocial children would be at greater risk than late starters for both early police arrest and for chronic arrests during adolescence. The longitudinal data collected for the OYS provided strong support for both hypotheses (Patterson, Crosby, & Vuchinich, 1992; Patterson & Yoerger, 1993).

The findings for the late starters' intraindividual growth in antisocial behavior suggest that some of the variance not accounted for in stability estimates may be generated by systematic increases in aggression for subgroups of young adolescents.

ANALYSES OF QUALITATIVE SHIFTS

It was hypothesized that over time there are two major qualitative changes in problem behaviors that accompany the antisocial trait. One shift is in the form of the antisocial acts; the other involves the addition of nonantisocial problem behaviors. The assumption being tested is that these qualitative shifts are quantifiable and that they define an emerging second-order deviancy factor.

The Addition of New Problem Behaviors

Coercive and antisocial acts elicit predictable reactions from the social environment, adding qualitatively new problems to the developmental trajectory (Patterson et al., 1992). The additions occur in an identifiable sequence of reactions by members of the child's social environment. The sequence is initiated by the entrance of the antisocial child into the school setting. In that setting, the child's coercive interpersonal style produces an immediate reaction. Coie and Kupersmidt (1983) showed that, in a newly formed group, other children began to label the antisocial child as "disliked" within 2 or 3 hours of contact. The second reaction to the child's behavior is from the teacher. The child's obdurate noncompliance to implicit and explicit rules means she or he spends less time on tasks when in the classroom and less time on homework assignments. The child's academic failure is probably evident to him or her early on. By grades 3 or 4, the antisocial child has failed in two fundamentally important tasks: peer relations and academic skills. Patterson and Capaldi (1990) hypothesized that the effect of this dual failure is increased frequency of depressed moods. School failure, peer rejection, and depressed mood constitute a cascade of qualitative problems that add to the child's burden. The link between prior antisocial behavior and academic failure and peer rejection has been examined by SEM in a series of analyses summarized by Patterson and Yoerger (1993). The relation between dual failure and depressed mood has been replicated in three SEM studies detailed by Patterson and Capaldi (1990) and Patterson and Stoolmiller (1991).

Developmental Changes in Form of Antisocial Acts

The stability studies reviewed earlier imply that the antisocial acts of a five-year-old may be prototypic of the acts of the delinquent adolescent. It is evident, however, that there are profound changes over time in the form of coercive (e.g., noncompliance, threats, temper tantrums) and antisocial (e.g., stealing, lying) acts. How do we move from the five-year-old's noncompliance and temper tantrums to the adolescent's substance abuse, burglary, and shoplifting? We believe that many crucial changes in the form of antisocial acts occur during early adolescence, and the primary agents of change for these qualitative shifts are members of the deviant peer group. During early adolescence, the training is fairly intensive and may involve multiple antisocial acts. If this is so, several new forms of antisocial behavior might change in a similar fashion over time. To test this hypothesis, data were examined for the changes in substance use and in truancy at grades 4 through 9. Substance use was defined by a single item, "uses alcohol or drugs" (never, sometimes, very often), from the Child Behavior Checklist (CBCL) (Achenbach & Edelbrock, 1983) filled out by one or more teachers at each grade. The truancy variable was based on ratings for a single item, "skips school" (not true, sometimes true, often true), from the CBCL. The ratings were made by mothers in single-parent families and by both parents in intact families. For both variables, there was about a fivefold increase from grade 4 to grade 9; much of the growth occurred between grades 7 and 8. The key hypothesis is that the individuals who show growth in one form will also be at significant risk for growth in the other.

The results of the two-parameter LGM are summarized in Figure 3.3. The initial phases of the growth were characterized by a very high incidence of zero values. This violation of the assumption of normal distributed variables is a major cause for concern. Although the assumption of equal error variance could not be met, setting the error as proportional to variance proved successful. The probability value of .15 for the chi-square value of 34.59 (df = 27) showed an acceptable fit of the a priori model to the data set.

Only a few boys showed positive initial scores for the truancy and substance use constructs. As shown by the path coefficient of .34, there was a significant likelihood that these early starters were involved with deviant peers. The timing of the involvement with deviant peers seems to be critical, as evidenced by the path coefficient of .58 between early involvement (age 10) and later growth in the new forms of antisocial behavior: the earlier the onset, the greater the future growth. However, increasing involvement with deviant peers also contributed significantly to individual difference variance in growth. Note that the timing and the growth in deviant peer involvement made significant contributions of the same magnitude. Increased wandering also contributed significantly. Taken together, the information from the three covariates accounted for 54% of the variance in the slope factor.

Quantifying Qualitative Shifts

The behaviors that define the antisocial trait may serve as determinants for a host of new problems such as peer rejection, academic failure, and depressed mood. New forms (e.g., truancy, substance abuse, police arrest) are constantly being

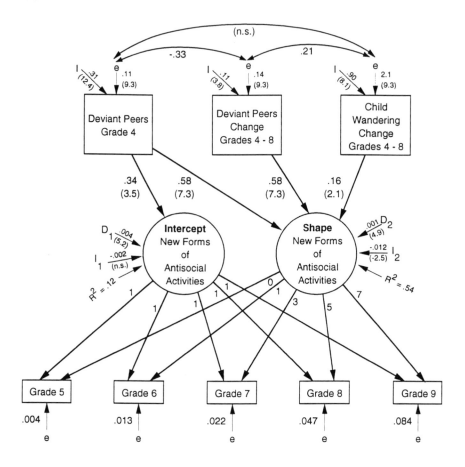

FIG. 3.3.   A growth model for changes in form.

added. This raises the question of whether these changes themselves form an orderly pattern of change over time. One way of thinking about this problem is to consider each qualitative change as contributing to a second-order deviancy factor that has the antisocial trait as its core. As each qualitatively new problem emerges and the prevalence becomes noticeable, it should appear as a newly significant factor loading on a second-order deviancy factor. At younger ages, indicators for qualitative shifts such as substance abuse and arrest would describe so few members of the sample that the factor loadings would be nonsignificant.

Repeated factor analyses at early and midadolescence should show that each qualitative shift eventually loads significantly on the second-order deviancy factor. Each addition is but a new branch of what is essentially the same thing.

By way of illustration, four qualitative shift variables from the OYS were each measured at three points in time. Two of the variables—antisocial behavior and academic failure—were latent constructs; the other two—police arrests and teacher ratings of substance use—were new forms. The findings for the data collected at grades 4, 6, and 8 are summarized in Figure 3.4. At each point in time, the antisocial construct serves as the core defining variable; the estimated factor loadings for waves 1 through 3 were 1.0, 1.0, and .89 respectively. Over time, the academic skills construct makes an increasing contribution to the deviancy factor; the loadings shifted from .32 at the beginning of the process to a substantial .43, and then .60. The other variables representing qualitative shifts (substance use and police arrest) also showed increased loadings on the deviancy factor. The data sets at all three points in time provide a good fit to the model, as shown by the nonsignificant chi-square values.

The findings demonstrate that the factor structure defining deviancy is altered

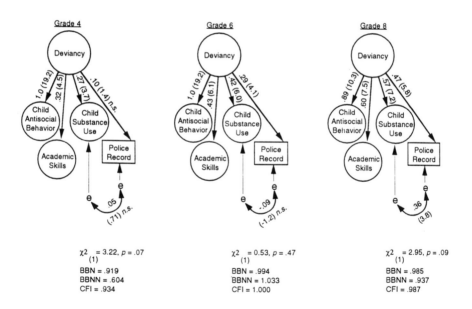

Listwise N = 185

FIG. 3.4. Changes in the structure of deviancy over time.

significantly between age 10 and age 17. However, the second-order factor analyses suggest that these qualitative changes represent a pattern of orderly change over time.

THE TRAIT AS A CHIMERA

The antisocial trait defines an interpersonal style that may maximize short-term gains but adds to long-term increases in misery (Patterson et al., 1992). An understanding of the trait requires both a short-term and a long-term perspective. The second-order deviancy factor is one means for expressing in quantitative terms the nature of some of these long-term changes and demonstrating that the changes are systematic.

The chimera metaphor implies that these qualitative changes are analogous to tissue grafts. The Greeks described the chimera as a fire-breathing creature that was part goat, part lion, and part snake. As shown in Figure 3.5, from a developmental perspective, the chimera begins as a goat and always retains its goatlike essence. This is analogous to seeing the antisocial trait as the underlying essence for the deviancy factor. Academic failure and peer rejection components constitute the addition of the lionesque countenance to what is essentially still a goat. By midadolescence, the additions of substance use and police arrest produce an aroused society and complete the conversion of a simple goat to a fire-breathing monster with the tail of a snake.

IMPLICATIONS

In summary, a developmental approach to the study of antisocial behavior requires not only longitudinal data and a theory but also a sensitive application of statistical analyses that consider intraindividual growth over time. The concept of growth must be expanded to include quantitative changes in mean level over time as well as qualitative changes generated by the same process. A trait is generalizable across time and across settings but, in a very real sense, it reflects an underlying dynamic process.

ACKNOWLEDGMENTS

I gratefully acknowledge the contribution of Grant No. MH 37940 from the Center for Studies of Antisocial and Violent Behavior, NIMH, U.S. PHS, in collecting and processing the longitudinal data sets for the OYS. I also wish to acknowledge the support from MH 46690 from the Prevention Research Branch, NIMH, U.S. PHS, which made possible much of the analyses.

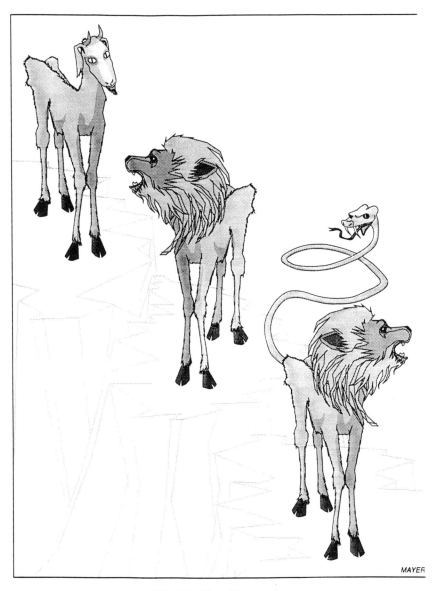

FIG. 3.5. The chimera effect.

I am very grateful for the exchanges with my colleagues Karen Yoerger and Mike Stoolmiller. Without those exchanges, this manuscript simply would not have come about. I wish to thank Beverly Fagot and Lew Bank for their critiques of an earlier version of the manuscript.

REFERENCES

Achenbach, T. M., & Edelbrock, C. S. (1983). *Manual for the child behavior checklist and the revised child behavior profile.* Burlington, VT: Thomas M. Achenbach.

Bentler, P. M. (1980). Multivariate analysis with latent variables: Causal modeling. *Annual Review of Psychology, 31,* 419–455.

Cairns, R. B., & Cairns, B. D. (1991). Social cognition and social networks: A developmental perspective. In D. J. Pepler & K. H. Rubin (Eds.), *The development and treatment of childhood aggression* (pp. 249–278). Hillsdale, NJ: Lawrence Erlbaum Associates.

Capaldi, D. M., & Patterson, G. R. (1987). An approach to the problem of recruitment and retention rates for longitudinal research. *Behavioral Assessment, 9,* 169–177.

Capaldi, D. M., & Patterson, G. R. (1989). *Psychometric properties of fourteen latent constructs from the Oregon youth study.* New York: Springer-Verlag.

Coie, J. D., & Kupersmidt, J. B. (1983). A behavioral analysis of emerging social status in boys' groups. *Child Development, 54,* 1400–1416.

Collins, L. M., & Horn, J. L. (1991). *Best methods for the analysis of change.* Washington, DC: American Psychological Association.

Conger, R. D., Patterson, G. R., & Gé, X. (1995). It takes two to replicate: A mediational model for the impact of parents' stress on adolescent adjustment. *Child Development, 66,* 80–97.

Dishion, T. J., Patterson, G. R., & Kavanagh, K. A. (1992). An experimental test of the coercion model: Linking theory, measurement, and intervention. In J. McCord & R. Tremblay (Eds.), *The interaction of theory and practice: Experimental studies of intervention* (pp. 253–282). New York: Guilford.

Eddy, J. M., Heyman, R. E., & Weiss, R. L. (1991). An empirical evaluation of the dyadic adjustment scale: Exploring the differences between marital "satisfaction" and "adjustment." *Behavioral Assessment, 13,* 199–220.

Farrington, D. (1986). What have we learned from major longitudinal surveys? In D. P. Farrington, L. E. Ohlin, & J. Q. Wilson (Eds.), *Understanding and controlling crime: Towards a new researching strategy.* New York: Springer-Verlag.

Farrington, D. P., & Hawkins, J. D. (1991). Predicting participation, early onset, and later persistence in officially recorded offending. *Criminal Behaviour and Mental Health, 1,* 1–33.

Forgatch, M. S. (1991). The clinical science vortex: A developing theory of antisocial behavior. In D. Pepler & K. H. Rubin (Eds.), *The development and treatment of childhood aggression* (pp. 291–315). Hillsdale, NJ: Lawrence Erlbaum Associates.

Gollob, H. F., & Reichardt, C. S. (1987). Taking account of time lags in causal models. *Child Development, 58,* 80–92.

Nesselroade, J. R., & Baltes, P. B. (Eds.). (1979). *Longitudinal research in the study of behavior and development.* New York: Academic Press.

Olweus, D. (1979). Stability of aggressive reaction patterns in males: A review. *Psychological Bulletin, 86,* 852–875.

Patterson, G. R. (1988). Family process: Loops, levels, and linkages. In N. Bolger, A. Caspi, G. Downey, & M. Moorehouse (Eds.), *Persons in context: Developmental processes* (pp. 114–151). Cambridge, MA: Cambridge University Press.

Patterson, G. R. (1992). Developmental changes in antisocial behavior. In R. D. Peters, R. J.

McMahon, & V. L. Quinsey (Eds.), *Aggression and violence throughout the life span* (pp. 52–82). Newbury Park, CA: Sage.

Patterson, G. R., & Bank, L. (1987). When is a nomological network a construct? In D. R. Peterson & D. B. Fishman (Eds.), *Assessment for decision* (pp. 249–279). New Brunswick, NJ: Rutgers University Press.

Patterson, G. R., & Bank, L. (1989). Some amplifying mechanisms for pathologic processes in families. In M. R. Gunner & E. Thelen (Eds.), *Systems and development: The Minnesota Symposia on Child Psychology* (vol. 22, pp. 167–209). Hillsdale, NJ: Lawrence Erlbaum Associates.

Patterson, G. R., & Capaldi, D. M. (1990). A mediational model for boys' depressed mood. In J. Rolf, A. S. Masten, D. Cicchetti, K. H. Nuechterlein, & S. Weintraub (Eds.), *Risk and protective factors in the development of psychopathology* (pp. 141–163). Cambridge: Press Syndicate of the University of Cambridge.

Patterson, G. R., Crosby, L., & Vuchinich, S. (1992). Predicting risk for early police arrest. *Journal of Quantitative Criminology, 8,* 335–355.

Patterson, G. R., DeBaryshe, B. D., & Ramsey, E. (1989). A developmental perspective on antisocial behavior. *American Psychologist, 44,* 329–335.

Patterson, G. R., Reid, J. B., & Dishion, T. J. (1992). *A social learning approach: IV. Antisocial boys.* Eugene, OR: Castalia.

Patterson, G. R., & Stoolmiller, M. (1991). Replications of a dual failure model for boys' depressed mood. *Journal of Consulting and Clinical Psychology, 59,* 491–498.

Patterson, G. R., & Yoerger, K. (1993). Developmental models for delinquent behavior. In S. Hodgins (Ed.), *Crime and mental disorder* (pp. 140–172). Newbury Park, CA: Sage.

Rogosa, D. (1979). Causal models in longitudinal research: Rationale, formulation, and interpretation. In J. R. Nesselroade & P. B. Baltes (Eds.), *Longitudinal research in the study of behavior and development* (pp. 263–301). New York: Academic.

Rogosa, D. R., & Willett, J. B. (1985). Understanding correlates of change by modeling individual differences in growth. *Psychometrika, 50,* 203–228.

Stoolmiller, M. (1990). *Latent growth model analysis of the relation between antisocial behavior and wandering.* Unpublished doctoral dissertation, University of Oregon, Eugene.

Stoolmiller, M., & Patterson, G. R. (1995). *Predicting the onset and frequency of official offending for male delinquents.* Unpublished manuscript available from Oregon Social Learning Center, Eugene, OR.

Stoolmiller, M., & Bank, L. (in press). Autoregressive effects in structural equation models: We see some problems. In J. Gottman & G. Sackett (Eds.), *The analysis of change.* Hillsdale, NJ: Lawrence Erlbaum Associates.

Sullivan, J. L. (1974). Multiple indicators: Some criteria of selection. In H. M. Blalock (Ed.), *Measurement in the social sciences* (pp. 93–156). Chicago: Aldine.

4

Using Latent Growth Curve Models to Study Developmental Processes

Mike Stoolmiller
Oregon Social Learning Center

In this chapter Stoolmiller tells us how to use commercially available structural equations software packages to estimate latent growth curve models for the analysis of repeated measures. He discusses the interpretation of model parameters with the two-points-in-time model. Various special cases are discussed, and an illustration is presented of the growth in intelligence scores.

—Editor

The analysis of change over time has been the subject of ongoing debate in the social sciences. Some writers (e.g., Rogosa, Brandt, & Zimowski, 1982; Rogosa & Willet, 1985b) have strongly advocated growth curve methodology as the best way to study change. Others (e.g., Gollob & Reichardt, 1987; Kessler & Greenberg, 1981; Maccoby & Martin, 1983) have advocated using autoregressive panel models to analyze change. In this chapter we briefly discuss some of the issues surrounding the use of growth curve (GC) and latent growth curve (LGC) methodology to study change. Estimation of GC models is demonstrated using commercially available structural equation software such as LISREL (Jöreskog & Sörbom, 1989) and EQS (Bentler, 1989).

The intended audience of this chapter is applied researchers with some knowledge of structural equation modeling (SEM) techniques and a basic understanding of regression methodology. Mathematically sophisticated readers may want to study more advanced treatments of this subject, such as Meredith and Tisak (1990) or Tisak and Meredith (1990). The development here will draw heavily from the above-mentioned sources, but the presentation will be much less technical. Although many important ideas here are expressed mathematically, they are stated nonmathematically. In this way, readers without detailed knowledge of the statistical theory or matrix algebra of SEM techniques will not be at a disadvantage in terms of grasping the overall concepts of GC methodology.

It is our hope that we stimulate the substantive application of GC models to psychological phenomena. We believe the study of individual GCs in one form or another can only lead to a greater understanding of how developmental processes unfold over time and of what variables influence the course of development. For more discussion of this and other philosophical perspectives on development and their implications for the study of GCs, see Burchinal and Appelbaum (1991).

GC methodology is not new, nor is its application confined to the social sciences. One of the earliest demonstrations of the usefulness of the statistical modeling of GC's was Wishart's (1934) study of weight gain in bacon pigs. Rao (1958) and Tucker (1958) were perhaps the first to suggest that factor-analytic techniques could be used to develop statistical models for individual GCs. An early application was Scher, Young, and Meredith's (1960) factor analysis of electrocardiograms. More recently, Meredith and Tisak (1990) and Tisak and Meredith (1990) have demonstrated the analysis of individual GCs using currently available SEM programs. They have termed this approach *latent growth curve analysis*. McArdle (1988) and McArdle and Epstein (1987) have applied LGC models to study growth in intelligence test scores.

As motivation for the study of GC methodology, consider the suggestion that the study of the repeated measures describing a single individual's trajectory over time are the proper focus of a developmental model (Baltes & Nesselroade, 1979; Rogosa, Brandt, & Zimowski, 1982; Rogosa & Willet, 1985b). To follow this suggestion, we need a model that somehow captures individual differences in these trajectories over time. For example, if the developmental process plotted against time produced a collection of straight lines for a sample of individuals, we would want our developmental model to reflect individual differences in the slopes (amount of vertical change per unit horizontal change) and intercepts (point where the line intercepts the vertical axis) of those lines. We then want to be able to study predictors of those individual differences, in slope for example, to answer questions about which variables exert important effects on the rate of development.

At the same time, we want our model to capture the important group statistics in a way that allows us to study development at the group level. For example, we might want to know what sort of trend best describes the group means over time.

Finally, we want our model to be flexible enough to allow us to examine and compare multiple populations, and to incorporate multiple method or informant measurement strategies to allow corrections for measurement error.

LGC models meet all of the above criteria. Statistical tests on overall model fit and the significance of individual model parameters are available if the measured variables are multinormally distributed (Tisak & Meredith, 1990).

Clearly, a fundamental assumption of GC methodology is that change for each individual on the phenomena under study is systematically related to the passage of time. If change is only weakly or not at all systematically related to the passage of time, studying individual trajectories over time will not be very informative. In this case, a repeated-measures regression approach such as the generalized estimating equations framework of Zeger and Liang (1986) might be more useful. Evaluating the extent to which a particular growth model is capable of describing the observed pattern of change with respect to time is an important part of growth model testing. This includes evaluating the possibility that, although change may be occurring, it is not systematically related to the passage of time.

LGC METHODOLOGY, MEASUREMENT, AND DESIGN ISSUES

In order to study growth at the individual level, it is important that the measurement and scaling processes produce scores in which individual change is meaningful. Scores that are assumed to be measured on at least an interval-level scale are required. If the measurement process does not meet this requirement, for whatever reason, then LGC methodology is probably not appropriate. For example, measuring height or weight over time for growing children would produce scores appropriate for LGC. The meaningfulness of individual change on simple physical measurements is rarely an issue. With more abstract psychological constructions, however, this is not so true.

Consider, for example, growth in intelligence test scores over time for children. If we thought the process of measuring intelligence produced scores for which it made sense to talk about individual change over time in units of intelligence, then LGC methodology would be appropriate. If we thought the intelligence test scores were only useful to rank order a given sample of children from highest to lowest, then it becomes far less clear how to proceed. One strategy employed by McArdle and Epstein (1987) in modeling intelligence test scores was simply to count the number of questions the child correctly answered at each point in time, and model growth in percent correct responses. See Burchinal and Appelbaum (1991) for more discussion of this issue.

Scaling details are also important when using LGC methodology. First of all, it is important that the repeated measures over time are kept in their raw metric. Because this represents a departure from usual path analytic or SEM techniques, it merits some additional discussion.

Repeated measures ANOVAs are basically a special case of LGC (Meredith & Tisak, 1990). Therefore, the two methods share the same requirements concerning the appropriate types of data.

If the variables being studied are scale scores (i.e., composites made up of multiple items), then care should be taken in constructing the total scale score to preserve the raw metric. The scale score should be computed in the same fashion at each point in time. Experienced users of SEM may feel that this is very restrictive, but in order to talk meaningfully about growth it is important that changes in the scale scores under study are actually due to growth and not to changes in scaling procedures.

Another practice with multitrait and multiagent assessment batteries that is less than optimal when studying growth is standardizing items before computing scale scores. This procedure has the attraction of equalizing the variances of all the items and ensures that the contribution of each item to the total variance of the scale score is not affected by arbitrary scaling differences across items. Unfortunately, it also has the effect of artificially stabilizing the scale-score variances over time. This amounts to throwing away valuable information about the nature of development. If items are not standardized prior to combining them into scale scores, however, the scaling of items across informants and measurement instruments becomes an important consideration.

If all of the items are measured on the same scale (say, for example, five-point Likert scales), the problem is minimal. But if the items are mixtures of dichotomous items, three-point scales, five-point scales, etc., it becomes far less clear how to combine into one scale score. One way of proceeding in this case would be to recode the items so they all have zero for a lower anchor point, then multiply or divide each scale by an appropriate constant so all the scales have the same numerical upper anchor point. Good planning prior to data collection can save a lot of work and data analysis headaches when using LGC methodology.

Another important issue is the number and spacing of assessment points. It is difficult to give general advice because knowing something about the phenomena under study is crucial to making good decisions about the number and spacing of assessments. Another important consideration is which research questions will be addressed. If the questions focus on the form of growth over time, then, in general, more points will be necessary than if the focus is on predictors of rates of change or on amount of change (D. Rogosa, personal communication, May 24, 1991), but see also Rogosa and Willet (1985b) for potential pitfalls of studying amount of change versus rates of change. Rogosa (personal communication, May 24, 1991) has suggested as a rough rule of thumb that four to five points will allow the researcher to determine if growth is straight line during an interval. More complicated curvilinear forms would require more assessments. This is an area of GC methodology that needs further development.

The last issue considered here is missing data. The application of SEM programs to estimate LGC models depends on data, at least ideally, that are obtained when all subjects are observed at about the same time and when the number and spacing of assessment times are the same for all subjects. Longitudinal panel data are typical of this sort of design. Ware (1985) refers to these kinds of data as *balanced on time*. This requirement is actually no different than standard SEM techniques for panel models. The most common way of dealing with missing data within this format is to use only those subjects for whom complete data are available (i.e., listwise deletion). For a more complete discussion of the issue of missing data within SEM, see Bollen (1989). If the time of assessment, the number of time points, and the spacing between time points vary across individuals, other GC techniques are available. See, for example, Hui and Berger (1983), Kleinbaum (1973), or Bryk and Raudenbush (1987). If the data are missing by design, as in a cohort sequential design, see McArdle and Anderson (1989).

LATENT GROWTH CURVE MODELS FOR LINEAR GROWTH

The simplest LGC model to begin studying is for straight-line growth. The observed, raw data corresponding to a straight-line LGC is a collection of approximately straight lines, one for each subject measured at, say, four evenly spaced points in time. An example of such raw data is shown in Figure 4.1 for some variable of interest, say v. Because straight lines are completely characterized by a slope and an intercept, our LGC model will need to capture individual differences in slopes and intercepts. Our strategy will be to set up a model in which two latent factors will capture these individual differences. We can extend the model by adding other fixed-in-time variables or other GCs. This allows us to test hypotheses about which individuals grow the fastest, whether individual differences in growth rates on one variable are significantly related to individual differences in growth rates on another variable, or both.

The simple straight-line LGC model with one fixed-in-time covariate is shown in diagrammatic form in Figure 4.2, using Bentler's (1989) notation.

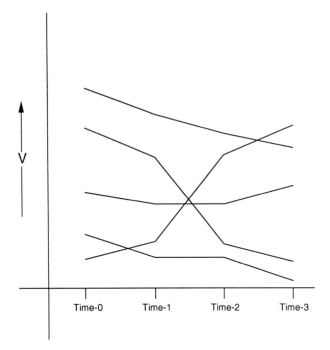

FIG. 4.1. Example growth curves for four individuals across four points in time.

Latent variables are shown by circles and measured variables by squares. Double-headed arrows signify covariances between variables, and single-headed arrows signify regression paths. The weights for the regression of the observed variables on the latent factors, the Ls, are referred to as *loadings*.

In standard SEM models, the es and ds are usually deviation-from-predicted-value variables; hence, the variance of the es and ds usually represents regression residual or error variance. By convention, the es are usually associated with the vs, which are the measured variables, and the ds are usually associated with the fs, which are the latent factors.

The Is are a new parameter. In our simple LGC, they represent the means of the latent factors. We go into more detail on new parameters and new interpretations after previewing the entire model.

In Figure 4.2, the first factor (f_1) is labeled the *intercept*. The intercept is the starting point for the growth of any given individual and makes a constant contribution to the scores on the observed variables across time, hence, the 1s for factor loadings on the repeated measures. The mean, I_1, and variance, $\text{var}(d_1)$, of the intercept factor across the whole sample can be estimated from the data.

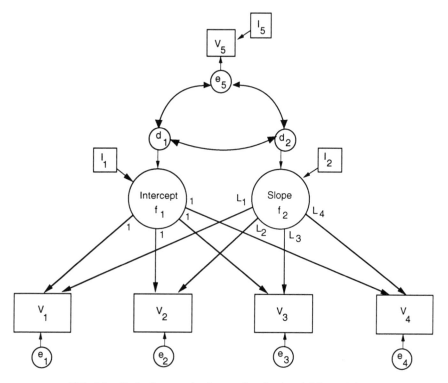

FIG. 4.2.   Path diagram for four-points-in-time LGC model.

The second factor (f_2, labeled *slope*) represents the slope of an individual's trajectory, which in this case is simply the slope of the straight line determined by the repeated measures. The slope factor loadings are fixed at 0, 1, 2 and 3 to represent straight-line growth over four evenly spaced time intervals. The slope factor has a mean, I_2, and variance, var(d_2), across the whole sample; like the intercept mean and variance, the slope factor mean and variance can be estimated from the data. The slope and intercept factors are allowed to covary; the double-headed arrow between d_1 and d_2 represents this covariance, which can also be estimated from the data.

The variances of the error variables, e_1 through e_4, represent variance not accounted for by the growth factors that could be due to systematic, time-specific influences or more random measurement error. The variances of e_1 through e_4 can also be estimated.

Finally, a fixed-in-time, observed covariate, v_5, is shown with a mean, I_5, a variance, var(e_5), and covarying with both the intercept factor and the slope factor, all of which can be estimated from the data. We turn now to more details on new parameters and new interpretations for standard parameters.

Using SEM programs to model GCs depends on incorporating means into the standard SEM model. Generalization of SEM to include means is discussed in Bentler (1989), Jöreskog and Sörbom (1989), and Sörbom (1974). Our development will draw heavily from Bentler (1989). Incorporating means in the standard SEM model introduces some new parameters and additional interpretations for some of the more standard parameters.

Figure 4.2 shows that the latent factor scores, f_1 and f_2, can be expressed as an additive combination of the factor means, I_1 and I_2, and the latent deviation variables, d_1 and d_2. In this case, d_1 and d_2 are really latent deviation-from-the-mean variables. This implies that the variances of d_1 and d_2 are actually the variances of the intercept and slope factors, respectively. Using equations, we are saying $f_1 = I_1 + d_1$ and $f_2 = I_2 + d_2$. To make this concrete, say a subject has a latent slope score, f_2, of 3, and the mean of f_2 is equal to 1. In this case, the deviation-from-the-mean score is 2 and the full equation is $f_2 = 1 + 2 = 3$. We note by way of contrast that in traditional SEM, the means of the factor scores are assumed to be zero, leaving only the deviation-from-the-mean score.

An equivalent expression for the factor scores is $f_1 = 1I_1 + d_1$ and $f_2 = 1I_2 + d_2$. The 1s in the equations are just constant variables, variables for which all individuals get the score 1. In other words, the Is can be thought of as latent factor means or as the beta weights for the regression of the latent factors on the constant variable 1. For notational convenience, we will usually suppress the 1 and just use I to represent the regression of a variable on the constant 1. This same line of reasoning can also be applied to measured variables such as v_5 in Figure 4.2, but now $v_5 = I_5 + e_5$. I_5 is the mean of v_5, and e_5 is the deviation-from-the-mean variable, implying that the variance of e_5 is the variance of v_5.

Thinking of the I term as representing the regression of a variable on the constant 1 is not always standard practice, but within the SEM format it has the advantage of allowing incorporation of means into the model regardless of whether the particular software package is set up to deal with structured means. In addition to Bentler (1989), McArdle (1988) and McArdle and Epstein (1987) have employed the use of the constant 1 to incorporate means into LGC models.

In particular, when the only predictor in a regression equation is the constant 1, the beta weight for 1 is equal to the mean of the dependent variable, what we are calling I. The variance of the deviation-from-the-mean variable, what we are calling d or e, is just the variance of the dependent variable. This is not true in general, however, and when additional predictor variables are in the equation these three parameters have different interpretations.

In this case, the d or e variable is more generally a deviation-from-predicted-value variable, sometimes referred to as a disturbance term, and represents unexplained or residual variation. The I term is usually called the regression intercept or constant, and could be thought of as representing that part of the dependent variable mean that is not explained by the predictor variables. We refer to I as a regression constant or mean to avoid confusion with factor scores that represent the collection of intercepts from the LGCs in our sample.

Turning now to details on the factor loadings, consider the equations for the measured variables, vs, implied by the model shown in Figure 4.2 for the ith individual. Further, assume that for individual i, their latent intercept score, f_1, is 2, their latent slope score, f_2, is 3, and their latent time-specific scores, e_1 through e_4 are all equal to 0.

$$v_{1i} = 1f_{1i} + 0f_{2i} + e_{1i} = 2 + 0 + 0 = 2,$$
$$v_{2i} = 1f_{1i} + 1f_{2i} + e_{2i} = 2 + 3 + 0 = 5,$$
$$v_{3i} = 1f_{1i} + 2f_{2i} + e_{3i} = 2 + 6 + 0 = 8,$$
$$v_{4i} = 1f_{1i} + 3f_{2i} + e_{4i} = 2 + 9 + 0 = 11.$$

Notice that the equations for individual i imply a straight-line trajectory, which in slope-intercept notation is given by $y = 3x + 2$. It is also apparent that the intercept factor is equivalent to v_1 when there is no time-specific error at time 1 and when the first factor loading on the slope factor is fixed at 0. In general, the factor loadings play three important roles. First, they determine the form of growth. For example, squaring the loadings on the slope factor would produce quadratic-shaped trajectories. Second, they control the scaling of the individual differences on both factors. For example, doubling the factor loadings on both factors would require halving the factor scores for individual i in order to obtain the same values for the vs. Third, they define the intercept factor. In the above example, by fixing the first factor loading to zero, the intercept was defined to be equal to v_1. Some other pattern of loadings on the slope factor that still produces straight-line growth (e.g., 1, 2, 3, 4 or 3, 2, 1, 0) would completely redefine the intercept factor. We will clarify how this happens shortly.

Finally, to complete the model, we will make several more, standard assumptions: the means of the error variables, the e and d variables, are all zero; the e and d variables have a joint multivariate normal distribution; the constant 1 variable has a mean of 1, a variance arbitrarily set to 1, and a covariance of zero with the e and d variables. Since the observed variables are linear combinations of the e and d variables, they will also have a joint multivariate normal distribution, and the use of normal theory maximum likelihood estimation procedures is justified.

Before estimation of model parameters can proceed, however, we must show that the model is identified. Identification of parameters in SEM is a complicated issue; readers should refer to Bollen (1989) for more details. For two-factor models such as our straight-line LGC with fixed 1s as factor loadings on the intercept factor, one way of identifying the model is to fix at least two factor loadings on the slope factor to two different values (McArdle, 1988; Meredith & Tisak, 1990). In our example with all slope factor loadings fixed, we achieve overidentified status. The model has 13 estimated parameters as it is shown. We have $p(p + 3)/2 = 20$ (where $p = 5$ is the number of variables) pieces of information with which to estimate the model (10 covariances, 5 variances, and 5 means). Before we actually estimate the model, we turn to some algebraic details to clarify how the interpretation of estimated model parameters depends on the way the model is set up or parameterized.

To simplify matters algebraically, we present equations only for the two-points-in-time, just-identified, straight-line LGC model. This model is easily obtained from the model in Figure 4.2 by dropping v_3 and v_4. Readers should keep in mind that with more time points, the relations we demonstrate still hold, but the model is overidentified (i.e., there is more than one way to solve for some model parameters). Notationally, we use the expectation, variance, and covariance operators (symbolized E, *var*, and *cov* respectively). For readers unfamiliar with these operators, they can be thought of as roughly equivalent to the mean, variance, and covariance, respectively, that might be computed on collected data. In this case, the operators are being applied to hypothetical random variables instead of actual collected data. The operators have algebraic rules governing their application to linear combinations of random variables that can be found in most statistics texts (e.g., Kirk, 1982). We use these algebraic rules to generate expressions that help in the interpretation of model parameters.

In all of the equations that follow for the two-points-in-time LGC model, the error variables, e_1 and e_2, are assumed to be fixed. In the simplest case, if errors of measurement were thought to be negligible, e_1 and e_2 could be set to zero. Alternatively, a reliability estimate from prior research could be used to set the values of the error terms. In addition, the intercept factor loadings are not shown in the equations because they are assumed to be fixed to 1. With e_1, e_2, and all the factor loadings fixed, the two-points-in-time model is just identified. We note that this model is equivalent to the *improved-difference-score model* of Rogosa et al. (1982).

The usual purpose of mean and covariance structure models is to reproduce the actual observed means and covariances as closely as possible with the model parameters. Equations 4.1 through 4.9 in Appendix A show how the observed means, variances, and covariances are a function of the fixed and freely estimated model parameters. Equations 4.10 through 4.18 show how the freely estimated model parameters are a function of the observed means, variances, covariances, and the fixed model parameters. Equations 4.19 through 4.27 are derived from Equations 4.10 through 4.18 and represent the simplifications that result when the factor loadings on the slope factor are fixed. In this case, L_1 is set equal to 0 and L_2 is set equal to 1. We suggest readers begin with the description of the third set and save the first two sets for later reference.

Equation 4.19 indicates that the mean of the intercept factor is just the mean of v_1 or the mean of initial status on v_5. Equation 4.20 shows the mean of the slope factor is the mean of the difference scores, $v_2 - v_1$. Equation 4.21 indicates that the mean of v_5 is simply I_5. Equation 4.22 shows that variance of the intercept factor is the true-score variance of initial status on v. Equation 4.23 indicates that the variance of the slope factor is the true-difference-score variance. Equation 4.24 shows that the variance of v_5 is simply the variance of e_5. Equation 4.25 shows that the covariance between the slope and intercept factors is just the covariance between true initial status and true change. Equation 4.26 indicates that the covariance of v_5 with f_1 is just the covariance of v_5 with initial status on v. Finally, Equation 4.27 shows that the covariance of v_5 with f_2 is just the covariance of v_5 with change on v from time 1 to time 2.

Equations Set 3 $(L_1 = 0, L_2 = 1)$

$$I_1 = E(f_1) = E(v_1), \tag{4.19}$$

$$I_2 = E(f_2) = E(v_2 - v_1) = E(v_2) - E(v_1), \tag{4.20}$$

$$I_5 = E(v_5), \tag{4.21}$$

$$\text{var}(d_1) = \text{var}(f_1) = \text{var}(v_1) - \text{var}(e_1), \tag{4.22}$$

$$\text{var}(d_2) = \text{var}(f_2) = \text{var}(v_1) - \text{var}(e_1) + \text{var}(v_2)$$
$$- \text{var}(e_2) - 2\,\text{cov}(v_1, v_2), \tag{4.23}$$

$$\text{var}(e_5) = \text{var}(v_5), \tag{4.24}$$

$$\text{cov}(d_1, d_2) = \text{cov}(f_1, f_2) = \text{cov}(v_1, v_2) - [\text{var}(v_1) - \text{var}(e_1)], \tag{4.25}$$

$$\text{cov}(d_1, e_5) = \text{cov}(f_1, v_5) = \text{cov}(v_1, v_5), \tag{4.26}$$

$$\text{cov}(d_2, e_5) = \text{cov}(f_2, v_5) = \text{cov}(v_2, v_5) - \text{cov}(v_1, v_5). \tag{4.27}$$

Given the basic LGM equations, we can explore the effects of choosing different values for fixed factor loadings on the slope. First of all, notice in Appendix A in Equations 4.11, 4.14, and 4.18—equations for the slope factor mean, variance, and covariance with v_5—that the slope factor loadings appear only in the denominators, not in the numerators of the expressions. This implies that for different choices of L_1 and L_2 we are just rescaling these parameters by a fixed amount, $L_2 - L_1$. This rescaling by constants does not alter the fundamental meaning or interpretation of the parameters or any of the significance tests on these parameters.

However, in Equations 4.10, 4.13, and 4.17—equations for the intercept factor mean, variance and covariance with v_5—the slope factor loadings appear in the numerators and denominators. Different choices of L_1 and L_2 affect the fundamental meaning, interpretation, and significance tests of these parameters. One way to think about the difference in invariance to choice of factor loadings between the slope and intercept factors is to consider the fact that for any given straight line, the slope is invariant to shifting the coordinate system by a fixed amount horizontally, while the intercept is, in general, not. In this case, picking different values for L_1 and L_2 is equivalent to horizontal shifts of the time axis and can result in a different intercept for any individual GC. This implies that for horizontal shifts of the time axis, the collection of intercepts can also have a different mean, variance, and rank order of highest to lowest, which would affect the value of the covariance of the intercept with predictor variables such as v_5. To see this more concretely, look at Figure 4.1 and notice, as you move horizontally, that for any given cross section the mean, the spread (variance), and the rank order of the data are changing.

If we choose $L_1 = -1$ and $L_2 = 0$, representing a shift of the horizontal time axis backward, the intercept factor now becomes equivalent to the time-2 measure of v, corrected for measurement error. If we choose $L_1 = 1$ and $L_2 = 2$, representing a shift of the horizontal time axis forward, the intercept factor becomes equivalent to v at one time unit before time 1, call it time 0, corrected for measurement error. This basically represents an extrapolation of the individual GCs backwards in time.

The last set of factor loadings we will consider are obtained from orthogonal polynomial contrast coefficients. In this case, $L_1 = -1$ and $L_2 = 1$. The intercept factor is now equivalent to the average across time of v_1 and v_2, corrected for measurement error. The slope factor is scaled by $L_2 - L_1 = 2$, making it half the value in all the previous examples. In this chapter we only consider models in which the intercept factor is equivalent to initial status on v (labeled *initial status* models) or the average over time of v (labeled *time-averaged* models). We do this primarily because of the ease of interpreting model parameters under these two conditions. In general, the orthogonal polynomial coefficients that are usually tabled in statistics texts (e.g., Kirk, 1982) are given in terms of whole numbers. These coefficients have the property that (a) for an even number of time points, the slope factor would be half the value obtained in an *initial status* model, and (b) for an odd number of points the two slope factors are the same. The reason for this is because, for even numbers of points, the coefficients for the straight-line trend for any two consecutive points in time differ by 2, whereas for odd numbers of points they differ by 1, the same as in an *initial status* model.

The last set of parameters to consider under different choices of factor loadings are the error terms for the measured variables, the e variables. Obviously, in the two-points-in-time model, the e variables are invariant because they are fixed. In the four-points-in time model, however, the e variables can be estimated from the data. For the straight-line LGC, the e variables are completely invariant to the choice of fixed factor loadings. Regardless of whether the model is *initial status* or *time averaged,* the error terms will converge to the same value.

Over all, *time-averaged* and *initial status* straight-line models are equivalent in the sense that they have the same degrees of freedom and the same chi-square, and the parameters from one model have a one-to-one relation with the parameters from the other model (Jöreskog & Sörbom, 1989; Stelzl, 1986). We will have more to say about the relation between the two types of models when we discuss higher-order polynomial models.

In summary, for a straight-line LGC model, the error terms are completely invariant to choice of factor loadings, the slope factor is invariant up to a constant determined by the fixed values of the loadings, and the meaning and interpretation of the intercept factor is completely dependent on the fixed values for factor loadings. We turn now to an example application.

THE STRAIGHT-LINE LGC MODEL FOR WISC SCORES

The data we use to demonstrate a straight-line LGC model were published by McArdle (1988) and McArdle and Epstein (1987). They presented an interesting LGC analysis of Wechsler Intelligence Scale for Children (WISC) (Wechsler, 1974) scores for 204 children from a longitudinal study carried out by Osborne between 1961 and 1965 (Osborne & Suddick, 1972). The WISC scores represent a percent correct of all the items that the child could have been presented with from eight different subscales: (a) information, (b) comprehension, (c) similarities, (d) vocabulary, (e) picture completion, (f) block design, (g) picture arrangement, and (h) object assembly (see McArdle & Epstein, 1987, for more details on the scaling of WISC scores).

The input data consists of the means, standard deviations, and correlation matrices for the four WISC scores and mother education (see Table 4.1). Skewness and kurtosis values are also shown. The data do not appear to violate the multinormality assumption, although lack of univariate skewness and kurtosis are necessary, but not sufficient, for demonstrating multivariate normality. Estimation was carried out by EQS (Bentler, 1989).

Figure 4.3 shows the results for both *initial status* and *time-averaged* versions of the model, with the *time-averaged* parameters shown below the *initial status* parameters when they are different. Starting with overall measures of fit, it can

TABLE 4.1
Means, Standard Deviations, Skewness, Kurtosis, and Correlations
for WISC Scores and Mother Education ($N = 204$)

	WISC-1	WISC-2	WISC-3	WISC-4	Mother Education
WISC-1	1.000				
WISC-2	.809	1.000			
WISC-3	.806	.850	1.000		
WISC-4	.765	.831	.867	1.000	
Mother Educ.	.520	.531	.448	.458	1.000
Mean	18.034	25.819	36.255	46.593	10.810
Std. dev.	6.374	7.319	7.796	10.386	2.700
Skewness	.176	.287	.151	−.049	—
Kurtosis	−.367	−.587	−.087	−.217	—

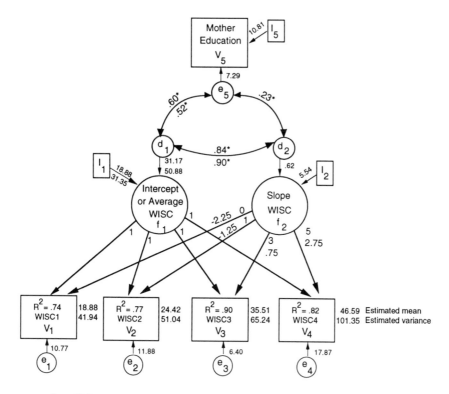

FIG. 4.3.   Linear initial status and time-averaged LGC models.

be seen by the chi-square test that the model does not fit: $\chi^2 = 69.67$ (df = 7); $p < .001$. The Bentler-Bonnet normed-fit index (bbn) and the comparative-fit index (cfi) are .922 and .929 respectively, which indicates a substantial improvement over the independence null model that postulates a set of uncorrelated variables (Bentler, 1989).

Looking at the model parameters in the *initial status* model, the fixed factor loadings represent straight-line growth over uneven measurement intervals starting from the first time point. In the *time-averaged* model, the fixed loadings represent orthogonal polynomial contrast coefficients for unevenly spaced intervals, with the loadings on the slope factor rescaled by 2 to match the *initial status* slope factor. See Appendix A for details on obtaining orthogonal contract coefficients for uneven time metrics. For the *initial status* model, the intercept factor represents true individual differences in WISC scores at time 1 and has a mean of 18.88 and a variance of 31.17. For the *time-averaged* model, the intercept factor represents true individual differences in average WISC scores over time and has a mean of 31.35 and a variance of 50.88. The slope factor mean and variance for both models are 5.54 and .62 respectively, substantially smaller than the corresponding parameters for the intercept factor in either model.

The error variances are the same for both models. The time-1 value is 10.77 and the estimated variance of v_1 is 41.94, meaning that the LGC factors explain about 74% of the variance of the time-1 WISC scores. Either model explains about 77%, 90%, and 82% of the estimated variances of the time-2, -3, and -4 WISC scores respectively. The percentages of variance explained by the model are relatively high and indicate that straight lines do well in terms of reproducing the observed GCs. We note that it is entirely possible to have a model that fits the data well by the chi-square test, but the size of the error terms indicates that most of the observed variance is either time specific, measurement error, or a combination of the two. In this case, LGC may not be appropriate and the repeated-measures regression approach of Zeger and Liang (1986) might be considered as an alternative.

Turning now to the correlations among the growth factors and mother education, Figure 4.3 shows that mother education is more highly related to initial status ($r = .60$) and to average value over time ($r = .52$) than to growth rate ($r = .23$). Both initial status and average value over time are highly related to growth rate: $r = .84$, and $r = .90$ respectively. Notice that the correlation of the slope factor with mother education is the same in both models. We can easily convert these correlations to regression weights to facilitate interpretation. The raw beta for the regression of the intercept factor in the *initial status* model on mother education is 1.24, measuring that, on the average, an increase of one year of mother education is associated with an increase of 1.24 percentage points on the initial WISC score. Mother education accounts for about 36% of the true variance in initial status on WISC scores. The raw beta for the regression of the intercept factor in the *time-averaged* model on mother education is 1.37, meaning that on the average, an increase of one year of mother education is associated with an increase of 1.37 percentage points on the average across-time WISC score. Mother education accounts for about 27% of the true variance in average-over-time WISC scores. The raw beta for the slope factor in either model is .07 (i.e., on the average, an increase of one year of mother education is associated with an increase of .07 percentage point in the rate of change of WISC scores). As can be seen from this simple example, some care must be taken in choosing fixed slope loadings if interpretation of the raw beta weights is important. Mother education accounts for about 5% of the true variance in growth rates of WISC scores for either model. Of the three GC parameters—initial status, average over time, and growth rate—initial status and average over time make the largest contributions to overall differences in WISC scores during this interval. In other words, there is only a weak tendency for children of more highly educated mothers to grow faster, but there is a rather strong tendency for them to begin their growth at a higher level and have higher across-time average WISC scores.

The straight-line LGC model did not fit the data by the chi-square test. The fit improvement indices suggest that significant improvement in fit would result if the slope factor loadings for the WISC at times 3 and 4 were freed. We turn now to exploring this *unspecified* model.

THE UNSPECIFIED TWO-FACTOR LGC MODEL
FOR WISC SCORES

Perhaps the best way to understand the unspecified two-factor model is to consider first generalizing the straight-line two-factor model. One way is by fixing the time-3 and time-4 slope factor loadings to values that reflect something other than a straight-line GC. In other words, if straight lines do not fit the data well, perhaps the collection of individual GCs could be modeled by "crooked lines" (i.e., a piecewise curve in which the successive straight-line pieces do not necessarily fall on the same overall straight line). An example of such a crooked line is the curve that results when we connect the four WISC means with straight lines. Such curves are sometimes called *linear splines* (Meredith & Tisak, 1990). Notice, however, that this linear spline we are proposing to use has three attributes: slope and intercept, as before with a straight line, and shape. Because we still have only two factors in the model, however, shape will be perfectly confounded with slope because the slope factor loadings carry the information about shape. To make this more concrete, consider the linear spline obtained from the mean WISC scores plotted in Figure 4.4. If we fix factor loadings on the slope factor at values to take the mean GC as our basic shape, hold the level of the intercept factor score constant, and plot the curves that result from varying the slope factor score from positive to negative, it is much more apparent how slope and shape are confounded. Large positive-slope scores produce exaggerations of the basic shape in a positive direction, zero-slope scores produce horizontal lines, and large negative-slope scores produce inverted exaggerations of the basic shape. In the case of fixing slope factor loadings to produce something other than a straight line, we are attempting to fit the collection of observed trajectories to an a priori linear spline in which the shape and slope are perfectly confounded. If, on the other hand, we freely estimate the last two loadings, we are determining the best-possible-fitting linear spline under the constraint that the shape and

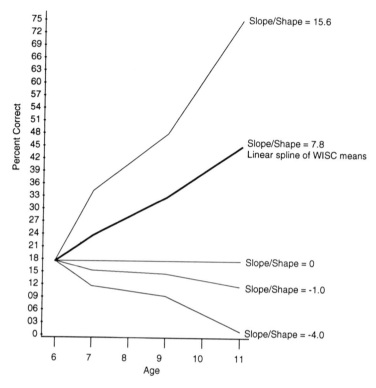

FIG. 4.4. Demonstrating the effect of confounding slope and shape in
linear spline models.

slope are confounded. We turn now to examples of these two approaches.

In the case of an a priori, two-factor, linear spline model, a natural choice
would be the linear spline of the WISC means. If, however, we simply fixed the
slope loadings at the values of the WISC means, we would essentially be shifting
the horizontal axis of our GCs forward, which would put the intercept factor
backwards in time. To keep the intercept factor representing initial status and
capturing the shape of the linear spline of the means requires some arithmetic.
The following formula can be used to generate factor loadings that will match the
linear spline of the means and keep the intercept factor representing initial status:

$$\frac{\bar{V}_i - \bar{V}_1}{\bar{V}_2 - \bar{V}_1} = L_i, \qquad i = 1, 2, 3, 4. \tag{4.28}$$

Substituting the appropriate WISC means in for the v variables in Formula 4.28
gives $L_1 = 0$, $L_2 = 1$, $L_3 = 2.21$, and $L_4 = 3.67$. It is apparent that v_1 must be
different from v_2 in order to get sensible results. If they are not different, then

some point other than v_2 should be used. It should be kept in mind that the slope factor will be rescaled even though the models are equivalent. If no two means are different, then something other than the two-factor, mean, linear spline model is probably more appropriate, such as a parallel or monotonic stability model. See the section on single-factor LGC models for more discussion of these models.

The overall fit of the mean linear spline model is substantially improved over the straight-line LGC model. The chi-square statistic is now 11.50 (df = 7), $p =$

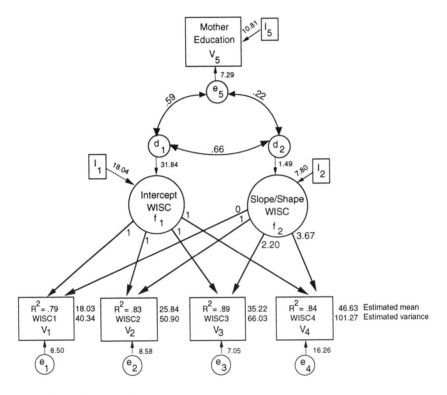

$\chi2_{(5)} = 11.48$, $p = .04$

BBN = .987
CFI = .993
N = 204

*Standardized values (i.e., correlations)

All parameters significant except where indicated.

Comparison to linear model: $\chi2_{(2)} = 58.19$, $p < .001$, BBN = .835, CFI = .897

FIG. 4.5.   Unspecified linear spline LGC model.

.12, which is nonsignificant, and the bbn and cfi for the comparison of this model to the independence null model are .987 and .995 respectively. As it turns out, there is not much difference between the mean linear spline model and the unspecified linear spline model. We will turn to the unspecified linear spline model for a more detailed look at model parameters.

The chi-square in Figure 4.5 for the unspecified linear spline model is 11.48 (df = 5), p = .04, and the bbn and cfi for comparison to the independence null model are .987 and .983 respectively. The difference chi-square for the unspecified linear spline model versus the straight-line model is 58.19 (df = 2), $p < .001$, indicating a substantial and highly significant improvement in fit. The bbn and cfi for the comparison of the straight-line model to the unspecified linear spline model are .835 and .897, respectively, also indicating a substantial improvement.

Comparing the parameter estimates in Figure 4.5 to the corresponding estimates in Figure 4.3, it is apparent that only the slope/shape factor and the time-1 and -2 error terms changed substantially. The unspecified linear spline model slope/shape factor has a mean of 7.80 and variance of 1.49, both larger than the corresponding values for the straight-line model. The correlation between initial

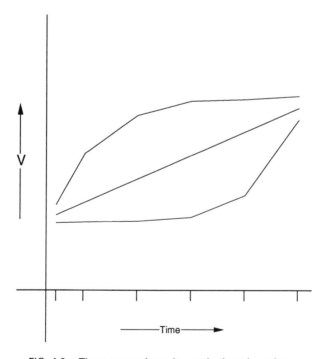

FIG. 4.6.   Three approximately quadratic trajectories.

status and rate of change ($r = .66$) is lower in the unspecified linear spline model, and the time-1 and time-2 error terms are also smaller. Notice, however, that the correlation of mother education with slope/shape and intercept scores stays substantially the same.

The unspecified linear spline model attempts to reproduce curvilinear trajectories under the constraint that the basic shape of the spline is confounded with slope. Although it works well for the WISC data, this approach can and does fail. For example, Figure 4.6 shows three approximately quadratic trajectories in which the shape of the curve varies for a constant value of slope and intercept. There is no single linear spline that we can use to simultaneously accommodate all three of these trajectories as long as shape and slope are confounded. In a case like this, we can add an extra quadratic factor to the straight-line model to adequately reproduce the observed trajectories. Although the unspecified linear spline model seems adequate for the WISC data, for the purposes of demonstration we will fit several higher-order polynomial models also.

HIGHER-ORDER POLYNOMIAL LGC MODELS
FOR WISC SCORES

Up to this point, we have considered both *time-averaged* and *initial status* straight-line models and discussed the differences between the model parameters. For higher-order polynomial models, the two models are still equivalent. The relations between corresponding model parameters across the two models become more complicated in higher-order models, especially if the time metric is uneven. It will generally be true that the parameters of a *time-averaged* model will be linear combinations of the parameters of the equivalent *initial status* model, and vice versa. The linear combinations will be given by matrix expressions involving the matrices of the factor loadings of the two models. The details are given in Appendix B.

The first attempt at fitting a *time-averaged* quadratic model resulted in a nonsensical negative variance estimate for the quadratic factor. In the second attempt, the quadratic factor variance was constrained at zero for these data. Besides the significant lack of fit by the chi-square test in both models, the nonsensical negative variance estimate for the quadratic factor variance indicates that this model is not appropriate.

The last higher-order polynomial model we will consider is the saturated, *time-averaged* cubic model. In order to estimate this model, we must fix the error terms. The WISC manual provides test-retest reliabilities for different age groups of children that can be used as rough estimates (Wechsler, 1974). The overall fit of this model is not at issue because of the lack of degrees of freedom. What is accomplished by this model is an interesting decomposition of the raw data into components of variance due to various polynomial components of growth and

	Average	Linear	Quadratic	Cubic	Mother Ed.
Average	1.00				
Linear	.66	1.00			
Quadratic	.20	.30	1.00		
Cubic	.29	.29	.08 (ns)	1.00	
Mother Education	.53	.20	.17 (ns)	.25	1.00
Mean	31.43	2.77	-.08	.15	10.81
Variance	54.22	.34	.08	.05	7.29

v	f_1 Average	f_2 Linear	f_3 Quadratic	f_4 Cubic	e Error
v_1	1	-4.5	3.86	-4.02	4
v_2	1	-2.5	-2.19	7.54	4
v_3	1	1.5	-5.29	-5.03	4
v_4	1	5.5	3.61	1.51	4
		factor loadings		error variance estimates	

All parameters significant except where indicated; $\chi2_{(0)} = 0$

FIG. 4.7. Cubic growth model for WISC scores: means, variances, and correlations among growth factors and mother education.

error. Figure 4.7 shows that the average level over time, the straight-line trend, and the cubic trend have significant positive means, but the quadratic trend has a significant negative mean. All growth components have significant variance. Interestingly, mother education is positively related to all the components, although the correlation with the quadratic component is not significant. This finding indicates that children of more highly educated mothers are growing faster in all respects in percent correct responses on the WISC.

It should be noted that the error variance estimates in the two-factor straight-line model range from 4.5 to 1.6 times the corresponding values from the test-retest reliability estimates used in the saturated cubic model. In effect, observed variance in the WISC scores that was being captured by the error terms in the straight-line model is now incorporated into the growth factors in the saturated cubic model. The other noteworthy comparison is the similarity between the average and straight-line trend factors in the straight-line model and the cubic model. The straight-line trend factor in the cubic model is scaled twice as large as the straight-line trend factor in the straight-line model. Once this scaling difference is taken into account, the two straight-line trend factors are quite similar in terms of their means, variances, and, perhaps most importantly, their correlation with mother education. This highlights a nice property of *time-averaged,* higher-order polynomial models. Even in the presence of higher-order factors, the straight-line trend factor still represents individual differences in the general

(a)

d1, d1	1.00								
d2, d1	-.13	1.00							
d2, d2	.01	-.13	1.00						
d3, d1	.09	-.96	.13	1.00					
d3, d2	-.01	.11	-.98	-.11	1.00				
d3, d3	.00	-.09	.93	.09	-.98	1.00			
d4, d1	-.03	.92	-.12	-.99	.11	-.09	1.00		
d4, d2	.00	.08	.96	.08	-.99	.99	-.08	1.00	
d4, d3	-.00	.06	-.89	-.06	.96	-.99	.06	-.98	1.00
d4, d4	.00	-.03	.84	.03	-.93	.98	-.03	.96	-.99	1.00

(b)

d1, d1	1.00								
d2, d1	.72	1.00							
d2, d2	.36	.72	1.00						
d3, d1	.21	.25	.17	1.00					
d3, d2	.12	.23	.29	.61	1.00				
d3, d3	.02	.04	.04	.21	.29	1.00			
d4, d1	.29	.27	.16	.07	.05	.01	1.00		
d4, d2	.17	.28	.27	.07	.08	.01	.61	1.00	
d4, d3	.04	.06	.06	.21	.20	.06	.15	.21	1.00
d4, d4	.04	.05	.04	.01	.01	.00	.29	.27	.06	1.00

FIG. 4.8. Correlations among parameter estimates for factor covariance matrix for (a) initial status and (b) time-averaged cubic models.

upward or downward straight-line trends of the individual GCs as it does in the straight-line model. Appendix C gives more details on the interpretations of higher-order polynomial factors in *time-averaged* models.

It has been our experience after fitting a number of these models to actual data that while the *time-averaged* and *initial status* models are theoretically equivalent, the parameter values tend to be better defined in the *time-averaged* models. By "better defined," we mean that the correlations among the parameter estimates tend to be smaller. For example, compare the correlations for the parameter estimates of the factor covariance matrix in Figure 4.8 for the two saturated cubic models. There are near-linear dependencies in the *initial status* model. The correlation between the estimate of the variance of the cubic factor and the estimate of the covariance between the cubic factor and the quadratic factor is $r = -.994$, essentially a perfect correlation. So while both of these two parameter estimates are algebraically identified, in this particular data set they are nearly linearly dependent, a situation commonly referred to as empirical underidentification (Kenny, 1979). Near-linear dependencies can create estimation problems for computer software packages in which the minimization algorithm fails to converge to a solution even after many iterations. Another typical, paradoxical result is that neither parameter involved in the near-linear dependency will be reliably different from zero, but if either or both is eliminated from the model the chi-square deteriorates significantly. In the *time-averaged* model, however, the highest correlation between two parameter estimates is .72.

Using orthogonal polynomial contrast coefficients basically amounts to *centering* the time scale about zero. Centering predictor variables is usually advocated in regression texts when dealing with higher-order product terms (Aiken & West, 1991). Centering usually reduces the covariance between a product variable and its individual components, which in turn reduces multicollinearity. Centering appears to have the same beneficial effects in LGC models.

THE SINGLE-FACTOR LGC MODEL

Our first LGC model for the WISC scores was a simple straight-line model in which we attempted to fit a straight line to each individual's trajectory. We return now to that basic idea, but consider models that might arise due to the characteristics of the straight lines that make up the collection of observed GCs. For example, consider what would happen to the straight-line LGC model if all the straight lines in the sample were parallel and flat but passed through different intercepts. In this case, the slope factor mean and variance would not be significantly different from zero. Tisak and Meredith (1990) have termed this model a *parallel stability model*. Or consider the case in which all the straight lines emanate from zero at the intercept with different slopes. Under this condition, the intercept mean and variance would not be significantly different from zero. Tisak and Meredith have termed this model the *monotonic stability model*. In both the above cases, because of the structure of the data, a single factor is adequate. The two preceding models can also be generalized to the case of unspecified linear spline models. The single-factor LGC has been used by McArdle and his colleagues (McArdle & Epstein, 1987; McArdle, 1988) and is probably more familiar to developmentalists than the multifactor approach outlined here. For this reason and also because it is not widely appreciated that the single-factor LGC is a special case of the unspecified linear spline approach, we will devote some time to discussing this model.

McArdle has termed the univariate single-factor LGC model a *curve model*. When examining the curve model analyses of the WISC data (McArdle & Epstein, 1987) it is not immediately obvious that it is nested or a special case within the unspecified linear spline model. Indeed, in a later, more thorough reanalysis of the same data that included various two-factor models, McArdle (1988) stated that the curve model was not nested within the unspecified linear spline model. Tisak and Meredith (1990), however, stated that the curve model was nested within the unspecified linear spline model. We will demonstrate now in terms of a sequence of model tests how the two models can be related and how the fit of the monotonic stability model can be compared to the more general unspecified linear spline model.

One way of understanding what it means to say one model is nested within another is to try to arrive at the nested model through a series of constraints on the parameters of the general model. Using this definition of nested models, the nested status is clear when either the slope or the intercept factor collapses (i.e., has a mean and variance not significantly different from zero). A complication arises, however, because of the fact that the intercept factor mean and variance depend on the choice of factor loadings fixed for identification in a nontrivial way. If it were found, for example, that the mean and variance of the intercept factor were not zero for some choice of factor loadings, might there be some other choice of loadings for which the intercept factor mean and variance are zero? According to Tisak and Meredith (1990), the intercept factor can be eliminated if it is zero (i.e., its mean and variance are zero) or if it is strictly proportional to the slope. The first of these two conditions is straightforward. The second condition, strict proportionality (in equation form, $f_1 = bf_2$), can be tested by changing the basic two-factor model so that the intercept factor is a linear function of the slope factor and the residual variance (disturbance term) and the regression constant for the intercept factor are constrained to zero. (Recall that when a factor becomes a dependent variable in the sense of being predicted by other factors, the *I* parameter that we have been calling the *factor mean* is now the regression constant.) If these constraints do not produce a significant increase in the chi-square statistic over the model in which they are freely estimated, the intercept factor scores are strictly proportional to the slope factor scores. In this case, the single-factor model will be an adequate representation of the data. Appendix D gives the algebraic details demonstrating the equivalence of the two models.

In addition to the reasons given above for focusing on one-factor models rather than two-factor models, premature adoption of a single-factor model can result in very different conclusions about the level of covariation between some predictor variable, say v_5, and the growth parameters. If the one-factor model fits the data well, then either the slope factor collapses, the intercept factor collapses, or the slope and intercept are perfectly correlated and strictly proportional. If the slope factor collapses, the level of correlation of v_5 with the intercept factor will stay about the same when the slope factor is eliminated from the model, and vice versa. If the slope and intercept correlation is not significantly different from 1, v_5 correlates about the same with both, and the level of correlation will not change much when the slope and intercept are collapsed together in a single-factor model. If the single-factor model is not a good model for the data, however, the level of covariation of v_5 with the single factor in the single-factor model can be quite different than with the slope factor in the two-factor model.

In order to see this, we need only point out that the single factor in the curve model is just initial status, $v_1 = f_3 + e_1$, corrected for measurement error. It follows, then, that if v_5 has a significantly different correlation with initial status than it does with change, premature adoption of a single-factor model will be misleading about the relation of v_5 with change. The implication of the term *monotonic stability model* should be clearer now. If monotonic stability holds, the rank order of the observations stays the same over time, and therefore the correlation of v_5 with initial status will be the same as the correlation of v_5 with any other time point. In addition, the correlation of v_5 with change will be the same as the correlation of v_5 with initial status because initial status (intercept) is strictly proportional (i.e., perfectly correlated) to change (slope). Monotonic stability puts severe demands on the structure of the means, variances, and covariances of the observed variables, and we feel that the model should be adopted only when (a) it makes sense theoretically, and (b) the data seem to warrant it.

We have discussed some special cases in which one of the two factors collapses. In particular, we have shown how the single-factor curve model is nested within the more general unspecified linear spline model. Finally, we have shown the consequences of prematurely adopting a single-factor model when the data do not seem to warrant it. We turn now to an example application of evaluating single-factor LGC models of the WISC data.

Figure 4.9 shows the constrained two-factor version of the single-factor model. The overall chi-square is 82.80 (df = 8, $p < .001$), indicating a statistically significant lack of fit. The bbn and the cfi for comparison to the null model of independence are .908 and .916. More importantly, the nested chi-square for comparison to the unconstrained, unspecified linear spline model is 71.32 (df = 3), $p < .001$, indicating a very large decrement in fit associated with the single-factor model. The bbn and cfi for improvement in fit over the single-factor model

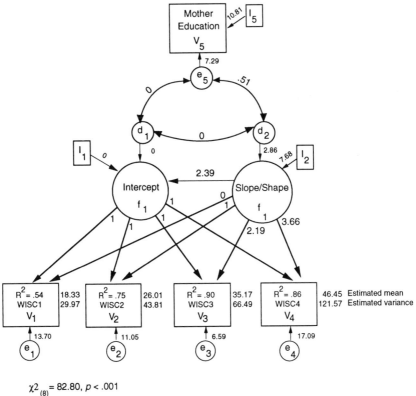

FIG. 4.9. Monotonic stability model: constrained two-factor version.

are .861 and .913 respectively. Clearly, the unspecified linear spline model fits the data better than the single-factor model. The other noteworthy feature of the model is the correlation of mother education with the single factor, $r = .51$. This correlation is much closer to the correlation of mother education with the intercept factor than the slope/shape factor in the unspecified linear spline model.

OTHER CURVILINEAR LGC MODELS

We should point out that, although it is possible to keep adding factors in a *time-averaged* polynomial LGC model until a satisfactory fit to the data is obtained,

LGC modeling in general is more powerful if a small number of factors can adequately describe the data. In several of our examples, there was no parsimony to our models because there were as many factors as there were variables. With larger numbers of time points and many factors, the factors may become difficult to interpret. With curvilinear trajectories in general, we have no guarantee that a small number of factors will be adequate to describe the data. The question of how many factors it takes to represent a given curvilinear growth form or how well a small number of factors approximates any particular type of curvilinear trajectory is an issue that is beyond the scope of this chapter. Interested readers should consult Burchinal and Appelbaum (1991), Tisak and Meredith (1990), or Tucker (1958).

Although at first glance this might appear to be a serious shortcoming to LGC methodology, the utility of simple linear models to describe a wide variety of phenomena is well documented. Furthermore, many initially curvilinear relationships can be suitably transformed so that linear models are valid. Finally, many relationships that are curvilinear over their entire range can be well approximated by linear models over smaller intervals of interest. We will mention some additional papers readers may want to consult for more information on some specific curvilinear forms. Tucker (1958) shows how one factor is adequate to model simple exponential growth. If the trajectories were a collection of simple exponential curves, we would find that the intercept factor is strictly proportional to the slope/shape factor in an unspecified linear spline model and hence could be eliminated. Meredith and Tisak (1990) demonstrate the usefulness of the two-factor unspecified model in modeling negative exponential growth trajectories over 14 repeated measures.

CONCLUSION

In summary, the examples demonstrate some of the highlights of LGC methodology. To keep the presentation simple, we avoided discussing more complicated curvilinear growth forms.

We think that the widespread availability of SEM software, the relative abundance of multiwave, longitudinal panel data, and the power and flexibility of polynomial LGCs and the unspecified two-factor approach to deal with a wide spectrum of developmental phenomena make LGC methodology a promising data-analytic technique. With the judicious choice of factor loadings to identify the unspecified linear spline model, the intercept and shape factors have straightforward interpretations of initial status and change, respectively. Using this parameterization, investigators can study predictors of change separately from correlates of initial status. While interpretations of higher-order polynomial factors might be more difficult, *time-averaged* polynomial models still have the attractive feature of decomposing the GCs into their constituent trends (straight line, quadratic, etc.), which can then be studied separately.

LGC is a valuable methodology that is currently underused. The more popular alternative for multiwave panel data, the autoregressive panel model, has some serious shortcomings as a general approach to the analysis of change (Rogosa & Willet, 1985a). These shortcomings are especially obvious when growth is monotonically stable (Stoolmiller & Bank, Chapter 8, this volume). We also question the soundness of the routine practice of controlling for autoregressive effects when evaluating predictors of change. In contrast, we believe that as developmentalists begin to use LGC models, they will have greater success in identifying important predictors of change.

ACKNOWLEDGMENTS

Support for this research was provided by Grant Nos. RO1 MH 38318 Prevention Research Branch, Division of Epidemiology and Services Research, National Institute of Mental Health (NIMH) U.S. PHS; P50 MH 46690, Prevention Research Branch, NIMH, U.S. PHS; and R37 MH 37940, Center for Studies of Violent Behavior and Traumatic Stress, NIMH, U.S. PHS.

The author can be contacted at the Oregon Social Learning Center, 207 E. 5th Ave., Suite 202, Eugene, OR 97401.

REFERENCES

Aiken, L. S., & West, S. G. (1991). *Multiple regression: Testing and interpreting interactions.* Newbury Park, CA: Sage Publications.

Baltes, P. B., & Nesselroade, J. R. (1979). History and rationale of longitudinal research. In J. R. Nesselroade & P. B. Baltes (Eds.), *Longitudinal research in the study of behavior and development.* New York: Academic Press.

Bentler, P. M. (1989). *EQS structural equations program manual.* Los Angeles, CA: BMDP Statistical Software, Inc.

Bollen, K. A. (1989). *Structural equations with latent variables.* New York: Wiley.

Bryk, A. S., & Raudenbush, S. W. (1987). Application of hierarchical linear models to assessing change. *Psychological Bulletin, 101*(1), 147–158.

Burchinal, M., & Appelbaum, M. I. (1991). Estimating individual developmental functions: Methods and their assumptions. *Child Development, 62,* 23–43.

Gollob, H. F., & Reichardt, C. S. (1987). Taking account of time lags in causal models. *Child Development, 58,* 80–92.

Hui, S. L., & Berger, J. O. (1983). Empirical Bayes estimation of rates in longitudinal studies. *Journal of the American Statistical Association, 78,* 753–760.

Jöreskog, K., & Sörbom, D. (1989). *LISREL7: A guide to the program and applications* (2nd ed.) Chicago: SPSS Inc.

Kenny, D. A. (1979). *Correlation and causation.* New York: Wiley.

Kessler, R. C., & Greenberg, D. F. (1981). *Linear panel analysis: Models of quantitative change.* New York: Academic Press.

Kirk, R. E. (1982). *Experimental design: Procedures for the behavioral sciences* (2nd ed.). Monterey, CA: Brooks/Cole.

Kleinbaum, D. G. (1973). A generalization of the growth curve model which allows missing data. *Journal of Multivariate Analysis, 3,* 117–124.

Maccoby, E. E., & Martin, J. A. (1983). Socialization in the context of the family: Parent-child interaction. In E. M. Heatherington (Ed.), *Handbook of child psychology: Vol. IV. Socialization, personality and social development* (4th ed.) (pp. 1–101). New York: Wiley.

McArdle, J. J. (1988). Dynamic but structural equation modeling of repeated measures data. In J. R. Nesselroade & R. B. Cattel (Eds.), *Handbook of multivariate experimental psychology* (2nd ed.) (pp. 561–614). New York: Plenum.

McArdle, J. J., & Anderson, E. (1989). Latent growth models for research on aging. In J. E. Birren & K. W. Schaie (Eds.), *The handbook of the psychology of aging. Vol. III* (pp. 21–44). New York: Academic Press.

McArdle, J. J., & Anderson, E. (1990). *Handbook of the psychology of aging* (3rd ed.). New York: Academic Press.

McArdle, J. J., & Epstein, D. (1987). Latent growth curves within developmental structural equation models. *Child Development, 58,* 110–133.

Meredith, W. & Tisak, J. (1990). Latent curve analysis. *Psychometrika, 55,* 107–122.

Norusis, M. J. (1990). *SPSS advanced statistics 4.0.* Chicago, IL: SPSS Inc.

Osborne, R. T., & Suddick, D. E. (1972). A longitudinal investigation of the intellectual differentiation hypothesis. *The Journal of Genetic Psychology, 121,* 83–89.

Rao, C. R. (1958). Some statistical methods for comparison of growth curves. *Biometrics, 14,* 1–17.

Robson, D. S. (1959). A simple method for constructing orthogonal polynomials when the independent variable is unequally spaced. *Biometrics, 15,* 187–191.

Rogosa, D. R., Brandt, D., & Zimowski, M. (1982). A GC approach to the measurement of change. *Psychological Bulletin, 92*(3), 726–748.

Rogosa, D. R., & Willet, J. B. (1985a). Satisfying a simplex structure is simpler than it should be. *Journal of Educational Statistics, 10*(2), 99–107.

Rogosa, D. R., & Willet, J. B. (1985b). Understanding correlates of change by modeling individual differences in growth. *Psychometrika, 50*(2), 203–228.

Scher, A. M., Young, A. C., & Meredith, W. M. (1960). Factor analysis of the electrocardiogram. *Circulation Research, 8,* 519–526.

Sörbom, D. (1974). A general method for studying differences in factor means and factor structure between groups. *British Journal of Mathematical and Statistical Psychology, 27,* 229–239.

Stelzl, I. (1986). Changing a causal hypothesis without changing the fit: Some rules for generating equivalent path models. *Multivariate Behavioral Research, 21,* 309–331.

Tisak, J., & Meredith, W. (1990). Descriptive and associative developmental models. In A. von Eye (Ed.), *New statistical methods in developmental research.* New York: Academic Press.

Tucker, L. R. (1958). Determination of parameters of a functional relation by factor analysis. *Psychometrika, 23*(1), 19–23.

Ware, J. H. (1985). Linear models for the analysis of longitudinal studies. *American Statistician, 39,* 95–101.

Wechsler, D. (1974). *Wechsler intelligence scale for children* (rev. ed.). New York: The Psychological Corporation.

Wishart, J. (1934). Growth-rate determinations in nutrition studies with the bacon pig, and their analysis. *Biometrika, 30,* 16–28.

Zeger, S. L., & Liang, K. (1986). Longitudinal data analysis for discrete and continuous outcomes. *Biometrics, 42,* 121–130.

APPENDIX A

Equations Set 1

$$E(v_1) = E(f_1) + L_1 E(f_2), \tag{4.1}$$

$$E(v_2) = E(f_1) + L_2 E(f_2), \tag{4.2}$$

$$E(v_5) = I_5, \tag{4.3}$$

$$var(v_1) = var(f_1) + L_1^2 var(f_2) + 2L_1 cov(f_1, f_2) + var(e_1), \tag{4.4}$$

$$var(v_2) = var(f_1) + L_2^2 var(f_2) + 2L_2 cov(f_1, f_2) + var(e_2), \tag{4.5}$$

$$var(v_5) = var(e_5), \tag{4.6}$$

$$cov(v_1, v_2) = var(f_1) + L_1 L_2 var(f_2) + (L_1 + L_2) cov(f_1, f_2), \tag{4.7}$$

$$cov(v_1, v_5) = cov(f_1, v_5) + L_1 cov(f_2, v_5), \tag{4.8}$$

$$cov(v_2, v_5) = cov(f_1, v_5) + L_2 cov(f_2, v_5). \tag{4.9}$$

Equations Set 2

$$I_1 = E(f_1) = \frac{L_2 E(v_1) - L_1 E(v_2)}{L_2 - L_1} \tag{4.10}$$

$$I_2 = E(f_2) = \frac{E(v_2 - v_1)}{L_2 - L_1}, \tag{4.11}$$

$$I_5 = E(v_5), \tag{4.12}$$

$$var(d_1) = var(f_1) = \frac{L_1^2[var(v_2) - var(e_2)] + L_2^2[var(v_1) - var(e_1)] - 2L_2 L_1 cov(v_1, v_2)}{(L_2 - L_1)^2} \tag{4.13}$$

$$var(d_2) = var(f_2) = \frac{[var(v_1) - var(e_1)] + [var(v_2) - var(e_2)] - 2cov(v_1, v_2)}{(L_2 - L_1)^2}, \tag{4.14}$$

$$var(e_5) = var(v_5), \tag{4.15}$$

$$cov(d_1, d_2) = cov(f_1, f_2)$$
$$= \frac{L_2(cov(v_1, v_2) - [var(v_1) - var(e_1)]) + L_1(cov(v_1, v_2) - [var(v_2) - var(e_2)])}{(L_2 - L_1)^2}, \tag{4.16}$$

$$cov(d_1, e_5) = cov(f_1, v_5) = \frac{L_2 cov(v_1, v_5) - L_1 cov(v_2, v_5)}{L_2 - L_1}, \tag{4.17}$$

$$cov(d_2, e_5) = cov(f_2, v_5) = \frac{cov(v_2, v_5) - cov(v_1, v_5)}{L_2 - L_1}. \tag{4.18}$$

APPENDIX B: SOLVING FOR *TIME-AVERAGED* FACTOR SCORES IN TERMS OF *INITIAL STATUS* FACTOR SCORES

In the notation we have been using, the matrix equation for factor analysis over n individuals observed for t time periods using t factors in the model is $v = fL + e$, where v is the $n \times t$ matrix of observed variable scores for n individuals over t time periods, f is the $n \times t$ matrix of factor scores for n individuals and t factors, L is the $t \times t$ factor loading matrix, and e is $n \times t$ matrix of error variable scores. For simplicity we will use a just-identified model. This implies that the factor-loading and error-variance matrices will be fixed. In this case we need two versions of the standard equation, one for the *initial status* model and one for the *time-averaged* model.

Let S be the matrix of *initial status* factor scores, and let T be the factor-loading matrix that carries the *initial status* time metric values, so that $v = ST + e$.

Let A be the *time-averaged* factor scores, and let O be the factor-loading matrix that carries the *time-averaged* time metric values, so that $v = AO + e$; O is also a rowwise orthogonal polynomial contrast coefficient matrix.

Since the rows of O are orthogonal, $OO' = D$, where D is a diagonal matrix with the sums of the squares of the rows of O on the main diagonal. Also, $O^{-1} = O'^{-1}D$. Let $On^{-1} = DO$ so that On is a rescaled version of O. Equating the two expressions for v gives $ST = AO$, where the e variables cancel. Solving for A gives

$$A = STO^{-1} = STO'^{-1}D = STOn' = vOn'.$$

Solving for S gives

$$S = ADO'^{-1} = AOn'^{-1} T^{-1} = AOT^{-1} = vT^{-1}.$$

Although we assumed the number of factors was equal to the number of time points, the relations given by the above and following expressions still hold with fewer factors than time points. In other words, these relations hold for overidentified models such as the straight-line or quadratic model. In addition, these relations generalize to uneven time metrics. For an uneven time metric, O is obtained from $O*$ where $O*$ is the rowwise orthogonal polynomial contrast coefficient matrix for the total number of time points. The columns of $O*$ that correspond to missing time points are deleted, and rows are deleted from $O*$ off the bottom of the matrix until the matrix is once again square. The remaining rows that make up O are now no longer orthogonal so the Gram-Schmidt procedure can be used to restore orthogonality. A simple alternative procedure is outlined in Robson (1959). The SPSS MANOVA procedure (Norusis, 1990) can also be used to obtain orthonormal contrast coefficients for uneven time metrics. While it represents more arithmetic, normalizing the contrast coefficients has the additional attraction of scaling all the factors similarly. This places less of a computational burden on software programs if the numbers to be dealt with are all within one or two orders of magnitude of each other (Bentler, 1989, p. 20). The above formulas still hold using the new rowwise orthogonal O for unevenly spaced time points. The linear combinations that convert A to S, and vice versa, of course will, in general, be different than the evenly spaced case.

In growth modeling using SEM, we do not deal directly with the factor scores but with their means, variances, and covariances. Therefore it is also important to specify how the means, variances, and covariances of the two sets of factor scores will be related. The means are straightforward because the expected value of a linear combination of random variables is just the linear combination of the expected values. Therefore the means of the two sets of scores will be related in the same way the raw scores are. The variance of a linear combination of random variables is more complicated. The matrix equations for the vector of means of A, $E(A)$, and the covariance matrix of A, VAR(A), are

$$
\begin{array}{cccc}
t \times 1 & t \times t & t \times t & t \times 1 \\
E(A) = & T & On' & E(S)
\end{array}
$$

$$
\begin{array}{cccccc}
t \times t & t \times t & t \times t & t \times t & t \times t & t \times t \\
\text{VAR}(A) = & On & T' & \text{VAR}(S) & T & On',
\end{array}
$$

where the dimension of a given matrix is shown above the matrix.

APPENDIX C: THE INTERPRETATION OF THE *TIME-AVERAGED* FACTOR SCORES IN HIGHER-ORDER POLYNOMIAL MODELS

For *time-averaged* models, the factors have straightforward interpretations. Each factor represents individual differences in orthogonal polynomial trends in the GCs. For example, the straight-line trend of an individual GC is just the value of the regression coefficient (or some constant multiple of it) for the straight-line regression of v on time, controlling for the regression constant in the following model:

$$v = b_0 + b_1(\text{time}) + e.$$

The quadratic trend is the value of the regression coefficient (or some constant multiple of it) for the quadratic regression of v on time, controlling for the straight-line trend and the regression constant in the following model:

$$v = b_0 + b_1(\text{time}) + b_2(\text{time})^2 + e.$$

The interpretations for higher-order polynomial factors are similar. Here are the results of successive regression models demonstrating how orthogonal polynomial trends can be obtained for an individual GC using the mean WISC GC as an example. The raw data consists of the four values of time for the independent

variable (0, 1, 3, and 4) and the four mean levels for the WISC scores for the
dependent variable (18.03, 25.82, 36.26, and 46.59). First, we compute the
first-order polynomial model for the straight-line trend:

$$\text{wisc} = b_0 + b_1(\text{time}) + e \quad \{b_0 = 18.96, b_1 = 5.59\}.$$

The straight-line trend is equal to 5.59. Second, we compute the quadratic
model:

$$\text{wisc} = b_0 + b_1(\text{time}) + b_2(\text{time})^2 + e$$
$$\{b_0 = 18.44, b_1 = 6.86, b_2 = -.25\}.$$

The quadratic trend is equal to $-.25$. Notice that b_1 in this model differs from b_1
in the previous model. The b_1 obtained in this model should not be confused with
the b_1 for the straight-line trend obtained in the previous model. Last, we compute the cubic model:

$$\text{wisc} = b_0 + b_1(\text{time}) + b_2(\text{time})^2 + b_3(\text{time})^3 + e$$
$$\{b_0 = 18.03, b_1 = 9.15, b_2 = -1.53, b_3 = .17\}.$$

The cubic trend is equal to .17. Notice that b_1 and b_2 in this model differ from b_1
and b_2 in the previous two models. In summary, the orthogonal straight-line,
quadratic, and cubic trends for the mean WISC GC are, respectively, 5.59,
$-.25$, and .17. These values would be obtained by a simultaneous regression
with the following data:

WISC	Straight Line	Quadratic	Cubic
18.03	−9/4	152/59	−480/199
25.82	−5/4	−86/59	900/199
36.26	3/4	−208/59	−600/199
46.59	11/4	142/59	300/199

The values in the straight-line, quadratic, and cubic columns are orthogonal
polynomial contrast coefficients for the four unevenly spaced points in time, 0,
1, 3, and 5. The uneven time metric is what creates the odd-looking fractional
values.

In reality, we have 204 individual GCs not just 1, but each individual GC has
scores on all the components of growth from average to cubic. The factor scores
represent the individual differences of these polynomial components of growth.

APPENDIX D: DEMONSTRATING THE EQUIVALENCE
OF THE MONOTONIC STABILITY MODEL AND THE
CONSTRAINED TWO-FACTOR UNSPECIFIED MODEL

Demonstrating the equivalence of the single-factor model and the equivalent
constrained version of the unspecified two-factor model is most conveniently

accomplished by using two-points-in-time models. The equivalence still holds in overidentified models with more time points.

We can write the linear equations for the single factor model as $v_1 = f_3 + e_1$ and $v_2 = Lf_3 + e_2$, where we assume that e_1 and e_2 are fixed, and the factor loading for v_1 on f_3 is fixed to 1. The factor loading for v_2 on f_3 is a freely estimated parameter as are the factor mean and variance. Actually, there are enough degrees of freedom to estimate e_1 and e_2 in the single-factor model, but if we did estimate these two parameters the single-factor model would no longer be nested within the unspecified two-factor model. This consideration is peculiar to the two points in time situation. With more time points, error terms can be estimated in both the single-factor and the unspecified two-factor model, and the single-factor model will be nested within the two-factor unspecified model. Using expectation and covariance algebra, we can generate expressions for the expectations and variance of the measured variables in terms of the single-factor model parameters:

$$E(v_1) = E(f_3), \tag{4.29}$$

$$E(v_2) = LE(f_3), \tag{4.30}$$

$$\text{var}(v_1) = \text{var}(f_3) + \text{var}(e_1), \tag{4.31}$$

$$\text{var}(v_2) = L^2 \, \text{var}(f_3) + \text{var}(e_2), \tag{4.32}$$

$$\text{cov}(v_1, v_2) = L \, \text{var}(f_3). \tag{4.33}$$

For two points in time, the unspecified two-factor model is just a simple straight-line LGC model. Recalling that for the two-points-in-time straight-line LGC model the variances of e_1 and e_2 are fixed, and assuming $L_1 = 0$ and $L_2 = 1$ are fixed, we can write the linear equations for the constrained two-factor version of the single-factor model as $v_1 = f_1 + e_1$, $v_2 = f_1 + f_2 + e_2$, and $f_1 = bf_2$. Expectations and variances of the measured variables in terms of model parameters are

$$E(v_1) = E(f_1) = bE(f_2), \tag{4.34}$$

$$E(v_2) = E(f_1) + E(f_2) = bE(f_2) + E(f_2) = (b + 1)E(f_2), \tag{4.35}$$

$$\text{var}(v_1) = \text{var}(f_1) + \text{var}(e_1) = b^2 \, \text{var}(f_2) + \text{var}(e_1), \tag{4.36}$$

$$\begin{aligned} \text{var}(v_2) &= \text{var}(f_1) + \text{var}(f_2) + 2 \, \text{cov}(f_1, f_2) + \text{var}(e_2) \\ &= b^2 \, \text{var}(f_2) + \text{var}(f_2) + 2b \, \text{var}(f_2) + \text{var}(e_2) \\ &= (b + 1)^2 \, \text{var}(f_2) + \text{var}(e_2), \end{aligned} \tag{4.37}$$

$$\begin{aligned} \text{cov}(v_1, v_2) &= \text{var}(f_1) + \text{cov}(f_1, f_2) = b^2 \, \text{var}(f_2) + b \, \text{var}(f_2) \\ &= b(b + 1) \, \text{var}(f_2). \end{aligned} \tag{4.38}$$

If we substitute $b = 1/(L - 1)$, $\text{var}(f_2) = (L - 1)^2 \, \text{var}(f_3)$, and $E(f_2) = (L - 1) E(f_3)$ into Equations 4.34–4.38 and simplify, we see that they are equivalent to Equations 4.29–4.33 indicating that the models are equivalent. Alternatively, we could make the substitutions $L = (b + 1)/b$, $\text{var}(f_3) = b^2 \text{var}(f_2)$, and $E(f_3) = bE(f_2)$ into Equations 4.29–4.33 and simplify to show that the models are equivalent. Either way it should be clear that the models are equivalent and the only changes in parameter values are due to the rescaling that is given in the substitutions.

5

Accelerating and Maximizing Information from Short-Term Longitudinal Research

Edward R. Anderson
Texas Tech University

In longitudinal research, the use of short-term studies with multiple cohorts may provide one means for accelerating the process of studying change. In this chapter Anderson demonstrates the use of cohort-sequential designs for longitudinal research using convergence analysis.

—Editor

When studying human development, we often wish to understand whether specific variables generally increase or decrease across age, as well as to identify whether this change remains constant. For example, we know that the variable *height* increases most rapidly during the first two years of life, then changes more slowly throughout childhood, but accelerates again during adolescence (Brooks-Gunn & Reiter, 1990). Although there is a great deal of variation in this pattern—some individuals reach their peak height much earlier or more rapidly than others—the average pattern of change still provides an important descriptor of the population.

Two broad approaches address these fundamental questions about age changes: individuals of different ages are studied at only one point in time (i.e., cross-sectional), or the same group of individuals are assessed at more than one—and preferably many—points in time (i.e., longitudinal). Advantages and disadvantages of these research designs are widely known, and often discussed as costs versus benefits (see Nesselroade & Baltes, 1979). For example, in cross-sectional studies, a wide age range can be obtained, but ideas about change within individuals cannot be tested. In longitudinal studies, ideas about change may be tested, but require intensive monitoring of the same individuals over a lengthy period of time. Fortunately, cohort-sequential designs provide a solution to this cost-benefit dilemma. Such designs allow for estimating a single developmental curve by linking together small, overlapping segments of data about varying age groups—a technique termed "convergence" by Bell (1953, 1954). By using convergence analysis with cohort-sequential designs, we can obtain information about a long age range in a short period of time—an acceleration of longitudinal information.

Ironically, researchers commonly collect data compatible with cohort-sequential designs, but use approaches which fail to maximize the potential information. Because I believe this method offers many advantages, this chapter therefore provides a primer for researchers interested in applying convergence analysis to cohort-sequential designs. Toward this aim, advantages of this approach are first outlined, followed by a discussion of design considerations. Next, explicit instruction in programming convergence analysis is provided. Finally, this approach is demonstrated using data from a study by Mavis Hetherington and her colleagues (1992).

CONVERTING TO CONVERGENCE

Historically, researchers often have collected cohort-sequential data, but have used longitudinal approaches rather than convergence analysis. Longitudinal procedures not only reduce the amount of information available, but may also give misleading results. This section demonstrates these errors and shows how using convergence analysis may overcome them.

Consider the longitudinal study (Hetherington et al., 1992) displayed in Table 5.1. We see that in 1984, 1985, and 1986, a group of children between the ages of 9 and 13 were interviewed about frequency of involvement in mutual activities with their mothers (e.g., playing games, building something). To analyze this data, we could calculate means on this variable for each wave of measurement, as children averaged ages 11, 12, and 13. Because the mean values decrease over time, we might be tempted to conclude that participation in mutual activities decreases between the ages of 11 and 13. This, conclusion, however, is inappropriate because we are ignoring differences about age and collapsing all children ages 9 to 13 into a single category. Thus, the mean corresponding to age 11 contains 13-year-olds as well. Instead of studying age, this procedure is in fact, unwittingly studying time.

Alternatively, this same study can comprise a cohort-sequential design, with Figure 5.1 displaying the reformatted data for mutual activity. A dashed line through the middle of the data represents a single growth curve estimated from the information provided by the separate curves. Now the mean calculated for 11-year-olds represents data on all children as they reached 11 years of age, regardless of the year in which it occurred.

Across the ages studied, the general pattern shows decreasing scores for all groups, as in the first analysis. With a cohort-sequential design, however, change in participation in mutual activity is documented for a period of seven years. The former approach collapsed seven potential years of data into three by calculating a mean across ages. Furthermore, because the data took only two years to collect, cohort-sequential procedures are a more efficient strategy than following one group of individuals for the entire time. In sum, cohort-sequential studies approximate a complete longitudinal study by using convergence analysis to describe a single developmental growth curve.

Convergence analysis not only extends longitudinal information, but also

TABLE 5.1
Means on a Measure of Mutual Activity
for a Two-Year Longitudinal Study

Age of Child	Year of Data Collection		
	1984	1985	1986
9	1.89	2.16	2.00
10	1.86	1.75	1.65
11	1.96	1.92	1.56
12	2.02	1.52	1.76
13	1.67	1.64	1.31
Mean age	11	12	13
Mean value	1.88	1.78	1.65

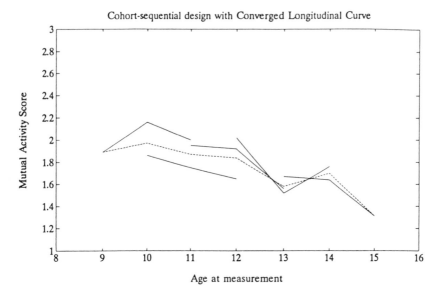

FIG. 5.1.   Cohort-sequential design with converged longitudinal curve.

uncovers misleading results when data are grouped according to year instead of age. In the previous example, information provided by different age groups converged on the same line, with the longitudinal estimation providing an approximation to convergence analysis results. In the same study, a measure of internalizing produced means of .379, .488, and .317, when averaged at each wave of the study, suggesting that internalizing peaks at age 12. When this data are organized by specific age cohort, however, the results are as displayed in Figure 5.2. Scores on internalizing behavior now appear to be changing as a function of time of measurement rather than age: the highest scores are obtained at the second assessment for all groups (except the 10-year-olds) regardless of age. By collapsing across age groups for each time of measurement, we fail to correctly identify change as a function of time. In fact, the children whose scores are displayed in Figure 5.2 are a subsample who had all experienced a parent's remarriage at the first time of measurement. Their scores on internalizing peak about a year after parental remarriage.

    Thus, when cohort-sequential data are analyzed with longitudinal methods, researchers lose not only the possibility of describing a longer age span, but also inadvertently may ascribe change to time rather than age. In a statistical sense, such researchers assume that different age groups converge on the same information. Convergence analysis overcomes this statistical limitation by first testing for this assumption of convergence across age groups. Then, hypotheses about different patterns of change are tested. The next section describes basic consider-

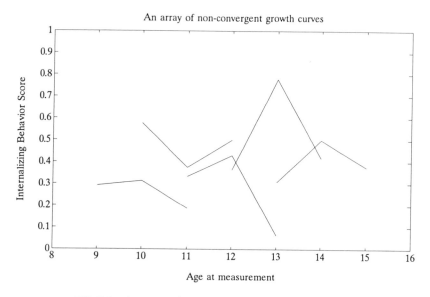

FIG. 5.2.   An array of nonconvergent growth curves.

ations in cohort-sequential designs, with the goal of yielding data amenable to convergence analysis.

BASICS OF COHORT SEQUENTIAL DESIGNS

Design Considerations

When designing cohort-sequential studies for the purpose of conducting convergence analysis, researchers need to consider two primary issues: sufficiency of overlap between age cohorts, and efficiency of data collection.

Sufficiency of Overlap

Appropriate use of convergence analysis rests on using age groups which are appropriately "staggered," where some information about development is overlapping. By what criteria, then, can we determine how much overlap should occur among groups?

Essentially, we need enough overlap in data points to be confident that adjacent groups follow the same developmental pattern. Related to longitudinal studies, David Rogosa (e.g., Rogosa, 1988) has consistently called for an increase in the number of measurements taken, so the pattern of change can be reliably identified. For example, if a longitudinal study comprises just two measurements, the only pattern of change which can be described is a straight line. In fact, because two points *exactly* describe a straight line, there is no way to determine if the data diverge from a straight line. Instead, the addition of a third time point allows for detecting variation from a straight line. Thus, with three or more data points, hypotheses about linear growth patterns become testable.

Extending this reasoning to cohort-sequential data, if three data points allow for increased confidence about the pattern of a single group, the same rationale can be applied to adjacent groups. In other words, three data points allow for detecting a linear pattern regardless of whether that change is within one group or between groups. Furthermore, the nature of cohort-sequential designs allows for detection of even more complex overall patterns, as long as change between adjacent groups is less complex. Note, for example, that in Figure 5.3, although the overall pattern appears complex, overlapping segments between ages 9 and 11 are linear. The third measurement point between adjacent groups allows us to test whether a linear segment links these two groups. Overlapping segments between 10 and 12 are quadratic, however; with just three overlapping measurements, hypotheses about a quadratic curve between these two groups remains untestable. Unless some a priori reason exists to expect something more complex than a straight line between adjacent groups, *as a general principle, three overlapping measurements between adjacent groups should be sufficient for most research.*

Efficiency of Data Collection

Efficiency provides a compelling reason for conducting cohort-sequential research as opposed to complete longitudinal studies. That is, researchers desire to

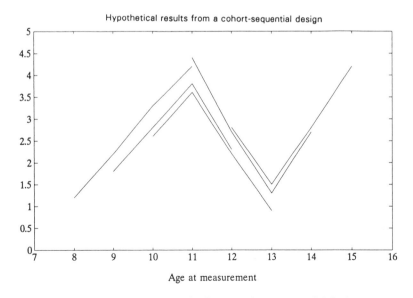

FIG. 5.3.   Hypothetical results from a cohort-sequential design.

gain knowledge about a longer period of the life span in a shorter amount of time. Such a goal should be addressed when designing cohort-sequential studies. The question then becomes, how long should data be collected to maximize efficiency?

One useful way to define efficiency is as a ratio of the range of ages to the length of data collection. In the Hetherington et al. (1992) study, childrens' ages ranged from 9 to 15, for an age span of seven years. These data took two years to collect, with children initially measured and followed at yearly intervals for two more times. This study, therefore, achieved a ratio of age span covered to data collection time of 7:2, for an efficiency of 3.5. Efficiency (measured against the length of time for data collection, for a variety of different numbers of age groups) is graphed in Figure 5.4.

As can be seen, efficiency decreases as the length of data collection increases. Another way to think about this efficiency measure is to consider that the primary goal of a cohort-sequential design is to approximate a longitudinal study in a shorter period of time. As the time for data collection increases, the design of the study approaches a complete longitudinal study, and thus becomes a less efficient substitute for a longitudinal study. The efficiency of a complete longitudinal study is given in Figure 5.4 as the dashed line. From this line, we can see that after the first year of a longitudinal study efficiency is at a maximum: the age span length is 2—the beginning and end points of the study—and this information took one year to collect, yielding an efficiency value of 2. A reasonable

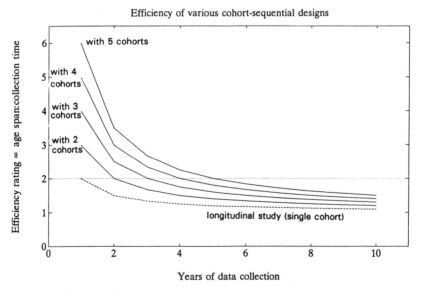

FIG. 5.4.   Efficiency of various cohort-sequential designs.

principle derived from this graph is that researchers using cohort-sequential studies should strive for an efficiency value of at least two (shown as the dotted line in the figure), so that they gain improvement over a complete longitudinal study.

Using this measure of efficiency, cross-sectional studies are the most efficient, because any age span may be covered at one point in time. Further, because data collection length comprises the total time *between* data collection points, cross-sectional studies have an effective data collection length of zero, thus earning an efficiency rating of infinity. In other words, cross-sectional studies are infinitely efficient as longitudinal approximations, because an entire age span may be collected in no time at all.

Of course, cross-sectional studies cannot test for the possibility of convergence across age groups. We are left, then, to balance the principle of efficiency against the principle of sufficient overlap between age groups, to test whether groups follow the same developmental pattern. In achieving this balance, researchers should generally strive to collect data until the youngest cohort reaches the age the oldest cohort was at the first time of measurement. By doing so, this strategy will guarantee an efficiency value of greater than 2.

Alternately, collecting data for a longer period of time decreases efficiency, and the study approaches a complete longitudinal design. Further, a smaller age difference between cohorts also works against efficiency, with a larger age difference working against sufficiency of overlap. For example, if children ages 9, 10, and 11 are assessed each year for a period of five years, the total age range spans from 9 to 16, or 8 years. But the efficiency of such a study is 8/5, or 1.6. By adding three more age groups of children, efficiency increases to 2.2, because the age range would then span 11 years. Collecting information on still more groups increases efficiency further, but then no overlap in information will exist between the youngest and oldest cohorts.

In sum, when designing cohort-sequential studies, a researcher should consider two basic principles: *efficiency of data collection,* and *sufficiency of overlap.* I believe that a proper balance between these two principles can be achieved by ensuring that (1) at least three data points overlap between adjacent groups, and (2) the youngest age group is followed until they reach the age of the oldest group at the first measurement.

Analytical Goals

The main goal with convergence analysis is to estimate an average curve from a limited set of information. Figure 5.5 shows the curve which has been fit to the data in Figure 5.1. Several features of this curve can be tested statistically.

First, we might test for the general form of the curve. In other words, we want to test whether the apparent overall decrease in mutual activity over the entire age span is significant or whether the growth curve is essentially flat. Second, we might investigate whether the slight bends in the pattern are significant in a statistical sense or whether the pattern of change can be reduced to a simple straight line. For the case presented in Figure 5.1, for example, it appears that mutual activity scores decline more sharply between ages 12 and 13 than the years immediately before or after. This apparent acceleration in change, however, may be unsubstantial and fail to be significantly different from a constant rate of change across the age span.

CONDUCTING CONVERGENCE ANALYSIS

Building the Convergence Model

Assume for a moment that the scores displayed in Figure 5.1 are measured without error. How could we best summarize the resulting curve?

First, we would calculate average scores where information from different groups overlaps. It is reasonable to assume, for example, that all 10-year-olds should receive the same average score, regardless of the year in which they reached 10. In other words, the 9-year-old group should score similarly to the 10-year-old group when both groups are 10 unless the entire cohort of 9-year-olds experienced an event which increased or decreased their scores before turning 10. Once a single mean is calculated for all individuals who would be age 10 in the sample, we could simply connect these points to form a single curve across the age ranges, as seen in Figure 5.5. Underlying such a process is a testable

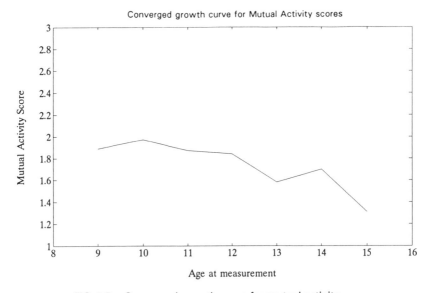

FIG. 5.5.   Converged growth curve for mutual activity.

TABLE 5.2
Weights Describing the Converged Growth Curve

Age of Measurement	Weight	* Slope	= Amount of Change
9	0	−.58	0
10	−.135	−.58	.08
11	.05	−.58	−.03
12	.11	−.58	−.06
13	.51	−.58	−.30
14	.40	−.58	−.23
15	1.0	−.58	−.58

hypothesis that this particular pattern of change would match results from studying a single group of children across the entire age range.

Continuing along, the slope of this curve is defined as the amount of change which has occurred across the length of the age span: the difference between the average score at the oldest age and the average score at the youngest age. In this case, the average score at age 15 is 1.31, and the average score at age 9 is 1.89, for a difference of −.58 points. This slope value, when multiplied by the weights presented in Table 5.2, produce the amount of change occurring by a particular age.

In Table 5.2, the weight associated with an age represents the proportion of change that has occurred by that age. Thus, between ages 9 and 11, average scores decreased by .03 point. This represents 5% of the total amount of change (decrease) between 9 and 15, and the corresponding weight for age 11 is .05. Scores decrease −.06 between 9 and 12, therefore 11% of the total decrease occurs by the age of 12. Note that in all cases except age 10, the weights are positive. Scores increase slightly at age 10, so the weight associated with that age is negative, indicating a change opposite to the general pattern over the age span. Similarly, at age 14, scores increase slightly compared to age 13, so the proportion of change by age 14 is slightly less than at 13. The weight, however, is positive because, relative to age 9, age 14 scores are lower. The weights, then, are always interpreted as relative to the total difference in change between the beginning and end of the study.

Note also, that if a term representing the initial level is added to the amount of change, the original score results. The initial level corresponds to the intercept term in a regression equation (see Table 5.3).

Recall that for this example, we assumed that these scores contained no measurement error. This assumption is equivalent to believing that any bends in the curve, however slight, are meaningful. We can test this belief against an alternative hypothesis that the data follow a straight line, which is an hypothesis that the rate of growth across this age span is constant. By examining Figure 5.6, it is clear that the data do not fall *exactly* on a straight line, but only approximate

TABLE 5.3
Adding an Intercept Term

Age of Measurement	Amount of Change	+ Initial Level	= Score
9	0	1.89	1.89
10	.08	1.89	1.97
11	−.03	1.89	1.86
12	−.06	1.89	1.83
13	−.30	1.89	1.59
14	−.23	1.89	1.66
15	−.58	1.89	1.31

it. If we estimate a straight line from these same scores, we obtain an error term, or the deviation from constant change. These estimates are given in Table 5.4. Note that slope and intercept change slightly here, because we are estimating a best-fitting regression line.

The difference between the original scores and the estimated scores corresponds to our error of measurement under the hypothesis that the data follow a straight line. The weights in this case show us how much change *should have occurred* if growth were constant. In other words, the age difference between 11 and 9 is two years, and six years of change take place across the study, so two-sixths of the change (.333 of the total) should occur between 9 and 11 if growth is

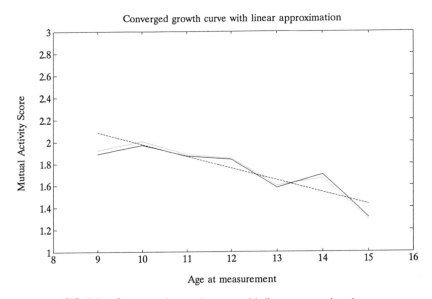

FIG. 5.6. Converged growth curve with linear approximation.

TABLE 5.4
Estimating a Linear Growth Curve

Age of Measurement	Weight	* Slope	+ Initial Level	= Estimated Score
9	0	−.65	2.08	2.08
10	.167	−.65	2.08	1.97
11	.333	−.65	2.08	1.86
12	.500	−.65	2.08	1.76
13	.667	−.65	2.08	1.65
14	.833	−.65	2.08	1.54
15	1.0	−.65	2.08	1.43

constant. Thus, making a theoretical statement that growth is constant allows us to make explicit predictions about growth at each age. Because our data may deviate from this prediction, the linear model represents a testable hypothesis.

Of course, *any* set of weights we choose can be made into a testable hypothesis. Consider the weights given in Table 5.5. These weights also make a prediction about the form of an average growth curve. In this case, the prediction is a negative quadratic pattern, in which the lowest scores are expected to occur at age 12. The proportion of change that occurs by the end of the age span is zero—the growth curve returns to the initial level. Total change, then, is theoretically expected to occur by age 12. A choice of weights, therefore, corresponds to an hypothesis or theoretical statement about the particular form of an average growth curve. Such hypotheses allow for statistical testing.

Adding Statistical Tests

Thus far we have conceptualized a set of points as a product of a slope and a series of weights, with each point calculated as the proportion of total change

TABLE 5.5
An Alternative Hypothesis About the Form of the Growth Curve

Age of Measurement	Weight	* Slope	+ Initial Level	= Estimated Score
9	0	−.200	1.89	1.89
10	.250	−.200	1.89	1.84
11	.500	−.200	1.89	1.79
12	1.00	−.200	1.89	1.69
13	.500	−.200	1.89	1.79
14	.250	−.200	1.89	1.84
15	0	−.200	1.89	1.89

from initial levels that has occurred by that age. With a constant proportion of change, the following regression equation applies:

$$\text{predicted score}_t = \text{level} + \text{slope}\left(\frac{\text{age}_t\text{-age}_0}{\text{age}_T\text{-age}_0}\right) \quad (5.1)$$

Note that in Equation 5.1, every increase in years corresponds to a proportional increase in the predicted score. The predicted score at age 10 is therefore the score at age 9 (i.e., the level) plus the total change across the age span studied (i.e., the slope) multiplied by the proportion of change expected to occur by age 10 (i.e., (10-9)/(15-9) = 1/6).

Alternatively, with nonconstant growth, the following equation applies in which each age obtains a unique weight:

$$\text{predicted score}_t = \text{level} + (\text{slope})b_{\text{age}}. \quad (5.2)$$

The Latent Growth Curve Model

McArdle (McArdle, 1987; McArdle & Anderson, 1990; McArdle & Epstein, 1987) describes this nonconstant growth equation as essentially a factor analysis of time, and terms this approach the *latent growth curve model* because predicted scores for each age derive from latent variable factors. Specifically, McArdle conceptualizes the regression equations at each age in path analytic terms with the two latent factors being level (i.e., intercept) and slope. For example, in Figure 5.7, both the level and slope factor values are multiplied by their respective regression coefficients and then totaled to derive a score for a particular age. In other words,

$$\text{age score} = \text{level score} \times 1 + \text{slope score} \times \text{weight for that age}. \quad (5.3)$$

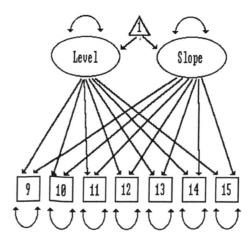

FIG. 5.7. A RAM-path diagram of a latent growth curve model.

Note that when calculating a score for the youngest age, the formula reduces to only a level score, because no change has occurred at the first time of measurement.

Loadings on the level factor are constant (a value of 1) for each age because each age score depends equally on the intercept term. Loadings on the slope factor provide information about the shape of change. In a linear model, the loadings on the slope factor correspond to the linear weights described in Table 5.4. In a nonlinear (or nonconstant) model, the loadings on the slope factor indicate the proportion of change that occurs by that age, as given in Table 5.2.

This approach comprises a general representation of growth curve models. For example, in the analysis of individual growth curves (e.g., Rogosa, Brandt, & Zimowski, 1982; Rogosa & Willett, 1985), individuals each receive a slope score derived from their respective data. Data in Table 5.4, for example, might represent a single subject's scores, with a calculated slope of $-.65$ as the best-fitting value *under the hypothesis of a linear growth pattern.*

This calculated slope value is, in fact, interpreted in the same manner as a factor score. In traditional factor analysis, the underlying phenomenon comprises a psychological construct, with measured variables representing various aspects of the construct. Alternatively, growth curve analysis focuses on an underlying phenomenon of pattern of growth, with ages revealing aspects of this pattern. In both cases, therefore, a single score summarizes a group of variables. In growth curve analysis, the single slope score summarizes growth information.

Analyzing a Latent Growth Curve Model

Analyzing a latent growth curve model involves two other considerations. First, because we are interested in making predictions about mean values, this information needs to be included in the path model. Mean values are represented by the closed triangle in Figure 5.7. Second, adding specific variance for each time point and residual covariances for each latent factor are necessary. With this additional information, the path model in Figure 5.7 now allows predictions for both mean scores and covariances. A structural equation modeling program such as LISREL allows comparisons between a predicted covariance structure and actual data. Because mean values are used, the covariance structure becomes a moment or raw cross-product structure.

The latent growth curve model must simultaneously account for all variances and covariances among the variables in addition to the mean scores at each age. When variances and covariances are included, the loadings on the slope factor differ slightly from the proportional weights given in Table 5.2. In Figure 5.6, for example, the dotted line represents the nonconstant growth curve estimated using variances and covariances. This dotted line deviates slightly from the solid line connecting the means.

Testing for Linear Change

A nonconstant latent growth curve model is then tested against a more restrictive model, such as one that depicts a linear change. The statistical test of whether the curve drawn from these points deviates significantly from a straight line involves comparing the goodness-of-fit statistics obtained from these two models. The chi-square for the linear or constant model for this data is 55 (df = 39); the chi-square for the nonconstant model is 45 (df = 34). A difference of 10 (df = 5) is nonsignificant at $p < .05$. The nonconstant growth curve model is therefore an insignificant improvement over the constant or linear latent growth curve model. In other words, apparent bends in the average line fail to deviate from a straight-line approximation in this case.

In sum, a structural equation model called the latent growth curve model tests the shape of an average growth curve. Importantly, this procedure provides a method for testing growth curves in cohort-sequential designs when complete longitudinal information is unavailable. The next section demonstrates how latent growth curve models are used to test for hypotheses about convergence.

Statistical Tests of Convergence

Convergence hypotheses can be tested using a latent growth curve model because the nonoverlapping sections of the growth curve are treated as missing data. We identify the level and slope factors by constraining the overlapping means to be equal across age groups. The statistical test of convergence compares the structural model of equal values for the level and slope on all age groups against a structural model allowing different values for level and slope. If age groups significantly differ on the overlapping means, a nonconvergent model will provide the better fit. Alternatively, if age groups have similar values, a convergent model provides the better fit. Using data from Figure 5.1, the chi-square test for the convergent model yields a value of 55 (df = 39) versus 40 (df = 23) for the nonconvergent model. With a difference of 15 (df = 16, $p > .05$), there is no significant improvement gained from estimating different levels and slopes across age groups. In other words, with no evidence that the groups follow statistically different patterns, we accept the null hypothesis that the groups converge on the same pattern. Readers will next learn how to program such convergence analysis using the LISREL program.

Programming a Convergence Analysis with LISREL

McArdle and colleagues (McArdle & Anderson, 1990; McArdle, Anderson, & Aber, 1987) devised a way to conduct convergence analysis with LISREL. To do so requires using RAM notation (McArdle & McDonald, 1984), in which researchers first specify the pattern of regression equations, next the pattern of residual (co)variances, and finally label each variable as either *manifest* (i.e., observed), or *latent* (i.e., unobserved). For purposes of diagramming a RAM path analysis, *regression equations* are represented as single-headed arrows denoting an asymmetrical or directional relation between two variables. Additionally, *residual (co)variances* consist of bidirectional arrows, or "slings," representing a symmetrical relation (i.e., either a residual variance, or a nondirectional covariance between two variables). Finally, *manifest and latent variables* are represented by squares and circles, respectively.

Figure 5.7 is a completely specified RAM path model for the growth curve in Figure 5.5. Transcribing this path model into the LISREL program consists of creating three matrices within LISREL, to identify locations of first arrows (the LISREL "beta" matrix) and next slings (the LISREL "psi" matrix). The third matrix is used to identify latent and manifest variables (the LISREL "Lambda-Y" matrix). In the path model, there are a total of nine variables, seven of which are manifest variables corresponding to the seven ages of measurement and two of which are latent variables corresponding to the level and slope factors. The matrix in Table 5.6 distinguishes between the latent and manifest variables.

The columns in Table 5.6 correspond to each of the nine total variables in the path diagram. Under each of the columns representing the seven measured ages, a 1 is placed to indicate that this variable is manifest. The columns representing the two latent variables consist of only zeros.

When specifying a convergence model in LISREL, we use a multiple-group program, with each age group containing a different pattern of manifest and latent variables. In our cohort-sequential design, each age group contributes only three manifest variables, with the remaining six variables latent. The matrices used to represent the manifest and latent variables for each of the age groups are given in Table 5.7. Note in this table that the columns in which the 1 appears differ across groups. This arrangement corresponds to the staggering of information across age groups. These matrices are specified in LISREL as completely fixed and can be ignored when they appear on the printout.

TABLE 5.6
The RAM "Filter" Matrix for the Example Data

| | Variables Displayed in the RAM Path Diagram | | | | | | | | |
	9	10	11	12	13	14	15	Level	Slope
Data 1	1	0	0	0	0	0	0	0	0
Data 2	0	1	0	0	0	0	0	0	0
Data 3	0	0	1	0	0	0	0	0	0
Data 4	0	0	0	1	0	0	0	0	0
Data 5	0	0	0	0	1	0	0	0	0
Data 6	0	0	0	0	0	1	0	0	0
Data 7	0	0	0	0	0	0	1	0	0

TABLE 5.7
Staggered Filter Matrices for the Example Data

	9	10	11	12	13	14	15	Level	Slope
				Filter for Group 1					
Data 1	1	0	0	0	0	0	0	0	0
Data 2	0	1	0	0	0	0	0	0	0
Data 3	0	0	1	0	0	0	0	0	0
				Filter for Group 2					
Data 1	0	1	0	0	0	0	0	0	0
Data 2	0	0	1	0	0	0	0	0	0
Data 3	0	0	0	1	0	0	0	0	0
				Filter for Group 3					
Data 1	0	0	1	0	0	0	0	0	0
Data 2	0	0	0	1	0	0	0	0	0
Data 3	0	0	0	0	1	0	0	0	0
				Filter for Group 4					
Data 1	0	0	0	1	0	0	0	0	0
Data 2	0	0	0	0	1	0	0	0	0
Data 3	0	0	0	0	0	1	0	0	0
				Filter for Group 5					
Data 1	0	0	0	0	1	0	0	0	0
Data 2	0	0	0	0	0	1	0	0	0
Data 3	0	0	0	0	0	0	1	0	0

USING CONVERGENCE ANALYSIS

Convergence analysis will be demonstrated using data from Hetherington et al.'s (1992) study, which examined childrens' adjustment to the custodial mother's remarriage, using divorced and nondivorced comparison groups. Each family contained a target child between the ages of 9 and 13, with boys and girls about equally represented. Although a battery of self-report and observational data were collected, this chapter uses only four selected measures. Specifically, mothers provided information for two measures of child behavior problems: Aversive and Internalizing Behavior, derived from the Child Behavior Checklist (Achenbach & Edelbrock, 1983) and the telephone interview of Patterson (1982). Additionally, children provided information on two variables of perceived warmth with their mothers: Mutual Activities and Positive Verbal Exchange, both derived from the Expression of Affection measure (Patterson, 1982). Table 5.8 shows the staggered means by age group and variable across the entire sample. The previous examples using Mutual Activities was based on a subsample of intact families.

Descriptive Results

Tests of Convergence

With convergence analysis, we first test whether separate age groups converge on a single pattern. With just two overlapping time points for adjacent

TABLE 5.8
Age Group Means for Measures of Child Behavior
and Mother's Warmth

	Age at Measurement						
Age Group	9	10	11	12	13	14	15
			Aversive Behavior				
9	.596	.571	.515				
10		.563	.554	.429			
11			.539	.550	.343		
12				.477	.490	.373	
13					.610	.457	.410
			Internalizing				
9	.420	.465	.395				
10		.551	.497	.429			
11			.359	.354	.203		
12				.457	.384	.246	
13					.429	.22	.367
			Mutual Activity				
9	2.16	2.05	1.86				
10		2.01	1.84	1.85			
11			1.98	1.79	1.78		
12				2.12	1.78	1.67	
13					1.73	1.86	1.77
			Positive Verbal				
9	3.40	3.76	3.37				
10		3.72	3.72	3.90			
11			3.59	3.78	3.79		
12				3.81	3.78	3.61	
13					3.72	4.16	3.88

groups in this sample, recall that only a linear convergence curve can be tested. Therefore, loadings on the slope factor were set equal to their corresponding linear proportions of change (i.e., 0, .167, .333, .5, .667, .833, 1). Two structural equation models were then fit to the data for each variable of interest.

In the first model, values for mean level and mean slope and respective variances were constrained to be equivalent across age groups. In the second model, mean level, mean slope, and respective residual variances were estimated separately for each group. Note that these two models comprise an extreme test of the nonconvergent hypothesis. Rather than all groups differing, we might find that only one age group follows a unique developmental trajectory. This extreme nonconvergent hypothesis, however, serves as an omnibus test for detecting any differences between age groups.[1]

We see from Table 5.9 that positive verbal behavior, mutual activity, and aversive behavior each show convergence across age groups (at $p < .05$). Thus, a single longitudinal growth curve can be estimated for these variables—garnering a seven-year age span from only two years of data collection. Internalizing behavior, in contrast, demonstrates nonconvergence: different cohorts in our study change in unique ways on internalizing behavior. The next step in convergence analysis is describing the form of growth in these converged curves.

Testing the Form of Growth

When determining the form of growth, the first test examines whether *any* change occurs in these variables across the age span studied. Therefore, we compare two structural models: one in which the slope of change equals zero (i.e., no change in average scores across the period), and a second in which the slope is estimated.

Results of these models, given in Table 5.10, indicate that for the variables of aversive behavior and mutual activity, adding an estimate of slope results in a significant improvement in fit. In other words, mutual activity and aversive behavior scores demonstrate a significant change—a decrease in this case— between the ages of 9 and 15. Ironically, just as children report declines in mutual activities with their mothers, mothers perceive improvements in their offspring's aversive behavior.

Interestingly, earlier analysis of these data (reported in Anderson, 1993) revealed slight increases in aversive or externalizing behavior across this age span, in contrast to the current results. Those earlier analyses used composite measures of both self-report and observations. Because observational data when analyzed

---

[1]The models used for these examples also constrain the residual variance at each age to be equal. This is not a necessary requirement of the latent growth curve model. It is possible that different ages have smaller or larger residual variance. Because specific variance here is used to represent measurement error, there was no a priori reason to expect unequal measurement over age.

TABLE 5.9
Statistical Tests of Convergence

Variable	Convergent df = 39	Nonconvergent df = 23	Difference df = 16
Aversive behavior	70	45	25
Internalizing	78	41	37*
Mutual activity	55	30	25
Positive verbal	43	28	15

*Two models are significantly different at $p < .05$.

separately indicate a substantial increase in externalizing, combining across methods attenuates this increase. It appears, then, that across these analyses, observed behavior becomes more coercive and disruptive with age, but mothers perceive improvements. Perhaps spending less time together, as evidenced by the childrens' reports of involvement, reduces the level of perceived coercion. For positive verbal behavior, however, the model of "no slope" cannot be rejected; thus, positive verbal behavior shows essentially no change in average scores across this age span.

Once it has been determined that significant change has occurred, researchers can now examine whether the nature of this change is constant or nonconstant across the age span. By comparing a linear model to a nonlinear model, we can assess for any bends in the line which would indicate nonconstant change. For the example data, only mutual activity and aversive behavior showed significant change. The difference in chi-square value between the linear and nonlinear models fails to achieve significance for both aversive behavior ($X2 = 3$, df = 5) and mutual activity ($X2 = 4$, df = 5), indicating a constant rate of change. A summary of the results of the descriptive analyses is presented in Table 5.11.

In sum, we examined the variables of aversive behavior, internalizing, mutual activity, and positive verbal exchange. Three of these variables—mutual activity, aversive behavior, and positive verbal exchange—demonstrated convergence, a single pattern of change over age groups. Regarding the nature of this pattern of

TABLE 5.10
Testing for Significant Change in Average Scores

Variable	No Slope df = 40	Slope df = 39	Difference df = 1
Aversive behavior	97	70	27*
Mutual activity	66	55	11*
Positive verbal	45	43	2

*Indicates two models are significantly different at $p < .05$.

TABLE 5.11
Summary of Convergence Tests

Variable	Are the Curves Convergent?	Does the Curve Show Change?	Does the Curve Show Nonlinearity?
Aversive behavior	Yes	Yes	No
Internalizing	No	—	—
Mutual activity	Yes	Yes	No
Positive verbal	Yes	No	—

change, aversive behavior and mutual activity show a significant linear decrease over this age period, while positive verbal behavior displays no change in average scores. Interpretation becomes more difficult when a test of convergence fails, as in the case of internalizing. In the next section, we turn our attention to this task.

Interpreting Nonconvergence

It is of course possible that the test of convergence will fail, as in the case of internalizing. There are at least two possible explanations when convergence fails.

First, an age-by-cohort interaction may exist, indicating multiple trajectories in the data. The data in Figure 5.8 show the staggered age group means on

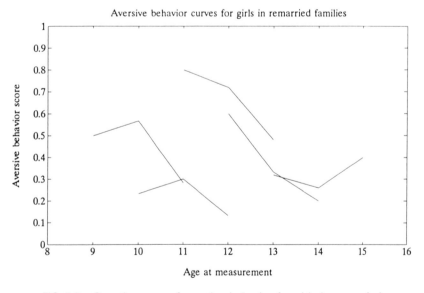

FIG. 5.8. Growth curves of aversive behavior for girls in remarried families.

aversive behavior for the subsample of girls from remarried families. The display here indicates that two curves, rather than one, are necessary to describe this array, depending on age at remarriage. Specifically, there appear to be two distinct groups: those who experienced their parent's remarriage before the age of 11 and those who experienced their parent's remarriage after age 11. The difference in chi-square values between a model allowing separate curves for these two groups and one in which a single curve is estimated is 10 (df = 4, $p < .05$). Thus, there is evidence that 11-, 12-, and 13-year-olds follow a different trajectory than do 9- and 10-year-olds. It can be concluded that at least two separate developmental patterns exist for girls in remarried families. This interaction with age and time of remarriage would have been overlooked without an initial test of convergence.

A second possibility when convergence fails is that chronological age is not the correct metric by which to measure change. An alternative to chronological age, such as puberty (i.e., "biological age"), or time since a critical event (i.e., "social age") offer possibilities. For example, Figure 5.9 shows growth curves of internalizing for children in remarried families, where groups are staggered by the number of years since parental divorce. Age in this particular example is years since parental divorce rather than chronological age.

When using "divorce age" rather than chronological age, the convergence analysis indicates that a single longitudinal curve can be drawn from the array of growth curves in Figure 5.9, since the difference between the converged and nonconverged models is 13 (df = 20, $p > .05$). A test of convergence may fail,

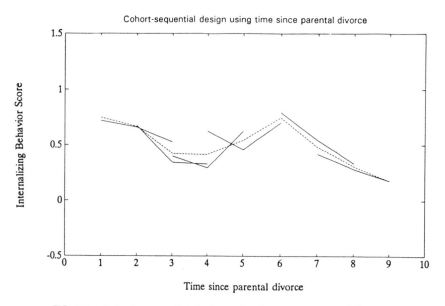

FIG. 5.9. Cohort-sequential design using time since parental divorce.

therefore, because chronological age may not be the time scale on which changes take place. In this example, "divorce age" appears to be a better time scale on which to measure changes in internalizing behavior for children experiencing their parent's remarriage.

SUMMARY AND CONCLUSIONS

This chapter illustrated the use of convergence analysis for cohort-sequential data. Cohort-sequential designs provide a means for accelerating longitudinal information. Researchers may already collect cohort-sequential forms of data in short-term longitudinal designs, but they have historically failed to use convergence analysis in understanding change across development. Consequently, resulting analyses are prone to misleading conclusions about age-related changes.

Convergence analysis allows the researcher not only to extend developmental information over a longer age range, but also to investigate age-by-cohort interactions. In the Hetherington et al. (1992) study, convergence analyses identified the presence of a critical age in girls' adjustment to their custodial mother's remarriage. Although perceived levels of aversive behavior declined significantly over time for all girls regardless of age at remarriage, girls experiencing remarriage around the age of 12 exhibited higher initial levels than their counterparts with remarriage occurring at other ages. With analysis other than convergence, such information remains unknown.

Cohort-sequential studies are not limited to chronological age for conducting convergence analysis. In the Hetherington et al. (1992) study, age since divorce, rather than chronological age, appeared to be a better ruler for measuring change in internalizing behavior. Researchers studying change can thus use convergence analysis to investigate appropriate developmental markers. In designing future developmental studies, researchers should consider how best to use convergence analysis to maximize and accelerate their short-term longitudinal information.

AUTHOR NOTES

The research reported in this chapter was supported by a grant from the John D. and Catherine T. MacArthur Foundation to E. Mavis Hetherington and W. G. Clingempeel.

I express my appreciation to Jack McArdle, Mavis Hetherington, Dick Bell, Shannon Greene, and Glenn Clingempeel.

REFERENCES

Achenbach, T. M., & Edelbrock, C. S. (1983). *Manual for the child behavior checklist and revised child behavior profile*. New York: Queen City Publishers.

Anderson, E. R. (1993). Analyzing change in short term longitudinal research using cohort-sequential designs. *Journal of Consulting and Clinical Psychology, 61,* 929–940.

Bell, R. Q. (1953). Convergence: An accelerated longitudinal approach. *Child Development, 24,* 145–152.

Bell, R. Q. (1954). An experimental test of the accelerated longitudinal approach. *Child Development, 25,* 281–286.

Brooks-Gunn, J., & Reiter, E. O. (1990). The role of pubertal processes. In S. S. Feldman & G. R. Elliott (Eds.), *At the threshold: The development adolescent* (pp. 16–53). Cambridge, MA: Harvard University Press.

Hetherington, E. M., Clingempeel, W. G., Anderson, E. R., Deal, J. E., Hollier, E. A., Lindner, M. S., & Stanley-Hagan, M. (1992). Coping with marital transitions: A family systems perspective. *Monographs of the Society for Research in Child Development, 57* (2–3, Serial No. 227).

McArdle, J. J. (1987). Dynamic but structural equation modeling of repeated measures data. In J. R. Nesselroade and R. B. Cattell (Eds.), *The handbook of multivariate experimental psychology.* New York: Plenum Press.

McArdle, J. J., & Anderson, E. R. (1990). Latent variable growth models for research on aging. In J. E. Birren and K. W. Schaie (Eds.), *Handbook of the psychology of aging* (3rd ed., pp. 21–44). San Diego: Academic Press.

McArdle, J. J., Anderson, E. R., & Aber, M. S. (1987). Convergence hypotheses modeled and tested with linear structural equations. *Data for an aging population.* Proceedings of the 1987 Public Health Conference on Records and Statistics. Hyattsville, MD: DHHS Pub. No. (PHS)88-1214.

McArdle, J. J., & Epstein, D. (1987). Latent growth curves within developmental structural equation models. *Child Development, 58,* 110–133.

McArdle, J. J., & McDonald, R. P. (1984). Some algebraic properties of the Reticular Action Model for moment structures. *British Journal of Mathematical and Statistical Psychology, 37,* 234–251.

Nesselroade, J. R., & Baltes, P. B. (1979). *Longitudinal research in the study of behavior and development.* New York: Academic Press.

Patterson, G. R. (1982). *Coercive family process.* Eugene, OR: Castalia.

Rogosa, D. R. (1988). Myths about longitudinal research. In K. W. Schaie, R. T. Campbell, W. Meredith, & S. C. Rawlings (Eds.), *Methodological issues in aging research* (pp. 171–210). New York: Springer.

Rogosa, D., Brandt, D., & Zimowski, M. (1982). A growth curve approach to the measurement of change. *Psychological Bulletin, 92,* 726–748.

Rogosa, D. R., & Willett, J. B. (19858). Understanding correlates of change by modeling individual differences in growth. *Psychometrika, 50,* 203–228.

6

Hierarchical Linear Models to Study the Effects of Social Context on Development

Stephen W. Raudenbush
Michigan State University

In this chapter Raudenbush explores the use of hierarchical linear models for the study of repeated observations. He tackles the problem that repeated observations are often nested within social contexts such as families, classrooms, schools, neighborhoods, etc. By adding a third level to the analysis, it is possible to study the effects of social contexts on individual development. Concepts are illustrated using data from the National Youth Survey. The work is expanded to include the situation in which individuals are cross-classified across social contexts. Generalization to binary data is also considered in this chapter.

—Editor

BACKGROUND AND RATIONALE

In studies of individual development it is natural to employ a panel design in which the researcher samples subjects at a particular age and then follows those subjects for several years. When the outcome is continuously measured, researchers have conventionally applied univariate or multivariate analysis of variance (ANOVA) to such repeated measures data. Methodologists have generally recommended the multivariate approach because it allows more general assumptions about the correlation structure of the repeated-measures data than does the univariate approach (Bock, 1975). However, as Ware (1985) pointed out, even the multivariate approach is of limited use when there are missing data, unbalanced designs, time-varying covariates, or continuous predictors of rates of change. Such characteristics are common in large-scale longitudinal studies, so more flexible analytic approaches are quite broadly needed.

The essential statistical problem is that when time-series designs vary across subjects, efficient estimation of linear model parameters requires some type of iterative procedure. Standard ANOVA methods do not fill the bill. However, with the advent of procedures such as the EM algorithm (Dempster, Laird, & Rubin, 1977), implemented on increasingly powerful computers, iterative computational techniques have become widely available, making accessible to researchers broadly applicable models for studying psychological growth.

The Two-Level Model for Repeated-Measures Data

Laird and Ware (1982) and Strenio, Weisberg, and Bryk (1983), working independently, proposed essentially identical approaches to the analysis of repeated-measures data, both employing the EM algorithm. In this approach, each subject's growth curve is characterized by a set of person-specific parameters. For example, in a linear growth model, the parameters might be an "initial status" and a rate of growth. However, these parameters are themselves viewed as randomly sampled from a population of persons. Hence, the model may be viewed as having two levels: a within-subjects level and a between-subjects level. Laird and Ware (1982) refer to this kind of model as a "random effects model," though it differs from classical random effects models in allowing covariation between growth parameters. Hence, Dempster, Rubin, and Tsutakawa (1981) referred to related models as "covariance components" models. Strenio et al. (1983) applied the term "hierarchical linear model" reflecting the important influence of Lindley and Smith (1972), whose pioneering work on hierarchical models inspired many of the subsequent developments.

Bryk and Raudenbush (1987) reconsidered decades-old dilemmas in the measurement of change from the standpoint of the hierarchical linear model. They showed how the model could be employed to assess the psychometric properties of an instrument for measuring characteristics of the growth curve such as the status of a subject at a time point, the linear rate of growth, or the rate of acceleration. They showed how to formulate and test alternative models for mean growth and how to assess the extent of individual variation around the mean growth curve. To assess correlates of growth, they conceived each set of individual growth parameters as a multivariate outcome to be predicted by measured characteristics of the person's background and environment. They viewed this work as building directly on the contributions of Rogosa, Brand, and Zimkowski (1982) and Rogosa and Willett (1985), who saw the formulation of explicit models for individual growth as essential in understanding the problems of measuring growth or change.

Longitudinal applications of hierarchical linear models in education and psychology include papers by Bryk and Raudenbush (1987, 1988), Goldstein (1989), and Willms and Jacobson (1990). Huttenlocher et al. (1991) used this approach to shed new light on vocabulary development during early childhood. Francis, Fletcher, Stubting, Davidson, and Thompson (1991) considered the potentially broad applicability of this approach in the context of clinical studies with an illustration from data on recovery from brain injury. Raudenbush and Chan (1992) applied the model by reanalyzing data from the National Youth Survey (NYS), and we build on their results in our first example below.

Incorporating Effects of Social Context

After reviewing the two-level model, this chapter considers extensions of the basic two-level model to incorporate the effects of shared social contexts, such as families, classrooms, schools, communities, and therapy groups. There are several types of research setting in which it becomes essential to represent social contextual effects in the analysis of longitudinal data.

1. In "cluster randomization trials" intact groups such as communities, classrooms, or therapy groups—rather than individuals—are assigned at random to experimental treatments (Hopkins, 1982). Moreover, the treatments are administered to those intact groups rather than to persons individually. It can be assumed that the responses of persons who share membership in these groups will be correlated by virtue of the common experience they share in those settings.

2. Social contextual effects on growth also arise in settings where one or more treatments are implemented within each of many contexts. An example is the recent "immersion study" (Ramirez, Yuen, Ramey, & Pasta, 1991), a federally funded evaluation of three alternative approaches to the instruction of children having limited English proficiency. At first glance, the design suggested a two-level hierarchical model in which level 1 represents the growth of a subject over time and level 2 represents the effect of treatment group membership plus person-specific random effects. The evaluators' goal was to compare the mean linear growth rates of the three treatment groups, controlling for relevant covari-

ates. However, the students within each group were nested within school districts during the course of the longitudinal study. Because many districts experienced all three treatments, it was possible to assess the variability in the treatment effect across districts, that is, the context specificity of the treatment effect.

3. Finally, one might take the proactive view that the clustering within natural social settings of persons who are changing over time represents *an opportunity to integrate psychological and sociological perspectives in the study of human development*. The Program on Human Development and Criminal Behavior (Tonry, Ohlin, & Farrington, 1991) has adopted this approach, and the purpose of the methodological research reported in this chapter is to develop, test, and refine statistical modeling approaches that faithfully represent this conceptualization.

Farrington (1993) persuasively argues the case for simultaneously including psychological and sociological perspectives in the study of antisocial behavior. He raises the provocative question: "Have any individual or ecological effects on offending been conclusively established?" His answer is negative. It is not that individual risk factors such as temperamental and cognitive orientations, personality traits, early social learning, hormonal configurations, or economic well-being have been ignored as predictors of antisocial outcomes. Nor have researchers ignored the normative and organizational characteristics of neighborhoods and schools as correlates of antisocial outcomes. The problem, Farrington argues, is that researchers have assessed individual and ecological sources of variation in separate studies. In fact, these two sources are *correlated* and they *interact* to shape development.

Individual and ecological factors *are correlated* because of the selective migration of persons into and out of neighborhoods and schools.

They *interact* in that a social context can either endanger or protect its members so that the consequences of a given "profile of individual risk" may vary across social settings.

Thus, studies that assess only the main effects of personal characteristics or the main effects of social context are likely to be misleading for two reasons: (1) By ignoring the confounding of the two sources, main-effect estimates may be biased. (2) By ignoring the statistical interaction between the two, main effects may mislead even if estimated without bias.

For example, persons predisposed to antisocial development may have a propensity to reside in neighborhoods lacking social cohesion and control (correlation of individual and social influence); and the realization of potential for antisocial development may depend on the social setting (interaction between individual and social influence). Ignoring statistical interaction distorts understanding of individual risk. For example, a study that estimated the effect of temperament on adolescent offending—ignoring neighborhood—would report the average of the temperament effects across the neighborhoods sampled. Such an average effect might apply poorly to any particular neighborhood. The variation in the effects of temperament across neighborhoods, arguably the most interesting feature of the data, would be attributed to random error, reducing the explanatory power of the model.

Clearly, the problems of confounding and interaction between the person and the social context arise quite generally outside the study of antisocial behavior. Thus, the consequences of poverty or minority status may vary across high schools (Lee & Bryk, 1989), and a secondary school teacher's sense of efficacy may vary across the several classes she is assigned to teach as a function of the academic track of the class and her level of preparation to teach the subject matter of the class (Raudenbush, Rowan, & Cheong, 1992). These two examples involve cross-sectional data on person-context interactions. In this chapter, we consider longitudinal data relevant to the study of such interactions.

Implications for Design and Statistical Modeling

How individual and social factors operate independently and jointly to shape development can be adequately studied only in the context of longitudinal research. The conception evolving from this analysis is that personal characteristics create propensities favoring certain kinds of developmental trajectories but development is realized over time in a social context. An adequate conception of individual development must apparently take into account the main effects of age (as suggested, for example, in the literature on the age-crime curve of Gottfredson and Hirschi, 1990), the main effects of both psychological and social-contextual influences, and interactions involving age, psychological variables, and social context descriptors. Individual-level developmental curves apparently depend on personal and social influences and their interaction, and neither the shape of these curves nor the influence of such variables on them can be inferred from cross-sectional data.

To render the discussion more concrete, we refer to Figure 6.1. The figure shows the fitted "age-crime curve" for a randomly sampled subject; specifically, the estimated probability that such a subject will commit serious theft during a year (vertical axis) as a function of age (horizontal axis) based on the National Youth Survey (Raudenbush, 1993a).[1] Notice that the curve has exactly the age-crime characteristics described in the criminological literature: age of onset is captured by an accelerating rate early in adolescence; a decelerating trend occurs a little later, leading to a peak age and, finally, a rapidly falling rate ("desistance").

Figure 6.2 presents results from a more fine-grained analysis in which the

---

[1]Seven overlapping cohorts of data spanning ages 11–21 were fitted. Each subject had five years of data, with the presence or absence of serious theft observed each year. A generalized linear model with random effects was estimated by means of maximum quasi-likelihood as suggested by Schall (1991).

Probability of Theft

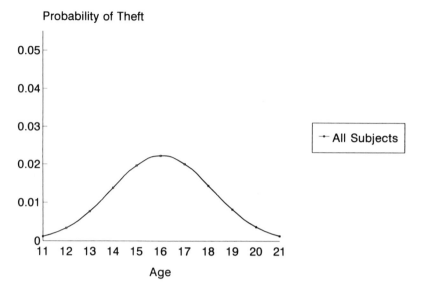

FIG. 6.1. Expected probability of serious theft per year (vertical axis) as a function of age (horizontal axis) based on the National Youth Survey.

Probability of Theft

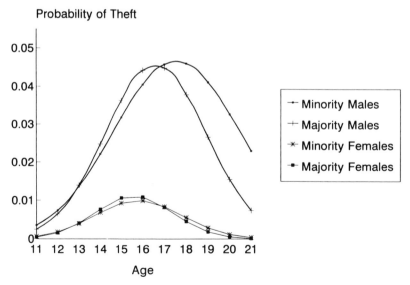

FIG. 6.2. Expected probability of serious theft per year (vertical axis) as a function of age (horizontal axis), by sex and ethnicity, controlling income (based on the National Youth Survey).

age-crime curve is predicted by sex and ethnicity, controlling for income. Notice that sex differences are not just rate differences at different ages. Moreover, ethnic differences are manifest not simply as rate differences. Indeed, the figure shows clear evidence of similar peak rates for minority and majority males; however, the rate of desistance is slower for minority than for majority males, giving rise to provocative hypotheses about how inequalities in social opportunity delay desistance.

This type of curve defines one of the most important objects of study in modern research on crime and deviance. In principle, every youth has a "personal" curve with respect to this kind of outcome, and it is each person's entire curve, including rate of acceleration early, rate of deceleration later, peak age, and rate of desistance, that requires investigation. The parameters of each curve can be viewed as a vector of latent outcomes to be predicted by early temperamental and family characteristics as well as by time-varying covariates (e.g., parental separation, arrest, incarceration). Moreover, we seek to understand how the organizational characteristics of schools and communities interact with the psychological characteristics of persons inhabiting them to influence the shape of each person's curve.

The conceptual framework we have constructed can be represented faithfully in terms of the parameters of a hierarchical linear statistical model, also referred to as a multilevel model or a covariance components model (Goldstein, 1987; Bryk & Raudenbush, 1992). In particular, the link between psychological predispositions and subsequent development can be represented by a two-level hierarchical model. Effects of the social contexts of communities or schools can be incorporated either as nested random effects in a three-level model or as crossed random effects, depending on the structure of the data.

We begin by describing and illustrating the two-level model using data from the National Youth Survey. Adding a third level to the model incorporates social context effects in those studies where persons are nested within one and only one social context during the course of the study, and this approach is illustrated with data on the academic learning of students who are nested within schools. The data were collected as part of a recent evaluation of U.S. compensatory education (Carter, 1984). However, persons will often migrate across social contexts during the course of a study. The three-level model is not adequate to represent the effects of the multiple contexts a person experiences during such a study, and for this reason we introduce a cross-classification model. A paradigmatic example involves the movement of U.S. primary school students from teacher to teacher as they advance from grade to grade. In effect, the students are cross-classified with teachers. We illustrate this approach using data from a recent national evaluation of bilingual education (Ramirez et al., 1991). The chapter briefly considers extensions of the model to discrete outcome data, and it concludes by emphasizing issues of statistical conclusion validity that arise in these studies.

THE TWO-LEVEL MODEL FOR REPEATED-MEASURES DATA

Raudenbush and Chan (1992, 1993) utilized a two-level hierarchical linear model to study growth in pro-deviant attitudes during adolescence based on the U.S. National Youth Survey. Their analysis serves as a useful example for introducing the logic of the model.

Data

For simplicity we focus on the youngest NYS cohort of 239 11-year-olds sampled in 1976 and followed until 1980 so that subjects with complete data were observed on five occasions. The outcome variable for this analysis is a nine-item scale assessing attitudes favorable to deviant behavior. Subjects were asked how wrong they believe it is for someone their age to cheat on school tests; purposely damage or destroy property that does not belong to him or her; use marijuana or hashish, steal something worth less than $5.00, hit or threaten someone without any reason; use alcohol; break into a vehicle or building to steal something; sell hard drugs such as heroin, cocaine, and LSD; or steal something worth more than $50.00. In each case, subjects were asked to choose one of four categories: "very wrong," "wrong," "a little bit wrong," or "not wrong at all." This scale was administered annually for five years.[2] Of our total sample, 68.2% had complete data at all five points of data collection; 18.2% had data at four time points, 6.7% had three waves of data, 3.9% had two waves, and 3.0% had only one wave. Our analytic method utilizes any data available, so no subjects were eliminated. A logarithmic transformation of the outcome substantially reduced skewness. The descriptive statistics provided in Table 6.1 (under "cohort 1") are in this logarithmic metric.

Predictors

Sex, race, income, and exposure to deviant peers were initially employed as predictors. However, race and income proved unuseful in predicting deviance and so were dropped from the analysis. Sex (1 = female; 0 = male) is, by definition, time invariant. "Exposure to deviant peers" was based on a nine-item scale that was administered every year and so is a time-varying predictor.

The scaling of exposure closely paralleled the scaling of deviance. Subjects were asked how many of their friends engaged in the nine activities mentioned above. Responses were coded on a five-point Likert scale (from "all of them" to "none of them"). Item responses were averaged (Chronbach's alpha = .80) and

---

[2]For simplicity, we refer to this outcome as "deviance," keeping in mind that it measures attitudes and not behavior.

TABLE 6.1
Descriptive Statistics for the Log of Attitude Toward Deviance
and the Log of Exposure to Delinquent Peers by Age, Cohort, and Sex

	Age	11	12	13	14	15	16	17	18
				Log of Attitude Toward Deviance					
Cohort 1									
Male	m	.24	.27	.36	.45	.49	—	—	—
N = 122	sd	.21	.21	.28	.27	.27	—	—	—
Female	m	.19	.21	.29	.36	.40	—	—	—
N = 117	sd	.17	.22	.25	.31	.33	—	—	—
Cohort 2									
Male	m	—	—	—	.41	.51	.56	.55	.55
N = 140	sd	—	—	—	.30	.31	.30	.27	.28
Female	m	—	—	—	.36	.44	.46	.46	.51
N = 105	sd	—	—	—	.27	.26	.26	.24	.27
				Log of Exposure to Delinquent Peers					
Cohort 1									
Male	m	.39	.36	.43	.48	.49	—	—	—
	sd	.29	.26	.32	.32	.32	—	—	—
Female	m	.20	.23	.31	.38	.41	—	—	—
	sd	.18	.22	.27	.32	.33	—	—	—
Cohort 2									
Male	m	—	—	—	.52	.57	.60	.61	.61
	sd	—	—	—	.32	.34	.31	.33	.31
Female	m	—	—	—	.48	.54	.56	.54	.53
	sd	—	—	—	.30	.32	.29	.26	.26

transformed into a logarithmic metric. Means and standard deviations appear in
Table 6.1 (under "cohort 1").

Goals of the Analysis

The presentation seeks to clarify how researchers may specify the appropriate
shape of the mean and individual change functions, interpret the extent of intersubject variation in person-specific change parameters, assess the reliability of
the estimates of these person-specific change parameters, estimate effects of
time-invariant covariates, and incorporate the effects of time-varying covariates.

Shape of the Mean and Individual Change Curves

Level-1 Model

We begin with a simple linear model for individual change. According to this
model, there is a tendency for the deviance score of each subject to change at a

steady rate from age 11 to age 15. The age variable is deviated from age 13 according to the following table:

Age	11	12	13	14	15
Age − 13	−2	−1	0	1	2

The level-1 model is

$$Y_{it} = \pi_{0i} + \pi_{1i}(\text{AGE} - 13)_{it} + e_{it}, \qquad (6.1)$$

where

Y_{it} = deviance score for subject i at time t, $i = 1, \ldots, 239$, $t = 1, \ldots, 5$

$(\text{AGE} - 13)_{it}$ = age of subject i at time t minus 13 so that $(\text{AGE} - 13)_{it}$ is −2, −1, 0, 1, or 2 at ages 11, 12, 13, 14, and 15 respectively, corresponding to times $t = 1, 2, 3, 4,$ and 5

π_{0i} = intercept of subject i, so that, given the coding of (AGE − 13), π_{0i} is the expected deviance of subject i at age 13, π_{1i} is the expected rate of increase per year in the deviance score for subject i, and e_{it} is the random within-subject error of prediction for subject i at time t, conditional on that subject's change parameters π_{0i} and π_{1i}. These within-subject errors are assumed mutually independent and normally distributed with mean of zero; i.e., $e_{it} \sim N(0, \sigma^2)$

Level-2 Model

Equation 6.1 characterizes each subject's trajectory from age 11 to 15 by two parameters: π_{0i} and π_{1i}. Our current interest focuses on the distribution of these parameters across subjects. We expect that the average rate of increase is positive during these early adolescent years, but that there will also exist substantial variation across subjects in these rates. To examine these hypotheses, we formulate a simple *level-2* model

$$\pi_{0i} = \beta_{00} + u_{0i}, \qquad \pi_{1i} = \beta_{10} + u_{1i}, \qquad (6.2)$$

where

β_{00} = grand mean deviance score at age 13
β_{10} = grand mean rate of increase in deviance
u_{0i} = random effect of person i on deviance at age 13
u_{1i} = random effect of person i on the rate of increase in deviance

The random effects (u_{0i}, u_{1i}) are assumed bivariate normal with zero means, variances τ_{00}, τ_{11}, and covariance τ_{01}. The regression coefficients β_{00} and β_{10}

are termed fixed effects. When Equations 6.1 and 6.2 are combined, the resulting equation may be written

$$Y_{it} = \beta_{00} + \beta_{10}(\text{AGE} - 13)_{it} + \epsilon_{it}, \tag{6.3}$$

where $\epsilon_{it} = u_{0i} + u_{1i}(\text{AGE} - 13)_{it} + e_{it}$. Two aspects of the error ϵ_{it} render Equation 6.3 inappropriate for estimation via ordinary least-squares regression. First, these errors are correlated within subjects by virtue of the fact that every time-series observation for subject i shares random effects u_{0i} and u_{1i}. Second, the errors are heteroscedastic, given the dependence of their variance on $(\text{AGE} - 13)_{it}$. Under these conditions, and with balanced data, ordinary least-squares estimates of the fixed effects β_{00} and β_{10} would be efficient in the case of Equation 6.3, but the standard error estimates would not. When the data are unbalanced (as they are here) and/or when time-varying covariates are added to the model, ordinary least-squares regression would yield inefficient estimates of the fixed effects as well. To solve these problems, a variety of algorithms can be employed that produce maximum-likelihood estimates of all the parameters of Equation 6.3, including the variances and covariances. We utilized the HLM program of Bryk, Raudenbush, Seltzer, and Congdon (1988) to compute such estimates. Raudenbush (1988) provides a review of the theory underlying this approach and of applications of this methodology in education and psychology, so we will not consider estimation theory further in this chapter.

Results

Let us first consider the results for the fixed effects (Table 6.2, Model 1). We see, first, that the mean growth rate β_{10} is estimated to be .063, $t = 12.55$, indicating a highly significantly positive average rate of increase in deviance during ages 11–15. In terms of the standard deviation of the outcome at age 13 (see Table 6.1), this is equivalent to an expected increase of about a quarter of a standard deviation per year.

The fixed-effects results provide information about average change across all subjects. The variance components results provide information about individual differences in change. Specifically, we see from Table 6.2, Model 1 that the estimated variance in subjects' intercepts (expected deviance at age 13) is

$$\text{Estimated Var}(\pi_{0i}) = \hat{\tau}_{00} = 0.0345.$$

The table also provides a test of the hypothesis of intersubject homogeneity with respect to these intercepts, that is, a test of the hypothesis

$$H_0: \tau_{00} = 0.$$

The resulting statistic of 1504.8, when compared to the percentiles of chi-square distribution with 223 degrees of freedom, indicates significant intersubject variation in intercepts, $p < .001$. See Bryk and Raudenbush (1992, 3) for the details of this test.

Similarly, Table 6.2 provides the estimated variance in rates of change, $\hat{\tau}_{11} = .0030$ and the associated chi-square statistic of 469.8, $p < .001$. The results imply that subjects vary significantly not only in terms of deviance at age 13 but also in rates of change during the age interval 11 to 15.

A Test for Quadratic Effects

Equation 6.1 specifies that changes in deviance are strictly linear during ages 11–15. However, it could be that change is curvilinear. For example, it could be that deviance is accelerating or decelerating on average during these ages; and it could be that rates of acceleration or deceleration vary across subjects. To study these possibilities, Equation 6.1 was elaborated to include a quadratic contrast. The results indicated, however, that there was no significant tendency for mean growth to be quadratic, and the estimated variance component for quadratic effects was very small. These findings suggest that a linear change or "growth" structure is adequate to describe change in deviance for cohort 1.

Interpreting the Intersubject Variance in Rate of Change

Though our results indicate a distinct samplewide increase in pro-deviant attitudes from age 11 to 15, they certainly do not imply that every subject is increasing in deviance. As mentioned, Table 6.2 (Model 1) provides the estimate $\hat{\tau}_{11} = .0030$ of the variance across subjects in rates of change. The estimated standard deviation of the change rates is then $\sqrt{.0030} = .055$. To interpret this statistic, consider two subjects, one with a rate of change two standard deviations below the average of $\hat{\beta}_{00} = .063$, and one with a rate of increase two standard deviations above average. The predicted growth rates for these two subjects would be $.063 \pm 2(.055) = (-.047, .173)$. Thus, it would be possible to find a subject with no increase or even a decrease in pro-deviant attitudes during this age interval; and it would be possible also to find a subject with pro-deviant attitudes increasing at the rate of .17 per year. Given a standard deviation of .28 of the outcome at age 13, a linear rate of increase of .17 would be $.17/.28$ or 61% of a standard deviation per year, a substantial increase.

Assessment of Reliability of Measures of Growth and Status

Our analysis indicates that the linear growth model is adequate to represent individual change from 11 to 15. Hence, each person's "growth trajectory" is described by two parameters: an intercept, representing status at age 13, and a linear rate of change. In essence, these are the two quantities we seek to "measure" in this study of change. The question therefore naturally arises: How reliable are our measures of these two quantities?

TABLE 6.2
Hierarchical Linear Model Results for Cohort 1

(a) Fixed Effects

Predictor	Model 1: No Covariates			Model 2: Sex as a Covariate			Model 3: Sex and Exposure as Covariates		
	Coefficient	SE	t Ratio	Coefficient	SE	t Ratio	Coefficient	SE	t Ratio
For base rate, π_{0i}									
Intercept, β_{00}	0.329	0.013	—	0.3649	0.0179	—	0.3463	0.0150	—
Sex, β_{01}				−0.0741	0.0258	−2.88	−0.0311	0.0216	−1.44
For linear change, π_{1i}									
Intercept, β_{10}	0.063	0.005	12.55	0.0679	0.0069	9.84	0.0606	0.0062	9.74
sex, β_{11}				−0.0112	0.0100	−1.12	−0.0230	0.0092	−2.50
For exposure effect, π_{2i}									
Intercept, β_{20}							0.2935	0.0316	9.28
Sex, β_{21}							0.0831	0.0508	1.64

(b) Variance Components

Parameter[a]	Estimate	Chi-Square	df	Estimate	Chi-Square	df	Estimate	Chi-Square	df
$Var(\pi_{0i}) = \tau_{00}$	0.0345	1504.8*	223	0.0333	1473.1*	222	0.0213	902.0*	219
$Var(\pi_{1i}) = \tau_{11}$	0.0030	469.8*	223	0.0030	468.7	222	0.0017	377.1	219
$Var(e_{it}) = \sigma^2$	0.0262			0.0262			0.0243		

[a]Degrees of freedom are based on the number of persons with sufficient data for ordinary least-squares estimation of person-specific parameters. All estimates are based on all the data, including persons with insufficient data for OLS estimation.

*$p < .001$

To answer this question, Bryk and Raudenbush (1987) reasoned as follows. Suppose we use each subject's data to estimate that subject's intercept and slope. The estimate for the intercept would simply be the sample mean; that is, for a subject with five observations,

$$\hat{\pi}_{0i} = \bar{Y}_{i\cdot} = \sum \frac{Y_{it}}{5},$$

and the sampling variance of $\hat{\pi}_{0i}$ is

$$\text{Var}(\hat{\pi}_{0i} - \pi_{0i}) = \sigma^2/5,$$

where, according to Table 6.2, σ^2 is estimated to be .0262, so that the estimated sampling variance of $\hat{\pi}_{0i}$ is $.0262/5 = .00524$. Similarly, the least-squares estimator of the slope for subject i is

$$\hat{\pi}_{1i} = \frac{\Sigma(\text{AGE} - 13)_{it}(Y_{it} - \bar{Y}_{i\cdot})}{\Sigma(\text{AGE} - 13)_{it}^2}$$

with sampling variance

$$\text{Var}(\hat{\pi}_{1i} - \pi_{1i}) = \frac{\Sigma^2}{\Sigma(\text{AGE} - 13)_{it}^2}$$

where $\Sigma(\text{AGE} - 13)_{it}^2 = 10$, so that the estimated sampling variance of $\hat{\pi}_{1i}$ is $.0262/10 = .00262$. Hence, each subject's data supplies estimates of the two unknown quantities, the mean and the slope. Part of the variation in these quantities is "noise," that is, sampling variance, and we have estimates of the noise in each case. However, our analysis also supplies estimates of the "variance of the true intercepts," that is, $\hat{\tau}_{00} = .0345$, as well as the "variance of the true slopes," that is $\hat{\tau}_{11} = .0030$. We can use these to construct reliability estimates having the form

$$\text{reliability} = \frac{\text{``true score'' variance}}{\text{``observed score'' variance,}}$$

which, for the mean and the slope, respectively, are

$$\text{reliability}(\hat{\pi}_{0i}) = \frac{.0345}{.0345 + .00524} = .87,$$

$$\text{reliability}(\hat{\pi}_{1i}) = \frac{.0030}{.0030 + .00262} = .53.$$

The formulas make it clear that reliability depends on two factors: the degree of intersubject variability in the growth parameter (i.e., τ_{00} and τ_{11}) and the sample size per subject (the length of the study): the greater the heterogeneity among subjects and the larger the sample size per subject, the higher the reliability.

Our results suggest that the data contain substantial "signal" for detecting differences among subjects in their means with less signal for detecting slope differences. This does not mean that we shall forsake entirely the possibility of predicting slope differences because our earlier hypothesis testing revealed statistically significant intersubject heterogeneity on slopes as well as means.

These reliability results are based on the assumption that a subject has five time points. To see how the sample size per subject affects reliability, let us consider those subjects with only the first four time points. The reliability estimates computed as above for such a subject are .84 for the intercept and .36 for the slope. Note that the loss of one data point reduces the reliability of the slope (from .53 to .36) more than it does the reliability of the intercept (.87 to .84).

One might wonder how the varying sample sizes in this study affect the precision of estimation of the fixed effects, that is the grand mean at age 13, $\hat{\beta}_{00}$, and the average slope, $\hat{\beta}_{10}$. We find that when the sample size per subject varies, the effective within-subject sample size is, to a close approximation, the harmonic mean

$$T(\text{harmonic}) = \frac{n}{\Sigma(1/T_i)},$$

where n is the number of subjects and T_i is the number of time points for subject i. In our case, 163 subjects have five data points, 44 have four, 16 have three, 9 have two, and 7 have one. Hence, the harmonic mean is

$$T(\text{harmonic}) = \frac{239}{163/5 + 44/4 + 16/3 + 9/2 + 7} = 3.96.$$

For example, for balanced designs, the estimated standard error for $\hat{\beta}_{00}$ is

$$SE(\hat{\beta}_{00}) = \sqrt{\frac{\hat{\tau}_{00} + \sigma^2/T}{J}}.$$

Substituting the harmonic mean

$$SE(\hat{\beta}_{00}) = \sqrt{\frac{.0345 + .0262/3.96}{239}} = .013,$$

which reproduces the result reported in Table 6.2. Using the harmonic mean as an effective sample size makes it quite simple to assess power when sample sizes are unequal.

Specification of a Between-Subjects (Time-Invariant) Covariate

Our results so far indicate significant variation among subjects both in terms of intercepts (rates of deviance at age 13) and rates of increase in deviance, encouraging a search for differences in subject background that might account for this variation. In this illustrative analysis, we utilized race, income, and sex as predictors, but found that only sex was related to the intercept or rate of change.

Using the variable sex as an example, we now illustrate how time-invariant predictors ("covariates"), either discretely or continuously measured, may be incorporated in the model.

The level-1 model of Equation 6.1, which accounts for variation within subjects over time, remains unchanged. However, the level-2 model (Equation 6.2) is elaborated:

$$\pi_{0i} = \beta_{00} + \beta_{01}X_i + u_{0i},$$
$$\pi_{1i} = \beta_{10} + \beta_{11}X_i + u_{1i}, \tag{6.4}$$

where

$X_i = 1$ if female, 0 if male

$\beta_{00} =$ expected deviance at age 13 for males

$\beta_{01} =$ difference in deviance between females and males at age 13

$\beta_{10} =$ expected rate of change in deviance for males

$\beta_{11} =$ mean difference in rate of change between females and males

$u_{0i} =$ random effect of person i on deviance at age 13 after accounting for sex differences

$u_{1i} =$ random effect of person i on the rate of increase in deviance after accounting for sex differences

The results (Table 6.2, Model 2) imply that females have significantly lower levels of deviance at 13, $\hat{\beta}_{01} = -.074$, $t = -2.88$. However, there is no significant sex difference in rates of increase, $\hat{\beta}_{11} = -.011$, $t = -1.12$. These results are graphed for males and females in Figure 6.3 (see solid lines above ages 11 through 15).

Specification of a Within-Subjects (Time-Varying) Covariate

The researcher may also wish to control for covariates that change with time. Examples might include changes in family status, movement to a new neighborhood, or loss of a job. We shall utilize exposure to deviant peers which we expect to change over time. Of course, such exposure cannot be viewed as exogenous to deviance because those who are initially high in deviance may seek out deviant peers, and this new set of friendships may lead to further increases in deviance. It is nonetheless interesting to discover whether controlling for exposure to deviant peers partially or even completely accounts for growth in deviance between 11 and 15. If not, other mechanisms may be at work that explain interpersonal differences in rates of change.

Level-1 Model

Recall that to incorporate between-subjects (time-invariant) covariates required elaboration of the level-2 model. In contrast, specification of within-

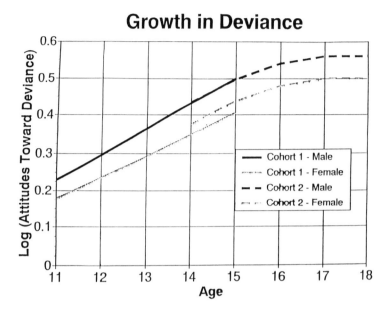

FIG. 6.3. Expected logarithm of the attitudes toward deviance (vertical axis) as a function of age (horizontal axis) for cohort 1 (solid line)
and cohort 2 (dashed line) based on separate analyses for each cohort.

subjects (time-varying) predictors requires elaboration of the level-1 model
(Equation 6.1), which now becomes

$$Y_{it} = \pi_{0i} + \pi_{1i}(\text{AGE} - 13)_{it} + \pi_{2i}(\text{EXPOSURE})_{it} + e_{it}, \qquad (6.5)$$

where $(\text{EXPOSURE})_{it}$ represents the level of exposure to deviant peers of subject
i at time t, π_{2i} is the partial effect of exposure, controlling for age, and both the
intercept, π_{0i}, and the linear age effect (rate of change), π_{1i}, are adjusted for
exposure.

Level-2 Model

Three parameters (the π's) now characterize the trajectory of each subject.
The level-2 model must now specify how those are viewed as varying across
subjects. That model becomes

$$\begin{aligned}
\pi_{0i} &= \beta_{00} + \beta_{01}X_i + u_{0i}, \\
\pi_{1i} &= \beta_{10} + \beta_{11}X_i + u_{1i}, \\
\pi_{2i} &= \beta_{20} + \beta_{21}X_i,
\end{aligned} \qquad (6.6)$$

where X_i remains the indicator for sex (1 if female, 0 if male). Note that we have
constrained the random effect of subjects on the exposure slope (π_{2i}) to be zero.

A prior analysis revealed that the exposure random effect was quite collinear with the age random effect, so the exposure effect was fixed.

Results

Table 6.2 (Model 3) reveals several interesting results. First, we see that exposure is strongly and positively related to deviance, $\hat{\beta}_{20} = .293$, $t = 9.28$. The causal status of this effect remains unclear, though, as mentioned, the relationship between exposure and deviance is probably reciprocal. Second, once exposure is controlled, the mean difference in deviance at age 13 between males and females become nonsignificant, $\hat{\beta}_{01} = -.031$, $t = -1.44$. Apparently males are more likely to be exposed to deviant peers and this higher propensity helps account for the higher deviance among males. Third, once exposure has been controlled, sex differences in rates of change become significant, $\hat{\beta}_{11} = -.023$, $t = -2.50$. If exposure is held constant, the rate of increase in deviance tends to be faster for males than for females.

Subsequent Analyses

Raudenbush and Chan (1992) replicated the logic of the analysis described above using data from a second cohort of youth who were 14 at the outset of the study (in 1976) and 18 at the termination of data collection (descriptive statistics for cohort 2 are listed in Table 6.1). Results for this older cohort were quite different from those for the 11–15-year-old cohort reported above. Specifically, a significant negative quadratic trend, manifest both for males and females, appeared in the 14–18-year-old data. Such a trend may be interpreted as evidence of a deceleration in the rate of increase of pro-deviant attitudes during later adolescence. Figure 6.3 displays the mean trajectories by sex for the two cohorts. Cohort 1, aged 11–15 (solid line) exhibits a comparatively rapid rate of increase in pro-deviant attitudes, and the relationship between age and the outcome during these early adolescent years is linear. In contrast, the rate of increase is slower in cohort 2's data (dashed line), and a curvilinear effect is apparent, with the rate of increase nearing zero at around age 17.

There are several alternative explanations for the differences between results for cohorts 1 and 2 displayed in Figure 6.3. First, the comparatively rapid increase in deviance during early adolescence, followed by deceleration later in adolescence, could indicate an underlying developmental phenomenon in which deviant propensities increase rapidly during early adolescence and then decelerate later, achieving a peak in late adolescence and then declining during early adulthood. In contrast, it could be that demographic differences between the two cohorts interact with age, and that if we had data on cohort 1 from age 15 to 18 we would see, for example, a continuing linear increase in pro-deviant attitudes. According to this explanation, the comparatively smaller rate of increase manifest in cohort two's data reflects the different personal backgrounds or experiences of that cohort and has nothing to do with their older age. Interactions between age and period could also arguably account for the different trajectories of the two cohorts.

To distinguish among these potential explanations, Raudenbush and Chan conducted a further analysis that merged the data from the two cohorts and tested for a cohort effect and an age-by-cohort interaction. In effect, they were testing the null hypothesis that the two cohorts have the same mean and rate of growth at the times their data overlap, that is, at ages 14 and 15. If these effects were found null, the weight would fall on the developmental explanation. This kind of analysis is potentially important in longitudinal studies using a multiple-cohort design in which subjects of varying age are sampled at a single time point and then followed for several years. The goal of such an analysis is to describe development over a comparatively long interval of the life course by collecting data over a comparatively short interval of time (Tonry et al., 1991), and so this design has been labeled an "accelerated longitudinal design." In the current example, one hopes to learn about development over nine years (between ages 11

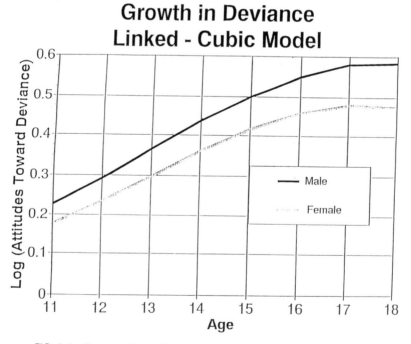

FIG. 6.4.   Expected logarithm of the attitudes toward deviance (vertical axis) as a function of age (horizontal axis) for all subjects in cohorts 1 and 2, based on an analysis that links data from the two cohorts.

and 18) even though data were collected on only five occasions, from 1976 to 1980. The two-level hierarchical linear model is well suited to analyzing data merged across cohorts because the model readily incorporates unbalanced data. An important result of Raudenbush and Chan's analysis was that no significant cohort effects were found on the deviance base rate, π_{0i}, or on the linear rate of change in deviance, π_{1i}. This result implies that both the base rate in deviance and the rate of change in deviance at age 14.5 are not significantly different across the two cohorts. Thus, it appears, the same mean growth trajectory appears to apply to both cohorts (Figure 6.4), reinforcing the inference that, although young people become increasingly pro-deviant in their thinking during early adolescence, on average, the rate of increase diminishes, with pro-deviant thinking reaching a peak around the age of 17. Thus, the typical trajectory of pro-deviant thinking as a function of age is similar in shape to the trajectory of the propensity to commit serious theft shown in Figure 6.1.

INCORPORATING THE EFFECTS OF SOCIAL CONTEXT

In the pair of illustrative examples below, the designs involve time-series data collected on persons who are members of social contexts (schools or communities). The models must therefore incorporate both interindividual and intercontextual variation in the shape of development. Characteristics of persons and contexts that jointly shape development may be represented in the model as time-invariant covariates. Responses of the environment over time are represented as time-varying covariates. Unpredictable components of variation at the personal and contextual level are represented as random effects. Extension to nonnormal data and nonlinear models is quite straightforward, and we consider this issue briefly in closing.

Suppose that during the course of the investigation, each subject is a member of one and only one social context such as a school or community. Then the design would involve time-series data collected on subjects nested within social contexts. A three-level hierarchical model is appropriate for such a design, and we describe application of this model below. However, in most settings, subjects will migrate across social contextual boundaries during the course of the investigation. In this case, subjects are crossed rather than nested within social context. We shall consider hierarchical models in which each time-series observation is nested within a cell created by the cross-classification of subjects and contexts. We begin, however, with the simpler three-level model for nested data.

Three-Level Models

Let us return to the curves plotted in Figure 6.4 that describe the characteristic relationship between age and pro-deviant attitudes for males and females in the

United States between 1976 and 1980. These plots represent estimated mean
growth curves for males and females. However, Table 6.2 indicates that significant interpersonal variation exists; both the base levels of the outcome and the
linear rate of increase vary insignificantly from subject to subject. In essence,
each subject has a personal growth curve, and the plots in Figure 6.4 represent
the average of these personal trajectories.

Let us suppose that the subjects of our study were nested within communities
during the course of the investigation. Time-invariant community covariates
could be used to predict the intercept, linear, quadratic, and cubic change components in a way quite analogous to the use of sex as a covariate in Equation 6.4.
Time-varying covariates measured at the community level could be incorporated
in the same way as we incorporated exposure to deviant peers as a time-varying
covariate in Equation 6.5. However, we need also to incorporate the unmeasured
(random) effects of communities. To do so, we add a third level to the model.

Unfortunately, the NYS data do not include information about the membership of young people in ecologically meaningful community or neighborhood
contexts, and so we turn to an example from educational research in order to
illustrate application of the model.

Example: Growth of Children Nested
Within Primary Schools

Bryk and Raudenbush (1988) analyzed a subset of the Sustaining Effects Study
data (Carter, 1984) in which 618 students nested within 86 schools were followed
during the first three years of primary school. Test scores in mathematics and
reading were collected at five points: spring of grade 1, fall and spring of grade
2, and fall and spring of grade 3. The California Tests of Basic Skills were the
outcome measure. These have been equated across forms to reveal growth. The
existence of an interval scale over the ages under study is a critical element in
modeling change and we shall return to this issue in closing.

Level-1 Model

Children's growth in math and reading tends to be well-described by a linear
model during these grades; however, some accommodation must be made for the
effect associated with their receiving no instruction during the summer. Hence,
we formulate a model for change over time that includes an intercept, a linear
rate of change, and the effects of a time-varying covariate indicating whether the
previous period was the summer or the academic year. The metrics of the two
level-1 predictors are given in the following table:

| | Grade 1 | Grade 2 | | Grade 3 | |
	Spring	Fall	Spring	Fall	Spring
TIME POINT	0	1	2	3	4
SUMMER DROP	0	1	0	1	0

$$Y_{tij} = \pi_{0ij} + \pi_{1ij}(\text{TIME POINT})_{tij}$$
$$+ \pi_{2ij}(\text{SUMMER DROP})_{tij} + e_{tij}, \tag{6.7}$$

where

$$Y_{tij} = \text{outcome at time } t \text{ for child } i \text{ in school } j$$

$(\text{TIME POINT})_{tij} = 0, 1, 2, 3,$ and 4 at the five time points, respectively

$(\text{SUMMER DROP})_{tij} = 1$ in the fall and 0 in the spring

$\pi_{0ij} =$ expected value of the outcome when both TIME POINT and SUMMER DROP are zero and, hence, represents the "initial status" of child ij, that is, the status of the child at spring of first grade

$\pi_{1ij} =$ linear rate of increase in learning per year

$\pi_{2ij} =$ summer effect on the outcome for that subject

$e_{tij} =$ random error assumed independently normally distributed with variance σ^2; i.e., $e_{tij} \sim N(0, \sigma^2)$

According to the model, child i in school j will gain π_{1ij} in achievement during the calendar year, $\pi_{1ij} + \pi_{2ij}$ during the summer, and $\pi_{1ij} - \pi_{2ij}$ during the academic year. Hence, three parameters describe the growth of each child: an initial status, π_{0ij}, a yearly learning rate, π_{1ij}, and a summer drop-off effect, π_{2ij}.

Level-2 Model

Within each school, each of the three child-specific growth parameters π_{pij}, $p = 0, 1, 2$, is now modeled as varying around a school mean, i.e.,

$$\pi_{pij} = \beta_{p0j} + u_{pij}, \tag{6.8}$$

where β_{p0j} is the mean value of growth parameter p within school j and u_{pij} is a random child effect. These school effects are assumed to have a trivariate normal distribution with variances $\text{Var}(u_{pij}) = \tau_{\pi pp}$ and covariances $\text{Cov}(u_{pij}, u_{p'ij}) = \tau_{\pi pp'}$ to be estimated. Thus, each school is characterized by a mean initial status, a mean growth rate, and a summer drop-off effect. Within each school, children's growth parameters vary randomly. In fact, a preliminary analysis revealed little evidence that the summer drop-off effect varied much among children within schools, and so this variance and the associated covariances were constrained to be null.

Level-3 Model

The three β's that characterize typical growth within a school are now viewed as varying randomly across the entire population of schools according to the model

$$\beta_{p0j} = \gamma_{p00} + v_{p0j} \tag{6.9}$$

where γ_{p00} is the grand mean of the growth parameter p, and v_{p0j} represents a random school effect for parameters $p = 0, 1, 2$. The three school effects are assumed to vary across schools according to a trivariate normal distribution with variances $\text{Var}(v_{p0j}) = \tau_{\beta pp}$ and covariances $\text{Cov}(v_{p0j}, v_{p'0j}) = \tau_{\beta pp'}$.

Results

Figure 6.5 displays the mean growth curves in both reading and mathematics. The figure indicates that, for mathematics, as expected, there is a positive growth rate during the academic year and essentially no growth during the summer. For reading the results are a bit different. There is some growth during summer, though certainly less than during the academic year.

Of course we assume that the growth curves vary from child to child within schools and from school to school. In essence, each child and school can be characterized by a growth function of the type displayed in Figure 6.5, and, in fact, empirical Bayes methods can be used to estimate such functions for each of the 86 schools and each of the 618 children.[3]

Table 6.3 provides the results for the math outcome. The mean growth curve is described by the mean initial status, $\hat{\gamma}_{000} = 403.27$, the mean calendar-year learning rate, $\hat{\gamma}_{100} = 28.51$, and the mean summer drop-off effect, $\hat{\gamma}_{200} = -27.78$. Note that the mean summer learning rate is $\hat{\gamma}_{000} + \hat{\gamma}_{100} = 28.51 - 27.78$ is near zero as indicated in Figure 6.5.

Perhaps more interesting are the variance component estimates. Variance components estimates for initial status are 1033.05 within schools and 173.04 between schools, implying that only $173.04/(173.04 + 1033.05)$, or 14.3%, of the variation in initial status lies between schools. In contrast, the variance in growth rates between schools is estimated at 19.08, and the variance within schools at 3.97, implying that the lion's share of 82.8% of the variance lies between schools! The implication of these results for school-effects research is potentially important. Most studies of school effects have compared schools by comparing the status of the students in them and found that school differences

---

[3]These empirical Bayes estimates are produced routinely by the computer software used in these examples (Bryk et al., 1988).

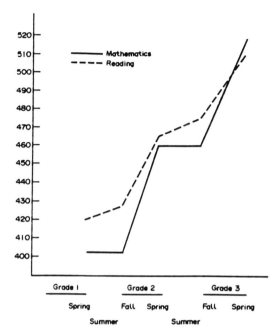

FIG. 6.5.   Expected growth functions in math and reading based on three-level model analysis of data from the Sustaining Effects Study.

TABLE 6.3
Three-Level Results from Sustaining Effects Data

(a) Fixed Effects

Predictor	Coefficient	SE	t Ratio
Average initial status, γ_{000}	403.27	2.28	—
Average learning rate, γ_{100}	28.51	0.62	46.05
Average summer drop, γ_{200}	−27.78	1.23	−22.60

(b) Variance Components

Parameter	Estimate	Chi-Square	df	p
Level 1				
σ^2	613.10			
Level 2				
Initial status, $\tau_{\pi00}$	1033.05	2148.80	532	.000
Learning rate, $\tau_{\pi11}$	3.98	694.17	532	.000
Level 3				
Initial status, $\tau_{\beta00}$	173.04	154.51	85	.000
Learning rate, $\tau_{\beta11}$	19.08	235.85	85	.000
Summer drop, $\tau_{\beta22}$	44.60	121.58	85	.000

account for only a fraction of the total variance. Bryk and Raudenbush's (1988) results imply that if investigators study school differences in *learning rates* rather than status, especially in subjects learned only in school, such as mathematics, they are likely to discover much more significant effects of school differences than have previously emerged from school-effects research. We caution that these effects would not appear as important as they are had we used *observed* learning rates as the criterion. The observed rates are likely to be highly fallible as a result of sampling and measurement error, which contribute much more to the within-school variation than to the between-school variation, leading to an underestimate of the school contribution. The results presented in Table 6.3 are maximum likelihood estimates of variances of the "true" or "latent" learning rates, giving a larger and more realistic estimate of the importance of school difference than would appear had the observed rates been assessed.

Incorporating Covariates

The model we have presented so far includes two time-varying predictors (TIME POINT and SUMMER DROP). However, it includes no child-level or school-level predictors. Such covariates can be readily included in the model. For example, the level-2 model could be expanded so that

$$\pi_{pij} = \beta_{p0j} + \sum \beta_{pqj} X_{qij} + u_{pij}, \tag{6.10}$$

where each X_{qij} is a child-level predictor (e.g., sex, socioeconomic status, etc.). The school-specific coefficients β_{pqj} could be allowed to vary randomly over the population of schools, to be constrained to be equal across schools, or to be themselves predicted by school-level covariates. Also, the level-3 model of Equation 6.9 can be expanded so that the school-level growth parameter β_{pqj} can be predicted by school-level covariates. The level-three model may therefore be written

$$\beta_{pqj} = \gamma_{pq0} + \sum \gamma_{pqs} W_{qsj} + v_{pqj}, \tag{6.11}$$

for coefficients β_{pqj}, $p = 0, 1, \ldots, P$ and $q = 0, 1, \ldots, Q_p$ where p indexes the growth parameters in the level-1 model and q indexes the child-level covariates used to predict a growth parameter. The variables W_{qsi}, $s = 1, \ldots, S_{pq}$, are school-level covariates that are hypothesized to influence the magnitude of the school-specific coefficient β_{pqj}. Bryk and Raudenbush (1992) provide a thorough exposition on three-level models in general and on their application to the Sustaining Effects Data, including specification of child-level and school-level covariates.

Parallels with the Two-Level Model

In our discussion of the two-level model, we considered the mean growth trajectory, the degree of individual variability around that mean, the reliability of measures of status and rate of change, and the incorporation of time-invariant and time-varying covariates. Each of these concepts is relevant in the three-level model as we indicate below.

Each school as well as each student now has a growth curve, and the *mean growth curve* is now a weighted average of the school-specific growth curves while each school's growth curve is a weighted average of individual growth curves.

Variability about the mean growth curve now exists at two levels: variability of school-specific growth curves about the mean growth curve and variability of the individual growth curves about the school-specific growth curve.

It is now possible to estimate two types of *reliability:* reliability for distinguishing among schools in status or rate of change, and reliability for distinguishing among students within schools in status or rate of change.

Time-invariant covariates are incorporated at level 2 if those covariates are characteristics of persons (e.g., student sex), and at level 3 if they are characteristics of schools (e.g., school size).

Time-varying covariates, as before, are incorporated at level 1. In fact, SUMMER DROP was a time-varying covariate.

Summary and Extrapolation to the Study of Deviance

A three-level model is useful for studying the individual change of subjects nested within social contexts. The level-1 model specifies a change or growth function for each individual. At level 2, the individual change parameters vary across persons sharing the same social context as a function of context-specific parameters plus error. At level-3, the context-specific parameters vary across contexts as a function of population-wide parameters plus error. Time-varying covariates are specified at level 1, person-specific covariates at level 2, and context-specific covariates at level 3. The variance-covariance structure of the data is decomposed into variance-covariance structures within persons, between persons with contexts and between contexts.

The most obvious application of such three-level models in studying deviance involves formulating a model for change in antisocial behavior or attitudes over time for each person at level 1. The level-1 model would specify the outcome as a function of age and possibly time-varying covariates. That is, the level-1 model specifies the "age-deviance" curve for a particular subject as well as allowing the incorporation of time-varying environmental interventions that may modify that curve. At level-2, person-specific covariates are included. These may represent the investigator's theory regarding the constellation of individual-level characteristics viewed as shaping later development with respect to deviant behavior or attitudes. Time-invariant community-level predictors are specified at level 3. However, community characteristics that change over time may represent important environmental interventions. These will be specified as time-varying predictors at level 1. The social context need not be the community; in some cases school context may be more relevant. It is also possible to employ this model in studying the development of siblings nested within families or of married persons over time.

The Two-Way Crossed Random Effects Model

The three-level nested random effects model facilitates an elegant representation of individual development within a social context. Its application, however, is constrained by the assumption that each person under study will inhabit one and only one social context (e.g., community) during the course of the investigation. If, instead, subjects migrate across social context during the course of the study, a rigid adherence to the three-level model would require one of the following undesirable decisions: (2) ignoring the migration; (b) discarding the data of those who migrate; or (c) ignoring the social context altogether. If the frequency of migration is small, it may make sense to treat the context of origin as the context throughout (ignoring migration). Discarding data is not to be recommended, and ignoring social context defeats the purpose of this chapter.

A more generally satisfactory solution is to regard subjects as crossed with context. Each time-series observation is viewed as nested within a cell defined by the cross-clarification of persons and social contexts. We formulate a model for individual development as in the level-1 models above. However, this model includes a series of indicator variables, one for each social context, conceived as time-varying covariates. In general there will be many such social contexts, and it will be unparsimonious to treat each context effect as a fixed effect in the model. Instead, we view the context effects as random realizations from a probability distribution, and we estimate the parameters of that distribution. As in the three-level model, the context effects are therefore random, though now they vary within subjects. This approach is illustrated in another example from research on cognitive growth, with results borrowed from Raudenbush (1993b).

Example: The Effects of Teachers on Children's Growth in Mathematics

Studying teacher effects on children's growth during the primary grades yields the kind of data structure displayed in Figure 6.6 where each row represents a child and each column a teacher. The data constitute a subsample from the "Immersion Study" (Ramirez et al., 1991), a national evaluation of alternative programs for children in the United States having limited English proficiency. The outcome measure is again the California Tests of Basic Skills. The investigators aimed to test each child during the spring of each year from grade 1 to grade 4. However, attrition was very high, and most children have fewer than four data points.

Each X indicates an Observation

Grade	Grade 1					Grade 2					Grade 3					Grade 4			
Teacher	1	3	5	7	9	11	13	15	17	19	21	23				25	27		
	2	4	6	8	10	12	14	16	18		20	22	24			26			Totals

Student

	1	2	3	4	5	6	7	8	9	10	11	12	13	14	15	16	17	18	19	20/21	22/23	24	25	26	27	Totals
5003	X										X															2
5005		X									X															2
5006	X																									1
5007		X										X														2
5009			X									X								X			X			4
5010			X			X																				2
5011	X					X														X						3
5013		X																								1
5014							X													X						2
5015			X									X								X						3
.																										.
.																										.
.																										.
5232				X																						1
5234			X				X													X						3
5236		X						X												X						3
5237		X				X																				2
5238		X				X																				2
5241				X																						1
5242			X														X			X						2
5243	X								X																	2
5245		X							X																	2
5246		X					X												X	X						4

| Totals | 5 | 15 | 14 | 13 | 10 | 2 | 10 | 13 | 6 | 11 | 12 | 3 | | | | 11 | 1 | | | | | | | | | |
| | 13 | 18 | 15 | 13 | 7 | 9 | 11 | 4 | 15 | | 12 | 3 | 2 | | | 2 | | | Totals | | | | | | | |

FIG. 6.6. Organization of data in a subsample from the Immersion Study.

In Figure 6.6, the first row describes the data for child 5003, who was assigned teacher 2 during first grade and teacher 11 during grade 2 and was not available for testing during grades 3 or 4. The figure gives the data pattern for the first and last 10 of the 123 children who provided a total of 250 observations and encountered 27 teachers. The data are quite sparse for estimating both child and teacher effects. There are from 1 to 4 data points per child and from 2 to 18 data points per teacher. The analytic approach uses all of the data to estimate these effects, though inferences must be made with extreme caution given the likely nonrandomness of the missing data.

A Two-Level Growth Analysis

We first consider how the data might be analyzed, ignoring teacher effects. At level-1 (within-children) we would model the math outcome for each child via a linear regression with a predictor a_{it} = grade $-$ 1, as described by the following table:

Grade	1	2	3	4
a_{it}	0	1	2	3

Thus, we have the level-1 model

$$Y_{it} = \pi_{0i} + \pi_{1i}a_{it} + e_{it}, \qquad e_{it} \sim N(0, \sigma^2), \qquad (6.12)$$

where

Y_{it} = math outcome for child i at time t, $i = 1, \ldots, 4$; $i = 1, \ldots, 123$
a_{it} = grade $-$ 1, so that $a_{it} = 0$ at grade 1
π_{0i} = expected outcome at first grade for child i
π_{1i} = expected gain per year for child i
e_{it} = within-child error

At level 2, we might view the intercept and rate of change of each child as varying randomly over the population of children; i.e.,

$$\pi_{0i} = \beta_{00} + u_{0i}, \qquad \pi_{1i} = \beta_{10} + u_{1i} \qquad (6.13)$$

where β_{p0}, $p = 0$, 1, are, respectively, the population mean outcome at grade 1 and the population mean rate of change; and the errors u_{pr} are viewed as realizations from a bivariate normal distribution defined on the population of children. In fact, results of estimation based on a two-level hierarchical linear model are displayed in Table 6.4, column 1.

Crossed Random Effects Analysis

We now modify the level-1 model (Equation 6.12) to incorporate the effects of teachers as "time-varying covariates" via the model

$$Y_{it} = \pi_{0i} + \pi_{1i}a_{it} + \sum_{q=1}^{Q} \alpha_q Z_{qit} + e_{it}, \qquad e_{it} \sim N(0, \sigma^2), \qquad (6.14)$$

where

Z_{qit} = indicator variable taking on a value of 1 if child i encounters teacher q at time t and 0 otherwise
α_q = effect associated with teacher q

and the other terms retain the same definitions as in Equation 6.12, controlling, of course, for the teacher effects. Variation between children is modeled exactly as in the previous level-2 model (Equation 6.13).

It would clearly be unparsimonious to estimate 27 regression coefficients, one for each teacher, defined in Equation 6.14. Instead, we conceive of the teacher effects a varying randomly around a mean of zero:

$$\alpha_q \sim N(0, \delta^2), \qquad (6.15)$$

TABLE 6.4
Modeling Results for Immersion Data

(a) Fixed Effects

Predictor	Model 1: Teacher Variance Ignored			Model 2: Teacher Variance Estimated			Model 3: Teacher Variance Prediced		
	Coefficient	SE	t Ratio	Coefficient	SE	t Ratio	Coefficient	SE	t Ratio
Expected first grade status	256.54	2.51	—	257.53	1.71	—	257.66	1.86	—
Expected linear growth rate	47.28	2.24	21.00	45.48	1.48	30.74	44.90	1.65	27.20
Effect of masters' degree							5.37	3.62	1.48

(b) Variance Components

Parameter	Estimate	Estimate	Estimate
Initial status: $\mathrm{Var}(\pi_{0i}) = \tau_{00}$	484.22	442.82	437.04
Growth rate: $\mathrm{Var}(\pi_{1i}) = \tau_{11}$	133.58	94.63	90.74
Covariance, initial status, and growth rate: $\mathrm{Cov}(\pi_{0i}, \pi_{1i}) = \tau_{01}$	28.02	92.87	92.37
Teacher effect: $\mathrm{Var}(v) = \delta^2$		79.49	68.71
Residual error: $\mathrm{Var}(e_{it}) = \sigma^2$	319.60	274.37	279.75

(see column 2 of Table 6.4). In a second analysis, we shall add teacher level of education as a predictor

$$\alpha_q = \gamma W_q + V_q, \qquad v_q \sim N(0, \delta^2),$$

where W_q takes on a value of 1 if teacher q has received a masters or doctoral degree, 0 if not.

A comparison of results between the two-level model that ignores teachers and the crossed random effects model produces some interesting results (second panel of Table 6.4). Estimation of the teacher effect variance of $\hat{\delta}^2 = 79.5$ is accompanied by reductions in the estimates of variance attributable to variation among children in intercepts ($\hat{\tau}_{00}$ of 442.8 in column 2 versus 484.2 in column 1), variance among children in slopes ($\hat{\tau}_{00}$ of 94.6 versus 133.6), and variance within children ($\hat{\sigma}^2$ of 274.4 versus 319.6).

These results illustrate the kinds of benefits that can be expected when social contexts are explicitly incorporated into the model. First, it is apparent that taking teacher effects into account changes our opinion about the extent of individual differences in rates of growth. Part of the variation in these growth rates that is assigned to individual differences is now assigned to the classroom context, as indicated by the reduction in growth rate variance from 133.6 to 94.6 after the teacher indicators were incorporated into the model.

Second, the reduction of within person variance from 319.6 to 274.4 shows that some of the variability attributable to temporal instability in the model that ignores classrooms is now assigned to classrooms. The varying effects of the classroom experiences during a child's primary school career appear as noise in the model that ignores classrooms.

The analysis, then, illustrates the kinds of gains in understanding that can be expected when explicitly incorporating the changing social context effects that occur as persons move across contexts during development. A strong note of caution, however, is in order. As mentioned, these data are quite sparse and exhibit substantial attrition. More generally, however, our interpretations are strongly dependent on the validity of the assumption that students are not assigned to teachers each year on the basis of current achievement. If they were, we would be falsely assigning to classrooms part of the variance accountable by prior growth. Thus, the analyst needs to assess whether systematic selection into classrooms is occurring. Fortunately, the data at hand reveal no evidence of such selection, implying that assignment to classrooms is essentially arbitrary.

To account for variability between classrooms, we added teacher education as a predictor. The addition of the teacher education indicator to the model (column 3) resulted in a small reduction in the teacher-level variance component of $\hat{\delta}^2$ from 79.5 to 68.7. The effect of higher education was in the expected direction, $\hat{\gamma} = 5.37$, but nonsignificant, $t = 1.48$.

Comparison with Two- and Three-Level Models

Like the two- and three-level nested model, the two-way crossed random effects model begins with a model for individual change. However, because social context can vary within a person over time, social context effects are formulated as time-varying covariates. Because the social context effects are numerous and often are assumed to represent a large population, they are specified as random variables. These variables may have a mean of zero, or their means may depend on covariates defined at the context level. Although our example includes only random main effects of context, it is also possible to define regression coefficients that vary over context. For example, it may be that the effect of a teacher depends on student aptitude, in which case the effect of student aptitude on the outcome could be defined as randomly varying over teachers.

As in the case of the three-level nested model, the crossed random effects model allows specification of covariates that are time varying or time invariant. The time-invariant covariates can be defined on persons or contexts. In fact, the crossed random effects model can be shown to be more general than the three-level nested model in that any nested-model results can be reproduced by the crossed random results. However, the crossed random effects analysis is more computationally intensive, so that the nested analysis is preferable when justified.

Parallels with the Two-Level Model

As before, it may help to summarize parallels between the crossed random effects model with respect to common analytic goals.

The *mean growth curve* in a crossed random effects analysis will tend to be very similar to that found in a two-level analysis, as indicated in our example. This mean curve averages over the effects of teachers, and the teacher effects are assumed to have a mean of zero.

Individual variability about the mean growth curve in a crossed random effects analysis is variability net the effect of teachers; it has been adjusted for the teachers encountered by the children.

It is possible to estimate two types of *reliability:* reliability for distinguishing among children in status or rate of change; and reliability for distinguishing among teachers in their effects on children.

Time-invariant covariates are incorporated at level 2 as in the two-level analysis.

Time-varying covariates, as before, are incorporated at level 1. Note that all teacher characteristics (e.g., education, gender, experience) are time-varying covariates.

These principles readily generalize to studies of migration across other types of context such as neighborhoods.

CONCLUSIONS

Two-level, three-level, and crossed random effects models provide a reasonably flexible family of analytic approaches to modeling individual development and social context effects. Each of these models is founded on a model for individual change over time. Each person's development is described by a set of person-specific parameters, and these parameters, in turn, are viewed as varying randomly across the population of persons and, in the cases discussed here, social contexts. Time-varying or time-invariant covariates—and their interactions—may be incorporated at the appropriate levels. In general, time-invariant personal characteristics may be specified as predicting the entire trajectory of later development. Environmental responses may be incorporated as time-varying covariates.

Missing data, unbalanced designs, and unequal spacing of time points across subjects pose no difficulties for the analyses, though the investigator must carefully study the sources of attrition and imbalance to insure that these do not give rise to erroneous inference. The capacity of the method to handle unbalanced data suits it well to application in accelerated longitudinal designs, as indicated in the example from the National Youth Survey.

The metric of the dependent variable is of critical importance in studies of quantitative change. In each of the examples illustrated in this chapter, the dependent variable was measured on an interval scale having the same definition over time. It is on this scale that terms like "early acceleration" in deviant propensity, "peak age," and "rate of desistance" become meaningful. In the educational examples the concepts of "summer drop-off" in learning rate and "proportion of variation in learning rates between schools" similarly depend on the existence of a meaningful interval scale over the ages under study. The standardization of such dependent variables within ages or their transformation to percentile ranks are fatal to the characterization of development in these meaningful and dynamic terms.

The examples provided here have employed outcomes measured continuously and predicted by linear models with normal errors. Progress on nonlinear, nonnormal models for discrete outcomes is now rapid. Raudenbush (1993a) has presented preliminary results based on this kind of model (see Figures 6.1 and 6.2), and a subsequent paper will consider their application to the study of individual development in a social context. The logic of the two-level model in this case of binary outcomes is as follows, using theft as an example.

Level-1 Sampling Model

Given the underlying probability that person i will commit theft at time t, the outcome (theft versus no theft) for that person at that time is viewed as a Bernoulli random variable.

Level-1 Structural Model

The logit of the probability of theft (i.e., the log-odds of theft) for a person at a given time is viewed as a polynomial function of age.

Level-2 Structural Model

The parameters defined at level 1 (e.g., linear rate of increase or acceleration rate of increase in the log-odds of theft) become outcome variables to be explained by measured characteristics of the person plus person-specific random effects.

Level-2 Sampling Model

The person-specific random effects are assumed multivariate normally distributed over the population of persons.

The reader will note that, aside from the level-1 sampling model and the logit ("log-odds") transformation, the above model is identical to the two-level model for continuous outcomes described earlier in this chapter. Thus, extensions to a three-level nested model or a crossed random effects model are similar as well.

When the outcome is a behavioral count, the level-1 sampling model assumes that the number of thefts committed, given a person's latent underlying "rate" of theft at time t, is Poisson distributed. The level-1 sampling model relates the log of the rate of that person at that time to a polynomial function of age. The model for counts is otherwise identical to the model for binary outcomes.

Violations of the model assumptions may be quite likely whether the data are continuous or discrete. For example, level-1 observations may be autocorrelated even after controlling for the person-specific random effects. And the level-2 random person effects may not be normal. Zeger, Liang, and Albert (1988) discuss a strategy for insuring the robustness of inferences about the fixed effects of the model to such violations, and this strategy is employed by Raudenbush (1993a), who used a modification of software for hierarchical linear model analysis.

Interpretation of results of models based on link functions such as the logit or log must be made with some care, as the above references indicate, though this issue goes beyond the scope of this chapter.

What appears most crucial in the nonnormal case as well as the normal case, however, is the formulation of explicit models that reflect the conceptualization of the psychological and ecological correlates of development and that are appropriate to the design of the data collection. The basic principles of modeling elucidated here will then apply to a broad class of outcome measures, personal characteristics, and conceptions of social context.

REFERENCES

Bock, R. D. (1975). *Multivariate statistical methods in behavioral research.* New York: McGraw-Hill.

Bryk, A. S., & Raudenbush, S. W. (1987). Application of hierarchical linear models to assessing change. *Psychological Bulletin, 101*(1), 147–158.

Bryk, A. S., & Raudenbush, S. W. (1988). Toward a more appropriate conceptualization of research on school effects: A three-level hierarchical linear model. *American Journal of Education, 97*(1), 65–108.

Bryk, A. S., & Raudenbush, S. W. (1992). *Hierarchical linear models in social and behavioral research: Applications and data analysis methods.* Newbury Park, CA: Sage.

Bryk, A. S., Raudenbush, S. W., Seltzer, M., & Congdon, R. (1988). *An introduction to HLM: Computer program and users manual.* University of Chicago Department of Education.

Carter, L. F. (1984). The sustaining effects study of compensatory and elementary education. *Educational Researcher, 13*(7), 4–13.

Dempster, A. P., Laird, N. M., & Rubin, D. B. (1977). Maximum likelihood from incomplete data via the EM algorithm. *Journal of the Royal Statistical Society, Series B, 39,* 1–8.

Dempster, A. P., Rubin, D. B., & Tsutakawa, R. K. (1981). Estimation in covariance components models. *Journal of the American Statistical Association, 76,* 341–353.

Farrington, D. (1993). Have any individual, family, or neighborhood influences on offending been demonstrated conclusively? In Farrington, D. E., Sampson, R. J., & Wikstrom, P-O. *Integrating individual and ecological aspects of crime.* Stockholm: National Council for Crime Prevention.

Francis, D. J., Fletcher, J. M., Stubting, K. K., Davidson, K. C., & Thompson, N. M. (1991). Analysis of change: Modeling individual growth. *Journal of Consulting and Clinical Psychology, 39*(1), 27–37.

Goldstein, H. (1987). *Multilevel models in educational and social research.* London: Oxford University Press.

Goldstein, H. (1989). Models for multilevel response variables with an application to growth curves. In R. D. Bock (Ed.), *Multilevel analysis of educational data.* New York: Academic Press.

Gottfredson, M., & Hirschi, T. (1990). *A general theory of crime.* Stanford: Stanford University Press.

Hopkins, K. D. (1982). the unit of analysis: Group means versus individual observations. *American Educational Research Journal, 19*(1), 5–18.

Huttenlocher, J. E., Haight, W., Bryk, A. S., & Seltzer, M. (1991). Early vocabulary growth: Relation to language input and gender. *Developmental Psychology, 27*(2), 236–249.

Laird, N. M., & Ware, J. H. (1982). Random-effects models for longitudinal data. *Biometrika, 65*(1), 581–590.

Lee, V., & Bryk, A. S. (1989). A multilevel model of the social distribution of high school achievement. *Sociology of Education, 62,* 172–192.

Lindley, D. V., & Smith, A. F. M. (1972). Bayes estimates for the linear model. *Journal of the Royal Statistical Society, Series B, 34,* 1–41.

Ramirez, D., Yuen, S., Ramey, R., & Pasta, D. (1991). *The immersion study: Final report.* Washington, DC: U.S. Office of Educational Research and Improvement.

Raudenbush, S. W. (1988). Educational applications of hierarchical linear models: A review. *Journal of Educational Statistics, 13*(2), 85–116.

Raudenbush, S. W. (1993a). *Posterior modal estimation for hierarchical generalized linear models with application to dichotomous and count data.* Unpublished manuscript, College of Education, Michigan State University.

Raudenbush, S. W. (1993b). A crossed random effects model for unbalanced data with applications in cross-sectional and longitudinal research. *Journal of Educational Statistics, 18*(4), 321–349.

Raudenbush, S. W., & Chan, W. S. (1992). Growth curve analysis in a longitudinal accelerated design. *Journal of Research on Crime and Delinquency, 29*(4), 387–411.

Raudenbush, S. W., & Chan, W. S. (1993). Application of a hierarchical linear model to the study of deviance in an overlapping cohort design. *Journal of Clinical and Consulting Psychology, 61,* 6, 941–951.

Raudenbush, S. W., Rowan, B., & Cheong, Y. F. (1992). Contextual effects on the self-perceived efficacy of high school teachers. *Sociology of Education, 65,* 150–167.

Rogosa, D. R., Brand, D., & Zimowski, M. (1982). A growth curve approach to the measurement of change. *Psychological Bulletin, 90,* 726–748.

Rogosa, D. R., & Willett, J. B. (1985). Understanding correlates of change by modeling individual differences in growth. *Psychometrika, 90,* 726–748.

Strenio, J. L. F., Weisberg, H. I., & Bryk, A. S. (1983). Empirical Bayes estimation of individual growth curves parameters and their relationship to covariates. *Biometrics, 39,* 71–86.

Tonry, M., Ohlin, L. E., & Farrington, D. P. (1991). *Human development and criminal behavior: New ways of advancing knowledge.* New York: Springer-Verlag.

Ware, J. H. (1985). Linear models for the analysis of longitudinal studies. *American Statistician, 39*(2), 95–101.

Willms, J. D., & Jacobson, S. (1990). Growth in mathematics skills during the intermediate years: Sex differences and school effects. *International Journal of Educational Research, 14,* 157–174.

Zeger, S. L., Liang, K-Y., & Albert, P. S. (1988). Models for longitudinal data: A generalized estimating equation approach. *Biometrics, 44,* 1049–1060.

7

Investigating Onset, Cessation, Relapse, and Recovery: Using Discrete-Time Survival Analysis to Examine the Occurrence and Timing of Critical Events

John B. Willett
Judith D. Singer
Harvard University

The use of survival analysis is introduced in this chapter by Willett and Singer. The data are discrete information on event occurrence, such as we might have with onset, relapse, and recovery in clinical applications, or particular events of importance (e.g., adjudication for delinquent acts, death, divorce, graduation) in longitudinal studies.

—Editor

Researchers in psychology often pose questions about the occurrence and timing of particular events; they ask *whether* and, if so, *when* a variety of events occur. Researchers investigating the course of affective illness for instance, have examined: when the disease first strikes (Rice, Reich, Andreasen, Endicott et al., 1987; Turnbull, George, Landerman, Swartz, & Blazer, 1990), the length of time between onset and entry into treatment (Monroe, Simons, & Thase, 1991), the length of initial illness spells (Zito, Craig, Wanderling, & Siegel, 1987), how long treated patients remain free of symptoms (Frank, Kupfer, & Perel, 1989; Krantz & Moos, 1988), whether people with a history of affective disorder tend to relapse (Suppes, Baldessarini, Faedda, & Tohen, 1991), how long successfully treated people remain well before relapse (Prien, Kupfer, Mansky, Small et al., 1984), and how long second and subsequent illness spells last (Shapiro, Quitkin, & Fleiss, 1989).

Similar questions arise in investigations of the occurrence and timing of a broad range of psychologically interesting events. They arise, for instance, in research on the

- Onset, treatment, and recurrence of other illnesses (anxiety disorder, obsessive-compulsive disorder, suicidality, seasonal affective disorder, sexual dysfunction)
- Onset and relapse of undesirable behaviors (antisocial behavior, criminal activity, smoking, drug use, gambling, alcohol abuse, unsafe sexual practices, marital distress)
- Efficacy of particular types of treatment (self-help, social support, telephone counseling, behavior modification, psychotherapy, pharmacotherapy hospitalization)
- Attainment of developmental milestones (first step, first word, particular cognitive, moral and interpersonal stages, menarche, menopause)
- Occurrence and timing of important behaviors (learning to drive, first sexual experience, pregnancy)

With a little thought, the list seems to become almost endless.

In the past, answering questions about the occurrence and timing of events was difficult, if not analytically intractable. Thankfully, however, there are new statistical techniques—the methods of *survival analysis*—that are ideally suited to answering these questions about "whether" and "when." Since the 1972 publication of Cox's seminal paper on these new and innovative methods, survival techniques have enjoyed increasing popularity in many disparate disciplines, including archaeology (Bleed, 1991), industrial product testing (Lawless, 1982), economics (Heckman & Singer, 1985), education (Willett & Singer, 1991), sociology (Tuma & Hannan, 1984), and wildlife management (Murphy, Singer, & Nichols, 1990).

Despite their suitability for answering important questions in psychological research, however, survival methods are only now beginning to make an impact in this domain. Recently, for instance, the *Journal of Consulting and Clinical Psychology* has published a nontechnical introduction to continuous-time survival methods (Greenhouse, Stangl, & Bromberg, 1989) and several empirical applications (see, for instance, Cooney, Kadden, Litt, & Getter, 1991; Hall, Havassy, & Wasserman, 1991; Hart, Kropp, & Hare, 1988; Sorenson, Rutter, & Aneshensel, 1991; Stevens & Hollis, 1989; Weisz, Walter, Weiss, Fernandez, & Mikow, 1990). In this chapter, we use examples drawn from some of these sources to enrich and illuminate our presentation.

If survival methods lend themselves so naturally to important questions in psychological research, why have they yet to be routinely employed? While we cannot know for certain, we believe that this dearth stems from the misconception that these methods are analytically complex and practically intractable. Add some ominous and foreboding terminology (such as "survival" and "hazard") and perhaps clinical researchers cannot be blamed for choosing alternative analytic routes (Wainer, 1990).

But recent methodological developments, along with improvements in statistical computing, promise to change this state of affairs. Several articles published during the past five years have demonstrated the utility of survival methods for exploring psychological and psychiatric phenomena (Fichman, 1988; Gardner & Griffin, 1989; Morita, Lee, & Mowday, 1989; Singer & Willett, 1991, 1992) and social phenomena (Hutchison, 1988a, 1988b; Willett & Singer, 1989, 1991, 1994). Most statistical packages for both mainframe and personal computers now include some form of program for analyzing survival data and for fitting at least one type of survival model, usually the "proportional-hazards" model for continuous-time data (Goldstein et al., 1989; Harrell & Goldstein, 1992). And in addition to the classic references (Cox & Oakes, 1984; Kalbfleisch & Prentice, 1980; Miller, 1981), many excellent methodological introductions to the new methods are now available (Allison, 1982; Blossfeld, Hamerle, & Mayer, 1989; Harrington & Fleming, 1991; Yamaguchi, 1991).

In this chapter, we introduce a subclass of survival methodology, called *discrete-time survival analysis,* that we believe has much relevance for research in psychology and the social sciences. To facilitate our presentation, we begin by distinguishing between discrete- and continuous-time survival methods and by commenting on the advantages of the latter over the former for social and psychological research. Our presentation then continues heuristically, as we use real data from the psychological research literature to motivate our arguments and substantiate the need for the specialized analytic methods that we subsequently outline. We describe the foundations of discrete-time survival analysis and we review, also via concrete example, the different types of effects that can be easily explored within the framework of discrete-time survival analysis. Throughout our chapter, we comment on important issues in data analysis and we provide examples of easy ways that investigators can interpret the findings of their discrete-time survival analyses for the colleague, the layperson, the clinician, and the policymaker.

WHY EMPHASIZE A DISCRETE-TIME APPROACH?

There is a critical distinction that must be observed in survival analysis between *continuous-time* and *discrete-time* methods. The definition of the fundamental parameters, the construction and interpretation of the central statistical models, and the statistical methods for model fitting and parameter estimation differ critically between the two approaches. In our opinion, parameter definition, model structure, statistical analysis, and interpretation are considerably simpler and more comprehensible in the discrete-time case. Furthermore we believe that initial mastery of the discrete-time approach facilitates the transfer of analytic expertise to the continuous-time framework, if it should be required. We explore these and further advantages below.

When event occurrence is being investigated in any form of survival study, times-to-event must be measured for everyone in the sample. And, as the label implies, the use of continuous-time survival analysis requires that these measurements be recorded as continuous data. Discrete-time survival analysis, on the other hand, requires only that the investigator know in which of several discrete time periods the event of interest occurred. Consequently, when observing event occurrence in discrete-time survival analysis, we behave as though time has been partitioned into a sequence of continuous discrete time periods.

Although there is no mathematical reason for these time intervals to be of the same duration as each other, it is usually extremely convenient from an interpretative perspective to ensure that all discrete time periods are of equal duration. Typically, they may each represent a day, a week, a month, a year, or whatever time period is prudent for the process under investigation. When the event of interest is likely to occur very rapidly after the beginning of data collection, it may be best to observe people quite frequently—recording event occurrence on an hourly or daily basis. If the event is likely to occur less frequently, then perhaps monthly or yearly observations are sufficient. In either case, the investigator must trade off the costs of extra observation against the benefits of more finely tuned information on event occurrence. For instance, when Havassy, Hall, and Wasserman (1992) decided to investigate relapse among former cocaine abusers following treatment, their knowledge of the research literature on drug abuse convinced them that "high relapse rates are common across all classes of abused drugs" (Havassey et al., 1992). They therefore concluded that, since most former cocaine abusers would probably relapse quite soon after treatment, monthly or yearly observation of the former drug abusers would be too coarse a time frame for data collection and would simply disguise interesting variation in time-to-relapse across people. Consequently, the authors made the sensible decision to collect discrete-time event-history data by assessing their subjects weekly for the 12 weeks following treatment.

Why Is Discrete-Time Survival Analysis Preferred in Clinical Research?

In this chapter, we focus on *discrete-time survival analysis* because we believe that this subclass of methods offers several unique advantages to researchers in psychology and the social sciences. First and foremost, we believe that discrete-time methods are simply more appropriate for much of the event-history data that are currently collected because, for logistical and financial reasons, observations are often made in discrete time. For instance, rather than observing everyone continuously, Young, Watel, Lahmeyer, and Eastman (1991) asked their patients with seasonal affective disorder to reconstruct a weekly life history. Baer and Lichtenstein (1988) collected data on time-to-relapse by telephoning former smokers 1 month, 2 months, 3 months, and 12 months after treatment. A study of the impact of early intervention on marital distress by Markman, Floyd, Stanley, and Storaasli (1988) collected event histories over a period of years.

Second, we believe that not only is discrete-time survival analysis intrinsically more comprehensible than its continuous-time cousin but that mastery of discrete-time methods facilitates a transition to the continuous-time approach (if that should be required). In both types of survival analysis, the principal quantity being modeled (referred to as "hazard") describes the risk of event occurrence over time. However, when time has been measured discretely, hazard has a conceptually satisfying and straightforward interpretation as a probability. When time has been measured continuously, on the other hand, hazard must be redefined as a *rate*, a quantity that has less intuitive appeal and is more difficult to interpret when research findings are being communicated to the lay reader, the broad clinical audience or the policymaker.

A third advantage is concerned with the ease with which *time-varying predictors* can be included in discrete-time survival analyses. In most research, measurements of the outcome variable are not the sole interest; investigators are often more interested in what *predicts* the outcome. Thus, in survival analysis, prime analytic interest often focuses on the predictors of "whether" and "when." However, when longitudinal event history data are being collected, it is natural that many of the interesting predictors will have values that fluctuate over time. With discrete-time methods it is easy to incorporate such time-varying predictors into the statistical analyses. In continuous-time survival analysis, on the other hand, time-varying predictors can present analytic (and programming) problems for the data analyst. In their recent review of software for personal computers, for instance, Goldstein, Anderson, Ash, Craig, Harrington, and Pagano (1989) note that only one continuous-time survival analysis package (BMDP2L) can handle time-varying predictors, and, even then, the researcher must write an accompanying FORTRAN subroutine to implement the procedure.

Fourth, in addition to investigating how selected predictors influence the risk of event occurrence over time, discrete-time survival analysis fosters inspection of how the pattern of risk shapes up over time. Why is this important? Because the shape of the temporal profile of risk directly answers the central research question. It shows how the chances of event occurrence vary from time period to time period and therefore indicates whether and when an event is most likely to occur. The most popular continuous-time survival analysis strategy (known as Cox regression; Cox, 1972), however, is described as *semiparametric* because it ignores the shape of the temporal risk profile in favor of estimating only the influence of predictors on risk, under a restrictive assumption of "proportionality" that we discuss later in the chapter.

A fifth and related advantage concerns the manner in which discrete-time methods facilitate the testing of the proportionality assumption that underpins (and is ignored) in most continuous-time analyses. Under the discrete-time approach, the proportionality assumption is easily checked by adding interactions between selected predictors and time to the statistical models, in much the same way that interaction terms are added to regular multiple-regression models. In fact, in discrete-time, "nonproportional" hazard models are so easily fitted and interpreted that researchers need not sidestep this important issue at all. Discrete-time survival analysis facilitates the fitting of a broader class of statistical models and thereby allows researchers to represent the world in a more comprehensive and realistic fashion.

Finally, in discrete-time survival analysis, all of the required statistical estimation can be carried out straightforwardly using standard methods of logistic regression analysis. This avoids any reliance on the "black box" of dedicated (and often esoteric) computer software that is usually required for continuous-time survival analyses. Why is this important? We believe that the use of familiar techniques and well-worn software encourages investigators to do a better job. It makes their data analyses more familiar and allows them to bring all of their existing analytic and interpretive skills to bear on the problem. Ultimately, it leads to research findings that are more trustworthy, to published research accounts that are correct and convincing, and to public policy and patient care that is more well informed.

WHY ARE SPECIAL ANALYTIC METHODS NEEDED FOR STUDYING THE OCCURRENCE AND TIMING OF EVENTS, ANYWAY?

Unfortunately, dangerous methodological reefs await unwary researchers adrift on the stormy seas of event history. The core problem is that, no matter when data collection begins and no matter how long it lasts, some people may never experience the target event during the period of observation. Some people may not consider suicide, some patients may not recover from depression, some former patients may not relapse, some children may not take their first step, some adolescents may not reach the specified developmental milestone.

When someone does not experience the event of interest during the targeted period of data collection, they are said to have a *censored* history or lifetime.[1] Censoring can occur whether data are collected either prospectively or retrospectively. Less censoring will occur if the event of interest is very likely to happen during the period of observation. For instance, when Glasgow, Klesges, Klesges, and Somes (1988) followed ex-smokers for half a year to observe whether the event of "smoking relapse" occurred, they report that only 15% of the original participants did not relapse in the period of observation. Since we do not know how long these 15% ultimately remained abstinent, their "smoking cessation" histories are censored. On the other hand, in studies of rarer events, censoring will be greater because fewer participants will experience the event. In their investigation of relapse into high-risk sexual behavior after counseling among gay men, for instance, Kelly, Lawrence, and Brasfield (1991) report that almost two-thirds of the initial sample were "safe" (and therefore censored) 16 months later.

Although censoring can be minimized via research design, it can rarely be eradicated completely. When data are collected prospectively, a researcher without temporal, financial, or logistical constraints could reduce censoring by following a random sample of people from a common point in time for as long as necessary. Adolescents could be tracked into adulthood and old age. Former patients followed in perpetuity. However, in practice, researchers cannot afford to track people indefinitely, and censoring is the natural consequence. When data are collected retrospectively, on the other hand, people are asked to remember whether (and when) the event of interest has happened to them. Asking such questions at a later time (to reduce censoring), will lead to flimsier recall and noisier event-occurrence data. And whether data are collected prospectively or retrospectively, when the occurrence of rare events is being studied, lengthier data collection will not necessarily eliminate censoring entirely because some people may simply never experience the target event at all (or never have experienced, in the case of a retrospective study).

When lifetimes are censored, the researcher necessarily possesses incomplete information about "Whether" and "When". When someone's event time is censored, the researcher knows only that, if the person ever experiences the event,

---

[1]We are referring here, and throughout the rest of the chapter, to the process of *right censoring* where the *endpoints* of the careers of a proportion of the sample are unknown. The reader must be careful to distinguish this from *left censoring*, where the career *start points* are unknown. This latter type of censoring is more analytically intractable.

TABLE 7.1
What Do Survival Data Look Like? Age at First Suicide Ideation
for 417 College Students

	Number Who			Proportion of	
Age	Had Not Yet Thought About Suicide at the Beginning of the Year	Onset During the Year	Were Censored at the End of the Year	All Students Who Had Not Onset by the End of the Year	Students Who Had Not Yet Thought About Suicide Who Onset During This Year
6	417	2	0	0.9952	0.0048
7	415	3	0	0.9880	0.0072
8	412	13	0	0.9568	0.0316
9	399	8	0	0.9376	0.0201
10	391	24	0	0.8801	0.0614
11	367	9	0	0.8585	0.0245
12	358	45	0	0.7506	0.1257
13	313	44	0	0.6451	0.1406
14	269	31	0	0.5707	0.1152
15	238	37	0	0.4820	0.1555
16	201	21	2	*0.4317*	0.1045
17	178	17	11	*0.3904*	0.0955
18	150	18	23	*0.3436*	0.1200
19	109	11	31	*0.3089*	0.1009
20	67	3	23	*0.2951*	0.0448
21	41	1	40	*0.2879*	0.0244

Source: Data kindly provided by Bolger, Downey, Walker, & Steininger (1989).

he or she can only do so after data collection ends. The researcher knows neither *when* the event will occur nor even *whether* it will ever happen at all for this person—and, unfortunately, these are the very issues of interest. All the investigator knows is that, by the end of data collection (a time that is probably arbitrary with respect to the underlying event history process), the event had not yet occurred.

Censoring's toll can be seen in Table 7.1, which presents data describing the ages at which college-bound preadolescents and adolescents report having experienced a critical event—their first thoughts of suicide. Bolger, Downey, Walker, and Steininger (1989) collected these suicide ideation data retrospectively from a sample of undergraduates at a major university, who were asked via anonymous questionnaire whether they had ever thought of committing suicide.[2] In an interesting and trend-setting paper, Bolger and his colleagues report the results of survival analyses that answer their research questions. Alarmingly, they discov-

[2]We would like to thank Niall Bolger, and his colleagues, for providing these data and for their kind permission to use the data in this chapter.

ered that the risks of suicide ideation were very common among college-bound children and adolescents (more than two-thirds of the sample had considered suicide at least once) and that these risks were higher in middle to late adolescence. There were statistically significant effects of critical demographic variables: (a) gender—girls were consistently at higher risk than boys, and (b) race—minority students were less likely to have considered suicide. In addition, although children with absent parents were more likely in general to have contemplated suicide, parental absence had a markedly greater influence on suicide ideation during preadolescence.

The entries in Table 7.1 can be used to investigate whether and, if so, when the 417 adolescents in the sample first thought of committing suicide. The first column lists the chronological age of the adolescents in discrete years. The next three columns tally the number of youths who had not yet thought of suicide at the beginning of each age period, the number who contemplated suicide during each period, and the number whose histories were censored at the end of the period. Notice that all of the censoring occurred in the later age periods (16 years and older). This distributional phenomenon is often found in studies that collect data retrospectively. In such studies, the event histories are usually censored at the moment of data collection when, in age-heterogeneous samples, adolescents are of different ages. In the case of the Bolger study, a total of 287 adolescents had considered suicide by the interview date and 130 had not (31% of the sample) and were therefore censored.

How can we best describe the distribution of age at first suicide ideation in this sample of college-bound youth (and hence get to grips with questions about whether and when)? Researchers faced with similar data structures have used a variety of ad hoc strategies, none completely satisfactory. Some have decided to focus exclusively on those people with noncensored event histories (see, for instance, Lelliott, Marks, McNamee, & Tobena, 1989; Litman, Eiser, & Taylor, 1979). Implementing this strategy in Table 7.1, using data from only the 287 adolescents who had actually experienced thoughts of suicide by the date of the interview, yields an estimate of the average age of first suicide ideation of 13.5 years. But excluding the 130 censored adolescents obviously distorts the complete distribution of age-at-first-ideation. The "average" age at first suicide ideation for all college-bound adolescents must be greater than 13.5 because this estimate uses data from only those youths who experienced such thoughts "early" in their lives (i.e., before the interview). To determine when the age at which first thoughts of suicide occur in general among college-bound youth, both the censored and the uncensored cases must be included in the computation. Censored histories provide information too, especially about the probability that age-at-first suicide ideation may be greater than the age at which censoring occurred. The censored adolescents must not be excluded, even though we do not know when, or even whether, any of them will ever experience the target event.

Cognizant of these concerns, some investigators incorporate the censored cases in their analyses by imputing the unknown event times. The most popular approach is to assign censored cases the age or duration value they possess when data collection ends. This strategy is frequently used in studies of relapse into undesirable behavior such as smoking (Harackiewicz, Sansone, Blair, Epstein, & Manderlink, 1987; Ossip-Klein, Giovino et al., 1991), alcohol abuse (Nathan & Skinstad, 1987), drug abuse, and so forth. Using this approach in our example (e.g., assigning an age-at-first-ideation of 16 to the two students who were censored at age 16, and so forth), yields an estimated age at first suicide ideation of 15.4 years. While suitably longer than our first underestimate of 13.5 years, this estimate, too, must surely be wrong. Imputing event times for censored cases changes a "nonevent" (the interview) into an "event" (contemplation of suicide) and it further assumes that all these new "events" occur at the earliest ages possible!

Given these inescapable errors, many researchers choose a more conservative approach. Rather than attempting to impute missing data, they choose to abandon the "when?" question entirely by sacrificing their knowledge of duration. They simply dichotomize the event histories at some particular (and often arbitrary) event time so that they ask only *whether* the event occurs by that time (e.g., Sargeant, Bruce, Florio, & Weissman, 1990; Norris, Kaniasty, & Scheer, 1990; Rice, Quinsey, & Harris, 1991), or by each of several successive points in time (e.g., Marlatt, Curry, & Gordon, 1988; Myers, McCauley, Calderon, & Treder, 1991). In the case of the data in our table, one might ask, for instance, whether first suicide ideation tends to occur by, or after, the age of 14.

Although better than data elimination or incorrect imputation, dichotomization does not resolve the censoring dilemma; it simply obscures it from view. First, sample dichotomization eliminates potentially meaningful variation in event history by clustering everyone into two groups: those who experience the event before the chosen cutoff, and those who have the experience after. Children who experience their first suicide ideation at six years, for example, may differ systematically from those who experience it at age 12; yet these groups would be combined in an analysis that dichotomized at age 14. Second, any particular dividing criterion, even one ostensibly relevant to the process under study, is arbitrary. Why should 14 years be selected as the age of dichotomization rather than 13 or 15? Third, seemingly contradictory conclusions can result from nothing more than variation in the time chosen for dichotomization. Fourth, if different people are censored at different ages, dichotomization discards information. Were we to dichotomize the data in Table 7.1 at the end of 14 years, for example, we would ignore the known ages at first suicide ideation of the 108 adolescents who contemplated suicide after age 14 and before the date of the interview. Fifth, once data are dichotomized, a researcher can no longer answer key research questions such as "At what age does the average college-bound adolescent first contemplate suicide?"

Introducing the Sample Survivor and Hazard Functions

Clearly a better analytic strategy is needed and in the next section, we begin to formulate one. But before doing so, let us continue heuristically, by returning to Table 7.1 and speculating about meaningful ways of summarizing the distribution of age at first suicide ideation, even in the face of censoring.[3]

The fifth column of Table 7.1 presents one such summary—the proportion of all children who had *not* first contemplated suicide by the end of each age period. The survival analysis literature uses the term *survival probability* to refer to the proportion of an initial population that do not experience the event of interest through each of several successive time periods and the term *survivor function* to refer to the chronological pattern of these probabilities over time.

Examining the sample survivor function listed in the fifth column of Table 7.1, we see the proportion of the sample that had not experienced their first thoughts of suicide by end of each of the listed age periods. For instance, 88% of the adolescents had not contemplated suicide for the first time by the end of the tenth year, 86% had not thought about it by the end of the 11th year; 48% by the end of the 15th year. Unfortunately, in our example, we cannot directly compute the sample survivor function beyond age 15 because we do not know whether the two children who were censored at age 16 ever contemplated suicide or not. Fortunately, however, the remaining sample survival probabilities can be estimated indirectly by an alternative method that we will describe below and these estimates are included in italics in the bottom half of column 5 of the table.

Computational simplicity and intuitive interpretability have fostered the occasional appearance of sample survivor functions in the research literature on psychology. Sample survivor functions have been used to summarize whether, and when, former alcohol abusers will relapse (Cooney et al., 1991), former smokers will relapse (Stevens & Hollis, 1989), released prisoners will be reconvicted (Hart et al., 1988), and violent individuals will be first arrested (Weisz et al., 1990). Censoring, however, has made it difficult for researchers to move beyond these simple sample descriptions to formal models relating predictors to event occurrence.

The sixth column of Table 7.1 presents another useful summary of an event-history process—the proportion of adolescents who had not first contemplated suicide at the beginning of each age period but who did consider it by the end of the age period. Defining the *risk set* as the group of people known to be eligible to experience the event in a particular time period (the group "at risk"), the survival analysis literature uses the term *hazard probability* to refer to the propor-

---

[3]While it is somewhat unorthodox to present sample estimators of population quantities not yet defined, we have chosen this approach here because of its pedagogic value.

tion of this risk set who experience the event in that time period and the term *hazard function* to refer to the chronological profile of these probabilities over time.

Examining Table 7.1, we see that all of the children in the sample were members of the risk set at age six because none of them had ever considered suicide prior to this age. Of the 417 children thus eligible to experience the event of interest (i.e., those at risk of "first suicide ideation"), only 2 first considered suicide in this age period, leaving 415 children remaining in the risk set at age 7. The corresponding age-6 hazard probability is therefore 2/417, or .0048. Then, of the 415 children remaining in the risk set, 3 first contemplated suicide at age 7, leading to a sample hazard probability for this period to 3/415, or .0072, and reducing the risk set further to 412. This computational process continues through each successive year. By the beginning of the 14th year, for instance, there remained only 269 children who had not yet considered suicide and, of these, about 11.5% did so during their 14th years.

Unlike the sample survivor function, however, we can continue to compute the hazard probability in every time period regardless of censoring—we simply remove any censored people from inclusion in the appropriate risk set, therefore reducing the denominator of the computed hazard quotient. This can be illustrated by considering the transition between ages 17 and 18 in Table 7.1. Of the 178 adolescents who had not yet experienced their first thoughts of suicide by the beginning of their 17th year, 17 did so during this year and 11 were censored. Thus, the hazard probability at age 17 was 17/178 (or .0955). However, neither the 17 "ideators" nor the 11 "censorees" were eligible to continue as members of the risk set into the 18th year because they had either experienced the event of interest (first suicide ideation) or their fates were unknown (censored) at age 17. Therefore, only 150 youths (= 178 − 17 − 11) remained at risk at age 18, providing the denominator of the age-18 hazard computation. In the top panel of Figure 7.1, we have plotted the complete discrete-time hazard function for our sample of adolescents (following Miller's, 1981, suggestion, on the plot, we have interpolated linearly between discrete sample hazard probabilities, rather than plotting the hazard profile as a step function).

Basing hazard on the known risk set ensures that we can compute hazard in every time period even in the face of extreme censoring. Of course, the credibility of this definition rests upon the assumption that censoring is unrelated to event occurrence, which the survival analysis literature refers to as *independent censoring*. If censoring is independent, the subsample making up each year's risk set—those definitely known to have not yet contemplated suicide by that age—is representative of all adolescents in that age group; those who are censored do not differ from those who have yet to experience the event. This allows us to generalize the behavior of people in the risk set back to the entire sample and hence back to the original population. If censoring is not independent, people in the risk set differ systematically from those who are censored and the generalization may be incorrect. For these reasons, we generally cross our fingers and hope, as others do, that censoring is independent of event occurrence!

The discrete-time hazard function has many appealing properties that, taken together, explain why it—and not the survivor function—forms the cornerstone of survival analysis. First and foremost, it assesses exactly what we want to know—*whether* and, if so, *when* are events are likely to occur. Its size in each time period indicates the risk of event occurrence in that period—the higher the hazard, the greater the risk. Examining the sample hazard function in Figure 7.1, for example, we see that adolescents were most likely to first contemplate suicide between the ages of 12 and 16 years.

A second important advantage of the hazard function is that it incorporates information from both the noncensored and the censored cases. In our example in Table 7.1, for instance, adolescents were included in the hazard computations up until they either first contemplated suicide or were censored. The hazard function does not discard people nor does it arbitrarily impute their event times even when the ultimate outcome of their event history is unknown.

Third, the sample hazard function can be computed directly in every time period for which event occurrence is recorded. Information on variation in the timing of events is not ignored or pooled, as it was in the case of the dichotomization strategy described above.

Last but not least, under the assumption of independent censoring, the sample hazard function can be used to estimate the sample survivor function indirectly in those time periods in which censoring precludes the latter's direct computation. We can do this because there is an inextricable link between discrete-time survival and hazard probabilities. We will illustrate this linkage using data from ages 15 and 16 in Table 7.1. From the survival probability estimate in the age-15 row, we know that 48.2% of all children will not first contemplate suicide up to, and including, their 15th years. From the row corresponding to age 16, where the sample hazard probability is 10.45%, we know that 89.55% (= 100% − 10.45%) of the entering 16th year risk set will not first contemplate suicide in this year. So, putting these two things together, we can estimate that, at the end of the 16th year, 89.55% of the entering 48.2% will probably not have experienced the event of interest. Therefore, an estimate of the survival probability at the end of 16th year is simply (.8955)(.4820), or .4317%. In other words, the sample survival probability in any time period is simply 1 minus the hazard probability for that period multiplied by the sample survival probability from the previous period. Providing censoring is independent of event occurrence, this computational algorithm can be used to fill in the sample survival probabilities in Table 7.1 for years 16 through 21 (shown in italics). We have plotted the obtained sample survivor function in the lower panel of Figure 7.1.

Once the complete sample survivor function has been obtained, it is often convenient to summarize it with a simple statistic—the *median lifetime*. When

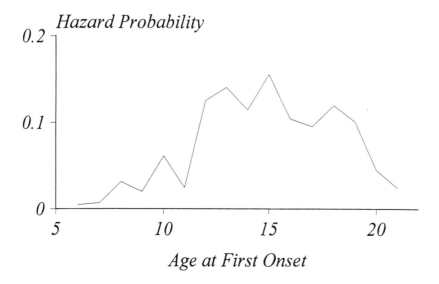

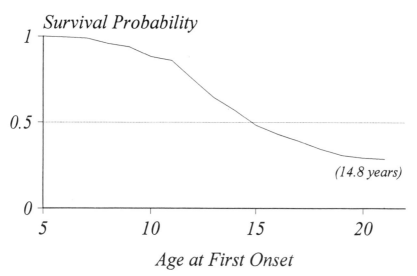

FIG. 7.1.   Sample survivor and hazard functions describing age-at-first-suicide-ideation for 417 college-bound adolescents, with estimated median lifetime in parentheses on the plot of the sample survival function. Data kindly provided by Dr. Niall Bolger and his colleagues (Bolger, Downey, Walker, & Steininger, 1989).

the sample survivor function has fallen to .50, half of the children in the sample will have experienced the event of interest (i.e., will have thought about committing suicide for the first time), half will have not. For instance, from the lower panel of Figure 7.1 (using linear interpolation between years, see Miller, 1981), the estimated median age at which children in this sample first contemplate suicide is 14.8 years. Unlike our earlier biased estimate of the average age at first suicide ideation, the estimated median lifetime correctly answers the initial descriptive question "On average, at what age does a college-bound adolescent first contemplate suicide?", and it does so meaningfully in the metric of time using all the data from both noncensored and censored cases alike.

The close correspondence among the hazard function, the survivor function, and the median lifetime permits intuitive interpretation of survival analyses in empirical work. Statistical models built using discrete-time survival analysis actually involve the modeling of hazard probabilities, not survival probabilities nor event times. However, the simple relationships among the three quantities allows all the findings obtained in one metric to be translated into either of the other two. This greatly facilitates the communication of research results to a lay audience.

FORMALIZING THE STATISTICAL UNDERPINNINGS OF DISCRETE-TIME SURVIVAL ANALYSIS

So far, we have proceeded heuristically. We have simply used a sample of data to present some intuitive ways of describing event-history data and to introduce three critical concepts crucial to the understanding of survival analysis. We have not distinguished the sample from the population, we have not specified models and identified parameters, we have ignored model fitting and the process of statistical inference. However, as in all statistical analyses, our ultimate intention is not only to summarize sample information in a reasonable way but also to use that information to make thoughtful inferences about an underlying problem. In order to do this, we need a formal statistical structure for discrete-time survival analysis. In this section, we describe that structure.

Temporal Patterns of Risk and the Population Hazard Function

In a discrete-time survival study we draw a sample from a population of individuals, each of whom is at risk of experiencing a single target event—the onset of a disease or a behavior, relapse into drug abuse, ultimate recovery, and so forth. For the moment, we will assume that each person in the population can experience the target event only once; once it occurs, it cannot occur again. Then, when analytic methods have been developed for this simple case, they can be generalized to the case of repeated event occurrence. Readers interested in the survival analysis of repeated events should also consult Allison (1984), Tuma and Hannan (1984), Willett and Singer (1995), and Yamaguchi (1991).

As we have noted earlier, research interest centers on whether and, if so, when (i.e., in which time period) an event occurs. Notice that because each person can experience the target event only once, event occurrence is inherently *conditional*. Any person can experience the event in one particular time period only if he or she did *not* already experience it any of the earlier time periods. Similarly, once a person experiences the event, he or she cannot experience it again in a later time period.

As we have noted in the discussion following Table 7.1, we can succinctly summarize event occurrence in terms of the "risk" that the event will occur in each time period under study. If the event is very likely to occur, then risk in that period is high; if it is not likely to occur, then the risk is low. In discrete-time survival analysis these risks are described by the population *hazard probabilities*, which can take on a different value in each time period under study. And, because event occurrence is intrinsically conditional, hazard is also defined conditionally—for each discrete time period, hazard is the probability that a randomly selected person in the population will experience the event of interest in that period *given that the event has not already occurred to the person in an earlier time period*. As a probability, the value of hazard always lies between 0 and 1.[4]

The population period-by-period hazard probabilities are the fundamental parameters underpinning event occurrence. Together, they are referred to as the *hazard function*. The population hazard function can be visualized as a plot, against time, of the population risk of the event occurring in each time period, conditional on the event having not occurred earlier. Depending upon the distribution of these risks over time, the hazard function takes on a different shape. In Table 7.1, and in all our subsequent survival analyses, we spend much energy trying to estimate the population hazard probabilities and infer the shape of the population hazard function.

Does the Pattern of Event Occurrence Depend on Other Factors?

In most applications, however, research interest centers not only on estimating the population hazard function but also on determining whether this temporal

---

[4]If time were measured continuously, we would know the particular instant when events occur, and we would define hazard differently because the probability that any event occurs at a single "infinitely thin" instant of time tends to zero (by definition). Continuous time hazard is defined as the instantaneous rate of event occurrence, given that the event has not already occurred until the immediately prior instant. It can assume any value greater than or equal to zero.

profile of risk differs systematically for different types of people. In the case of first onset of major depression, for instance, we might ask: Is the hazard function describing the risk of depression different for men and women? Does the pattern of risk differ for members of minority and majority groups? For those in different counseling programs, or undergoing different types of drug therapy?

When we pose such questions, we are asking whether there is a relationship between the hazard function (which describes the temporal pattern of risk) and critical attributes of people's background, treatment and training. In fact, conceptually, we are treating the entire hazard function as an *outcome* and variables such as gender, minority-group membership, type of counseling program or drug therapy as *predictors* of that outcome. To answer our research questions, we must carry out statistical analyses designed to expose the relationship between the outcome and the predictors.

However, as in regular regression analysis or any other form of statistical analysis, before we can move ahead we must first quantify our research question by specifying a statistical model to represent the hypothesized population relationship that we intend to investigate. Such a model gives algebraic form to the link between the hazard function and the chosen predictors. Once the population model is specified and its parameters are defined, we can proceed. We can test to see whether the model fits our data and, if it does, we can estimate and interpret its parameters.

But, exactly what is an appropriate statistical model for representing the population relationship between a hazard function and its predictors? Is a linear model suitable, as in simple regression analysis or analysis of variance? Or is a more complex nonlinear statistical model required? What functional form should such a model take? What special problems arise because the outcome—the hazard function—is a temporal profile rather than a single number?

Soon, we will propose a formal statistical model to represent the hypothesized population relationship between the discrete-time hazard function and predictors. Understanding how this model functions is critical to the thoughtful use of discrete-time survival analysis. If the reader understands the algebraic "shape" of the model and the function of its several unknown parameters, then future interpretation of the fitted model is facilitated. In fact, one might be tempted to say that understanding how a statistical model represents reality is the most important facet of learning to use any type of statistical analysis. All else is simply estimation.

However, because the statistical model that is used to represent the discrete-time hazard function as a function of predictors is a little unusual, we have decided to presage our specification of the model by examining a further real data example. We do this to motivate the construction of the statistical model and to clarify the meaning of the fundamental parameters in the model. In the new example, we make use of data that were analyzed previously in an interesting and thoughtful study by Sorenson et al. (1991) in which the event of interest was the age of first onset of a major depressive disorder.[5] Because major depression is an event that has relatively low prevalence, the study required a large number of participants—the community-based sample included 3,131 adults between the ages of 18 and 97 who were interviewed and their event histories constructed retrospectively (for a discussion of sample size in survival studies see Singer & Willett, 1991). There were about equal numbers of men and women, and Hispanic and non-Hispanic Americans in the sample. The authors used survival analysis to show that several important variables, including gender and ethnicity, were critical predictors of the temporal profile of depressive risk. We will use these sample data to motivate a population representation for the hypothesized relationship between a single predictor—gender—and the hazard function that describes the temporal profile of risk of first onset of depression.

We expect that, if a person's gender is related to the risk of first onset of major depression, then the hazard function describing the risk of onset for men must differ in some systematic way from the hazard function for women. But exactly how do these profiles differ? Perhaps we can educate ourselves about the possible form of the dependence of the hazard profile on patient gender by inspecting hazard functions estimated separately in subsamples of men and women. In Figure 7.2, we use the depression data to plot sample risk summaries in three distinct but related ways.

The top panel of Figure 7.2 presents the "raw" sample hazard profiles, estimated separately by gender. For both men and women, the overall magnitude of the hazard probabilities is low confirming that depression occurs quite rarely in the general population. Sorenson and her colleagues (1991, p. 543) report that, overall, less than 6% of the sample ever experienced major depression in their entire lifetimes. Notice also that the estimated risk of first onset of depression is almost negligible when a person is very young or very old, but rises to a jittery peak between ages 20 and 35. Similarly shaped risk profiles have been reported for the first onset of major depression by other authors (see, for instance, the review by Lewinsohn, Duncan, Stanton, & Hautzinger, 1986).

However, there is nothing sacrosanct about probability. It is just one way of representing the chances of event occurrence. The same risks can be equally well described using *odds*—a related quantity that describes the chance of experiencing an event versus not experiencing it. In many types of statistical analysis (including survival analysis), it is odds rather than probabilities that provide the preferred metric. There is, however, a simple one-to-one relationship between probabilities and odds. For instance, suppose that the sample hazard probability was .20 in a particular time period. Then we would know that there was probability of .20 that the event of interest *would* occur in that period, and a probability of .80 that it would not occur (given no previous occurrence in prior time

---

[5]We would like to thank Susan B. Sorenson and her colleagues for providing us with, and granting us permission to use, these data.

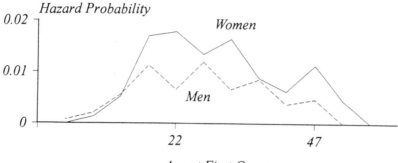

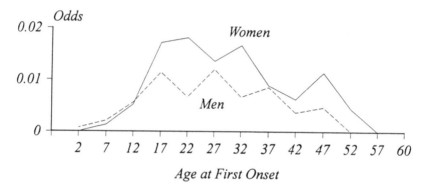

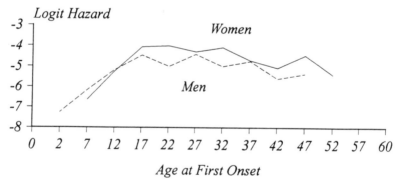

FIG. 7.2. Sample hazard functions describing the lifetime risks of onset of lifetime depressive disorder for men and women, plotted on
three vertical scales: (a) top panel—raw hazard, (b) middle panel—
odds, and (c) bottom panel—log-odds ("logit-hazard"). Data kindly
provided by Dr. Susan B. Sorenson and her colleagues (Sorenson,
Rutter, & Aneshensel, 1991).

periods). Because of this, we could say that the odds of event occurrence in this period were ".20 to .80" or "1 in 4" (this is usually written as $1/4$ or .25). In other words, odds are easily computed from hazard probabilities by the simple formula, odds = hazard/(1 − hazard).

In the middle panel of Figure 7.2, using this algorithm, we have converted the sample hazard profiles into sample odds profiles with each point in the latter indicating the odds that men and women will experience major depression in each period versus not experience it (given no prior occurrence). Interestingly enough, the hazard and odds profiles in the top and middle panels of Figure 7.2 appear almost identical to each other. This "equivalence" oddity holds only when hazard probability is small (less than .15, say) because a small number divided by one minus the same small number is then approximately equal to the original number.[6] When events occur more frequently and risks are higher, the equality will be disrupted because the values of the corresponding probabilities and odds diverge when hazard probability is higher. For this reason, and because we will ultimately frame the discrete-time hazard model in terms of the odds of event occurrence, we will persist with this "probability-to-odds" transformation here and in Figure 7.2.

In the lower panel of Figure 7.2, we have displayed the natural logarithm of the sample odds profiles that were displayed in the middle panel. Traditionally, the natural logarithm has been used as a reasonable and effective transformation for odds, in order to symmetrize their range. The resulting quantity has been referred to as "logit" rather than "log-odds." Thus, in discrete-time survival analysis, we refer to the log-odds of event occurrence in any time period (given no earlier occurrence) as "logit-hazard" and this is how we have labeled the vertical axis in the lower panel of Figure 7.2.

Regardless of the specific vicissitudes of the particular mathematical transformation used, however, do not lose sight of the fact that all three panels in Figure 7.2 convey identical information, albeit on different scales. Within any panel, men's and women's profiles of risk have basically similar shapes as each other, whether they are expressed in the metric of hazard probability, of odds, or of logit-hazard. For both genders, the risk of first onset of major depression is highest in the 20's and early 30's. And, despite an early crossover in pre-adolescence and some haphazard zigzagging that subsequent analysis attributes to sampling variation, there appears to be a vertical separation between the male and female sample profiles. Across most of the lifetime, in fact, the sample hazard function for women is "higher" than the men's, and so are the corresponding sample odds and log-odds profiles. So, in nearly every year of their lives, women in the sample are at greater risk of suffering the onset of major depression than are men.

---

[6]This claim can be proven mathematically by using a Taylor series expansion of the expression for odds, $h/(1 − h)$, when h is small (where the symbol h represents discrete-time hazard probability).

When we make statements like these—one about the shape of the *general profile of risk over time* and another about the *difference* in the net level of risk between the two groups—we are essentially ascribing variation in hazard to two components: a "baseline" temporal profile of risk and a "shift" in risk profile associated with variation in gender. Even in the absence of formal model, we can systematize this partition further by defining a dichotomous predictor FEMALE (with value 0 for men, 1 for women) in order to think further about how variation in the values of the predictor is associated with variation in the conceptual outcome—the entire hazard profile.

One approach is to treat the entire hazard function for men (i.e., the profile when FEMALE has the value 0) as a "baseline" pattern of risk—the risk profile for a baseline group of people—those sharing the predictor value of 0, which in this example happens to be men. Having done so, think of estimating a parameter that describes the way in which the baseline hazard function "shifts" when the value of FEMALE changes from 0 to 1 leading, as it happens in this case, to the risk profile for women.

Conceptually at least, although we have ignored minor variations in the shapes of the male and female risk profiles for the moment, we seem to have been drawn toward a specification for a statistical model of hazard in which variation in the predictor acts to "displace" an entire baseline hazard function "vertically," yielding another entire function. While admittedly coarse, this conceptualization nevertheless captures the two essential attributes that are required of a decent discrete-time hazard model. It must include algebraic terms to represent a "baseline" temporal profile of risk, and it must incorporate a "shift" parameter that captures the effect of a predictor on the baseline profile.

For mathematical convenience, Cox (1972) proposed that the discrete-time hazard model should be framed in terms of logit-hazard (the log-odds of event occurrence) rather than directly in terms of probabilities (also see Allison, 1982; Brown, 1975; Efron, 1988; Laird & Olivier, 1981; Thompson, 1977). However, the similarities among the plots in the three panels of Figure 7.2 should reassure the reader that this is not unreasonable and, in the final analysis, results can always be transformed back into hazard probabilities for interpretive purposes. We provide concrete examples of this conversion later.

Taking all of these requirements into account, a statistical model that represents the dependence of the risk profile for onset of depression on the single predictor, FEMALE, looks like this:

$$\log_e \left(\frac{h_j}{1 - h_j} \right) = \text{logit}_e(h_j) = [\alpha_1 D_1 + \alpha_2 D_2 + \cdots + \alpha_J D_J] + \beta_1 \text{FEMALE}.$$

$$(7.1)$$

Remember that Equation 7.1 is a *population discrete-time hazard model*. In many ways the model is similar to a regular regression model. It represents the hypothesized population linear relationship between logit-hazard and several predictors, one of which is easily recognizable (FEMALE, the respondent gender) and some of which have mysterious purposes $(D_1, D_2, \ldots, D_J)$. In every case, however, each predictor is multiplied by an unknown "slope" parameter (β_1 and $\alpha_1, \alpha_2, \ldots, \alpha_J$ respectively) that ultimately will be estimated and interpreted. We will introduce and explain these different facets of the model separately.

First, let us examine the left-hand side of the equation—here is where the "outcome," logit-hazard, is found. We have used subscript j to index the discrete time-periods ($j = 1, 2, 3, \ldots, J$), with J indicating the last time period observed for anyone in the sample. So, for instance, h_1 represents the population hazard probability in the first discrete time period, h_2 is the hazard probability in the second period, h_3 is the hazard in the third, . . . and so on, until h_J represents the population risk in the last period. Together, the parameters $h_1, h_2, h_3, \ldots$, h_J make up the entire discrete-time population hazard function. They constitute the central focus of our survival analyses representing, as they do, the lifetime risks of onset of major depressive disorder.

Now consider the set of terms in parentheses immediately to the right of the equals sign in Equation 7.1. To understand the action of these terms, first notice that the discrete-time hazard model contains no single stand-alone intercept, as might be anticipated in a regular regression analysis. In fact, because of the way that the predictors $D_1, D_2, \ldots, D_J$ are defined, the several alpha parameters α_1, $\alpha_2, \ldots, \alpha_J$ act as multiple intercepts, one per time period. The predictors D_1, $D_2, \ldots, D_J$ are a set of dichotomous dummy variables that, by taking on values of 0 and 1, reference the different discrete time periods. For instance, in the first time period (i.e., when $j = 1$), D_1 takes on a value of 1 and all the other "time dummies" have value zero. Thus, the model in Equation 7.1 reduces to

$$\text{logit}_e(h_1) = \alpha_1 + \beta_1 \text{FEMALE}, \qquad (7.2)$$

and the unknown parameter α_1 acts as the intercept in time period 1. In the second time period (i.e., when $j = 2$), the next time dummy D_2 has value 1 and all the other time dummies are set to zero. Then α_2 becomes the intercept in time period 2. Similarly, α_3 is the intercept in the third period, α_4 is the intercept in the fourth period, and so on:

$$\text{logit}_e(h_2) = \alpha_2 + \beta_1 \text{FEMALE},$$
$$\text{logit}_e(h_3) = \alpha_3 + \beta_1 \text{FEMALE},$$
$$\vdots \qquad (7.3)$$
$$\text{logit}_e(h_J) = \alpha_J + \beta_1 \text{FEMALE}.$$

So we see that, by inspection of the submodels in Equations 7.2 and 7.3, because of the way the "time dummies" are defined the set of multiple intercept parameters taken together capture what we have referred to earlier as the "baseline" hazard function, albeit on an inhospitable logistic scale. When the value of

FEMALE is set to zero in these equations (representing men), the $\alpha_1, \alpha_2, \ldots, \alpha_J$ parameters are simply the population logit-hazard probabilities for men in each time period and, since men are the defined "baseline" group, they define the baseline logit-hazard function. In our data example on depression, for instance, α_1 represents the log-odds that a man will experience the first onset of depression in the first time period; α_2 represents the log-odds that a man experiences depression in the second period (given that he did not experience it in the first, and so on.

The final term remaining to the right of the parentheses in Equation 7.1 represents the hypothesized influence of respondent gender on the population logit-hazard function. We can illustrate its function by reexamining Equations 7.2 and 7.3 and evaluating the impact of changing the value of FEMALE from 0 (representing men) to 1 (representing women) in each time period. In Equation 7.3, the presence of the additional "slope" parameter permits an identical increase ("vertical shift") of magnitude β_1 in logit-hazard in every time period when FEMALE equals 1. It is as though the model has taken the logit-hazard function for men (denoted by $\alpha_1, \alpha_2, \ldots, \alpha_J$ alone) and shifted it "upward" by an amount β_1 for women. The model is working in the way that our inspection of the sample depression data suggested that a decent discrete-time hazard model should work. We can interpret β_1 as the difference in population logit-hazard per unit difference in FEMALE. Of course, in this particular case, because FEMALE is coded as a dichotomy with 0 representing men and 1 representing women, β_1 summarizes the differential risk of depression for women over men. If the model were fitted to the sample data in Figure 7.2, for instance, the obtained estimate of β_1 would be positive because women are generally at greater risk of the onset of depression.

Notice that we are interpreting these parameters on a *logit-hazard* scale. Our discrete-time hazard model does not actually posit that the hazard function for women is a vertically shifted version of the baseline hazard function for men, as was initially suggested by the sample plots in the top panel of Figure 7.2. The "shifts" actually occur in the transformed world of logit-hazard. If we were to antilog these logit-hazard profiles to yield profiles describing the conditional *odds* of event occurrence at different values of the predictors then, because of the nature of the log transformation, the odds profiles would be *magnifications* or *diminutions* of one another—they would be *proportional*. We return to this property of proportionality later when we discuss the fundamental assumptions of the discrete-time hazard model.

It is an easy task to extend the simple discrete-time hazard model in Equation 7.1 to include several predictors. For instance, like Sorenson and her colleagues, we might want to examine the influence of ethnicity on the hazard function controlling for the effects of gender. To achieve this we would simply include the predictors FEMALE and HISPANIC (coded 0 for non-Hispanic, 1 for Hispanic) in the model simultaneously:

$$\text{logit}_e(h_j) = [\alpha_1 D_1 + \alpha_2 D_2 + \cdots + \alpha_J D_J] + \beta_1 \text{FEMALE} +$$

$$\beta_2 \text{HISPANIC}. \tag{7.4}$$

In Equation 7.4, the parameter β_1 captures the influence of gender and β_2 the influence of ethnicity, each effect being controlled for the other. As in the case of regular multiple-regression analysis, within the limits imposed by identification and power, any number of predictors can be added to the discrete-time hazard model. And, although we have only alluded to dichotomous predictors so far, both dichotomous and continuous predictors are equally acceptable. It is also possible to examine the synergistic effect of several predictors by including statistical interactions among them. Appropriate cross-product terms are simply added to main-effects models in the same way as when interactions are examined in multiple-regression models.

Finally, one additional important generalization is permitted for discrete-time hazard models that distinguishes them from multiple-regression models. When event-history data are collected the values of critical predictors often fluctuate naturally over time, differing in different time periods. Such *time-varying predictors* can easily be included in discrete-time hazard models, often allowing one developmental attribute to be predicted by another. In a longitudinal study of the first onset of depression, for instance, a participant may undergo drug therapy in some time periods but not in others. If this were the case, the value of the THERAPY variable would vary from time period to time period. We can record its value in each time period and use it as a time-varying predictor in a discrete-time hazard model:

$$\text{logit}_e(h_j) = [\alpha_1 D_1 + \alpha_2 D_2 + \cdots + \alpha_J D_J] + \beta_3 \text{THERAPY}_j. \tag{7.5}$$

In order to understand the action of this time-varying predictor, the discrete-time hazard model can be broken down into its period-by-period components, as before:

$$\text{logit}_e(h_1) = \alpha_1 + \beta_3 \text{THERAPY}_1,$$
$$\text{logit}_e(h_2) = \alpha_2 + \beta_3 \text{THERAPY}_2,$$
$$\cdot$$
$$\cdot \tag{7.6}$$
$$\cdot$$
$$\text{logit}_e(h_J) = \alpha_J + \beta_3 \text{THERAPY}_J.$$

The value of logit-hazard in each period is now made up of two parts: the baseline part (represented by the α) and a THERAPY effect of magnitude β_3. However, the interpretation is slightly different from that offered for the time-invariant effect of FEMALE in Equation 7.3.

What is that interpretation? Don't forget that THERAPY is time varying. If the patient is in therapy in the first time period, then THERAPY$_1$ will equal 1; if not, then THERAPY$_1$ will equal 0. If the patient is in therapy in the second time period then THERAPY$_2$ will be 1, otherwise 0. Similarly, THERAPY$_3$, THERAPY$_4$, . . . , THERAPY$_J$ can each take on a value of 1 or 0, depending on whether the patient is in or out of therapy in time periods 3 through J. Notice how this affects the logit-hazard profile being portrayed in Equation 7.6. In each time period that the person is in therapy, the value of THERAPY will become 1 and the effect of therapy will "kick in" for this period only, vertically shifting the logit-hazard function by an amount β_3.

Notice how this interpretation is different from the interpretation offered previously for the action of FEMALE in Equation 7.3. In that model, FEMALE was time invariant, retaining its value from time period to time period. Therefore, it acted to shift the logit-hazard function equally by β_1 across the board in all time periods. Here, as patients pass in and out of therapy, the effect of the time-varying THERAPY predictor mirrors this scheduling variation by *shifting the logit-hazard function only in those periods in which the patient was in therapy.* The critical point to remember is that we have built a discrete-time hazard model that tolerates the inclusion of time-varying predictors, allowing them to act only when there is a need. This is an important advantage indeed.

This has been a long and important section. In it, we have attempted to "unpack" a discrete-time hazard model so that its fundamental workings could be appreciated and its suitability for our research questions be understood. By beginning this extended technical argument with a real data example, we have shown how the mathematical form that was chosen for the hazard model permits it to represent realistic risk profiles in a natural and meaningful way. We have shown how the many "intercepts" contained in the model are required because the conceptual "outcome" in our research questions is an entire temporal profile of hazard. We have demonstrated how different types of predictor—both time invariant and time varying—can be added to the basic model in order to investigate how other factors affect the risks of event occurrence. In the rest of the chapter, we demonstrate how this hazard model can easily be fitted to discrete event-history data using widely available and standard software and we offer examples of data analysis and interpretation.

To set the stage for some of these forthcoming interpretations, we close this section by emphasizing that all of the "logit-hazard" models that we have cited here have an alternative "hazard-based" formulation. In fact, by straightforward algebraic manipulation of any of the models, the hazard probability—rather than logit-hazard—can be made the "subject of the formula." It is easy to show, for instance, that Equation 7.1 is the same as

$$h_j = \frac{1}{1 + e^{-\{[\alpha_1 D_1 + \alpha_2 D_2 + \cdots + \alpha_J D_J] + \beta_1 \text{FEMALE}\}}} . \tag{7.7}$$

The reader familiar with logistic regression analysis will recognize this as a standard logistic regression model with the intercept term slightly modified. In fact, a general discrete-time hazard model with multiple predictors (here labeled $X_1, X_2, \ldots , X_p$) can be written

$$h_j = \frac{1}{1 + e^{-\{[\alpha_1 D_1 + \alpha_2 D_2 + \cdots + \alpha_J D_J] + [\beta_1 X_1 + \beta_2 X_2 + \cdots + \beta_p X_p]\}}}, \qquad (7.8)$$

And, of course, the X's can be continuous or dichotomous, time invariant or time varying, main effects or interactions, in the manner that we have described. We will return to this general representation later, when we compute estimated hazard profiles from discrete-time hazard models fitted to sample data.

FITTING THE DISCRETE-TIME HAZARD MODEL TO DATA

To fit any statistical model, data are required. Ideally, these data are measurements on a representative sample of people drawn at random from the population of interest. Because they are representative of the underlying population, we will be able to make inferences about the population from the sample analyses. We have already proposed a discrete-time hazard model to represent the population relationship between the hazard function and predictors. But, how can we fit this model to data? In this section and the next, we describe the typical structure of a sample of event-history data and we show how the parameters of our discrete-time hazard model can be estimated from those data.

The Structure of Discrete Event-History Data

Discrete event-history data are not usually obtained in a format appropriate for subsequent data analysis. For conveniences and efficiency, data are usually collected and recorded in a "person-oriented" format and then converted to a "person-period" format prior to analysis.

In Figure 7.3, we illustrate the transformation of a person-oriented dataset (top panel) into a person-period dataset (bottom panel) using data on three former cocaine abusers in the 12 weeks following treatment in one of several intensive chemical-dependency programs. The research question being posed is: Whether, and when, do treated cocaine abusers tend to relapse into further cocaine usage? Our example is taken from a larger dataset that contains weekly prospective event-history data on 104 cocaine patients. The data were previously analyzed using survival methods and the findings written up in a thoughtful and interesting paper by Hall, Havassy, and Wasserman (1991).[7]

---

[7]We would like to thank Sharon M. Hall and her colleagues for providing us with these data and for permitting us to use them in this chapter.

Original Person Data Set

ID	SLIPWEEK	CENSOR	NASAL	M_1	M_2	M_3	M_4	M_5	M_6	M_7	M_8	M_9	M_{10}	M_{11}	M_{12}
01	03	0	0	23	18	13	.	.	.	.	.	.	.	.	.
02	12	1	1	27	30	35	29	36	32	27	22	28	30	24	26
03	12	0	1	38	48	48	48	44	47	48	43	42	44	46	14

Converted Person-Period Data Set

ID	D_1	D_2	D_3	D_4	D_5	D_6	D_7	D_8	D_9	D_{10}	D_{11}	D_{12}	NASAL	MOOD	RELAPSE
01	1	0	0	0	0	0	0	0	0	0	0	0	0	23	0
01	0	1	0	0	0	0	0	0	0	0	0	0	0	18	0
01	0	0	1	0	0	0	0	0	0	0	0	0	0	13	1
02	1	0	0	0	0	0	0	0	0	0	0	0	1	27	0
02	0	1	0	0	0	0	0	0	0	0	0	0	1	30	0
02	0	0	1	0	0	0	0	0	0	0	0	0	1	35	0
02	0	0	0	1	0	0	0	0	0	0	0	0	1	29	0
02	0	0	0	0	1	0	0	0	0	0	0	0	1	36	0
02	0	0	0	0	0	1	0	0	0	0	0	0	1	32	0
02	0	0	0	0	0	0	1	0	0	0	0	0	1	27	0
02	0	0	0	0	0	0	0	1	0	0	0	0	1	22	0
02	0	0	0	0	0	0	0	0	1	0	0	0	1	28	0
02	0	0	0	0	0	0	0	0	0	1	0	0	1	30	0
02	0	0	0	0	0	0	0	0	0	0	1	0	1	24	0
02	0	0	0	0	0	0	0	0	0	0	0	1	1	26	0
03	1	0	0	0	0	0	0	0	0	0	0	0	1	38	0
03	0	1	0	0	0	0	0	0	0	0	0	0	1	48	0
03	0	0	1	0	0	0	0	0	0	0	0	0	1	48	0
03	0	0	0	1	0	0	0	0	0	0	0	0	1	48	0
03	0	0	0	0	1	0	0	0	0	0	0	0	1	44	0
03	0	0	0	0	0	1	0	0	0	0	0	0	1	47	0
03	0	0	0	0	0	0	1	0	0	0	0	0	1	48	0
03	0	0	0	0	0	0	0	1	0	0	0	0	1	43	0
03	0	0	0	0	0	0	0	0	1	0	0	0	1	42	0
03	0	0	0	0	0	0	0	0	0	1	0	0	1	44	0
03	0	0	0	0	0	0	0	0	0	0	1	0	1	46	0
03	0	0	0	0	0	0	0	0	0	0	0	1	1	14	1

FIG. 7.3. Converting a person-oriented dataset into a person-period dataset prior to discrete-time hazard modeling by logistic regression. Data kindly provided by Dr. Sharon M. Hall and her colleagues (Hall, Havassy, & Wasserman, 1991.)

The person-oriented dataset usually contains a single record for each person in the sample. In addition to identification information, this "line" of data typically records:

- *Duration*. The length of each person's event history is recorded by noting the last time period in which he or she was assessed. In Figure 7.3, SLIP-WEEK records the week in which a former addict relapsed or was censored.

- *Censoring*. CENSOR records whether the event of interest actually occurred (in the time period given by SLIPWEEK) or whether the event history was censored (0 = not censored, 1 = censored).

- *Selected predictors.* The values of the predictors are recorded in each time period that they were assessed. In Figure 7.3, we display the values of one time-invariant predictor and "one" time-varying predictor. For the time-invariant predictor only a single value is recorded, applying uniformly across all time-periods. In Figure 7.3, time-invariant NASAL denotes the primary route of cocaine administration used by the addict prior to treatment (1 = nasal administration, 0 = all other methods). Time-varying predictors, on the other hand, may take on a different value in each period and so time-varying predictor MOOD, for instance, is represented by 12 variables, $M_1, M_2, \ldots , M_{12}$, one for each week observed. Each of these is a continuous variable that record patients' weekly scores on the positive mood subscale of Ryman, Biersner, and La Rocco's (1974) mood questionnaire. When a person's history is terminated before the end of data collection, subsequent unknown values of any time-varying predictor are set to "missing," here recorded as a dot (see person 01).

After dataset conversion, each person has multiple records in the person-period dataset, each one pertaining to a different time period. Person 1, who was observed for three weeks, has three records. Former addicts 2 and 3, who were observed for 12 weeks, have 12. All person-period records are made up of identical variables, denoting the state of each person in each period:

- *Time dummies.* These dichotomous variables take on values that identify the particular time-period being referenced. In Figure 7.3, the 12 time dummies identify each of the discrete weeks in the prospective data collection. D_1 has value 1 in the record corresponding to the first time period, D_2 is 1 in the record for the second time period, D_3 is 1 in the third, and so on, with all other values being set to 0.
- *Predictors.* In each record, the predictors contain values appropriate for that time period. The time-invariant predictor, NASAL, has the same value in the several records that describe each former addict; thus, person 3, who formerly preferred the nasal method of cocaine administration, has the value 1 recorded in all 12 of her person-period records. The original 12 mood predictors $M_1, M_2, \ldots , M_{12}$ become a single column of values called MOOD, with values appropriate to each time period. Thus, in the three records for person 1, the values of MOOD are 23, 18, and 13 corresponding to the values of M_1, M_2, and M_3 in the original person-oriented dataset.
- *Event indicator.* The event indicator variable records whether the event of interest occurred for each person in each discrete period (0 = no event, 1 = event occurred). In Figure 7.3, RELAPSE describes whether each former cocaine abuser experienced relapse in each week. Because we are concerned with a single, nonrepeatable event, RELAPSE has zero values in all weeks except the last, where its value indicates whether the target event

occurred or whether the career was censored. For example, former addicts 2 and 3 each have 12 values of RELAPSE with the first 11 values being zero. In the 12th week, however, addict 2 was censored and so the value of RELAPSE is 0 (indicating that there was no relapse into cocaine abuse in the final week of observation). On the other hand, the event history of person 3 is not censored and so relapse must have been observed in the final week of observation. So, in the 12th week, RELAPSE has value 1 for addict 3.

Estimating the Unknown Parameters in the Discrete-Time Hazard Model

In discrete-time survival analysis, the relationship between event occurrence (relapse into cocaine abuse, in this case) and predictors is investigated using the person-period dataset. To fit a discrete-time hazard model, one simply regresses the event indicator RELAPSE on the selected predictors (including all of the time dummies) using logistic regression analysis (Cox, 1970; Cox & Snell, 1989; Hosmer & Lemeshow, 1989). No dedicated software is needed. Allison (1982) describes this process and provides a worked example (see also Brown, 1975; Laird & Olivier, 1981; Yamaguchi, 1991). Singer & Willett (1992) list computer code (in SAS, Version 6) for transforming a person-oriented into a person-period dataset, fitting hazard models, and reconstructing fitted discrete-time hazard and survivor profiles.[8]

The regression coefficients obtained under this logistic regression strategy are maximum likelihood estimates of the parameters in the discrete-time hazard model such as those proposed in Equations 7.1 through 7.8 (Singer & Willett, 1992). These estimates are "consistent, asymptotically efficient, and asymptotically normally distributed" (Allison, 1984, p. 82). Furthermore, despite the apparent lack of independence among the observations in the person-period dataset and the seeming sample-size inflation, the obtained standard errors appropriately estimate the sampling variation in the parameter estimates (Allison, 1984, p. 82). Consequently, the standard errors and model goodness-of-fit statistics are exactly those required for testing hypotheses about discrete-time hazard.

Finally, in a technical investigation of the convergence of discrete- and continuous-time survival methods, Efron (1988) showed that the estimated discrete-time survival profiles obtained by this method approach the well-known Kaplan-Meier estimates as the overall time interval is more finely discretized. He demonstrated, in addition, that the information loss on discretization is inversely related to the square of the number of discrete intervals and therefore declines rapidly with increasing discretization. In the following section, we provide examples of discrete-time hazard models that were fitted to data using the logistic regression strategy, and we demonstrate methods of data analysis and interpretation.

---

[8]Updated copies of this code can be obtained directly from the authors.

FITTING AND INTERPRETING FITTED DISCRETE-TIME HAZARD MODELS

Researchers fit statistical models so that they can address their substantive questions clearly and persuasively. Once discrete-time hazard models have been fitted, substantive interpretation is facilitated by examining analytic results using three complementary strategies: (a) by computing numerical summaries of effect size, (b) by graphically displaying the magnitude and direction of the effects, and (c) by evaluating how likely it is that we would have obtained our sample results if the null hypothesis of zero effect were really true (determining "statistical significance"). In this section, we illustrate this three-pronged approach by interpreting the results of fitting discrete-time hazard models to Hall et al.'s (1991) cocaine relapse data introduced in Figure 7.3.

Table 7.2 presents the results of fitting three hazard models to these data. The table contains output from PROC LOGISTIC in SAS Version 6, having regressed the event indicator, RELAPSE, in the person-period data set, on three "predic-

TABLE 7.2

Parameter Estimates and Goodness-of-Fit Statistics for Three Hazard Models Fitted to the Cocaine Relapse Data: (A) Main Effect of Time Indicators; (B) Main Effects of Time Indicators and Time-Invariant Route of Administration (1 = nasal only, 0 = all others); and (C) Main Effects of Time Indicators and Time-Varying Positive Mood Count (centered at 30)

	Parameter Estimate		
Predictor	Model A	Model B	Model C
D_1	−1.8608	−1.5914	−2.0194
D_2	−2.0794	−1.7871	−2.3108
D_3	−2.1547	−1.8307	−2.4507
D_4	−2.5802	−2.2576	−2.9167
D_5	−2.6912	−2.3662	−2.9858
D_6	−2.2336	−1.8647	−2.6562
D_7	−3.2581	−2.8560	−3.5543
D_8	−2.5055	−2.1035	−2.9577
D_9	−2.7300	−2.3120	−3.1651
D_{10}	−3.8286	−3.3772	−4.1986
D_{11}	−3.0910	−2.6438	−3.6345
D_{12}	−3.0445	−2.6178	−3.6869
NASAL		−1.0511	
MOOD-30			−0.0806
−2LL	412.17	400.06	381.52
Change in		12.11	30.63
−2LL (df)		(1)	(1)
p		<.001	<.0001

Source: Data kindly provided by Hall, Havassy, & Wasserman (1991).

tors": the time indicators D_1-D_{12}, time-invariant prior mode of administration (NASAL), and the patient's time-varying weekly MOOD. Other logistic regression routines, such as those available in SPSS-X, BMDP, STATA, and SYSTAT, provide comparable summary information. The top portion of the table presents parameter estimates; the bottom portion presents associated goodness-of-fit statistics. We now show how to use the parameter estimates to compute maximum-likelihood estimates of the hazard function, the survivor function, and the median lifetime, and how to use the goodness-of-fit statistics to conduct hypothesis tests for the parameters of the model (the α's and the β's).

An Initial Hazard Model

Fitting Model A in Table 7.2, the simplest possible discrete-time hazard model, provides an important first step during discrete-time survival analysis. Because the model contains no substantive predictors (such as NASAL or MOOD) that distinguish members of the sample from each other, this initial hazard model describes the behavior of the *entire* sample, assuming a homogeneous population. As we have noted earlier, the model contains as many "intercept" terms as there are time periods under study. Because Hall et al. assessed cocaine use for up to 12 weeks after treatment ended, Model A includes 12 intercepts, α_1, $\alpha_2, \ldots, \alpha_{12}$, which are coefficients of the 12 time dummies, D_1-D_{12}:

$$\text{logit}_e(h_j) = [\alpha_1 D_1 + \alpha_2 D_2 + \cdots + \alpha_{12} D_{12}]. \tag{7.9}$$

In writing Equation 7.9, we bracket the 12 terms involving the intercepts and the time dummies because, as a group, they describe the overall temporal profile of risk of relapse and therefore represent the effect of a single conceptual predictor, *the main effect of* TIME. By referring to these 12 terms as the main effect of TIME, we highlight an apparent paradox in hazard modeling: TIME, the conceptual *outcome,* is the fundamental *predictor* of the hazard profile. This seeming anomaly arises because of our reformulation of the question "When does the event occur?" to "What is the risk of event occurrence in each time period?" This mathematically convenient reexpression sacrifices nothing intellectually because, as we show below, we can easily use summary statistics to answer not only this second question, but the original question as well.

The initial hazard model serves three purposes. First, it provides a benchmark against which to compare the goodness of fit of more complex models, a procedure we describe when examining the results of fitting Models B and C. Second, inspection of $\hat{\alpha}_1, \hat{\alpha}_2, \ldots, \hat{\alpha}_{12}$ tells us what the overall logit-hazard profile looks like and therefore provides a first suggestion of the temporal shape of the overall pattern of risk in the sample. If the risk of event occurrence were unrelated to time, the hazard function would be flat and $\hat{\alpha}_1, \hat{\alpha}_2, \ldots, \hat{\alpha}_{12}$ would be approximately equal. If risk of event occurrence were to decrease over time, parameter estimates for the early time periods would be large (i.e., closer to zero) and subsequent estimates would be smaller. If the risk of event occurrence increased over time, early parameter estimates would be small (i.e., far from zero) and later estimates would be larger. The steady decrease in the magnitudes of the parameter estimates across time for Model A in Table 7.2 suggests that among these former cocaine abusers, the risk of relapse declines over time.

Third, we can use the parameter estimates to obtain maximum-likelihood estimates of the population hazard probabilities themselves in each discrete time period by substituting back into Equation 7.8. Examination of the fitted hazard probabilities provides direct answers to substantive questions such as: How soon after the end of treatment are cocaine patients likely to relapse? Is the risk of relapse highest immediately after treatment ends, or later, after a period of abstinence? Does the risk of relapse increase or decrease over time? Is there a safe period after which previously unrelapsed patients rarely relapse?

Computation of the maximum-likelihood estimate of the hazard function is relatively straightforward because we have represented TIME as a series of time dummies, one per period. To understand the computation, reexamine the discrete-time hazard model in Equation 7.9. Recall that in the first week after treatment, $D_1 = 1$ and all other time indicators, $D_2, D_3, \ldots, D_{12}$ are zero. In addition, in this initial model, no other predictors are included (i.e., there are no other X's). As a result, if we substitute into Equation 7.9, only the term involving α_1 and D_1 remains. We therefore estimate h_1 to be

$$\hat{h}_1 = \frac{1}{1 + e^{-(-1.8608 \times 1)}} = .1346. \qquad (7.10)$$

The fitted hazard probability of .1346 indicates that among all cocaine treatment patients who successfully completed treatment, we estimate 13% risk of relapse in the first week. In the second week after treatment ($j = 2$), $D_2 = 1$ and all other time indicators are zero. By similar substitution of -2.0794 ($\hat{\alpha}_2$, the estimated coefficient for D_2), we estimate h_2 to be $1/(1 + e^{-(-2.0794 \times 1)}) = 0.1111$. This tells us that among treated patients who remain abstinent for one week, there is an 11% chance of relapse in the second week. We can estimate the remaining hazard probabilities—$h_3, h_4, \ldots, h_{12}$—using the same strategy. We display these estimated probabilities in Table 7.3 and as a fitted hazard function in the top panel of Figure 7.4.

Examination of the profile of fitted hazard probabilities confirms the pattern suggested by our initial inspection of the parameter estimates: The risk of relapse to cocaine use is greatest immediately after the end of treatment; over time successfully abstinent individuals are less and less likely to relapse. In each of the first three weeks after treatment, the risk of relapse exceeds 10%. After 5 weeks of successful abstinence, the risk of relapse falls below 10% and after 10 weeks of successful abstinence, it falls below 5%.

We may also summarize our results via the corresponding fitted survivor function. Maximum-likelihood estimates of this function can be obtained by

TABLE 7.3
Estimated Logistic Regression Parameters, Hazard Function,
and Survivor Function for a Baseline Discrete-Time Hazard
Model Fit to the Cocaine Relapse Data

Week	Parameter Estimate	Estimated Hazard Probability	Estimated Survival Probability
1	−1.8608	0.1346	0.8654
2	−2.0794	0.1111	0.7692
3	−2.1547	0.1039	0.6893
4	−2.5802	0.0704	0.6408
5	−2.6912	0.0635	0.6001
6	−2.2336	0.0968	0.5420
7	−3.2581	0.0370	0.5219
8	−2.5055	0.0755	0.4826
9	−2.7300	0.0612	0.4530
10	−3.8286	0.1213	0.4434
11	−3.0910	0.0435	0.4241
12	−3.0445	0.0454	0.4048

Source: Data kindly provided by Hall, Havassy, & Wasserman
(1991).

cumulating the maximum-likelihood estimates of the hazard probabilities using the method introduced earlier. To understand this calculation, recall that in the beginning, when all the patients have just completed treatment, everyone is abstinent, and so the survivor probability S_0 is 1. The estimated survivor probability in each subsequent time period is simply the estimated survivor probability in the prior time period decremented proportionally by the estimated fraction of people who relapse in that period ($\hat{h}_j$):

$$\hat{S}_j = \hat{S}_{j-1}(1 - \hat{h}_j) \tag{7.11}$$

Equation 7.11 simply formalizes the method of survivor function calculation that we introduced without substantiation when we examined the age of first onset of suicide ideation in Table 7.1.

Applying Equation 7.11 to the estimated hazard probabilities obtained above yields the estimated survivor function presented in Table 7.3 and in the bottom panel of Figure 7.4. Substituting $\hat{h}_1$ as computed in Equation 7.10 into Equation 7.11, for example, we estimate that 87% (= 1 − .1346) of the treated patients remain abstinent for more than one week. By a similar process, we estimate that 77% remain abstinent for more than two weeks, 52% remain abstinent for more than seven weeks, 48% remain abstinent for more than eight weeks. After 12 weeks, when Hall et al. suspended weekly data collection, an estimated 40% of the treated cocaine patients remained abstinent.

Having computed the maximum-likelihood estimates of the survivor function,

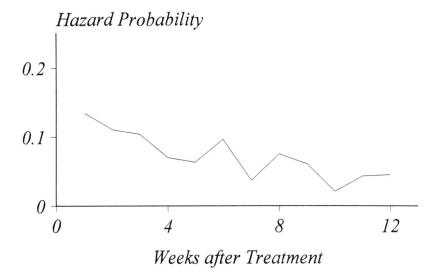

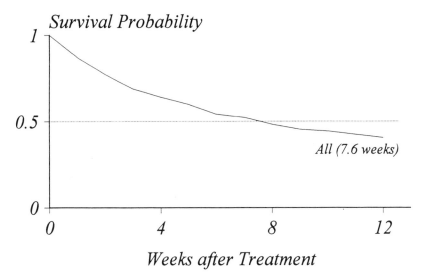

FIG. 7.4. Fitted hazard function (top panel) and survivor function (bottom panel) describing the risks of relapse for 104 former cocaine abusers following treatment. Plots derived from a hazard model containing only the main effect of TIME (estimated median lifetime in parentheses). Data kindly provided by Dr. Sharon M. Hall and her colleagues (Hall, Havassy, & Wasserman, 1991).

we can now calculate perhaps the most easily understood summary statistic available in survival analysis—the estimated median lifetime. Following the recommendation of Miller (1981), we estimate the median lifetime by linearly interpolating between the two time periods for which the survivor function brackets .50. In the cocaine relapse data, we linearly interpolate between the fitted values of $\hat{S}_7 = 0.5219$ and $\hat{S}_8 = 0.4826$, which yields an estimated median lifetime of 7.6 weeks. This tells us that, in this sample at least, the "average" treated former cocaine abuser started using cocaine again 7.6 weeks after treatment ended.

Estimated median lifetimes are intuitively appealing summaries of research results and are communicable to broad audiences. A clinician who knows little about survival analysis can understand what it means for the average time to relapse among treated cocaine patients to be 7.6 weeks. The fact that we have taken a somewhat circuitous analytic path—from event occurrence to hazard model to fitted survivor function to estimated median lifetime—does not detract from the comprehensibility of this statistic. Yet the use of sound mathematical principles and appropriate statistical models ensures that summary statements can withstand stringent methodological scrutiny. Nevertheless, we must always remind ourselves that any numeric summary of a distribution's center invariably ignores important variation about that average. The estimated median lifetime of 7.6 weeks only tells us that half the sample relapsed within 7.6 weeks of quitting. It does not highlight the fact that another 10% of the sample relapsed by the end of the 12th week and the remaining 40% of the sample either relapsed after 12 weeks or remain abstinent to this day. To emphasize such variation, we therefore recommend supplementing estimates of median lifetimes with graphical displays of fitted hazard and/or survivor functions (as presented in Figure 7.4).

Main Effect of a Time-Invariant Predictor

Model B adds the main effect of the single time-invariant predictor NASAL to the main effect of TIME:

$$\text{logit}_e\,(h_j) = [\alpha_1 D_1 + \alpha_2 D_2 + \cdots + \alpha_{12} D_{12}] + \beta_1 \text{NASAL}. \quad (7.12)$$

Because a discrete-time hazard model represents the relationship between predictors and the entire hazard profile, deriving a comprehensible vehicle for interpreting effect sizes can be a formidable task. As we show below, however, $\hat{\beta}_1$, the parameter estimate associated with the time-invariant predictor NASAL, can be interpreted in much the same way as we interpret estimated coefficients in multiple-regression models. Similarly, we can evaluate the "statistical significance" of this coefficient in much the same way as we do when fitting ordinary logistic regression models.

First, let us consider the size of the effect associated with the predictor NASAL. The estimated coefficient for NASAL, $\hat{\beta}_1$, is -1.05. Because NASAL is a dichotomy, which takes on the value 0 for individuals who formerly smoked or injected cocaine and the value 1 for individuals who formerly used cocaine intranasally, the coefficient's negative sign indicates that, in every week after treatment, intranasal users are less likely than all other users to relapse. The coefficient's magnitude (1.05) estimates the size of this differential in the metric of *logit-hazard* or log-odds. It indicates that the vertical separation between the two logit-hazard functions for these groups is -1.05.

Few of us find the metric of log-odds intuitively understandable. For this reason, as when examining the parameter estimates of any logistic regression model, we recommend that researchers antilog parameter estimates and interpret them in the more familiar metric of *odds* (Agresti, 1990; Hosmer & Lemeshow, 1989). In Model B, antilogging the fitted value of $\hat{\beta}_1$ yields $e^{-1.0511} = 0.35$. This tells us that the estimated odds of relapse for former intranasal users in any given week after treatment are about one third of the odds of relapse for former addicts who administered the drug by other routes. Because NASAL is a dichotomy, we may also express its effect by taking the inverse of its antilogarithm, $1/0.35 = 2.86$. This tells us that the estimated odds of relapse in any given week are nearly three times the odds of relapse for people who either smoked or injected cocaine as compared with those who used it intranasally.

This transformation strategy enabled Shapiro et al. (1989) to document the vast superiority of lithium over imipramine in reducing the recurrence of manic episodes in a group of patients with a history of affective disorders. After adjusting for the presence of several other predictors, including patient gender and psychological history, the authors obtained a parameter estimate of 2.378 for a dummy predictor representing type of drug therapy (see their Table 2, p. 403). They interpreted the antilog of this estimate ($e^{2.378} = 10.8$), by commenting that "patients with a manic index episode taking imipramine were at almost 11 times the risk for recurrence of those taking lithium" (p. 403). Other studies that have used a similar method of reporting the findings of their survival analyses include investigations of: adult outcomes of childhood and adolescent depression (Harrington, Fudge, Rutter, Pickles, & Hill, 1990a, 1990b), demographic and clinical factors associated with the risk of first suicide attempt (Pfeffer, Klerman, Hurt, Lesser, Peskin, & Siefker, 1991), the efficacy of interpersonal psychotherapy as a maintenance treatment of recurrent depression (Frank, Kupfer, Wagner, McEachran, & Cornes, 1991), and the onset of suicide ideation in childhood and adolescence (Bolger et al., 1989).

Although we agree that it is easier to interpret parameters expressed in the metric of odds in comparison to those expressed in the metric of log-odds (as in Table 7.2), the effects of many predictors can be better and more easily understood by simply presenting hazard and survivor functions fitted at substantively important, or prototypical, values of the predictors. We recommend this approach for the same reason that we recommend presenting fitted plots when conducting ordinary regression analyses—it is easier to ascertain an effect when it is presented graphically as opposed to numerically (Wainer, 1990). And as we will show in the next section, the utility of fitted plots expands when the predictors in a hazard model are continuous because, then, statements about odds must be expressed not in terms of group differences but in terms of differences in odds per unit difference in the value of the predictor (!).

We illustrate the "fitted-plots" approach in Figure 7.5, which presents fitted hazard and survivor functions for the treated cocaine users by their route of cocaine use prior to entry into treatment. We derived the fitted hazard functions in the top panel by substituting the parameter estimates from Model B in Table 7.2 into Equation 7.8. We then derived the fitted survivor functions in the bottom panel by substituting the estimates of hazard into Equation 7.11. Having computed the fitted survivor function, we then linearly interpolated to estimate the median lifetimes for the two groups. As with Figure 7.4, we present the fitted hazard function above the fitted survivor function to emphasize that it was recovered first.

Comparison of the two fitted hazard functions in Figure 7.5 demonstrates the large differential in risk of relapse associated with route of administration. According to Model B, in every week after treatment, intranasal users are far less likely than other users to relapse. These fitted functions have the same basic shape and one appears to be a magnification of the other.[9] Were we to replot these hazard functions on a log-odds scale they would have a constant vertical separation. The functions have been constrained to appear this way by the "proportional-odds" assumption built into the hazard model as written in Equations 7.1 through 7.8. In the next section we show how to determine whether this proportional-odds assumption is tenable in practice.

The fitted survivor plots in the bottom panel of Figure 7.5 show the cumulative effects of the large weekly differentials in risk. Unlike the fitted hazard functions that emphasize large and consistent differences in risk, the fitted survivor functions condense the effects of these weekly risk differentials together to reveal a substantial difference between the groups. Focusing on the last fitted survival probability, for example, we estimate that 12 weeks after treatment ended, 63% of the intranasal users remained abstinent as compared with 28% of other users.

A third perspective on the divergent relapse patterns of these two groups comes from comparison of the estimated median lifetimes displayed in the bottom panel of Figure 7.5: more than 12 weeks for intranasal users versus 5.1 weeks for all other users. Even though censoring prevents us from estimating a median lifetime precisely for intranasal users, the large difference between these "average" relapse times powerfully communicates the analytic results.

No discussion of the magnitude of a predictor's effect is complete unless we

---

[9]Strictly speaking, this apparent magnification of one hazard profile into the other is approximate in the discrete-time hazard model and only holds when h_j is small. For further discussion, see our section on the proportionality assumption.

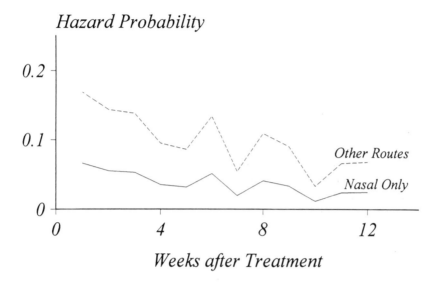

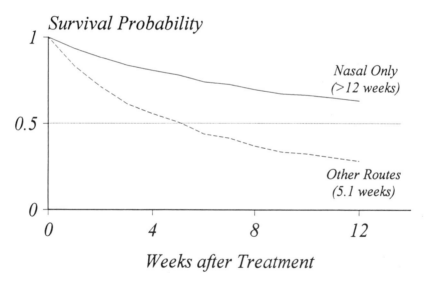

FIG. 7.5. Fitted hazard functions (top panel) and survivor functions (bottom panel) describing the risks of relapse for 104 former cocaine abusers following treatment, by route of cocaine administration prior to treatment (intranasal versus all others). Plots derived from a fitted hazard model containing the main effect of TIME and the main effect of time-invariant NASAL as predictors (estimated median lifetimes in parentheses). Data kindly provided by Dr. Sharon M. Hall and her colleagues (Hall, Havassy, & Wasserman, 1991).

consider the very real possibility that the estimate obtained in our single sample may not reflect an underlying population relationship. We address the issue of inference by comparing goodness-of-fit statistics for hierarchically nested discrete-time hazard models. As when fitting any logistic regression model, standard decrement-to-chi-square testing, based on the known asymptotic distributional properties of -2 times the log-likelihood statistic (listed as "$-2LL$" in computer printouts and Table 7.2) can be used to evaluate the effect of additional predictors by comparing the goodness of fit of an extended model to that of a reduced model. If the additional predictors are not associated with logit-hazard, the fit of the extended model will not be much better than the fit of the reduced model and the corresponding chi-square statistic will not decline substantially. If the additional predictors are associated with risk, there will be a statistically significant decline in the value of the chi-square statistic. Decrement-to-chi-square testing thereby allows us to identify important influences on risk.

We illustrate this procedure by comparing the two goodness-of-fit statistics presented for Models A and B in Table 7.2. Model A is nested within Model B because the sole difference between the two models is the inclusion of the single time-invariant predictor NASAL. When NASAL is added to the initial model containing only the main effect of TIME, the goodness-of-fit statistic decreases from 412.17 to 400.06, indicating a better fit for Model B. Because we have added only a single predictor, this improvement of 12.11 comes with a loss of 1 degree of freedom, which yields an associated p-value less than .001. This indicates that the addition of NASAL to the initial discrete-time hazard model has significantly improved the overall fit. We therefore reject the null hypothesis that the predictor NASAL has no effect on the population hazard profile, H_0: $\beta_1 = 0$, and conclude that there is a relationship between NASAL and risk of relapse. Of course, when adding a single predictor like this, the same conclusion can be reached by comparing the magnitude of the parameter estimate to its asymptotic standard error.

Main Effect of a Time-Varying Predictor

Identical methods of interpretation, display, and inference are used to examine the effects of time-varying predictors. We illustrate these methods using Model C in Table 7.2, which adds the main effect of the time-varying predictor MOOD to the baseline model that includes only the main effect of TIME:

$$\text{logit}_e \ (h_j) = [\alpha_1 D_1 + \alpha_2 D_2 + \cdots + \alpha_{12} D_{12}]$$
$$+ \ \beta_2 (\text{MOOD}_j - 30). \qquad (7.13)$$

The value of MOOD in each time period reflects the individual's positive mood score at that time. Because a person's mood can fluctuate naturally over time, the values of the predictor MOOD may differ from week to week. For ease of interpretation, we have centered the variable MOOD at 30, the approximate sample mean.

Notice that when we write the discrete-time hazard model in Equation 7.13, we include the subscript j on the variable name MOOD$_j$. This reminds us that the values of this variable—this *time varying predictor*—can fluctuate from week to week. The person-period data set easily captures this natural fluctuation because each individual has a separate data record for each discrete time period when data were collected. The model specifies that the risk of relapse in each week depends upon the person's mood *in that particular week*. The protective benefit of a high score accrues only in those weeks when the individual scores high; the potential liability of a low score takes its toll only in those weeks when the individual scores low.

The discrete-time hazard model in Equation 7.13 specifies that each of the many possible combinations of mood levels over time produces a different profile of risk over time. But the model also postulates that, although the *values* of MOOD may fluctuate over time, its *effect* on logit-hazard remains constant. A one-point decline on the positive mood scale "kicks in" the same amount of risk whenever the mood decrease occurs. Similarly, a one-point improvement on the positive mood scale "kicks out" the same amount of risk whenever the mood change occurs. Because the *effect* of MOOD does not vary over time (even though its values do), we say that *the time-varying predictor* (MOOD) *has a time-invariant effect*.

β_2 in Equation 7.13 captures this time-invariant main effect of time-varying MOOD on the population logit-hazard profile. As shown in Table 7.2, in this sample, we estimate β_2 to be $-.0806$. The negative sign indicates that higher scores on the positive mood scale are associated with a decreased risk of relapse. To determine the magnitude of this effect, we antilog the parameter estimate by computing $e^{-.0806}$, which yields 0.92. This antilogged estimate indicates that for each one-point increase in the positive mood scale, the odds of relapse are lower, being multiplied by 0.92.

When we attempt to evaluate the magnitude of an effect associated with a continuous predictor, we run into the difficulty of interpreting odds ratios that do not compare well-defined groups of people. Predictors that represent permanent group membership (such as sex) or time-varying group membership (such as in therapy or not) yield antilogged parameter estimates amenable to easy interpretation. We evaluated the size of the effect associated with administration route in Model B, for example, by antilogging the parameter estimate -1.05 and concluding that the odds of relapse for intranasal users were one third of the odds among other users.

With continuous predictors such as MOOD, however, comparative odds ratios are less than compelling. We therefore recommend that researchers display the results of fitting discrete-time hazard models with continuous predictors by plotting fitted hazard and survivor functions computed at substantively meaningful values of the continuous predictor.

What values of the continuous predictor are substantively meaningful? Because the predictor MOOD is nearly continuous (it ranges between 1 and 48), we could draw as many as 48 fitted hazard and survivor functions corresponding to the 48 possible values of MOOD. To avoid overkill and clutter, we have selected three values, 20, 30, and 40, which correspond roughly to the 10th, 50th, and 90th percentiles of its sample distribution. Figure 7.6 presents these three fitted survivor and hazard functions, produced by using Equation 7.8 and substituting in these three values for the time-varying predictor MOOD: one for individuals who had consistently low positive mood scores (20), one for individuals who had consistently average positive mood scores (30), and one for individuals who had consistently high positive mood scores (40).

As in Figure 7.5, which presented the main effect of NASAL, the three hazard functions in the top panel of Figure 7.6 share the same basic shape; each is simply a magnification of another.[10] In every week after treatment, cocaine patients who report more positive moods are less likely to relapse than their peers who report fewer positive moods. The two extreme profiles can be regarded as an "envelope" containing the hazard profiles for treated cocaine users in various possible combinations of mood levels over time, varying from approximately the 10th percentile (with a score of 20) to the 90th percentile (with a score of 40). Because most people's moods fluctuate over time, these three hazard functions do not correspond to specific individuals in the sample, but rather circumscribe an envelope within which most people's hazard profiles fall. The fitted hazard profile for individuals who first report many positive moods and then report few positive moods, for example, would initially follow the bottom hazard function and then move higher as the score on the positive mood scale decreased.

The fitted survivor functions and estimated median lifetimes displayed in the bottom panel of Figure 7.6 summarize these risk differentials across the 12-week period. The uppermost fitted survivor function represents our best estimate of what would happen to individuals whose mood levels were consistently high (at 40): 12 weeks after treatment ends, we predict that 74% would remain abstinent. The middle fitted survivor function represents our prediction for individuals whose mood levels were consistently moderate (at 30): 12 weeks after treatment ends, we predict that 51% would remain abstinent. But it is for patients who report consistently negative moods that the relapse rates appear grimmest. For a group of treated patients whose moods were consistently low (at 20), we estimate that the average time to relapse is 3.5 weeks. In making these summary statements, however, we hasten to add that these are predictions for prototypical individuals whose values of MOOD remain constant over time. A different pattern

---

[10]Again, the apparent magnification is approximate, applying only for small h_{ij}. For further discussion, see our section on the proportionality assumption.

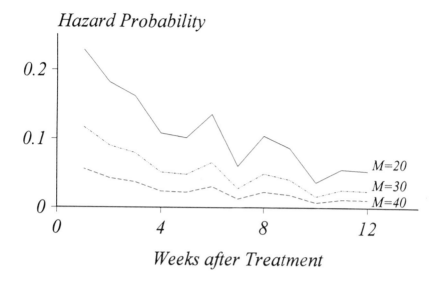

Weeks after Treatment

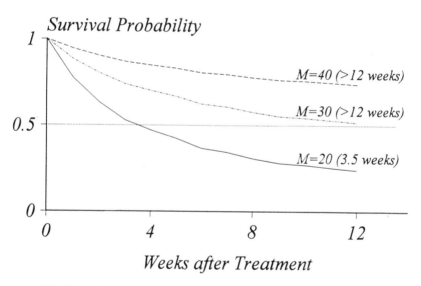

Weeks after Treatment

FIG. 7.6. Fitted hazard functions (top panel) and survivor functions (bottom panel) describing the risks of relapse for 104 former cocaine abusers following treatment, by level of positive mood. Plots fitted at the sample 10th, 50th, and 90th percentiles of MOOD and derived from a fitted hazard model containing the main effect of TIME and the main effect of time-varying MOOD as predictors (estimated median lifetimes in parentheses). Data kindly provided by Dr. Sharon M. Hall and her colleagues (Hall, Havassy, & Wasserman, 1991).

of mood levels over time, and in particular one that shifted over time, would generate a different fitted survivor function.

How do we determine whether this sample risk differential associated with the predictor MOOD likely reflects a relationship in the population? The methods for drawing a statistical inference about a time-varying predictor are identical those for drawing an inference for a time-invariant predictor. We evaluate whether the addition of MOOD to our initial hazard model has significantly improved the prediction of the risk profile by comparing the goodness-of-fit statistics ($-2LL$) for Models A and C. On the addition of MOOD to Model A, the chi-square goodness-of-fit statistic declines by 30.63 for a loss of 1 degree of freedom ($p <$ .0001) indicating a considerable improvement in fit and telling us that we can reject H_0: $\beta_2 = 0$. We therefore conclude that MOOD is a statistically significant predictor of the risk of relapse.

THE PROPORTIONALITY ASSUMPTION

In the discrete-time hazard models that we have presented so far, we have made three important assumptions. (1) the linear-logistic model is a valid representation of reality—that *equal differences* in the values of a predictor correspond to *equal vertical displacements* of the logit-hazard profile (the *linearity* assumption); (2) the model requires no "error" term—that all heterogeneity across people is accounted for by variation in the values of the predictors (the *no unobserved heterogeneity* assumption); (3) the logit-hazard profiles corresponding to all possible values of every predictor are distinguished only by their relative elevation (the *proportionality* assumption). In this section, we focus attention on the third assumption, which is unique to survival analysis and is often violated in practice. For a discussion of the other two assumptions, consult Singer and Willett (1993).

Most standard specifications of continuous-time and discrete-time hazard models invoke a *proportionality* assumption. The discrete-time hazard model proposed in Equation 7.12, for example, implicitly embodies such an assumption. It postulates that the entire family of logit-hazard profiles represented by all possible values of NASAL share a common shape and are mutually parallel, being shifted only vertically for different values of NASAL.

Why is this referred to as a "proportionality" assumption? The answer is straightforward, but not immediately obvious. Because discrete-time hazard is a (conditional) probability, points on the logit-hazard function describe the *log-odds* of event occurrence in each time period (given no earlier occurrence). If we antilog these logit-hazard profiles, we obtain profiles describing the conditional *odds* of event occurrence at different values of the predictors. And, because of the nature of the logarithmic transformation, these new odds profiles are magnifications or diminutions of one another—they are *proportional*. It is this "proportional-odds" consequence of the discrete-time hazard model that we refer to as the *proportionality* assumption. As noted in Singer and Willett (1993), the proportionality assumption in survival analysis resembles the assumption of parallel regression slopes in the traditional analysis of covariance.

When the magnitude of the hazard probabilities is small (as in Figures 7.1 and 7.2, for instance), the *odds* of an event occurring is approximately equal to the *probability* of its occurring (i.e., $h_j \approx h_j/(1 - h_j)$ when h_j is small, the equality improving rapidly as h_j gets smaller). Thus, in many settings, the discrete-time proportional-odds assumption underwrites an approximate discrete-time "proportional-hazards" assumption in which the hazard profiles corresponding to different values of the predictors also appear to be magnifications and diminutions of one another (see, as we have noted earlier, Figures 7.5 and 7.6). In continuous-time survival analysis, where *log* hazard rate (rather than *logit*-hazard probability) is modeled as a linear function of predictors, the proportionality assumption is not a proportional-odds assumption but a *proportional-hazards* assumption.

There is a simple graphical method for verifying the proportionality assumption. In preliminary analyses, if logit-hazard profiles estimated separately within important strata (as defined by the values of potential predictors) are approximately parallel, then the assumption is met; if they are not, it is violated. Unfortunately, in practice, it is often difficult to separate true nonproportionality from the vagaries of sampling variation. For instance, Figure 7.2 shows hazard profiles estimated separately for subsamples of men and women. Even though statistical testing confirms that the proportional-odds assumption is actually met in this case, sampling idiosyncrasy ensures minor differences in shape between the profiles that may fool the eye.

We hasten to add that we have found, in a wide variety of settings including not only our own work on teachers' careers (Murnane, Singer, & Willett, 1989; Murnane, Singer, Willett, Kemple, & Olsen, 1991; Singer, 1993a, 1993b) but also others' work on child mortality (Trussel & Hammerslough, 1983), duration of breastfeeding (Tognetti, 1990), time to undergraduate degree (Lopez, 1990), time to doctorate (Civian, 1990), and age at first suicide ideation (Bolger et al., 1989), that violations of the proportionality assumption seem to be the rule rather than the exception. In many real-world situations, logit-hazard profiles corresponding to different values of the predictors are not simply shifted versions of the same baseline shape; many predictors do more than vertically displace the logit-hazard profile; they also alter its shape.

Ignoring potential violations of the proportionality assumption may challenge the integrity of your findings. To avoid this, we suggest that researchers routinely adopt a more skeptical approach at the outset. They should assume the very real possibility of a nonproportional relationship between hazard and the chosen predictors and test to confirm whether this is the case. If the proportionality assumption is violated, then terms can be included in the hazard model to represent the nonproportional effects. Nonproportional relationships can be investigated straightforwardly in discrete-time survival analysis by examining statistical interactions between substantive predictors and TIME, a procedure that we now describe in greater detail.

NONPROPORTIONAL HAZARDS MODELS

An interesting phenomenon that is easily checked with discrete-time hazard models is whether the *effect* of a predictor fluctuates with time or whether it is constant. Hazard models that do not include an interaction between the predictor and TIME (i.e., all of the proportional-odds models that we have fit so far) implicitly assume that a predictor has an identical effect in each time period. When modeling the effect of mood on cocaine relapse, for example, the proportional-odds assumption implies that the vertical shift in the logit-hazard function corresponding to a one-point difference in the mood scale is the same regardless of whether it was a former user's 1st or 10th week after treatment.

But not all predictors work only as main effects. The *effects* of both time-invariant and time-varying predictors can themselves fluctuate over time. Some predictors may primarily affect early hazards, causing the hazard profiles to be widely separated in the beginning and narrower later. Other predictors may primarily affect late hazards, having little effect at the beginning and widening the distance between the hazard functions as time passes.

As in ordinary least-squares regression analysis, we can easily explore whether the effect of any predictor varies over time by including the statistical interaction between TIME and the predictor in our hazard model. An interaction between a predictor and TIME implies that the effect of the predictor on the hazard profile differs from time period to time period. In other words, the vertical displacement in logit-hazard per unit difference in the predictor is no longer the same in every time period. When this occurs the *shapes* of the logit-hazard functions corresponding to different values of the predictor are no longer identical and the proportional-odds assumption has been violated.

Interactions between predictors and TIME are not simply methodological nuisances. Substantive interpretations of interactions with time often lead to a richer understanding of the relationships between predictors and hazard. From this upbeat perspective, we urge researchers to explore interactions with time systematically and consistently in their work. In addition, we recommend that researchers and methodologists refer to failures of the proportional-odds assumptions as an "interaction with time." Unfortunately, there are several other terms used in the literature to describe the same concept, including "time-dependent effect" (Cox & Oakes, 1984) and the misleading "time-varying effect." We prefer the "interaction with time" label because we believe that it helps distinguish this concept from the unrelated concept of whether the values of the predictor itself are time varying or time invariant.

Interactions between a predictor and TIME are easily incorporated in discrete-time hazard models. The researcher must simply form appropriate cross-products in the person-period dataset between the several time indicators and the chosen predictor and then include these cross-products, along with the relevant main effects, as a group of predictors in the ensuing logistic regression analysis.

We illustrate the inclusion of interactions with time by returning to the data on age at first onset of suicide ideation (Bolger et al., 1989) that were introduced in Figure 7.1. In their review of the literature on suicide and suicide ideation, Bolger and his colleagues noted that the Centers for Disease Control report that nationally, the suicide rate for Whites is twice that of non-Whites. This led them to hypothesize that White college students in their sample would be more likely to report having considered suicide. In Figure 7.7, we present the results of having fit two discrete-time hazard models to these data: one that included only the main effect of time-invariant predictor representing race, called WHITE ($0 =$ non-White; $1 =$ White), and a second that includes its interaction with TIME. We would use the same procedure to examine the interaction between a time-varying predictor and time.

The top panel of Figure 7.7 presents fitted hazard functions derived from a model that included only the main effects of TIME and WHITE. The odds that a White college student had considered suicide are 22% higher than for a non-White student, although the effect is not statistically significant at conventional levels ($p = .2961$). Because this top panel reflects the results of fitting a main-effects model (and because hazard probabilities are small—see previous section), the upper hazard function, for White students, is forced to be an (approximate) magnification of the lower one, for non-White students. Had we used a logit scale on the vertical axis, the two functions would be parallel and equidistant. This parallelism is a feature of the main-effects model—it forces the shapes of the two hazard functions to be similar.

Now consider a model in which WHITE interacts with time. Although we could have included this interaction in the hazard model by using a series of cross-product terms between the time dummies and WHITE, consideration of developmental stages led Bolger and colleagues to suspect that the interaction would be simpler, varying only by developmental stage. Following their lead, we simplify the interaction term by creating a new summary variable LATE that distinguishes childhood and early adolescence (LATE $= 0$, for children of ages 6 to 12) from later adolescence (LATE $= 1$, for children of ages 13 and older). We may therefore write the "interactive" discrete-time hazard model as

$$\text{logit}_e(h_j) = [\alpha_6 D_6 + \cdots + \alpha_{21} D_{21}] + \beta_1 \text{ WHITE} + \beta_2 (\text{LATE} \times \text{WHITE}).$$
(7.14)

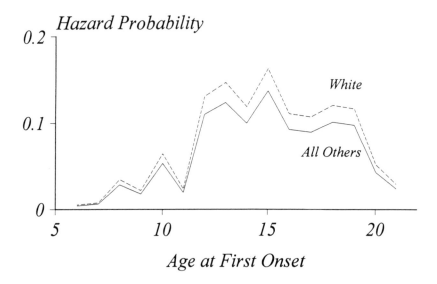

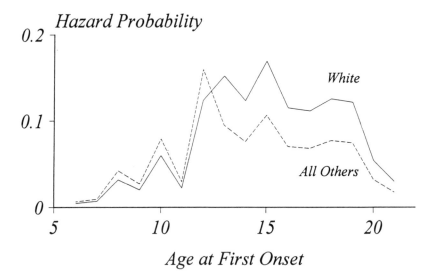

FIG. 7.7.   Fitted hazard functions describing the risks of onset of first suicide ideation for 417 college-bound adolescents by ethnicity, from a hazard model containing (a) top panel—the main effect of TIME and the main effect of ethnicity, and (b) bottom panel—the main effect of TIME, the main effect of ethnicity, and the two-way interaction between TIME and ethnicity. Data kindly provided by Dr. Niall Bolger and his colleagues (Bolger, Downey, Walker, & Steininger, 1989).

The inclusion of the two-way interaction between LATE and WHITE allows the effect of WHITE to differ between early and late adolescence.

Statistical comparison of the goodness of fit of two discrete-time hazard models—one in which WHITE is included as a main effect and one in which WHITE interacts with LATE—reveals that the addition of the interaction significantly improves the prediction of hazard. The model chi-square goodness-of-fit statistic declines by 4.64 between the main-effects and interaction models, for a loss of 1 degree of freedom ($p < .05$); we can reject the null hypothesis that the addition of the WHITE by LATE interaction makes no difference. Thus, the interaction between WHITE and LATE must be included in the model and the proportional-odds assumption has been violated.

The bottom panel of Figure 7.7 presents the fitted hazard functions for the interaction model. Notice the failure of the proportional-odds assumption. Comparing the fitted hazard functions from the interaction model to the pair from the main-effects model (in the top panel) illustrates the influence of the interaction between WHITE and time. In the top panel, the two hazard functions have similar shapes, with the hazard function for Whites being consistently above the hazard function for non-Whites. In the bottom panel, the hazard functions *cross*. Among children under 13, Whites are at lower risk of suicide ideation, but among adolescents age 13 and older Whites are at *higher* risk. Instead of having a constant vertical separation in logit-hazard space, the relative positions of the hazard functions reverse.

Because of the closer coincidence in hazard among younger children, the estimated median lifetimes for two groups computed from the interaction model are virtually identical (14.6 among White children; 15.4 among non-White children). Comparison of the main-effects model with the interaction model, however, documents the untenability of the assumption that the effect of race is constant over time and the degree to which a researcher can be misled by unthinking acceptance of the proportionality assumption. Had we estimated only the main-effects model, we would have erroneously concluded that the logit-hazard functions for the groups did not differ ($p = .2961$). As the lower panel shows, the hazard functions do differ, but the direction of the difference varies across time.

When the effect of a predictor—either time invariant or time varying—varies over time, the proportionality assumption is violated. If the assumption is violated, proportional-odds models are inappropriate. Serious analytic consequences await anyone who blindly fits proportional-odds models without examining the tenability of the model's assumptions. Had we stopped at the main-effects model here, for instance, we would have erroneously concluded that there was no race differential in the risk of suicide ideation. The interaction model shows that the risk patterns of the two groups are nearly identical during childhood and diverge sharply during adolescence.

The ability to examine the proportionality assumption precisely, instead of relying solely on the visual examination described earlier, makes discrete-time hazard modeling a particularly attractive analytic approach. Within this framework, it is easy to test the proportionality assumption by adding interactions with time to a baseline main-effects model. If the proportionality assumption is violated, the models easily support inclusion of the necessary interactions with time, ensuring the appropriate estimation of effects.

IS DISCRETE-TIME SURVIVAL ANALYSIS FOR YOU?

Discrete-time survival analysis permits researchers to answer questions about *whether,* and if so *when,* critical events occur. The method is powerful, flexible, and applicable to many questions arising in psychology and the social sciences. Although increasing numbers of researchers in this domain are using survival analysis, a review of the literature shows that many others studying onset, duration, recovery, recidivism, relapse, and recurrence have yet to exploit the new analytic tool.

We believe that one reason why survival methods have not yet become the method of choice for questions about event occurrence in this domain is that many researchers still wonder whether survival analysis is really necessary. Although few researchers explicitly state this view, reading between the lines suggests that many of them believe that traditional analytic approaches can suffice.

Of course, some skepticism is certainly healthy. After all, why bother with complexity if an equally valid answer can be obtained by using simpler methods? Because we agree that the use of any statistical method requires justification, we conclude by describing five ways in which traditional methods can obscure important information about event occurrence, information that is sensitively and assuredly revealed by methods available within the survival analysis framework.

First, answers obtained by researchers using traditional methods are inextricably linked to the particular time frame chosen for data collection and analysis; yet in psychological inquiry, these time frames are rarely substantively motivated. Researchers comparing six-month, one-year, or five-year relapse rates for individuals receiving different modes of therapy, for example, are simply describing *cumulative* differences in behavior until these times. All other variation over time in the risk of relapse is lost. The literature is filled with examples of disparate risk profiles that lead to comparable relapse rates at specific points in time (see, e.g., Figure 1 of Carpenter et al., 1991; Figure 1 of Prien et al., 1984; Figure 3 of Coryell, Keller, Lavori, & Endicott, 1990). Just because two groups of individuals have identical rates of event occurrence at one point in time does not mean that they followed similar trajectories to get there—most of those in one group might have experienced the event in the first month while those in the other might have been equally likely to experience it at all points in time. The six-month, one-year, and five-year cutpoints used in the past are convenient, but not purposeful. By documenting variation in risk over time, and by discovering what predicts variation in risk, we can better understand when events occur. Traditional methods disregard this information; with survival methods, variation in risk becomes the primary analytic focus.

Disregard for variation in risk over time leads to a second problem with traditional methods; seemingly contradictory conclusions can result from nothing more than variations in the particular time frames studied. Had Coryell et al. (1990) computed only 40-week, 80-week, or 200-week recovery rates when comparing patients with psychotic major depressive disorder (PMDD) and schizoaffective depressive disorder (SADD), for example, they would have reached three different conclusions: the 40-week rates would have shown that SADD patients were more likely to recover, the 80-week rates would have shown no difference, and the 200-week rates would have shown that PMDD patients were more likely to recover. By thoughtfully presenting survivor functions, they showed that SADD patients were more likely to recover early on but PMDD were more likely to recover subsequently. Researchers using traditional methods must constantly remind themselves that conclusions can change as the time frame changes. While such caveats usually appear in the "Methods" section of an article, they often disappear by the "Discussion" section. In survival analysis, the time frame itself is integral to the answer; it highlights, rather than obscures, variation over time.

Third, traditional analytic methods offer no systematic mechanism for incorporating censored observations in the analyses. If all the censored observations occur at the same point in time, traditional data analysis can collapse the sampled individuals into two groups: those who experienced the event before the censoring point and those who did not. Using a sample of adults with major depressive disorder who had been treated with one of three different modes of psychotherapy, Gallagher-Thompson, Hanley-Peterson, & Thompson (1990), for example, compared patients who relapsed and patients who did not one year (and two years) after cessation of treatment. But if the first weeks following cessation are the hardest, individuals who relapse soon after cessation may differ systematically from those who relapse subsequently. Dichotomization conceals such differences; survival methods, which focus on the risk of event occurrence over time, bring such differences to light.

If censoring does not occur at the same time point for every individual under study (as when researchers follow cohorts of patients admitted over time until a single fixed point in time), traditional methods create a fourth problem: If censoring times vary across people, the risk periods vary as well. People followed for longer periods of time have more opportunities to experience the target event than do those followed for shorter periods of time. This means that observed differences in rates of event occurrence might be attributable to nothing more than research design. In Goldstein, Black, Nasrallah, & Winokur's (1991) study of suicidality among 1,906 Iowans with affective disorders, the follow-up period ranged from 2 to 13 years. As they note, "The highly variable period of follow-up is also a potential limitation, because those patients followed up for the shortest periods may not have been given the opportunity for their suicidal outcome to emerge" (p. 421). Had the researchers used survival methods, they would have been better able to address this concern because each person who did not commit suicide would simply have been censored at follow-up.

Fifth, traditional analytic methods offer few mechanisms for including predictors whose values vary over time or for permitting the effects of predictors to fluctuate over time. To overcome this limitation, researchers studying the effects of time-varying variables tend to use predictor values corresponding to a single point in time, the average of predictor values over time, or the rate of change in predictor values over time. This is not necessary in survival analysis. The analytic effort is identical whether including predictors that are static over time or predictors that change over time; so, too, it is easy to determine whether the *effects* of predictors are constant over time or whether they differ over time. There is no need to create a single-number summary of the temporal behavior of a changing predictor. Traditional methods force researchers into building static models of dynamic processes; survival methods allow researchers to model dynamic processes dynamically.

We encourage researchers in psychology and the social sciences to investigate the design and analytic possibilities offered by survival methods. When these methods were in their infancy and statistical software was either not available or not user friendly, researchers reasonably adopted other approaches. But experience elsewhere in medicine and in the social sciences shows that these methods, originally developed to model human lifetimes, lend themselves naturally to the study of other phenomena as well. While software lags behind, this is an area of active research with rapidly improving options.

Researchers rarely ask questions that they do not have the analytic methods to answer. We suspect that many researchers interested in the occurrence of events have modified their research questions because they did not know how to build statistical models appropriate for the original questions. We hope that our presentation of survival analysis will help researchers reframe these modified questions and provide them with strategies for answering those questions as simply and as directly as possible.

ACKNOWLEDGMENTS

The order of the authors was determined by randomization. This chapter is an expanded version of a paper that appeared in the *Journal of Consulting and Clinical Psychology* (1994). Correspondence concerning the chapter can be addressed to either author at the Harvard University Graduate School of Education,

Appian Way, Cambridge, MA 02138. The authors wish to thank the *National Science Foundation* and the *American Statistical Association* for their support during their research fellowship at the *National Center for Education Statistics*.

REFERENCES

Agresti, A. (1990). *Categorical data analysis*. New York: Wiley.

Allison, P. D. (1982). Discrete-time methods for the analysis of event histories. In S. Leinhardt (Ed.), *Sociological methodology* (pp. 61–98). San Francisco: Jossey-Bass.

Allison, P. D. (1984). *Event history analysis: Regression for longitudinal event data*. Sage University Paper Series on Quantitative Applications in the Social Sciences, Series Number 07-046. Beverly Hills, CA: Sage Publications.

Baer, J. S., & Lichtenstein, E. (1988). Classification and prediction of smoking relapse episodes: An exploration of initial differences. *Journal of Consulting and Clinical Psychology, 56*(1), 104–110.

Bleed, P. (1991). Operations research and archaeology. *American Antiquity, 56*, 19–36.

Blossfeld, H. P., Hamerle, A., & Mayer, K. U. (1989). *Event history analysis: Statistical theory and application in the social sciences*. Hillsdale, NJ: Lawrence Erlbaum.

Bolger, N., Downey, G., Walker, E., & Steininger, P. (1989). The onset of suicide ideation in childhood and adolescence. *Journal of Youth and Adolescence, 18*, 175–189.

Brown, C. C. (1975). On the use of indicator variables for studying the time-dependence of parameters in a response-time model. *Biometrics, 31*, 863–872.

Carpenter, W. T., Kurz, R., Kirkpatrick, B., Hanlon, T. E., Summerfelt, A. T., Buchanan, R. W., Waltrip, R. W., & Breier, A. (1991). Carbamazepine maintenance treatment in outpatient schizophrenics. *Archives of General Psychiatry, 48*, 69–72.

Civian, J. T. (1990). *Using proportional hazards models to examine time to doctorate*. Unpublished doctoral dissertation, Harvard University Graduate School of Education.

Cooney, N. L., Kadden, R. M., Litt, M. D., & Getter, H. (1991). Matching alcoholics to coping skills or interactional therapies: Two-year follow-up results. *Journal of Consulting and Clinical Psychology, 59*(4), 598–601.

Coryell, W., Keller, M., Lavori, P., & Endicott, J. (1990). Affective syndromes, psychotic features, and prognosis. *Archives of General Psychiatry, 47*, 651–662.

Cox, D. R. (1970). *The analysis of binary data*. London: Chapman and Hall.

Cox, D. R. (1972). Regression models and life tables. *Journal of the Royal Statistical Society, Series B, 34*, 187–202.

Cox, D. R., & Oakes, D. (1984). *Analysis of survival data*. London: Chapman and Hall.

Cox, D. R., and Snell, E. J. (1989). *Analysis of binary data* (2nd ed.). London: Chapman and Hall.

Efron, B. (1988). Logistic regression, survival analysis, and the Kaplan-Meier curve. *Journal of the American Statistical Association, 83*, 414–425.

Fichman, M. (1988). Motivational consequences of absence and attendance: Proportional hazard estimation of a dynamic motivation model. *Journal of Applied Psychology, 73*, 119–134.

Frank, E., Kupfer, D. J., & Perel, J. M. (1989). Early recurrence in unipolar depression. *Archives of General Psychiatry, 46*, 397–400.

Frank, E., Kupfer, D. J., Wagner, E. F., McEachran, A. B., & Cornes, C. (1991). Efficacy of interpersonal psychotherapy as a maintenance treatment of recurrent depression. *Archives of General Psychiatry, 48*, 1053–1059.

Gallagher-Thompson, D., Hanley-Peterson, P., & Thompson, L. W. (1990). Maintenance of gains versus relapse following brief psychotherapy for depression. *Journal of Consulting and Clinical Psychology, 58*, 371–374.

Gardner, W., & Griffin, W. A. (1989). Methods for the analysis of parallel streams of continuously-recorded social behaviors. *Psychological, 105*, 446–455.

Glasgow, R. E., Klesges, R. C., Klesges, L. M., & Somes, G. R. (1988). Variables associated with participation and outcome in a worksite smoking control program. *Journal of Consulting and Clinical Psychology, 56*(4), 617–620.

Goldstein, R., Anderson, J., Ash, A., Craig, B., Harrington, D., & Pagano, M. (1989). Survival analysis software on MS/PC-DOS computers. *Journal of Applied Econometrics, 4*, 393–414.

Goldstein, R. B., Black, D. W., Nasrallah, A., & Winokur, G. (1991). The prediction of suicide: Sensitivity, specificity, and predictive value of a multivariate model applied to suicide among 1906 patients with affective disorders. *Archives of General Psychiatry, 48*, 418–422.

Greenhouse, J. B., Stangl, D., & Bromberg, J. (1989). An introduction to survival analysis methods for analysis of clinical trial data. *Journal of Consulting and Clinical Psychology, 57*, 536–544.

Hall, S. M., Havassy, B. E., & Wassermann, D. A. (1991). Effects of commitment to abstinence, positive moods, stress, and coping on relapse to cocaine use. *Journal of Consulting and Clinical Psychology, 59*(4), 526–532.

Harackiewicz, J. M., Sansone, C., Blair, L. W., Epstein, J. A., Manderlink, G. (1987). Attributional processes in behavior change and maintenance: Smoking cessation and continued abstinence. *Journal of Consulting and Clinical Psychology, 55*(3), 372–378.

Harrell, F. E. Jr., & Goldstein, R. (in press). A survey of micro-computer survival analysis software: The need for an integrated framework. *The American Statistician.*

Harrington, D. P., & Fleming, T. R. (1991). *Counting processes and survival analysis.* New York: Wiley.

Harrington, R., Fudge, H., Rutter, M., Pickles, A., & Hill, J. (1990a). Adult outcomes of childhood and adolescent depression. I: Psychiatric status. *Archives of General Psychiatry, 47*, 465–473.

Harrington, R., Fudge, H., Rutter, M., Pickles, A., & Hill, J. (1990b). Adult outcomes of childhood and adolescent depression. II: Links with antisocial disorders. *Journal of the American Academy of Child and Adolescent Psychiatry, 30*(3), 434–439.

Hart, S. D., Kropp, P. R., & Hare, R. D. (1988). Performance of male psychopaths following conditional release from prison. *Journal of Consulting and Clinical Psychology, 56*(2), 227–232.

Havassy, B. E., Hall, S. M., & Wasserman, D. A. (1991). Social support and relapse: Commonalities among alcoholics, opiate users, and cigarette smokers. *Addictive Behaviors, 16*(3), 235–246.

Heckman, J., & Singer, B. (Eds.). (1985). *Longitudinal analysis of labor market data.* New York: Cambridge University Press.

Hosmer, D., & Lemeshow, S. (1989). *Applied logistic regression.* New York: Wiley.

Hutchison, D. (1988a). Event history and survival analysis in the social sciences. I: Background and introduction. *Quality and Quantity, 22*, 203–219.

Hutchison, D. (1988b). Event history and survival analysis in the social sciences. II: Advanced applications and recent developments. *Quality and Quantity, 22*, 255–278.

Kalbfleisch, J. D., & Prentice, R. L. (1980). *The statistical analysis of failure time data.* New York: Wiley.

Kelly, J. A., St. Lawrence, J. S., & Brasfield, T. L. (1991). Predictors of vulnerability to AIDS risk behavior relapse. *Journal of Clinical and Consulting Psychology, 59*(1), 163–166.

Krantz, S. E., & Moos, R. H. (1988). Risk factors at intake predict nonremission among depressed patients. *Journal of Clinical and Consulting Psychology, 56*(6), 863–869.

Laird, N., & Oliver, D. (1981). Covariance analysis of censored survival data using log-linear analysis techniques. *Journal of the American Statistical Association, 76*, 231–240.

Lawless, J. F. (1982). *Statistical methods for lifetime data.* New York: Wiley.

Lelliott, P., Marks, I., McNamee, G., & Tobena, A. (1989). Onset of panic disorder with agoraphobia. *Archives of General Psychiatry, 46,* 1000–1004.

Lewinsohn, P. M., Duncan, E. M., Stanton, A. K., & Hautzinger, M. (1986). Age at first onset for nonbipolar depression. *Journal of Abnormal Psychology, 95,* 378–383.

Litman, G. K., Eiser, J. R., & Taylor, C. (1979). Dependence, relapse and extinction: A theoretical critique and a behavioral examination. *Journal of Clinical Psychology, 35,* 192–199.

Lopez, P. F. (1990). *Mexican-Americans and graduation from college.* Unpublished doctoral dissertation, Graduate School of Education, Harvard University, Cambridge, MA.

Markman, H. J., Floyd, F. J., Stanley, S. M., & Storaasli, R. D. (1988). Prevention of marital distress: A longitudinal investigation. *Journal of Consulting and Clinical Psychology, 56,* 210–217.

Marlatt, G. A., Curry, S., & Gordon, J. R. (1988). A longitudinal analysis of unaided smoking cessation. *Journal of Consulting and Clinical Psychology, 56*(5), 715–720.

Miller, R. G. (1981). *Survival analysis.* New York: Wiley.

Monroe, S. M., Simons, A. D., & Thase, M. E. (1991). Onset of depression and time to treatment entry: Roles of life stress. *Journal of Consulting and Clinical Psychology, 59*(4), 566–573.

Morita, J. G., Lee, T. W., & Mowday, R. T. (1989). Introducing survival analysis to organizational researchers: A selected application to turnover research. *Journal of Applied Psychology, 74,* 280–292.

Murnane, R. J., Singer, J. D., & Willett, J. B. (1989). The influences of salaries and "opportunity costs" on teachers' career choices: Evidence from North Carolina. *Harvard Educational Review, 59*(3), 325–346.

Murnane, R. J., Singer, J. D., Willett, J. B., Kemple, J., & Olson, R. (1991). *Who will teach?: Policies that matter.* Cambridge, MA: Harvard University Press.

Murphy, E. L., Singer, F. S., & Nichols, L. (1990). Effects of hunting on survival and productivity of Dall sheep. *Journal of Wildlife Management, 54,* 284–329.

Myers, K., McCauley, E., Calderon, R., & Treder, R. (1991). The three-year longitudinal course of suicidality and predictive factors for subsequent suicidality in youths with major depressive disorder. *Journal of the American Academy of Child and Adolescent Psychiatry, 30*(5), 804–810.

Nathan, P. E., & Skinstad, A. H. (1987). Outcomes of treatment for alcohol problems: Current methods, problems, and results. *Journal of Consulting and Clinical Psychology, 55*(3), 332–340.

Norris, F. H., Kaniasty, K. Z., & Scheer, D. A. (1990). Use of mental health services among victims of crime: Frequency, correlates, and subsequent recovery. *Journal of Consulting and Clinical Psychology, 58*(5), 538–547.

Ossip-Klein, D. J., Giovino, G. A., Megahed, N., Black, P. M., Emont, S. L., Stiggins, J., Shulman, E., & Moore, L. (1991). Effects of a smokers' hotline: Results of a 10-county self-help trial. *Journal of Consulting and Clinical Psychology, 59*(2), 325–332.

Pfeffer, C. R., Klerman, G. L., Hurt, S. W., Lesser, M., Peskin, J. R., & Siefker, C. A. (1991). Suicidal children grow up: Demographic and clinical risk factors for adolescent suicide attempts. *Journal of the American Academy of Child Adolescent Psychiatry, 30*(4), 609–616.

Prien, R. F., Kupfer, D. J., Mansky, P. A., Small, J. G., Tuason, V. B., Voss, C. B., & Johnson, W. E. (1984). Drug therapy in the prevention of recurrences in unipolar and bipolar affective disorders. *Archives of General Psychiatry, 41*(Nov.), 1096–1104.

Rice, M. E., Quinsey, V. L., & Harris, G. T. (1991). Sexual recidivism among child molesters released from a maximum security psychiatric institution. *Journal of Consulting and Clinical Psychology, 59*(3), 381–386.

Rice, J., Reich, T., Andreasen, N. C., Endicott, J., Van Eerdewegh, M., Fishman, R., Hirschfeld, R. M. A., & Klerman, G. L. (1987). The familial transition of bipolar illness. *Archives of General Psychiatry, 44,* 441–447.

Ryman, D. H., Biersner, R. J., & LaRocco, J. M. (1974). Reliabilities and validities of the mood questionnaire. *Psychological Reports, 35,* 479–484.

Sargeant, J. K., Bruce, M. L., Florio, L. P., & Weissman, M. M. (1990). Factors associated with 1-year outcome of major depression in the community. *Archives of General Psychiatry, 47*, 519–526.

Shapiro, D. R., Quitkin, F. M., & Fleiss, J. L. (1989). Response to maintenance therapy in bipolar illness: Effect of index episode. *Archives of General Psychiatry, 46*, 401–405.

Singer, J. D. (1993a). Are special educators' careers special?: Results from a 13-year longitudinal study. *Exceptional Children, 59*, 262–279.

Singer, J. D. (1993b). Once is not enough: Former special educators who return to teaching. *Exceptional Children, 60*(1), 58–72.

Singer, J. D., & Willett, J. B. (1991). Modeling the days of our lives: Using survival analysis when designing and analyzing longitudinal studies of duration and the timing of events. *Psychological Bulletin, 110*(2), 268–290.

Singer, J. D., & Willett, J. B. (1992). A practical guide to survival analysis in research. In M. Fava & J. Rosenbaum (Eds.), *Research design and methods in psychiatry, Techniques in the behavioral and neural sciences* (Vol. 9, pp. 37–83). Amsterdam: Elsevier.

Singer, J. D., & Willett, J. B. (1993). It's about time: Using discrete-time survival analysis to study duration and the timing of events. *Journal of Educational Statistics, 18*, 155–195.

Sorenson, S. B., Rutter, C. M., & Aneshensel, C. S. (1991). Depression in the community: An investigation into age of onset. *Journal of Consulting and Clinical Psychology, 59*(4), 541–546.

Stevens, V. J., & Hollis, J. F. (1989). Preventing smoking relapse, using an individually tailored skills-training program. *Journal of Consulting and Clinical Psychology, 57*(3), 420–424.

Suppes, T., Baldessarini, R. J., Faedda, G. L., & Tohen, M. (1991). Risk of recurrence following discontinuation of lithium treatment in bipolar disorder. *Archives of General Psychiatry, 48*, 1082–1088.

Thompson, W. A., Jr. (1977). On the treatment of grouped observations in life studies. *Biometrics, 33*, 463–470.

Tognetti, J. (1990). *The role of employment versus the role of attitudes and beliefs in maternal infant feeding behavior in Bangkok, Thailand.* Unpublished doctoral thesis, Harvard University Graduate School of Education.

Trussel, J., & Hammerslough, C. (1983). A hazards-model analysis of the covariates of infant and child mortality in Sri Lanka, *Demography, 20*, 1–26.

Tuma, N. B., & Hannan, M. T. (1984). *Social dynamics: Models and methods.* New York: Academic Press.

Turnbull, J. E., George, L. K., Landerman, R., Swartz, M. S., & Blazer, D. G. (1990). Social outcomes related to age of onset among psychiatric disorders. *Journal of Consulting and Clinical Psychology, 58*(6), 832–839.

Wainer, H. (1990). Discussant's comment at the annual meeting of the American Educational Research Association, Boston, MA.

Weisz, J. R., Walter, B. R., Weiss, B., Fernandez, G. A., & Mikow, V. A. (1990). Arrests among emotionally disturbed violent and assaultive individuals following minimal versus lengthy intervention through North Carolina's Willie M Program. *Journal of Consulting and Clinical Psychology, 58*(6), 720–728.

Willett, J. B., & Singer, J. D. (1989). Two types of question about time: Methodological issues in the analysis of teacher career path data. *International Journal of Educational Research, 13*(4), 421–437.

Willett, J. B., & Singer, J. D. (1991). From whether to when: New methods for studying student dropout and teacher attrition. *Review of Educational Research, 61*(4), 407–450.

Willett, J. B., & Singer, J. D. (1994). New methods for investigating the occurrence and timing of educational events using survival analysis. In T. Husen & T. N. Postlethwaite (Eds.), *The international encyclopedia of education* (2nd ed.). Oxford: Pergamon Press.

Willett, J. B., & Singer, J. D. (1995). It's deja-vu all over again: Using multiple-spell discrete-time survival analysis. *Journal of Educational Statistics.*

Yamaguchi, K. (1991). *Event history analysis.* Newbury Park, CA: Sage.

Young, M. A., Watel, L. G., Lahmeyer, H. W., & Eastman, C. I. (1991). The temporal onset of individual symptoms in winter depression: Differentiating the underlying mechanisms. *Journal of Affective Disorders, 22,* 191–197.

Zito, J. M., Craig, T. T., Wanderling, J., & Siegel, C. (1987). Pharmacoepidemiology in 136 hospitalized schizophrenic patients. *American Journal of Psychiatry, 144,* 778–782.

8 Autoregressive Effects in Structural Equation Models: We See Some Problems

Mike Stoolmiller
Lew Bank
Oregon Social Learning Center

What happens when data are quite regular over time? How can these autoregressive effects be included in structural equations models? Stoolmiller and Bank review current suggestions for dealing with this problem and suggest that growth curve methodology can deal with problems that the inclusion of autoregressive terms can not deal with.

—Editor

The focus of this chapter is on how structural equation modeling (SEM) that includes autoregressive effects can obscure the detection of important predictors of change or growth. For our purposes, autoregressive means the effect of the time-1 measure of a variable on the time-2 measure of the same variable. The two-wave linear panel model so frequently seen in the psychological and sociological literature is a common example of an autoregressive model.

Consider the study of the development of antisocial behavior in grade-school boys within the context of SEM. Antisocial behavior has been found to be extremely stable over several years (Olweus, 1980), about as stable as IQ scores. This high stability has made it extremely difficult to identify correlates of change using SEM when controlling for initial levels of antisocial behavior. It appears that the prior level of the behavior is the only important determinant of the current level, even over a period of several years.

Controlling for initial levels or including autoregressive effects of a variable has been advocated by developmentalists (Maccoby & Martin, 1983) and methodologists alike (Dwyer, 1983; Gollob & Reichardt, 1987) as important to avoid biased estimates of path weights for potential covariates of change. Thus, when some interesting developmental phenomenon seems to be highly stable over time when using SEM, it is difficult to demonstrate that change is correlated with some third, outside variable. Given that many developmental processes worthy of study exhibit this kind of stability in any given sample, the routine recommendation for including autoregressive effects in SEM models poses a serious problem.

Here, we first compare simple difference score (SDS) models to autoregressive (AR) models in terms of the patterns of change that can be detected. For readers who cringe at the idea of using difference scores, we recommend a close reading of Rogosa, Brandt, and Zimowski (1982). This paper offers a complete account of the statistical and psychometric properties of differences or change scores and dispels the negative myths surrounding their use.

Second, we consider the plausibility of the underlying assumption of the AR model that time-1 values of a variable can have a direct causal effect on time-2 values of the same variable. Finally, we advocate SDS models and growth curve approaches as an alternative strategy in studying developmental processes in psychology.

SIMPLE DIFFERENCE SCORE VERSUS AUTOREGRESSIVE MODELS

Figure 8.1 depicts an AR model and an SDS model with variables $X1$ and $X2$ and one additional predictor labeled Y. The AR model in Figure 8.1 can also be interpreted as a residual change score model (Kessler & Greenberg, 1981). Thus, both models can be viewed as models of change from time 1 to time 2.

Simple Autoregressive Model

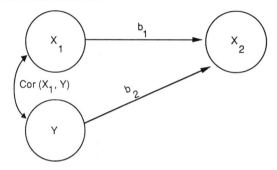

Simple Difference Score Model

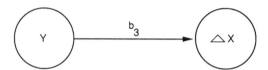

FIG. 8.1. Simple autoregressive and difference score models.

AR effects are based on stability correlations. Correlations, in general, are known to be primarily sensitive to correspondence in rank order, and to a lesser extent, correspondence in shape of distribution (Gorsuch, 1983, p. 304). This implies significant growth can be taking place as a result of changes in other covariates, but if it does not involve changes in the rank order or shape of the distribution of X it will largely be attributed to the AR effect. If the rank order of X does not change, Y will be correlated with $X1$ and $X2$ at about the same level and Y is unlikely to enter the equation because it would not compete with large stability correlation of X.

As an illustration, consider the plot of three subjects' scores on X at two time points, shown in Figure 8.2. The rank order of the observations and the mean stay the same, but the variance (spread) increases from time 1 to time 2. This increase in variance depicted in Figure 8.2, coupled with high-rank-order stability, is sometimes known as a fan-spread growth pattern. Further, suppose that the increase for Subject 3 is associated with a high score on Y, the intermediate score for Subject 2 is associated with an intermediate score on Y, and the decrease for Subject 1 is associated with a low score on Y. In this example, Y would be a potent predictor of change in the SDS model. In the AR model, however, this same situation appears to be just as well and more parsimoniously explained by the subjects' initial status on $X1$. That is, in Figure 8.2, perhaps Subject 3 increased on X simply because he was high on X at time 1, and likewise for Subjects 1 and 2.

We can be more precise about the above assertions by examining the two equations for $b3$, $b2$, and $b1$ in Figure 8.1. In the equations that follow, we will demonstrate that the magnitude of individual differences (variance) in change over time can play a key role in determining whether the AR or SDS model detects the effect of a predictor of change. We will assume, consistent with the focus on constructs that show high-rank-order stability over time, that $\text{cor}(X1,X2)$ is one of the largest, if not the largest, correlation in the matrix. Further, without loss of generality, we will assume that all correlations are positive.

$$b3 = \frac{(b1 - 1)\text{cor}(X1,Y)\text{std}(X1)}{\text{std}(Y)} + b2, \tag{8.1}$$

$$b1 = \frac{\text{std}(X2)[\text{cor}(X1,X2) - \text{cor}(X1,Y)\text{cor}(X2,Y)]}{\text{std}(X1)[1 - \text{cor}^2(X1,Y)]}. \tag{8.2}$$

In Equation 8.1 we have shown that $b3$, the path weight for Y predicting the simple difference score, $X2 - X1$, is $b2$, the path weight for Y in the AR model plus an additional quantity. Because of the assumption of a positive correlation matrix, whether or not the additional quantity that will be added to $b2$ to obtain $b3$ is positive or negative depends only on whether $b1$ is greater or less than 1. To determine whether $b1$ exceeds 1, we need to examine Equation 8.2.

In Equation 8.2, all the terms in the denominator must be positive. The term in the numerator in the brackets must be positive whenever $\text{cor}(X1,X2)$ is the largest correlation in the matrix. It might be positive even if $\text{cor}(X1,X2)$ is not the largest, but then it depends on $\text{cor}(X1,Y)$ and $\text{cor}(X2,Y)$. If it is positive, which is typically the case when studying highly stable phenomena over time, then $b1$ gets larger and larger and eventually exceeds 1 as the variance of X increases from time 1 to time 2. The larger the quantity in brackets in the numerator in Equation 8.2, the smaller the variance increase required to push $b1$ over 1 and, conversely, the smaller the quantity in brackets the bigger the variance increase required to push $b1$ over 1.

A special case of interest which highlights an important difference between

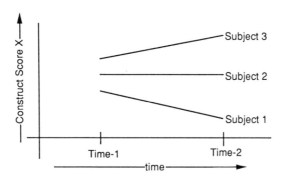

FIG. 8.2. Fan-spread growth pattern for three subjects.

the two models is one in which $b2$, the effect of Y in the AR model, is equal to zero. This occurs only if the correlation of Y with $X2$ is equal to the product of the correlation of $X1$ with $X2$ and the correlation of $X1$ with Y. In equation form this condition is

$$cor(X2,Y) = cor(X1,X2) \, cor(X1,Y).$$

In this case, Equation 8.1 simplifies to

$$b3 = \frac{std(X2)cor(X2, \, Y) \, - \, std(X1)cor(X1, \, Y)}{std(Y)}. \qquad (8.3)$$

Notice in Equation 8.3 that for fixed values of $cor(X2,Y)$ and $cor(X1,Y)$, the magnitude of $b3$ goes up as the standard deviation of X increases over time. Thus, for the special case of $b2$ equal to zero, it is easy to see that with an increase in variance, for example fan-spread growth from time 1 to time 2, Y can be a significant predictor of simple change in the SDS model while not predicting change after controlling for initial status in the AR model.

A second special case of interest is one in which $b3$, the effect of Y in the SDS model, is equal to zero. This occurs only if the ratio of the correlation of Y with $X1$ to Y with $X2$ is equal to the ratio of the standard deviation of $X2$ to $X1$. In equation form this condition is

$$\frac{cor(X1,Y)}{cor(X2,Y)} = \frac{std(X2)}{std(X1)}.$$

In this case Equation 8.1 simplifies to

$$b2 = \frac{[std(X1) \, - \, std(X2)cor(X1,X2)]cor(X1,Y)}{[1 \, - \, cor^2(X1,Y)]std(Y)} \qquad (8.4)$$

Notice in Equation 8.4 that for fixed values of $cor(X1,X2)$ and $cor(X1,Y)$, the magnitude of $b2$ goes up as the standard deviation of X shrinks over time. Thus, for the special case of $b3$ equal to zero, it is easy to see that with stable or decreasing variance, Y can be a significant predictor of change after controlling for initial status in the AR model, while not predicting simple change. Lord (1967), using an example of weight gain, made the same point we make in Equation 8.4 almost 30 years ago. His example eventually gained notoriety as Lord's Paradox.

Figure 8.3 shows actual data in which a fan-spread growth pattern with high stability in intelligence test scores for 204 children produced a significant path weight for the predictor variable of mother education in the SDS model but a nonsignificant path weight in the AR model. The data were taken from Osborne and Suddick (1972, as cited in McArdle & Epstein, 1987).

Figure 8.4 shows actual data in which a stable-variance growth pattern with high stability in antisocial trait scores for 203 children produced a significant

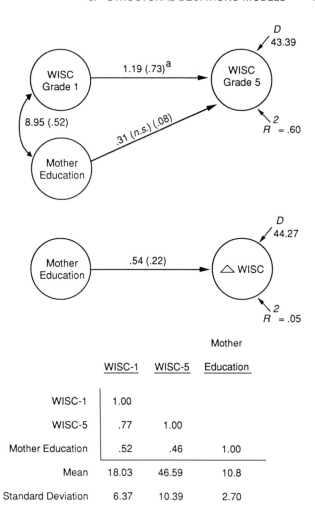

	WISC-1	WISC-5	Mother Education
WISC-1	1.00		
WISC-5	.77	1.00	
Mother Education	.52	.46	1.00
Mean	18.03	46.59	10.8
Standard Deviation	6.37	10.39	2.70

[a]Standardized values shown in parantheses.

FIG. 8.3. Autoregressive and difference score models for growth in WISC scores.

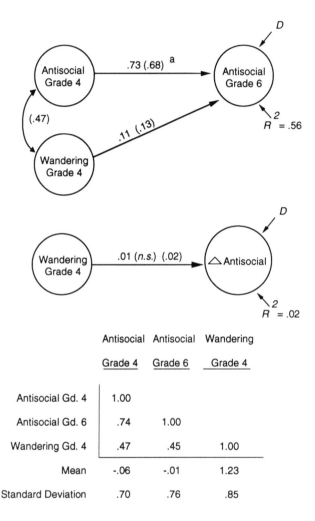

Antisocial Antisocial Wandering

Grade 4   Grade 6   Grade 4

	Antisocial Grade 4	Antisocial Grade 6	Wandering Grade 4
Antisocial Gd. 4	1.00		
Antisocial Gd. 6	.74	1.00	
Wandering Gd. 4	.47	.45	1.00
Mean	-.06	-.01	1.23
Standard Deviation	.70	.76	.85

[a] Standardized value shown in parentheses

FIG. 8.4. Autoregressive and difference score models for growth in antisocial behavior scores.

path weight for the predictor variable of unsupervised wandering in the AR model but a nonsignificant path weight in the SDS model. The data were taken from Stoolmiller (1990).

In summary, AR and SDS models can yield quite different conclusions about the importance of predictors of change. These differences in the case of moderate to high stability correlations can be related to whether individual differences (variance) are increasing or decreasing over time. For a given pattern of correlations, increasing individual differences can yield significant predictors of simple change and nonsignificant predictors of residual change while the reverse is true when individual differences are stable or decreasing. Note that increasing individual differences implies larger individual differences in change than in the case when individual differences are stable or decreasing. Thus, an alternative way of stating the conclusions above is to say that when individual differences in change are large relative to individual differences at time 1, SDS models may be more useful for detecting predictors of change. Conversely, when individual differences in change are small, the AR model may be more useful. In light of the twin facts that (1) large individual differences in change can occur and be completely undetected in AR models and (2) AR models are routinely recommended as the proper way to study predictors of change (Dwyer, 1983; Gollob & Reichardt, 1987), it is disturbing that these two ways of studying predictors of change can yield such drastically different results.

For example, in Figure 8.2 the data provide no basis for choosing between Y and $X1$ as the true cause of change or in Figure 8.3 for choosing between grade-1 WISC scores or mother education. Part of the difficulty of doing correlational research is the problem of competing hypotheses. The question then becomes, is there any way on the basis of logical or scientific arguments to favor one hypothesis over the other?

Gollob and Reichardt (1987) provide a very clear and concise account of how to proceed with SEM given that one is willing to accept initial status as a plausible cause of change. What they demonstrate is that except under special circumstances, one is obligated to include initial status in all SEM models of change. In essence, to find significant relationships, one must study change that cannot be accounted for by initial status which is primarily rank-order change.

Therefore, the implications of accepting initial status as a plausible direct cause of change are important in terms of the type of change that can be studied. We believe that to routinely and uncritically entertain this notion is a serious mistake.

THE PLAUSIBILITY OF THE AUTOREGRESSIVE EFFECT FOR WISC SCORES

We can begin exploring the plausibility of the AR effect as a true direct causal effect by examining the interpretation of the AR model in Figure 8.3. Kessler and Greenberg (1981) have demonstrated how a static regression equation can be manipulated to clearly show the effects of the predictors on change. In the context of the WISC example, start by writing the equation for the jth individual (with subscripts for individuals suppressed):

$$b0 + b1 \text{ WISC1} + b2 \text{ Mom Ed} + e = \text{WISC5}. \qquad (8.5)$$

Next, we subtract WISC1 from both sides of Equation 8.5 to get an expression in terms of WISC difference scores:

$$b0 + b1 \text{ WISC1} - \text{WISC1} + b2 \text{ Mom Ed} + e = \text{WISC5} - \text{WISC1}. \qquad (8.6)$$

Simplifying Equation 8.6 we get

$$b0 + (b1 - 1)\text{WISC1} + b2 \text{ Mom Ed} + e = \text{WISC5} - \text{WISC1}. \quad (8.7)$$

In Figure 8.3, $b2$ is not significantly different from zero, so our interpretation of the model is that controlling for grade-1 WISC scores, Mom Ed(ucation) does not predict change in WISC scores. Usually the interpretation stops here, but for the purpose of critically examining the plausibility of grade-1 WISC scores as a direct cause of change in WISC scores, we will continue. We found $b1 = 1.19$, implying that the effect of grade-1 WISC scores on change in WISC scores is .19 (see Figure 8.3). The standard error for $b1$ indicates that the estimate of .19 is significantly different from zero. Therefore, holding Mom Education constant, the change in WISC scores is, on the average, .19 times the grade-1 WISC score. At the individual level, the answer to the question of why a given child changed by 4.8 (4.8 = 25(.19)) WISC points from grade 1 to grade 5 is because the child scored 25 WISC points in the first grade.

We find this sort of explanation for change in WISC scores implausible. Why should a static WISC score at grade 1 imply change at all? The simplest thing to assume given a single set of grade-1 WISC scores is that they will stay the same over time. If change does occur, it is the change that needs to be explained, and using a part of the data necessary to determine the amount of change (initial status) as an explanation for that change seems tautological.

TWO PHILOSOPHICAL PERSPECTIVES

Bollen (1989) has offered a perspective on studying causality within SEM. In his view, the definition of cause has three components: isolation, association, and the direction of influence. The first component, isolation, is never really achieved, but ideally means that X and Y, for example, are isolated from all other potential causal influences. The second component, association, means that changes in Y covary with changes in X. The last component, direction of association, is necessary because isolation and association still do not pinpoint whether Y causes X, X causes Y, or X and Y reciprocally cause each other. It is the isolation part of this argument that we want to focus on.

Bollen (1989) points out that isolation is necessary for certainty in causal inference. However, isolation never exists in reality, making certain causal inference impossible. Even though complete isolation is practically impossible, to examine the plausibility of the AR effect we can create a "thought experiment," in which we completely and totally isolate variable X away from all other causal influences. We observe X at time 1, let time pass, and observe again at time 2. At that point, the problem with the AR effect becomes apparent. $X1$ is just X measured at time 1, $X2$ is X measured again at time 2; but, if X is isolated from all other causal influences, how could X change with the mere passage of time? In order to have X change from time 1 to time 2, we need a causal agent that is logically distinct from X itself; otherwise we are supposing that X can change for no reason. Does the passage of time make $X2$ logically distinct from $X1$ in a way that makes $X1$ a plausible cause of $X2$? We find this notion difficult to accept.

Mulaik (1987) expressed a very similar idea within the philosophical framework of the language of objects. He argued that spontaneous change of an object is rejected. A reason for the change must be something other than that which it explains. If there is a second object, however, logically distinct from the first, a change in the second object can be the reason for the change in the first object. While the changes in the second object can go unexplained, it stands as the reason for the change in the first object.

To make the above discussion more concrete, consider a simple experiment designed to study growth of money left in bank accounts. Suppose we deposit a range of sums of money in each of several banks paying a range of interest rates on deposits. In an AR model with the initial sum of money and the interest rate as predictors of the amount of money at time 2, we would typically find that initial amount was a very strong predictor of money at time 2. But clearly if we follow the procedure suggested by Bollen and isolate the money at time 1 away from all suspected causal forces, (e.g., in a shoebox under a bed), we will find at time 2, much to our dismay, that the money has failed to grow.

Despite the fact that AR effects would be large in the bank example, they are not true direct causal effects. Interest causes money to grow, not initial amount of money. It so happens in this case that bankers pay interest as a percentage of the amount currently deposited and this creates autoregressive effects. Bankers, however, could decide to pay interest using a flat rate or some other functional rule that may or may not involve the initial amount deposited. To discard interest as a predictor of change because it failed to compete with initial amount of money in an AR model would be an error. It is our contention that SDS models or individual growth curve models are a more useful alternative to studying situations such as these. We are not, however, arguing that AR models should never be used, only that they should not be considered the only or even technique of first choice for identifying predictors of change. The fact that at times they detect effects that would not be detected by SDS models makes them interesting and potentially useful. We do believe, however, that (1) the meaning and interpretation of AR effects should be carefully considered, and (2) the meaning and interpretation of predictors of change that depend on controlling for initial level for their significance should be carefully considered (Lord, 1967, 1969). We turn now to exploring how predictors of change are handled within a growth curve framework.

THE AUTOREGRESSIVE MODEL COMPARED
TO A LINEAR GROWTH MODEL

Few authors, even among those who advocate a growth curve approach to the study of development have explicitly criticized the AR model. The papers of Rogosa and Willet (1985a, 1985b) are, to our knowledge, the exceptions. In these papers, AR models are criticized on the grounds that (1) they are not explicit models for individual change (Rogosa & Willet, 1985a), (2) they do not generalize to more than two points in time except by essentially breaking the models down into a series of two-points-in-time designs (Rogosa & Willet, 1985a), and (3) the input data are usually just the covariance matrix, which is a severe and inadequate summary of longitudinal data (Rogosa & Willet, 1985b).

Consider a simple growth model in which the plot of the theoretical construct of interest against time is a straight line for any given individual. The formula according to Rogosa and Willet (1985a) for this type of growth model for, say, the jth person (with subscripts for individuals suppressed) at the ith time period is the familiar linear equation:

$$X_{ti} = X_{t0} + b(t_i - t_0).$$

This equation states that the value of X at any time, t_i, is equal to the value of X initially at t_0, plus b for person j multiplied by $t_i - t_0$ time units. Assuming time starts at 0, for $t = 1$, the equation is

$$X_{t1} = X_{t0} + 1b,$$

for $t = 2$ the equation is

$$X_{t2} = X_{t0} + 2b,$$

etc.

Both initial status, X_{t0}, and slope, b, play a role in determining the value of X at any time t, but we do not interpret either as a causal force for any given individual. Instead, the causal forces produce variation in initial status and slope across individuals in the sample. This in turn produces the observed individual differences in development, in this case according to a simple linear growth function. For a given individual, the initial value and the slope are constants that define the model so that, assuming the model is accurate, the X value for any later time t, could be computed. In the language of differential equations, such constants are known as initial or boundary conditions. Once the boundary conditions are supplied, a numerical solution can be obtained for a given individual.

The boundary conditions themselves, however, are not the cause or explanation of developmental variation. According to Kuhn (1977), "If boundary conditions supply the cause, then cause ceases to be explanatory" (p. 26). Rather, important predictors of individual variation in boundary conditions of the growth equation are the explanation or causes of developmental variation.

Now consider the equation for say, the jth person (with subscripts for individuals suppressed) for a simple AR model:

$$X_{t+1} = b_t X_t + e_t.$$

Individual j's value at time $t + 1$ is equal to his or her X value at time t weighted by a group defined regression weight, b_t, plus an error term unique to individual j at time t. Actually the AR model is not well defined for a single individual because the b weight used to predict later time scores can only be computed for a group of individuals. There is no explicit model for change at the individual level without reference to some population of which the individual is thought to be a part.

However, we believe that the crux of the problem with the routine use of the AR model is that it blurs the distinction between boundary conditions and causal forces. Within an AR model, any additional predictor must compete with the boundary condition of initial status as an explanation of change. Since we do not routinely consider boundary conditions as explanations for developmental variation, we see the routine use of the AR model as a questionable way of identifying important predictors of change.

We believe that a large part of the appeal of AR models in the social sciences comes from the idea that the rate of growth of something can depend on its current level as in the bank account example. Old cliches such as the rich get richer and the poor get poorer succinctly capture this idea. From inspecting the equation for the AR model, it can be seen that, on the average, the greatest change from time 1 to time 2 will indeed by awarded to those who start at the highest initial level, assuming a positive b weight. In contrast, in the simple linear growth model the rate of change, b, is not necessarily or functionally related to current or initial status. Growth models can be formulated, however, in which the rate of change does depend on current status; we believe this approach is superior to the AR approach when it comes to identifying important predictors of change. Such models tend to be mathematically more complicated because the rate of change for an individual is not constant. For example, following Rogosa and Willet (1985a), a linear state-dependence model for learning could specify that the rate of learning for an individual is proportional to the amount yet to be learned. The implicit growth curve exhibits negatively accelerated growth that eventually levels off at some ceiling value. This type of growth curve is sometimes referred to as negative exponential growth.

The important point even with negative exponential growth is that initial status does not compete with other variables to explain individual variation in growth. Just as with the simple linear growth model, there are parameters that control the shape of the negative exponential growth curve, initial status being one of them. It is the variation in these parameters across individuals that produces developmental variation. This is the variation that our explanatory variables need to account for.

A HYPOTHETICAL EXAMPLE: ARRESTED SOCIALIZATION

The idea behind arrested socialization is that aversive and antisocial behaviors are a normal part of the behavioral repertoire of infants. Part of the task of socialization is to teach children more appropriate and acceptable ways of achieving their goals. For some children, however, this process fails, perhaps due to unskilled or inept parenting. As a result, they do not outgrow their tantrums. This sets the stage for the development of more serious forms of antisocial behavior as the children get older.

Thinking about this theory in terms of growth models implies, for a sample of children observed at three or more occasions, a set of developmental trajectories. The trajectories of children who receive adequate parenting should tend downward on measures of aversive or antisocial behavior, while the trajectories of children with inept parents should decrease less, perhaps staying flat or even increasing. If we suspected that initial or current levels of aversive child behavior were related to parenting which, in turn, affected the rate of socialization, we could build this into our growth model.

The antithesis of this approach would be to observe the children and parents at only two occasions and then use a two-wave linear panel model with autoregressive effects to analyze the data. If it happened that the relative ranking of the children on the antisocial behavior measured remained constant from time 1 to time 2, we would probably be hard-pressed to show that parenting had anything to do with socialization, even if the children's trajectories perfectly matched our theoretical expectations.

CONCLUSION

We believe that the routine inclusion of AR effects in SEM is problematic for two reasons. The AR model fails when change is accompanied by high-rank-order stability over time. The second is the questionable nature of the assertion that time-1 values of a variable can have a direct causal effect on time-2 values of the same variable. The AR model blurs the important distinction in models of change or growth between boundary or initial values of the system and parameters representing causal forces.

We believe that the exclusive and uncritical use of the AR model in developmental psychology is really unwarranted, given the growing development of growth modeling techniques. At the very least, we hope that researchers begin to fit some of these growth models to their data, in addition to the usual AR models. We also hope that reviewers of journal articles will stop insisting that models contain autoregressive effects before they are published.

ACKNOWLEDGMENTS

Support for this research was provided by Grant Nos. RO1 MH 38318 Prevention Research Branch, Division of Epidemiology and Services Research, National Institute of Mental Health (NIMH) U.S. PHS; P50 MH 46690, Prevention Research Branch, NIMH, U.S. PHS; and R37 MH 37940, Center for Studies of Violent Behavior and Traumatic Stress, NIMH, U.S. PHS. The authors can be contacted at the Oregon Social Learning Center, 207 E. 5th Ave., Suite 202, Eugene, OR 97401.

REFERENCES

Bollen, K. A. (1989). *Structural equations with latent variables*. New York: Wiley.

Dwyer, J. H. (1983). *Statistical models for the social and behavioral sciences*. New York: Oxford University Press.

Gollob, H. F., & Reichardt, C. S. (1987). Taking account of time lags in causal models. *Child Development, 58,* 80–92.

Gorsuch, R. L. (1983). *Factor analysis* (2nd ed). Hillsdale, NJ: Lawrence Erlbaum.

Kessler, R. C., & Greenberg, D. F. (1981). *Linear panel analysis: Models of quantitative change.* New York: Academic Press.

Kuhn, T. S. (1977). *The essential tension: Selected studies in scientific tradition and change.* Chicago: University of Chicago Press.

Lord, F. M. (1967). A paradox in the interpretation of group comparisons. *Psychological Bulletin, 68,* 304–305.

Lord, F. M. (1969). Statistical adjustments when comparing preexisting groups. *Psychological Bulletin, 70,* 336–337.

Maccoby, E. A., & Martin, J. A. (1983). Socialization in the context of the family: Parent-child interaction. In E. M. Hetherington (Ed.), *Handbook of child psychology: Vol. 4. Socialization, personality and social development* (pp. 1–101). New York: Wiley.

McArdle, J. J., & Epstein, D. (1987). Latent growth curves within developmental structural equation models. *Child Development, 58,* 110–133.

Mulaik, S. A. (1987). Toward a conception of causality applicable to experimentation and causal modeling. *Child Development, 58,* 18–32.

Olweus, D. (1980). Familial and temperamental determinants of aggressive behavior in adolescent boys: A causal analysis. *Developmental Psychology, 16,* 644–660.

Rogosa, D., Brandt, D., & Zimowski, M. (1982). A growth approach to the measurement of change. *Psychological Bulletin, 92,* 726–748.

Rogosa, D., & Willet, J. B. (1985a). Satisfying a simplex structure is simpler than it should be. *Journal of Educational Statistics, 10,* 99–107.

Rogosa, D. R., & Willet, J. B. (1985b). Understanding correlates of change by modeling individual differences in growth. *Psychometrika, 50,* 203–228.

Stoolmiller, M. (1990). *Parent supervision, child wandering and child antisocial behavior: A latent growth curve analysis.* Unpublished doctoral dissertation, School of Education, Division of Counseling and Educational Psychology, University of Oregon, Eugene, OR.

II
ANALYZING CHANGE IN A SINGLE SUBJECT OR AN INTERACTING SYSTEM

This section of the book is concerned with analyzing change in single subjects, or in a single type of interacting system. It includes several methods. The first method is sequential analytic methodology for analyzing sequences of social interaction. Here we have the contributions of Bakeman, Griffin, and Gardner. The second method is time-series analysis. Here we have the contributions of Crosbie and Priestley. The third method is dynamic modeling, or the use of mathematical models using nonlinear differential equations. Here we have the contributions of Murray and Baker.

9

Lags and Logs: Statistical Approaches to Interaction (SPSS version)*

Roger Bakeman
Lauren B. Adamson
Peter Strisik
Georgia State University

This chapter casts sequential analyses of interaction in log-linear terms. Log-linear analysis is not widely known among investigators who study social interaction but seems remarkably well-suited to their concerns. Several examples of log-linear analyses of interaction are presented, along with the SPSS statements required to effect them, including issues of groups differences, rare events, stationarity and autocorrelation.

---

*This chapter originally appeared in M. H. Bornstein & J. Bruner (Eds.), 1989, *Interaction in human development*, Hillsdale, NJ: Lawrence Erlbaum Associates. Unlike the 1989 version, this version of the chapter contains SPSS examples. We would like to thank Jeffrey Cohn, Daryl Nenstiel, Bruce Dorval, Josephine Brown, David Baldwin, Marguerite Stevenson, and William Griffin for their useful comments on an earlier draft.

279

INTRODUCTION

Much has been written recently about how sequential analysis may help researchers preserve and manipulate the events in a stream of observed behavior (e.g., Bakeman & Gottman, 1986, 1987; Sackett, 1987). These works celebrate the elegant match between recent ideas about the process of social interaction and quantitative methods for documenting such patterns. Yet for many, these festivities may seem marred by impenetrable technical discussions. Our intent in this chapter is to present sequential statistical approaches to interaction in a way that is relatively free of complex terminology and intimidating notation.

One insight greatly facilitates this endeavor. When sequential problems are cast in log-linear terms, their analysis becomes almost straightforward. Moreover, the basic approach should seem familiar to researchers previously schooled in traditional approaches to data analysis and hypothesis testing. First, we will attempt to demonstrate this happy state of affairs. Then, we will present specific examples of log-linear solutions to common sequential analytic problems.

BASIC CONCEPTS

In this first section we discuss how sequential data should be structured for sequential analysis, distinguishing between dimensions (or variables) of interest and their mutually exclusive and exhaustive levels (or codes). We also note the difference between event and time sequences and between sequences that permit and do not permit codes to repeat (i.e., follow themselves). Then we discuss how sequential data can be arranged in contingency tables, make some introductory comments about log-linear analysis, and show how the familiar chi-square is simply a special case of a log-linear analysis.

Event and Time Sequences

One way to capture interactive phenomena is to code successive events. What constitutes an event can vary, as we discuss later on, but at the very least it is a bounded "unit" that can be segregated from the passing stream of behavior. Following definitions and rules specified by the investigator, trained observers then categorize the event. It seems reasonable to call data that result from this process of coding sequential events "event sequences" or *event sequential data*.

Often events are coded on just one dimension. (A *dimension* is a categorical variable; the codes associated with it represent the permissible *levels* that the dimension can assume.) For example, Bakeman and Adamson (1984) defined five mutually exclusive and exhaustive codes that they used to characterize the dimension of infants' engagement:

   a. Engagement state (five levels)
     1. Unengaged
     2. Onlooking
     3. Person engagement
     4. Object engagement
     5. Joint engagement

In this case, the events coded were engagement states and the coding allowed Bakeman and Adamson to represent mother-infant interaction as sequences of such states.

Events can also be coded on more than one dimension. For example, simplifying the Marital Interaction Coding System (Hops, Willis, Patterson, & Weiss, 1971) somewhat, we could code turns of talk on two dimensions, function and speaker:

   a. Function of successive turns (five levels)
     1. Complains
     2. Emotes
     3. Approves
     4. Empathizes
     5. Negates
   b. Speaker for each turn (two levels)
     1. Husband
     2. Wife

Because the codes that can be assigned to a dimension are sometimes confused with the dimension itself, we use letters to identify dimensions and numbers for codes, as above, or else we simply separate permissible codes with slashes—e.g., Yes/No—and assume that the name of the dimension is understood from context.

A second way to represent data dealing with interactive phenomena is as a series of coded time intervals. In this case, the events coded are time intervals, and so it seems reasonable to call such data "time sequences" or *time-sequential data*. The intervals used are often short, for instance, a 5- or 10-s interval is common, but both shorter and longer intervals are also used. As with events, time intervals can be coded on more than one dimension.

For example, influenced by Parten (1932), Bakeman and Brownlee (1980) trained observers to code a toddler's predominant play state (one dimension) for successive 15-second intervals of videotaped observations made during a free-play period:

   a. Play state (five levels)
     1. Unoccupied

2. Solitary
3. Together
4. Parallel
5. Group

A more complex example is provided by Vietze, Abernathy, Ashe, and Faulstich (1978). Their observers coded successive 1-second intervals on two dimensions:

a. Infants' behavior (five levels)
   1. Vocalize
   2. Look
   3. Smile
   4. Cry
   5. None
b. Mothers' behavior (four levels)
   1. Vocalize
   2. Look
   3. Touch/Play
   4. None

A still more complex example is suggested by the work of Konner (1977). He coded each successive 5-second interval of !Kung mother-infant interaction for the

1. Presence or
2. Absence

of a number of different behaviors. In this case, each behavior served as a dimension. Examples of some of the dimensions he used are (a) infant vocalization, (b) caretaker vocalization, (c) adult response to fret, (d) infant and mother face-to-face, and (e) infant smile.

As these examples demonstrate, event sequences and time sequences are really the same. Only the coding "unit"—events versus time intervals—distinguishes between them. Both event and time-sequential data consist of strings of numbers (or other symbols) representing the codes assigned to successive events or intervals, for one or more dimensions. Thus, it should be no surprise that the analyses described subsequently apply equally to either kind of sequence.

We have distinguished between event and time sequences here because the terms appear frequently in the literature and because organizing the examples this way makes it easier, we think, for readers to recognize in them something that applies to their own work. The important point is to note the essential similarity between event and time sequences (actually time sequences can be regarded as a particular kind of event sequence) and to realize that any collection of coding schemes can be, and for sequential analysis should be, structured as sets of mutually exclusive and exhaustive codes, each set representing a dimension of interest.

Repeatable and Nonrepeatable Codes

A second distinction, one that has important implications for subsequent analyses, is between sequences that allow codes to repeat (i.e., to follow themselves) and those that do not. The requirement that adjacent codes be different applies to so many coding schemes in actual use that some writers (e.g., Sackett, 1987) suggest that all event sequences are so restricted. But in fact only some are. For example, successive turns of talk could be, and often are, assigned the same code (see, e.g., Dorval & Eckerman, 1984).

The distinctions between event and time sequences and between sequences that allow codes to repeat and those that do not yield the four possibilities presented in Table 9.1. If the unit coded is a time interval, there seems no reason to prohibit an interval from being assigned the same code as the immediately previous one, and so we regard the time-interval/nonrepeatable-code possibility as a null or empty category. Time sequences, then, always allow codes to repeat. Event sequences are a different matter. If the unit coded is a "state," then by definition codes cannot repeat—any repeated code would just be a continuation of the same state, not a new code. For other kinds of events, however, like turns of talk, codes may be, and often are, allowed to repeat.

The importance of this distinction is that analytic procedures are somewhat different for sequences that do and do not allow codes to repeat. In fact, applying procedures appropriate for sequences of repeatable codes to sequences of nonrepeatable codes can yield incorrect results. Moreover, and very much to the point given the general thrust of this chapter, procedures for dealing with nonrepeatable code sequences are easily handled in a log-linear context.

TABLE 9.1
Examples of Different Types of Sequences

Unit Coded	Adjacent Codes	
	Repeatable	Nonrepeatable
Event	Hops' marital turns of talk	Bakeman & Adamson's engagement states
Time interval	Vietze's mother and infant codes	No example, null category

Lags

A common question asked by researchers who study interaction is "What follows what?" When an infant smiles, does the mother vocalize? When one spouse complains, does the other spouse offer sympathy or respond with a complaint? Do spouses in general, or perhaps just certain groups of spouses, respond to negative behavior with reciprocal negative behavior? The general question is, is there any systematic relation between adjacent (or near-adjacent, or even concurrent) behavior?

A useful word to indicate displacement in time is "lag." In common usage, lag indicates that something (like a laggard) has fallen behind, but more specifically a lag may be defined as any interval between events. Sometimes this can be confusing: One convention is to identify the consequent event with an index of zero and antecedent events with negative indices; another convention—and the one we follow—is to identify the first antecedent event of interest with an index of zero and subsequent events with positive indices. Thus, if we think of later events (or intervals) as lagging earlier events and if we say that the earlier event (often called the criterion, or given, or antecedent event) occupies lag position 0 and later events (often called target or consequent events) occupy lag positions 1, 2, etc., then the general question becomes, does behavior at lag position 0 affect behavior at lag 1? at lag 2? at lag 8? etc.

We might ask, for example, if a baby is coded Cry at lag 0, is he or she likely to be coded Cry at lag 1? at lag 2? at lag 8? etc. Or, concerned with reciprocal relationships, we might ask, if a toddler is coded Unoccupied at lag 0 is he or she likely to be coded Solitary at lag 1? And similarly, if coded Solitary at lag 0, is he or she likely to be coded Unoccupied at lag 1? Finally, given a concern with concurrent relationships, we might ask, is a mother more likely to vocalize at lag 0 if her baby is also vocalizing at lag 0?

Contingency Tables

The first step in answering questions such as those just posed usually involves organizing the sequential data into frequency or contingency tables (Castellan, 1979). If just two dimensions are of interest, then the resulting table is easy to visualize. For example, if an investigator were interested in adjacent (lag 0–lag 1) relationships and if successive turns of talk had been coded using the simplified Marital Interaction Coding System (MICS) defined earlier, then a two-dimensional 5 × 5 table would be defined. The rows could represent lag 0 and the columns lag 1 behavior; the five rows and columns would represent the five permissible MICS codes (see Table 9.2).

Next, each successive *pair* of adjacent codes would be categorized and a tally added to the appropriate cell. For example, imagine the following coded se-

TABLE 9.2
Example Tallies for the MICS

Lag 0	Lag 1					Totals
	Compln	Emote	Approv	Empthz	Negate	
Complain	/	/		/	/	4
Emote				//		2
Approve				/	/	2
Empathize	//		/	/		4
Negate	/	/			//	4
Totals	4	2	1	5	4	16

quence (1 = Complains, 2 = Emotes, 3 = Approves, 4 = Empathizes, 5 = Negates):

3 4 1 4 1 1 5 2 4 4 3 5 5 5 1 2 4

and imagine further a "moving window" that operates as follows:

(3 4) 1 4 1 1 5 2 4 4 3 5 5 5 1 2 4
3 (4 1) 4 1 1 5 2 4 4 3 5 5 5 1 2 4
3 4 (1 4) 1 1 5 2 4 4 3 5 5 5 1 2 4
etc.

The first window would result in a tally being added to the cell in the third row and fourth column (the Approves-Empathizes cell), the second a tally to the cell in the fourth row and first column (the Empathizes-Complains cell), etc. The total N would indicate the number of adjacent code pairs (which would be 16 in this case because there were 17 codes total) and each cell would indicate how often each transition occurred—e.g., how often Empathizes was followed by Complains. The final tallies resulting from this small segment of data are given in Table 9.2.

It is important to stress how general such tables can be. Rows might represent codes for an infant's lag-0 behavior, and columns codes for the mother's lag-0 (or lag 1, etc.) behavior. Or rows might represent an infant's lag-0 behavior and columns the infant's lag-1 (or lag 2, lag 3, etc.) behavior. Moreover, such tables are not confined to the two dimensions of rows and columns. Triplets of codes instead of pairs of codes could be tallied, and in such cases dimensions 1, 2, and 3 might correspond to lag-0 (rows), lag-1 (columns), and lag-2 behavior respectively (this third dimension could be visualized as slices of a cube). In this case, the first, or (3 4 1), window from the data segment given in the previous paragraph would cause us to add one tally to the cell in the third row, the fourth column, and the first slice of a $5 \times 5 \times 5$ cube.

In addition, not all dimensions need refer to lag positions. For example, dimension 1 could be the spouse (Husband/Wife); dimension 2, lag-0 codes for that spouse; and dimension 3, the other spouse's lag-1 response. For the MICS code, this would result in a 2 × 5 × 5 table: one 5 × 5 slice would indicate the husband's responses to his wife, whereas the other 5 × 5 slice would indicate the wife's response to her husband. This table would allow us to test whether husbands and wives respond to each other in a similar way. In sum, because dimensions can encode any categorical research factor (male/female, old/young, preterm/full-term, partner 1/partner 2, clinic/normal, mother/father/adolescent, 3-month/6-month/9-month, etc.), subsequent analyses of such tables can investigate not just sequential effects, but effects of other research factors as well as any interactions between them.

Logs and Logits

Given appropriately constructed contingency tables, log-linear methods allow researchers to answer questions like, "What interactive patterns characterize these individuals/dyads/families?" and "Are interactive patterns different for different kinds of individuals/dyads/families?" Yet, in spite of their considerable advantages (see Kennedy, 1983; Wickens, 1989), log-linear methods, with just a few notable exceptions (e.g., Cohn & Tronick, 1987; Stevenson, Ver Hoeve, Roach, & Leavitt, 1986), are seldom used by behavioral researchers.

True, the theoretical work is relatively new (e.g., Bishop, Fienberg, & Holland, 1975; Goodman & Kruskal, 1954) and too often couched in intimidating notation. Easy to use and widely available computer programs (like SPSS' LOG-LINEAR: Norusis, 1985; SPSS, 1986) and texts intended specifically for social scientists (e.g., Haberman, 1978, 1979; Kennedy, 1983; Upton, 1978) and non-statisticians (e.g., Fienberg, 1980) have appeared only recently. Even the name can be intimidating. However, just as a skillful driver need not know how to fix an engine, and just as a conceptually correct user of multiple regression need not know how to invert a matrix, so too proper use of log-linear methods does not require that a user even know exactly what a logarithm, logit, or odds ratio is.

The log-linear approach may seem more foreign to psychologists and other social science researchers than it actually is. As several writers have noted (e.g., Kennedy, 1983), the conceptual overlap with traditional analysis of variance and multiple regression is considerable. This is especially true for logit models, which form an important and useful subclass of log-linear models. Moreover, for simple problems, familiar chi-square and log-linear analyses are almost identical. In the next section we compare chi-square, log-linear, and logit approaches, stressing their common features.

Note. It is possible to view a log-linear or logit analysis as a division of responsibilities between investigator and computer. It is the investigator's responsibility to specify terms for various models, to state which dimensions and which interactions might affect the distribution of outcome responses. After a model is specified, it is then the computer program's responsibility to compute coefficients for each term in the model and to determine how well the cell counts generated by the model fit the observed data. Typically, more than one model is specified. Thus, it is the investigator's responsibility in the end to decide which model best fits the data. As we demonstrate in subsequent sections, there is much to be learned both from models that do and do not fit the observed data.

Chi-Square: Taking the Log View

A Chi-Square Analysis

Imagine that we had recorded conversations between spouses and had subsequently coded the content for each turn of talk using the simplified MICS described previously. Imagine further that we are interested in negative reciprocity —defined as the tendency to respond to a negative statement with another one (this example is inspired by Cousins & Power, 1986)—and that classifying pairs of adjacent turns of talk for the Negate code (lag 0 Negate/Other, lag 1 Negate/Other) resulted in the tallies given in Table 9.3. To test whether there is a relation between lag-0 and lag-1 Negate codes, we could simply compute a chi-square, using the data in Table 9.3 and the standard chi-square formula:

$$X^2 = \sum \frac{(\text{obs} - \text{exp})^2}{\text{exp}}$$

Because the chi-square for Table 9.3 is 35.7, $p < .001$, and because the expected frequency for the lag 0 Negate/lag 1 Negate cell is 31.9, whereas the observed frequency is 62, we would conclude that Negate follows Negate more often than one would expect, given the base rate for Negate. Thus, these data apparently reflect a pattern of negative reciprocity.

A Log-Linear Model

The chi-square analysis just presented can easily be recast in log-linear terms. When we compute expected cell frequencies from the row and column totals, we

TABLE 9.3
Counts for Negative Reciprocity

Lag 0	Lag 1		Totals
	Negate	Other	
Negate	62	235	297
Other	236	2243	2479
Totals	298	2478	2776

are, in effect, guided by a model. The model assumes that cell frequencies reflect the overall (or marginal) distributions of lag-0 and lag-1 responses and nothing more. If this model, which assumes that row and column variables are independent, generates cell frequencies fairly similar to those actually observed, then chi-square will be small and we can accept the relatively parsimonious model that includes just a lag-0 (row) and a lag-1 (column) effect.

If chi-square is large, however, then we would reject the simple two-term, [LAG0] [LAG1], model just presented. In order to generate tallies that fit the observed data, a three-term [LAG0] [LAG1] [LAG0 LAG1], model is required, in which the third term represents the association (or interaction) between lag-0 and lag-1 codes. (Terms are enclosed in brackets; here all terms are listed, even lower-order terms implied by higher-order ones.)

In the case of a two-dimensional table, adding this third term results in a "saturated" model (a model that contains all possible effects). By definition, a saturated model generates tallies identical to those observed, and so it always fits the data perfectly. In substantive terms, if only the three-term model generates expected scores that fit the observed data, then categories for adjacent turns are associated and not independent. The chi-square analysis yielded the same result; the advantage of a log-linear approach, although not demonstrated by this simple example, is that the effects of more than just two variables (or dimensions) can be considered concurrently.

Almost always, log-linear analyses require computers. One popular and widely used set of programs is provided by SPSS (see also Bakeman & Robinson, 1994). Because we think some readers may find demonstrations showing exactly how problems like these would be run helpful, we have included the SPSS specifications for most of our examples. For the present case, the independence (no row × column association) and the saturated models would be specified as follows:

```
DATA LIST /LAG0 1 LAG1 3 COUNT 5-8
WEIGHT BY COUNT
VALUE LABELS LAG0 LAG1 1 'NEGATE' 2 'OTHER'
LOGLINEAR LAG1 LAG0 (1,2)
   /PRINT DEFAULT ESTIM
   /DESIGN = LAG1   LAG0
   /DESIGN = LAG1   LAG0   LAG1 BY LAG0
BEGIN DATA
1 1    62
1 2   235
2 1   236
2 2  2243
END DATA
```

The DATA LIST statement names the variables and notes which columns they occupy in the data. The LOGLINEAR command specifies a log-linear analysis of a table with two dimensions, LAG0 and LAG1, and notes that each dimension can assume values 1 and 2 (defined as Negate and Other respectively by the VALUE LABELS statement). The program will PRINT observed and expected cell frequencies and percentages and raw, standardized, and adjusted residuals (by DEFAULT) as well as ESTIMated coefficients and their standard errors, standardized values, and confidence limits for each term in the model. The first DESIGN specifies a model with two terms, LAG1 and LAG0; the second DE-SIGN specifies the saturated model, which includes in addition the LAG1 BY LAG0 term.

A Logit Model

For our purposes, logit models have two major advantages. First, unlike the more general log-linear models, logit models require that response (or criterion or dependent) variables be segregated from explanatory (or predictor or independent) variables. Asking "How is this (dependent) variable affected by these (independent) variables?" is faithful to the way we typically conceptualize questions and is a familiar way of summarizing multiple regression and analysis of variance (ANOVA) results as well. Second, at a more practical level, a logit model is specified with fewer terms than a corresponding log-linear model, and those terms correspond to ANOVA-like main effects and interactions.

For the current example, a logit analysis would identify lag 1 as the response and lag 0 as the explanatory variable. The no-effect model (which corresponds to the log-linear independence model) would consist of a single term, [LAG 1], whereas the main-effect model (corresponding to the log-linear interaction model) would consist of two terms, [LAG1] [LAG1 LAG0]. The first term is analogous to the grand mean in an ANOVA design, whereas the second term indicates that the distribution of scores at lag 1 is affected by events at lag 0. If the first model generated scores that did not fit the data, whereas the second did, a main effect for lag 0 would be indicated.

In SPSS terms, the logit analysis would be specified as follows (in this and following examples, only the LOGLINEAR statement is shown):

```
LOGLINEAR LAG1 (1,2) BY LAG0 (1,2)
    /PRINT DEFAULT ESTIM
    /DESIGN = LAG1
    /DESIGN = LAG1    LAG1 BY LAG0
```

LAG1, the dimension to the left of BY, is the response (or dependent) variable, and LAG0, the dimension to the right, is the explanatory (or independent) variable. As before, the numbers in parentheses indicate that each dimension can assume the values 1 to 2. The first DESIGN specifies just the response variable. This is a no-effect model (independence); it is constrained to generate data that fit the observed distribution of the response variable and (by design) the explanatory variable, but that is all. The second DESIGN specifies that the response variable is affected by the explanatory variable. This model specifies a main effect for LAG0 and, with just one explanatory variable, will be saturated. Specifically, the LAG1 BY LAG0 term indicates that LAG1 is affected by LAG0.

The ease of a logit compared to a log-linear model is more evident as the number of dimensions increases. For example, a saturated loglinear model for a three-dimensional table would involve the following terms:

$$[A]\ [B]\ [C]\ [A\ B]\ [A\ C]\ [B\ C]\ [A\ B\ C]$$

whereas the corresponding saturated logit model, with dimension C as the dependent variable, would require just

$$[C]\ [A\ C]\ [B\ C]\ [A\ B\ C]$$

In this case, the first term, [C], is analogous to the grand mean, whereas the [A C] term represents a main effect for A, the [B C] term, a main effect for B, and the [A B C] term, the A $\times$ B interaction.

Let us now consider what the output for a logit analysis of the data in Table 9.3 would look like. First consider the output for the [LAG1] [LAG1 LAG0] model. Because it is saturated, the expected counts generated by the model for each of the four cells of Table 9.3 are identical with the observed. As a result, the chi-square goodness-of-fit statistics are zero, as are the *residuals* (the differences between observed and expected counts for each cell). More interesting are the estimated parameter *coefficients*. The coefficient associated with the [LAG1 LAG0] term is .23, its standard error is .040, and its z value is 5.8. This significant z value ($p < .001$) suggests that the main effect of LAG0 on LAG1 is significant and that a model without the [LAG1 LAG0] term would generate expected counts quite discrepant from those observed; in other words, eliminating the [LAG1 LAG0] term from the saturated model would result in an ill-fitting model.

As a general rule, instead of adding terms until a "fitting" model is found, it often makes sense to begin interpretation of a logit analysis with an examination of the parameter coefficients computed for the saturated model precisely because these coefficients indicate which terms are important and which terms can be eliminated. Moreover, these coefficients can be interpreted in a manner analogous to regression coefficients (see SPSS, 1986, pp. 576–579).

Next consider the output associated with the [LAG 1] or no-effect model. As expected, given the coefficients for the saturated model, the chi-square goodness-of-fit statistics are large and significant, indicating poor fit. (Likelihood ratio chi-square = 29.7, Pearson chi-square = 35.7, $df = 1$ and $p < .001$ for both; because these statistics only approximate chi-square, values for the two may be different; if there is a conflict, usually the likelihood ratio chi-square is favored.) These significant chi-squares, coupled with large residuals, convinces us to regard the no-effect model as inadequate. (If most residuals were small, e.g., <2, we might accept a model even if its associated chi-squares were significant). Thus the traditional chi-square, the log-linear, and the logit analysis all lead us to conclude that whether or not the antecedent turn is negative significantly affects whether or not the consequent turn will be negative. As noted earlier, these data appear to reflect a pattern of negative reciprocity.

Residuals and z-Scores

For other than saturated models, expected counts will usually be different from observed. But how should the differences between observed and expected values (the residuals) be evaluated? In other words, when is it appropriate to claim that the observed count for a particular cell is significantly different from the count generated by a particular model?

There are at least three reasons why such information is valuable. First, as noted earlier, if all or most residuals are insignificant, it often makes sense to accept the model in question even if the goodness-of-fit statistics are significant. Second, a single large residual can indicate an outlier, which might be an error. Third, and perhaps most important for devotees of sequential analysis, the analysis of residuals indicates which patterns or sequences occur with greater than chance frequency. This becomes a more interesting question when tables larger than the current 2×2 are considered.

A number of statistics, most distributed approximately as z, have been proposed for the analysis of residuals. One early suggestion, applied to sequential analysis (Bakeman, 1978; Sackett, 1979), used the computation appropriate for a binomial test, but, as Allison and Liker (1982) pointed out, this assumes that probability estimates used in the computation represent true values when in fact they are observed values subject to sampling error. Another suggestion is the *standardized residual,* which is simply the residual divided by the square root of its expected value (Bishop et al., 1975, pp. 136–137; Haberman, 1973). This has the merit of being easy to compute, but it tends to underestimate the true value. Another suggestion is the *adjusted residual,* which, according to Haberman, is a better approximation to z (1978, pp. 77–79). It is also equivalent to the computation suggested by Allison and Liker (1982). In addition, for 2×2 tables, all four adjusted residuals are equivalent, which makes intuitive sense, whereas the standardized residuals are not. (See Table 9.4; as a general rule, the approxima-

TABLE 9.4
Residuals for No-Effect Logit Model (Negative Reciprocity)

LAG0 Code	LAG1 Code	Obs. Count	Exp. Count	Residual	Std. Residual	Adj. Residual
Negate	Negate	62	31.9	30.1	5.33	5.97
Other	Negate	236	266.1	−30.1	−1.85	−5.97
Negate	Other	235	265.1	−30.1	−1.85	−5.97
Other	Other	2243	2212.9	30.1	0.64	5.97

tion to z for standardized residuals is less adequate when the number of levels for variables is small.) For all these reasons, we recommend the adjusted residual as the best index of how much observed cell values deviate from their expected values.

COMMON PROBLEMS

In the previous two sections we analyzed data from a single 2×2 contingency table. Our intent was to demonstrate, in the context of an admittedly simple example, how easily a log-linear approach to sequential analysis might proceed. In the following sections we demonstrate further how a number of common problems in sequential analysis can be solved by applying log-linear methods to the appropriate contingency tables. In addition, we show how sequential effects and effects of other research factors can be investigated concurrently. First, however, we address the fundamental question of whether there is enough relatedness in the data even to justify further exploration.

Omnibus Tests of Sequential Constraint

Unless one plans a priori to examine only a few specified patterns, so many different patterns can be tested during an exploratory sequential analysis that the risk of finding some significant by chance alone (type I error) is high. For example, with only five codes on one dimension, 25 different two-event sequences (lag 0–lag 1 pairings) could be tested for significance, given repeatable codes, and 20, given nonrepeatable ones. Before individual two-event sequences are tested, however, the investigator should first determine whether adjacent codes are related in general. Only if they are does it make sense to proceed with an examination of particular pairs.

Such an omnibus test is easily accomplished with an appropriate logit model. Consider, for example, the modified MICS defined earlier. Using a 5×5 table like the one portrayed in Table 9.2, all two-event sequences would be tallied. SPSS specifications could be as follows:

```
LOGLINEAR LAG1 (1,5) BY LAG0 (1,5)
    /DESIGN = LAG1
    /DESIGN = LAG1    LAG1 BY LAG0
```

If the data generated by the first DESIGN (the no-effect model) failed to fit the observed tallies (as indicated by goodness-of-fit statistics significantly different from zero), we would infer that lag-1 events are indeed affected by lag-0 ones. Only then would we proceed to individual tests of two-event sequences—just as analysis of variance users would proceed to post hoc tests of differences between pairs of group means only in the presence of a significant group main effect.

The SPSS statements for the omnibus test would be somewhat different if sequences of nonrepeatable codes were involved. As an example, we use Bakeman and Adamson's (1984) study of infants' engagement state. Recall that their codes were

1. Engagement state (five levels)
    1. Unengaged
    2. Onlooking
    3. Person engagement
    4. Object engagement
    5. Joint engagement

Typically when the events coded are conceptualized as "states," adjacent codes cannot be the same because, if they were, they would represent a single event or state. Thus the number of transitions from a particular state at lag 0 to the same state at lag 1 would be zero, not because the transition did not occur (an empirical matter), but because by definition it could not occur (a structural matter).

The existence of such *a priori* or *structural zeros* on the diagonal of the lag 0–lag 1 contingency table must be communicated to the program, which could be done as follows:

```
LOGLINEAR LAG1 (1,5) BY LAG0 (1,5)
   /CWEIGHT = (0 1 1 1 1
               1 0 1 1 1
               1 1 0 1 1
               1 1 1 0 1
               1 1 1 1 0
   /DESIGN = LAG1
   /DESIGN = LAG1   LAG1 BY LAG0
```

The CWEIGHT statement indicates that cells on the diagonal are structurally zero, allowing the program to adjust degrees of freedom and expected counts accordingly. Again, if the goodness-of-fit statistics associated with the no-effect model (the first DESIGN) were significantly large, meaning that only the second model fit the data, we would conclude that lag-1 events were affected by lag-0 events and that we are justified in investigating particular two-event sequences further.

Testing for Particular Patterns

Usually investigators want to know more than just whether adjacent codes are related in general. They want to know about particular patterns, such as, Do married couples demonstrate negative reciprocity? Is parallel play a bridge to group play for toddlers? Do mothers respond to their infants' cries by picking them up? How are infants engaged just prior to becoming jointly engaged with their mothers?

The information needed to answer these questions is produced by the omnibus tests just described; specifically, it is part of the output associated with the no-effect model. As noted earlier, adjusted residuals are distributed approximately as z, thus adjusted residuals greater than 1.96 (or less than -1.96) indicate significant patterns ($p < .05$), pinpointing precisely which cells bear responsibility for the no-effect model's failure to fit the data. The larger the total number of tallies and the larger the expected count for a particular pattern, the better the approximation will be; but in general, and recognizing the need for occasional caution, large residuals indicate sequences that occur significantly more (or less) often than the base rates for their individual components would suggest.

Readers familiar with the sequential analysis literature may wonder how any of this is different from the various z-score approaches to individual-cell goodness-of-fit commonly discussed. For sequences involving *repeatable* codes, as previously noted, an analysis of adjusted residuals and z-scores computed as recommended by Allison and Liker (1982) gives identical results. The merit of casting the discussion in terms of adjusted residuals is that sequential analysis is thereby integrated into a coherent statistical tradition.

For sequences involving *nonrepeatable* codes, however, the situation is more complex. Allison and Liker (1982) discuss only sequences involving repeatable codes and are silent about the special considerations sequences of nonrepeatable codes require. Other writers, including ourselves (e.g., Bakeman & Gottman, 1986), note the problem but suggest a solution that we now believe to be problematic since it is not obvious how expected counts that preserve marginal frequencies should be computed when codes cannot follow themselves. Given a log-linear frame, however, the solution seems simple. Structural zeros are specified for the diagonal, indicating that these cells are necessarily zero as a consequence of not permitting codes to follow themselves. The usual iterative procedures will then be invoked by the program to produce expected counts based on this model.

Let us return to the Bakeman and Adamson (1984) study of infants' engagement state to show how this works. Their counts for pairs of adjacent engagement states observed for 15-month-old infants with their mothers are given in Table 9.5 and the appropriate SPSS statements for analyzing this table, including the critical CWEIGHT statement, were given in the previous section. The results from the first DESIGN (the no-effect model) are given in Table 9.6. This analysis suggests that infants rarely proceeded directly from an Unengaged to a Joint engagement state (the adjusted residual is -3.96), instead infants moved first from Unengaged to Onlooking ($z = 3.48$) and then from Onlooking to Joint engagement ($z = 2.73$). After Joint engagement, Object play was likely ($z =$

TABLE 9.5
Observed Counts for Infant's Engagement State

Lag 0	Lag 1					Totals
	Uneng	Onlook	Object	Person	Joint	
Unengaged	—	36	38	10	11	95
Onlooking	25	—	107	8	95	235
Object	39	120	—	20	147	326
Person	8	15	14	—	12	49
Joint	25	61	170	11	—	267
Totals	97	232	329	49	265	972

TABLE 9.6
Residuals for No-Effect Model (Infants' Engagement)

LAG0 Code	LAG1 Code	Obs. Count	Exp. Count	Raw Residual	Std. Residual	Adj. Residual
Unengaged	Unengaged	0	0	0	0	0
Onlook	Unengaged	25	23.1	1.86	.39	.47
Object	Unengaged	39	42.0	−2.98	−.46	−.67
Person	Unengaged	8	3.9	4.08	2.06*	2.20*
Joint	Unengaged	25	28.0	−2.96	−.56	−.71
Unengaged	Onlook	36	22.5	13.53	2.85*	3.48*
Onlook	Onlook	0	0	0	0	0
Object	Onlook	120	119.1	.90	.08	.16
Person	Onlook	15	11.1	3.89	1.17	1.37
Joint	Onlook	61	79.3	−18.32	−2.06*	−3.27*
Unengaged	Object	38	41.4	−3.41	−.53	−.77
Onlook	Object	107	121.0	−13.96	−1.27	−2.42*
Object	Object	0	0	0	0	0
Person	Object	14	20.5	−6.48	−1.43	−1.95
Joint	Object	170	146.2	23.8	1.97*	4.07*
Unengaged	Person	10	3.8	6.16	3.14*	3.34*
Onlook	Person	8	11.2	−3.23	−.96	−1.13
Object	Person	20	20.4	−.37	−.08	−.11
Person	Person	0	0	0	0	0
Joint	Person	11	13.6	−2.56	−.70	−.85
Unengaged	Joint	11	27.3	−16.28	−3.12*	−3.96*
Onlook	Joint	95	79.7	15.32	1.72	2.73*
Object	Joint	147	144.6	2.44	.20	.42
Person	Joint	12	13.5	−1.49	−.41	−.49
Joint	Joint	0	0	0	0	0

*$p < .05$.

4.07), Onlooking unlikely ($z = -3.27$). In addition, there was some suggestion of reciprocal movement between Unengaged and Person engagement (z's = 3.34 and 2.20), but the small expected counts cause us to regard this result with caution.

Testing for Group Differences

As Castellan (1979), Allison and Liker (1982), and others have noted, an advantage of the contingency table or log-linear approach is that it can easily be generalized to more complicated situations. For example, a follow-up question for the analysis just presented might be, "Does the Onlooking-to-Joint engagement pattern characterize older infants as well?" Indeed, often investigators want to know not only which interactive patterns occur in their data, but whether different groups of infants, dyads, couples, etc., manifest different patterns.

As an illustration of the log-linear approach to such questions, we use an example based on a study by Gottman (1980) and reanalyzed by Allison and Liker (1982). Two questions posed by Gottman were: "Is a wife's acting or not dependent on whether her husband has just acted?" And, "Is the degree of this dependency different for distressed and nondistressed couples?" The tallies Allison and Liker used are given in Table 9.7 and the SPSS statements we used to analyze these data are as follows (WIFE1 indicates whether the wife acted at lag 1, HUSB0 whether the husband acted at lag 0, and GROUP whether the couple was distressed):

```
LOGLINEAR WIFE1 (1,2) BY HUSB0 GROUP (1,2)
   /DESIGN = WIFE1   WIFE1 BY HUSB0   WIFE1 BY GROUP
   /DESIGN = WIFE1   WIFE1 BY HUSB0   WIFE1 BY GROUP
      WIFE1 BY HUSB0 BY GROUP
```

TABLE 9.7
Counts for Wife's Acts

Husband Lag 0	Wife Lag 1		Totals
	Act	No-Act	
A. Distressed Couples			
Act	76	100	176
No-Act	79	200	279
Totals	155	300	455
B. Nondistressed Couples			
Act	80	63	143
No-Act	43	39	82
Totals	123	102	225

As noted earlier, first we examine the output for the second DESIGN because coefficients for the saturated model suggest which terms should be retained and which, in the interest of parsimony, can be eliminated. In this case, coefficients for all terms but the WIFE1 BY HUSB0 BY GROUP interaction differed significantly from zero. (The standardized or z-values for each coefficient are given in Table 9.8.) The significant WIFE1 term merely tells us that the probabilities for the wife's two responses at lag 1 (Act/No-Act) were not equal. The significant WIFE1 BY HUSB0 term signals a husband main effect: wives acted 49% of the time when their husbands had just acted but only 34% of the time when their husbands had not. The log-linear analysis suggests that this difference is significant.

Similarly, the significant WIFE1 BY GROUP term indicates a group main effect: distressed wives acted 34%, and nondistressed wives 55%, of the time. However, the degree of dependency was not significantly different for distressed and nondistressed groups. If it were, then the husband by group interaction (indicated by the WIFE1 BY HUSB0 BY GROUP term) would be significant. Indeed, the model without this term (the first DESIGN in the last set of SPSS statements) generated expected counts not significantly different from those observed (likelihood ratio chi-square = 2.23, Pearson chi-square = 2.24, $df = 1$, $p = .135$ for both), verifying that the effect of the husband on the wife did *not* interact with type of couple. This is the same conclusion Allison and Liker reached.

For a second example of the ease with which log-linear analyses combine sequential and other variables, let us return to the notion of negative reciprocity discussed by Cousins and Power (1986). Recall that turns of talk were recoded as Negate or Other; Table 9.3 gives tallies for all two-event sequences so coded. However, some sequences began with the wife, others with the husband speaking, and some couples were categorized as moderately adjusted and others as very highly adjusted. Thus the data in Table 9.3 could be reclassified into four 2 × 2 tables: one table for each type of couple would tally sequences that began with the wife, the other sequences that began with the husband. Combining these four tables results in a four-dimensional 2 × 2 × 2 × 2 table. This table is not easy to visualize, but its four dimensions are

TABLE 9.8
Coefficients for Saturated Logit Model (Wife's Acts)

Term	Coefficient	z-Value
WIFE1	−.108	−2.52
WIFE1 BY HUSB0	0.99	2.32
WIFE1 BY GROUP	−.192	−4.48
WIFE1 BY HUSB0 BY GROUP	.064	1.49

a. Lag 0 (Negate/Other)
b. Lag 1 (Negate/Other)
c. Initiator (Husband/Wife)
d. Adjustment (Moderate/High)

The saturated model for this table is defined as follows:

```
LOGLINEAR LAG1 (1,2) BY LAG0 INI ADJ (1,2)
    /DESIGN = LAG1    LAG1 BY LAG0    LAG1 BY INI    LAG1 BY ADJ
      LAG1 BY LAG0 BY INI    LAG1 BY LAG0 BY ADJ
      LAG1 BY INI BY ADJ    LAG1 BY LAG0 BY INI BY ADJ
```

As before, a significant coefficient associated with the first term indicates only that the two LAG1 response categories are not equally probable. The next three terms indicate main effects and answer the following questions: Is the probability of Negate at lag 1 affected by whether the lag-0 code is Negate or not (LAG1 BY LAG0, suggesting negative reciprocity)? by whether the initiator is the husband or wife (LAG1 BY INI)? and by whether the couples are moderately or highly adjusted (LAG1 BY ADJ)?

The following three terms indicate two-way interactions and address an interesting series of questions: Is one spouse more likely than the other to elicit negative reciprocity (LAG1 BY LAG0 BY INI)? Is one adjustment group more likely than the other to manifest negative reciprocity (LAG1 BY LAG0 BY ADJ)? Is the likelihood that one spouse more than the other will elicit a negative response different for the two adjustment groups (LAG1 BY INI BY ADJ)?

The final term (LAG1 BY LAG0 BY ADJ BY INI) indicates a three-way interaction. If a "fitting" model required it, interpretation would depend on the data. The immediate point of this example, however, is to show how easily other variables can be incorporated with sequential ones in a single log-linear design so that the analysis of appropriate logit models can answer substantive questions concerned both with sequential patterns and with group differences in the manifestation of those patterns.

The Problem of Rare Events

At this point, we would like to discuss four specific problems that are commonly encountered in sequential analysis. These problems illustrate particular applications of the general techniques just discussed. The first concerns rare events that investigators feel are important, profoundly affecting the events that follow. Yet, if these influential events occur only rarely, too few tallies may be accumulated for a reliable analysis.

A solution is to treat the occurrence of the rare event as a point of demarcation, a point in time when the "rules" may change. Then all other events, in addition to their other dimensions, are coded Before/After, depending on their position relative to the rare event. If only one rare event could occur during an observation session, all events before it might be coded Before; all after it, After. If more than one rare event could occur, then it might make sense to code some number of events on each side of the rare event on the Before/After dimension.

For example, imagine that discussions among a mother, a father, and their adolescent son or daughter were recorded and that each person's turn of talk was coded as either:

1. Enabling (defined as accepting, explaining, problem solving, showing empathy, etc.) or
2. Constraining (defined as devaluing, distracting, judging, withholding, etc.).

(See Hauser, Powers, Noam, Jacobson, Weiss, & Follansbee, 1984.) Imagine further that parents rarely ridicule their sons or daughters overtly, but when they do we suspect it will have a chilling effect. Before the rare event of ridicule, mutual enabling might be the rule (adolescents respond to their parents Enabling statements with Enabling statements of their own); whereas after ridicule, adolescents might no longer respond in a systematic way to their parents Enabling comments or might actually respond with Constraining statements.

In order to test whether a rare event like ridicule has this effect, two 2×2 tables would be constructed—one for sequences before the event, one for sequences after. The three dimensions for the resulting $2 \times 2 \times 2$ table are

a. Parent's lag-0 statement (Enabling/Constraining)
b. Adolescent's lag-1 statement (Enabling/Constraining)
c. Position relative to the rare event (Before/After)

Models to test the importance of the rare event are as follows:

```
LOGLINEAR ADOL1 BY PARENT0 RARE
    /DESIGN = ADOL1
    /DESIGN = ADOL1    ADOL1 BY PARENT0
    /DESIGN = ADOL1    ADOL1 BY PARENT0    ADOL1 BY RARE
    /DESIGN = ADOL1    ADOL1 BY PARENT0    ADOL1 BY RARE
       ADOL1 BY PARENT0 BY RARE
```

If the first no-effects model fits the data, we would conclude that the adolescents' responses were not affected by their parents' statements. If the first failed but the second model fit, we would conclude that the adolescent's responses were in fact affected by their parents' statements. If the second failed but the third fit, we would conclude in addition that the probabilities that an adolescent would make an Enabling or a Constraining statement were different before and after the rare event. But only if the third failed, requiring the fourth or saturated model, would we conclude that the relation between parents' and adolescents' statements was affected by the rare event, that the "rule" connecting parents' and adolescents' statements was changed by the rare event. This provides us with a clear way to test the importance of rare events.

Testing for Stationarity

When conducting a sequential analysis, we assume that the data collected were generated by an underlying process. Thus pooling data generated by more than one process together is a serious matter. Such data lack "stationarity," which means that the process or rule responsible for generating the data has changed midstream. This makes it difficult if not impossible to uncover the generating rules.

If we regard the point at which the rules change, if such occurs, as a rare event, then the test procedure for stationarity is the same as that for rare events. For example, if sequences derived from an hour of observation were tallied, the table could be split into two half-hour tables. If only the appropriate saturated model fits, then we would conclude that these data lack stationarity across the two half-hours and we would be reluctant to proceed with further analyses. Such tests are recommended whenever researchers have reason to think that processes of interest may change within an observation session or across different sessions that have been pooled for analysis.

Controlling for Individual Differences

A related problem concerns observations derived, not from different parts of a session or different sessions, but from different individuals. It is not uncommon for researchers to draw on observations from several individuals, dyads, etc., when constructing tables for sequential analysis. Such pooling of data across individuals is routine among animal behaviorists but tends to make students of human behavior uncomfortable. The fear is that some individuals may contribute more tallies than others, thereby unduly influencing the results.

A simple and elegant solution to this problem is exemplified by Stevenson et al. (1986). Using codes similar to those of Vietze et al. (1978) described earlier, they observed 25 mother-infant dyads. One matter of concern to them was whether mothers responded vocally to their infants' vocalization. Thus they constructed 2 × 2 tables in which rows coded infant events (Vocalize/Not-Vocalize) and columns coded the following mother event (Vocalize/Not-Vocalize). However, not just one, but 25 such tables were constructed, one for each dyad.

SPSS statements that could have been used to analyze these data are as follows:

```
LOGLINEAR MOM1 (1,2) BY BABYO (1,2) DYAD (1,25)
   /DESIGN = MOM1    MOM1 BY DYAD
   /DESIGN = MOM1    MOM1 BY DYAD    MOM1 BY BABYO
   /DESIGN = MOM1    MOM1 BY DYAD    MOM1 BY BABYO
      MOM1 BY BABYO BY DYAD
```

The key concern is not whether these models fit the data, but whether the second model represents a significant improvement in fit over the first. If it does, then the *difference* between the likelihood ratio chi-squares for the first and second models (which is distributed as chi-square with 1 degree of freedom) will be significantly large. In this case, the second model provided a significantly better fit and the coefficient associated with the MOM1 BY BABYO term was significant (its standardized parameter estimate was 4.7). Hence, controlling for differences in vocalization rate (which is what the MOM1 BY DYAD term does), these mothers were significantly more likely to vocalize, given that their infants just had. As Stevenson et al. (1986) note, this approach allows analysis of data from several subjects without requiring either separate analysis of each subject's data or the pooling of data across all subjects (for a critique of this approach, see Wickens, 1993). However, it does require sufficient data so that reasonable expected counts will be generated for at least most of the cells in the individual tables. It also controls only for individual differences in rates, not transition frequencies; if this were desired, the second and third models would need to be compared.

Controlling for Autocorrelation

Past behavior, psychologists are fond of saying, is the best predictor of present behavior. A corollary is that an individual's present behavior is often best predicted from that individual's past, not from someone else's past. Thus as Allison and Liker (1982) and others (e.g., Gottman & Ringland, 1981) have pointed out, before concluding that one individual influences another (e.g., a mother, her child; a husband, his wife), it is often important first to control for the other's past.

As an illustration, let us again use an example based on Gottman (1980) and reanalyzed by Allison and Liker (1982). Recall that one of Gottman's questions was, Is a wife's acting or not dependent on whether her husband has just acted? But an additional question is, Is a wife's acting or not dependent on whether she herself has just acted. The tallies Allison and Liker used to address this question are given in Table 9.9 and the SPSS statements we used to analyze these data are as follows:

TABLE 9.9
Counts for Wife's Acts Controlling for Wife's Previous Act

Wife	Husband	Wife Lag 1		Totals
Lag 0	Lag 0	Act	No-Act	Totals
Act	Act	577	139	716
Act	No-Act	222	76	298
	Totals	799	215	1014
No-Act	Act	169	1089	1258
No-Act	No-Act	149	839	988
	Totals	318	1928	2246

```
LOGLINEAR WIFE1 (1,2) BY WIFE0 HUSB0 (1,2)
  /DESIGN = WIFE1
  /DESIGN = WIFE1    WIFE1 BY WIFE0    WIFE1 BY HUSB0
  /DESIGN = WIFE1    WIFE1 BY WIFE0    WIFE1 BY HUSB0
    WIFE1 BY WIFE0 BY HUSB0
```

The coefficients for the saturated model are given in Table 9.10 and can be interpreted as follows. Clearly, the best predictor of whether the wife will act in the current interval is whether or not she acted in the previous interval (WIFE1 BY WIFE0 term). If the wife acted in the lag-0 interval, she acted 79% of the time in the lag-1 interval as well; but if she did not act in the lag-0 interval, she acted in the lag-1 interval only 14% of the time. Thus, we agree with Allison and Liker that, when the autodependence is partialed out, the apparent cross-dependence (found when models do not include terms including WIFE0) is greatly attenuated. But it does not disappear. True, there is no main effect for the husband's behavior at lag 0 (the WIFE1 BY HUSB0 term is not significant). Instead, HUSB0 interacts with WIFE0 (the WIFE1 BY WIFE0 BY HUSB0 term). (The second model, which includes both wife and husband main effects

TABLE 9.10
Coefficients for Saturated Logit Model
(Wife's Acts, Controlling for Autocorrelation)

Term	Coefficient	z-Value
WIFE1	−.137	−5.39
WIFE1 BY WIFE0	.761	29.94
WIFE1 BY HUSB0	.027	1.07
WIFE1 BY WIFE0 BY HUSB0	.061	2.39

but no interaction, did not fit the data (likelihood ratio chi-square $= 5.65$, Pearson chi-square $= 5.74$, $df = 1$, $p = .017$ for both), whereas the third or saturated model, which includes the interaction, of course did.)

Apparently the husband's influence was largely confined to intervals when the wife was already acting. If the wife acted at lag 0, the probability that she would act at lag 1, given that her husband did not act at lag 0, was .74. This probability increased to .81 if her husband acted at lag 0. However, if the wife did not act at lag 0, corresponding probabilities were .15 and .13, suggesting little influence for the husband's previous act when the wife was not already acting.

The example just presented assumed time sequential data coded on two dimensions—husband's behavior and wife's behavior. This is a common data format when mutual influence is under consideration. Still, as Sackett (1987) reminds us, it can also be important to control for autocorrelation even when events or intervals are coded on just one dimension. The example Sackett presents is based on work by Vietze et al. (1978), who studied mother-infant communication in normal and developmentally delayed dyads.

One dimension Vietze et al. investigated was

  a. infants' signals (five levels)
    1. Vocalize
    2. Look
    3. Smile
    4. Cry
    5. None

(Appropriate hierarchy rules—e.g., a sequence coded Vocal and Look initially was recoded Vocal—ensured that each 1-second interval was assigned just one code.)

Sackett first asked whether the no signal or None code evidenced any cyclicity within an 8-lag range. In effect, he constructed eight 2×2 tables: rows and columns were labeled None/Not-None, rows represented lag 0, and columns represented lag 1 for the first table, lag 2 for the second, etc. (See Figure 16.1, Sackett, 1987, p. 866.) The z-scores associated with these tables indicated that None followed itself well above base rate at lags 1 and 6 and well below base rate at lags 3 and 8.

This is interesting information in itself, but it complicates answering the question, After None at lag 0, and independent of any autocorrelation for None, are some signals more likely than others at lag 1, lag 2, etc.? Consider the lag 0– lag 1 tallies given in Table 9.11. Because the tendency for None to follow itself is so strong (80% of lag 0 None's are followed by None at lag 1), all other patterns (None-Voc, None-Look, None-Smile, None-Cry) appear relatively weak. Given None's autocorrelation, there is essentially no chance that other patterns would be deemed significant.

TABLE 9.11
Counts for Infants' Signaling Behavior

| | Lag 1 | | | | | |
Lag 0	None	Voc	Look	Smile	Cry	Totals
None	221	19	15	5	16	276
Not-None	55	94	75	25	74	323
Totals	276	113	90	30	90	599

A solution, suggested by Sackett (1987), is to remove the biasing tallies before analyzing the table. In this case, removing the None column from Table 9.11 removes the source of bias—sequences ending in None. Applying a logit no-effect model to the resulting 2 × 4 table yielded small and insignificant adjusted residuals. For these data, none of the particular behaviors coded (Vocalization, Look, Smile, Cry) was especially likely after an interval coded None. But if we had not removed the autocorrelation bias, we probably would have concluded that at least some of these patterns (None-Vocalize, None-Look, etc.) were significantly unlikely.

Given sequential data coded on one dimension, and assuming sequences of repeatable codes as in the previous example, there is a second way to remove autocorrelation bias. This second approach may even be preferable to the one just presented, depending on the nature of the data and the exact questions the investigator seeks to answer. Let us assume time-sequential data and the Vietze et al. coding scheme. The complete uncollapsed table for tallying lag 0–lag 1 sequences would consist of 25 cells, 5 rows and 5 columns. (Our example assumes lag 1, but the logic applies to other lags as well.)

The diagonal cells represent transitions from a particular code to the same code, whereas the off-diagonal cells represent changes from one code to another. If we are concerned, not with how long behavior represented by the various codes lasted, but with how behavior changed, then it makes sense to ignore the tallies in the diagonal cells (see Bakeman & Brownlee, 1980). This removes all autocorrelative influence, not just that due to one code as in the previous example, for the lag indicated. All that remains is to apply the procedures described earlier for testing particular patterns in sequences of nonrepeatable codes (replacing diagonal cells with zeros, using models that specify structural zeros).

CONCLUSIONS

In the course of writing this chapter, we have become passionately committed to the log-linear approach. First, it provides a simple, single, unified way of treating most common sequential analysis problems. Investigators need only construct contingency tables, labeled and lagged in ways that reflect their substantive concerns. Nothing more, except for some clear thinking (and a computer program like SPSS' LOGLINEAR), is needed. Second, other variables (e.g., clinic/nonclinic, parent/child, 3-month/6-month/9-month) can easily be combined with sequential variables in a single design. This results in straightforward analyses that can reflect an investigator's substantive concerns with considerable fidelity. In addition, log-linear analyses have a number of technical advantages. For example, they are statistically efficient and make few assumptions about the data.

We recognize that analyses can be carried out using any of several different computer programs and that some of these programs differ in fitting algorithm used. We have used SPSS LOGLINEAR for our examples because of its wide availability and because of our own familiarity with it, and because it is available in both recent and earlier releases of SPSS. Alternatives include SPSS, HILOGLINEAR and ILOG (Bakeman and Robinson, 1994).

Throughout this chapter, we have stressed the simplicity of the log-linear approach as well as its conceptual overlap with topics more familiar to behavioral investigators, such as analysis of variance. We should further stress, however, that—as simple as we think log-linear analyses may be—our discussion has left a number of useful and technical topics untouched. We encourage interested readers to consult both local experts and the references cited here (e.g., Bakeman & Robinson, 1994; Kennedy, 1983; Norusis, 1985; Wickens, 1989) for further advice and information. Still, the information provided here should allow readers to begin with relatively simple log-linear sequential analyses almost immediately.

REFERENCES

Allison, P. D., & Liker, J. K. (1982). Analyzing sequential categorical data on dyadic interaction: A comment on Gottman. *Psychological Bulletin, 91*, 393–403.

Bakeman, R. (1978). Untangling streams of behavior: Sequential analyses of observation data. In G. P. Sackett (Ed.), *Observing behavior: Vol. 2. Data collection and analysis methods* (pp. 63–78). Baltimore: University Park Press.

Bakeman, R., & Adamson, L. B. (1984). Coordinating attention to people and objects in mother-infant and peer-infant interaction. *Child Development, 55*, 1278–1289.

Bakeman, R., & Brownlee, J. R. (1980). The strategic use of parallel play: A sequential analysis. *Child Development, 51*, 873–878.

Bakeman, R., & Gottman, J. M. (1986). *Observing interaction: An introduction to sequential analysis*. New York: Cambridge University Press.

Bakeman, R., & Gottman, J. M. (1987). Applying observational methods: A systematic view. In J. Osofsky (Ed.), *Handbook of infant development* (2nd ed., pp. 818–854). New York: Wiley.

Bakeman, R., & Robinson, B. F. (1994). *Understanding log-linear analysis with ILOG*. Hillsdale, NJ: Lawrence Erlbaum Associates.

Bishop, Y. M. M., Fienberg, S. R., & Holland, P. W. (1975). *Discrete multivariate analysis: Theory and practice*. Cambridge, MA: MIT Press.

Castellan, N. J., Jr. (1979). The analysis of behavior sequences. In R. B. Cairns (Ed.), *The analysis of social interactions: Methods, issues, and illustrations* (pp. 81–116). Hillsdale, NJ: Erlbaum.

Cohn, J. F., & Tronick, E. Z. (1987). Mother-infant face-to-face interaction: The sequence of dyadic states at 3, 6, and 9 months. *Developmental Psychology, 23*, 68–77.

Cousins, P. C., & Power, T. G. (1986). Quantifying family process: Issues in the analysis of interaction sequences. *Family Process, 25*, 89–105.

Dorval, B., & Eckerman, C. O. (1984). The development of conversation. *Monographs of the Society for Research in Child Development, 49* (2).

Fienberg, S. E. (1980). *The analysis of cross-classified categorical data* (2nd ed.). Cambridge, MA: MIT Press.

Goodman, L. A., & Kruskal, W. H. (1954). Measures of association for cross-classifications. *Journal of the American Statistical Association, 49*, 732–764.

Gottman, J. M. (1980). *Marital interaction: Experimental investigations*. New York: Academic Press.

Gottman, J. M., & Ringland, J. T. (1981). The analysis of dominance and bidirectionality in social development. *Child Development, 52*, 393–412.

Haberman, S. J. (1973). The analysis of residuals in cross-classified tables. *Biometrics, 29*, 205–220.

Haberman, S. J. (1978). *Analysis of qualitative data* (Vol. 1). New York: Academic Press.

Haberman, S. J. (1979). *Analysis of qualitative data* (Vol. 2). New York: Academic Press.

Hauser, S. T., Powers, S. I., Noam, G. G., Jacobson, A. M., Weiss, B., & Follansbee, D. J. (1984). Family contexts of adolescent ego development. *Child Development, 55*, 195–213.

Hops, H., Willis, T. A., Patterson, G. R., & Weiss, R. L. (1971). Marital Interaction Coding System, Eugene, OR: University of Oregon and Oregon Research Institute (order from ASIS/NAPS, Microfiche Publications, 305 E. 46th St., New York, NY 10017).

Kennedy, J. J. (1983). *Analyzing qualitative data: Introductory log-linear analysis for behavioral research*. New York: Praeger.

Konner, M. (1977). Infancy among the Kalahari Desert San. In P. H. Leiderman, S. R. Tulkin, & A. Rosenfeld (Eds.), *Culture and infancy: Variations in the human experience* (pp. 287–327). New York: Academic Press.

Norusis, M. J. (1985). *SPSSX advanced statistics guide*. New York: McGraw-Hill.

Parten, M. B. (1932). Social participation among preschool children. *Journal of Abnormal and Social Psychology, 27*, 243–269.

Sackett, G. P. (1979). The lag sequential analysis of contingency and cyclicity in behavioral interaction research. In J. Osofsky (Ed.), *Handbook of infant development* (1st ed., pp. 623–649). New York: Wiley.

Sackett, G. P. (1987). Analysis of sequential social interaction data: Some issues, recent developments, and a causal inference model. In J. Osofsky (Ed.), *Handbook of infant development* (2nd ed., pp. 855–878). New York: Wiley.

SPSS (1986). *SPSSX user's guide* (2nd ed.). New York: McGraw-Hill.

Stevenson, M. B., Ver Hoeve, J. N., Roach, M. A., & Leavitt, L. A. (1986). The beginning of conversation: Early patterns of mother-infant vocal responsiveness. *Infant Behavior and Development, 9*, 423–440.

Upton, G. J. G. (1978). *The analysis of cross-tabulated data*. New York: Wiley.

Vietze, P. M., Abernathy, S. R., Ashe, M. L., & Faulstich, G. (1978). Contingent interaction between mothers and their developmentally delayed infants. In G. P. Sackett (Ed.), *Observing behavior: Vol. 1. Theory and application in mental retardation* (pp. 115–132). Baltimore: University Park Press.

Wickens, T. D. (1989). *Multiway contingency table analysis for the social sciences.* Hillsdale, NJ: Lawrence Erlbaum Associates.

Wickens, T. D. (1993). Analysis of contingency tables with between subjects variability. *Psychological Bulletin, 113,* 191–204.

10

Assessing State Changes in Microsocial Interaction: An Introduction to Event-History Analysis

William A. Griffin
Arizona State University

Griffin shows how event-history analysis can be used to analyze sequential data. The methodology and examples also show how these methods can be used across multiple subjects.

—Editor

INTRODUCTION

Suppose that you want to determine what measurable factors influence the likelihood of marital conflict occurring and how rapidly the dyad moves from the conflict state to the nonconflict state. Similarly, you might ask what factors influence how rapidly a family moves to a conflict state if they are currently in a neutral state having previously been in a positive state? Until recently, such questions were typically either not asked or duration information was separated from the probability information and averaged by variable, and then a comparison procedure determined the presence of statistically significant differences across variables. Aside from the crudeness of such a procedure, an additional problem is that it portrays the interaction between time and behavior as static, not dynamic (Tuma & Hannan, 1984). This dynamic interdependence between time and behavior during social interaction is at the core of several contemporary theories of marital and family processes (see e.g., Fincham & Bradbury, 1991; Gottman, 1990; Patterson, 1982; Reiss, 1981). Fortunately, recent developments in the application of statistical theory, and the advent of the computers have made it possible for investigators to integrate time into their models to better represent this dynamic interdependence. At present, the most accessible data analytic procedure integrating time and state change is event-history analysis.

This chapter is intended to encourage investigators with microsocial data to consider event-history analysis as a means of exploring the dynamic interdependence between time in state, either psychological or behavioral, and the outcome of the state. To facilitate this consideration, this chapter provides some definitions and a general guideline for analyzing microsocial data using event-history analysis. Second, because this chapter is intended as a general introduction to the method and application of microsocial data, depth is sacrificed for breadth, and references to more detailed texts are amply provided. Within this chapter microsocial data refers to discrete behaviors or cognitive or affective states that occur during the interaction of at least two individuals (Griffin & Gottman, 1990; Patterson & Reid, 1984). These individuals may or may not be related, and the data can be obtained either by observation or self-report.

IS KNOWING RATE OF CHANGE IMPORTANT?

Publications about event-history analysis, such as this chapter, imply that measuring rate of change is important. And writers of these works, such as myself, often assume that the reader will appreciate knowing a data analytic method for assessing rate of change. Yet investigators often legitimately ask, "how will knowing *when* a state change is most likely to occur add substantially to understanding a process above and beyond simply knowing that a change occurred?"

This question reflects the fact that, until recently, most investigators of social processes have not included duration as a key ingredient in the formulation of how interactions evolve and change. Most theoretical formulations have simply left time in state out of the equation. Leaving time in state out of the study of a process might imply that, for example:

- Time does not add additional information about the state's contribution to the process being investigated.
- The length of time an individual spends in a state does not influence process outcome.
- The length of time an individual spends in a state does not reflect its intensity.
- There is not a relationship between duration and state; that is, a short fight is as detrimental as a long fight, or an extended romantic interlude has no more effect on a relationship than does a perfunctory one. It is the act, not the duration, that has the impact on the process.

Seen in the light of these rhetorical statements it is evident that sequence alone, without time information, intuitively lacks the breath to fully explain complex and dynamic microsocial processes. An effective and comprehensive model of such processes should address both the temporal and sequential patterning in microsocial interactions (Gottman, 1982; Vuchinich, Teachman, & Crosby, 1991). These are interdependent components of any behavioral pattern. Sequence provides structure, duration adds the contextual meaning. It is the combination of state and duration that forms the basis of complex structures. Moreover, and with some speculation, it might be suggested that to the interactant it is the behavioral act and its *duration* that forms the subjective impression of the process. For example, work examining negative state transitions during family conflict suggests that time in conflict influences the likelihood of a physically abusive outcome (Reid, 1986). Or, as Vuchinich et al. (1991) found, family conflicts are extended when additional family members become involved in the original two-person conflict.

If the utility of duration as a dimension in the study of a microsocial phenomia is self-evident, why then has it not been included until recently? There are at least two practical reasons. First, until videocamera and time-data generator overlays became readily available, recording time was difficult, inexact, and available only at a crude level (e.g., minutes instead of seconds, or hand-held watch rather than time overlays). Second, even if duration were recorded and accessible, appropriate data analytic methods were generally unavailable to most investigators. However, recent developments in video hardware, statistical theory, and the concurrent evolution of appropriate software and computers now warrants the inclusion of time in the theory and in the data analysis.

DEFINITIONS AND EXAMPLES

Even for experienced statistical analysts the initial foray into event-history analysis requires learning a lexicon unique to this analytic approach. Below are definitions of some of the most important terms necessary for comprehension of issues and recommendations. Immediately following most of the definitions is a short example that illustrates the concept being defined. All examples are taken from Griffin's (1993b) study of gender differences in affect change during marital interaction. In his investigation, self-report of negative affect was gathered in real time from 19 couples immediately following a positive and a negative interaction. Event-history analysis was used to determine covariate influence on how quickly males and females differentially change from negative affect to nonnegative affect during a marital conversation. Additional details can be found in Griffin (1993b).

Event-History Analysis

Initially developed for insurance company actuarial tables and for individuals in the medical field that studied health risk, this body of work was fully developed in biostatistics under the name of *survival analysis.* Biostatisticians want to know whether an individual at risk of dying will survive over some given period of time. Like human beings, machines stop functioning, and engineers are interested in assessing the risk that a machine will quit during some specified interval of time. In engineering this investigation of breakdown rate is referred to as *reliability analysis.* The term *event-history analysis* is usually associated with sociology. Sociologists are interested in an individual's status change (e.g., single to married). The major contribution to this area by sociologists is their refinement of regression models to describe the change process.

Each discipline using this analytic method is concerned with the same issues: What is the likelihood that the event of interest will occur, how rapidly it will occur, and what factors influence that likelihood? The strategy is to model the probability of changing from one state to another in the next increment of time. There are several ways to conceptualize this change. The investigator may be interested in the likelihood of immediately leaving the present state in the next small interval of time or conversely, not leaving the present state in the next small interval of time. It is also possible to examine the likelihood of leaving a state that is between two identified states (i.e., the intervent interval). This latter option examines how quickly events of interest reoccur.

Moreover, it is possible to collect frequency data (i.e., number of visits to a state), and substitute the value for duration in event-history analysis. This provides information about the general process until a specified event occurs (i.e., state change), except that one substitutes the number of events for the traditional ticks on the clock.

Several introductory articles (Hutchinson, 1988a, 1988b; Singer & Willett, 1991; Willett & Singer, 1993) and texts (Allison, 1984; Blossfeld, Hamerle, & Mayer, 1989) provide greater detail to readers interested in this methodology. Also, several articles have been written illustrating event-history analysis using microsocial data (Gardner & Griffin, 1989; Griffin, 1993a, 1993b; Griffin & Gardner, 1989; Vuchinich, Teachman, & Crosby, 1991).

Multiepisode Models

In event-history literature, multiepisode generally refers to repeatable, yet infrequent events (e.g., marriage, job mobility). In contrast, events examined in microsocial data are typically a small cross section of an ongoing behavior stream. Within this stream are state shifts which have occurred hundreds or even thousands of times prior. Hence, with microsocial data we are modeling covariate influence on multiple transition processes that typically are not unique, where outcomes probably reflect the general trend of such transactions. In other words, these event outcomes reflect behavioral organization in the individual, the dyad, or the family. Because of redundancy in behavioral organization, each outcome will not uniquely determine the course of subsequent events. Stated differently, each unique event (i.e., the state change or transition) is affected by the general condition of the social relationship which reflects the accumulative outcomes of the previous tens, hundreds, or thousands of similar events. Thus, event-history analysis with repeatable events using microsocial data seeks to describe the transitional process as affected by the covariates, with the acknowledgment that each event is not unique but reflective of a general process.

Example. A general event-history path of negative affect for three male subjects during the first 200 seconds of a 12-minute conversation with their spouses is illustrated in Figure 10.1. As evident, each subject provides numerous episodes. Each small line represents a unique negative affect episode, and line length reflects episode duration. This figure also shows that across the subjects are three episodes with the same duration (9 seconds); these duration ties are indicated by the double lines.

Hazard Rate

Irrespective of how specific research questions are framed, event-history analysis addresses the risk of changing states. This risk is assumed to be affected by known and unknown factors. Known factors are used as covariates, and regression models are used to estimate the covariate influence. Risk of change is expressed through the hazard rate, the unobserved dependent variable, and is modeled by taking the natural logarithm of the hazard before setting it equal to a linear function of the covariates (Allison, 1984).

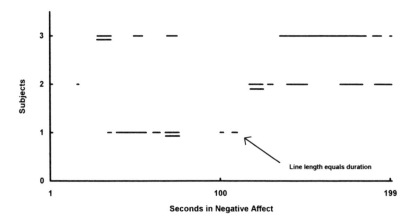

FIG. 10.1.   Event history path for three subjects experiencing multiple episodes of negative affect during 200 seconds of marital conversation (line length = duration; double lines show tied events; see text).

Depending on the discipline, and whether or not there are competing states in the data, the hazard rate is sometimes called the hazard, the hazard function, the transition intensity, or the transition rate and can be indicated symbolically at time t by $h(t)$, $r(t)$, or $\lambda(t)$. If we let T be a random variable for duration of the risk period for an event, then the hazard rate $h(t)$ is given as

$$h(t) = \lim_{\substack{\Delta t \to 0 \\ \Delta t > 0}} \frac{1}{\Delta t} P(t \le T < t + \Delta t \mid T \ge t). \qquad (10.1)$$

In the continuous-time model the hazard rate expresses the instantaneous probability of the observed individuals exiting (i.e., changing) the state in the interval $[t,\ t + \Delta t]$, given that the individuals have not yet exited the state.

For discrete-time analysis, the hazard is the conditional probability that the state will end during a particular interval, given that state had not ended prior to the beginning of the interval. Whether time is measured continuously or in discrete units, in general, the hazard rate represents the degree of risk for changing the state at each point in time. As such, high hazard rates reflect shorter state durations compared to low hazard rates. More formal definitions can be found in Kalbfleisch and Prentice (1980) or Blossfeld, Hamerle, & Mayer (1989).

It is also possible, especially with microsocial data, to look for changes in the hazard over the period of observation. Although one assumes stationarity in the change likelihood, the hazard profile (i.e., duration distribution) may change as the observation period continues. This implies, for example, that the hazard profile for the first 10 minutes of an interaction may be different than the last 10 minutes. A tendency for the hazard rate to increase over the period of observation means that episodes are ending quicker over time. Conversely, if the hazard rates become lower over the period of observation, episodes are less likely to end immediately and thus tend to have longer durations. If this variation is suspected, the investigator can divide the observation period and compare distributions across subdivisions, or include as a covariate some measure of time in observation (see, e.g., Griffin, 1993b).

If the investigator is interested only in a two-state process (e.g., negative, not negative) the hazard rate reflects the general likelihood of leaving the current episode (e.g., not negative). If however there are more than two states, (e.g., negative, neutral, positive) and the investigator is looking at the rate of leaving positive, then separate hazard rates are computed for moving from positive to negative and from positive to neutral. Stated generally, on exiting the current state, one of multiple other states will be entered, and within the event-history literature these multiple states are said to be competing for entry. Hence the model is called a competing risks model. It logically follows that states with higher risks are entered more often. Unique hazard rates for competing states are often referred to as transition rates or transition intensities (Gardner & Griffin, 1989; Tuma & Hannan, 1984).

An integral part of event-history analysis is plotting the risk of change (or not changing). As such, it is common practice to plot some form of the hazard rate. Given that the hazard rate expresses the relative risk at each moment over the period of observation, this moment-to-moment estimation of the hazard rate shows wide variability and, as such, interval by interval plots are difficult to interpret. One solution is to smooth (interpolate) the data, resulting in a more interpretable line (see Singer & Willett, 1991; Willett & Singer, 1993). When interpreting the hazard, the analyst looks for general trends in the rate: For example, does it appear to increase or decrease over time? One can also look for peak hazard points—that is, points of highest risk over the observation period. Alternatively, if the data are stratified by some covariate level, it is possible to determine whether and where the groups differ.

Example.   To visually grasp the hazard process it is necessary to plot the hazard, yet because of its variability, some writers suggest that examining the hazard is of limited value (see Figure 10.2). This variability is evident in Figure 10.2, although it is possible to discern a slight downward trend in the hazard over time for these males leaving negative affect. As an alternative, many investigators use the integrated (cumulative) hazard (see Figure 10.3). The cumulative hazard is useful in determining if duration dependency exists (i.e., does the hazard rate change over time; see Hannan & Freeman, 1989). If the hazard is constant (i.e., there is no duration dependency), then the line in this plot should form a slope of 1. Conversely, a line that does not show a slope of 1 indicates duration dependence. Figures 10.2 and 10.3 are plotted from the same data, and suggest, at least visually, that duration dependency exists in these data. A good

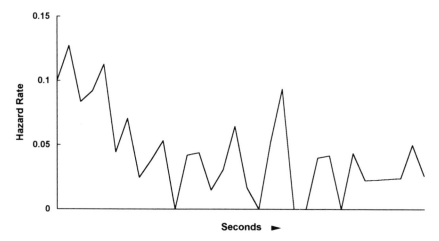

FIG. 10.2.   Illustration of a non-smoothed hazard rate.

discussion and illustration of the diagnostic property of the cumulative hazard plot is given by Hannan and Freeman (1989). Good examples of general plotting techniques are found in Blossfeld et al. (1989), Lawless (1982), or Nelson (1982).

Survivor Function

While the hazard rate expresses the likelihood of changing, in both continuous- and discrete-time analysis the survivor function represents the probability of not

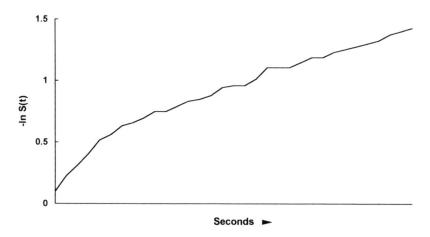

FIG. 10.3.   Cumulative hazard rate.

changing (surviving) over the period of observation. It is highest initially at time zero (t_0) and decreases monotonically from 1. In continuous time the survivor function expresses the probability that someone occupying the state remains in the state until time t, given that the episode is continuing and the individual has not yet left the state. Modified for discrete time, it is defined as the probability of not exiting the state (surviving) during time interval t, given that an exit has not occurred up until the beginning of the time interval. Concepts about surviving and various interpretations of the survivor function are best developed in the biomedical field (see, e.g., Kalbfleisch and Prentice, 1980).

The hazard rate provides information about the relative risk of changing states over the observed period, whereas the survivor function expresses the likelihood of no change. Most investigators using microsocial data generate hypotheses that address the risk of changing rather than not changing. As such, the hazard rate is typically the preferred way to conceptualize change (Yamaguchi, 1991), although the survivor function is very useful to graphically illustrate within-group strata differences or mean and median differences between groups.

Example. In Griffin (1993b), different event-history models were generated for males and females. These different models were constructed initially based on theoretical assumptions; these assumptions were later empirically supported when it was shown that males and females generate different hazard rates. Their respective survivor functions are seen in Figure 10.4. As seen in Figure 10.4, although the shape of the curves are similar, the husbands' curve is always below the wives', implying that husbands are continuously at higher risk of immediately leaving negative affect. Note further the vertical lines indicating the

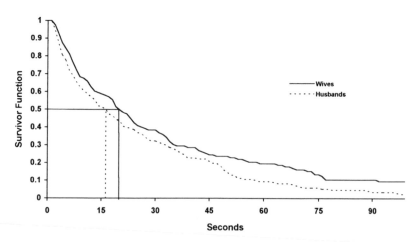

FIG. 10.4.   Survivor function by gender showing differences in median change duration.

median duration (50% have exited negative affect) for males and females. The horizontal distance between these lines as they cross the x axis reflect a 3.8-second difference.

Parametric Model Versus Proportional Hazards (Cox) Model

Parametric

In a parametric model the investigator specifies how the hazard rate changes during time in state. This specification forces the investigator to classify the form of duration dependency according to families of known curves, either monotonic (e.g., Weibull) and nonmonotonic (e.g., log-logistic). The investigator may ask, for example, do state changes tend to occur early and then slow down, or do they remain constant for some period before increasing or decreasing. If the investigator is interested in the specific hazard rate path (i.e., shape over time), then the parametric model is clearly preferred over the proportional hazards model. While parametric models have been advocated as the desired approach in event-history analysis (Singer & Willett, 1991; Vuchinich et al., 1991), others note that social science data seldom readily fit existing curves (Yamaguchi, 1991). Further, it may be extremely difficult to empirically distinguish between curves (see, e.g., Arminger, 1987), resulting in a misspecified model, thus leaving the investigator with minimal confidence in the regression coefficients.

Semiparametric or Proportional Hazards (Cox) Model

Initially developed by D. R. Cox (1972; Cox & Oakes, 1984), the estimation procedure in the proportional hazards model is divided into two components, one which estimates the form of the duration dependency and one which estimates the impact of the covariates. The Cox procedure utilizes only the regression coefficient estimates and, in effect, ignores the shape of the duration dependency. Since the estimation procedure (partial likelihood (PL)) used for the proportional hazards model only estimates covariate influences it is often referred to as the *semi-* or *partial parametric* approach, this in contrast to the maximum-likelihood (ML) estimation procedure used in the parametric model (see Kalbfleisch & Prentice, 1980).

In at least two respects the proportional hazards model is more flexible than the parametric model. First, unlike the parametric model, it requires no assumptions about the functional form of duration dependency. Second, it handles time-dependent covariates easier than the parametric model.

Although more flexible, there is one major assumption that underlies this model: covariate level proportionality. Proportionality implies that two individuals having unique values on the covariate will show hazard rates that are constant (i.e., proportional) over time. In regression terms, proportionality implies no interaction between covariate level and time. Testing this assumption is a necessary first step when using this model. Tests of proportionality can be incorporated into the regression model by creating an interaction term expressing the product of the covariate and some function of time (e.g., covariate $*$ Ln(time)), where time represents duration in state. If the interaction term is significant, then the variable can be used as a stratification variable (discussed in subsequent sections of this chapter) or left in the model, which then becomes a nonproportional hazards model. A good introduction of the proportional hazards model is found in Allison (1984), Blossfeld et al. (1989), Hutchison (1988a, 1988b), and Yamaguchi (1991); a more advanced treatment of this method is in Cox and Oakes (1984) and Kalbfleisch and Prentice (1980). Illustrations can be found in Griffin (1993b) and Yamaguchi (1991).

In summary, if the hypotheses specifically require information about covariate influence without concern about duration dependency, then the proportional hazards model is the procedure of choice. Conversely, if the research question specifically addresses the shape of the hazard rate over time then the parametric model should be used.

Example.   In Griffin (1993b), the initial analysis of husbands' state transitions from negative affect indicated that four covariates did not meet the assumption of proportionality, namely Previous State, Marital Satisfaction, Education, and Communication Orientation. A series of models was run where each nonproportional variable was used as a stratification variable while the three remaining variables were entered as time-dependent covariates. Time-dependent covariates were entered in the model as interaction terms with time (specifically, $\log_e$ time) representing duration in negative affect. The single best model (comparing log-likelihood estimates) was with Previous State (neutral, positive) as the stratification variable. Results from this model can be seen in Table 10.1.

This stratified nonproportional hazards model contains three interaction terms: Marital Satisfaction $\times$ Ln(time), Education $\times$ Ln(time), and Communication $\times$ Ln(time). Among these, Education $\times$ Ln(time) had the greatest influence on the hazard rate, and in conjunction with the Education covariate influence this interaction could be interpreted as follows: as Education increases the immediate likelihood of exiting negative affect increases (shorter durations), and this influence increases over time. In other words, the longer the negative affect state has existed, the greater the effect of education on the likelihood of immediately leaving the negative state.

States

In the study of microsocial interaction, and in particular with event-history analysis, one of the most important decisions is to determine "what constitutes a

TABLE 10.1
Regression Coefficients for Husbands Changing from Negative Affect, $n = 265$[a]

Model Variables	β	SE	Std. t	≈ % Change[b]
Previous duration	−.0031	.0038	−0.81	
Time in task	.0004	.0004	0.88	
Task (D)[c]	−.5616	.1870	−3.00*	57
Marital length	.0003	.0010	0.38	
Spouse rating	.0506	.0653	0.77	
Tally	−.0276	.0277	−0.99	
Ac.f. 1	.5497	.5167	1.06	
Marital satisfaction	−.0040	.0036	−1.10	
Marital sat. × Ln(Time)	−.0102	.0028	−3.64*	−1
Education	.1374	.0449	3.06*	15
Education × Ln(Time)	.0764	.0263	2.90*	8
Communication	.0020	.0120	0.17	
Communication × Ln(Time)	.0139	.0080	1.72	
Log-likelihood	−986.72			

[a]Stratification by Previous State (neutral, positive).
[b]% change indicates the approximate % change in the hazard rate for a one-unit change in the explanatory variable; for Task (D) it is the relative hazard for negative task compared to positive task.
[c]Task is dummy coded (D): 0 = positive, 1 = negative.
*$p < .01$.

state?" States should represent discrete entities that imply a categorical shift in the phenomena when they change. To permit strong conclusions, states should be internally logical and represent distinct shifts in the behavioral process. States may be discrete behaviors, composite behavioral sets, or unique pattern sequences. They, for example, may reflect status changes (e.g., married versus divorced) or microbehavioral states like unidirectional or bidirectional dyadic eye gaze (Gardner & Griffin, 1989), microsocial dyadic states like conflict versus no conflict (Vuchinich et al., 1991), or even self-reported internal affect states (Griffin, 1993b).

States must be mutually exclusive and exhaustive, and there must be a minimum of two. These states must have clear onset and offset times, and the duration of the state begins anew with each onset. If possible, the phenomena should be recorded in sufficiently fine time increments to avoid duration ties in the data. Strategies for handling ties are discussed later in this chapter.

States can reflect either discrete or continuous phenomena. Affect rating, for example, can range from extreme negative to extreme positive along a continuum. In general, data in this continuous form is better suited for time-series analysis (see, e.g., Griffin & Greene, 1994), and, as such, to be useful for event-history analysis the phenomena must be cleaved into distinct categorical states.

Griffin (1993b), for example, reduced his original nine-point affect scale to three distinct states: positive, neutral, and negative. Obviously such a reduction assumes that the important features of the data are retained after its form is altered.

Most microsocial data represent complex behavioral or psychological patterns involving multiple states. Multiple states (>2) pose no serious problem for event-history analysis. The only additional work on the part of the analyst involves changing the censoring information as a function of which state is not being entered. Specifically, states not being entered into are considered censored (discussed subsequently), and a separate model is estimated for each type of transition. For example, suppose that there are three states A–C, and that the investigator is interested in all transitions from state A. A separate model is estimated for A–B and A–C transitions. For the A–B transition model, all A–C transitions are coded as censored; similar censoring is done for the A–B transitions when estimating the A–C model. As noted in the definitions section of this chapter, this is called a competing risks model, and transition specific hazard rates are often referred to as transition intensities. This method works well unless some states are rarely visited, creating inefficient estimates because of the small N relative to the censored observations. In this case, it would probably be better to collapse the state into another, logically adjacent state.

Example. Figure 10.5 shows the continuous affect rating for a husband (Subject 2 in Figure 10.1) during the first 200 seconds of a conversation with his wife. A low rating (≤ 3) reflects positive affect, and a rating greater than 4 indicates negative affect. The double lines in Figure 10.5 indicate negative states and are consistent with the discrete pattern for this subject in Figure 10.1. As noted, this reduction assumes that the important features of the data are retained

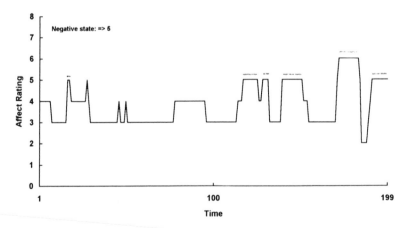

FIG. 10.5. Converting continuous-time negative affect rating to discrete-time state data.

after its form is altered. Negative affect is the most potent discriminator of marital satisfaction in dyads according to the marital interaction literature; hence the reduction, in effect, highlights the important episodes in the interaction.

Censoring

Censoring refers to incomplete information about the subject over time relative to the beginning or ending of each episode. *Left censoring* implies that the subject being monitored entered the relevant state prior to the observation period; thus onset time is not available. Left censoring poses unique data reconstruction problems, but, fortunately, microsocial data seldom have left censoring. In *right censoring* the episode is considered censored if an event has not ended when observation stops.

Censored data are necessary in order to calculate the risk of change per interval of time. Discarding this information inflates the estimated hazard rate. In fact, handling censored data is an important advantage event-history analysis has over classical multiple regression.

All event-history analysis software require that censoring be specified for each record in the dataset; the usual convention is to assign 1 if the event occurred and 0 if the event was censored. Censored observations are rare in most microsocial data; the maximum should be one per subject per observation period. Detailed discussion of censoring can be found in Blossfeld et al. (1989), Tuma and Hannan (1984), and Yamaguchi (1991).

Example. Appendix A illustrates censoring for continuous-time and discrete-time analysis. For now ignore the differences in record format; they are discussed later. Instead note that in the continuous-time format (left section of the page) of the nine episodes shown, three are censored. A 0 in the censor column indicates that the subject was still in that particular state when the observation ended; hence we have no information about the state's complete duration other than it was as long as the last second of observation.

Covariates

Continuous Versus Categorical

Either continuous or categorical variables can be included in the regression model. In some respects, categorical variables are easier to interpret than continuous variables; they permit logical stratification and more relevant graphical or numerical comparisons. Hence, many investigations convert variables from continuous to categorical. Depending on the questions being asked and the number of categories, this conversion to categorical intervals permits a good approximation to the continuous form of the variable. A good example of how this can be done is illustrated by Yamaguchi (1991).

Time Dependent Versus Time Independent

Covariates are also classified as time varying or time invariant. *Time-invariant* (time-independent) covariates have values that do change throughout the period of risk. Most covariates are this type, especially for microsocial data. Variables of this type include, for example, information about age, number of children, and marital satisfaction.

Time-varying (time-dependent) covariates can change their value over the period of observation. Time-varying covariates are possible in discrete- and continuous-time models, and they are less cumbersome to include in proportional hazards models than in parametric models. Yamaguchi (1991) provides a detailed discussion of time-varying covariates, and Blossfeld et al. (1989) illustrate several strategies for including this type of covariate into both parametric and proportional hazards models. However, because most microsocial events are recorded in seconds, aside from testing for nonproportionality or to include them as interaction terms, most models using microsocial data do not contain time-varying covariates.

Example.   As noted in the example for the proportional hazards model, Table 10.1 has three interaction terms, and each is a time-varying covariate included because of its failure to meet the assumption of proportionality. All other variables are time invariant. Also included in Table 10.1 is the categorical Task; all others are continuous.

Unobserved Heterogeneity

Explanatory variables are included in classical regression models to account for variance in the dependent variable. Analogously, covariates are included in event-history analysis to account for their influence on the hazard rate. Unfortunately, in reality, all relevant covariates are seldom included in the model, resulting in estimation bias in the regression of coefficients (Yamaguchi, 1991).

This inability to account for sources of hazard rate influence is called unobserved population heterogeneity. Unobserved heterogeneity has the distinct effect of making the hazard rate appear to decrease over time. While it is possible that the hazard may actually decrease over time, the decrease may also be an artifact of at least two subgroups having distinct hazard rates. Specifically, one group might have a high hazard and thus change quickly ("the movers"), and another group, the "stayers," would have a much lower hazard rate, thus exiting only at the extreme of the observed period. Their composite hazard would appear to be decreasing over time. This problem is illustrated and discussed in detail in Blossfeld et al. (1989).

Several strategies have been proposed to handle this problem. The simplest and most straightforward is to include covariates in the model that identify relevant subgroups. A second, more controversial, method is to include a random effects term representing a disturbance on the hazard. If, however, the distribution term (most often a gamma) is misspecified, the model may produce grossly inadequate estimates for the true hazard rate. Detailed discussions of this problem can be found in Blossfeld et al. (1989), Heckman and Singer (1984), Heckman and Walker (1987), Trussell and Richards (1985), Tuma and Hannan (1984), and Yamaguchi (1986). Blossfeld et al. (1989) and Hannan and Freeman (1989) provide examples of adding a disturbance term to their parametric models.

Example. Since sources of heterogeneity are often unknown (unobserved) and known (observed), the investigator is obligated to include all potential sources of influence on the hazard. Their selection may be determined by theory, or they may simply be practical features describing data collection. For example, Griffin (1993b) included *Tally* as a covariate in his models. It referred to the cumulative number of prior negative states within the positive or negative task. It was included to determine if the number of events has an effect on the hazard rate. Although within each marital dyad these transitions from negative affect may have occurred hundreds or thousands of times, within the context of the experimental design its influence was unknown. Although found to have substantive value as a stratified variable in the wife model (see his Table 10.1), Tally's initial inclusion was to control for unobserved heterogeneity.

Autocorrelation

Multiple observations from the same subject, typical of microsocial data, create the potential problem of intercorrelation between entries. Unless this correlation is accounted for within the statistical model, it is likely to bias the test of regression coefficients (Allison, 1984; see Rogosa & Ghandour, 1991, however, for a different conclusion). In general, an effort should be made by the investigator to include covariates that can account for the correlation structure in the data (Allison, 1984).

Example. For example, Griffin (1993b) included as a covariate the lag-1 autocorrelation function (Ac.f.1) of negative affect. It was included as a measure of general serial dependency for duration. Ac.f.1 provided a measure of if and how consistency in transitioning behavior (i.e., duration) influences the likelihood of immediately exiting the current negative state. All estimates for Ac.f.1 were done using the correction for small samples recommended by Huitema and McKean (1991). For wives the range was from $-.27$ to .59 ($M = .05$, $SD = .15$), and for husbands it was from $-.34$ to .50 ($M = .03$, $SD = .16$); only one subject, a wife, had a significant Ac.f.1 ($t = 2.53$, $p < .05$). In order to derive reasonable estimates of Ac.f.1, only individuals having at least five negative episodes ($n = 31$) were involved in the calculations; the remaining seven subjects were assigned Ac.f.1 = 0. Finding only one significant t using this conservative estimation procedure suggests that negative state durations were only nominally autocorrelated.

Coefficient Interpretation

Both maximum-likelihood (ML) and partial-likelihood (PL) estimation procedures provide a regression coefficient estimate for each covariate, similar to the estimate provided in OLS regression. The ratio of this coefficient estimate to its standard error is a standardized t. If the value of this ratio exceeds 1.96, the covariate is statistically significant ($p < .05$) and indicates an influence on the hazard rate. Analogous to linear regression, a positive regression coefficient indicates that as the covariate increases the hazard increases; an increase in the hazard rate denotes a decrease in state duration (i.e., change occurs quicker). Conversely, a negative regression coefficient indicates that as the covariate increases the hazard decreases and state duration lengthens.

Covariate influence, specified as percent change in the hazard rate per one unit change in the covariate, is obtained by subtracting 1 from the exponentiated regression coefficient multiplied by 100 ($\exp(\beta) - 1 * 100 = \%$ change; see Allison, 1984, or Blossfeld et al., 1989). For dummy coded covariates this interpretation is slightly different; the exponentiated coefficient ($\exp(\beta)$) gives the relative hazard for the groups corresponding to the covariate dummy values (Allison, 1984). See Allison (1984) for heuristic examples and Yamaguchi and Kandel (1987) for substantive examples of coefficient interpretations.

Example. In Table 10.1 there are four significant covariates, of which two demonstrate especially powerful influence on the hazard. For the first, Task, exponentiating the coefficient for this dichotomous variable ($\beta = -.561$) yields .57, indicating that the hazard rate for exiting negative affect during the negative interaction was approximately 57% of the hazard rate during positive interaction. Viewed differently, the hazard rate for exiting negative affect was 75% ($1/.57 = 1.75$) larger in the positive interaction task than in the negative interaction task. For Education, a continuous variable, the coefficient was positive, indicating that education increased the hazard rate, thereby shortening durations in negative affect. Each additional year of education increased the hazard by about 15% ($\exp(.1374) - 1 * 100 = 14.72$).

Model Testing

Much like log-linear analysis or any other analytic procedure that provides coefficient estimates generated by the maximum-likelihood estimation procedure, it is possible to test for improvement in the model (lower log-likelihood values) by comparing it to another model, when one model is considered a special case of the other (Allison, 1984). Likelihood estimation procedures produce log-likelihood estimates that reflect the fit between the observed and expected data given the specified model. Adding or removing covariates or changing the duration dependency parameters (curves) produces a value change in the log-likelihood.

Differences between models are determined by taking twice the absolute difference in the log-likelihoods and referring the value to a chi-square distribution, with the *df* equal to the differences in the number of parameters in the two models. In most cases, the *df* will represent the addition or removal of covariates across the models. In general, lower log-likelihood values suggest a better fit to the data. In parametric models it is not possible to compare across curves that are not within the same family of curves (e.g., monotonic versus nonmonotonic). Details about model testing can be found in Blossfeld et al. (1989), Hannan and Freeman (1989), and Yamaguchi, 1991. Substantive examples are provided by Hannan and Freeman (1989) and Yamaguchi (1991).

Example. In Table 10.1 the final husband model is shown from Griffin (1993b). Along with Education, Task is the most potent covariate in the model (see the Coefficient Interpretation section above). To illustrate its potency I re-fit the model excluding Task. In the reduced model the log-likelihood rose to -991.23, this in contrast to -986.72 in the complete model shown in Table 10.1. Taking twice the absolute value from the log-likelihoods yields 9.02, which is significant at .01 with 1 *df*. This indicates, as expected, that the model containing Task better fit the observed data than the model excluding Task. Most event history analysis software also permit model development using classical stepwise regression methods. A brief discussion of available software programs for event history analysis is in Griffin (1993a, Appendix C) or Allison (1984, Appendix C).

ASSESSING CHANGE IN MICROSOCIAL EVENTS: AN EVENT HISTORY ANALYSIS PROCEDURAL CHECKLIST

As evident from the definitions provided, the analyst is faced with a barrage of new terms and several important data analytic choices at each step of the analysis. Figure 10.6 contains a decision tree useful in determining what analytic choices are available, both within and across continuous- and discrete-time models. This decision tree is a skeleton of the analysis process envisioned by me, and as such, reflects selective readings and idiosyncratic ideas about the smoothest path through a set of data.

First, collect data in continuous real time as opposed to discrete time. Although appropriate, collecting data in large discrete units would limit the type of subsequent analyses to discrete-time models. Conversely, by collecting data in

328   GRIFFIN

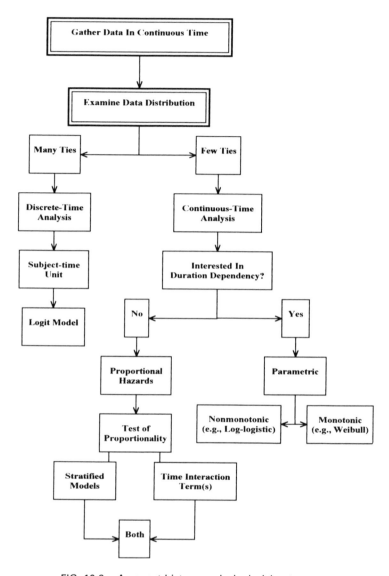

FIG. 10.6.   An event history analysis decision tree.

continuous time, the investigator has the option of later collapsing the data into
larger intervals, or, if ties dictate, discrete-time analysis can be used to approximate the continuous model.

Next, the investigator examines the distribution of durations over the period of
observation. Relevant pieces of information about the event-history process are
available from standard event-history software; these include time, hazard rate,

survivor function, and proportion failing per interval. Blossfeld et al. (1989) and Yamaguchi (1991) provide detailed suggestions about what information should be extracted from an output file in order for the investigator to make good decisions about model fit and subsequent analyses. When a model has been fit, the output file contains several relevant pieces of information: regression coefficient estimates, standard errors, log-likelihood (or variant), and an omnibus test of covariate influence (e.g., Wald test) (see Griffin, 1993a: his Appendix B shows an output file). Initially, however, the important features to examine are sample size, amount of censored data, and the number of ties per interval of time. Censored data should not consist of more than 30–50% of the data, and as the number of censored data increase so should the sample size. Similarly, as the number of possible states and covariates increase so should the sample size. Simply put, since sample size influences coefficient estimates, the analyst must account for the proportion of censored data, the number of covariates, and the number of states in determining the appropriate sample size. Singer and Willett (1991) provide a nice discussion of sample size issues.

The next issue is duration ties. Typically event-history durations are collected in real time and with sufficient measurement exactness to avoid ties. Ties occur when two or more events have the same duration. For example, Figure 10.1 depicts the duration history of multiple events across three subjects. There are multiple ties in these data, their location is indicated by the double horizontal lines. In this illustration of actual data, there are three state changes that occurred at 9 seconds. As evident from these data, even when time is continuously measured there is a chance of ties. This chance increases if time intervals are large or there are only a few time intervals. For example, on average, microsocial events measured at minute intervals will have more ties than events measured in seconds, or if the phenomenon is being observed for 15 minutes, 5 three-minute measurement intervals will produce more ties than 15 one-minute measurement intervals.

As discussed here, ties do not refer to the absolute number of ties in the data but rather to the number of state changes relative to the number at risk per interval of time. At issue, what proportion of the population, relative to those at risk, changed states at each interval of time? It is obvious intuitively that model parameters based on extreme loading of failures across a few intervals will produce inefficient coefficient estimates.

More formally, since the initial papers which established the asymptotic properties of the estimators in hazard rate models assume that ties occur with zero probability (see Hamerle, 1987), then, strictly speaking, continuous-time models are inappropriate if ties occur (Blossfeld et al. 1989; Kalbfleisch & Prentice, 1980). Moreover, because the proportional hazards model uses the temporal order of event durations to generate estimates (PL estimation procedure), it is especially sensitive to ties, even with Breslow's commonly employed method to correct for ties (Breslow, 1974). If the ties are too frequent, then the investigator is advised to use discrete-time models. Unfortunately, what constitutes too many ties has not been established in the literature.

Given that there is not an established criteria in the literature for the optimal maximum proportion of state changes per interval (i.e., ties), it is difficult to recommend a basis for the decision to analyze with either the continuous- or discrete-time model. However, a general conservative (yet admittedly arbitrary) guideline for *large samples* might be: If across all time intervals, the proportion exiting (ties) for any given interval is less than 5% of the population, then continuous-time analysis is appropriate; and if the proportion exiting varies from 5% to 15% over only a few intervals with the remainder having relative few ties, then continuous-time analysis would probably be adequate; finally, if the distribution shows a pattern other than these two, it would probably be better to use a discrete-time model. Good discussions of this issue can be found in Allison (1982), Blossfeld et al. (1989), Cox and Oakes (1984), Hamerle, (1987), and Kalbfleisch and Prentice (1980).

DISCRETE-TIME MODELS

Discrete-time analysis is appropriate if state changes are proportionally high per interval (i.e., ties), and then only if the conditional probabilities of changing states are consistently less than .1 per interval (Yamaguchi, 1991). Since the discrete-time model generates parameter estimates that converge with those generated by the continuous-time model as the intervals get smaller, this default to the discrete-time hazard should not be perceived as somehow being a second tier analysis (see Willett & Singer, 1993, or Yamaguchi, 1991, for a discussion). Moreover, another benefit of the discrete-time model other than its ability to handle ties is that it can be estimated using standard statistical software. Although there are several methods to estimate the discrete-time model, most users of this model agree that the logistic regression format is the easiest (see Allison, 1982; Hamerle, 1987; Cox & Oakes, 1984; Yamaguchi, 1991).

However, before hazard estimates can be generated using the logit regression model, the data must first be transformed to meaningfully represent the hazard process. This data transformation requires that each event be transformed from the usual single-subject, single-record format to a single-subject, multiple-record format, where the number of records equals the number of time units spent in the state (illustrated in Appendix A). For example, a noncensored 4-second episode for Subject A requires a single record in a continuous-time dataset, whereas in a discrete-time dataset this must be transformed into four records for Subject A, each containing identical information, except that the first three records are listed as censored (0) and the final record is listed as noncensored (1). In the logistic regression model the censoring represents the dependent variable where nonoccurrence (censored) = 0 and occurrence = 1. Although altering the subject-time unit appears to artificially inflate the sample size and thus create a downward bias in the standard errors, Allison (1982) demonstrated the estimated standard errors are consistent estimators of the true standard errors.

With a dichotomous dependent variable, the fitted model estimates the *log-odds* (representing the hazard) of the event occurring within the time interval, given the covariate values, assuming that the event has not yet occurred (see discrete-time hazard definition). Stated differently, the logistic model allows an investigator to estimate the log-odds of event occurring during an interval of time as a function of the covariate values. This strategy can be extended to a polytomous dependent variable using a multinomial logit model.

Allison (1982, 1984), Willett and Singer (1993), and Yamaguchi (1991) provide excellent overviews of the assumption, data construction methods, and illustrations of the discrete-time model. Hamerle (1987) and Yamaguchi (1990) provide an advanced treatment of the model.

CONTINUOUS-TIME MODELS

If the frequency of ties is inconsequential then the continuous-time model is appropriate. Within continuous-time models the first decision is whether the investigator's research questions need information about the shape of the baseline hazard rate over time. Specifically, are hypotheses formed in such a way that it is necessary to know whether the baseline hazard rate increases over time or initially increases then decreases? If so, then the parametric model is appropriate. On the other hand, if the investigator is simply interested in the effect of covariate values on the hazard rate, then the proportional hazards model is adequate.

Assuming that the investigator is interested in hazard change over time, then assessing the presence of duration dependency is the first of many steps necessary to determine the functional form of the time dependency. The initial step would be to take a nonparametric estimate (e.g., Kaplan-Meier, 1958) of the survivor function ($S(t)$), then take the negative of the natural log of that function and plot it against time. This $-Ln(S(t))$ is an estimate of the cumulative hazard illustrated in Figure 10.3, and, as noted in the description of that figure, if the line has a slope of 1, indicating a constant hazard, then duration dependence is not evident, but a slope away from 1 suggest duration dependency. In most cases there is evidence of duration dependency.

After duration dependency has been demonstrated it becomes much more difficult to determine the appropriate parametric model. The first step is to fit an exponential regression model with covariates. The exponential model is almost always untenable because it assumes a constant hazard rate, and there are probably few naturally occurring social processes that have a constant hazard. Next, the flexible Weibull model with covariates is fit to the data, and since the exponential is a special case of the Weibull a comparison of log-likelihoods is appropriate, and if a significant difference is found, as is usually the case, the exponential model is abandoned. After the exponential model has been rejected, the investigator must next model the data using existing curves. Unfortunately, heuristic examples by Blossfeld et al. (1989) and substantive findings by Hannan and Freeman (1989) illustrate the difficulty in distinguishing not only within a family of curves (e.g., monotonic (Weibull versus Gomperz) or nonmonotonic (log normal versus log logistic)) but also the difficulty determining fit across types of curves (e.g., monotonic versus nonmonotonic). In fact, it is possible that a *best-fitting* model can be completely misspecified (see Arminger, 1987). To aid the investigator determine the appropriate form of the duration dependency, researchers have developed numerous numerical and plotting methods. For example, Blossfeld et al. (1989) provide an overview of the numerical methods, and they also illustrate how, by varying the time scale on the x axis, the plot of the cumulative hazard, used as an estimate of the residual, can be used to determine the data's fit in parametric models. Lawless (1982) and Nelson (1982) also provide good illustrations of plotting methods.

Two points yet need to be emphasized: first, it has been repeatedly noted that social science data may not readily fit known distributions; second, for most substantive questions about social and especially microsocial processes the shape of the baseline hazard is not as important as determining general covariate influence. As such, the analyst using microsocial data may waste valuable time attempting to specify the duration dependency form (see Allison, 1984; Hutchison, 1988a; Yamaguchi, 1991).

An alternative approach is to ignore the shape of the baseline hazard and examine only the influence of the covariates. This is the Cox proportional hazards model. Several points should be made about the proportional hazards model relative to the definition provided previously. First, the proportional hazards model is sensitive to sample size because of the way the partial-likelihood estimation procedure (PL) uses the temporal order of durations to generate parameter estimates. The discrepancies between parameter estimates generated by the maximum-likelihood method and those generated by the partial-likelihood method tend to decrease as sample size increases. Thus efforts should be made to secure a large sample in order to have confidence in the parameter estimates.

Second, the Cox model is sensitive to ties. An investigator must be cautious interpreting parameter estimates generated by data exceeding the proportion of ties discussed in the guidelines recommended previously. Aside from these caveats, the proportional hazard models is generally considered the bet all-around method for analyzing event histories (Allison, 1984; Hutchison, 1988a).

As noted (see definitions), the proportional hazards rate factors the likelihood function into basically two parts, one estimates the covariate influences, and the other estimates the shape of the duration dependency. The Cox model ignores the information about the shape of the baseline hazard. To employ this factorization an assumption must be made: for any two individuals having unique covariate scores, the ratio of their hazards is a constant (proportional) at any point in time.

Although this model is somewhat robust to the violation of this assumption, if a variable is nonproportional it is preferable to stratify the variable in order to estimate the best model (Blossfeld et al., 1989). Stratifying splits the covariate into multiple levels (e.g., gender). By stratifying, the semiparametric model permits a general estimate of the covariate influence across different levels of the covariate, but the baseline hazard is allowed to vary, and yet remain unspecified (Cox & Oakes, 1984).

Each covariate should be tested for proportionality before retaining it in the model. To determine proportionality, an interaction term is created by multiplying the covariate with duration or Ln(duration), and included in the initial model without stratification. If this interaction term is significant then a new model is specified using the covariate as a stratification variable, this is referred to as a stratified proportional hazards model. Or the significant interaction term can remain in the model, and the larger model is called a nonproportional hazards model (see Yamaguchi, 1991). Finally, if one covariate is being used as the stratification variable, additional interaction terms can be included in the general model (see, e.g., Table 10.1). For most analyses the interaction terms can be generated using covariate $*$ [Ln(duration) $-$ Ln(average duration)] (see Blossfeld et al., 1989, pp. 147–148; Yamaguchi, 1991, p. 107).

In conjunction with the above statistical method for determining proportionality, an analyst can also plot the natural log of the cumulative hazard against time to provide a visual means of examining the proportionality of a stratified covariate (Kalbfleisch & Prentice, 1980). Since, as noted, minus the natural log of the survivor function ($-$Ln $S(t)$) is an estimate of the cumulative hazard, this plot (Ln $-$ Ln $S(t)$) is often called the log minus log plot, or the log minus log survivor function plot (see Griffin, 1993b, Figure 2). It is useful for examining where along the time axis the interaction occurs.

In summary, data should be collected in continuous time using the smallest unit of time possible relative to the phenomena being studied. If ties occur frequently per interval of time, then the investigator should consider discrete-time models. If ties are not abundant, then the next step is determined by the structure of the research questions. Specifically, to adequately test the hypotheses is it necessary to determine the shape of the baseline hazard rate. If the answer is yes, then a parametric model is appropriate, an if the answer is no then the Cox proportional hazard model is most appropriate.

CONCLUSION

This chapter is a general overview of how event-history analysis can be used to examine state changes using microsocial data. An attempt was made to address major terms and concepts without burdening the reader with too much detail. Some relevant event-history analysis information was purposely omitted in an effort not to confuse or discourage the potential user of this method. For additional study the reader is referred to the papers and texts listed in Griffin (1993a, Appendix A). Finally, this chapter is intended to encourage investigators using microsocial data to consider this methodology if their research questions warrant an examination of the interdependence between time and state change.

ACKNOWLEDGMENTS

I extend my thanks to Bill Gardner, with whom I have had many enlightening conversations about applying event-history analysis to microsocial data, and to John Gottman for providing a work environment that permitted these conversations to bear fruit. I also want to thank Sonia Krainz for her comments on an earlier version of this chapter. Appendix A and Figure 10.6 were previously published in the *Journal of Family Psychology* and are reprinted here with the permission of the American Psychological Association. Correspondence should be sent to Marital Interaction Lab, Department of Family Resources and Human Development, YHE 2502, Arizona State University, Tempe, AZ 85287.

REFERENCES

Allison, P. D. (1982). Discrete-time methods for the analysis of event histories. In S. Leinhardt (Ed.), *Sociological methodology 1982* (pp. 61–98). San Francisco: Jossey-Bass.

Allison, P. D. (1984). *Event history analysis: Regression for longitudinal event data.* Beverly Hills, CA: Sage.

Arminger, G. (1987). Testing against misspecification in parametric rate models. In K. U. Mayer and N. B. Tuma (Eds.), *Applications of event history analysis in life course research* (pp. 679–699). Madison: University of Wisconsin Press.

Blossfeld, H. P., Hamerle, A., & Mayer, K. (1989). *Event history analysis: Statistical theory and application in the social sciences.* Hillsdale, NJ: Erlbaum.

Breslow, N. E. (1974). Covariance analysis of censored survival data. *Biometrics, 30,* 89–100.

Cox, D. R. (1972). Regression models and life-tables (with discussion). *Journal of the Royal Statistical Society B, 34,* 187–220.

Cox, D. R., & Oakes, D. (1984). *Analysis of survival data.* London: Chapman and Hall.

Fincham, F. D., Bradbury, T., & Scott, C. K. (1991). Cognition in marriage. In F. D. Fincham & T. N. Bradbury (Eds.), *The Psychology of Marriage* (pp. 118–149). New York: Guilford.

Gardner, W., & Griffin, W. A. (1989). Methods for the analysis of parallel streams of continuously recorded social behaviors. *Psychological Bulletin, 105,* 446–455.

Gottman, J. M. (1990). How marriages change. In Gerald R. Patterson (Ed.), *Family social interaction: Content and methodological issues in the study of aggression and depression* (pp. 75–101). Hillsdale, NJ: Lawrence Erlbaum.

Gottman, J. M. (1982). Temporal form: Toward a new language for describing relationships. *Journal of Marriage and the Family, 44,* 943–962.

Griffin, W. A. (1993a). Event history analysis of marital and family interactions: A practical introduction. *Journal of Family Psychology, 6*(3), 211–229.

Griffin, W. A. (1993b). Transitions from negative affect during marital interaction: Husband and wife differences. *Journal of Family Psychology, 6*(3), 230–244.

Griffin, W. A., & Gardner, W. (1989). Analysis of behavioral durations in observational studies of social interaction. *Psychological Bulletin, 106*, 497–502.

Griffin, W. A., & Gottman, J. M. (1990). Statistical methods for analyzing family interaction. In G. R. Patterson (Ed.), *Family social interaction: Content and methodological issues in the study of aggression and depression* (pp. 131–168). Hillsdale, NJ: Lawrence Erlbaum Associates.

Griffin, W. A., & Greene, S. (1994). Social interaction and symptom sequences: A case study of orofacial bradykinesia exacerbation in Parkinson's disease during negative marital interaction. *Psychiatry, 57*, 269–274.

Hamerle, A. (1987). Regression analysis for discrete event history or failure time data. In K. U. Mayer and N. B. Tuma (Eds.), *Applications of event history analysis in life course research* (pp. 609–627). Madison: University of Wisconsin Press.

Hannan, M. T., & Freeman, J. (199). *Organizational ecology.* Cambridge, MA: Cambridge University Press.

Heckman, J. J., & Singer, B. (1984). A method for minimizing the impact of distributional assumptions in econometric models for duration data. *Econometrica, 52*, 271–320.

Heckman, J. J., & Walker, J. (1987). Using goodness of fit and other criteria to choose among competing duration models: A case study of Hutterite data. In C. Clogg (Ed.), *Sociological methodology 1987* (pp. 247–307). San Francisco: Jossey-Bass.

Huitema, B. E., & McKean, J. W. (1991). Autocorrelation estimation and inference with small samples. *Psychological Bulletin, 110*, 291–304.

Hutchison, D. (1988a). Event history and survival analysis in the social sciences: I. Background and introduction. *Quality & Quantity, 22*, 203–219.

Hutchison, D. (1988b). Event history and survival analysis in the social sciences: II. Advanced applications and recent developments. *Quality & Quantity, 22*, 255–278.

Kalbfleisch, J. D., & Prentice, R. L. (1980). *The statistical analysis of failure time data.* New York: Wiley.

Kaplan, E. L., & Meier, P. (1958). Nonparametric estimation from incomplete observations. *Journal of the American Statistical Association, 53*, 457–481.

Lawless, J. F. (1982). *Statistical models and methods for lifetime data.* New York: Wiley.

Nelson, W. (1982). *Applied life data analysis.* New York: Wiley.

Patterson, G. R. (1982). *Coercive family process.* Eugene, OR: Castalia.

Patterson, G. R., & Reid, J. B. (1984). Social interactional processes within the family: The study of the moment-by-moment family transactions in which human social development is imbedded. *Journal of Applied Developmental Psychology, 5*, 237–262.

Reid, J. B. (1986). Social-interactional patterns in families of abused and nonabused children. In C. Zahn-Waxler, E. M. Cummings & R. Iannotti (Eds.), *Altruism and aggression: Biological and social origins* (pp. 239–255). New York: Cambridge University Press.

Reiss, D. (1981). *The family's construction of reality.* Cambridge: Harvard University Press.

Rogosa, D., & Ghandour, G. (1991). Statistical models for behaviors observations. *Journal of Educational Statistics, 16*, 157–252.

Singer, J. D., & Willett, J. B. (1991). Modeling the days of our lives: Using survival analysis when designing and analyzing longitudinal studies of duration and the timing of events. *Psychological Bulletin, 110*(2), 268–290.

Trussell, J., & Richards, T. (1985). Correcting for unmeasured heterogeneity in hazard models using the Heckman-Singer procedure. In N. B. Tuma (Ed.), *Sociological methodology 1985* (pp. 242–276). San Francisco: Jossey-Bass.

Tuma, N. B., & Hannan, M. (1984). *Social dynamics: Models and methods.* New York: Academic Press.

Vuchinich, S., Teachman, J., & Crosby, L. (1991). Families and hazard rates that change over time: Some methodological issues in analyzing transitions. *Journal of Marriage and the Family, 53*, 898–912.

Willett, J. B., & Singer, J. D. (1993). Investigation onset, cessation, relapse, and recovery: Why you should, and how you can, use discrete-time survival analysis to examine event occurrence. *Journal of Consulting and Clinical Psychology, 61,* 952–965.

Yamaguchi, K. (1991). *Event history analysis.* Newbury Park, CA: Sage.

Yamaguchi, K. (1986). Alternative approaches to unobserved heterogeneity in the analysis of repeatable events. In N. Tuma (Ed.), *Sociological methodology 1986* (pp. 213–249). San Francisco: Jossey-Bass.

Yamaguchi, K. (1990). Logit and multinomial logit models for discrete-time event-history analysis: a causal analysis of interdependent discrete-state processes. *Quality & Quantity, 24,* 323–341.

Yamaguchi, K., & Kandel, D. B. (1987). Drug use and other determinants of premarital pregnancy and its outcome: A dynamic analysis of competing life events. *Journal of Marriage and the Family, 49,* 257–270.

APPENDIX A

Continuous Data Format					Discrete Data Format				
Single Subject, Single Record					Single Subject, Multiple Records				
					Time	ID	Censor	Session	Monitor
					1	1	0	−0.1637	−0.73
					2	1	0	−0.1637	−0.73
					3	1	0	−0.1637	−0.73
					4	1	0	−0.1637	−0.73
Duration	ID	Censor	Session	Monitor	1	1	0	−0.1637	−0.73
					2	1	1	−0.1637	−0.73
4	1	0	−0.1637	−0.73	1	1	0	−0.1637	−0.73
2	1	1	−0.1637	−0.73	2	1	0	−0.1637	−0.73
6	1	1	−0.1637	−0.73	3	1	0	−0.1637	−0.73
2	2	1	−1.4232	−2.199	4	1	0	−0.1637	−0.73
5	3	0	1.0957	−1.903	5	1	0	−0.1637	−0.73
1	4	0	−1.4232	−0.16	6	1	1	−0.1637	−0.73
2	4	1	−0.1637	−0.16	1	2	0	−1.4232	−2.199
4	4	1	1.0957	−0.16	2	2	1	−1.4232	−2.199
3	5	1	−1.4231	−0.223	1	3	0	1.0957	−1.903
					2	3	0	1.0957	−1.903
					3	3	0	1.0957	−1.903
					4	3	0	1.0957	−1.903
					5	3	0	1.0957	−1.903
					1	4	0	−1.4232	−0.16
					1	4	0	−0.1637	−0.16
					2	4	1	−0.1637	−0.16
					1	4	0	1.0957	−0.16
					2	4	0	1.0957	−0.16
					3	4	0	1.0957	−0.16
					4	4	1	1.0957	−0.16
					1	5	0	−1.4231	−0.223
					2	5	0	−1.4231	−0.223
					3	5	1	−1.4231	−0.223

As noted, data are arranged differently, depending on whether the investigator will use discrete- or continuous-time analysis. A sample dataset showing the two arrangements is given above. These data are from five subjects (note ID), two having multiple entries. Two standardized quantitative variables are included for illustration purposes. Note that the discrete-time dataset is larger because each unit of time receives a separate record. Connecting lines between the format columns show corresponding data. These formats are typical of the formatting required for most statistical packages (see Singer & Willett, 1991, for additional illustrations). Finally, observe the method of altering the censoring indicator (Censor) in the discrete-time format relative to the continuous-time format. In discrete, the indicator is zero except for the final time unit in each event when it is either 1 or zero, depending on whether the event ended or was censored, respectively.

11

On the Reliability of Sequential Data: Measurement, Meaning, and Correction

William Gardner
University of Pittsburgh

> *In this chapter, Gardner tackles the tricky problem of determining the proper estimates of reliability for sequential observational data.*
>
> —Editor

Many investigators are collecting data on social interaction through direct observation of behavior (for example, Patterson, 1982; for an application in the study of developmental change, see Graham, Collins, Wugalter, Chung, & Hansen, 1991). Techniques for the analysis of the temporal patterning of sequences of categorical data are known as sequential analysis (Gardner & Griffin, 1989; Gottman & Roy, 1990; Sackett, 1976, 1987). Because it is difficult to accurately classify social behaviors, the practical implementation of observational technologies has been extensively studied (see reviews and commentary in Cone, 1977; Cone & Foster, 1982; Foster & Cone, 1980; Hartmann, 1977; Hartmann & Wood, 1990). Sequential analysts (for example, Bakeman & Gottman, 1986) have stressed the importance of accurately classifying sequential categorical data and of frequently assessing the reliability of those measurements.

Few sequential analysts, however, seem to grasp the magnitude of the problems that inaccurate measurement can cause (Schwartz, 1985; for a rare example of statistical interest in this issue, see Rogosa & Ghandour, 1991). Similarly, the statistical properties of reliability measures for sequential analysis have received little attention. Sequential analysts frequently employ the κ statistic (Cohen, 1960) to measure the reliability of sequential data, perhaps because it has been widely recommended as a measure of the reliability of psychiatric diagnosis (Spitzer, Cohen, Fleiss, & Endicott, 1967). There have, however, been many criticisms of the use of κ to evaluate the reliability of diagnosis (for example, Grove et al., 1981; Siegel, Podgor, & Remaley, 1992), raising issues that may also apply to the use of κ in sequential analysis (see also Cicchetti & Feinstein, 1990; Feinstein & Cicchetti, 1990; and Uebersax, 1987, 1988).

This chapter describes how estimates of conditional probabilities of sequential behaviors are affected by inaccurate classifications of those behaviors. It also discusses the utility of κ as an assessment of the reliability of observation in sequential analysis. I begin with the presentation of a model for imperfectly measured categorical sequential data that distinguishes between latent (or true) and manifest (or observed) behavioral states. The sequence of latent states is generated by a stochastic process called the sequential process. The manifest states are generated from the latent states by another process called the measurement process. The probability model defined by the sequential and measurement processes is used to calculate expected values of conditional probabilities estimated from unreliable sequential data. It is shown that unreliably measured sequential systems, particularly those in which the base rates of critical behaviors are low, can generate inaccurate sequential statistics whose substantive interpretation contradicts the natural interpretation of the parameters of the sequential process.

In light of these problems, how should we measure the reliability of sequential data? The chapter illustrates how κ depends not only on the accuracy with which coders record behaviors, but also on the base rates of the latent behaviors, and it discusses the problems of interpretation this may cause. As an alternative to κ, it is recommended that sequential analysts assess the accuracy of classification by comparing coded observations against a true criterion. When feasible, this approach offers more information about the location of measurement problems and a clearer indication of how serious they could be than can be obtained from calculating κ alone. A formula for correcting manifest sequential statistics for unreliability is presented. This formula can be used to check the sensitivity of the results of a sequential analysis to reliability problems. Unfortunately, in many cases it will be impractical or impossible to compare coder's classification with a true criterion. In these cases, researchers must find means of assessing the accuracy of sequential data from agreements between observers. The chapter concludes with a suggestion about how methods for this purpose might be developed using techniques from latent structure analysis (Goodman, 1974).

UNRELIABILITY IN SEQUENTIAL DATA

Latent and Manifest Behavioral States

Latent Sequential States

Measurement problems in sequential analysis are probably most severe in data sets with large numbers of codable behavioral states, some of which will undoubtedly have small base rates. However, these problems can also be studied in data based on simple, dichotomous codes, and the statistics of such systems are much easier to understand. Suppose that we are observing a conversation between a wife and husband and we code the emotional valence of each alternating turn as positive or negative. The four possible true or latent states in the interaction are labeled h_+, h_-, w_+, and w_-, that is, husband true positive, husband true negative, and so on. Because turns alternate, h_+ can only be followed by w_+ or w_-, and similarly for the other states (see Figure 11.1). The process being observed, then, consists of a single, long stream of alternating husband and wife states.[1] These states are either positive or negative through a realization of a stochastic process. Assume that this true process is a Markov process (Çinlar, 1975), meaning that the probability distribution of the current behavioral state is conditional only on the immediately preceding state. Although this may not be a realistic assumption in many social interactive systems, it is tacitly assumed in most sequential analyses. Let p_{ab} be the probability that a latent state b will occur, given that it was preceded by a state a, so that $p_{w_+h_-}$ is the conditional

---

[1] In most research projects sequences from many dyads would be observed. Accounting for individual differences among sequences of social interactive data is important, but introduces complexities that cannot be addressed here. See Gardner (1990, 1993) and Gottman and Roy (1990) for further discussion.

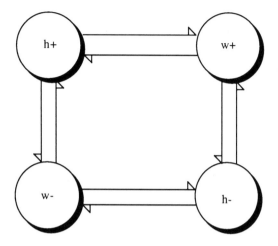

FIG. 11.1.   A state-space diagram for the marital example. An arrow from one state to another indicates that sequential transitions between states are possible.

probability that a husband true negative will follow a wife true positive. These conditional probabilities are the raw materials for much of sequential analysis (Bakeman & Gottman, 1986; Gottman & Roy, 1990).

The behaviors in the sequence are coded by observers and the resulting sequence of codes are the manifest sequential states. The manifest states will be labeled $\dot{h}_+$, $\dot{h}_-$, and so on, to distinguish them from the corresponding latent states. The data used to estimate the conditional probabilities are the counts of transitions from one step to the next. In the following excerpt from a stream of codes, $\ldots \dot{w}_-\dot{h}_-\dot{w}_+\underline{\dot{h}_-\dot{w}_+}\dot{h}_+ \ldots$, the fourth transition is a husband negative $\rightarrow$ wife positive transition. The estimated conditional probability that a husband true negative will follow a wife true positive will be

$$\hat{p}_{w_+h_-} = \frac{f_{\dot{w}_+h_-}}{f_{\dot{w}_+h_+} + f_{\dot{w}_+h_-}}, \qquad (11.1)$$

where f_{ab} is the count of the times that manifest state b is observed to follow state $\dot{a}$. This formula assumes that the counts are random but correct in the sense that, for example, every latent h_+ in the sample stream was correctly classified as a manifest husband positive ($\dot{h}_+$).

Analysts use estimated conditional probabilities like Equation 11.1 to describe social interactive processes. For example, the conditional probability that a wife negative will occur given a prior husband negative could be compared to the base rate negativity of the wife, where the base rate is the proportion of the total wife behavioral states in which she is negative. If the conditional probability is higher than the base rate, it suggests that the wife reciprocates the negative affect of the husband. In the following we will investigate how estimated conditional probabilities, and the inferences that may be drawn from them, are affected by the accuracy of measurement and the probability distribution of the latent sequential states.

The Sequential Process

To study the properties of the estimated conditional probabilities, we need to define a statistical model for the latent sequential states and their measurement. Suppose for the moment that coding is perfectly accurate, so that $f_{ab} = f_{ab}$, where f_{ab} is the count of (typically unobservable) latent $a \to b$ transitions. Let g_{ab} be the unconditional probability of an $a \to b$ transition, where $\Sigma_a \Sigma_b g_{ab} = 1$. Then

$$E[\hat{p}_{ab}] = p_{ab} = \frac{g_{ab}}{\pi_a},$$ (11.2)

where $\pi_a = \Sigma_b g_{ab}$ is the unconditional probability of the latent state a occurring in the chain (Anderson & Goodman, 1957). We place these probabilities in a vector $\pi' = [\pi_{h_+} \quad \pi_{h_-} \quad \pi_{w_+} \quad \pi_{w_-}]$. Also, the p_{ab} conditional probabilities are placed in a matrix.

$$P = \begin{bmatrix} 0 & 0 & p_{h_+w_+} & p_{h_+w_-} \\ 0 & 0 & p_{h_-w_+} & p_{h_-w_-} \\ p_{w_+h_+} & p_{w_+h_-} & 0 & 0 \\ p_{w_-h_+} & p_{w_-h_-} & 0 & 0 \end{bmatrix}$$

The rows of P are identified with the antecedent latent states in the order h_+, h_-, w_+, and w_-, and the columns are similarly identified with the consequent latent states.

The unconditional probabilities of the latent states (that is, π) are determined when P is given.[2] Then the unconditional probabilities of transitions between latent states are in

---

[2]One can find π from P as follows. First, label the blocks in P,

$$P = \begin{bmatrix} 0 & A \\ B & 0 \end{bmatrix}.$$

Let $\pi' = [\pi_h' \quad \pi_w']$, where $\pi_{h_+} + \pi_{h_-} = \pi_{w_+} + \pi_{w_-} = 1/2$. Systems like the one described in Figure 11.1 are periodic Markov chains, in this case with period 2, meaning that the chain alternates between discrete classes of states. The matrix

$$P^2 = \begin{bmatrix} AB & 0 \\ 0 & BA \end{bmatrix}$$ (11.3)

contains the conditional probabilities describing two-turn transitions from husband state to husband state (AB) and wife state to wife state (BA). These matrices can be used to find the base rate distributions of the husband's and wife's behaviors. It can be shown (for example, in Çinlar, 1975) that in chains like (11.3), the base rate vectors will obey the relations $2\pi_w' AB = 2\pi_w'$ and $2\pi_h' BA = 2\pi_h'$. Hence $2\pi_w'$ is a row eigenvector of AB associated with an eigenvalue equal to 1 (and similarly for $2\pi_h'$ and BA), so that π is determined and calculable when P is specified. To calculate, for example, $2\pi_h$, note that $1'\pi_h = 1/2$ and $(I - A'B')\pi_h = 0$. Therefore we can write $C' = [I - BA \quad 1]$ and $\pi_h' C' = [0 \quad 1/2]$. Then as long as C has full column rank, $\pi_h' = [0 \quad 1/2] C(C'C)^{-1}$.

$$G = \text{Diag}(\pi)P, \tag{11.4}$$

where the elements of G are either g_{ab} or 0, corresponding to the pattern in P, and the function $\text{Diag}(\cdot)$ is a diagonal matrix where the diagonal is the argument vector.

The Measurement Process

The direct estimation of a conditional probability from the observed frequencies Equation 11.1 assumes that observers coded the latent states correctly. What happens to the estimates when coding is imperfect? To capture the fallibility of measurement, we assume that a coder's classifications are affected only by the present latent state, which means that they are independent of prior states or coding decisions. We also suppose that the accuracy of coding a wife's positive or negative states is the same as for the corresponding states of the husband. These are restrictive and possibly unrealistic assumptions about classification errors. A more realistic model might account for the possibility that coders' decisions are affected by their previous coding decisions. This means that the probability of coding positive depends not only on whether the coder is presently looking at a latent positive or negative state, but also on how the coder classified the previous state. If coder classifications are affected by prior classifications, it would mean that there is a time-dependent structure in the manifest states as well as the latent states.[3] But even if the model fails to include some important components of the processes that generate behavioral observations, it is far more realistic than the assumption implicit in everyday sequential analysis. When analysts use Equation 11.1 to estimate conditional probabilities, they are behaving as if there were no classification errors at all.

Suppose that an observer has a probability r_{++} of coding a positive state given that a positive latent state occurred, and $r_{+-} = 1 - r_{++}$ of classifying the positive as negative. Defining r_{--} similarly, let

$$R = \begin{bmatrix} r_{++} & r_{+-} \\ r_{-+} & r_{--} \end{bmatrix}.$$

Let $g_{\dot{a}b}$ be the unconditional probability that a coder will record an $\dot{a} \rightarrow b$ transition. Then the unconditional probability that a randomly sampled manifest transition will be a husband negative followed by a wife positive ($h_- \rightarrow w_+$) is

$$\begin{aligned} g_{h-\dot{w}+} &= (r_{+-}\pi_{h_+}p_{h_+w_+}r_{++}) + (r_{+-}\pi_{h_+}p_{h_+w_-}r_{-+}) + \\ & (r_{--}\pi_{h_-}p_{h_-w_+}r_{++}) + (r_{--}\pi_{h_-}p_{h_-w_-}r_{-+}). \end{aligned}$$

The first term of the sum is the probability that a latent husband positive occurred, was misclassified as a negative, and was followed by a correctly classi-

---

[3]The key idea is that observer expectations create sequential dependencies between manifest behaviors over and above the dependencies that derive from the underlying latent process. Ideas about how this might be modeled are in Hagenaars (1988).

fied latent wife positive. Thus when coding is fallible, the manifest frequency of (for example) husband negative to wife positive transitions is likely to include portions of latent $h_- \rightarrow w_-$, $h_+ \rightarrow w_+$, and $h_+ \rightarrow w_-$ transitions that have been misclassified as $\dot{h}_- \rightarrow \dot{w}_+$. Notice that when reliability is perfect, that is $r_{++} = r_{--} = 1$, then $g_{h_-\dot{w}_+} = \pi_h\,p_{h_-w_+} = g_{h_-w_+}$. Modifying Equation 11.4 to include fallible measurement gives

$$\dot{G} = (I \otimes R)^t \mathrm{Diag}(\pi) P (I \otimes R). \tag{11.5}$$

The next section uses Equation 11.5 to find the expected values of the estimated probabilities (that is, $\hat{P}$) when measurement is unreliable.

Estimating Conditional Probabilities from Unreliable Data

Next we examine the bias in the estimation of P induced by inaccurate measurement. As (11.5) implies, the expected value of an estimated conditional probability $\hat{p}_{ab}$ involves every parameter of the latent sequential process and many measurement parameters suggesting that $E[\hat{p}_{ab}]$ may differ substantially from p_{ab}. It is straightforward to use Equations 11.2 and 11.5 to calculate the expected value of $\hat{P}$ for specific values of P and R.

To make these calculations more easily interpretable, I rewrite P in terms of more interesting parameters.[4] The conditional probabilities describing wife responses are rewritten as functions of new parameters ϕ_w and β_w. The ϕ_w parameter $(-1 \leq \phi_w \leq 1)$ indexes the reciprocity of the wife: $\phi_w > 0$ means that the wife responds positively to a husband positive and negatively to a husband negative, $\phi_w < 0$ means that she responds to positives with negatives and to negatives with positives, and $\phi_w = 0$ means that she responds noncontingently. The β_w parameter $(0 < \beta_w < 1)$ determines the wife's underlying emotional valance, in the sense that it would be the base rate of positives she would exhibit

---

[4]Here is how to write P in terms of the base rate and reciprocity parameters. Let $\beta_h = p_{w_-h_+}/(p_{w_-h_+} + p_{w_+h_-})$. Let $\phi_h = 1 - p_{w_-h_+} - p_{w_+h_-}$. Then $[\beta_h \quad 1 - \beta_h]$ is the row eigenvector of B associated with the eigenvalue 1 and ϕ_h is the second eigenvalue of B. Define β_w and ϕ_w similarly in terms of A. Substitution then gives

$$P = \begin{bmatrix} 0 & 0 & \phi_w + \beta_w - \phi_w\beta_w & (1 - \phi_w)(1 - \beta_w) \\ 0 & 0 & \beta_w(1 - \phi_w) & 1 - \beta_w + \phi_w\beta_w \\ \phi_h + \beta_h - \phi_h\beta_h & (1 - \phi_h)(1 - \beta_h) & 0 & 0 \\ \beta_h(1 - \phi_h) & 1 - \beta_h + \phi_h\beta_h & 0 & 0 \end{bmatrix} \tag{11.6}$$

In Figure 11.3, the ϕ and β parameters are identical for husband and wife. This means that in Equation 11.3 $A = B$ and that P is identical to Equation 11.6 but with the subscripts dropped from all terms. Then $2\pi_h^t A^2 = 2\pi_h^t = 2\pi_w^t A^2 = 2\pi_w^t$. It can be shown that the row eigenvector associated with A^2 that solves these equations has the form $[c_{21}/(c_{21} + c_{12}) \quad c_{12}/(c_{21} + c_{12})]$. Replacing c_{12} and c_{21} with the corresponding elements from A^2 and simplifying, we find that $2\pi_h^t = 2\pi_w^t = [\beta \quad 1 - \beta]$. This shows that β will be the base rate of positive behaviors for both husband and wife in Figure 11.3.

if she interacted with someone exactly like herself. We reparameterize the rows describing the husband's responses similarly with β_h and ϕ_h.

These new parameters of the sequential process and the measurement parameters were then varied to explore their effects on the estimated conditional probabilities. The following example illustrates the central finding. Suppose that the husband has a strongly tit-for-tat interactive style ($\phi_h = .4$) and would be negative half the time if he interacted with someone like himself ($\beta_h = .5$). Luckily for him, however, he is married to a very positive woman ($\beta_w = .9$) who tends not to retaliate ($\phi_w = .1$). Then the conditional probabilities describing transitions among the latent states are

$$P = \begin{bmatrix} 0 & 0 & .91 & .09 \\ 0 & 0 & .81 & .19 \\ .7 & .3 & 0 & 0 \\ .3 & .7 & 0 & 0 \end{bmatrix} \tag{11.7}$$

In this dyad the husband will respond positively 65% of the time, more than the 50% implied by $\beta_h = .5$, because he is reciprocating the behaviors of his positively disposed wife. She responds positively 87.5% of the time, less than the 90% implied by β_w because she occasionally reciprocates the negativity of her husband.

Now suppose that the accuracy of measurement is $r_{++} = r_{--} = .8$, a discouragingly low value, but possibly representative of the accuracy of classification for some social behaviors or expressions of affect. The expected values of the conditional probability estimates calculated from unreliable data will be $E[\hat{p}_{ab}] = g_{ab}/\Sigma_b g_{ab}$. Then for our example,

$$E[\hat{P}] = \begin{bmatrix} 0 & 0 & .739 & .261 \\ 0 & 0 & .705 & .295 \\ .612 & .388 & 0 & 0 \\ .533 & .467 & 0 & 0 \end{bmatrix} \tag{11.8}$$

In this example, the effect of the unreliability is, first, that in the sequential process 11.7, $\hat{p}_{h_+w_+} < p_{h_+w_+}$, $\hat{p}_{h_-w_+} < p_{h_-w_+}$, and $\hat{p}_{w_+h_+} < p_{w_+h_+}$. In each case, a distribution of conditional probabilities that was sharply skewed is less skewed in the manifest data. The primary problem is that misclassification of sequential behaviors obscures how the conditional probabilities of a subject will vary as a function of the antecedent behavior of the spouse. Consider, for example, the wife's responses to husband negative behaviors (the second row of Equation 11.8). If 1,000 transitions had been observed, we would expect 175 latent husband negatives, followed by 141.75 latent wife positive and 33.25 latent wife negative responses. As Table 11.1 illustrates, when these latent wife responses are classified by coders who are equally unreliable for positive and negative states, many more latent positive responses are misclassified as negatives than vice versa. Therefore, wife negative responses are more common in the manifest

TABLE 11.1
Classifications of Wife Responses
to Latent Husband Negative Behaviors

| Latent Responses | Manifest Responses[a] | | |
	$\dot{\omega}_+$	$\dot{\omega}_-$	Total
ω_+	113.4	28.35	141.75
ω_-	6.65	26.6	33.25
Total	120.05	54.95	175

[a]Numbers are expected frequencies.

data than they should be, reducing the true difference between her rates of negative and positive responding conditional on a husband behavior.

This phenomenon departs from intuitions about the effects of unreliability that many researchers will have acquired during the study of classical psychometric theory (see, for example, Crocker & Algina, 1986). In that theory errors appear as symmetrically distributed random shocks that increase the sampling variance of, for example, sample means, without affecting their expected value. In this case, however, the effect of unreliability is to bias the estimation of a primary sequential statistic, and the size of the bias will be proportional to the skew in the baserates (Rogosa, personal communication, May 25, 1991).

The second effect of misclassifications is even more disturbing. In the latent sequential process 11.7, $p_{w\_h\_}$ is significantly larger than $p_{w\_h\_+}$, meaning that the husband reciprocates negatives for negatives. The reversal of the pattern of a person's responding conditional on the other's behavior is the essence of the tit-for-tat style. But in the conditional probabilities estimated from the manifest data (Equation 11.8) $\hat{p}_{w\_h\_} < \hat{p}_{w\_h\_+}$. In the manifest data, it looks as though the husband usually responds positively whatever the wife does, whereas in the latent data he is very negative in response to her negatives. Using the unreliable manifest data we are likely to substantially misinterpret the husband's interactive style.

To explain why this happens, we continue the numerical example presented above. The expected number of latent wife positives and negatives will be 437.5 and 62.5 respectively. Table 11.2 shows how these wife antecedents would be classified. Misclassified latent wife positives are so common that they constitute the *majority* (63.6%) of the manifest wife negative states. Most of the time a wife positive occurred, the husband responded positively and most of these husband responses were correctly coded as positives. So the reason that the husband's responses to his wife's ostensibly negative behaviors appear (falsely) to resemble his response to her positive behaviors is that in most of these cases he *is*

TABLE 11.2
Classifications of Wife Antecedents

Latent Responses	Manifest Responses[a]		
	$\dot{\omega}_+$	$\dot{\omega}_-$	Total
ω_+	350.0	87.5	437.5
ω_-	12.5	50.0	62.5
Total	362.5	137.5	500

[a]Numbers are expected frequencies.

responding to a wife positive behavior that was misclassified as a negative behavior.

Consequences of Unreliability

This example demonstrates that particular combinations of parameter values in the sequential and measurement processes can result in dramatic differences between expected values of conditional probabilities calculated from unreliable manifest data and their true values. There are other combinations of values for which the problems appear to be less severe, and it is likely that, particularly in systems that are more complex than dichotomous data, there may be phenomena quite different than the one illustrated above. Nevertheless, it is clear that the effects of misclassifications in the analysis of sequential categorical data can be more serious than the effects of random shocks in the analysis of quantitative data. In the analysis of quantitative data, the principal costs of unreliability are the inflation of standard errors and the loss of power in significance testing. Random shocks will not, however, introduce a bias in the expected value of the mean under ordinary circumstances.[5] Misclassifications in sequential categorical data will also reduce statistical power and increase the standard errors of estimated conditional probabilities (Rogosa & Ghandour, 1991). In addition, misclassifications will bias the expected values of the conditional probabilities that describe the social interaction, possibly affecting the substantive interpretation of the social interactive system. Moreover, although collecting many sequential data will increase power and reduce the standard errors of conditional probabilities, it will not remedy the bias.

---

[5]Biases *can* easily be introduced in the estimation of a mean if the assumption of normally distributed observations is not met. For example, in a test with a ceiling, an increase in the unreliability of the test will tend to lower the expected value of the test for a person who scores near the ceiling.

MEASURING THE RELIABILITY OF SEQUENTIAL DATA

The κ Statistic

The reliability of sequential data is frequently measured by having pairs of observers code sections of a stream of events and then calculating the percentage of times they agree. One problem with using the percentage of agreement as a measure of the accuracy of coding is that a high-percentage agreement need not imply that the data are accurately coded. For example, two coders who frequently recalibrate their observations through measurements of percentage agreement might both drift away from the true definition of a classification, maintaining agreement but coding inaccurately. There is also a concern that when the baserates of codes are highly skewed, a high-percentage agreement could be achieved by chance alone. For example, suppose two coders observed an interaction and both entered positive codes for 95% of the turns. Moreover, they agreed on whether a particular conversational turn was positive or negative for 91% of the turns. This level of agreement is not necessarily impressive, however, because if each coder had randomly and independently assigned positive codes to 95% of the turns, they would attain a 90.5% agreement by chance alone.

To address this problem, it is frequently recommended (for example, Fleiss, 1975) that researchers recalibrate the percentage agreement by calculating

$$\kappa = \frac{p_o - p_e}{1 - p_e},\tag{11.9}$$

where p_o is the proportion of coded events in which two observers recorded the same code and p_e is the proportion of agreements expected by chance. What κ measures is recondite: it is the improvement of percentage agreement above chance, expressed as a proportion of the possible improvement above chance.

Although the argument that a raw percentage agreement is uninformative is well-founded, it is troubling that κ measures reliability by comparing percentage agreement to a hypothetical level of agreement that is premised on an unrealistic model of the measurement process (Grove et al., 1981; Maxwell, 1977). How could two observers independently conclude that 95% of the turns in a conversation were positive, while having no information about *which* turns were positive and negative? This unrealistic model may encourage a significant misunderstanding of the low-base-rate problem in sequential analysis. Conversations with investigators who use κ suggest that many believe that the problem with highly skewed baserates is that skewed base rates make it harder to reject the null hypothesis that observers are coding independently. This mistakes the symptom for the cause. The problem with small base rates is that statistics pertaining to rare events are vulnerable to being swamped by misclassifications, leading to severe biases in estimation (this is not the only problem: statistics calculated from small base rates are subject to great sampling fluctuation). These qualms about κ motivate an investigation of the behavior of the statistic as a function of both the distribution of the latent sequential states and the accuracy of their measurement.

Because κ is a transformed measure of the agreement between observers, we must extend the combined sequential and measurement model of Equation 11.5 to cover the case where measurement involves two coders. Now the manifest states are pairs of codes, for the husband, for example, they are $(\dot{h}_+, \dot{h}_+)$, $(\dot{h}_+, \dot{h}_-)$, $(\dot{h}_-, \dot{h}_+)$, and $(\dot{h}_-, \dot{h}_-)$. Suppose that for a given husband $\rightarrow$ wife transition, the coders agree that the husband's turn was negative but disagree about the wife's. Let $g_{(\dot{h}_-, \dot{h}_-)(\dot{w}_+, \dot{w}_-)}$ be the proportion of doubly coded transitions of this kind. Once again, this set of manifest transitions could include portions of four types of latent transitions:

$$g_{(\dot{h}_-, \dot{h}_-)(\dot{w}_+, \dot{w}_-)} = (r_+^2 - \pi_{h_+} p_{h_+ w_+} r_{++} r_{+-}) + (r_+^2 - \pi_{h_+} p_{h_+ w_-} r_{-+} r_{--})$$
$$+ (r_-^2 - \pi_{h_-} p_{h_- w_+} r_{++} r_{+-})$$
$$+ (r_-^2 - \pi_{h_-} p_{h_- w_-} r_{-+} r_{--}). \tag{11.10}$$

The first term of the sum is the probability that a latent $h_+ \rightarrow w_+$ transition occurred, that the husband's behavior was misclassified as negative by both coders, and that the wife's behavior was correctly classified by one coder and misclassified by the other.

After calculating the unconditional probabilities of double coded transitions as in Equation 11.10, the base rate probabilities of double codes were calculated as $\pi_{(\dot{a}, \dot{b})} = \Sigma_c \Sigma_d g_{(\dot{a}, \dot{b})(\dot{c}, \dot{d})}$. These base rates were then used to find the expected proportion of turns in which coders will agree, $p_o = \Sigma_a \pi_{(\dot{a}, \dot{a})}$ and the proportion in which they are expected to agree by chance, $p_e = \Sigma_a \pi_a^2 = \Sigma_a (\Sigma_b \pi_{(\dot{a}, \dot{b})})^2$. These expressions for p_e and p_o were then used to express κ as a function of the base rate, reciprocity, and measurement accuracy parameters. The behavior of κ was then examined as a function of variation in accuracy of measurement (that is, the parameters of the measurement process) and reciprocity and base rate positivity (the parameters of the sequential process).

First, we consider the response of κ to variation in the accuracy of measurement (see Figure 11.2). The accuracy of coding, $r_{++} = r_{--} = r$, was varied between .5, where observers are guessing, and 1, where they are perfectly accurate in discriminating positive and negative states. The reciprocity parameters of the sequential process were fixed at $\phi_w = \phi_h = \phi = .05$.[6] Curves are

---

[6]Given these simplifications, we can easily write an expression for r in terms of β and κ. Set $\beta_w = \beta_h = \beta$, $r_{++} = r_{--} = r$, and $\phi_w = \phi_h = 0$. Then using the formulae for p_o and p_e in the text, the proportion of agreements between observers will be $p_o = 1 - 2r + 2r^2$, while the proportion expected given that coders decisions were at the observed base rates but were independent of the latent states is $p_e = p_o(1 - 2\beta)^2 + 6\beta(1 - \beta)$. Then Equation 11.9 can be rewritten as $p_o - p_e - \kappa(1 - p_e) = 0$, an equation which is quadratic in r, and which has a solution

$$r = \frac{1}{2}\left(1 + \sqrt{1 - \frac{1 - \kappa}{\kappa + 4(\beta - \beta^2)(1 - \kappa)}}\right).$$

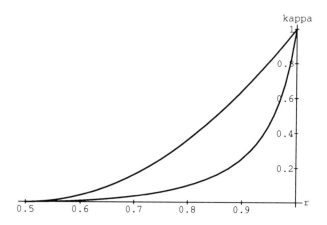

FIG. 11.2. The value of κ as a function of the accuracy of observer coding (r_{++} and r_{--}). The upper and lower curves are calculated for β = .5 and .95 respectively.

plotted for two values of $\beta_h = \beta_w = \beta$.[7] As would be expected, κ = 0 at $r_{++} = r_{--} = .5$, where coders are guessing, and κ = 1 at $r_{++} = r_{--} = 1$, where coding is infallible. Notice, however, that when the latent base rates are highly skewed (β = .95), κ remains low except when the accuracy of measurement is very high (r is nearly 1).

Next we consider the effect of varying the components of the sequential process, with the accuracy of measurement held constant. Varying the reciprocity (φ) parameters did not affect κ, but the effect of variation in the latent base rates (β) is presented in Figure 11.3 for three levels of coding accuracy (r). The reciprocity parameters (ϕ_w and ϕ_h) were set at .05, and the base rate parameters ($\beta_w = \beta_h = \beta$) were varied from .5 up to nearly 1 (a dichotomous variable would not vary at 1). Figure 11.3 shows that κ declines as the base rates of the latent states grow more skewed.

Figures 11.2 and 11.3 suggest that many combinations of accuracies of measurement and latent base rates are consistent with any value of κ. To illustrate this, the reciprocity parameters were set to zero, in which case one can solve for r as a function of β and κ (see Appendix). Figure 11.4 graphs the relationship between r and β for several levels of fixed κ. Notice that r is always high for high values of κ, but that a wide range of values for r are consistent with a small κ. A high κ implies accurate measurement, but a low κ does not imply inaccurate measurement.

---

[7]Under these conditions, β is the base rate of positive latent states for both the husband and the wife; that is,

$$2\pi_h^t = 2\pi_w^t = [\beta \quad 1 - \beta].$$

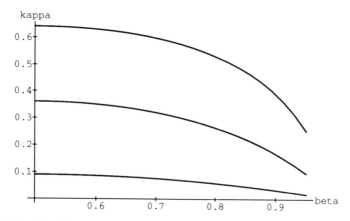

FIG. 11.3.   The value of κ as a function of the base rate parameters (β_h and β_w). The top, middle, and bottom curves represent r = .65, .8, and .9 respectively.

The sensitivity of κ to skewness in the base rates of the latent states is a desirable behavior, because as the previous discussion of $\hat{P}$ indicates, highly skewed latent base rates in the presence of unreliable measurement contribute to estimation problems in sequential analysis. The finding that κ is sensitive to base rates *appears* to follow from the definition of κ (11.9), in that the statistic corrects the percentage agreement by a factor calculated from the observed base rates. It is important to recall, however, that the base rates used to calculate κ are the manifest base rates which, as we have seen, are different from the latent base rates manipulated in Figure 11.3. The base rate for manifest husband positives, for example, is determined by the latent base rates for positive behaviors and the

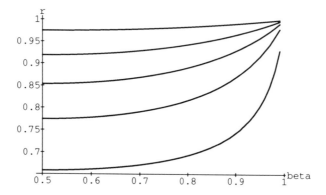

FIG. 11.4.   Relationship between r and β for constant κ = .1, .3, .5, .7, and .9. The higher curves correspond to higher values of κ.

accuracies of measurement of both positive and negative states. Thus the size of a manifest base rate is a symptom of measurement problems, not a cause. Moreover, the size of the latent base rate cannot be recovered without an independent assessment of the accuracy of measurement, that is, an estimate of R.

The important message is that unless κ is high, there is no necessary relationship between κ and the accuracy of measurement, because a low or moderate κ is consistent with wide range of measurement accuracies. This problem with κ has been frequently discussed in the context of psychiatric diagnosis (Carey & Gottesman, 1979; Grove et al., 1981; Spitznagel & Helzer, 1985) and is implicit in the classic discussion of the psychometrics of diagnosis by Meehl and Rosen (1946). In defense of κ, Shrout and his colleagues (Shrout, Spitzer, & Fleiss, 1987) note that *all* reliability measures are affected by the base rates of the conditions that are to be diagnosed, and hence are specific to the populations in which assessments are made. It remains true, however, that κ provides little help for researchers who need information about the accuracy of their measurement procedures and lack an independent means of measuring the latent base rates. Although a low κ correctly informs an investigator of problems in a sequential analytic study, κ by itself will not indicate whether the source of those problems is inaccurate measurement or skewed latent base rates. If the former, the measurement procedure should be modified so as to improve its accuracy. If the latter, the problem is in the sample of persons or settings of observation, or some other aspect of the design. The researcher must then seek means whereby small latent base rates can be increased: for example, by observing subjects in a context that might elicit more examples of a rare behavior, or by merging a rare code with a conceptually-related larger category.

ALTERNATIVE APPROACHES TO SEQUENTIAL ANALYSIS OF UNRELIABLE DATA

A critical task for sequential analysis is the development of (a) a means of obtaining more detailed and useful information about the accuracy of sequential data and (b) a means of calculating unbiased estimates of the parameters of the latent sequential process. Unfortunately, the parameters of a statistical model of inaccurately classified sequential states like Equation 11.5 cannot be estimated from the data it models. The problem with Equation 11.5 is that it has too many parameters compared to the degrees of freedom in a table of transition frequency counts. The possible directions for developing a statistical model for unreliable sequential data depend on the strategy used to obtain data on the quality of measurement. We present one possible approach in which information about the accuracy of observation is obtained by comparing observers' codings against a true criterion, and a second in which it is obtained from the agreements and disagreements between pairs of coders.

Criterion-Based Reliability Measurement

The problem with Equation 11.5 is that we do not have enough information to separately identify R, which determines the probability distribution of the manifest states conditional on the latent states, and P, which determines the distribution of the latent states. When observers code videotapes, however, it might be possible to obtain an independent estimate of R from data on observers' codings of standard videotapes where the correct classification of the latent behavioral sequence has been established by expert observers. We then would have a set of manifest sequential states corresponding to known latent states and R could be estimated directly from the data: $\hat{r}_{++}$, for example, would be the number positive codings of positive latent states, divided by the total number of latent states.

Given $\hat{R}$, we could calculate a reliability-corrected estimate of P. First we calculate a reliability-corrected estimate of G, the matrix of unconditional probabilities of latent variable transitions. Let $\dot{F}$ be a matrix of the f_{ab} counts of manifest transitions, arranged just as in P. A matrix estimating G, that is, the unconditional probabilities of the manifest transitions, is just $n^{-1}F$, where n is the number of transitions in the behavioral stream. Then from Equation 11.5 we have

$$\tilde{G} = (I \otimes \hat{R}^{-1})^t n^{-1} \dot{F} (I \otimes \hat{R}^{-1}), \tag{11.11}$$

which is a reliability-corrected estimate of G. Given $\tilde{G}$, we calculate $\tilde{P}$, a reliability-corrected estimate of P, from the relation in Equation 11.1.

The primary reason to calculate $\tilde{P}$ would be to check the sensitivity of an ordinary sequential analysis to reliability problems. If the ordinary estimates of conditional probabilities (Equation 11.1) differ substantially from $\tilde{P}$, there would be substantial reason for concern. But although calculation of $\tilde{P}$ could provide a useful way to check the sensitivity of an analysis to measurement error, it would not provide estimates of the conditional probabilities that could be used for making statistical inferences. The problem is that Equation 11.11 assumes that we have correctly estimated the reliability of the data, whereas $\hat{R}$ is subject to sampling variation. If information about the quality of the estimate $\hat{R}$ is not included in the analysis, we will overestimate the precision of an error-corrected estimate of P and introduce a bias toward rejection of the null hypothesis.

It might be possible to remedy this, however, by extending the idea in Equation 11.11. First, write a likelihood for the stream of unreliable single-observer manifest data using the $\dot{G}$ unconditional probabilities for manifest transitions in unreliable sequential data (Equation 11.5). This likelihood would depend on both P and R and, as previously discussed, neither matrix would be identifiable from the manifest transitions. We could also, however, write a likelihood for the observers' codings of the criterion videotape that would depend on R only, and in which R would be identified. If we combined these likelihoods and maximized them simultaneously, it is possible that both P and R would be identified and could be estimated. Moreover, standard errors for estimated values of P and R might be obtained from the information matrix of the likelihood model, opening a route to statistical inferences using reliability-corrected estimates of the conditional probabilities of latent sequential transitions.

This strategy is feasible, however, only in the case where it is possible to estimate R accurately. This will require investigators to find a large sample of sequential behaviors and code them to criterion, to provide the standard against which observers could be tested. The criterion-based approach will require a good estimate of $\hat{R}$. This will require many criterion-based reliability data. To obtain these data, researchers must be able to authoritatively code a long and representative stream of social interactive behavior. Under the restrictive assumptions of our measurement model, the standard error of $\hat{r}_{++}$ will be $\sqrt{\hat{r}_{++}\hat{r}_{+-}/n_{+}}$, where n_{+} is the number of latent positive states in the criterion sample. If $r_{++} = .8$, we would need $n_{+} = 246$ to have 95% confidence that the true r_{++} was between .75 and .85. This is not unreasonable for a behavior with a large latent base rate, but for small base rate behaviors it could require as much criterion coding as the research project for which the instrument is being calibrated.

Agreement-Based Reliability Measurement and Estimation

If accuracy cannot be measured against a criterion, it may be possible to make inferences about R using measurements of agreement between observers and use that information to improve the estimation of P. This might be accomplished by applying some of the recent techniques for inferring latent classes from multiple categorical indicators of such classes (Clogg & Goodman, 1984; Goodman, 1974; Uebersax & Grove, 1990) to sequential data (Dillon, Madden, & Kumar, 1983). A variant of this technique called latent Markov theory (Bye & Schecter, 1986; van de Pol & de Leeuw, 1986; van de Pol & Langeheine, 1990) has been developed for the study of repeated measurements using unreliable categorical data, and may be extensible to sequential analysis. The idea is to have two observers code the entire behavioral stream. This would give us a table of the counts of manifest transitions between pairs of codes. Given the assumption that the underlying latent process is Markov, there would appear to be enough degrees of freedom to simultaneously estimate R and P from the double-coded data using a maximum-likelihood technique.

DISCUSSION

These results suggest that inaccurate measurements pose serious threats to the interpretability of sequential data. In quantitative data where errors are described by the classical reliability model, unreliability in a dependent variable will not bias parameter estimates within the general linear model. In that context there is a choice of means for attacking the problem: one can either improve the quality of measurement or increase the size of the sample. In sequential analysis, however, inaccurate measurement biases parameter estimates in a way that cannot be remedied by increasing sample size. It was shown that these problems depend on both the accuracy of measurements and the base rates of latent sequential states (and possibly other attributes of the latent process in behavioral systems more complex than the one studied here). A study of κ revealed that although this statistic is an improvement on the raw percentage agreement, a low κ does not inform researchers about whether the difficulty lies in the accuracy of measurement or the latent base rates of the behaviors under observation.

Experience with observational coding (for example, Gardner & Rogoff, 1990) teaches the lesson that are hard upper limits on the accuracy that can be obtained in direct observation of many behaviors. It is imperative, then, to develop methods for unbiased estimation of sequential statistics from unreliable data. There are two profitable directions for the development of such techniques, using criterion-based or agreement-based reliability information. These possibilities share the characteristic that data from several observers (or the same observers coding criterion and ordinary tapes) are combined to identify a latent sequential process and a measurement process that produce sequential observations. In practice, either approach will require a significant increase in both analytical and observational effort by observational researchers.

ACKNOWLEDGMENTS

An earlier version was presented to the Conference on the Analysis of Change, University of Washington, Seattle, WA, May 24, 1991. Address correspondence to William Gardner, Law & Psychiatry Research, Department of Psychiatry, University of Pittsburgh School of Medicine, Pittsburgh, PA 15213. Thanks to John Gottman for comments at the conference and to Edward P. Mulvey and David Rogosa for criticisms of a written version.

REFERENCES

Anderson, T., & Goodman, L. (1957). Statistical inference about Markov chains. *Annals of Mathematical Statistics, 28,* 89–110.

Bakeman, R., & Gottman, J. (1986). *Observing interaction: An introduction to sequential analysis.* New York: Cambridge University Press.

Bye, B., & Schechter, E. (1986). A latent Markov approach to the estimation of response errors in multiwave panel data. *Journal of the American Statistical Association, 81,* 375–380.

Carey, G., & Gottesman, I. (1979). Reliability and validity in binary ratings. *Archives of General Psychiatry, 35,* 1454–1459.

Cicchetti, D. V., & Feinstein, A. R. (1990). High agreement but low kappa: II. Resolving the paradoxes. *Journal of Clinical Epidemiology, 43,* 551–558.

Çinlar, E. (1975). *Introduction to stochastic processes.* Englewood Cliffs, NJ: Prentice-Hall.

Clogg, C., & Goodman, L. (1984). Latent structure analysis of a set of multidimensional contingency tables. *Journal of the American Statistical Association, 79,* 762–771.

Cohen, J. (1960). A coefficient of agreement for nominal scales. *Educational and Psychological Measurement, 20,* 37–46.

Cone, J. (1977). The relevance of reliability and validity for behavioral assessment. *Behavior Therapy, 8,* 411–426.

Cone, J., & Foster, S. (1982). Direct observation in clinical psychology. In P. Kendall & J. Butcher (Eds.), *Handbook of research methods in clinical psychology.* New York: Wiley.

Crocker, L., & Algina, J. (1986). *Introduction to classical and modern test theory.* New York: Holt, Rinehart, & Winston.

Dillon, W., Madden, T., & Kumar, A. (1983). Analyzing sequential categorical data on dyadic interaction: A latent structure approach. *Psychological Bulletin, 94,* 564–583.

Feinstein, A. R., & Cicchetti, D. V. (1990). High agreement but low kappa: I. The problems of two paradoxes. *Journal of Clinical Epidemiology, 43,* 543–549.

Fleiss, J. (1975). Measuring agreement between two judges on the presence and absence of a trait. *Biometrics, 31,* 651–659.

Foster, S., & Cone, J. (1980). Current issues in direct observation. *Behavioral Assessment, 2,* 313–338.

Gardner, W. (1990). Analyzing sequential categorical data: Individual variation in Markov chains. *Psychometrika, 55,* 263–275.

Gardner, W. (1993). Hierarchical continuous-time sequential analysis: A strategy for clinical research. *Journal of Consulting and Clinical Psychology, 61,* 975–983.

Gardner, W., & Griffin, W. (1989). Methods for the analysis of parallel streams of social interactions. *Psychological Bulletin, 105,* 446–455.

Gardner, W., & Rogoff, B. (1990). Children's deliberateness of planning according to task circumstances. *Developmental Psychology, 26,* 480–487.

Goodman, L. (1974). The analysis of systems of qualitative variables when some of the variables are unobservable: I. A modified latent structure approach. *American Journal of Sociology, 79,* 1179–1259.

Gottman, J., & Roy, A. (1990). *Sequential analysis: A guide for behavioral research.* New York: Cambridge University Press.

Graham, J. W., Collins, L. M., Wugalter, S. E., Chung, N. K. (J.), & Hansen, W. B. (1991). Modeling transitions in latent stage-sequential processes: A substance abuse prevention example. *Journal of Consulting and Clinical Psychology, 59,* 48–57.

Grove, W., Andraesen, N., McDonald-Scott, P., Keller, M., & Shapiro, R. (1981). Reliability studies of psychiatric diagnosis: Theory and practice. *Archives of General Psychiatry, 38,* 408–413.

Hagenaars, J. (1988). Latent structure models with direct effects between indicators. *Sociological Methods and Research, 16,* 215–231.

Hartmann, D. (1977). Considerations in the choice of interobserver reliability estimates. *Journal of Applied Behavior analysis, 10,* 103–116.

Hartmann, D., & Wood, D. (1990). Observational methods. In A. Bellack, M. Hersen, & A. Kazdin (Eds.), *International handbook of behavior modification and therapy* (2d ed., pp. 107–138). New York: Plenum.

Maxwell, A. (1977). Coefficients of agreement between observers and their interpretation. *British Journal of Psychiatry, 130,* 79–83.

Meehl, P., & Rosen, A. (1946). Antecedent probability and the efficiency of psychometric signs, patterns, and cutting scores. *Psychological Bulletin, 30,* 525–564.

Patterson, G. (1982). *Coercive family process.* Eugene, OR: Castalia Press.

Rogosa, D., & Ghandour, G. (1991). Statistical models for behavioral observations. *Journal of Educational Statistics, 16,* 157–252.

Sackett, G. (1976). *Observing behavior. Vol. 2: Data collection and analysis methods.* Baltimore: University Park Press.

Sackett, G. (1987). Analysis of sequential social interaction data: Some issues, recent developments, and a causal inference model. In J. Osofsky (Ed.), *Handbook of infant development.* (2d ed., pp. 878–885). New York: Wiley.

Schwartz, J. (1985). the neglected problem of measurement error in categorical data. *Sociological Methods and Research, 13,* 435–466.

Shrout, P., Spitzer, R., & Fleiss, J. (1987). Quantification of agreement in psychiatric diagnosis revisited. *Archives of General Psychiatry, 49,* 172–177.

Siegel, D. G., Podgor, M. J., & Remaley, N. A. (1992). Acceptable values of kappa for comparison of two groups. *American Journal of Epidemiology, 135,* 571–578.

Spitzer, R., Cohen, J., Fleiss, J., & Endicott, J. (1967). Quantification of agreement in psychiatric diagnosis. *Archives of General Psychiatry, 17,* 83–87.

Spitznagel, E., & Helzer, J. (1985). A proposed solution to the base rate problem in the kappa statistic. *Archives of General Psychiatry, 44,* 172–177.

Uebersax, J. (1987). Diversity of decision-making models and measurement of interrater agreement. *Psychological Bulletin, 101,* 140–146.

Uebersax, J. (1988). Validating inferences from interobserver agreement. *Psychological Bulletin, 104,* 405–416.

Uebersax, J., & Grove, W. M. (1990). Latent class analysis of diagnostic agreement. *Statistics in Medicine, 9,* 559–572.

van de Pol, F., & de Leeuw, J. (1986). A latent Markov model to correct for measurement error. *Sociological Methods and Research, 15,* 118–141.

van de Pol, F., & Langeheine, R. (1990). Mixed Markov latent class models: From description toward explanation. In C. Clogg (ed.), *Sociological methodology 1990* (pp. 213–247). Oxford: Blackwell.

12

Interrupted Time-Series Analysis with Short Series: Why It Is Problematic; How It Can Be Improved

John Crosbie
West Virginia University

Crosbie's chapter has solved a very difficult problem in using time-series models to assess change. While more complex models are possible, Crosbie outlines with short time-series, which is quite typical, how to use simple autoregressive models to assess changes in level and slope following an event of interest, such as a planned intervention.

—Editor

One of the enduring problems for behavior analysts is how to assess change with single-subject data. The use of repeated observations with one subject controls intersubject variability, permits the subject to adapt to the experimental situation, and, ideally, establishes a stable baseline against which behavior in subsequent phases can be compared (Barlow, Hayes, & Nelson, 1984; Hersen & Barlow, 1976; Sidman, 1960). Unfortunately, such data are difficult to analyze. The present chapter describes the difficulties inherent in analyzing single-subject data and how a new interrupted time-series analysis procedure can be used effectively to assess change with typical applied behavioral data.

AUTOCORRELATION

The principal reason that time-series data are difficult to analyze is because successive scores are not independent (i.e., they are autocorrelated). Independence of scores is an important assumption of all inferential procedures, including visual inspection. Conceptually, lag-1 autocorrelation is computed by correlating score 1 with score 2, score 2 with score 3, score 3 with score 4, etc., until the complete series is included. Longer lags can also be considered. For example, a lag-3 autocorrelation is computed from score 1 with score 4, score 2 with score 5, etc. The formula for lag-n autocorrelation is

$$r_n = \frac{\sum_{i=1}^{N-1} (X_i - \bar{X})(X_{i+n} - \bar{X})}{\sum_{i=1}^{N} (X_i - \bar{X})^2}, \tag{12.1}$$

where N is the number of scores in the series, n is the lag, X_i is the ith score, and $\bar{X}$ is the mean of the series. The numerator of Equation 12.1 shows that, if X_i and X_{i+n} are both consistently on the same side of $\bar{X}$, r_n is positive. If they are consistently on opposite sides of $\bar{X}$, r_n is negative. If, however, they are not consistently on the same or opposite sides of $\bar{X}$, r_n is zero. Figure 12.1 shows these three autocorrelation patterns. Positive autocorrelation data were obtained by setting score 1 to 10, and all other scores to .9 times the previous score. Negative and zero autocorrelation were produced by changing the order of these scores.

VISUAL INFERENCE

Traditionally, single-subject data were obtained with laboratory animals in situations of tight experimental control for many sessions, or at least until the data

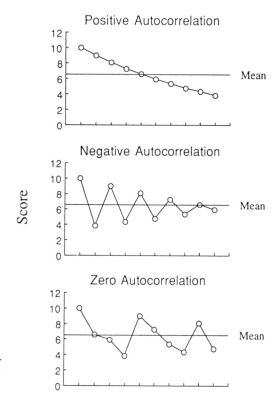

Positive Autocorrelation

Negative Autocorrelation

Score

Zero Autocorrelation

FIG. 12.1. Time series with positive, negative, and zero lag-1
autocorrelation.

appeared stable (i.e., there was no increasing or decreasing trend and minimal variability; Killeen, 1978; Sidman, 1960). Visual inspection was the recommended method of analysis. A change was considered significant if it was large, abrupt, and sustained; if change was not obvious, the effect was too small or experimental control inadequate. Visual inference was proposed as a conservative test which made behavior analysis strong because only robust reliable effects survived (Baer, 1977; Kazdin, 1982; Parsonson & Baer, 1978, 1986). With the long stable baselines typically obtained in animal laboratories, visual inference may indeed be reliable and conservative. However, with the short baselines typically reported with human subjects in applied behavioral journals (median baseline length is between 5 and 10; Sharpley, 1987), visual inference can be problematic.

For example, DeProspero and Cohen (1979) constructed graphs showing single-subject data in an ABAB design (A = baseline, B = intervention), and asked 114 reviewers and editors of behavioral journals to rate each graph in terms of the experimental control shown. Even with such experienced judges, interrater reliability was only .61. In another study, 11 experienced visual analysts were shown graphs which had been published in the *Journal of Applied Behavior Analysis,* and reported whether any change had occurred (Jones, Weinrott, & Vaught, 1978). Interrater reliability was .39. Several other studies have also shown that visual inference is unreliable (Furlong & Wampold, 1982; Matyas & Greenwood, 1990; Ottenbacher, 1986; Wampold & Furlong, 1981; White, 1972).

In addition to the problems of unreliability, visual inference also has an excessive risk of Type I error (i.e., an erroneous inference of a significant difference between phases). Matyas and Greenwood (1990) constructed AB graphs which differed in terms of autocorrelation amongst data points, variability, and increase in level from phase 1 to phase 2 (between 0 and 10 standard deviations). There was no programmed slope. Graduate students in a single-subject design and analysis course rated each graph by reporting whether there was an intervention effect. Type I error rates (i.e., the proportion of graphs with no change in level which were rated as showing an intervention effect) ranged from 16% to 84%, and were highest for graphs with increased variability and positive autocorrelation. In contrast, Type II error rates (i.e., the proportion of graphs with a change in level which were rated as showing no intervention effect) were 0% to 22% with most rates less than 10%. Clearly, with the short series, variability, and autocorrelation found in typical applied behavioral data (Matyas & Greenwood, 1991), visual inference is unreliable and cannot control Type I error.

ANOVA

Analysis of variance (ANOVA) has been proposed to assess change with single-subject data because it is reliable, and, when its assumptions are satisfied, maintains Type I error at the desired level. Proponents of ANOVA with single-subject data (e.g., Gentile, Roden, & Klein, 1972) maintained that baseline observation for a single subject constitute one group of scores, and observations during the intervention phase constitute another independent group of scores. Hence, change can be assessed with a between-groups ANOVA or *t* test. This proposal has received considerable criticism (e.g., Hartmann, 1974; Thoresen & Elashoff, 1974; Toothaker, Banz, Noble, Camp, & Davis, 1983).

The fundamental problem with using ANOVA in this way is that the independent observations assumption is violated. Although ANOVA is robust with respect to violations of some of its assumptions, it cannot accommodate violation of the independent observations assumption (Padia, 1975; Scheffé, 1959, chap. 10). Consider the independent-groups *t* test. The *t* statistic is calculated from the difference in the group means divided by the error variance. When data are positively autocorrelated, observations are more similar to each other than would occur by chance (see Figure 12.1). Hence, the error variance is artificially deflated, and the t value is artificially inflated. This means that positive autocorrelation increases the probability of making a Type I error. In contrast, negatively autocorrelated data are more dissimilar to each other than would occur by chance, which inflates the error variance and thereby deflates the t value and the probability of making a Type I error.

To demonstrate the effects of autocorrelation on Type I error rate with the t test, the following Monte Carlo analysis was performed on series with a range of lag-1 autocorrelation but no programmed slope or change between phases. One thousand two-phase series (with the same number of observations per phase) were produced for the first-order autoregressive process

$$Y_i = \rho Y_{i-1} + E_i, \qquad (12.2)$$

where Y_i is the ith observation in the series, ρ is the autoregressive parameter, and E_i is the ith normalized random error term. Random error terms were

TABLE 12.1
For the t Test, Empirical Probabilities
for 1000 Replications with Each Series
Length (N) and First-Order Autoregressive
Parameter (ρ). The Data Have No
Programmed Slope or Change from Phase
1 to Phase 2

	N			
ρ	10	20	30	40
.9	.35	.55	.59	.59
.8	.31	.51	.49	.49
.7	.26	.42	.40	.41
.6	.22	.34	.31	.33
.5	.18	.28	.26	.25
.4	.14	.21	.20	.19
.3	.11	.15	.14	.15
.2	.08	.12	.10	.12
.1	.07	.08	.07	.09
0	.05	.06	.05	.05
−.1	.04	.04	.03	.03
−.2	.03	.03	.02	.02
−.3	.02	.02	.01	.01
−.4	.01	.01	.01	.01
−.5	.01	.01	.00	.00
−.6	.01	.00	.00	.00
−.7	.00	.00	.00	.00
−.8	.00	.00	.00	.00
−.9	.00	.00	.00	.00

Note. The nominal alpha is .05.

produced by obtaining uniform random deviates and transforming them to nor- malized ($M = 0$, $SD = 1$) random deviates by the polar method (respectively, RAN3 and GASDEV in Press, Flannery, Teukolsky, & Vetterling, 1989; see Knuth, 1981, for a comprehensive discussion of these procedures). Series had a length of 10, 20, 30, or 40 scores, and ρ ranged from .9 to $-.9$ in steps of .1; all series were therefore stationary (see Gottman, 1981, for a discussion of sta- tionarity conditions).

Table 12.1 shows the empirical probability of rejecting H_0 for the t test with a nominal alpha of .05. When $\rho = 0$ the Type I error rate is close to the nominal alpha. As positive autocorrelation increases, however, the probability of Type I error exceeds the nominal alpha, and as negative autocorrelation increases, the probability of making a Type I error is lower than the nominal alpha.

Because applied behavioral data are often positively autocorrelated (Matyas & Greenwood, 1985, 1990, 1991), ANOVA cannot control Type I error, and conse- quently is invalid, with such data.

BINOMIAL TEST

Although parametric statistical procedures such as ANOVA are invalid with autocorrelated data, several authors have suggested a nonparametric alternative which employs the binomial test to determine whether the trend observed in one phase continues through the next phase. There are two versions of this procedure: the split middle (White, 1972, 1974), in which the phase-1 trend is computed from median scores, then raised or lowered to ensure that half of the phase-1 scores are above and half below the trend line; and the celeration line (Bloom & Fischer, 1982), in which the trend line is computed from means and not adjusted. Apart from minor computational differences, these procedures are very similar: Both compute the phase-1 trend and project it through phase 2; then a binomial test (Siegel, 1956) is used to compare the proportion of phase-2 scores that fall above the trend line with the probability of a phase-1 score falling above the line. If the trend is maintained across the two phases, it is assumed that the probability of a score falling above the trend line will be similar during each phase.

Figure 12.2 shows how the split-middle trend line is computed. The first step is to divide phase 1 in half by drawing a vertical line at the median number of sessions for the phase (in Figure 12.2 this is shown as the dashed vertical line between sessions 5 and 6); if there is an odd number of sessions in this phase the line is drawn through the data point for the median session. Next, each of the phase-1 halves is halved by drawing a vertical line through its median session (in Figure 12.2 these are shown as the dashed vertical lines through sessions 3 and 8). Then, for each of the phase-1 halves the median score is computed, and a horizontal line is drawn through this median score to intersect with the median session line. The two intersections are then joined to produce a trend line (dashed

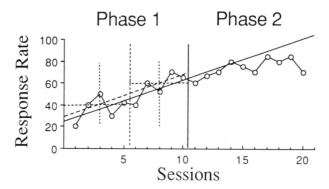

FIG. 12.2. Hypothetical two-phase data and the split-middle trend line computed from them.

in Figure 12.2) which is moved up or down (with the slope held constant) until there are as many phase-1 data points above the line as there are below the line. The resultant line is the split-middle trend line. In Figure 12.2 the preliminary (dashed) trend line has four data points above and six below it, so the line is moved down until there are five scores above and five below it, and the (solid) split-middle trend line is the result. Because the trend line is computed such that half of the phase-1 scores fall above it, if the trend continues in phase 2 the probability of a phase-2 score falling above the line should be close to .5. To determine whether there is a statistically significant difference between phases, a binomial test is used to compare the number of phase-2 scores that fall above the line with the total number of phase-2 scores that fall either above or below the line. Of the 10 phase-2 scores in Figure 12.2, one score falls above the line, and the two-tailed probability of such an extreme result is $< .05$.

The binomial test of the observed trend procedure is conceptually and computationally simple, and can be performed with as few as five phase-2 data points. Bloom and Fischer (1982) have also asserted that this technique "appears to resolve any of the problems brought on by autocorrelation" (p. 448), and recommended that "if the data are autocorrelated, your first choice would be the use of the celeration line" (p. 457). Despite Bloom and Fischer's enthusiastic support for the procedure, it is based on dubious statistical premises, and therefore its validity is suspect. The binomial test assumes that the probability of a success is constant; that is, on any trial the outcome is unaffected by outcomes of previous trials. If the outcome on a trial could be predicted from previous outcomes, then any inferential statistical assessment would require conditional probability instead of the constant probability used in the binomial test. Autocorrelation (the problem that the binomial test is supposed to overcome), means that a score can be predicted from its predecessors, so when the binomial test is used with autocorrelated data its assumptions are violated.

There is an additional statistical problem with this procedure. The assumption implicit in a comparison with an observed trend is that, with no intervention, a trend that develops during phase 1 will continue during phase 2. If this assumption is invalid (which seems likely with random data), inflated Type I error rates would be expected. Furthermore, the probability that a point falls above the trend line is constant only for the population trend line; use of the sample trend line offers no such assurance, and therefore is problematic.

Crosbie (1987) assessed the Type I error rates of this procedure with autocorrelated data which had no programmed slope or change between the phases. One thousand two-phase series (with the same number of observations per phase) were produced for the first-order autoregressive process $Y_i = \rho Y_{i-1} + E_i$. Series had a length of 10 or 100 scores, and ρ ranged from $-.8$ to $.8$ in steps of $.4$; all series were therefore stationary. In addition to assessing the binomial test of observed trend (split middle; SM), the binomial test was also assessed for the programmed trend of zero (TOPT). The difference in empirical Type I error between SM and TOPT showed the effect of employing an observed trend.

Table 12.2 shows that, when $\rho = 0$, the test of programmed trend (TOPT) has a Type I error rate close to the nominal alpha for both series lengths. For other values of ρ, however, the results are similar to those obtained with ANOVA: Type I error increases as autocorrelation becomes more positive, positive autocorrelation produces Type I error rates greater than the nominal alpha, and negative autocorrelation produces Type I error rates less than the nominal alpha. Hence, for the binomial test of programmed trend, nonzero autocorrelation in the data seriously affects Type I error. For the split middle (SM), Type I error also increases as autocorrelation becomes more positive. Unfortunately, Type I error is unacceptably high for all levels of autocorrelation; even with very short series and zero autocorrelation, the Type I error rate is nearly 10 times the nominal alpha.

TABLE 12.2
For the Test of Programmed Trend (TOPT) and Split Middle (SM), Empirical Probabilities for 1000 Replications with Each Series Length (N) and First-Order Autoregressive Parameter(ρ). The Data Have No Programmed Slope or Change from Phase 1 to Phase 2

| Test | N | ρ | | | | |
		$-.8$	$-.4$	0	$.4$	$.8$
TOPT	10	.00	.02	.07	.17	.43
	100	.00	.03	.07	.18	.46
SM	10	.26	.39	.49	.55	.60
	100	.47	.54	.64	.76	.84

Note. The nominal alpha is .05.

Although it has been asserted that a binomial test of observed trend can overcome the problems posed by autocorrelation (Bloom & Fischer, 1982), violation of the independent-scores assumption has similar adverse consequences for the binomial test as it has for ANOVA. Furthermore, the split-middle procedure compounds these difficulties by comparing phase-2 scores with the trend observed during phase 1. When combined, these two sources of error ensure that the split middle is invalid for all data. This analysis also shows the potential problems for visual inference if phase-2 performance is compared with the phase-1 trend (e.g., as advocated by Barlow et al., 1984, pp. 197, 213).

C STATISTIC

Tryon (1982) proposed a simple procedure to determine whether there is a statistically significant change in a time series. He maintained that it can be employed legitimately with as few as eight phase-1 observations, and that it overcomes problems posed by autocorrelation. The first step is to compute the C statistic with the following formula:

$$C = 1 - \frac{\displaystyle\sum_{i=1}^{N-1} (X_i - X_{i+1})^2}{2 \displaystyle\sum_{i=1}^{N} (X_i - \bar{X})^2}, \tag{12.3}$$

where X_i is the ith point in a time series, $\bar{X}$ is the mean of the series, and N is the number of points in the series. The C value is then divided by its standard error

$$SE_C = \sqrt{\frac{N - 2}{N^2 - 1}} \tag{12.4}$$

to produce a Z statistic which is normally distributed with 25 or more data points, and approximately normally distributed with 8–24 data points (Young, 1941). From the C formula it can be seen that, if the data have a trend or slope, the squared mean deviations (i.e., the denominator) will be greater than the squared consecutive difference (i.e., the numerator), and therefore the C value will be large. This is the essence of Tryon's use of C for time-series analysis. A statistically significant C is taken as evidence of trend or instability in the data, and a nonsignificant C as evidence that the data are stable. Tryon (1982) proposed the following conditional procedure: (i) perform the C test for phase 1; (ii) if it is nonsignificant, append phase 2 to phase 1, then perform the C test on the combined series; or (iii) if it is significant, subtract from each phase-2 score the corresponding phase-1 score (or corresponding point on the phase-1 trend line), then perform the C test on the modified phase 2. If the final C is significant, it is assumed that the phase-2 scores are significantly different from the phase-1 scores. If there are more data points during phase 2 than during phase 1, "modest extrapolation of the first phase trend line can provide a basis for adding a few more data points to the comparison series, thereby enhancing the power of the test" (Tryon, 1982, p. 426). Tryon asserted that the order of decreasing power for these procedures is nonsignificant phase 1, subtracted phase-1 trend, and subtracted phase-1 scores, respectively.

Crosbie (1989) assessed the Type I error rates of the various C tests with autocorrelated data which had no programmed slope or change between the phases. One thousand two-phase series (with the same number of observations per phase) were produced for the first-order autoregressive process $Y_i = \rho Y_{i-1} + E_i$. Series had lengths of 10, 20, or 40 scores, and ρ ranged from 0 to .8 in steps of .2; all series were stationary.

Table 12.3 shows the assessments of Type I error. With undifferentiated series and zero autocorrelation, the rate of Type I error is close to the nominal alpha. As positive autocorrelation increases, however, Type I error increases in the same way as is found with ANOVA and the binomial test. Therefore, although there was no programmed slope or change in the data, the C test was statistically significant when the data were positively autocorrelated. Despite Tryon's enthusiastic support for the C test with a nonsignificant phase 1, this procedure

TABLE 12.3
For the C Test, Empirical Probabilities for 1000 Replications
with Each Series Length (N) and First-Order Autoregressive
Parameter (ρ). The Data Have No Programmed Slope
or Change from Phase 1 to Phase 2

	ρ				
N	0	.2	.4	.6	.8
	Undifferentiated Series				
10	.042	.133	.235	.381	.557
20	.057	.192	.487	.775	.903
40	.058	.318	.761	.966	.995
	Nonsignificant Phase 1				
20	.038	.128	.340	.626	.820
40	.033	.221	.570	.885	.971
	Subtracted Trend				
20	.233	.365	.517	.677	.807
40	.122	.343	.638	.869	.948
	Subtracted Scores				
20	.177	.272	.417	.565	.736
40	.239	.399	.606	.790	.917

Note. The nominal alpha is .05.

produces levels of Type I error that are only slightly less than those obtained with undifferentiated series. When the data are uncorrelated this procedure has an acceptable probability of Type I error, but, with nonzero autocorrelation, Type I error rate is excessive. In contrast to the nonsignificant phase-1 procedure, when the phase-1 data have a significant C and subtracted series or trends were used, Type I error rates are unacceptably high for all levels of autocorrelation, even zero.

The analyses in the preceding sections have shown that autocorrelated data pose insurmountable problems for ANOVA, the binomial test, and the C procedure. Autocorrelation must be removed, or Type I error will not be controlled.

TMS

Interrupted time-series analysis (ITSA) is a technique which controls autocorrelation then employs a t test to assess change. TMS (Bower, Padia, & Glass, 1974; Glass, Willson, & Gottman, 1975) was an early ITSA procedure which is still popular. Conceptually it has five steps: (a) remove slope by differencing or detrending the data; (b) identify the model (i.e., assess the pattern of autocorrelations and partial autocorrelations to determine the number of autoregressive and moving-average parameters that best explain the data); (c) obtain least-squares estimates of the autoregressive and moving-average parameters; (d) subtract from the original scores terms based on the estimated autoregressive and moving-average parameters to remove autocorrelation; and (e) employ the *General Linear Model* (GLM) and associated t tests to determine whether the uncorrelated phase-1 scores differ significantly in level or slope from the uncorrelated phase-2 scores.

Removal of Slope

With TMS, phase-1 slope must be removed or the t test will be invalid. For example, if scores are increasing with a constant slope of 1 and there is no change between the phases, phase-2 scores will necessarily be larger than phase-1 scores because of the slope, and a t test will therefore report a significant increase in level. One way to remove slope is to difference the data. The first difference is obtained with the formula

$$X_i = Y_{i+1} - Y_i, \tag{12.5}$$

where X_i is the ith differenced score, and Y_i is the ith original score. The second difference is obtained by repeating this operation with the scores produced by the first difference:

$$Z_i = X_{i+1} - X_i. \tag{12.6}$$

The first difference removes linear trend, and the second difference removes quadratic trend. For example, the series 1, 2, 3, 4, 5, 6 has a linear trend with a slope of 1. The first difference of this series is 1, 1, 1, 1, 1 which has no trend. Similarly, the series 1, 4, 9, 16, 25 has a quadratic trend (Score = Position^2), the first difference 3, 5, 7, 9 has a linear trend, and the second difference 2, 2, 2 has no trend. Alternatively, the data can be detrended by computing a linear regression equation for phase 1, then subtracting from each score the value predicted by the regression equation.

Model Identification

TMS considers two main models of time-series data: autoregressive, and moving average. Autoregressive models have the form

$$Y_i = L + \sum_{j=1}^{n} p_j(Y_{i-j} - L) + E_i, \qquad (12.7)$$

where Y_i is the ith term in the series, L is the level, n is the number of autoregressive parameters (usually ≤ 3; Glass et al., 1975), p_j is the jth autoregressive parameter, and E_i is the ith random error term. Autoregressive models assume that each score is affected by some proportion of a specified number of previous scores. Moving-average models have the form

$$Y_i = L - \sum_{j=1}^{n} a_j E_{i-j} + E_i, \qquad (12.8)$$

where n is the number of moving-average parameters (usually ≤ 3), and a_j is the jth moving-average parameter. Moving-average models assume that each score is affected by some proportion of a specified number of previous error terms. The first task in model identification is to determine the number of autoregressive and moving-average parameters which best describe the data. This is achieved by assessing the pattern of autocorrelations and partial autocorrelations (i.e., autocorrelations produced after various lagged terms have been partialed out; see Gottman, 1981, pp. 141–143). Pure moving-average processes have autocorrelations which cut off after a certain lag, and the cutoff lag indicates the number of moving-average parameters. For example, if the last nonzero autocorrelation is for lag 2, the data have two moving-average parameters. Similarly, pure autoregressive processes have partial autocorrelations which cut off after a certain lag, and that lag indicates the number of autoregressive parameters. If neither the autocorrelations nor the partial autocorrelations cut off, the model has both moving-average and autoregressive parameters, and estimation is complicated. With real data, model identification is much more complex than the present simplified description suggests, and is more of an art than a science (Gottman, 1981).

Parameter Estimation

Autoregressive and moving-average parameters are estimated by performing a sequential grid search to obtain those values which minimize error variance (Glass et al., 1975). For example, if there is one autoregressive parameter, all values of this parameter within the stationarity region (i.e., from $-.98$ to $.98$ in steps of $.02$) are tested to determine which value produces the minimum error variance. This value is therefore the least-squares estimate of the autoregressive parameter. If more than one parameter is modeled, step size is increased to $.05$ or $.1$ to save time, and all values of the parameters are assessed.

Removal of Autocorrelation

When the autoregressive and moving-average parameters have been estimated, autocorrelation can be removed. Consider the following second-order autoregressive process which has parameters of $.6$ and $.3$, and a level of 10:

$$Y_i = 10 + .6(Y_{i-1} - 10) + .3(Y_{i-2} - 10) + E_i. \qquad (12.9)$$

Autocorrelation can be removed by subtracting the following terms from each score: 10, $.6$ times the previous score $- 10$, and $.3$ times the score two steps back $- 10$. Each score in the resultant subtracted series

$$Y_i - 10 - .6(Y_{i-1} - 10) - .3(Y_{i-2} - 10) = E_i \qquad (12.10)$$

is therefore uncorrelated with previous scores. Moving-average terms can be similarly removed. Hence, a t test can be legitimately employed with these uncorrelated data to assess change between the phases.

Analysis of Change

TMS assumes that there is no slope during phase 1, and an abrupt and constant change in level and slope in phase 2. Figure 12.3 shows stylized data for such a pattern. If, for example, no moving-average parameters are identified and one autoregressive parameter of $.6$, phase-1 scores would be modeled by

$$Y_i = L_1 + .6(Y_{i-1} - L_1) + E_i, \qquad (12.11)$$

and phase-2 scores by

$$Y_i = L_1 + L_{CH} + S_{CH}(i - n1) + .6(Y_{i-1} - L_1) + E_i, \qquad (12.12)$$

where L_1 is the phase-1 level, L_{CH} is the change in level, and S_{CH} is the change in slope. If L_1 and the autoregressive terms are subtracted from each score, the equations become

$$Z_i = E_i, \qquad (12.13)$$

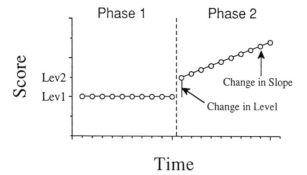

FIG. 12.3. Stylized data showing the parameters estimated by TMS. Change in level is the difference between the level at the end of phase 1 and the level at the start of phase 2. Change in slope is equal to the phase-2 slope because phase-1 slope is zero.

and

$$Z_i = L_{CH} + S_{CH}(i - n1) + E_i, \tag{12.14}$$

for phase 1 and phase 2, respectively. These equations can be written in matrix form as $\mathbf{Z} = \mathbf{X}\,\mathbf{Beta} + \mathbf{E}$:

$$
\begin{matrix}
\mathbf{Z} & \mathbf{X} & \mathbf{Beta} & \mathbf{E}
\end{matrix}
$$

$$
\begin{vmatrix}
Z_1 \\
\cdot \\
\cdot \\
\cdot \\
Z_{n1} \\
\hline
Z_{n1+1} \\
\cdot \\
\cdot \\
\cdot \\
Z_{n1+n2}
\end{vmatrix}
=
\begin{vmatrix}
0 & 0 \\
\cdot & \cdot \\
\cdot & \cdot \\
\cdot & \cdot \\
0 & 0 \\
\hline
1 & 1 \\
\cdot & \cdot \\
\cdot & \cdot \\
\cdot & \cdot \\
1 & n2
\end{vmatrix}
\begin{vmatrix}
L_{Ch} \\
S_{Ch}
\end{vmatrix}
+
\begin{vmatrix}
E_1 \\
\cdot \\
\cdot \\
\cdot \\
E_{n1} \\
\hline
E_{n1+1} \\
\cdot \\
\cdot \\
\cdot \\
E_{n1+n2}
\end{vmatrix}
$$

where $\mathbf{Z}$ is the matrix of transformed scores, $\mathbf{X}$ is the design matrix, $\mathbf{Beta}$ is the parameter matrix, and $\mathbf{E}$ is the matrix of error terms. Least-squares estimates of parameters are obtained with the *GLM* formula

$$\mathbf{Beta} = (\mathbf{X'X})^{-1}\,\mathbf{X'Z}, \tag{12.15}$$

where $\mathbf{X'}$ is the transpose of $\mathbf{X}$, and $(\mathbf{X'X})^{-1}$ is the inverse of $\mathbf{X}$ multiplied by itself. The significance of a parameter is assessed by

$$t(df) = \frac{\text{Beta}_i}{SE \sqrt{a_{ii}}} \qquad (12.16)$$

where $df = n1 + n2 - 2$, Beta_i is the ith parameter, SE is the standard error, and a_{ii} is the ith element on the main diagonal of $(\mathbf{X}'\mathbf{X})^{-1}$.

Conclusion

TMS is superior to visual inference because it is reliable. It is also superior to ANOVA because it removes autocorrelation, and consequently can control Type I error. Unfortunately, it is not useful for most behavior analysts because considerable expertise and many data points (perhaps 50 to 100 per phase; Box & Jenkins, 1976; Glass et al., 1975) are required for its proper use. Because the slope and model need to be estimated from the data by considering autocorrelations and partial autocorrelations, many data points are required for accurate estimates to be obtained (Huitema & McKean, 1991). Even with 50 observations per phase, however, model identification is problematic (Velicer & Harrop, 1983, report only 36% accuracy with 50 observations per phase), and the consequences of misidentification are unknown. Hence, not only is this procedure technically demanding for the user, but accurate model identification, and therefore complete removal of autocorrelation, is virtually impossible with the short series commonly reported in applied behavioral journals.

ITSE

A major problem with TMS is that many observations are required to identify models accurately. Accurate model identification may not be required, however: Autoregressive models (which are unique and computationally simple) can be employed by default for all data because any moving-average model is mathematically identical to some autoregressive model (Gottman, 1981). It has been shown that a model need not be fitted correctly and that an autoregressive model with one to five parameters can be employed successfully with any data (Harrop & Velicer, 1985; Simonton, 1977; Velicer & McDonald, 1984). Model identification can therefore be eliminated, but many data points are still required to remove slope with TMS.

Gottman (1981) proposed a new ITSA procedure (ITSE: interrupted time-series experiment) which is simple to use, does not require the removal of slope or autocorrelation, and can be employed with the short series typically employed in applied settings. ITSE models data on the assumptions that scores are autocorrelated and that each phase has a different intercept and slope. The GLM is then employed to perform the following functions: (a) obtain least-squares estimates of the two intercepts, two slopes and autoregressive parameters; (b) determine

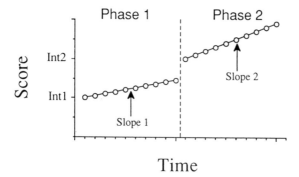

FIG. 12.4. Stylized data showing the parameters estimated by ITSE. Change in intercept is the difference between the value where the phase-2 line crosses the dashed line between phases and the value where the phase-1 line crosses the vertical axis. Change in slope is the difference between the two slopes.

whether there is any significant change in either intercept or slope from the first to the second phase; and (c) determine whether there is a significant difference between the two intercepts and between the two slopes. Figure 12.4 shows stylized data for ITSE.

IF three autoregressive parameters are employed, ITSE will model phase-1 data with the equation

$$Y_i = I_1 + iS_1 + \rho_1 Y_{i-1} + \rho_2 Y_{i-2} + \rho_3 Y_{i-3} + E_i, \qquad (12.17)$$

where Y_i is the ith score; I_1 is the intercept for phase 1; S_1 is the slope for phase 1; ρ_1, ρ_2, and ρ_3 are the three autoregressive parameters; and E_i is the ith normalized random error. Phase-2 data would be modeled with the equation

$$Y_i = I_2 + (i - n1)S_2 + \rho_1 Y_{i-1} + \rho_2 Y_{i-2} + \rho_3 Y_{i-3} + E_i, \qquad (12.18)$$

where I_2 and S_2 are respectively, the intercept and slope for phase 2, and $n1$ is the number of phase-1 scores. In matrix form these equations can be expressed as $\mathbf{Y} = \mathbf{X}\,\mathbf{Beta} + \mathbf{E}$.

$$
\begin{array}{c}
\mathbf{Y} \\
\begin{vmatrix}
Y_4 \\
Y_5 \\
\cdot \\
\cdot \\
Y_{n1} \\
\hline
Y_{n1+1} \\
Y_{n1+2} \\
\cdot \\
\cdot \\
Y_N
\end{vmatrix}
\end{array}
=
\begin{array}{c}
\mathbf{X} \\
\left|
\begin{array}{cccccc}
1 & 1 & 0 & 0 & Y_3 & Y_2 & Y_1 \\
\cdot & 2 & \cdot & \cdot & Y_4 & Y_3 & Y_2 \\
\cdot & \cdot & \cdot & \cdot & \cdot & \cdot & \cdot \\
\cdot & \cdot & \cdot & \cdot & \cdot & \cdot & \cdot \\
1 & n1-3 & 0 & 0 & Y_{n1-1} & Y_{n1-2} & Y_{n1-3} \\
\hline
0 & 0 & 1 & 1 & Y_{n1} & Y_{n1-1} & Y_{n1-2} \\
\cdot & \cdot & \cdot & 2 & Y_{n1+1} & Y_{n1} & Y_{n1-1} \\
\cdot & \cdot & \cdot & \cdot & \cdot & \cdot & \cdot \\
\cdot & \cdot & \cdot & \cdot & \cdot & \cdot & \cdot \\
0 & 0 & 1 & n2 & Y_{N-1} & Y_{N-2} & Y_{N-3}
\end{array}
\right|
\end{array}
\begin{array}{c}
\mathbf{Beta} \\
\begin{vmatrix}
\\
\\
I_1 \\
S_1 \\
I_2 \\
S_2 \\
\rho_1 \\
\rho_2 \\
\rho_3
\end{vmatrix}
\end{array}
+
\begin{array}{c}
\mathbf{E} \\
\begin{vmatrix}
E_4 \\
E_5 \\
\cdot \\
\cdot \\
E_{n1} \\
\hline
E_{n1+1} \\
E_{n1+2} \\
\cdot \\
\cdot \\
E_N
\end{vmatrix}
\end{array}
$$

The first analysis performed with ITSE is an omnibus test of any change from phase 1 to phase 2:

$$F(2, df) = \frac{(SS_0 - SS_1)/2}{SS_1/df}, \tag{12.19}$$

where $df = n1 + n2 - 4 = $ twice the number of autoregressive parameters, SS_1 is the error variance when all parameters are considered, and SS_0 is the error variance when the two phase-2 parameters (I_2 and S_2) are not considered. This test determines whether the addition of the two phase-2 parameters produces a significant reduction in error variance, which is directly analogous to the assessment of a change in R^2 for a multiple regression. In GLM assessments it is standard practice to employ the protected-t procedure of accepting a result as significant only if both the omnibus F and the appropriate t test are significant (Morrison, 1983, p. 79). With ITSE such protection is essential, because, with slope in the data, the t test for change in intercept will be significant even if there is no change between the phases. The omnibus F will not be misled, however, and will report no change. Hence, it is legitimate to perform the other tests only when the omnibus test is significant.

Beta is estimated in the usual way,

$$\textbf{Beta} = (\textbf{X}'\textbf{X})^{-1}\textbf{X}'\textbf{Y},$$

and the significance of individual parameters is assessed with the standard GLM test

$$t(df) = \frac{\textbf{Beta}}{SE\sqrt{a_{ii}}},$$

where $Beta_i$ is the ith parameter, SE is the standard error, and $a_{ii} = (\textbf{X}'\textbf{X})_i^{-1}$. The GLM test of the difference between parameters (e.g., the difference between intercepts, and the difference between slopes) follows directly from the test of individual parameters except that the standard error also incorporates the covariance of the parameters (Cliff, 1987, pp. 173–174; Morrison, 1983, p. 135):

$$t(df) = \frac{Beta_i - Beta_j}{SE\sqrt{(a_{ii} + a_{jj} - 2a_{ij})}}. \tag{12.20}$$

When Gottman first described ITSE (1981), he presented the following formula for this test:

$$t(df) = \frac{Beta_i - Beta_j}{SE\sqrt{df}} \tag{12.21}$$

Equation 12.21 is clearly wrong because it does not consider the variance and covariance of the parameters being assessed: all tests have the same denominator. To show the magnitude of the error obtained with Equation 12.21, a Monte Carlo

TABLE 12.4
For ITSE with Gottman's Original Formulas, Empirical Probabilities
for 1000 Replications with Each Series Length (N)
and First-Order Autoregressive Parameter (ρ). The Data Have
No Programmed Slope or Change from Phase 1 to Phase 2

N	ρ	SigI	SigS	SigF	SigF + I	SigF + S
	−.3	.598	.015	.058	.051	.015
20	0	.634	.022	.074	.065	.021
	.3	.683	.042	.114	.101	.039
	.6	.759	.092	.179	.170	.080
	−.3	.603	.000	.055	.047	.000
40	0	.624	.000	.072	.063	.000
	.3	.654	.000	.093	.084	.000
	.6	.713	.000	.142	.130	.000
	−.3	.615	.000	.049	.041	.000
200	0	.617	.000	.050	.042	.000
	.3	.619	.000	.053	.045	.000
	.6	.630	.000	.061	.053	.000

Note. The nominal alpha is .05. SigI is the test of change in intercept, SigS is the test of change in slope, SigF is the omnibus test of change, SigF + I is both a significant F plus a change in intercept, and SigF + S is both a significant F plus a change in slope.

analysis was performed with data with no slope or change between phases. Table 12.4 shows the results of this analysis. For all series lengths and levels of autocorrelation employed, the test of the difference between intercepts (SigI) has a Type I error rate at least 10 times the nominal alpha (Greenwood & Matyas, 1990, present similar data). Conversely, the test of the difference between slopes (SigS) has a Type I error rate lower than the nominal alpha for the longer series. The omnibus F test is closer to the nominal alpha (SigF), which ensures that the combination of a significant F plus a significant change in intercept (SigF + I) is not far above the nominal alpha for the longer series. Regardless of how closely SigF + I approaches the nominal alpha, however, Equation 12.21 is incorrect and should not be used. In Gottman's book (1981) and the computer programs which perform ITSE (Crosbie & Sharpley, 1989, 1991; Williams & Gottman, 1982), this erroneous formula (12.21) has recently been changed to the standard GLM formula (12.20).

In one step, ITSE estimates and statistically controls autocorrelation, estimates the two intercepts plus the two slopes, and determines whether there is any significant change in the intercepts or slopes. Because of its simplicity and reputed ability to accommodate slope and a small number of observations, ITSE seemed ideal for behavior analysts. Unfortunately, it is also problematic with short series.

Table 12.5 shows for ITSE with the appropriate GLM formula (12.20), the

TABLE 12.5
For ITSE, Empirical Probabilities for 1000 Replications with Each
Series Length (N) and First-Order Autoregressive Parameter (ρ). The
Data Have No Programmed Slope or Change from Phase 1 to Phase 2

	N							
	10		20		30		40	
ρ	$F + I$	$F + S$	$F + I$	$F + S$	$F + I$	$F + S$	$F + I$	$F + S$
.9	.10	.11	.19	.22	.21	.24	.20	.22
.8	.10	.12	.16	.19	.18	.19	.13	.14
.7	.10	.10	.13	.15	.14	.15	.10	.11
.6	.09	.10	.11	.13	.11	.12	.08	.09
.5	.08	.09	.09	.10	.07	.09	.06	.07
.4	.07	.08	.08	.09	.06	.08	.05	.06
.3	.06	.07	.06	.08	.05	.07	.04	.05
.2	.05	.06	.06	.07	.05	.06	.04	.05
.1	.05	.05	.05	.06	.04	.06	.04	.04
0	.04	.04	.04	.05	.04	.05	.03	.04
−.1	.04	.03	.03	.04	.04	.05	.03	.03
−.2	.04	.03	.03	.04	.04	.04	.03	.03
−.3	.03	.03	.03	.04	.03	.04	.03	.03
−.4	.03	.03	.03	.04	.03	.04	.03	.03
−.5	.03	.02	.02	.04	.03	.03	.03	.03
−.6	.02	.02	.02	.03	.02	.03	.03	.03
−.7	.02	.02	.02	.03	.02	.02	.03	.02
−.8	.02	.02	.02	.03	.02	.02	.02	.02
−.9	.02	.02	.02	.03	.02	.02	.02	.02

Note. The nominal alpha is .05. $F + I$ is the probability of obtaining both a significant omnibus F plus a significant change in intercept; $F + S$ is the probability of a significant F plus a significant change in slope.

empirical Type I error for a first-order autoregressive process with ρ between .9 and −.9, and lengths of 10, 20, 30, and 40 observations. When ρ is 0 or negative, Type I error is less than or equal to the nominal alpha for all N shown; as the magnitude of positive autocorrelation increases, however, Type I error becomes much greater than .05. This is the same pattern that was found with the t test, which suggests that ITSE does not remove all of the positive autocorrelation with short series.

ITSE's success rests on the accuracy of its autocorrelation estimate: an underestimate will produce inflated Type I error, an overestimate will produce inflated Type II error. Hence, with short series ITSE does not remove all of the positive autocorrelation, and consequently has an inflated risk of Type I error.

ITSACORR

It is clear from the previous sections that applied behavior analysts need a simple, reliable procedure to assess change with short autocorrelated series. Such a procedure must also be able to control Type I error for all levels of lag-1 autocorrelation up to .9. It is also clear that the available ITSA procedures have limitations when employed with typical applied behavioral data. In response to this need I developed a new ITSA procedure (ITSACORR) which is based on the ITSE model with modifications to provide better control of Type I error and acceptable power.

Autocorrelation Estimates with Short Series

Correction Formulas

The major problem faced by ITSE is that it underestimates positive autocorrelation (the most problematic for Type I error) with short series. This problem is not unique to ITSE, however; all measures of autocorrelation are similarly affected (Huitema & McKean, 1991; Matyas & Greenwood, 1991). Although underestimation of autocorrelation parameters with short series has only recently been discussed in the psychological literature (Huitema & McKean, 1991; Matyas & Greenwood, 1991), it has been described extensively in the statistical literature for 50 years (e.g., Anderson, 1942; Bartlett, 1946; Dixon, 1944; Kendall, 1954; Marrott & Pope, 1954; Moran, 1948; Shaman & Stine, 1988).

Figure 12.5 shows the relationship between programmed and estimated autocorrelation for 1000 replications of a first-order autoregressive process with programmed autocorrelation (ρ) between .9 and $-.9$ in steps of .1, and lengths of 10, 20, 30, 40, 50, and 100 observations. With $N = 100$, estimated and programmed autocorrelation are very similar for all values of ρ. With shorter series, however, autocorrelation is underestimated when ρ is positive, and the more positive values of ρ and the shorter series have the greatest underestimation.

ITSE and TMS assume that estimated autocorrelation (r_1) closely approximates the autocorrelation parameter (ρ_1). With the long series required by TMS this is correct, but with short series r_1 is biased as a function of N and ρ_1 (see Figure 12.5). A better approximation of ρ_1 (Huitema & McKean, 1991) is obtained with the formula

$$\rho_1^* = r_1 + 1/N. \qquad (12.22)$$

For example, with $N = 10$ and $\rho_1 = .9$, $r_1 = .4$, and $\rho_1^* = .5$ (i.e., $.4 + .1$). This value still underestimates ρ_1, but it is closer than r_1. One problem with this simple technique is that it does not work well with negative autocorrelation. With $N = 10$ and $\rho_1 = -.9$, $r_1 = -.72$, and $\rho_1^* = -.62$, which is an inferior estimate.

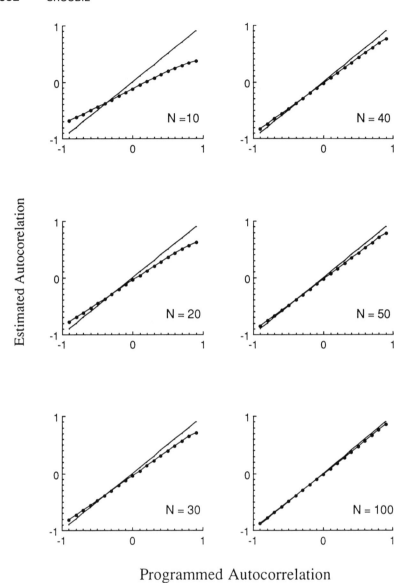

Programmed Autocorrelation

FIG. 12.5   Estimated autocorrelation as a function of programmed autocorrelation and number of observations (closed circles). The line of
perfect estimation is also shown.

When the mean of the scores is not necessarily zero (the normal situation with applied data), the relationship between r_1 and ρ_1 is approximately

$$r_1 = \rho_1 - \frac{1 + 3\rho_1}{N} \qquad (12.23)$$

(Marriott & Pope, 1954; Shaman & Stine, 1988). Following algebraic manipulation of Equation 12.23, a more accurate estimate of ρ_1 can be obtained with the formula

$$\rho_1^* = \frac{Nr_1 + 1}{N - 3} \qquad (12.24)$$

Compare the ρ_1^* estimates obtained with Equations 12.22 and 12.24. With $N = 10$ and $\rho_1 = .9$, $r_1 = .40$, ρ_1^* (12.22) $= .50$, and ρ_1^* (12.24) $= .71$. With $N = 10$ and $\rho_1 = -.9$, $r_1 = -.72$, ρ_1^* (12.22) $= -.62$, and ρ_1^* (12.24) $= -.89$. Hence, Equation 12.24 is more accurate for both positive and negative autocorrelation, and does not produce inferior estimates with negative autocorrelation. Similar theoretical formulas are available for autocorrelations up to lag 3 (Shaman & Stine, 1988), which extends the utility of this adjustment technique.

Estimation of Autocorrelation

If the data have no slope, r_1 can be calculated accurately with various formulas for lag-1 autocorrelation (see Huitema & McKean, 1991, for some of these formulas). When the data contain a slope in addition to positive autocorrelation, however, r_1 is inflated. As an example, consider the following Monte Carlo data:

$$Y_i = 5 + i + E_i, \qquad (12.25)$$

where Y_i *is the* ith score, i is the ordinal position of the score (between 1 and 20), and E_i is the ith normalized random error. This series has an intercept of 5, a slope of 1, and no autocorrelation. Using Equation 12.1 with this series, $r_1 = 45$, and ρ_1^* (12.24) $= .59$. Even though there is no autocorrelation in the data, a nonzero slope produces a large positive value for estimated autocorrelation. Clearly, slope must be controlled when estimating autocorrelation. This problem is avoided with TMS by first removing slope, and with ITSE by estimating r_1 above and beyond slope and intercept. ITSACORR employs a technique similar to ITSE and uses the GLM to estimate intercept, slope, and r_1 concurrently. Hence, r_1 is independent of slope. When ITSACORR is employed with the data from Equation 12.25, $r_1 = -.08$ and ρ_1^* (12.24) $= -.03$, which shows that its autocorrelation estimates are unaffected by slope.

If all scores are employed, a change in intercept or slope will inflate estimates of positive autocorrelation. With TMS, this problem is overcome, to some extent, by removing slope and employing long series. ITSE overcomes the problem by estimating autocorrelation independently of each intercept and slope. One possible way in which ITSACORR might circumvent this problem is to estimate autocorrelation from only one of the phases. Unfortunately, autocorrelation estimates obtained from single phases are considerably inferior to those obtained from both phases combined, and single-phase estimates produce excessive Type I error with the ITSACORR procedure described below. For this reason, ITSACORR estimates autocorrelation from all scores and thereby runs the risk of obtaining an inflated estimate of positive autocorrelation when there is a change between phases.

Control of Autocorrelation

After r_1 is estimated from all scores and adjusted with Equation 12.24, ITSACORR employs ρ_1^* to control autocorrelation. This is achieved by inserting ρ_1^* in the GLM parameter matrix via linear constraints (Searle, 1971; Theil, 1961), obtaining least-squares estimates of the two intercepts and the two slopes, then assessing change in intercept and slope.

Linear Constraints

Linear constraints is a GLM technique which permits additional information to be used so that least-squares estimates are obtained for parameters given the constraints imposed. Consider the following example of how linear constraints are employed. Five parameters were estimated (Intercept1, Slope1, Intercept2, Slope2, and lag-1 autocorrelation), and it was expected (on the basis of theory, the literature, or prior experience) that the following relationships would be found: (a) Intercept1 would be 10, (b) Slope1 would equal Slope2, and (c) lag-1 autocorrelation would equal .6. Least-squares estimates were then obtained for the five parameters so that the three conditions were satisfied. To achieve this a design matrix ($\mathbf{R}$) was constructed with one column for each parameter, and one row for each constraint (with fewer constraints than parameters). An array of constants ($\mathbf{r}$) was also produced, with one row for each constraint. The three constraints were therefore expressed in matrix form as $\mathbf{R}\,\mathbf{Beta} = \mathbf{r}$:

$$
\begin{array}{c}
\mathbf{R} \\
\begin{vmatrix}
1 & 0 & 0 & 0 & 0 \\
0 & 1 & 0 & -1 & 0 \\
0 & 0 & 0 & 0 & 1
\end{vmatrix}
\end{array}
\begin{array}{c}
\mathbf{Beta} \\
\begin{vmatrix}
I_1 \\
S_1 \\
I_2 \\
S_2 \\
r_1
\end{vmatrix}
\end{array}
=
\begin{array}{c}
\mathbf{r} \\
\begin{vmatrix}
10 \\
0 \\
.6
\end{vmatrix}
\end{array}
$$

Beta was estimated in the usual way, then adjusted with $\mathbf{R}$ and $\mathbf{r}$ to produce **B**, least-squares estimates of the parameters given the constraints (see Theil, 1961, for technical details of how **Beta** is adjusted to obtain **B**).

Monte Carlo data were then obtained with 10 phase-1 scores and 10 phase-2 scores produced with the formulas

$$Y_i = I_1 + S_1 i + .6Y_{i-1} + E_i, \tag{12.26}$$

and

$$Y_i = I_2 + S_2(i - n1) + .6Y_{i-1} + E_i, \tag{12.27}$$

where $I_1 = 10$, $I_2 = 12$, and $S_1 = S_2 = 0$. The phase-1 scores were 10.9, 14.5, 19.4, 21.7, 22.1, 24.2, 25.0, 25.1, 24.9, and 23.4; the phase-2 scores were 26.7, 27.1, 25.8, 26.4, 26.5, 29.9, 30.0, 29.2, 29.8, and 28.7. **Beta** was 8.60, $-.13$, 9.21, $-.01$, and .69. Without imposing any constraints, the parameter estimates were close, but not exactly equal, to the conditions assumed. **B** was 10, $-.02$, 11.62, $-.02$, and .60. Thus, all of the conditions were satisfied: I_1 was 10, S_1 was equal to S_2, and r_1 was .6. Parenthetically, the omnibus test of change was significant, $F(2, 17) = 8.71$, $p < .01$, as was the change in intercept, $t(17) = 3.30$, $p < .01$.

Linear constraints is essentially a way to produce designer matrices. It is also analogous to genetic engineering: the genetic structure of a cell is changed, and the organism is left to develop normally and produce the desired characteristic. For present purposes it is a useful way to insert more accurate estimates of autocorrelation into **Beta** so that the GLM can produce better estimates of slope and intercept.

Type I Error

The technique employed by ITSACORR is simple: (a) an ITSE data model is assumed, (b) r_1 is estimated for all scores with slope and intercept controlled, (c) r_1 is adjusted with Equation 12.24 to produce ρ_1^*, (d) ρ_1^* is inserted in **Beta** with linear constraints, and (e) the GLM is employed to assess change in intercept plus change in slope.

Table 12.6 shows the empirical Type I error for ITSACORR. For all N and ρ, ITSACORR has a risk of making a Type I error which is less than the nominal alpha. These results are substantially better than those obtained with the t test (Table 12.1) and ITSE (Table 12.5).

Table 12.6, however, also highlights a potential problem with the procedure: When $\rho = 0$ Type I error is approximately half the nominal alpha, which suggests that ITSACORR is conservative and may have insufficient power. The following analyses assessed this possibility.

Power

Visual inference in behavior analysis is based on the assumption that only large changes should be considered significant (Baer, 1977; Sidman, 1960). Conse-

TABLE 12.6

For ITSACORR, Empirical Probabilities for 1000 Replications with Each Series Length (*N*) and First-Order Autoregressive Parameter (ρ). The Data Have No Programmed Slope or Change from Phase 1 to Phase 2

	N							
	10		20		30		40	
ρ	*F + I*	*F + S*	*F + I*	*F + S*	*F + I*	*F + S*	*F + I*	*F + S*
.9	.03	.03	.03	.04	.02	.03	.02	.01
.8	.03	.03	.02	.03	.01	.01	.01	.00
.7	.03	.03	.02	.02	.00	.00	.01	.01
.6	.03	.02	.01	.01	.00	.00	.01	.01
.5	.02	.02	.01	.01	.00	.01	.01	.01
.4	.02	.02	.01	.01	.01	.01	.01	.01
.3	.02	.02	.01	.01	.01	.01	.01	.01
.2	.02	.03	.01	.01	.01	.02	.02	.02
.1	.02	.03	.01	.01	.02	.02	.02	.02
0	.02	.03	.01	.01	.02	.02	.02	.02
−.1	.02	.03	.01	.02	.02	.02	.02	.02
−.2	.02	.03	.01	.02	.03	.02	.02	.02
−.3	.03	.03	.02	.03	.03	.03	.02	.02
−.4	.03	.03	.02	.03	.03	.03	.02	.02
−.5	.03	.02	.02	.03	.03	.03	.03	.02
−.6	.03	.02	.03	.04	.03	.03	.03	.02
−.7	.03	.02	.03	.04	.02	.03	.03	.02
−.8	.02	.02	.03	.04	.02	.03	.03	.02
−.9	.02	.02	.03	.04	.02	.03	.03	.02

Note. The nominal alpha is .05. *F + I* is the probability of obtaining both a significant omnibus *F* plus a significant change in intercept; *F + S* is the probability of a significant *F* plus a significant change in slope.

quently, the changes reported in behavioral journals are typically large (a change in level of 5 standard deviations is the 25th percentile, and 10 standard deviations is the median change (Matyas & Greenwood, 1990). In the following power assessments, changes of 5 and 10 standard deviations were employed because they represent moderate changes for applied behavioral data; alpha was set at .05 and acceptable power at .80 (Cohen, 1977).

Table 12.7 shows the power of ITSACORR with a programmed change in intercept of five standard deviations, but no change in slope. *F + S* has a probability less than .80 for all *N* and ρ. *F + I*, however, varies systematically with *N* and ρ: for *N* = 10 power is inadequate (i.e., *F + I* < .80) for all levels of ρ, for *N* = 20 power is acceptable only when ρ is ≥ .5 or ≤ −.4, and for larger *N* power is acceptable for all levels of ρ. Hence, ITSACORR has the power to detect a modest change in intercept (i.e., the 25th percentile of typical applied behavioral data) for all levels of ρ only when $N \geq 30$.

Table 12.8 shows the power of ITSACORR with a programmed change in intercept of 10 standard deviations, but no change in slope. $F + I$ has acceptable power for all N and ρ except when $N = 10$ and ρ is between $-.1$ and $-.3$; in these three situations power is slightly less than .80. Hence, ITSACORR has the power to detect a moderate change in intercept (i.e., the 50th percentile of typical applied behavioral data) for all levels of N and ρ.

One limitation of ITSACORR is that, with a moderate change in intercept and high levels of positive autocorrelation, a spurious change in slope is reported (see Table 12.5). this occurs because a portion of the increased intercept is added to each phase-2 score, which produces an apparent increase in slope. Figure 12.6

TABLE 12.7

For ITSACORR, Empirical Probabilities for 1000 Replications with Each Series Length (N) and First-Order Autoregressive Parameter (ρ). The Data Have No Programmed Slope, but a Change in Intercept of 5 Standard Deviations from Phase 1 to Phase 2

	N							
	10		20		30		40	
ρ	$F + I$	$F + S$	$F + I$	$F + S$	$F + I$	$F + S$	$F + I$	$F + S$
.9	.58	.05	.99	.14	1.00	.27	1.00	.41
.8	.59	.10	.99	.37	1.00	.62	1.00	.73
.7	.59	.12	.97	.38	1.00	.56	1.00	.58
.6	.57	.12	.93	.30	.97	.35	.98	.29
.5	.54	.11	.85	.19	.93	.18	.92	.10
.4	.51	.09	.77	.09	.84	.07	.88	.03
.3	.47	.06	.69	.05	.81	.02	.87	.00
.2	.43	.05	.65	.02	.81	.01	.88	.00
.1	.40	.04	.65	.01	.83	.00	.91	.00
0	.38	.03	.66	.01	.87	.00	.94	.00
$-.1$	.36	.02	.69	.01	.90	.00	.97	.00
$-.2$	.37	.02	.74	.01	.93	.00	.98	.00
$-.3$	.38	.02	.79	.01	.95	.00	.99	.00
$-.4$	.40	.02	.83	.01	.97	.01	1.00	.00
$-.5$	.42	.03	.85	.01	.99	.01	1.00	.00
$-.6$	.43	.03	.88	.02	.99	.01	1.00	.00
$-.7$	.43	.03	.91	.02	1.00	.01	1.00	.01
$-.8$	.42	.03	.93	.03	1.00	.02	1.00	.01
$-.9$	.38	.02	.95	.03	1.00	.03	1.00	.02

Note. The nominal alpha is .05 and acceptable power is $\geq .80$. $F + I$ is the probability of obtaining both a significant omnibus F plus a significant change in intercept; $F + S$ is the probability of a significant F plus a significant change in slope.

TABLE 12.8

For ITSACORR, Empirical Probabilities for 1000 Replications with
Each Series Length (N) and First-Order Autoregressive Parameter
(ρ). The Data Have No Programmed Slope, but a Change in Intercept
of 10 Standard Deviations from Phase 1 to Phase 2

					N			
	10		20		30		40	
ρ	$F + I$	$F + S$	$F + I$	$F + S$	$F + I$	$F + S$	$F + I$	$F + S$
.9	1.00	.09	1.00	.42	1.00	.80	1.00	.96
.8	1.00	.31	1.00	.93	1.00	1.00	1.00	1.00
.7	.99	.45	1.00	.96	1.00	1.00	1.00	1.00
.6	.99	.38	1.00	.89	1.00	.98	1.00	.98
.5	.98	.28	1.00	.70	1.00	.81	1.00	.81
.4	.97	.20	1.00	.43	1.00	.50	1.00	.43
.3	.95	.13	1.00	.21	1.00	.21	1.00	.14
.2	.91	.08	.98	.08	.99	.07	.99	.03
.1	.86	.05	.96	.03	.98	.02	.99	.01
0	.83	.02	.95	.01	.98	.01	.99	.00
−.1	.79	.01	.94	.00	.98	.00	.99	.00
−.2	.78	.01	.94	.00	.98	.00	.99	.00
−.3	.79	.00	.95	.00	.98	.00	.99	.00
−.4	.80	.00	.95	.00	.99	.00	1.00	.00
−.5	.82	.01	.96	.00	.99	.00	1.00	.00
−.6	.84	.01	.97	.00	1.00	.00	1.00	.00
−.7	.86	.02	.98	.00	1.00	.00	1.00	.00
−.8	.86	.03	.98	.01	1.00	.00	1.00	.00
−.9	.84	.02	.99	.02	1.00	.01	1.00	.00

Note. The nominal alpha is .05 and acceptable power is $\geq$ .80. $F + I$ is the probability
of obtaining both a significant omnibus F plus a significant change in intercept; $F + S$
is the probability of a significant F plus a significant change in slope.

shows such a pattern with Monte Carlo data. The user is not greatly misled by
this, however, because $F + S$ is never larger than $F + I$, and the worst case is
that a significant change in slope is inferred in addition to a significant change in
intercept (see Tables 12.4 and 12.5). For most applications this is relatively
unimportant.

Clinical Examples

ITSACORR controls Type I error and has acceptable power with Monte
Carlo data, but how successful is it with real data? To answer this question,
ITSACORR was performed on two short data sets which evaluated the effects of

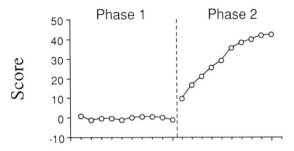

FIG. 12.6. Monte Carlo data produced with Intercept$_1$ = Slope$_1$ = Slope$_2$ = 0, Intercept$_2$ = 10, and programmed lag-1 autocorrelation = .8.

feedback on personal appearance, and a longer data set which showed the effect of chlorpromazine on perceptual speed.

Personal Appearance

McClannahan, McGee, MacDuff, and Krantz (1990) performed a single-subject assessment of the effects of providing feedback to parents concerning the personal appearance of their children at school. The children in the study (aged 8 to 16) displayed multiple, severe skill deficits and behavior problems, and their records showed evidence of moderate to profound retardation. These children had lived in an institution for several years before moving to group homes in which a maximum of five children lived with teaching parents. Childrens' personal appearance was recorded every day at school with the 20-item personal appearance index (PAI) which contained items such as hair clean, face clean, nose clean, shoes tied, and clothing fastened (see McClannahan et al., 1990, Table 1, for the complete list). For each item on the PAI, observers recorded a plus, minus, or not applicable for each child. A child's personal appearance score was obtained by dividing the number of items scored positive by the total number of items scored either positive or negative, and multiplying this quotient by 100. During baseline, teaching parents were unaware of any details concerning the measurement of child appearance. Baseline conditions were in effect for 6 sessions for Home 1, and 11 sessions for Home 2. Following baseline, teaching parents were provided with verbal and written feedback concerning the personal appearance of their children.

Figure 12.7 shows for Homes 1 and 2, the mean personal appearance score for each session (data were estimated from McClannahan et al., 1990, Figure 3). Given the variability, modest change, and slope in these data (especially in Home 2), visual inference is difficult. Home 2 provides a good example of the problems faced by visual inference: phase-2 scores are greater than those in phase 1, but the data are steadily increasing throughout, and it is not clear whether there is a

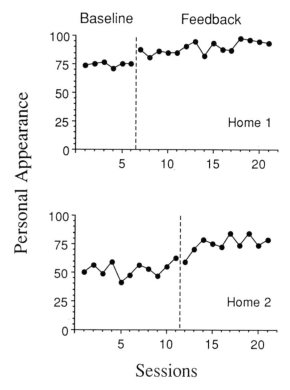

FIG. 12.7.   Mean personal appearance scores prior to and following feedback to teaching parents concerning their childrens' personal appearance.

change between phases or merely the continuation of a phase-1 trend. Furthermore, the data are quite variable which complicates visual analysis.

ITSACORR was performed on these data with a .05 significance level for all tests. For Home 1, there was a significant overall change from phase 1 to phase 2, $F(2, 16) = 4.60$, a significant increase in intercept, $t(16) = 2.16$, but no significant change in slope, $t(16) = .98$. For Home 2, there was no significant overall change from phase 1 to phase 2, $F(2, 16) = 1.06$, or change in intercept, $t(16) = 2.03$, or change in slope, $t(16) = .36$. Hence, with only 21 total observations and baseline lengths of 6 and 11, ITSACORR is able to discriminate between a significant change (as in Home 1) and no change (as in Home 2). Regardless of the small change in intercept in Home 1 (steady-state estimates of 74.81 and 82.67 for phase 1 and phase 2, respectively; see Gottman, 1981, for details of steady-state estimates), the omnibus F test and the t test for change in intercept both reported a change. In Home 2, however, there was more variability and slope during phase 1, and the omnibus F test found that the change was not significant.

Perceptual Speed

Glass et al. (1975, pp. 21, 219) presented data on the effects of chlor-promazine on the perceptual speed of a person with schizophrenia. There were 60 sessions of baseline before chlorpromazine was used, then 60 sessions during which the drug was administered. Figure 12.8 shows these data.

Because of the large number of observations, the perceptual speed data can be analyzed legitimately with TMS, ITSE, and ITSACORR. To demonstrate the similarities and differences of these three procedures, each was performed on these data.

TMS suggested that these data are best described by one moving-average parameter and one difference parameter (Glass et al., 1975, pp. 137–140). Fol-lowing the first difference, least-squares estimates of the moving-average param-eter, initial level, and change in level are .76, 54.06, and −21.83, respectively. Change in level is significant, $t(118) = −3.48$, $p < .05$.

ITSE found that the first autoregressive parameter is .17, and that there is a significant change (at the .05 level for all the following analyses) between phases, $F(2, 114) = 26.01$, and between slopes, $t(114) = −5.95$, but not between intercepts, $t(114) = −0.28$. Steady-state estimates of the two intercepts and the two slopes are 56.94, 55.97, 0.50, and −0.49, respectively. Each of these parameters is significant.

ITSACORR found that the first autoregressive parameter is .66, and that there is a significant difference between phases, $F(2, 115) = 6.41$, and between slopes, $t(115) = − 2.92$, but not between intercepts, $t(115) = −0.01$. Steady-state estimates of the intercepts and slopes are 59.59, 61.58, 0.47, and −0.65, respectively. Each of these parameters is significant.

All three procedures found an initial level or intercept between 50 and 60, plus a significant reduction in level or slope during phase 2. Hence, with a large

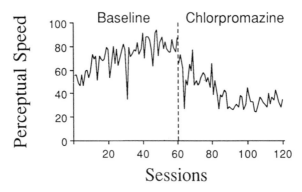

FIG. 12.8. Perceptual speed of a person with schizophrenia before and after administration of chlorpromazine.

number of scores, all three procedures reach the same conclusion. With short positively autocorrelated series, however, ITSACORR is superior.

CONCLUSION

The main conclusion to emerge from the present analyses is that the situation for behavior analysts is not hopeless. Although previously available procedures do not control Type I error adequately when series are short and have high levels of positive autocorrelation, ITSACORR can be used effectively with such data. Furthermore, ITSACORR is simple and the user requires no expertise: A computer program performs the entire analysis, reports whether there is a change in intercept or slope (with the exact probability for the F and t tests), and graphs the data with estimated steady-state trend lines.

Although ITSACORR works well, I hope it is soon superseded. Such rapid development would be invaluable for psychology because it would soon provide us with the high-quality precise tools that other scientists take for granted. For too long, researchers and clinicians have described the problems associated with statistical analysis of single-subject data, without suggesting solutions. It is important to appreciate the problems, but such an appreciation should not lead to learned helplessness. I hope that the present chapter will show that the problems are not insurmountable and will encourage researchers to spend time trying to obtain progressively better procedures which will provide a great leap forward for our science and clinical practice.

ACKNOWLEDGMENTS

The present research was supported by Deakin University Internal Research grants. I am grateful to Glenn Kelly, Brian Matthews, and Chris Sharpley for helpful comments on an earlier version of this manuscript. A program to perform ITSACORR is available from the author. Correspondence concerning this chapter should be sent to John Crosbie, who is now at the Department of Psychology, West Virginia University, Morgantown, West Virginia 26506-6040; Fax 304-293-6606.

REFERENCES

Anderson, R. L. (1942). Distribution of the serial correlation coefficient. *Annals of Mathematical Statistics, 13,* 1–13.

Baer, D. M. (1977). Perhaps it would be better not to know everything. *Journal of Applied Behavior Analysis, 10,* 167–172.

Barlow, D. H., Hayes, S. C., & Nelson, R. O. (1984). *The scientist practitioner: Research and accountability in clinical and educational settings.* New York: Pergamon.

Bartlett, M. S. (1946). On the theoretical specification of sampling properties of autocorrelated time series. *Journal of the Royal Statistical Society, B8,* 27–41.

Bloom, M., & Fischer, J. (1982). *Evaluating practice: Guidelines for the accountable professional.* Englewood Cliffs, NJ: Prentice-Hall.

Bower, C. R., Padia, W. L., & Glass, G. V. (1974). *TMS: Two FORTRAN IV programs for analysis of time-series experiments.* Boulder, CO: Laboratory of Educational Research, University of Colorado.

Box, G. E. P., & Jenkins, G. M. (1976). *Time series analysis: Forecasting and control.* San Francisco: Holden-Day.

Cliff, N. (1987). *Analyzing multivariate data.* San Diego, CA: Harcourt Brace Jovanovich.

Cohen, J. (1977). *Statistical power analysis for the behavioral sciences* (rev. ed.). New York: Academic Press.

Crosbie, J. (1987). The inability of the binomial test to control Type I error with single-subject data. *Behavioral Assessment, 9,* 141–150.

Crosbie, J. (1989). The inappropriateness of the *C* statistic for assessing stability or treatment effects with single-subject data. *Behavioral Assessment, 11,* 315–325.

Crosbie, J., & Sharpley, C. F. (1989). DMITSA: A simplified interrupted time-series analysis program. *Behavior Research Methods. Instruments, & Computers, 21,* 639–642.

Crosbie, J., & Sharpley, C. F. (1991). *The DMITSA 2.0 manual.* Melbourne, Australia: Monash University.

DeProspero, A., & Cohen, S. (1979). Inconsistent visual analyses of intrasubject data. *Journal of Applied Behavior Analysis, 12,* 573–579.

Dixon, W. J. (1944). Further contributions to the problem of serial correlation. *Annals of Mathematical Statistics, 15,* 119–144.

Furlong, M. J., & Wampold, B. E. (1982). Intervention effects and relative variations as dimensions in experts' use of visual inference. *Journal of Applied Behavior Analysis, 15,* 415–421.

Gentile, J. R., Roden, A. H., & Klein, R. D. (1972). An analysis-of-variance model for the intrasubject replication design. *Journal of Applied Behavior Analysis, 5,* 816–820.

Glass, G. V., Willson, V. L., & Gottman, J. M. (1975). *Design and analysis of time-series experiments.* Boulder, CO: University of Colorado Press.

Gottman, J. M. (1981). *Time-series analysis: A comprehensive introduction for social scientists.* Cambridge, England: Cambridge University Press.

Greenwood, K. M., & Matyas, T. A. (1990). Problems with the application of interrupted time series analysis for brief single-subject data. *Behavioral Assessment, 12,* 355–370.

Harrop, J. W., & Velicer, W. F. (1985). A comparison of alternative approaches to the analysis of interrupted time-series. *Multivariate Behavioral Research, 20,* 27–44.

Hartmann, D. P. (1974). Forcing square pegs into round holes: Some comments on an analysis of variance model for the intrasubject design. *Journal of Applied Behavior Analysis, 7,* 635–638.

Hersen, M., & Barlow, D. H. (1976). *Single case experimental designs: Strategies for studying change in the individual.* New York: Pergamon Press.

Huitema, B. E., & McKean, J. W. (1991). Autocorrelation estimation and inference with small samples. *Psychological Bulletin, 110,* 291–304.

Jones, R. R., Weinrott, M. R., & Vaught, R. S. (1978). Effects of serial dependency on the agreement between visual and statistical inference. *Journal of Applied Behavior Analysis, 11,* 277–283.

Kazdin, A. E. (1982). *Single-case research designs: Methods for clinical and research settings.* New York: Oxford University Press.

Kendall, M. G. (1954). Some notes on the estimation of autocorrelations. *Biometrika, 41,* 403–404.

Killeen, P. R. (1978). Stability criteria. *Journal of the Experimental Analysis of Behavior, 29,* 17–25.

Knuth, D. E. (1981). *The art of computer programming: Vol. 2. Seminumerical algorithms* (2nd ed.). Reading, MA: Addison-Wesley.

Marriott, F. H., & Pope, J. A. (1954). Bias in the estimation of autocorrelation. *Biometrika, 41,* 390–402.

Matyas, T. A., & Greenwood, K. M. (1985, July). *A survey of serial dependence in behavioural baselines.* Paper presented at the 8th National Conference of the Australian Behaviour Modification Association, Melbourne, Australia.

Matyas, T. A., & Greenwood, K. M. (1990). Visual analysis of single-case time series: Effects of variability, serial dependence, and magnitude of intervention effects. *Journal of Applied Behavior Analysis, 23,* 341–351.

Matyas, T. A., & Greenwood, K. M. (1991). Problems in the estimation of autocorrelations in brief time series and some implications for behavioral data. *Behavioral Assessment, 13,* 137–157.

McClannahan, L. E., McGee, G. G., MacDuff, G. S., & Krantz, P. J. (1990). Assessing and improving child care: A personal appearance index for children with autism. *Journal of Applied Behavior Analysis, 23,* 469–482.

Moran, P. A. P. (1948). Some theorems on time series: II. The significance of the serial correlation coefficient. *Biometrika, 35,* 255–260.

Morrison, D. F. (1983). *Applied linear statistical methods.* Englewood Cliffs, NJ: Prentice-Hall.

Ottenbacher, K. J. (1986). Reliability and accuracy of visually analyzing graphed data from single-subject designs. *American Journal of Occupational Therapy, 40,* 464–469.

Padia, W. L. (1975). *The consequence of model misidentification in the interrupted time-series experiment.* Unpublished doctoral dissertation, University of Colorado.

Parsonson, B. S., & Baer, D. M. (1978). The analysis and presentation of graphic data. In T. R. Kratochwill (Ed.), *Single-subject research: Strategies for evaluating change* (pp. 101–165). New York: Academic Press.

Parsonson, B. S., & Baer, D. M. (1986). The graphic analysis of data. In A. Poling & R. W. Fuqua (Eds.), *Research methods in applied behavior analysis: Issues and advances* (pp. 157–186). New York: Plenum Press.

Press, W. H., Flannery, B. P., Teukolsky, S. A., & Vetterling, W. T. (1989). *Numerical recipes in Pascal: The art of scientific computing.* Cambridge, England: Cambridge University Press.

Scheffé, H. (1959). *The analysis of variance.* New York: Wiley.

Searle, S. R. (1971). *Linear models.* New York: Wiley.

Shaman, P., & Stine, R. A. (1988). The bias of autoregressive coefficient estimators. *Journal of the American Statistical Association, 83,* 842–848.

Sharpley, C. F. (1987). Time-series analysis of behavioural data: An update. *Behaviour Change, 4,* 40–45.

Sidman, M. (1960). *Tactics for scientific research: Evaluating experimental data in psychology.* New York: Basic Books.

Siegel, S. (1956). *Nonparametric statistics for the behavioral sciences.* Tokyo: McGraw-Hill Kogakusha.

Simonton, D. K. (1977). Cross-sectional time-series experiments: Some suggested statistical analyses. *Psychological Bulletin, 84,* 489–502.

Theil, H. (1961). *Economic forecasts and policy* (2nd ed.). Amsterdam: North-Holland.

Thoresen, C. E., & Elashoff, J. D. (1974). An analysis of variance model for intrasubject replication designs: Some additional comments. *Journal of Applied Behavior Analysis, 7,* 639–641.

Toothaker, L. E., Banz, M., Noble, C., Camp, J., & Davis, D. (1983). $N = 1$ designs: The failure of ANOVA-based tests. *Journal of Educational Statistics, 8,* 289–309.

Tryon, W. W. (1982). A simplified time-series analysis for evaluating treatment interventions. *Journal of Applied Behavior Analysis, 15,* 423–429.

Velicer, W. F., & Harrop, J. (1983). The reliability and accuracy of time series model identification. *Evaluation Review, 7,* 551–560.

Velicer, W. F., & McDonald, R. P. (1984). Time series analysis without model identification. *Multivariate Behavioral Research, 19,* 33–47.

Wampold, B., & Furlong, M. (1981). The heuristics of visual inference. *Behavioral Assessment, 3,* 79–92.

White, O. R. (1972). *A manual for the calculation and use of the median slope—A technique of progress estimation and prediction in the single case.* Regional Resource Center for Handicapped Children, University of Oregon, Eugene, OR.

White, O. R. (1974). *The "split middle"—a "quickie" method of trend estimation.* Experimental Education Unit, Child Development and Mental Retardation Center, University of Washington.

Williams, E. A., & Gottman, J. M. (1982). *A user's guide to the Gottman-Williams time-series analysis computer programs for social scientists.* Cambridge, England: Cambridge University Press.

Young, L. C. (1941). On randomness in ordered sequences. *Annals of mathematical Statistics, 12,* 293–300.

13

Current Developments in Time-Series Modeling*

M. B. Priestley
University of Manchester Institute of Science and Technology, United Kingdom

Priestley's chapter is an update of current methods of time-series analysis, in particular using nonlinear models.

—Editor

*This chapter originally appeared in: Priestley, M. B. (1988). Current developments in time series modelling. *Journal of Econometrics*, *37*, 67–86. Copyright 1988 by North-Holland. Reprinted by permission of Elsevier Science S.A.

INTRODUCTION

Time series analysis is a strange subject. Its roots are firmly embedded in physics and engineering, yet its methodology is largely statistical, and its applications range from astrophysics to neurophysiology. It does not give rise to fierce arguments on the fundamental ideas of statistical inference (although Bayesian ideas do intrude from time to time), yet it has provoked some fierce battles on topics such as the Uncertainty Principle, the physical interpretation of time-dependent spectra, and the relative merits of various forecasting techniques, and it has often been said that if you present the same data to two time series analysts you will receive three different answers.

One of the areas in which time series methodology differs from that of the more conventional branches of statistics is in relation to the ideas and techniques of modelling. When we speak of a 'linear model' in conventional statistics we mean one in which the relationship between the observed variable and the explanatory variables is a linear function of the *parameters* of the model (a polynomial regression is, of course, still a linear model). However, within the context of time series modelling the term 'linear' is used in a sense which is much closer to its physical interpretation; a linear time series model is one in which the relationship between the present and the past is expressed in a linear form, i.e., the 'dynamics' of the process are of a linear form.

During the first fifty years of the development of modern methods of time series analysis linear models provided the dominant influence, and much of conventional time series analysis rests very heavily on this assumption. It may be of some interest therefore to consider some recent developments in the area of non-linear modelling, and to examine the way in which these ideas extend the well trodden areas of linear models.

Before embarking on a detailed discussion of these topics one or two general remarks may be in order. The subject of linear time series modelling has now reached a very refined state (in terms of both its theoretical structure and inferential aspects) and, by contrast, non-linear modelling is still very much in its infancy. When judged within the context of non-linear models, the subject of linear modelling appears to be almost trivial by comparison, and the availability of a complete theory is due essentially to the very neat and tidy theory of 'linear mathematics' (essentially, the theory of linear vector spaces). It is this feature which enables one to develop a very elegant theory of prediction, and which in turn leads to Akaike's superbly attractive geometrical interpretation of ideas such as 'state-space representation', 'minimal realisations' and, more importantly, the notion of the 'dimension' of a linear model [Akaike (1974a,b)]. There is of course no comparable comprehensive treatment of non-linear mathematics, and correspondingly the studies of non-linear time series models which have been conducted so far are essentially empirical in nature, although some degree of basic theory is beginning to emerge.

The subject matter of this paper is concerned with a fairly general class of non-linear models called 'state-dependent models', and the applications of these to the problem of identifying general forms of non-linear structure will be discussed in the following sections. Towards the end of the paper we will indicate a possible application of these ideas to the study of systems governed by non-linear differential equations.

THEORY OF LINEAR MODELS

All forms of time series modelling are based on the concept of a 'white noise' process, which henceforth we denote by $\{\epsilon_t\}$. In this context a white noise process is defined as a sequence of zero mean random variables, with constant variance σ_ϵ^2, i.e., $E\{\epsilon_t\} = 0$, $E\{\epsilon_t^2\} = \sigma_\epsilon^2$, $E\{\epsilon_s \epsilon_t\} = 0$, $s \neq t$, $s \neq t$.

Given a general discrete parameter time series $\{X_t; t = 0, \pm 1, \pm 2, \ldots\}$, a 'model' is specified by finding that function of future, present, and past observations which transforms the given series into a white noise process. Thus, we seek a function h which is such that

$$h(\ldots, X_{t-2}, X_{t-1}, X_t, X_{t+1}, X_{t+2}, \ldots) = \epsilon_t. \tag{13.1}$$

In particular, the class of *linear* models corresponds to the case where the function h is *linear*, so that 13.1 then takes the form

$$\sum_{u=-\infty}^{\infty} h_u X_{t-u} = \epsilon_t. \tag{13.2}$$

This is the general form of the non-linear model, but here X_t is allowed to depend on future values as well as on past values. In practice we would usually require X_t to depend only on past values, i.e., we would set $h_u = 0$, $u < 0$, and rewrite 13.2, the 'one-sided' form, as

$$\sum_{u=0}^{\infty} h_u X_{t-u} = \epsilon_t. \tag{13.3}$$

Introducing the backward shift operator B, defined by $BX_t = X_{t-1}$, etc., 13.3 can now be expressed in the form

$$H(B)X_t = \epsilon_t, \tag{13.4}$$

where

$$H(z) = \sum_{u=0}^{\infty} h_u z^u. \tag{13.5}$$

Equation 13.4 may be 'solved' to express X_t as a linear function of present and past values of ϵ_t. Thus, inverting 13.4 formally we may write

$$x_t = H^{-1}(B)\epsilon_t, \tag{13.6}$$

and if $H^{-1}(z)$ can be expanded as a convergent series for $|z| < 1$ [i.e., if $H(z)$ has no zeros inside the unit circle] we may write further

$$H^{-1}(z) = g_0 + g_1 z + g_2 z^2 + \ldots . \tag{13.7}$$

We may now write X_t explicitly as

$$X_t = \sum_{u=0}^{\infty} g_u \epsilon_{t-u}, \tag{13.8}$$

or

$$X_t = \Gamma(B)\epsilon_t, \tag{13.9}$$

where

$$\Gamma(z) = \sum_{u=0}^{\infty} g_u z^u. \tag{13.10}$$

Note that

$$\Gamma(z) \equiv H^{-1}(z) \text{ or } \Gamma(z)H(z) \equiv 1.$$

Equation 13.8 gives us an alternative formulation for the general (non-anticipative) linear model in which X_t is expressed as a linear combination of present and past values of a white noise process $\{\epsilon_t\}$.

AR, MA, and ARMA Models

The general linear model, as given by 13.3 or 13.8, involves an infinite number of parameters and cannot therefore be fitted directly to data unless further assumptions are made. In the context of practical time series model fitting we use a standard set of finite parameter models which arise as special cases of the general linear model 13.8. Thus, if we assume that $\Gamma^{-1}(z) \equiv H(z)$ may be approximated by a finite-order polynomial, say,

$$\Gamma^{-1}(z) = 1 + \alpha_1 z + \cdots + \alpha_k z^k, \tag{13.11}$$

then 13.8 reduces to the AR(k) (*autoregressive model of order k*) form

$$X_t + \alpha_1 X_{t-1} + \cdots + \alpha_k X_{t-k} = \epsilon_t. \tag{13.12}$$

On the other hand, if we approximate to $\Gamma(z)$ by a finite-order polynomial, say,

$$\Gamma_1(z) = 1 + \beta_1 z + \cdots + \beta_l z^l, \tag{13.13}$$

then 13.8 reduces to the MA(l) (*moving average of order l*) form

$$X_t = \epsilon_t + \beta_1 \epsilon_{t-1} + \cdots + \beta_l \epsilon_{t-l}. \tag{13.14}$$

If $\Gamma(zu)$ and $\Gamma^{-1}(z)$ are 'well-behaved' functions, we can, to an arbitrary degree of accuracy, approximate either by a finite polynomial of sufficiently high degree. It follows, therefore, that we can, in general, approximate a general linear model by either an AR or MA model of sufficiently high order. However, we can obtain a more 'parsimonious' finite parameter representation of $\Gamma(z)$ by approximating it by a *rational function*. If we take $\Gamma(z)$ to have the form,

$$\Gamma(z) = \frac{1 + \beta_1 z + \cdots + \beta_l z^l}{1 + \alpha_1 z + \cdots + \alpha_k z^k}, \tag{13.15}$$

then 13.8 reduces to the ARMA (k, l) [*mixed autoregressive/moving average of order(k, l)*] model,

$$X_t + \alpha_1 X_{t-1} + \cdots + \alpha_k X_{t-k} = \epsilon_t + \beta_1 \epsilon_{t-1} + \cdots + \beta_l \epsilon_{t-l}. \tag{13.16}$$

This model can be written in operator form as (with an obvious notation)

$$\alpha(B)X_t = \beta(B)\epsilon_t. \tag{13.17}$$

[The slightly more general ARIMA models, which have been studied, in particular, by Box and Jenkins (1970), correspond to the case where the operator $\alpha(B)$ in 13.17 contains a factor of the form $(1 - B)^d$. In this case $\Gamma(z) = [\beta(z)/\alpha(z)]$ contains a dth-order pole at $z = 1$ and consequently $\{X_t\}$ is no longer a stationary process—although its dth difference, $\Delta^d X_t$, would, in general, be stationary).

State-Space Representations

An alternative way of rewriting the general ARMA model 13.16 is based on the so-called '*state-space*' (or '*Markovian*') representation which provides a compact description of any finite-parameter linear model. The basic idea rests simply on the well-known result that any finite-order linear differential or difference equation can be expressed as a vector first-order equation. For example, if we take the AR(2) model

$$X_t + \alpha_1 X_{t-1} + \alpha_2 X_{t-2} = \epsilon_t, \tag{13.18}$$

and write $x_t^{(2)} = X_t$, $x_t^{(1)} = -\alpha_2 X_{t-1}[= -\alpha_2 X_{t-1}^{(2)}]$, then 13.18 may be rewritten as

$$\begin{bmatrix} x_t^{(1)} \\ x_t^{(2)} \end{bmatrix} = \begin{bmatrix} 0 & -\alpha_2 \\ 1 & -\alpha_1 \end{bmatrix} \begin{bmatrix} x_{t-1}^{(1)} \\ x_{t-1}^{(2)} \end{bmatrix} + \begin{bmatrix} 0 \\ 1 \end{bmatrix} \epsilon_t. \tag{13.19}$$

To recover X_t from the vector $[x_t^{(1)}, x_t^{(2)}]'$, we now write

$$X_t = (0, 1) \begin{bmatrix} x_t^{(1)} \\ x_t^{(2)} \end{bmatrix}. \tag{13.20}$$

The pair 13.18, 13.20 is completely equivalent to 13.18, but whereas 13.18 involves a two-stage dependence so that X_t is non-Markovian, 13.19 involves only a one-stage dependence so that $[x_t^{(1)}, x_t^{(2)}]'$ is a vector Markov process. [The device of expressing 3.18 in the form 13.19 may be viewed alternatively as a special case of the technique of writing certain types of non-Markov processes involving only finite-stage dependence as vector Markov processes.]

Exactly the same approach may be used to write the general ARMA model in the state-space form. thus, assuming that $l \le (k - 1)$ in 13.16), we first write 13.16 as

$$X_t + \alpha_1 X_{t-1} + \cdots + \alpha_k X_{t-k} = \epsilon_t + \beta_1 \epsilon_{t-1} + \cdots + \beta_{k-1} \epsilon_{t-k+1}, \tag{13.21}$$

where $\beta_j = 0$ $(j > l)$, and it is then easy to verify that 13.21 can be written in state-state form as

$$x(t + 1) = Fx(t) + G\epsilon_t, \tag{13.22}$$

$$X_t = Hx(t), \tag{13.23}$$

where the $k \times k$ matrix F is given by

$$F = \begin{bmatrix} 0 & 0 & \ldots & 0 & -\alpha_k \\ 1 & 0 & \ldots & 0 & -\alpha_{k-1} \\ 0 & 1 & \ldots & 0 & -\alpha_{k-2} \\ \multicolumn{5}{c}{\ldots\ldots\ldots\ldots\ldots} \\ 0 & 0 & \ldots & 1 & -\alpha_1 \end{bmatrix},$$

the $k \times 1$ matrix G by

$$G' = [\beta_{k-1}, \beta_{k-2}, \ldots, \beta_1, 1],$$

the $1 \times k$ matrix H by

$$H = (0, 0, \ldots, 0, 1),$$

and the $k \times 1$ vector $x(t)$ is partitioned as

$$x'(t) = (x_1(t), x_2(t), \ldots, x_k(t)).$$

[In fact, $x_k(t)$ is simply the variable X_t in 13.21, and $x_{k-1}(t), x_{t-2}(t), \ldots$ are defined recursively in terms of $x_k(t)$.] In this formulation $x(t)$ is called the *state vector*, F is called the *system matrix*, G the *input matrix, and* H the *observation matrix*. [Note that the condition for 13.21 to represent a stationary process is that $\alpha(z)$ has no zeros inside or on the unit circle—in which case the matrix F is 'stable', i.e., all its eigenvalues have modulus less than one, and consequently the process $x(t)$ is stationary.]

Akaike (1974a) has given a very general treatment of finite-order linear models and has shown, using a geometrical approach, that a *minimal* realisation (i.e., a state-space representation with $x(t)$ having the smallest possible dimension) can be derived by selecting the state vector $x(t)$ as any basis of the 'predictor space at time', $R(t + \mid t - 1)$, namely the space spanned by the linear least squares predictors of $X_t, X_{t+1}, X_{t+2}, \ldots$, given $\epsilon_t, \epsilon_{t-1}, \epsilon_{t-2}, \ldots$. The crucial feature of this space is that, for models described by finite-order difference equations, it has *finite dimensions*, k. A minimal realisation can now be constructed by choosing the state vector (at time t) as *any* basis of $R(t + \mid t -)$. If we think of the model as a physical stem with ϵ_t as the 'input' and X_t as the 'output', the above specification of the state vector is in complete accord with the physical interpretation of the 'state' of the system at time t_0 as that set of quantities which, together with the input for all time points $\geq t_0$, uniquely determines the output for all time points $\geq t_0$. (When, e.g., the relationship between input and output is described by a finite-order difference or differential equation, the 'state' at time t_0 is simply the set of 'initial conditions' required to determine the solution of the difference or differential equation for all $t \geq t_0$.) Intuitively, therefore, we may think of the state at any time point as the totality of information on the future output contained within the past input, and this is precisely the information contained within the set of predictors $\{X_t, X_{t+1|t}, X_{t+2|t}, \ldots \}$ or, equivalently, within any set of basis variables of the space spanned by these predictors.

GENERAL NON-LINEAR MODELS

We now return to the general model 13.1. If we impose the condition of 'physical realisability' on 13.1, we obtain a model of the form

$$h(X_t, X_{t-1}, X_{t-2}, \ldots) = \epsilon_t, \tag{13.24}$$

and if we assume that this model is 'invertible' [i.e., that 13.24 may be 'solved' to yield an expression for X_t in terms of $\epsilon_t, \epsilon_{t-1}, \epsilon_{t-2}, \ldots$], we then obtain, say,

$$X_t = f(\epsilon_t, \epsilon_{t-1}, \epsilon_{t-2}, \ldots). \tag{13.25}$$

From the standpoint of statistical analysis 13.25 is just as intractable as 13.1 but we may attempt to 'parametrise' 13.25 by assuming further that the function f is analytic, so that it can be expanded about some fixed point—say about the point $0 = (0, 0, 0, \ldots)$. This yields the formal expansion

$$X_t = \mu + \sum_{u=0}^{\infty} g_u \epsilon_{t-u} + \sum_{u=0}^{\infty} \sum_{v=0}^{\infty} g_{uv} \epsilon_{t-u} \epsilon_{t-v}$$

$$+ \sum_{u=0} \sum_{v=0} \sum_{w=0} g_{uvw} \epsilon_{t-u} \epsilon_{t-v} \epsilon_{t-w} + \dots , \qquad (13.26)$$

where we have written $\mu = f(\mathbf{0})$, $g_u = [\partial f/\partial \epsilon_{t-u}]_0, \dots$. This expansion is known as a *Volterra series* and was used by Wiener (1958) in his pioneering study of non-linear systems. Wiener's objective was to construct transformations of these series in which the successive terms are 'orthogonal' (i.e., uncorrelated)—rather like the use of orthogonal polynomials in regression analysis. However, there is clearly no possibility of fitting such a Volterra series to a finite stretch of data since the first term contains an infinite sequence of parameters, the second term a doubly infinite sequence of parameters, and so on. To circumvent this difficulty we may assume either (a) that the Fourier transforms of the sequences $\{g_u\}$, $\{g_{uv}\}$, $\dots$ possess certain 'smoothness' properties, or (b) that each of these transforms has a known functional form involving only a finite number of unknown parameters. Approach (a) leads to 'polyspectral analysis' [the Fourier analysis of the higher-order moments—see, e.g., Brillinger (1970)], but is feasible only when 13.26 is of 'homogeneous form' with only one term present. On the other hand, (b) leads to the development of special forms of non-linear schemes, three particularly important types being (i) *bi-linear models* (Granger and Andersen, 1978; Subba Rao, 1981), (ii) *threshold autoregressive models* (Tong and Lim, 1980) and (iii) *exponential autoregressive models* (Haggan and Ozaki, 1981). For example, a bilinear model takes the form

$$X_t + a_1 X_{t-1} + \dots + a_k X_{t-k}$$

$$= \epsilon_t + b_1 \epsilon_{t-1} + \dots + b_l \epsilon_{t-1} + \sum_{i=1}^{m} \sum_{j=1}^{p} c_{ij} \epsilon_{t-i} X_{t-j}, \qquad (13.27)$$

and is thus seen to be a generalisation of the (linear) ARMA model 13.16 in which a bi-linear form in $\{\epsilon_{t-i}\}$, $\{X_{t-j}\}$ has been added to the right-hand side. Threshold AR models are constructed by starting with the (linear) AR model 13.12 and allowing each of the coefficients $a_1, \dots, a_k$ to 'switch' between two different values according as to whether some past observation X_{t-d} falls below or above a given 'threshold' level. Exponential AR models are constructed by again starting with the AR model 13.12 and replacing each of the coefficients by exponential functions of X_{t-1}. Each of the special non-linear schemes describes, in its own way, a specific type of non-linearity; the threshold AR models can (with suitably chosen parameters) given rise to 'limit cycle' behaviour, while the exponential AR model can reproduce certain well-known features of non-linear random vibrations theory—such as 'amplitude-dependent frequency' and 'jump phenomena'. However, in practice it may be difficult to decide which, if any, of these special models is best suited to a given set of data. In the next section we describe a more general class of non-linear models, called '*state-dependent models*', which includes the bi-linear, threshold autoregressive, and exponential regressive models as special cases, but allows much greater flexibility in the characteristics of the non-linear structure. Although these 'state-dependent models' are of a general nature they are nevertheless amenable to statistical analysis and may be fitted to data. This approach offers two major advantages, namely (a) state-dependent models may be used directly in connection with, e.g., the prediction of future values, and (b) since they can be fitted to data without any specific prior assumptions about the form of non-linearity, they may be used to give us an 'overview' of the character of the non-linearity inherent in the data and thus indicate whether, e.g., a bi-linear threshold AR or exponential AR model is appropriate.

STATE-DEPENDENT MODELS

In developing the approach outlined at the end of the preceding section the basic difficulty which we encounter is that of striking a judicious balance between generality and tractability. To highlight this point we may note that the model 13.24 is completely general but totally intractable (as far as statistical analysis is concerned), whereas, e.g., the bilinear model 13.27 is certainly tractable but constrains us to a particular form of non-linear structure. Our approach is to start from the general model 13.24, and then impose further restrictions until we have reached the point at which statistical analysis may commence.

As it stands, the model 13.24 is 'infinite-dimensional'—in the sense that it involves a relationship between infinitely many variables. We now reduce this to a 'finite-dimensional' form by assuming that the relationship between X_t and the 'past history' of the series can be described in terms of finitely many values of past X_t's and ϵ_t's, so that we may write, say

$$X_t = h'(X_{t-1}, \ldots X_{t-k}, \epsilon_{t-1}, \ldots, \epsilon_{t-l}) + \epsilon_t. \qquad (13.28)$$

In this formulation ϵ_t plays the role of the 'innovations' process for X_t, and the function h describes the information on X_t contained in its past history. In the language of probability theory we may interpret h' as the 'projection' (i.e., conditional expectation) of X_t on $\mathcal{B}_{t-1}^{\epsilon}$, the Borel field generated by ϵ_{t-1}, $\epsilon_{t-2}, \ldots$. In postulating the model 13.28 we are saying, in effect, that *this 'projection' can be expressed* in terms of a finite number of functions of ϵ_{t-1}, $\epsilon_{t-2}, \ldots$. (Recall that, for each u, X_{t-u} is itself a function of $\epsilon_{t-1}, \epsilon_{t-2}, \ldots$.)

Assuming further that the function h' in 13.28 is analytic, we may expand the right-hand side of 13.28 about an arbitrary but fixed time point t_0. Using only a first-order expansion, we obtain

$$X_t = h'(x_{t_0}) + \sum_{u=1}^{k} f_u(x_{t-1})(X_{t-u} - X_{t_0-u})$$

$$+ \sum_{u=1}^{l} g_u(x_{t-1})(\epsilon_{t-u} - \epsilon_{t_0-u}), \text{ say,} \qquad (13.29)$$

where x_t denotes the 'state vector'

$$x_t = (\epsilon_{t-l+1}, \ldots \epsilon_t, X_{t-k+1}, \ldots X_t)', \qquad (13.30)$$

and f_u and g_u depend on the first-order partial derivatives of h'. We can now rewrite 13.29 in the form

$$X_t + \sum_{u=1}^{k} \phi_u(x_{t-1})X_{t-u} = \mu(x_{t-1}) + \epsilon_t + \sum_{u=1}^{l} \psi_u(x_{t-1})\epsilon_{t-u}. \qquad (13.31)$$

This is the basic model with which we now work, and we call 13.31 a '*state-dependent model of order (k, l)'*]. It has a natural interpretation as a *locally linear* ARMA model in which the evolution of the series at time $(t - 1)$ is governed by a set of AR coefficients $\{\phi_u\}$, a set of MA coefficients $\{\psi_u\}$, and a local mean μ, all of which depend on the 'state' of the series at time $(t - 1)$.

For each x_{t-1}, 13.31 may be interpreted geometrically as the *tangent plane* to the surface generated by $h'(x_{t-1})$. In this sense we may regard the SDM model as being formed by 'bending' the linear model around each point in the state-space.

It is easily seen that 13.31 includes as special cases all the special non-linear models described in the previous section. Thus, if we take μ and $\{\phi_u\}$ as constants and set

$$\psi_u(x_{t-1}) = b_u + \sum_{i=1}^{p} c_{uj}X_{t-j},$$

then 13.31 reduces to the bi-linear model 13.27 (with the value of l in 13.31 chosen as max(m, l), m and l being the corresponding parameters in 13.27). Similarly, if we take all the ψ_u to be zero, and let μ and the ϕ_u take the form of step functions, each switching between two levels, then 13.31 reduces to the AR threshold model, while setting all the ϕ_u to zero and taking each ϕ_u to be an exponential function of X_{t-1} gives the AR exponential model.

A formal state-space representation of the SDM model is easily obtained by augmenting the vector 13.30 with the additional element unity in the leading position. Specifically, if we re-define x_t as

$$x_t = (1, \epsilon_{t-l+1}, \ldots \epsilon_t, X_{t-k+1}, \ldots X_t)',$$

then it is not difficult to show that, with suitably defined matrices F and H, we can rewrite 13.31 as

$$x_{t+1} = F(x_t)x_t + \epsilon_{t+1},$$
$$x_t = Hx_t. \qquad (13.32)$$

If μ, ϕ_u, μ_u are each analytic functions of x_{t-1}, then 13.32 is a special case of the class of 'linear analytic' systems studied in the control theory literature [see, e.g., Brockett (1976)].

Identification of SDMs

We now consider the problem of estimating or 'identifying' the functional forms of the parameters $\mu(x_t)$, $\phi_u(x_t)$, $\mu_u(x_t)$ from observational data. The simplest assumption we can make about these parameters is that each is a linear function of the components of x_t so that, for example, we may write

$$\psi_u(x_t) = \psi_u^{(0)} + x_t'\beta_u,$$

$$\phi_u(x_t) = \phi_u^{(0)} + x_t'\gamma_u.$$

this form would be appropriate to bi-linear models (with $\gamma_u = 0$, all u), but it is unreasonable to suppose that all non-linear models can be approximated with sufficient accuracy with ψ_u and ϕ_u set as linear functions of x_t. However, if ψ_u and ϕ_u are 'smooth' functions of x_t, it would be reasonable to suppose that they may be represented *locally* as linear functions. This means that we can obtain a fairly general representation of these parameters by allowing both β_u and γ_u to be themselves state-dependent. We are then faced with the problem of specifying the functional forms of β_u and γ_u, but we can avoid this difficulty by simply letting β_u and γ_u 'wander' over time, i.e., we allow $\beta_u = \beta_u^{(t)}$ and $\gamma_u = \gamma_u^{(t)}$ to depend purely on the time parameters. This gives the SDM considerable flexibility, and if we now allow $\beta_u^{(t)}$ and $\gamma_u^{(t)}$ to 'wander' in the form of random walks, we can construct an estimation procedure which, for each t, determines those values of $\beta_u^{(t)}$, $\gamma_u^{(t)}$ which, in effect, minimises the discrepancy between X_{t+1} and its predictor $\tilde{X}_{t+1}$, computed from the model. The estimation procedure is thus based on a sequential type of algorithm, similar in nature to the '*Kalman filter*' algorithm.

The estimation algorithm involves some rather technical statistical features, and here we illustrate its operation simply by reference to the 'pure AR' SDM type of model. [For a full description, see Haggan, Heravi and Priestley (1984).] We consider the SDM model 13.31 in which $\psi_u = 0$, all u, and rewrite this in a different state-space form in which the state vector no longer represents the state of the series but now represents the current state of all the relevant parameters. Specifically, we defined the vector θ_t by

$$\theta_t = (\mu_{t-1}, \phi_{1,t-1}, \ldots, \phi_{k,t-1}, \alpha'^{(t)}, \gamma_1'^{(t)}, \ldots, \gamma_k'^{(t)})',$$

where, for brevity, we have written $\phi_{1,t-1}$ in place of $\phi_1(x_{t-1})$, and similarly for other parameters. Writing $H_t^* = (1, -X_{t-1}, \ldots, -X_{t-k}, 0, 0, \ldots, 0)$, we may now express 13.31 in the form

$$X_t = H_t^*\theta_t + \epsilon_t, \tag{13.33}$$

where $\mathbf{\theta}_t$ satisfies an evolution equation of the form

$$\mathbf{\theta}_t = \mathbf{F}^*_{t-1}\mathbf{\theta}_{t-1} + \mathbf{W}_t. \tag{13.34}$$

Equations 13.33 and 13.34 are now of the standard form to which the (extended) Kalman filter can be applied. If, on the basis of observations up to time $(t - 1)$, we have constructed an estimate $\hat{\mathbf{\theta}}_{t-1}$ of $\hat{\mathbf{\theta}}_{t-1}$, then given the next observation X_t, the updating equation for $\hat{\mathbf{\theta}}_t$ takes the form

$$\hat{\mathbf{\theta}}_t = \mathbf{F}_{t-1}\hat{\mathbf{\theta}}_{t-1} + \mathbf{K}^*_t[X_t - \mathbf{H}^*_t\mathbf{F}_{t-1}\hat{\mathbf{\theta}}_{t-1}].$$

where $\mathbf{K}^*_t$, the 'Kalman gain' matrix, may be evaluated from the standard recursive algorithm for the Kalman filter [see, e.g., Jazwinski (1970)]. Thus, at each time point we obtain a new estimate of each of the parameters μ, ϕ_1, . . . , ϕ_k, and these estimates can then be plotted against the corresponding state vector x_t. In this way we gradually build up a set of ordinates for each of the each of the parameter functions and these ordinates can then be transformed into smooth surfaces by applying one of the standard non-parametric function fitting routines [e.g., Priestley and Chao (1972)]. Once these surfaces have been constructed, we can then examine their shapes to gain insight into the non-linear structure of the model.

NUMERICAL EXAMPLES ON SIMULATED DATA

In order to examine the effectiveness of the SDM estimation technique, the application of the algorithm to simulated time series data of differing non-linear forms was studied. In all the cases, the estimated parameters were smoothed using the non-parametric function fitting technique of Priestley and Chao (1972) which employs a Gaussian smoothing kernel. This method is usually used to smooth equally-spaced ordinates into some functional form. However, in the SDM case, the ordinates are no longer equally spaced, since estimated parameter values are obtained at values of successive *states*, not successive time points. This can mean that if there are one or two outlying states in any set of data, excessive importance is attached to the parameter values at these states by the Gaussian smoothing kernel and spurious end effects can result. Difficulties can also arise from the 'transient effect' at the start of the recursion, where some anomalous parameter values may be obtained before the recursion settles down to a stable state. For these reasons, the first few parameter values in the recursion and the extreme edges of the parameter curves are ignored in the following analysis. Erratic behaviour at the ends of the range can arise also due to the presence of outliers in the original time series data. When an outlier occurs the algorithm tries to accommodate this observation by making large changes in the model parameters—which, in turn, leads to 'outliers' in the graphs of the estimated parameters.

Bilinear Model Simulation

The SDM algorithm was first applied to data simulated using a bi-linear scheme. The model chosen was

$$X_t + 0.4X_{t-1} = 0.5 + 0.4X_{t-1}\epsilon_{t-1} + \epsilon_t.$$

In all the models $\{\epsilon_t\}$ is a sequence of independent N(0, 1) variables, and 500 observations were simulated on each series. This type of model was chosen for simplicity, because the functional forms of most of the parameters are functions of one variable only. Hence, the shape of the parameter surface, being merely a curve, is much easier to determine. For each model, the recursion procedure described in the fourth section is carried out, fitting a linear ARMA model to the first 50 observations and starting the recursion at time origin $t = 25$. The original model fitting gave preliminary estimates.

$$\hat{\mu} = 0.8800, \quad \hat{\phi}_1 = 0.1777, \quad \hat{\psi}_1 = -0.1427, \quad \hat{\sigma}^2_\epsilon = 1.7663,$$

the variance–covariance matrix of $(\hat{\mu}_1, \hat{\psi}_1, \hat{\theta}_1)$ being

$$\hat{R} = \begin{bmatrix} 0.1197 & 0.1147 & 0.1134 \\ 0.1147 & 0.1157 & 0.1540 \\ 0.1134 & 0.1540 & 0.1711 \end{bmatrix}.$$

Figures 13.1 and 13.2 show the resulting graphs of the estimated parameters $\hat{\psi}_1$ and $\hat{\phi}_1$, respectively. The straight lines in these figures represent the true functional forms of ψ_1 and ϕ_1 for comparison.

As may be seen, the slopes of the graphs of the estimated parameters are very close to the slopes of the true parameters, and the intercept of $\hat{\phi}_1$ is also very close to the true value. The intercept of the graph of $\hat{\psi}_1$ is not so close to the true value, but both graphs clearly indicate linear trends in the parameters, and hence provide strong evidence that the series is generated by a bi-linear model.

It should be emphasized that the *SDM algorithm operates purely on the data* and has no a priori knowledge of the underlying model. Thus, based on the data only, the SDM algorithm has here pointed us very clearly in the direction of bi-linear models.

Exponential AR Model Simulation

The procedure becomes slightly easier in this case in that only an AR model fitting procedure is needed for the estimation of initial values. This means that, in general, it is relatively easy to obtain sufficiently accurate initial values using only a small number of observations at the start of the data set. 500 observations were simulated on the model

$$X_t + (-0.9 - 0.1e^{-X^2_{t-1}})X_{t-1} + (0.2 + 0.1e^{-X^2_{t-1}})X_{t-2} = \epsilon_t,$$

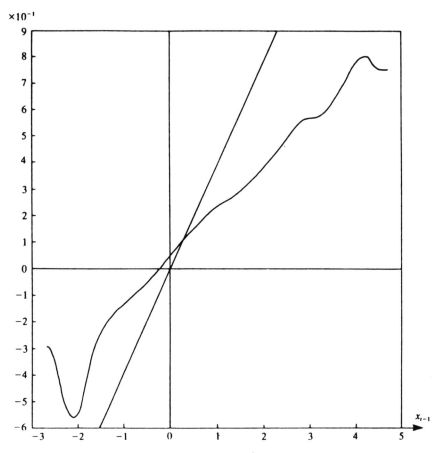

FIG. 13.1. Graph of the parameter $\hat{\psi}_1$ for bi-linear model.

where $\{\epsilon_t\}$ is a sequence of independent $N(0, 1)$ variables. To initialise the recursive estimation procedure, a linear AR model was fitted to the first 20 observations of each series to find estimates $\hat{\mu}$, $\hat{\phi}_1$, $\hat{\phi}_2$ and $\hat{\sigma}_\epsilon^2$ with which to start the recursion at $t = 10$. In this case the functional forms of ϕ_1 and ϕ_2 are given by

$$\phi_1 = -\frac{\partial h}{\partial X_{t-1}} = -0.9 - 0.1e^{-X_{t-1}^2} + 0.2\, X_{t-1}e^{-X_{t-1}^2},$$

and

$$\phi_2 = -\frac{\partial h}{\partial X_{t-2}} = 0.2 + 0.1e^{-X_{t-1}^2}.$$

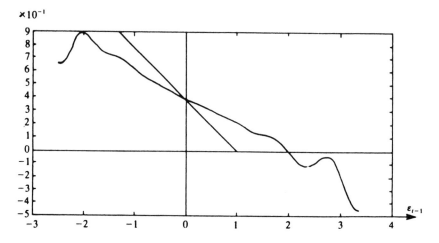

FIG. 13.2.   Graph of the parameter $\hat{\phi}_1$ against ϵ_{t-1} for bi-linear model.

The functional forms of ϕ_1 and ϕ_2 are shown graphically in Figures 13.3 and 13.4, respectively.

Preliminary estimates were

$$\hat{\mu} = 0.2879, \quad \hat{\hat{\phi}}_1 = -0.7001, \quad \hat{\hat{\phi}}_2 = -0.0330, \quad \hat{\sigma}_\epsilon^2 = 1.0087,$$

with variance–covariance matrix

$$\hat{\hat{R}} = \begin{bmatrix} 0.0622 & 0.0160 & -0.0066 \\ 0.0160 & 0.0559 & -0.0418 \\ -0.0066 & -0.0418 & 0.0491 \end{bmatrix}.$$

The graphs of the estimated values $\hat{\phi}_1$ and $\hat{\phi}_2$ are shown in Figures 13.5 and 13.6, respectively. As can be seen, the values of the estimated parameters are approximately correct and the shapes of the graphs are of a similar form to those

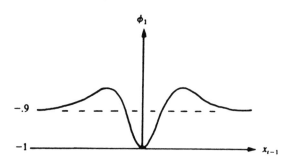

FIG. 13.3.   Graph of ϕ_1.

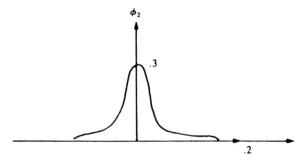

FIG. 13.4.   Graph of ϕ_2.

of the true graphs. $\hat{\phi}_1$ and $\hat{\phi}_2$ are clearly conspicuously different from what might be expected from a bi-linear model simulation. Similar results were obtained from several other simulations on this model. A particular feature of the estimated parameters is their approximately symmetric appearance.

SDM SCHEMES FOR NON-LINEAR SYSTEMS

It is well-known that a conventional linear time series model may be interpreted as a 'dynamical systems' model in which the observed series is regarded as the

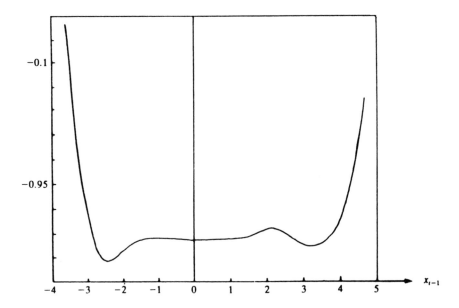

FIG. 13.5. $\hat{\phi}_1$ for exponential model.

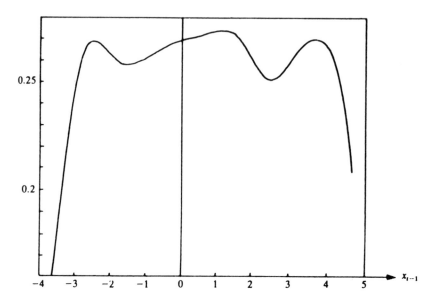

0.25

0.2

-4   -3   -2   -1   0   1   2   3   4   5 x_{t-1}

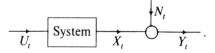

FIG. 13.6. $\hat{\phi}_2$ for exponential model.

output of a linear system 'driven' by an (unobservable) white-noise input, $\{\epsilon_t\}$. Thus, if we are dealing with a physical system in which the input $\{U_t\}$ and the output $\{X_t\}$ are both observable, we may adapt a linear time series model to this situation by replacing the white-noise process $\{\epsilon_t\}$ by the observable input process $\{U_t\}$ [see, e.g., Priestley (1981, ch. 10)]. The same approach may be applied to the non-linear SDM schemes. Consider the single-input/single-output system shown schematically in the diagram below:

$$\xrightarrow{\ \ U_t\ \ } \boxed{\text{System}} \xrightarrow{\ \ X_t\ \ } \bigcirc \xleftarrow{\ N_t} \xrightarrow{\ \ Y_t\ \ } .$$

Here U_t denotes the input, X_t the 'uncorrupted' output, N_t is an additive noise disturbance, and Y_t is the observed output. We assume that the system is operating in 'open-loop' form, so that it is reasonable to assume that $\{N_t\}$ and $\{U_t\}$ are uncorrelated processes. The 'systems' model corresponding to 13.28 takes the form

$$X_t = h(X_{t-1}, X_{t-2}, \ldots, X_{t-k}, U_{t-1}, U_{t-2}, \ldots, U_{t-l})$$
$$+ g(X_{t-1}, X_{t-2}, \ldots, X_{t-k}, U_{t-1}, U_{t-2}, \ldots, U_{t-l})U_t, \quad (13.35)$$

together with the observation equation

$$Y_t = X_t + N_t. \quad (13.36)$$

Equation 13.35 may now be re-written in SDM form as

$$X_t + \phi_1(x_{t-1})X_{t-1} + \cdots + \phi_k(x_{t-1})X_{t-k}$$
$$= \mu(x_{t-1}) + \psi_0(x_{t-1})U_t + \psi_1(x_{t-1})U_{t-1} + \cdots$$
$$+ \psi_l(x_{t-1})U_{t-l}, \tag{13.37}$$

where the state vector at time $t - 1$ is here given by

$$x_{t-1} = (U_{t-l}, \ldots, U_{t-1}, X_{t-k}, \ldots, X_{t-1})'. \tag{13.38}$$

(Note that since U_t is an observable process, the coefficient of U_t, ψ_0, is no longer unity but is now an additional parameter of the model.) If we augment the state vector by including the constant unity as an additional element; i.e., if we now write

$$x_{t-1} = (1, U_{t-l}, \ldots, U_{t-1}, X_{t-k}, \ldots, X_{t-1})', \tag{13.39}$$

then we can write 13.36 and 13.37 in the following state-space form:

$$x_{t+1} = \{F(x_t)\}x_t + \{G(x_t)\}U_{t+1}, \tag{13.40}$$

$$Y_t = Hx_t + N_t, \tag{13.41}$$

where the system matrix F is given by

$$\cdot \; F = \begin{bmatrix}
1 & 0 & 0 & \ldots & 0 & 0 & 0 & \ldots & 0 \\
0 & 0 & 1 & \ldots & 0 & 0 & 0 & \ldots & 0 \\
\cdots & & & & & & & & \cdots \\
0 & 0 & 0 & \ldots & 1 & 0 & 0 & \ldots & 0 \\
0 & 0 & 0 & \ldots & 0 & 0 & 0 & \ldots & 0 \\
\cdots & & & & & & & & \cdots \\
0 & 0 & 0 & \ldots & 0 & 0 & 1 & \ldots & 0 \\
0 & 0 & 0 & \ldots & 0 & 0 & 0 & 1\ldots & 0 \\
\cdots & & & & & & & & \cdots \\
0 & 0 & 0 & \ldots & 0 & 0 & 0 & 0\ldots & 1 \\
\mu & \psi_l & \psi_{l-1} & \cdots\cdots & \psi_1 & -\phi_k & -\phi_{k-1} & \cdots\cdots & -\phi_1
\end{bmatrix},$$

the input matrix G by

$$G = (0, 0, \ldots, 1\!:\!0, \ldots, \psi_0)',$$

and the observation matrix H by

$$H = (0, 0, \ldots, 0\!:\!0, \ldots, 1).$$

Assuming, as previously, that the coefficients μ, $\{\phi_u\}$ and $\{\psi_u\}$ may be represented as locally linear function of x_t, the 'up-dating' equations then take a similar form to that used for the 'pure' time series case.

Numerical Example

We illustrate the SDM systems model fitting procedure described above by applying this approach to simulated input/output data. In the simulation studies 500 observations were generated for the input and output processes. In each case the input process $\{U_t\}$ was generated from the stationary AR(1) model

$$U_t + 0.5U_{t-1} = \epsilon_t,$$

$\{\epsilon_t\}$ being a sequence of independent N(0, 1) variables, and the noise disturbance $\{N_t\}$ was also generated from a Gaussian white-noise process, with zero mean and unit variance.

The system chosen was generated by the bi-linear model

$$X_t - 0.4X_{t-1} = 0.8 + 0.4X_{t-1}U_t,$$
$$Y_t = X_t + N_t.$$

If X_t is written in the form of 13.35, it can be seen that the functional form of ϕ_1 is given by

$$\phi_1 = -\frac{\partial h}{\partial X_{t-1}} = -0.4,$$

and the functional form of ψ_0 is

$$\psi_0 = g(X_{t-1}) = 0.4X_{t-1}.$$

The preliminary estimates were

$$\hat{\mu} = 1.301, \quad \hat{\phi}_1 = -0.3436, \quad \hat{\psi}_0 = -0.8391, \quad \hat{\sigma}_N^2 = 1.768,$$

with

$$\hat{R} = \begin{bmatrix} 0.1276 & 0.0496 & 0.0200 \\ 0.0496 & 0.0273 & 0.0143 \\ 0.0200 & 0.0143 & 0.0326 \end{bmatrix}.$$

Graphs of ϕ_1 and ψ_0 (as functions of X_{t-1}) are given in Haggan et al. (1984), figs. 7 and 8, respectively. the straight line in fig. 8 represents the time functional form of ψ_0. Again, apart from the end effects, the estimated values of $\hat{\phi}_1$ are constant and very close to the value of -0.4 expected for this parameter. The graph of $\hat{\psi}_0$ shows a clear linear trend, with the slope very close to that of the expected functional form.

REFERENCES

Akaike, H. (1974a). Markovian representation of stochastic processes and its application to the analysis of autoregressive moving average processes. *Ann. Inst. Math.*, 26, 363–387.

Akaike, H. (1974b). Stochastic theory of minimal realisations, *IEEE Transactions on Automatic Control AC-19*, 667–673.

Box, G. E. P., & Jenkins, G. M. (1970). Time series analysis, forecasting and control. San Francisco, CA: Holden-Day.

Brillinger, D. R. (1970). The identification of polynomial systems by means of higher order spectra. *Journal of Sound Vib., 12*, 301–313.

Brockett, R. W. (1976). Volterra series and geometric control theory. *Automatica, 12*, 167–172.

Granger, C. W. J., & Andersen, A. P. (1978). An introduction to bilinear time series models. Göttingen: Vandenhoek and Ruprecht.

Haggan, V., & Ozaki, T. (1981). Modelling non-linear random vibrations using an amplitude-dependent autoregressive time series model. *Biometrika, 68*, 189–196.

Haggan, V., Heravi, S. M., & Priestley, M. B. (1984). A study of the application of state-dependent models in non-linear time series analysis. *Journal of Time Series Analysis, 5*, 69–102.

Jazwinski, A. J. (1970). Stochastic processes and filtering theory. New York: Academic Press.

Priestley, M. B. (1981). Spectral analysis and time series. London, England: Academic Press.

Priestley, M. B., & Chao, M. T. (1972). Non-parametric function fitting. *Journal of the Royal Statistical Society, B34*, 385–392.

Subba Rao, T. (1981). On the theory of bilinear time series models. *Journal of the Royal Statistical Society, B43*, 244–255.

Tong, H., & Lim, K.-S. (1980). Threshold autoregression, limit cycles and cyclical data. *Journal of the Royal Statistical Society, B42*, 245–292.

Wiener, N. (1958). Non-linear problems in random theory. Cambridge, MA: MIT Press.

Editor's Introduction to Chapters 14 and 15

Chapters 14 and 15 present some very new methods for modeling complex systems. These new methods involve using nonlinear discrete time or differential equations. These nonlinear models generally can not be solved exactly, but require numerical and graphical methods for envisioning solutions. The new graphical methods will introduce some new language for describing complex systems, such as "phase space plots," stable and unstable steady states,"null clines," "bifurcation diagrams," catastrophhes," "hysterisis, "and so on. To date, these methods have been remarkably successful in a wide range of sciences in describing very complex systems with relatively few parameters, although their application in the social sciences has been limited so far. The advantage that these types of models have over the statistical models previously introduced in this book is that they permit *simulations of the system under conditions different from those that generate the model.* In this way, these models make it possible to consider systematic experiments or interventions that will test and further refine the model, and help understand how the system changes as a function of system parameters, varying initial conditions, and so on.

14 Nonlinear Dynamics and Chaos

James D. Murray
University of Washington

Murray's chapter is a powerful overview on nonlinear dynamic models. These models have proved themselves highly successful in mathematical biology. In Murray's chapter he provides a succinct and practical data-based overview of how these models actually work in application. These models include logistic growth, catastrophe phenomena, delay models (which can be cyclic), models of two species in symbiosis, competition, or predatory-prey relationship. Discrete data and discrete models are also discussed, as is chaos.

—Editor

14.1. CONTINUOUS MODELS

During the last 20 years there has been a dramatic increase in the use of mathematical models in almost every scientific discipline. Their use in the social sciences will also inevitably increase as the models become more realistic. For example, in ecology and epidemiology these have helped us understand the dynamic processes involved in predator-prey and competition interactions, ecological control of pests, spread of disease (such as the sexually transmitted diseases like AIDS) and the development of control strategies, the spread of rumors and so on. The continually expanding list of applications is extensive. In psychology and physiology, for example, models have helped explain how the complex patterns resulting from hallucinogenic drugs are formed from a limited number of basic patterns, how nerve impulses are propagated along nerve fibers and how ocular dominance stripes in the visual cortex arise. In many applications mathematical models have been the key factor in explaining, or in highlighting, the important aspects. An extensive number of applications to a wide diversity of subjects such as the generation of butterfly wing patterns, the spatial spread of rabies, biological clocks, spiral waves of cortical depression in the brain, evolutionary aspects in cartilage development and so on, are described in the book by Murray (1989). A common thread in all of the models discussed is that they are nonlinear.

An assumption that a system is linear basically means that effects are simply additive. For example, if we take a given amount if a specific drug and achieve a certain quantifiable effect then twice as much of the drug will give twice the effect. Or, if a number of infectives are introduced into a susceptible population the spread of the disease will be twice as great if we introduce twice as many infectives. In these, and in almost all biomedical and social situations an assumption of linearity is simply invalid. In fact, if a model is linear it is, for almost all practical purposes, wrong.

Nonlinearity in recent years has been described as a new and important science. Nonlinear phenomena, such as the breaking of waves on a shore, were well known and studied in the 19th century by great mathematicians and physicists, such as James Clerk Maxwell, Henri Poincaré, and many others. In 1776 Daniel Bernoulli produced a nonlinear model for the effect of cowpox vaccination for the control of smallpox. Nonlinear models result in totally unexpected and fascinating phenomena even when these models are very simple. In this chapter, we shall consider a variety of different nonlinear mathematical models and demonstrate the richness in the phenomena which can arise. Little mathematical sophistication will be required. In Sections 14.1.1–3 an elementary knowledge of ordinary differential equations will be assumed: a good pedagogical introduction to such differential equations and their analysis is given in the textbook by Edelstein-Keshet (1988). In Sections 14.2.1–6 essentially no previous mathematical knowledge is required other than basic algebra. With these we can demonstrate simply the basic concepts of nonlinearity and chaos. These sections can be read independently of the others.

The aim of this chapter is to show how to construct deterministic, as opposed to stochastic, mathematical models for a variety of different problems and how to carry out the relevant analysis. One of the aims of this chapter is to show how we can get a qualitative feel for what models predict even if we cannot solve the equations analytically. In fact, one of the universal truths concerning nonlinear models is that they almost never can be solved analytically: the converse holds for many linear models.

14.1.1. Continuous Population Models for a Single Species

Although in most practical situations several interacting species are involved often some of them can be telescoped in one general species to get some idea of the gross features of the dynamics. We could, for example, group all the bird predators of field mice into one predator population. In many laboratory studies single-species models are of direct relevance, a single equation for the number of cells which become cancerous when subjected to different concentrations of UV light would be one (admittedly a simplistic one in this case). Consider a single population and let $N(t)$ be the population of the species at time t, then the rate of change of N:

$$\frac{dN}{dt} = \text{births} - \text{deaths} + \text{migration} \qquad (14.1.1)$$

is a *conservation equation* for the population. The species and situation determines how we model the form of the various terms on the right-hand side. The simplest model has no migration and the birth and death terms are proportional to N. That is

$$\frac{dN}{dt} = bN - dN = (b - d)N$$

where b and d are positive constants reflecting the birth and death rates respectively. On integrating this equation, given an initial population $N(0) = N_0$, we obtain

$$N(t) = N_0 e^{(b-d)t}.$$

Thus if $b > d$ the population grows exponentially while if $b < d$ it dies out. This approach, due to Malthus in 1798 but actually suggested earlier by Euler, is pretty unrealistic. However, if the species is the total world population from the 17th century to about 1990 it *is* essentially exponential. (Thomas Malthus was an English country curate and, by all accounts, rather a kindly and happy family man.)

There cannot, of course, be unlimited growth for all time; some adjustment must occur. Verhulst in 1836 proposed that a self-limiting process should operate when a population becomes too large. He suggested a more realistic form of the right-hand side, namely

$$\frac{dN}{dt} = rN\left(1 - \frac{N}{K}\right)$$
(14.1.2)

where r and K are positive constants. This, or rather the solution which we give below, is now referred to as *logistic growth* in a population. In this model the per capita birth rate is $r(1 - N/K)$; that is, it is dependent on the population N. The constant K is the *carrying capacity* of the environment.

With any model equation (or system of equations) we are primarily interested, mathematically and practically, in the temporal dynamics, whether or not there are any steady states, the stability of these steady states and whether there are oscillatory solutions. Steady states are where there is no rate of change, that is where $dN/dt = 0$. Setting the right-hand side in Equation 14.1.2 equal to zero, we see there are two *steady states* or *equilibrium states*, namely $N = 0$ and $N = K$.

When we talk of a steady-state population being stable we mean that any perturbation away from that steady state will decrease to zero. It can do this either monotonically or in an oscillatory manner. Let us consider first only small perturbations from the steady states and consider $N = 0$ to begin with. Let n be the small perturbation so that n^2 is negligible compared with n. Equation 14.1.2 then becomes, neglecting the term in n^2, $dn/dt \approx rn$, the solution of which is $n(t) = n_0 \exp[rt]$ where n_0 is the initial perturbation. So, this perturbation grows exponentially and hence $N = 0$ is unstable. The fact that we kept only linear terms in n, neglecting higher-order terms, n^2 here, means that we *linearized* the equation about the steady-state solution.

Now consider linear stability of the other steady state $N = K$. We linearize the equation now by setting $n = N - K$ and neglecting terms of second order; that is, terms in $(N - K)^2$ are neglected compared with $|N - K|$. This gives $d(N - K)/dt \approx -r(N - K)$ and so $N - K$ tends to zero exponentially, which means that $N \to K$ as $t \to \infty$. The carrying capacity, K, determines the size of the stable steady-state population while r is a measure of the rate at which it is reached; in other words, a measure of the dynamics. The parameter has dimension $1/\text{time}$ and so $1/r$ is a representative *time scale* of the response of the model to any change in the population. If $N(0) = N_0$ the solution of Equation 14.1.2, on separating variables, is given by

$$N(t) = \frac{N_0 K e^{rt}}{K + N_0(e^{rt} - 1)} \to K \qquad \text{as } t \to \infty$$
(14.1.3)

and is illustrated in Figure 14.1.1. With $N_0 < K/2$ note the typical sigmoid character.

Figures

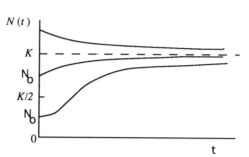

FIG. 14.1.1. Logistic population growth. Note the qualitative difference between the two
cases where the initial condition
N_0 satisfies $N_0 < K/2$ and $K > N_0$
$> K/2$.

Although population models for most species are, in specific detail, more
complex than this simple logistic model, it is more like a metaphor for a class of
population models with density dependent regulatory mechanisms—a kind of
compensating effect of overcrowding—and must not be taken too literally as the
equation governing the population dynamics. It can often be convenient when
seeking qualitative dynamic behavior in populations in which $N = 0$ is an
unstable steady state and $N(t)$ tends to a finite positive stable steady state. Let us
now generalize these qualitative (although in this case they are also quantitative)
results.

Consider a population to be governed by

$$\frac{dN}{dt} = f(N), \tag{14.1.4}$$

where typically $f(N)$ is a *nonlinear* function of N. Equilibrium solutions, N^* say,
are solutions of $f(N) = 0$, and unstable if $f'(N^*) > 0$. To see this we linearize
about N^* by writing

$$n(t) \approx N(t) - N^*, \qquad |n(t)| << 1$$

and Equation 14.1.4 becomes, on expanding $f(N^* + n(t))$ in a Taylor series about
$f(N^*)$,

$$\frac{dn}{dt} = f(N^* + n) \approx f(N^*) + nf'(N^*) + \ldots,$$

which to first order in $n(t)$ gives

$$\frac{dn}{dt} \approx nf'(N^*) \Rightarrow n(t) \propto \exp[f'(N^*)t]. \tag{14.1.5}$$

So n grows or decays according as $f'(N^*) > 0$ or $f'(N^*) < 0$. Thus linear
stability involves only the gradient of the growth dynamics function evaluated at

the steady state. The time scale of the response of the population to a disturbance is of the order of $1/|f'(N^*)|$: it is the time to change the initial disturbance by a factor e (cf. the role of r above).

Depending on the form of the dynamic growth function $f(N)$ there may be several equilibrium, or steady-state populations, N^*, which are solutions of $f(N) = 0$: it depends on the system $f(N)$ models. Plotting $f(N)$ against N immediately gives the equilibria. Not only that, the sign of the gradient $f'(N^*)$ at each steady state is obvious and it determines the linear stability.

The emphasis above was on linear stability. Linearly stable steady states may, however, be unstable to *finite* disturbances. Suppose, for example, that $f(N)$ is as illustrated in Figure 14.1.2. Where the curve cuts the N-axis gives the steady-state solutions. The gradients $f'(N)$ at $N = 0$, N_2 are positive, so these equilibria are linearly unstable while those at $N = N_1$, N_3 are stable to small perturbations: the arrows symbolically indicate stability or instability. If, for example, we now perturb the population from its equilibrium N_1 so that the new N is in the range $N_2 < N < N_3$ then $N \to N_3$ rather than returning to N_1. A similar perturbation from N_3 to a value in the range $0 < N < N_2$ would result in $N(t) \to N_1$. Qualitatively there is a *threshold perturbation* below which the steady states are always stable, and this threshold depends on the full nonlinear form of $f(N)$. For N_1, for example, the necessary threshold perturbation is $N_2 - N_1$.

14.1.2. An Insect Outbreak Model Which Displays a Cusp Catastrophe

A practical model which exhibits two positive, linearly stable, steady-state populations and a cusp catastrophe (which is discussed and defined below) is that governing the dynamics of the spruce budworm, a pest which, with great efficiency, destroys the balsam fir by eating the foliage. Ludwig et al. (1978) considered the budworm population dynamics to be governed by the equation

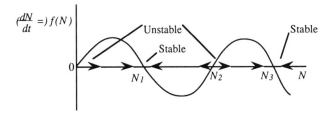

FIG. 14.1.2. An example of a population dynamics model $dN/dt = f(N)$ with several steady states. The gradient $f'(N)$ at each steady state, here $N = 0$, $N = N_i$, $i = 1, 2, 3$, that is where $f(N) = 0$, determines the linear stability simply by the sign of the gradient; if it is negative it is stable, while it is unstable if it is positive.

FIG. 14.1.3. Typical functional form of the predation in the spruce budworm model: note the sigmoid character. The population value N_c is an approximate threshold value. For $N <$ N_c predation is small, while for $N > N_c$ it is "switched on."

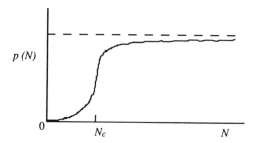

$$\frac{dN}{dt} = r_B N \left(1 - \frac{N}{K_B} \right) - p(N).$$

Here r_B is the linear birth rate of the budworm and K_B is the carrying capacity (amount of foliage) of the trees. The $p(N)$-term represents predation, generally by birds: the sigmoid-like qualitative form of it is important and is illustrated in Figure 14.1.3. Predation usually saturates, that is it tends to a constant maximum value, for large enough N. There is an approximate threshold value N_c, below which the predation is small, while above it the predation is close to its saturation value: such a form is like a switch with N_c being the critical switch value. For small population densities N, the birds tend to seek food elsewhere and so the predation term $p(N)$ drops more rapidly, as $N \to 0$, than a linear rate proportional to N. So as to be able to do some analysis we take the qualitatively reasonable form for $p(N) = BN^2/(A^2 + N^2)$ where A and B are positive constants. The dynamics of $N(t)$ is then governed by

$$\frac{dN}{dt} = r_B N \left(1 - \frac{N}{K_B} \right) - \frac{BN^2}{A^2 + N^2}, \qquad (14.1.6)$$

which has four parameters, r_B, K_B, B, and A, with A and K_B having the same dimensions as N, r_B has dimension $(\text{time})^{-1}$ and B has the dimensions of $N(\text{time})^{-1}$. A is a measure of the threshold budworm population where the predation is "switched on," that is N_c in Figure 14.1.3.

   In all modeling it is absolutely essential to express the model equation in *nondimensional* terms. That is, we measure the population, for example, as a fraction of some base population level. Nondimensionalizing has several important advantages. For one thing, the units used in the analysis are then unimportant, since everything is a ratio of units; the adjectives small and large have a definite relative meaning. It also always reduces the number of relevant parameters to dimensionless groupings which determine the dynamics. Here we introduce nondimensional quantities by introducing

$$u = \frac{N}{A}, \quad r = \frac{Ar_B}{B}, \quad q = \frac{K_B}{A}, \quad \tau = \frac{Bt}{A} \qquad (14.1.7)$$

Here, for example, the population is compared to the threshold switch size A: a value of $u = 3.2$ means that N is 3.2 times the size of the threshold value A. The specific units of N and A are irrelevant. If we now substitute Equation 14.1.7 into Equation 14.1.6, it becomes

$$\frac{du}{d\tau} = ru\left(1 - \frac{u}{q}\right) - \frac{u^2}{1 + u^2} = f(u; r, q), \qquad (14.1.8)$$

where $f(u;r,q)$ is defined by this equation. Whereas the original equation 14.1.6 has four parameters, this dimensional form has only two, namely r and q, which are pure numbers (the grouping of the dimensional parameters is dimensionless), as also is u of course. Now, for example, if $u \ll 1$ it means simply that $N \ll A$. In any model there are usually several different nondimensionalizations possible. The dimensionless groupings to choose depends on the aspects you want to investigate. The reasons for the particular forms 14.1.7 will become clear below.

The steady states are solutions of

$$f(u; r, q) = 0 \Rightarrow ru\left(1 - \frac{u}{q}\right) = \frac{u^2}{1 + u^2}. \qquad (14.1.9)$$

One solution is clearly $u = 0$ with other solutions, if they exist, satisfying

$$r\left(1 - \frac{u}{q}\right) = \frac{u^2}{1 + u^2}. \qquad (14.1.10)$$

The easiest way to determine the existence of solutions of Equation 14.1.10 is graphically as shown in Figure 14.1.4a where we have plotted the straight line, the left of Equation 14.1.10, and the function on the right of Equation 14.1.10; the intersections give the solutions. The actual algebraic expressions for the

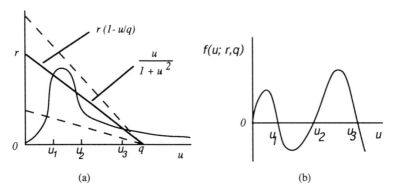

(a)   (b)

FIG. 14.1.4(a, b). Steady-state solutions for the population model 14.1.8. The positive solutions are given by the intersections of the straight line $r(1 - u/q)$ and the curve $u/(1 + u^2)$. With the solid straight line in (a) there are three steady states with $f(u; r, n)$ typically as in (b).

solutions are not important here but what is, however, is the existence of one, three, or again, one solution as r increases for a fixed q, as in Figure 14.1.4a, or, as also happens for a varying q and fixed r. When r is in the appropriate range, which depends on q, there are three steady states with a typical corresponding $f(u;r,q)$ as shown in Figure 14.1.4b. The two dimensionless parameters appear only in the straight-line part of Figure 14.1.4 and is particularly helpful in seeing how the solutions vary with the parameters: this was the motivation for the nondimensional form introduced in Equation 14.1.7. Recalling the correspondence between the sign of the gradient at a steady state and its linear stability we see, by inspection of Figure 14.1.4 that $u = 0$, $u = u_2$ are linearly unstable, since $df/du > 0$ at $u = 0$, $u = u_2$ while u_1 and u_3 are stable steady states since at these $df/du > 0$. There is a domain in the r,q parameter space where three roots of Equation 14.1.10 exist. This is shown in Figure 14.1.5: the analytical (rather algebraic) derivation of the boundary curves is left as an exercise.

This model exhibits a *hysteresis effect*. Suppose q, say, is fixed and r increases from zero along the path $ABCD$ in Figure 14.1.5. Then, referring also to Figure 14.1.4a, we see that if $u_1 = 0$ at $r = 0$ the u_1-equilibrium simply increases monotonically with r until C in Figure 14.1.5 is reached. For a larger r at this stage this steady state disappears and the equilibrium solution jumps to u_3. If we now reduce r again the equilibrium state is the u_3 one and it remains so until r reaches the lowest critical value B, where there is again only one steady state, at which point there is a jump from the u_3 to the u_1 state. In other words, as r increases along $ABCD$ there is a discontinuous jump up at C while as r decreases from D to A there is a discontinuous jump down at B. This is an example of a *cusp catastrophe* which is illustrated schematically in Figure 14.1.6 where the letters A, B, C, and D correspond to those in Figure 14.1.5. Figure 14.1.5 is the projection of the surface in Figure 14.1.6 onto the r, q plane with the shaded (three steady-state) region corresponding to the fold.

From field observation, parameters can be estimated and these are in the range where there are three possible steady states for the population. The smaller steady state u_1 is the *refuge* steady state, while u_3 is the *outbreak* steady state.

FIG. 14.1.5. The r, q parameter domain for the number of positive steady states for the budworm population model equation 14.1.8. The boundary curves (PCQ and PBR) are given parametrically by $r(a) = 2a^3/(a^2 + 1)^2$, $q(a) = 2a^3/(a^2 - 1)$ for $a \geq \sqrt{3}$, the value giving the cusp point P.

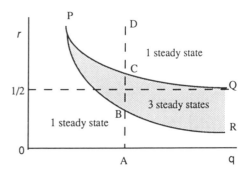

FIG. 14.1.6. The cusp catastrophe surface for the steady states in the $(u_{\text{steady state}}, r, q)$ parameters space. As r increases from A the path is ABC-CD, while as r decreases from D the path is $DCBBA$. The projection of this surface onto the r, q plane is given in Figure 14.1.5. Three equilibria or steady states exist where the fold is. (If a piece of paper is folded in this way and then flattened there are three layers where the fold is.)

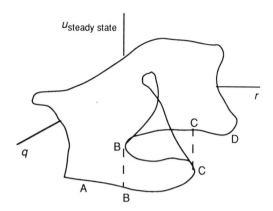

From a pest control point of view, it is best to keep the population at a refuge state rather than allow it to reach an outbreak situation. To see what we might do to achieve this we must relate the real parameters to the dimensionless ones, using Equation 14.1.7. For example, if the foliage was sprayed to discourage the budworm this would reduce q since K_B is reduced. If the reduction is large enough this could force the dynamics to have only one equilibrium: that is the parameters r and q do not lie in the shaded domain of Figure 14.1.5. Alternatively we could try and reduce the reproduction rate r_B or increase the threshold number of predators, since both reduce r which would be effective if it is below the critical value for u_3 to exist. Although these give preliminary qualitative ideas for control, it is not easy to determine the optimal strategy, particularly since spatial effects such as budworm dispersal must be taken into effect. Even though this is a simple model the results nevertheless highlight various control possibilities.

4.1.3. Delay Models

One of the deficiencies of single population models like Equation 14.1.4 for certain species is that the birth rate is considered to act instantaneously whereas there may be a time delay to account for the time to reach maturity, the finite gestation period, time to reproductive maturity and so on. Delays can be included in such models and result in equations of the form

$$\frac{dN(t)}{dt} = f(N(t), N(t - T)), \qquad (14.1.11)$$

where $T > 0$, the delay, is another parameter. To see what effect delay might have on the dynamics, consider an extension of the logistic growth model (14.1.2), namely

$$\frac{dN}{dt} = rN(t)\left[1 - \frac{N(t - T)}{K} \right], \qquad (14.1.12)$$

where r, K, and T are positive constants. This form says that the regulatory effect, that is the nonlinearity depends on the population at an earlier time, $t - T$, rather than the current time t.

The character of the solutions of Equation 14.1.12, and the type of boundary conditions required are quite different to those of Equation 14.1.2. Even with this simple-looking equation 14.1.12 the solutions almost always have to be found numerically. An important difference in computing the solution for $t > 0$ is that we require $N(t)$ to be given for *all* time $-T \leq t \leq 0$. However, in the spirit of getting some qualitative idea of the solutions without a numerical simulation we can use the following heuristic reasoning.

Refer to Figure 14.1.7 and suppose that for some $t = t_1$, $N(t_1) = K$, say, and that for some time $t < t_1$, $N(t - T) < K$. From Equation 14.1.12, since

$$1 - N(t - T)/K > 0 \Rightarrow dN(t)/dt > 0$$

and so $N(t)$ at t_1 is still increasing. When $t = t_1 + T$, $N(t - T) = N(t_1) = K$ and so $dN/dt = 0$. For the range $t_1 = T < t < t_2$, $N(t - T) > K$ and so $dN/dt < 0$ and $N(t)$ decreases until $t = t_2 + T$ since then $dN/dt = 0$ again because $N(t_2 + T - T)$ $= N(t_2) = K$. There is therefore the possibility of oscillatory behavior. If we consider the following particularly simple linear delay equation, it has an exact solution:

$$\frac{dN}{dt} = -\frac{\pi}{2T} N(t - T) \Rightarrow N(t) = A \cos \frac{\pi t}{2T},$$

which is periodic in time; it can be easily checked that it is a solution. How does this solution tend to the usual exponential one for this equation when T is identically zero?

In fact the solutions of Equation 14.1.12 can exhibit *stable limit cycle* periodic solutions for a large range of values if the product rT of the birth rate r and the delay $T > \pi/2$ (see, for example, Murray, 1989). If t_p is the period then $N(t + t_p)$ $= N(t)$ for all t. The point about *stable* limit cycle solutions is that if a perturbation is given the solution returns to the original periodic solution as $t \to \infty$, although possibly with a *phase* shift; that is the solution curve is displaced along the t-axis from the original curve. The periodic behavior, incidentally is independent of any initial data.

From Figure 14.1.7 and the heuristic argument above the period of the limit cycle periodic solutions might be expected to be of the order of $4T$. From numerical calculations this is the case for a large range of rT, which is a dimensionless grouping. For example, for $rT = 1.6$, the period $t_p \approx 4.03T$ and for $rT = 2.1$, $t_p \approx = 4.54T$. For large values of rT, however, the period changes considerably.

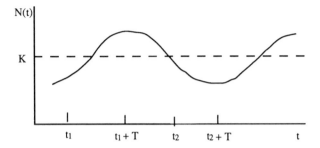

FIG. 14.1.7.   Schematic periodic solution of the delay equation population model 14.1.12.

It should perhaps be mentioned here that single (nondelay) differential equation models for population growth without delay, that is like $dN/dt = f(N)$, *cannot* exhibit limit cycle behavior. We can see this immediately as follows. Suppose this equation has a periodic solution with period T, that is $N(t + T) = N(t)$. Multiply the equation by dN/dt and integrate from t to $t + T$ to get

$$\int_t^{t+T} \left(\frac{dN}{dt} \right)^2 dt = \int_t^{t+T} f(N) \frac{dN}{dt} dt$$

$$= \int_{N(t)}^{N(t+T)} f(N) \, dN = 0,$$

since $N(t + T) = N(t)$. But the left-hand integral is positive since $(dN/dt)^2$ cannot be identically zero, so we have a contradiction. So, the single scalar equation $dN/dt = f(N)$ cannot have periodic solutions.

14.2. DISCRETE MODELS

14.2.1. Introduction: Simple Population Models

Differential equation models imply a continuous overlap of generations. Many species have essentially no overlap whatsoever between successive generations and so population growth is in discrete steps. For primitive organisms these steps can be quite short (for fruit flies, for example, it is 24 hours) in which case a continuous (in time) model may be good enough. However, with other species the step lengths can be relatively large: a year is common. In the models we discuss here we scale the time step to be 1 so models must relate the population at time $t + 1$, denoted by N_{t+1}, in terms of the population N_t at time t, or at an even earlier time $t - T$, where T is say the time to maturity. This leads us to consider difference equations, or discrete models, of the form

$$N_{t+1} = f(N_t) \qquad (14.2.1)$$

where $f(N_t)$ is a nonlinear function of N_t which reflects the dynamics of the population change. Except for rare, and usually contrived, examples, such equations are impossible to solve analytically but, as before, we can extract a considerable amount of information about the population dynamics without an analytical solution. From a practical computational point of view if we know the form of $f(N_t)$ it is a straightforward matter to evaluate N_{t+1} and subsequent generations by simply using Equation 14.2.1 recursively starting at N_0. Of course, whatever the form of $f(N_t)$, we are only interested in nonnegative populations.

The skill in modeling a specific population's growth dynamics is in determining the appropriate form of $f(N_t)$ to reflect known facts about the species. To do this with any confidence we must have a basic understanding of the major effects on the solutions of changes in the form of $f(N_t)$ and its parameters, and, crucially of course, also what solutions of Equation 14.2.1 look like for a few specimen examples. The mathematical problem is that of finding the solutions (or orbits or trajectories) as predicted by the model equation given a starting value $N_0 > 0$. We should note at the outset that there is no simple connection between difference equation models and what might appear to be the continuous differential equation analogue even though a numerical scheme for its solution gives a finite difference approximation, which is in effect a discrete equation. This will become clear below.

If we think of a typical population that can regulate its population to some extent we would expect the function $f(N_t)$ to increase initially and then to decrease after the population became too large, typically as in Figure 14.2.1. That is, it will exhibit some self-regulation. A variety of $f(N_t)$ have been used in practical biological situations (see, for example, the book by Hassell, 1978).

When we investigate discrete models analytically the algebra quickly gets out of hand. So, to highlight the remarkably rich behavior that solutions of these difference equations can exhibit we consider the simplest nontrivial (that is, nonlinear) model, which is often referred to as the discrete Verhulst model or a Verhulst process, namely

$$N_{t+1} = rN_t\left(1 - \frac{N_t}{K}\right), \qquad r > 0, \quad K > 0, \qquad (14.2.2)$$

which is a kind of discrete analogue of the continuous logistic growth model. As we shall see, however, the solutions and their dependence on the parameter r are dramatically different. We should point out here an obvious drawback of this specific model, namely that if $N_t > K$ then the next population generation, obtained from simply substituting this N_t into Equation 14.2.2 results in $N_{t+1} < 0$. If we had an $f(N_t)$ as in Figure 14.2.1 this would not happen: with it the populations are always positive if $N_0 > 0$.

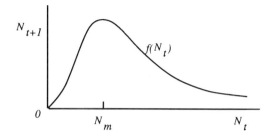

FIG. 14.2.1. Typical growth function for a discrete population model: after a certain size, N_m say, the growth rate starts to decrease.

A frequently used model, in keeping with the more realistic form in Figure 14.2.1, is

$$N_{t+1} = N_t \exp\left[r\left(1 - \frac{N_t}{K} \right) \right], \qquad r > 0, \quad K > 0, \qquad (14.2.3)$$

which we can think of as a modification of Equation 14.2.2 where there is a mortality factor $\exp(-r\,N_t/K)$ which is more severe (that is, the rate of increase is smaller), the larger N_t.

Since t increases by discrete steps there is, in a sense, an inherent *delay* in the population before it registers change. Thus, there is a certain heuristic basis for relating these difference equations to delay differential equations discussed in the above Section 14.2.1, which, depending on the length of the delay, we saw could have periodic solutions. Since we scaled the time step to be 1 in the general form (14.2.1) we should expect the other parameters to be the controlling factor as to whether or not solutions are periodic. With Equations 14.2.2 and 14.2.3 the determining parameter is r since K can be scaled out by introducing the dimensionless form N_t as $u = N_t/K$. Then dividing both sides by K we have an equation in u with the only parameter being r.

14.2.2. Cobwebbing: A Simple Graphical Solution Procedure

We can get a lot of information about the solution dynamics by simple graphical means. Consider (14.2.1) with the dynamics function $f(N_t)$ as in Figure 14.2.1. The steady states are solutions N^* of

$$N^* = f(N^*) \Rightarrow N^*. \qquad (14.2.4)$$

Graphically the steady states are intersections of the curve $N_{t+1} = f(N_t)$ and the straight line $N_{t+1} = N_t$ as shown in Figure 14.2.2a for a case where the maximum of the curve $N_{t+1} = f(N_t)$, at N_m say, has $N_m > N^*$. The evolution of the solution N_t of Equation 14.2.1 can be obtained graphically and very simply as follows.

Suppose we start at N_0 in Figure 14.2.2a. Then N_1 is given by simply moving along the N_{t+1} axis until we intersect with the curve $N_{t+1} = f(N_t)$, which gives N_1

$= f(N_0)$. The line $N_{t+1} = N_t$ is now used to start again but now, with N_1 in place of N_0. We then get N_2 by proceeding as before and then N_3, N_4 and so on: the arrows show the path sequence. The path is just a series of reflexions in the line $N_{t+1} = N_t$. We see that $N_t \to N^*$ as $t \to \infty$ and it does so monotonically as illustrated in Figure 14.2.2b. If we started at $N_0' > N^*$ in Figure 14.2.2a, then again $N_t \to N^*$ and monotonically but only after the first step. If we start close enough to the steady state N^* the approach to it is monotonic as long as the curve $N_{t+1} = f(N_t)$ crosses $N_{t+1} = f(N_t)$ appropriately. By appropriate we mean

$$ 0 < \left[\frac{df(N_t)}{dN_t} \right]_{N_t = N^*} = f'(N^*) < 1. \tag{14.2.5} $$

The derivative of $f(N_t)$ at the steady state, that is $f'(N^*)$, where the prime denotes the derivative with respect to N_t, is an important parameter as we shall

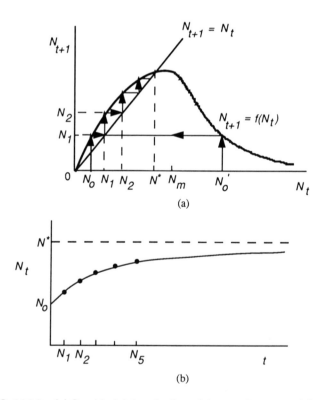

FIG. 14.2.2. (a) Graphical determination of the steady state and demonstration of how N_t approaches it in discrete steps in t. (b) Time evolution of the population growth using (a). We use a continuous curve joining up the population at different time steps for visual clarity: strictly the population changes abruptly at each time step.

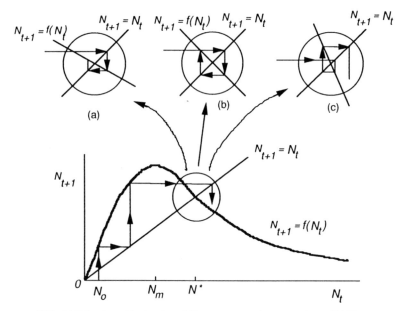

FIG. 14.2.3. Local behavior of N_t near a steady state where $f'(N^*) < 0$. The enlargements show the cases where: (a) $-1 < f'(N^*) < 0$; here N^* is stable with decreasing oscillations in any small perturbation from the steady state. (b) $f'(N^*) = -1$; here N^* is neutrally stable which means it stays on the orbit you start with. (c) $f'(N^*) < -1$; here N^* is unstable with growing oscillations.

see: it is the *eigenvalue* of the system at the steady state N^*. It is clear from the figure that if we perturb the steady state N^* by any amount—not just a small perturbation—the solution eventually r returns to the steady state so N^* is a *globally stable steady state*.

If the equilibrium $N^* > N_m$, as in Figure 14.2.3, then the dynamic behavior depends critically on the geometry of the intersection of the curves at N^* as seen from the inset enlargements in Figure 14.2.3a–c: these respectively have $-1 < f'(N^*) < 0$, $f'(N^*) = -1$, and $f'(N^*) < -1$. In all cases the solution N_t, as t increases, is oscillatory in the vicinity of N^*. If the oscillations decrease in amplitude and $N_t \rightarrow N^*$ then N^* is stable as in Figure 14.2.3a, while it is unstable if the oscillations grow as in Figure 14.2.3c. The case in Figure 14.2.3b exhibits oscillations which are periodic and suggest that periodic solutions to the equation $N_{t+1} = f(N_t)$ are possible. The steady state is strictly unstable if a small perturbation from N^* does not tend to zero. The population's dynamic behavior for each of the three cases in Figure 14.2.3 is illustrated in Figure 14.2.4.

The parameter $\lambda = f'(N^*)$, which determines the slope of the curve at the steady state, is called the *eigenvalue* of the equilibrium N^* of $N_{t+1} = f(N_t)$ and is

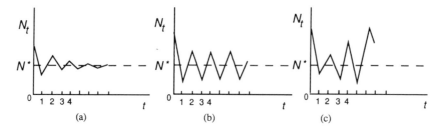

FIG. 14.2.4. Local temporal behavior of small perturbations about the equilibrium population N^* with (a), (b), and (c) corresponding to the situations illustrated in Figure 14.2.3a, b, and c, respectively: (a) is the stable case and (c) the unstable case.

crucially important in determining the local stability behavior of the steady state. The behavior is clear when $0 < \lambda < 1$ as in Figure 14.2.2a and $-1 < \lambda < 0$ as in Figure 14.2.3a. The equilibrium is stable if $-1 < \lambda < 1$; it is said to be an *attracting equilibrium*. The critical values, or *bifurcation* values, $\lambda = \pm 1$ are where the solution N_t changes its behavioral character. The case $\lambda = 1$ is where the curve $N_{t+1} = f(N_t)$ is tangent to $N_{t+1} = N_t$ at the steady state since $f(N_t) = 1$; it is called a *tangent bifurcation* for obvious reasons. The case $\lambda = -1$ is called a *pitchfork bifurcation*, the reason for the name will become clear below.

The reason for the description 'cobwebbing' for this graphical procedure is obvious particularly with the forms in Figures 14.2.3 and 14.2.5. It is a very simple and useful method for suggesting what the dynamic behavior of N_t will be for equations of the type (14.2.1). It is not just the local behavior near an equilibrium it describes, it also gives the quantitative global behavior. As an example suppose $\lambda = f'(N_t) < -1$, that is the local behavior near the unstable N^* is as in the case shown in Figure 14.2.3c. If we "cobweb" such a case we have a situation such as in Figure 14.2.5: the solution trajectory cannot tend to N^*. On the other hand, the population must be bounded by some maximum N_{max} in Figure 14.2.5a since there is no way we can generate a larger N_t unless, of course, we start with one. So, the solution is globally bounded but does *not* tend to a steady state. The solution seems to wander about in a random way if we look at it as a function of time in Figure 14.2.5b. Solutions which do this are called *chaotic* and the solution N_t exhibits *chaos*, which we discuss in more detail below.

The sensitivity of the solutions, hinted at by the special critical values of the eigenvalue λ, is indicated, or rather suggested, by the cobweb procedure and the resulting temporal solutions. We must now investigate such equations analytically. The results suggested by the graphical approach can be very helpful in the analysis but whether or not a solution really is chaotic or periodic has to be determined analytically. This we can do with the equation we now examine in detail.

14.2.3. Discrete Logistic Model: Chaos

Consider the nonlinear logistic model (14.2.2) which we rescale by writing $u_t = N_t/K$ so that the "carrying capacity" is 1. The specific equation we investigate is then

$$u_{t+1} = ru_t(1 - u_t), \qquad r > 0, \qquad (14.2.6)$$

where we take an initial value $0 < u_0 < 1$: if $u_0 > 1$ the first iteration would give $u_1 < 0$. We are only interested in solutions where $u_t \geq 0$. The steady states and corresponding eigenvalues λ (derivatives at the steady states) are

$$u^* = 0, \qquad \lambda = f'(0) = r,$$

$$u^* = \frac{r - 1}{r}, \qquad \lambda = f(u^*) = 2 - r. \qquad (14.2.7)$$

As r increases but with $0 < r < 1$, the only realistic, that is nonnegative, equilibrium or steady state is $u^* = 0$, which is stable since the eigenvalue $0 < \lambda < 1$. It is also clear from a cobwebbing of Equation 14.2.6 with $0 < r < 1$ or analytically from Equation 14.2.6 on noting that $u_1 < u_0 < 1$ and $u_{t+1} < u_t$ for all t, which in turn implies that $u_t \to 0$ as $t \to \infty$.

The first bifurcation, or change of behavior, comes when $r = 1$ since $u^* = 0$ becomes unstable because its eigenvalue, $\lambda > 1$ for $r > 1$, from the first of Equation 14.2.7. Now, however, the positive steady state $u^* = (r - 1)/r > 0$, for which its eigenvalue $-1 < \lambda < 1$ for $1 < r < 3$, is stable for this range of r. The second bifurcation occurs at $r = 3$ where $\lambda = -1$. Here $f'(u^*) = -1$, and so, locally near u^*, we have the situation in Figure 14.2.3b which exhibits a periodic solution.

To see what is happening when r passes through the bifurcation value $r = 3$ we first introduce a simplifying notation for the iterative procedure:

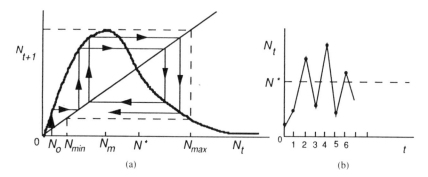

(a)   (b)

FIG. 14.2.5. (a) Cobweb for $N_{t+1} = f(N_t)$ where the eigenvalue $\lambda = f'(N_t) < -1$. (b) The corresponding population behavior as a function of time which is typical of a chaotic solution.

$$u_1 = f(u_0),$$

$$u_2 = f(f\, u_0) = f^2(u_0),$$

$$\vdots$$

$$u_t = f^t(u_0). \tag{14.2.8}$$

In the case of Equation 14.2.6 the first iteration is simply the equation itself, while the second iterate is

$$u_{t+2} = f^2(u_t) = r[ru_t(1 - u_t)]\, [1 - ru_t(1 - u_t)]. \tag{14.2.9}$$

Figure 14.2.6a illustrates the effect on the first iteration (and how the steady state varies) as r varies; the eigenvalue $\lambda = f'(u^*)$ decreases as r increases and $\lambda = -1$ when $r = 3$. If we now look at the second iteration (14.2.9) and ask if it has any equilibria, that is where $u_{t+2} = u_t = u_2^*$. A little algebra shows that u_2^* satisfies

$$u_2^*[ru_2^* - (r - 1)]\, [r^2 u_2^{*2} - r(r + 1)u_2^* + (r + 1)] = 0, \tag{14.2.10}$$

which has solutions

$$u_2^* = 0 \quad \text{or} \quad u_2^* = \frac{r - 1}{r} > 0 \quad \text{if } r > 1,$$

$$u_2^* = \frac{(r + 1) \pm [(r + 1)(r - 3)]^{1/2}}{2r} > 0 \qquad \text{if } r > 3, \tag{14.2.11}$$

from which we see that there are two more real positive steady states of $u_{t+2} = f^2(u_t)$ with $f(u_t)$ from Equation 14.2.6 if $r > 3$. This corresponds to the situation

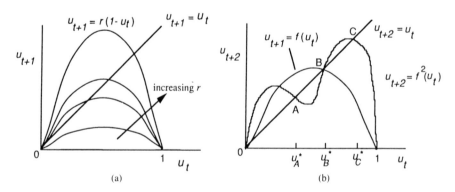

FIG. 14.2.6.   (a) First iteration as a function of r for $u_{t+1} = ru_t(1 - u_t)$, $u^* = r - 1/r$, $\lambda = f'(u^*) = 2 - r$. (b) Second iteration $u_{t+2} = f^2(u_t)$ as a function of u_t for $r = 3 + \epsilon$ where $0 < \epsilon << 1$. The single humped line reproduces the first iteration curve of u_{t+1} as a function of u_t; it passes through B, the unstable steady state.

in Figure 14.2.6b where A, B, and C are the positive equilibria u_2^*, with $B = (r - 1)/r$, lying between the two new solutions for u_2^* in Equation 14.2.11 which appear when $r > 3$.

We can think of (14.2.9) as a first iteration in a model where the iterative time step is 2 rather than 1 as in (14.2.6). The eigenvalues λ of the equilibria can be calculated at the points A, B, and C. Clearly $\lambda_B = f'(u_B^*) > 1$ from a visual inspection of Figure 14.2.6b where u_B^* denotes u_2^* at B and similarly for A and C. For r just greater than 3, such that $-1 < \lambda_A < 1$ and $-1 < \lambda_C < 1$ as can be seen visually (or, from Equation 14.2.9, by evaluating $\partial f^2(u_t)/\partial u_t$ at u_A^* and u_C^* given by the second iteration (14.2.9). Thus the steady states u_A^* and u_C^* of the second iteration are stable. What this means is that there is a stable equilibrium of the second iteration (14.2.9), which in turn means that there exists a stable *periodic solution of* period 2 of Equation 14.2.6. In other words if we start at A, for example, we come back to it after two iterations, that is $u_{A+2}^* = f^2(u_A^*)$ but $u_{A+1}^* = f(u_A^*) \neq u_A^*$. In fact $u_{A+1}^* = u_C^*$ and $u_{C+1}^* = u_A^*$.

As you increase r, the eigenvalues λ at A and C in Figure 14.2.6b pass through $\lambda = -1$ at which value these two-period solutions become unstable. At this stage we look at the fourth iterative and we find, as might now be expected, that u_{t+4} as a function of u_t will have four humps as compared with two in Figure 14.2.6b and so a four-cycle periodic solution appears. So as r passes through a series of bifurcation values (determined by the specific equation) the character of the solution, u_t, passes through a series of bifurcations, which here are reflected in period doubling of periodic solutions. The bifurcation situation is schematically illustrated in Figure 14.2.7a. As mentioned before, these bifurcations when $\lambda = -1$ are called *pitchfork bifurcations*. The reason for the name is

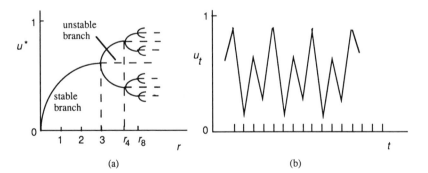

(a)   (b)

FIG. 14.2.7. (a) Stable solution branches (schematic) for the logistic model 14.2.6 as r passes through successive period doubling bifurcation values. At each bifurcation the previous state becomes unstable and is represented by the dashed lines. The sequence of stable solutions have periods 2, 2^2, 2^3, ... (b) A schematic example of a four-cycle periodic solution where $r_4 < r < r_8$; r_4 and r_8 are the bifurcation values for r for a four-period and eight-period solution respectively.

obvious from the bifurcation scenario they generate in Figure 14.2.7a. For example if $3 < r < r_4$, where r_4 is the bifurcation value to a four-period solution, then the periodic solution is between the two u^* in Figure 14.2.7a, which are the intersections of the vertical line through the specific r value and the bifurcation curve; that is with $r_4 < r < r_8$ the actual u_t values are given by the four intersections of the curve of equilibrium states with the vertical line through that value of r.

As r increases through successive bifurcations every even p-periodic solution branches into a $2p$-periodic solution and this occurs when the r makes the eigenvalue of the p-periodic solution passes through -1. The distance between bifurcations in r-space gets smaller and smaller: this is heuristically plausible since higher-order iterates imply more humps (compare with Figure 14.2.6b) all of which are fitted into the same unit interval (0, 1). There is thus a hierarchy of solutions of period 2^n for every integer n, and associated with each is a parameter interval in which the solution is stable. There is a limiting value r_c at which instability sets in for all periodic solutions of period 2^n and then for $r > r_c$ locally attracting cycles with periods k, $2k$, $4k$, . . . appear but where now k is *odd*.

This critical parameter value r_c in our model (14.2.6) is when a three-period solution is just possible. This happens when the third iterate has three steady states which are tangent to the line $u_{t+3} = u_t$: that is the eigenvalue is now $\lambda = 1$ at these steady states of the curve $u_{t+3} = f^3(u_t)$ in the space with axes u_{t+3} and u_t. This particularly critical situation is shown schematically in Figure 14.2.8. For the specific model Equation 14.2.6 the critical $r_c \approx 3.828$.

It can be proved that if a solution of $odd(\geq 3)$ period exists for a value $r = r_c$ then aperiodic or *chaotic solutions* exist for $r > r_c$. Such chaotic solutions simply oscillate in an apparently random manner. The bifurcation here, at r_c, is called a *tangent bifurcation:* where again, on looking at Figure 14.2.8, the name is suggestive of the situation.

Although we have concentrated here on the kind of solution behavior obtained with the logistic model (14.2.6) it is typical of discrete equation models with the dynamics like (14.2.1) and schematically illustrated in Figure 14.2.1. They all exhibit bifurcations to higher-order periodic solutions as some parameter varies, eventually leading to chaotic behavior at a specific parameter value. What is interesting is that if the parameter is increased, in Equation 14.2.6 for example, beyond the "chaos" value there is another critical value of r when the solution behavior again becomes *non*chaotic and the solution is a well-behaved periodic solution again. There is in fact a fractal type of behavior with these kinds of equations. By fractal I mean that a small section of the bifurcation scenario in Figure 14.2.7a is repeated but at a smaller scale (see, Murray, 1989, for a picture of this phenomenon). The interesting book by Peitgen and Richter (1986) shows a colorful selection of dramatic figures and fractal sequences which can arise from discrete models, particularly with two-dimensional models—that is, when there are coupled difference equations with two variables, say u_t and v_t.

There are two important questions to ask about models and data which arise

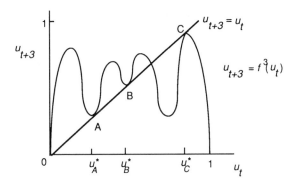

FIG. 14.2.8.   Schematic third iterate $u_{t+3} = f^3(u_t)$ for Equation 14.2.6 at $r = r_c$, the critical parameter value where the three steady states A, B, and C all have eigenvalue $\lambda = 1$; that is a tangent bifurcation.

from a discrete system. The first, about model equations, is how to determine whether or not a model can or cannot exhibit chaotic behavior. There is a simple practical way to show the existence of chaos. It can be proved that if, for some u_t and any $f(u_t)$, an *odd* integer n exists such that

$$f^n(u_t; r) < u_t < f(u_t; r)$$

then an *odd* periodic solution exists, which, from above, thus implies chaos. For example with

$$u_{t+1} = f(u_t; r) = u_t \exp\left[r(1 - u_t)\right]$$

if $r = 3.0$ and $u_0 = 0.1$ a computation of the first few terms shows

$$u_7 = f^5(u_2) < u_2 < f(u_2) = u_3;$$

that is, the odd integer $n = 5$ in the above inequality requirement. Hence this $f(u_t; r)$ with $r = 3$ is chaotic.

The second question, as to whether data is chaotic or not, is much more difficult. There are a variety of techniques which can often distinguish deterministic chaos (that is from a deterministic model) from random variation. Below, after we have discussed discrete delay models, we shall describe one based on the knowledge we have acquired from the above analysis.

14.2.4.   Stability, Periodic Solutions, and Bifurcations

All relevant ecological models involve at least one parameter, r say. It is straightforward to determine analytically the linear stability of the steady states of the general equation

$$u_{t+1} = f(u_t; r), \tag{14.2.12}$$

by a similar analysis to what we used above for a general single continuous (in time) equation. The solutions of such an equation will usually undergo bifurcations at specific values of r. From the cobweb type of graphical analysis, bifurcations occur when the relevant eigenvalues, λ, at the steady states pass through $\lambda = 1$ or $\lambda = -1$. For algebraic simplicity we shall often omit the r in $f(u_t; r)$ by writing $f(u_t)$ but the dependence on r will always be understood. Also the functions f we consider are qualitatively similar to that in Figure 14.2.1.

The steady states of Equation 14.2.12 are solutions of

$$u^* = f(u^*; r) \Rightarrow u^*(r). \tag{14.2.13}$$

To investigate the linear stability of u^* we write

$$u_t = u^* + v_t, \qquad \text{where } |v_t| << 1. \tag{14.2.14}$$

Substituting this into Equation 14.2.12 and expanding for small v_t, using a Taylor expansion, we get

$$\begin{aligned}
u^* + v_{t+1} &= f(u^* + v_t) \\
&= f(u^*) + v_t f'(u^*) + O(v_t^2), \qquad |v_t| << 1.
\end{aligned}$$

Since $u^* = f(u^*)$ the linear (in v_t) equation which determines the linear stability of u^* is then

$$v_{t+1} = v_t f'(u^*) = \lambda v_t, \qquad \lambda = f'(u^*),$$

where λ is the eigenvalue of Equation 14.2.12 at the steady state u^*. The solution of the last equation, obtained by substituting v_0 into it to calculate v_1 and so on, is

$$v_t = \lambda^t v_0 \rightarrow \begin{cases} 0 \\ \pm\infty \end{cases} \text{ as } t \rightarrow \infty \qquad \text{if } |\lambda| \begin{cases} <1, \\ >1. \end{cases}$$

So we see that

$$u^* \text{ is } \begin{cases} \text{stable} \\ \text{unstable} \end{cases} \text{if} \begin{cases} -1 < f'(u^*) < 1, \\ |f'(u^*)| > 1. \end{cases} \tag{14.2.15}$$

If u^* is stable, any small perturbation from this equilibrium decays to zero, monotonically if $0 < f'(u^*) < 1$, or with decreasing oscillations if $-1 < f'(u^*) < 1$. On the other hand, if u^* is unstable, the perturbation grows monotonically if $f'(u^*) > 1$, or by growing oscillations if $f'(u^*) < -1$. This is all as we deduced before by graphical arguments.

As an example consider the rescaled model Equation 14.2.3, which is

$$u_{t+1} = u_t \exp\left[r(1 - u_t)\right], \qquad r > 0. \tag{14.2.16}$$

for which the steady states are

$$u^* = 0 \qquad \text{or} \qquad 1 = \exp\left[r(1 - u^*)\right] \Rightarrow u^* = 1. \tag{14.2.17}$$

The corresponding eigenvalues are

$$\lambda_{u^*=0} = f'(0) = e^r > 1 \qquad \text{for } r > 0,$$

so $u^* = 0$ is unstable (monotonically) for all r (which realistically is always positive), and

$$\lambda_{u_*=1} = f'(1) = 1 - r. \qquad (14.2.18)$$

Hence the steady state $u^* = 1$ is stable for $0 < r < 2$ with an oscillatory behavior as it returns to the steady state if $1 < r < 2$. It is unstable by growing oscillations for $r > 2$. So $r = 2$ is the first bifurcation value. On the basis of the above we expect a periodic solution to be the bifurcation from $u^* = 1$ as r passes through the bifurcation value $r = 2$. Does the solution bifurcate to a periodic solution? We can see if this is probable if we look at Equation 14.2.16 with $|1 - u_t|$ small, but now we keep *quadratic* terms. In this case Equation 14.2.16 becomes

$$u_{t+1} \approx u_t[1 + r(1 - u_t)]$$

which we can transform into

$$U_{t+1} = (1 + r)U_t[1 - U_t] \qquad \text{where } U_t = \frac{ru_t}{1 + r},$$

which is the same form as the logistic model (14.2.6) with $r + 1$ in place of r. There a stable periodic solution with period 2 appeared at the first bifurcation so we deduce that the system 14.2.16 will also bifurcate to a periodic solution as r passes through the first bifurcation value. With example (14.2.16) chaotic behavior occurs for $r > r_c \approx 2.57$ with all the cascading periodic solution bifurcations occurring between $r = 2$ and this value. The sensitivity of the solutions to small variations when $r > 2$ is quite severe in this model; it is, in most of them in fact, at least for the equivalent of r beyond the first few bifurcation values. This technique of assuming perturbations are small about the steady state and keeping quadratic terms in the resulting equation can be very useful in getting some idea of the effect of the nonlinearity on the solutions near bifurcations.

After t iterations of u_0, $u_t = f^t(u_0)$, using the notation defined in (14.2.8). A *trajectory* or *orbit* generated by u_0 is the set of points $\{u_0, u_1, u_2, \ldots\}$ where

$$u_{i+1} = f(u_i) = f^{i+1}(u_0), \qquad i = 0, 1, 2, \ldots .$$

We say that a point is periodic of period m or *m-periodic* if

$$
\begin{aligned}
f^m(u_0; r) &= u_0, \\
f^i(u_0; r) &\neq u_0 \qquad \text{for } i = 1, 2, \ldots, m - 1,
\end{aligned}
\qquad (14.2.19)
$$

and in this case we say that the points $u_0, u_1, \ldots, u_{m-1}$ form an *m-cycle*. Stability of periodic solutions can also be defined, but it is a little more complicated (but not much), involving what is meant by an eigenvalue of a periodic solution. It is discussed in more, but not excessive, detail in Murray (1989).

In summary then a bifurcation occurs at a parameter value r_0 if there is a qualitative change in the dynamics of the solution for $r < r_0$ and $r > r_0$. From the above discussion we now expect it to be from one periodic solution to another with a different period. Also, when the sequence of even periods bifurcates to an odd-period solution, then solutions of every integer period exists, which implies chaos. Bifurcations with $\lambda = -1$ are the pitchfork bifurcations while those with $\lambda = 1$ are the tangent bifurcations.

14.2.5. Discrete Delay Models

In the discussion of continuous differential equation models we saw that the effect of delay could be very important. We can also include delay in these discrete models which up to now have been based on the assumption that the total population at time t contributes to the population at time $t + 1$. This is, of course, the case with most insects but is not so with many other animals where there can be a substantial maturation time to sexual maturity. In this situation the population model must include a delay effect: it is, in a sense, like incorporating an age structure. If this delay, to reproductive maturity say, is T time steps, then we are led to study difference delay models of the form

$$u_{t+1} = f(u_t; u_{t-T}).$$ (14.2.20)

In a model for baleen whales, which has been used by the International Whaling Commission T is of the order of several years; here the time step is a year.

We deal with the stability of these equations in much the same way as above. As an example we briefly consider the following simple model, which is nevertheless of practical interest:

$$u_{t+1} = u_t \exp[r(1 - u_{t-1})], \qquad r > 0.$$ (14.2.21)

This is a delay version of Equation 14.2.16. The steady states are again $u^* = 0$ and $u^* = 1$ obtained on setting $u_{t-1} = u_t = u_{t+1} = u^*$. The steady state $u^* = 0$ is unstable almost by inspection; a straightforward linearization about $u^* = 0$ immediately shows it. Linearizing about the other steady state is more interesting and somewhat more complicated since it involves some complex analysis.

We linearize about $u^* = 1$ by setting, in the usual way,

$$u_t = 1 + v_t, \qquad |v_t| \ll 1,$$

and substituting into 14.2.21 to get

$$1 + v_{t+1} = (1 + v_t) \exp[-rv_{t-1}] \approx (1 + v_t)(1 - rv_{t-1})$$

and so, retaining only the linear terms in v, we have

$$v_{t+1} - v_t + rv_{t-1} = 0.$$ (14.2.22)

We look for solutions of this kind of difference equation in the form

$$v_t = z^t \Rightarrow z^2 - z + r = 0$$

which gives two solutions (real or complex) for z, z_1 and z_2 say, where

$$z_1, z_2 = \tfrac{1}{2}[1 \pm (1 - 4r)^{1/2}], \quad r < \tfrac{1}{4},$$
$$z_1, z_2 = \rho e^{\pm i\theta}, \quad r > \tfrac{1}{4}, \tag{14.2.23}$$

with

$$\rho = r^{1/2}, \quad \theta = \tan^{-1}(4r - 1)^{1/2}, \quad r > \tfrac{1}{4}.$$

The solution of Equation 14.2.22 is then

$$v_t = A z_1^t + B z_2^t, \tag{14.2.24}$$

where A and B are arbitrary constants.

If $0 < r < \tfrac{1}{4}$, the solutions z_1 and z_2 are real, $0 < z_1 < 1$, $0 < z_2 < 1$ and so from Equation 14.2.24, $v_t \to 0$ as $t \to \infty$ and so $u^* = 1$ is a linearly stable steady stable. Furthermore, the return to this equilibrium after a small perturbation is monotonic.

If, however, $\tfrac{1}{4} < r$, z_1 and z_2 are complex with $z_2 = \bar{z}_1$, the complex conjugate of z_2. Also $z_1 z_2 = |z_1|^2 = \rho^2 = r$. Thus for $\tfrac{1}{4} < r < 1$, $|z_1|$ $|z_2| < 1$. In this case the solution is

$$v_t = A z_1^t + B \bar{z}_1^t$$

and, since the solution has to be real, we must have $B = \bar{A}$. So, with Equation 14.2.23, the real solution of the linear equation is

$$v_t = 2|A|\rho^t \cos(t\theta + \gamma), \quad \gamma = \arg A,$$
$$\theta = \tan^{-1}(4r - 1)^{1/2}. \tag{14.2.25}$$

We see that $v_t \to 0$ as $t \to \infty$ if $\rho < 1$ and so $u^* = 1$ is linearly stable. If $\rho > 1$ however the steady state is unstable by growing oscillations. As $r \to 1$, $\theta \to \tan^{-1}\sqrt{3} = \pi/3$. Let us now interpret what this means.

As r passes through the critical $r_c = 1$, $|z_1| > 1$ and so v_t grows unboundedly with time. Since $\theta \approx \pi/3$ for $r \approx 1$ and $v_t \approx 2|A| \cos(t\pi/3 + \gamma)$, which has a period of 6, we expect the solution of Equation 14.2.21, at least for r just greater than r_c, to exhibit a six-cycle periodic solution. With this example a six period cycle is clear for $r = 1.02$ but by the time $r = 1.4$ the solution is clearly chaotic.

As with continuous models, increasing the delay had a destabilizing effect so here it has a similar destabilizing effect in the discrete mode (14.2.21). In the logistic discrete model (14.2.6) the first bifurcation $r_c = 2$ and the solution bifurcates to a two-period solution, whereas in the above delay case at the critical value $r_c = 1$ the bifurcation is to a *six-period solution*. The longer the delay the greater the destabilizing effect. Higher-period solutions are often characterized by large population swings and if the crashback to low population levels from a previous high one is sufficiently severe, extinction is certainly a possibility.

14.2.6. Model Implications and Caveats

A major reason for modeling the dynamics of a population, or any dynamic problem, is to understand the main controlling features and to be able to predict the likely pattern of development consequent upon a change of parameter. In making a model we may have some knowledge of the species and observational data with which to compare the results of the model analysis. Although these models can be very helpful, it is essential to point out a few of their difficulties and limitations.

When a plausible model for a population's growth dynamics has been arrived at, the global dynamics can be determined. Using graphical methods the changes in the solutions as a major environment parameter varies can easily be seen. From Figure 14.2.5 for example, we see that if we start with a low population it simply grows for a while, then it can seem to oscillate quasi-regularly and then settle down to a constant state, or it can exhibit periodic behavior or just oscillate in a seemingly random way with large populations at one stage and crashing to very low densities in the following time step. Whatever the model, as long as it has a general form such as in Figure 14.2.5 the population density is always bounded.

This seemingly random dynamics poses serious problems from a modeling point of view. Are the data obtained which exhibit this kind of behavior generated by a deterministic model or by a stochastic situation? It is thus a problem to decide which is appropriate and it may not actually be one we can resolve in a specific situation. What modeling can do however is to point to how sensitive the population dynamics can be to changes in environmental parameters, the estimation of which is often difficult and almost always important.

One technique which often shows whether real data, which is chaotic and derives from a deterministic model, or is possibly stochastic is the following. Choose a point, call it u_{t+1} say, and plot the point (u_{t+1}, u_t) in the u_{t+1}-u_t plane. Do this with all the data points. If the curve joining these points is a smooth line this gives the graph of the function $f(u_t)$ and hence the data is generated by an equation of the form $u_{t+1} = f(u_t)$. The data could, of course, be derived from a deterministic discrete delay model. So, even if the graph of the points (u_{t+1}, u_t) do not result in a smooth curve the graph of (u_{t+1}, u_t, u_{t-1}) in three-dimensional space may do so. So even if data appears chaotic it is often possible to determine a smooth curve which has been generated by an equation of the form

$$u_{t+1} = f(u_t, u_{t-1}, u_{t-2}, \ldots).$$

There are other ways to investigate the "chaotic" character of data, but these cannot be dealt with here.

We can get some useful global results for the type of dynamics exhibited with, for example, $f(N_t)$ such as in Figure 14.2.5, which shows that the population is always bounded after a long time by some maximum N_{max} and minimum N_{min}:

the first few iterations can lie below $N_{\min}$ if N_0 is sufficiently small. With Figure 14.2.5 in mind the maximum $N_{\max}$ is given by the first iteration of the value where $N_{t+1} = f(N_t)$ has a maximum, N_m, say that is

$$\frac{df}{dN_t} = 0 \Rightarrow N_m, \qquad N_{\max} = f(N_m).$$

The minimum $N_{\min}$ is then the first iterative of $N_{\max}$ namely

$$N_{\min} = f(N_{\max}) = f(f(N_m)) = f^2(N_m). \tag{14.2.26}$$

These eventual limiting population sizes are easy to work out for a given model. For example, with

$$N_{t+1} = f(N_t) = N_t \exp\left[r\left(1 - \frac{N_t}{K} \right) \right], \qquad f'(N_t) = 0 \Rightarrow N_m = \frac{K}{r},$$

$$N_{\max} = f(N_m) = \frac{K}{r} e^{r-1},$$

$$N_{\min} = f(f(N_m)) = \frac{K}{r} \exp[2r - 1 - e^{r-1}]. \tag{14.2.27}$$

With a steeply decreasing behavior of the dynamics curve $N_{t+1} = f(N_t)$ for $N_t > N_m$ the possibility of the dramatic drop in the population to low values close to $N_{\min}$ brings up the question of *extinction* of a species. If the population drops to a value $N_t < 1$ the species is clearly extinct. In fact, extinction is almost inevitable if N_t drops to low values. At this stage a stochastic model is required which is outside the scope of this chapter. However an estimate of when the population drops to 1 or less, and hence extinction, can be obtained from the evaluation of $N_{\min}$ for a given model. The condition is, using Equation 14.2.26,

$$N_{min} = f^2(N_m) \le 1, \qquad \left[\frac{df}{dN} \right]_{N=N_m} = 0. \tag{14.2.28}$$

With the example in Equation 14.2.27 this condition is

$$\frac{K}{r} \exp[2r - 1 - e^{r-1}] \le 1.$$

So, if $r = 3.5$ say, and if $K < 1600$ approximately, the population will eventually become extinct.

An important phenomenon is indicated by the analysis of this model (14.2.27); the larger the reproduction parameter r the smaller is $N_{\min}$ and the more likelihood of a population crash which will make the species extinct. Note also that it will usually be the case that the population size immediately before the catastrophic drop is large. With the above example if $r = 3.5$ the population is almost 3500, from Equation 14.2.27.

Finally it should be emphasized here that the richness of solution behavior is a result of the nonlinearity of these models. It is interesting that many of the qualitative features can be found by remarkably elementary methods even though they present some sophisticated and challenging mathematical analytical problems.

When more species are involved which interact in a predator-prey or competition situation it is necessary to have coupled equations and deal with systems of equations. The mathematics becomes more complex, although in the case of two species it is still reasonable, but the dynamic behavior of the solutions is even more interesting.

14.3. CONTINUOUS MODELS FOR INTERACTING POPULATIONS

To get some idea of the complexities which can result when populations interact we shall consider here systems which involve two species, although the basic methods for studying these can be extended to more species with a corresponding increase in complexity of species behavior and mathematical difficulty. Population interactions, broadly speaking, are either predator-prey situations, competition situations or, if each population's growth rate benefits by the interaction it is called mutualism or symbiosis. With more than two species we could, for example, have one species the prey and the other two being in competition. With multispecies interaction there are clearly many other possibilities. We start by examining the classical, important, albeit now known to be unrealistic, Lotka-Volterra model. We shall use the method of analysis called phase-plane analysis which is described in elementary books on ordinary differential equations. A very brief summary is given in an appendix in Murray's (1989) book.

14.3.1. Predator-Prey Models: Lotka-Volterra Systems

In 1926 a mathematician, Volterra, put forward a model for the predation of one species by another as an explanation for the observed oscillatory levels of certain fish catches in the Adriatic. Defining $N(t)$ as the prey population and $P(t)$ that of the predator at time t, Volterra's model is

$$\frac{dN}{dt} = N(a - bP), \tag{14.3.1}$$

$$\frac{dP}{dt} = P(cN - d), \tag{14.3.2}$$

where a, b, c, and d are all positive constants. Let us motivate each of the terms in the model equations. (i) The prey, in the absence of any predation ($b = 0$), is assumed to grow exponentially, hence the aN term in Equation 14.3.1. (ii) The effect of the predation is to reduce the prey's per capita growth rate by a term proportional to the prey and predator populations; this is the $-bNP$ term. (iii) In the absence of any prey the predators simply die out, decaying exponentially, and this is represented by the $-dP$ term in Equation 14.3.2. (iv) The prey's contribution to the predators' growth rate is cNP; that is proportional to the available prey as well as to the size of the predator population. The NP terms can be thought of as representing the conversion of energy from one source to another: bNP is taken from the prey and cNP accrues to the predators. Although the model has serious drawbacks it has pedagogical importance and has been of considerable value in posing highly relevant practical ecological questions. The model (14.3.1) and (14.3.2) is known as the *Lotka-Volterra* model since the same equations were also derived by the chemist Lotka in 1920 for a hypothetical chemical reaction which he said could exhibit periodic behavior in the chemical concentrations.

As usual, we first nondimensionalize the system by writing

$$u(\tau) = \frac{cN(t)}{d}, \quad u(\tau) = \frac{bP(t)}{a}, \quad \tau = at, \quad \alpha = \frac{d}{a}, \quad (14.3.3)$$

and Equations 14.3.1 and 14.3.2 become

$$\frac{du}{d\tau} = u(1 - v), \quad \frac{dv}{d\tau} = \alpha v(u - 1). \quad (14.3.4)$$

In the u,v phase plane these give

$$\frac{dv}{du} = \alpha \frac{v(u - 1)}{u(1 - v)}, \quad (14.3.5)$$

which has singular points at $u = v = 0$ and $u = v = 1$. These singular points are the steady-state equilibrium points of the original differential equation system (14.3.4). For this special system (14.3.5) we can integrate it exactly to get the *phase trajectories* (which tell us how u and v vary together as time changes):

$$\alpha u + v - \ln u^{\alpha} v = H, \quad (14.3.6)$$

where H is a constant of integration. H has a minimum value for all possible u and v, namely $H_{min} = 1 + \alpha$, which occurs at $u = v = 1$. For a given H, the trajectories (14.3.6) in the u,v phase plane are closed curves as illustrated in Figure 14.3.1.

A closed trajectory in the u,v plane implies periodic solutions in τ, for u and v in Equation 14.3.4 since if you start at one point at a specific time you eventually return to it at some later time. The initial conditions, $u(0)$ and $v(0)$, determine the constant H in Equation 14.3.6 which in turn determines the phase trajectory in Figure 14.3.1. Typical periodic solutions are illustrated in Figure 14.3.2. The turning points (the maxima and minima) of u and v as functions of time, are given by setting the derivatives to zero. From Equation 14.3.4 we can see

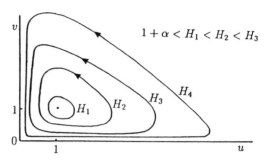

FIG. 14.3.1. Schematic phase plane trajectories, from Equation 14.3.6 with various H, for the Lotka-Volterra system 14.3.4. The arrows denote the direction of change with increasing time, τ.

immediately that u has a turning point when $v = 1$ and v has one when $u = 1$.

A major drawback of the Lotka-Volterra model is clear from Figure 14.3.1; the solutions are not structurally stable. To see what we mean by that, suppose $u(0)$ and $v(0)$ are such that u and v for $\tau > 0$ are on the trajectory H_4 which passes close to the u and v axes. Then, any small perturbation will move the solution onto another trajectory. Although the perturbation remains close to the original trajectory near where it was imposed it does not lie *everywhere* close to the original one, H_4. Thus, a small perturbation can have a very marked effect, at the very least on the amplitude of the oscillation. This is a problem with any system which has an integral, like Equation 14.3.6, which is a closed trajectory in the phase plane. Systems which are like this are called *conservative systems*. They are usually of little use as realistic models for real interacting populations (see one interesting and amusing attempt to do so below). However, the method of analysis of two species systems is in general the same, which we now do.

Returning to the form in Equation 14.3.4, a linearization about the steady states—the same as the singular points—determines the type of singularity and the stability of the steady states. The method is the same in principle as for single-equation models. A similar linear stability analysis has to be carried out on equivalent systems with any number of species equations. By inspection one steady state is $(u,v) = (0,0)$. Let us start with it and let x and y be small perturbations about $(0,0)$. If we keep only linear terms, Equation 14.3.4 becomes

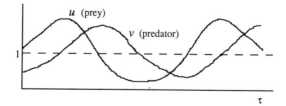

FIG. 14.3.2. Schematic periodic solutions for the prey, u, and predator, v, as functions of time, τ, for the Lotka-Volterra system 14.3.4.

$$\begin{aligned}\frac{dx}{d\tau}\\[4pt]\frac{dy}{d\tau}\end{aligned} \approx \begin{pmatrix} 1 & 0 \\ 0 & -\alpha \end{pmatrix}\begin{pmatrix} x \\ y \end{pmatrix} = A\begin{pmatrix} x \\ y \end{pmatrix}. \qquad (14.3.7)$$

the solutions of which are given by

$$\begin{pmatrix} x(\tau) \\ y(\tau) \end{pmatrix} = \mathbf{B}e^{\lambda\tau},$$

where $\mathbf{B}$ is an arbitrary constant column vector and the eigenvalues λ are given by the characteristic polynomial of the matrix A and thus are solutions of

$$|A - \lambda I| = \begin{vmatrix} 1 - \lambda & 0 \\ 0 & -\alpha - \lambda \end{vmatrix} = 0 \Rightarrow \lambda_1 = 1,\ \lambda_2 = -\alpha.$$

Since at least one eigenvalue $\lambda_1 > 0$, $x(\tau)$ and $y(\tau)$ grow exponentially and so $u = 0 = v$ is linearly unstable. Since $\lambda_1 > 0$ and $\lambda_2 < 0$ this is a *saddle point* singularity.

Linearizing about the other steady state $u = v = 1$ by setting $u = 1 + x$, $v = 1 + y$ with $|x|$ and $|y|$ small, Equation 14.3.4 becomes

$$\begin{aligned}\frac{dx}{d\tau}\\[4pt]\frac{dy}{d\tau}\end{aligned} \approx A\begin{pmatrix} x \\ y \end{pmatrix}, \qquad A = \begin{pmatrix} 0 & -1 \\ \alpha & 0 \end{pmatrix}, \qquad (14.3.8)$$

with eigenvalues λ given by

$$\begin{vmatrix} -\lambda & -1 \\ \alpha & -\lambda \end{vmatrix} = 0 \Rightarrow \lambda_1,\ \lambda_2 = \pm i\sqrt{\alpha}. \qquad (14.3.9)$$

Thus $u = v = 1$ is a *center* singularity since the eigenvalues are purely imaginary. Since Re $\lambda = 0$ the steady state is *neutrally stable* because the solutions neither grow nor decay, only oscillate. The solution of Equation 14.3.8 is of the form

$$\begin{pmatrix} x(\tau) \\ y(\tau) \end{pmatrix} = \mathbf{l}e^{i\sqrt{\alpha}\tau} + \mathbf{m}e^{-i\sqrt{\alpha}\tau}$$

where $\mathbf{l}$ and $\mathbf{m}$ are arbitrary column vectors. So, the solutions in the neighborhood of the singular point $u = v = 1$ are periodic in τ with period $2\pi//\sqrt{\alpha}$. In dimensional terms from Equation 14.3.3 this period is $T = 2\pi(a/d)^{1/2}$, that is the period is proportional to the square root of the ratio of the linear growth rate of the prey to the death rate of the predators. Even though we are only dealing with small perturbations about the steady state, we see how the period depends on the intrinsic growth and death rates. For example, an increase in the growth rate of the prey will increase the period: a decrease in the predator death rate does the same thing. Is this what you would expect intuitively?

In this ecological context the matrix in the linear equations (14.3.7) and (14.3.8) is the stability matrix, and its eigenvalues λ determine the stability of the steady states. If Re $\lambda > 0$ then the steady state is unstable while if both Re $\lambda < 0$ it is stable. The critical case Re $\lambda = 0$ is called neutral stability.

There have been many attempts to apply the Lotka-Volterra model to real-world oscillatory phenomena. In view of the system's structural instability, they must all fail to be of any quantitative practical use. However, they can be important by suggesting relevant practical questions. One interesting example was the attempt to apply the model to the extensive data on the Canadian lynx–snowshoe hare interaction in the fur catch records of the Hudson Bay Company from about 1845 until the 1930s where distinct periodic-like oscillations were observed. When the data was fitted to a Lotka-Volterra model and estimations were obtained for the parameters a reasonable-looking fit was obtained. Later when the corresponding phase-plane trajectories were plotted, it was found that, although it was a closed trajectory, it was like a figure eight with one part much smaller than the other. In this small part the arrows (cf. Figure 14.3.1) were reversed. This means that the predator lynx oscillation precedes the hare's, which is the opposite for a predatory-prey situation as in Figure 14.3.2. This implies that the hares are eating the lynx, which poses a considerable interpretation problem! It was suggested that perhaps the hares could kill the lynx if they carried a disease which they passed on to the lynx. It was a good try, but no such disease is known. One possible explanation offered is that fur trappers are the "disease" since in years of low population densities they did something else and only felt it worthwhile to return to trap when the hares were again sufficiently numerous. Since the lynx was more profitable to trap than the hare they possibly spent more time on the lynx than the hare. The moral of the story is that it is not enough simply to produce a model which exhibits oscillations but rather to provide a proper explanation of the underlying phenomenon which can stand up to scientific scrutiny.

Realistic Predator-Prey Models

Although the Lotka-Volterra model is unrealistic it shows that simple predator-prey interactions can result in oscillatory behavior in the populations. Reasoning heuristically this is not unexpected since if a prey population increases, it encourages growth of its predator. More predators, however, consume more prey, the population of which starts to decline. With less food around the predator population declines and when it is low enough, this allows the prey population to increase and the whole cycle starts over again. Depending on the detailed system such oscillations can grow or decay or go into what is called a *limit cycle* oscillation or even exhibit chaotic behavior, although in the latter case there must be at least three interacting species, or the model has to have some delay terms.

A limit cycle solution is a closed trajectory in the predatory-prey space which is not like a member of the family of closed trajectories such as the solutions of the Lotka-Volterra model in Figure 14.3.1. A stable limit cycle trajectory is such that any small perturbation from the trajectory decays to zero with the solution going back to the same limit cycle solution. A schematic example of a limit cycle trajectory in a two-species predator(P)–prey(N) interactions is illustrated in Figure 14.3.3. There are conditions that must be satisfied for the existence of such a solution: they are called the Poincaré-Bendixson conditions (see, for example, the brief appendix on phase-plane analysis in Murray, 1989).

14.3.2. Competition and Symbiotic Models

Competition is when two or more species compete for the same limited food source, prey or habitat or simply in some way they inhibit each others growth. Here we describe very briefly how a competition model can be constructed. The most basic competition model can demonstrate a fairly general principle which is observed to hold in nature, namely that when two species compete for the same limited resources one of the species usually (but not always) becomes extinct. This is called the *principle of competitive exclusion*.

We shall give here only the simple two-species Lotka-Volterra-equivalent competition model with each species N_1 and N_2 having logistic growth in the absence of the other. Inclusion of logistic growth in the Lotka-Volterra systems makes them much more realistic but to highlight the principle we consider the simpler model which nevertheless reflects many of the properties of more com-

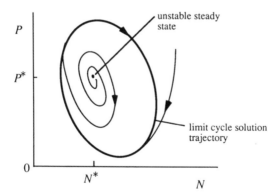

FIG. 14.3.3. Typical closed predator-prey solution trajectory which exhibits a limit cycle periodic oscillation. Any perturbation from the limit cycle tends to zero with time and the solution returns to the periodic solution trajectory.

plicated models, particularly as regards stability. With these model elements the Lotka-Volterra competition system is

$$\frac{dN_1}{dt} = r_1 N_1 \left[1 - \frac{N_1}{K_1} - b_{12} \frac{N_2}{K_1} \right],$$ (14.3.10)

$$\frac{dN_2}{dt} = r_2 N_2 \left[1 - \frac{N_2}{K_2} - b_{21} \frac{N_1}{K_2} \right],$$ (14.3.11)

where r_1, K_1, r_2, K_1, b_{12}, and b_{21} are all positive constants and, as before, the r's are the linear birth rates and the K's are the carrying capacities. The b_{12} and b_{21} measure the competitive effect of N_2 on N_1 and N_1 on N_2 respectively: they are generally not equal. The competition model 14.3.10 and 14.3.11 is not a conservative system like its predator-prey counterpart and so does not give periodic solutions.

To emphasize the importance of nondimensionalization we use this system as another example of how to do it. Here we introduce

$$u_1 = \frac{N_1}{K_1}, \quad u_2 = \frac{N_2}{K_2}, \quad \tau = r_1 t, \quad \rho = \frac{r_2}{r_1},$$

$$a_{12} = b_{12} \frac{K_2}{K_1}, \quad a_{21} = b_{21} \frac{K_1}{K_2},$$ (14.3.12)

and Equations 14.3.10 and 14.3.11 become

$$\frac{du_1}{d\tau} - u_1(1 - u_1 - a_{12} u_2) = f_1(u_1, u_2),$$

$$\frac{du_2}{d\tau} - \rho u_2(1 - u_2 - a_{21} u_1) = f_2(u_1, u_2).$$ (14.3.13)

The steady states, the phase-plane equilibria u_1^*, u_2^*, are the solutions of $f_1(u_1, u_2) = f_2(u_1, u_2) = 0$ which, from Equation 14.3.13, are

$$u_1^* = 0, \quad u_2^* = 0; \qquad u_1^* = 1, \quad u_2^* = 0; \qquad u_1^* = 0, \quad u_2^* = 1;$$

$$u_1^* = \frac{1 - a_{12}}{1 - a_{12} a_{21}}, \qquad u_2^* = \frac{1 - a_{21}}{1 - a_{12} a_{21}}.$$ (14.3.14)

The last of these is only of relevance if $u_1^* \geq 0$ and $u_2^* \geq 0$ are finite in which case $a_{12} a_{12} \neq 1$. The four possibilities are seen immediately, depending on whether a_{12} and a_{21} are greater than or less than 1. The competition acts to reduce the individual carrying capacity of each species.

The stability can be determined by graphical means (see Murray, 1989) or by analytical methods. To investigate the stability by analytical means we must linearize the system about the steady states and look at the eigenvalues of the stability matrix. The linearized matrix is

$$A = \begin{pmatrix} \dfrac{\partial f_1}{\partial u_1} & \dfrac{\partial f_1}{\partial u_2} \\[2mm] \dfrac{\partial f_2}{\partial u_1} & \dfrac{\partial f_2}{\partial u_2} \end{pmatrix}_{u_1^*, u_2^*}$$

$$= \begin{pmatrix} 1 - 2u_1 - a_{12}u_2 & -a_{12}u_1 \\ -\rho a_{21}u_2 & \rho(1 - 2u_2 - a_{21}u_1) \end{pmatrix}_{u_1^*, u_2^*} \qquad (14.3.15)$$

The first steady state in Equation 14.3.14 is unstable since the eigenvalues, λ, of the matrix, given from Equation 14.3.15 by

$$|A - \lambda I| = \begin{vmatrix} 1 - \lambda & 0 \\ 0 & \rho - \lambda \end{vmatrix} = 0 \Rightarrow \lambda_1 = 1, \lambda_2 = \rho,$$

are positive. This means that any perturbation from the steady state grows exponentially. For the second steady-state solution of Equation 14.3.14, namely (1,0), Equation 14.3.15 gives

$$|A - \lambda I| = \begin{vmatrix} -1 - \lambda & -a_{12} \\ 0 & \rho(1 - a_{21}) - \lambda \end{vmatrix} = 0 \Rightarrow \lambda_1 = -1, \lambda_2 = \rho(1 - a_{21}),$$

and so

$$u_1^* = 1, u_2^* = 0 \quad \text{is} \quad \begin{cases} \text{stable} \\ \text{unstable} \end{cases} \quad \text{if} \begin{cases} a_{21} > 1, \\ a_{21} < 1. \end{cases} \qquad (14.3.16)$$

Similarly, for the third steady state the eigenvalues are $\lambda = -\rho$, $\lambda_2 = 1 - a_{12}$ and so

$$u_1^* = 0, u_2^* = 1 \quad \text{is} \quad \begin{cases} \text{stable} \\ \text{unstable} \end{cases} \quad \text{if} \begin{cases} a_{12} > 1, \\ a_{12} < 1. \end{cases} \qquad (14.3.17)$$

Finally for the last steady state in Equation 14.3.14, when it exists (that is positive), the matrix A from Equation 14.3.15 is

$$A = (1 - a_{12}a_{21})^{-1} \begin{pmatrix} a_{12} - 1 & a_{12}(a_{12} - 1) \\ \rho a_{21}(a_{21} - 1) & \rho(a_{21} - 1) \end{pmatrix},$$

which has eigenvalues

$$\lambda_1, \lambda_2 = [2(1 - a_{12}a_{21})]^{-1} [[(a_{21} - 1) + \rho(a_{21} - 1)]$$

$$\pm \{[(a_{12} - 1) + \rho(a_{21} - 1)]^2 - 4\rho(1 - a_{12}a_{21})(a_{12} - 1)(a_{21} - 1)\}^{1/2}].$$
$$(14.3.18)$$

The sign of λ, or Re λ if it is complex, and hence the stability of the steady state, depends on the size of ρ, A_{12} and a_{21}. There are several cases to consider, namely (i) $a_{12} < 1$, $a_{21} < 1$, (ii) $a_{12} > 1$, $a_{21} > 1$, (iii) $a_{12} < 1$, $a_{21} > 1$, (iv) $a_{12} > 1$, $a_{21} < 1$, all of which have ecological implications which we discuss below. All of the cases are analyzed in a similar way.

Let us consider some of the ecological implications of these results. In case (i) where $a_{12} < 1$ and $a_{21} < 1$ there is a stable steady state where both species can exist. In terms of the original parameters from Equation 14.3.12 this corresponds to $b_{12}K_2/K_1 < 1$ and $b_{21}K_1/K_{2<1}$. For example if K_1 and K_2 are approximately the same and the *inter*specific competition, as measured by b_{12} and b_{21}, is not too strong, these conditions say that the two species simply adjust to a lower population size than if there was no competition. In other words the competition is not aggressive. This is the only case where extinction does not happen. On the other hand if the b_{12} and b_{21} are about the same and the K_1 and K_2 are different it is not easy to tell what will happen until we form and compare the *dimensionless* groupings a_{12} and a_{21}.

In case (ii), where $a_{12} > 1$ and $a_{21} > 1$, if the K's are about equal, then the b_{12} and b_{21} are not small. The analysis then says that the competition is such that all three nontrivial steady states can exist, but from Equations 14.3.16–14.3.18, only $(1,0)$ and $(0,1)$ are stable which is the situation where one or other of the species dies out. It can be a delicate matter which species ultimately wins out. It depends crucially on the starting advantage each species has.

Cases (iii) and (iv) in which the *inter*specific competition of one species is much stronger than the other, or the carrying capacities are sufficiently different so that $a_{12} = b_{12}K_2/K_1 < 1$ and $a_{21} = b_{21}K_1/K_2 > 1$ or alternatively $a_{12} > 1$ and $a_{21} < 1$, are quite definite in the ultimate result. In case (iii) the stronger dimensionless interspecific competition of the u_1-species dominates and the other species, u_2, dies out. In case (iv) it is the other way round and species u_1 becomes extinct.

Although all cases do not result in species elimination those in (iii) and (iv) always do and in (ii) it is probable due to natural fluctuations in the population levels. This early work led to the *principle of competitive exclusion* which was mentioned above. Note that the conditions for this to hold depend on the dimen*sionless* parameter groupings a_{12} and a_{21}: the growth rate ratio parameter ρ does not affect the gross stability results, just the dynamics of the system. Since $a_{12} = b_{12}K_2/K_1$, $a_{21} = b_{21}K_1/K_2$ the conditions for competitive exclusion depend critically on the interplay between competition and the carrying capacities as well as the initial conditions in case (ii).

Suppose for example we have two species comprised of large animals and small animals, with both competing for the same grass in a fixed area. Suppose also that they are equally competitive with $b_{12} = b_{21}$. With N_1 the large animals and N_2 the small, $K_1 < K_2$ and so $a_{12} = b_{12}K_2/K_1 < b_{21}K_2/K_1$. As an example if $b_{12} = 1 = b_{21}$, $A_{12} < 1$ and $a_{21} > 1$ then in this case $N_1 \to 0$ and $N_2 \to K_2$: that is the large animals become extinct.

The situation in which $a_{12} = 1 = a_{21}$ is special and, with the usual stochastic variability in nature, is unlikely to hold exactly in the real world. In this case the competitive exclusion of one or other of the species also occurs.

Mutualism or Symbiosis

There are many examples where the interaction of two or more species is to the advantage of all. Mutualism or symbiosis often plays the crucial role in promoting and even maintaining such species; plant and seed dispersers is but one example. Even if survival is not at stake the mutual advantage of mutualism or symbiosis can be very important. As a topic of theoretical ecology, even for two species, this area has not been as widely studied as the others even though its importance is comparable to that of predator-prey and competition interactions. This is in part due to the fact that simple models in the Lotka-Volterra vein give silly results. The simplest mutualism model equivalent to the classical Lotka-Volterra predator-prey one is

$$\frac{dN_1}{dt} = r_1 N_1 + a_1 N_1 N_2, \qquad \frac{dN_2}{dt} = r_2 N_2 + a_2 N_2 N_1$$

where r_1, r_2, a_1, and a_2 are all positive constants. Since $dN_1/dt > 0$ and $dN_2/dt > 0$, N_1 and N_2 simply grow unboundedly in, as has been aptly put, "an orgy of mutual benefaction."

Realistic models must at least show a mutual benefit to both species, or as many as are involved, and have some positive steady state or limit-cycle-type oscillation.

As a first step in producing a reasonable two-species model we can incorporate limited carrying capacities for both species and consider

$$\frac{dN_1}{dt} = r_1 N_1 \left(1 - \frac{N_1}{K_1} + b_{12} \frac{N_2}{K_1} \right),$$

$$\frac{dN_2}{dt} = r_2 N_2 \left(1 - \frac{N_2}{K_2} + b_{21} \frac{N_1}{K_2} \right), \qquad (14.3.19)$$

where r_1, r_2, K_1, K_2, b_{12}, and b_{21} are all positive constants. If we use the same nondimensionalization as in the competition model (the signs preceding the b's are negative there), namely (14.3.12), we get

$$\frac{du_1}{d\tau} = u_1(1 - u_1 + a_{12} u_2) = f_1(u_1, u_2),$$

$$\frac{du_2}{d\tau} = \rho u_2(1 - u_2 + a_{21} u_1) = f_2(u_1, u_2), \qquad (14.3.20)$$

where

$$u_1 = \frac{N_1}{K_1}, \quad u_2 = \frac{N_2}{K_2}, \quad \tau = r_1 t, \quad \rho = \frac{r_2}{r_1},$$

$$a_{12} = b_{12} \frac{K_2}{K_1}, \quad a_{21} = b_{21} \frac{K_1}{K_2}. \qquad (14.3.21)$$

Analyzing the model in the usual way we start with the steady states (u_1^*, u_2^*) which from Equation 14.3.20 are

$$(0, 0), \quad (1, 0), \quad (0, 1),$$

$$\left(\frac{1 + a_{12}}{\delta}, \frac{1 + a_{21}}{\delta} \right), \qquad \text{positive if } \delta = 1 - a_{12}a_{21} > 0. \qquad (14.3.22)$$

After calculating the stability matrix for Equation 14.3.20 and evaluating the eigenvalues λ for each of Equation 14.3.22, it is straightforward to show that $(0, 0)$, $(1, 0)$, and $(0, 1)$ are all unstable. If $1 - a_{12}a_{21} < 0$ there are only three steady states, the first three in Equation 14.3.22, and so the populations become unbounded. When $1 - a_{12}a_{21} > 0$ the fourth steady state in Equation 14.3.22 exists in the positive quadrant. Evaluation of the eigenvalues of the stability matrix shows it to be a stable equilibrium. Each species has increased its steady-state population from its maximum value in isolation.

This model has certain drawbacks. One is the sensitivity between unbounded growth and a finite positive steady state. It depends on the inequality $a_{12}a_{21} < 1$, which from Equation 14.3.12 in dimensional terms is $b_{12}b_{21} < 1$. So if symbiosis of either species is too large this last condition is violated and both populations grow unboundedly.

The purpose of this section is not to produce realistic models, which, in any case, require a knowledge of specific species, but rather to show how such models are constructed, give a few elementary principles, and show the basics of one method for analyzing the stability of the steady states. Even when we know what species interact we would like to model there can be no "correct" model for a given situation since many models can give qualitatively similar behavior. Getting the right qualitative characteristics is only the first step and must not be considered justification for a model. This is an important caveat for all models. What helps to make a model a good one is the plausibility of the growth dynamics based on observation, real facts and whether or not a reasonable assessment of the various parameters is possible and, finally, whether predictions based on the model are borne out by subsequent experiment and observation.

14.4. EPIDEMIC MODELS AND THE DYNAMICS OF INFECTIOUS DISEASES

The study of epidemics has a long history with a vast variety of models and explanations for the spread and cause of epidemic outbreaks. In this section we describe some very simple, but nevertheless practically useful, models for the population dynamics of the spread of infections. The practical use of such models relies on the realism put in the models. This does not mean the inclusion of all possible effects, but rather the incorporation of what appear to be the major components. Even simple models should, and frequently do, pose important questions with regard to the underlying process and possible means of control of the disease or epidemic. A fuller description of this kind of epidemic modeling is given in Murray (1989), where numerous other references are given.

14.4.1. Simple Epidemic Models and Practical Applications

Here we consider the total population to be constant. If a small group of infected individuals are introduced into a large population, a basic problem is to describe the spread of the infection within the population as a function of time. Of course this depends on many facts, including the disease involved, but as a first attempt at modeling directly transmitted diseases we make some reasonable general assumptions.

Consider a disease which, after recovery, confers immunity (which includes deaths: dead individuals are still counted). The population can then be divided into three distinct classes: the susceptibles, S, who can catch the disease; the infectives, I, who have the disease and can transmit it; and the removed class, R, who have either had the disease, or are recovered, immune, or isolated until recovered. The progress of individuals is schematically

$$S \rightarrow I \rightarrow R.$$

Such models are called *SIR* models.

The assumptions made about the transmission of the infection and incubation period are crucial in any model. With $S(t)$, $I(t)$, and $R(t)$ as the number of individuals in each class we assume for our purposes here that (i) the gain in the infective class is at a rate proportional to the number of infectives and susceptibles—that is, rSI, where $r > 0$ is a constant. The susceptibles are lost at the same rate. (ii) The rate of removal of infectives to the removed class is proportional to the number of infectives—that is, aI, where $a > 0$ is a constant. (iii) The incubation period is considered short enough to be negligible; that is a susceptible who contracts the disease is infective right away. We could include a delay in more sophisticated models.

We now consider the various classes as uniformly mixed (a gross assumption of course): that is every pair of individuals has equal probability of coming into contact with one another. The basic model mechanism is then represented by the differential equations

$$\frac{dS}{dt} = -rSI, \tag{14.4.1}$$

$$\frac{dI}{dt} = rSI - aI, \tag{14.4.2}$$

$$\frac{dR}{dt} = aI. \tag{14.4.3}$$

where $r > 0$ is the infection rate and $a > 0$ the removal rate of infectives. This is the classic Kermack-McKendrick (1927; see also 1932, 1933) model, whose work has had a similar influence in epidemiology as the Lotka-Volterra model has had in theoretical ecology. We are, of course, only interested in non-negative solutions for S, I, and R. This is a primitive model but we can still make some highly relevant general comments about epidemics and even adequately describe some specific epidemics with such a model. The usefulness of this specific modeling approach has been widely applied with considerable success (see Murray, 1989, for other examples and references).

The constant population size is built into the system 14.4.1–14.4.3 since on adding the equations and integrating we have

$$\frac{dS}{dt} + \frac{dI}{dt} + \frac{dR}{dt} = 0 \Rightarrow S(t) + I(t) + R(t) = N, \qquad (14.4.4)$$

where N is the total size of the population. Thus S, I, and R are all bounded above by N. The mathematical formulation of the problem 14.4.1–14.4.3 is completed given initial conditions such as

$$S(0) = S_0 > 0, \quad I(0) = I_0 > 0, \quad R(0) = 0, \qquad (14.4.5)$$

which means that we start with no removed class and some infectives (I_0) are introduced into a susceptible population (S_0).

Probably the first question to ask in any potential epidemic situation is, given r, a, S_0, and the initial number of infections, I_0, whether the infection will spread, and if it does, how it develops with time, and, of course, when it will start to decline. From Equation 14.4.2

$$\left[\frac{dI}{dt}\right]_{t=0} = I_0(rS_0 - a) \gtrless 0 \qquad \text{if } S_0 \gtrless \frac{a}{r} = \rho. \qquad (14.4.6)$$

Since, from Equation 14.4.1, $dS/dt \leq 0$, $S \leq S_0$ we have, if $S_0 < a/r$,

$$\frac{dI}{dt} = I(rS - a) \leq 0 \qquad \text{for all } t \geq 0, \qquad (14.4.7)$$

in which case $I_0 > I(t) \to 0$ as $t \to \infty$ and so the infection dies out: that is, no epidemic can occur. On the other hand if $S_0 > a/r$ then $I(t)$ initially increases and we have an epidemic. The term "epidemic" means that $I(t) > I_0$ for some $t > 0$: see Figure 14.4.1. We thus have a *threshold phenomenon*. If $S_0 > S_c = \rho$ (= a/r), there is an epidemic while if $S_0 < S_c$ there is not. The critical parameter $\rho = a/r$ is sometimes called the *relative removal rate* and its reciprocal σ (= r/a) the infection's *contact rate*.

We write

$$R_0 = rS_0/a,$$

where R_0 is the basic *reproduction rate* of the infection, that is, the number of secondary infections produced by one primary infection in a wholly susceptible

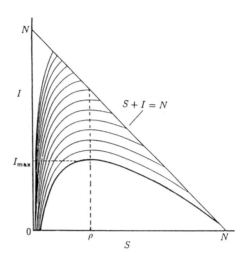

FIG. 14.4.1. Phase trajectories in the susceptibles (S)–infectives (I) phase plane for the SIR model epidemic system 14.4.1– 14.4.3. The curves are determined by the initial conditions $I(0) = I_0$ and $S(0) = S_0$. With $R(0) = 0$, all trajectories start on the line $S + I = N$ and remain within the triangle since $0 < S + I \leq N$ for all time. An epidemic situation formally exists if $I(t) > I_0$ for any time $t > 0$: this always occurs if $S_0 > \rho\, (= a/r)$ and $I_0 > 0$.

population. Here $1/a$ is the average infectious period. If more than one secondary infection is produced from one primary infection (that is, $R_0 > 1$), clearly an epidemic ensues. The whole question of thresholds in epidemics is obviously important.

We can derive some other useful analytical results from this simple model. From Equations 14.4.1 and 14.4.2

$$\frac{dI}{dS} = -\frac{(rS - a)I}{rSI} = -1 + \frac{\rho}{S}, \qquad \rho = \frac{a}{r} \quad (I \neq 0).$$

The singularities all lie on the $I = 0$ axis because if $I = 0$ we cannot cancel the I and dI/dS is undefined. Integrating the last equation gives the (I, S) phase-plane trajectories as

$$I + S - \rho \ln S = \text{constant} = I_0 + S_0 - \rho \ln S_0, \qquad (14.4.8)$$

where we have used the initial conditions 14.4.5 to determine the constant. The phase trajectories are sketched in Figure 14.4.1. Recall that because of Equation 14.4.5, all initial values S_0 and I_0 satisfy $I_0 + S_0 = N$ since $R(0) = 0$ and so for $t > 0$, $0 \leq S + I < N$.

If an epidemic exists we would like to know how severe it will be. From Equation 14.4.7 the maximum number of infectives I, $I_{\max}$, occurs at $dI/dt = 0$, that is where $S = \rho$. From Equation 14.4.8, with $S = \rho$,

$$I_{\max} = \rho \ln \rho - \rho + I_0 + S_0 - \rho \ln S_0$$

$$= I_0 + (S_0 - \rho) + \rho \ln \left(\frac{\rho}{S_0} \right)$$

$$= N - \rho + \rho \ln \left(\frac{\rho}{S_0} \right). \qquad (14.4.9)$$

For any initial values I_0 and $S_0 > S_c = \rho$, the phase trajectory starts with $S > \rho$ and we see that I increases from I_0, and hence an epidemic ensues. It may not necessarily be a severe epidemic as is the case if I_0 is close to I_{max}. It is also clear from Figure 14.4.1 that if $S_0 < \rho$ then I decreases from I_0 and no epidemic occurs.

Since the axis $I = 0$ is a line of singularities, on all trajectories $I \to 0$ as $t \to \infty$. From Equation 14.4.1, S decreases since $dS/dt < 0$ for $S \neq 0, I \neq 0$. From Equations 14.4.1 and 14.4.3

$$\frac{dS}{dR} = -\frac{S}{\rho}$$

$$\Rightarrow S = S_0 \exp\left[-\frac{R}{\rho}\right] \geq S_0 \exp\left[-\frac{N}{\rho}\right] > 0.$$

$$\Rightarrow 0 < S(\infty) \leq N. \tag{14.4.10}$$

In fact from Figure 14.4.1, $0 < S(\infty) < \rho$. Since $I(\infty) = 0$, Equation 14.4.4 implies that $R(\infty) = N - S(\infty)$. So, from Equation 14.4.10

$$S(\infty) = S_0 \exp\left[\frac{-R(\infty)}{\rho}\right] = S_0 \exp\left[-\frac{N - S(\infty)}{\rho}\right],$$

and so $S(\infty)$ is the positive root $0 < z < \rho$ of the transcendental equation

$$S_0 \exp\left[-\frac{N - z}{\rho}\right] = z. \tag{14.4.11}$$

We now get the total number of susceptibles who catch the disease in the course of the epidemic as

$$I_{total} = I_0 + S_0 - S(\infty), \tag{14.4.12}$$

where $S(\infty)$ is the positive solution z of Equation 14.4.11. An important implication of this analysis, namely that $I(t) \to 0$ and $S(t) \to S(\infty) > 0$, is that the disease dies out from a lack of *infectives* and *not* from a lack of susceptibles.

The threshold result for an epidemic is directly related to the relative removal rate ρ; if $S_0 > \rho$ an epidemic ensues whereas it does not if $S_0 < \rho$. For a given disease, the relative removal rate varies with the community and hence determines whether an epidemic may occur in one community and not in another. The number of susceptibles S_0 also plays a role, of course. For example, if the density of susceptibles is high and the removal rate, a, of infectives is low (through ignorance, lack of medical care, inadequate isolation and so on) then an epidemic is likely to occur. Expression 14.4.9 gives the maximum number of infectives, while Equation 14.4.12 gives the total number who get the infection in terms of $\rho (= a/r)$, I_0, S_0, and N.

In most epidemics it is difficult to determine how many new infectives there are each day since only those that are removed, for medical aid or whatever, can be counted. Public Health records generally give the number of infectives per day, week or month. So, to apply the model to actual epidemic situations in general, we need to know the number removed per unit time, namely dR/dt as a function of time.

From Equations 14.4.10, 14.4.4, and 14.4.3 we get an equation for R alone, namely

$$\frac{dR}{dt} = aI = a(N - R - S) = a\left(N - R - S_0 \exp\left[-\frac{R}{\rho} \right] \right),$$
$$R(0) = 0, \tag{14.4.13}$$

which can only be solved analytically in a parametric way: the solution in this form, however, is not very convenient. Of course, if we know a, r, S_0, and N it is a simple matter to compute the solution numerically. There are many simulation packages around for personal computers which cope with such equations very easily. Usually we do not know all the parameters and so we have to carry out a best-fit procedure, assuming, of course, the epidemic is reasonably described by such a model. In practice, however, it is often the case that if the epidemic is not large, R/ρ is small; at least we require $R/\rho < 1$. Following Kermack and McKendrick (1927) we can then approximate Equation 14.4.13 by

$$\frac{dR}{dt} = a\left[N - S_0 + \left(\frac{S_0}{\rho} - 1 \right) R - \frac{S_0 R^2}{2\rho^2} \right].$$

Factoring the right-hand side quadratic in R, we can integrate this equation to get, after some elementary but tedious algebra and integration, the solution

$$R(t) = \frac{\rho^2}{S_0}\left[N - S_0 + \left(\frac{S_0}{\rho} - 1 \right) + \alpha \tanh\left(\frac{\alpha a t}{2} - \phi \right) \right], \tag{14.4.14}$$

$$\alpha = \left[\left(\frac{S_0}{\rho} - 1 \right)^2 + \frac{2S_0(N - S_0)}{\rho^2} \right]^{1/2}, \qquad \phi = \frac{\tanh^{-1}(S_0/\rho - 1)}{\alpha}.$$

the removal rate is then given by

$$\frac{dR}{dt} = \frac{\alpha a^2 \rho^2}{2S_0} \operatorname{sech}^2\left(\frac{\alpha a t}{2} - \phi \right), \tag{14.4.15}$$

which involves only three parameters, namely $\alpha a^2 \rho^2 / 2S_0$, αa, and ϕ. With epidemics which are not large, it is this function of time which we should fit to the Public Health records. On the other hand, if the disease is such that we know the actual number of the removed class then it is $R(t)$ in Equation 14.4.14 we should use. If R/ρ is not small, however, we must use the differential equation 14.4.13 to determine $R(t)$.

This simple *SIR* model has been applied with some success to several quite different epidemic situations. The Bombay plague epidemic of 1905–1906 lasted for almost a year. Since most of the victims who got the disease died, the number removed per week, that is dR/dt is approximately equal to the number of deaths per week. On the basis that the epidemic was not severe (relative to the population size), Kermack and McKendrick (1927) compared the actual data with Equation 14.4.15, determined the best fit for the three parameters and got

$$\frac{dR}{dt} = 890 \text{ sech}^2 (0.2t - 3.4). \tag{14.4.16}$$

The fit is astonishingly good (see Murray, 1989).

Another quite different epidemic for which this model has been used was an influenza epidemic in an English Boarding School in 1978. In the March 4, 1978 issue of the *British Medical Journal* there is a report with detailed statistics of a flu epidemic in a boys boarding school with a total of 763 boys. Of these 512 were confined to bed during the epidemic, which lasted from January 22 to February 4, 1978. It seems that one infected boy initiated the epidemic. This situation has many of the requirements assumed in the model derivation. Here however, the epidemic is severe and the full system had to be used. In this situation, when a boy was infected he was put to bed, and so we have $I(t)$ directly from the data. Since in this case we have no analytical solution for comparison with the data, a best-fit numerical technique was used directly on Equations 14.4.1–14.4.3 for comparison of the data. The recent 1994 plague epidemic in India could probably be modeled in a similar way with an equally good fit. Figure 14.4.2 illustrates the resulting time evolution for the infectives, $I(t)$, together with the epidemic statistics. The R-equation 14.4.3 is uncoupled: the solution for $R(t)$ is simply proportional to the area under the $I(t)$ curve.

This *SIR* type of model has been used to model the outbreak of plague in the village of Eyam in England from 1665 to 1666. In this remarkable altruistic incident, the village sealed itself off when plague was discovered so as to prevent it spreading to the neighboring villages; it was successful. By the end of the epidemic only 83 of the original population of 350 survived. Thus here, $S(\infty) = 83$ out of an initial $S_0 = 350$. This is another example, like the school flu epidemic, where the epidemic was severe and where the disease died out because of lack of infectives and not as deduced above because of lack of susceptibles. Another use of the *SIR* model, when coupled to spatial dispersal has also been used (see Murray, 1989) to model the spread of rabies among foxes in the current epizootic in Europe and to predict the spread in England should it cross the English channel, as it inevitably will.

The point of using simple models for what are clearly complex issues is that they usually highlight key questions. They can also be used for examining control strategy ideas. This certainly was the case in the rabies situation where it was possible to suggest how wide, for example, a rabies "break" would have to be to stop the spatial spread.

Many diseases have a latent or incubation period when a susceptible has become infected but is not yet infectious. Measles, for example, has an 8–13 day

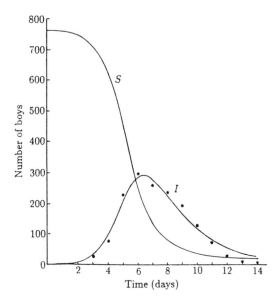

FIG. 14.4.2.   Influenza epidemic data (•) for a boys boarding school as reported in *British Medical Journal,* March 4, 1978. The continuous curves for the infectives (I) and susceptibles (S) were obtained from a best-fit numerical solution of the *SIR* system (19.1)–(19.3): parameter values $N = 763$, $S_0 = 762$, $I_0 = 1$, $\rho = 202$, $r = 2.18 \times 10^{-3}$/day. The conditions for an epidemic to occur, namely $S_0 > \rho$ is clearly satisfied and the epidemic is severe since R/ρ is not small.

latent period. The incubation time for AIDS, on the other hand, is anything from a few months to years after the patient has been shown to have antibodies to the human immunodeficiency virus (HIV). We can, for example, incorporate this as a delay effect, or by introducing a new class, $E(t)$ say, in which the susceptible remains for a given length of time before moving into the infective class. Such models give rise to integral equation formulations and they can exhibit oscillatory behavior as might be expected from the inclusion of delays. Finally age, a, is often a crucial factor in disease susceptibility and infectiousness. The models then become partial differential equations with independent variables (t, a).

There are many modifications and extensions which can and often must be incorporated in epidemic models; these depend critically on the disease. The book by Murray (1989) goes into some detail on the above and other examples of epidemic modeling: see also the references cited there.

Modeling Venereal Diseases

A different type of modeling, but which uses the above *SIR* ideas, has been applied to sexually transmitted diseases (STDs). The increasing incidence of sexually transmitted diseases, such as gonorrhea, chlamydia, syphilis, and, of course, AIDS, is a major health problem in both developed and developing countries. In the United States, for example, it is believed that more than 2 million people contract gonorrhea annually, while in the mid-1980s around 4 million Americans annually contracted chlamydia for which diagnostic techniques have only recently been sufficiently refined to make diagnosis more accurate and less expensive. Among reportable communicable diseases its incidence is far greater than the combined totals of syphilis, measles, tuberculosis, hepatitis plus others. The consequences of untreated STDs in general are extremely unpleasant.

STDs have certain characteristics which are different from other infections, such as measles or rubella (German measles). One difference is that they are mainly restricted to the sexually active community. Another is that often the carrier is asymptomatic until quite late on in the development of the infection. A third crucial difference is that STDs induce little or no acquired immunity following an infection. Equally important in viral infections is the lack of current knowledge of the parameters which characterize the transmission dynamics.

In this section we give a simple epidemic model which incorporates some of the basic elements in the heterosexual spread of venereal diseases. We have in mind such diseases as gonorrhea. For the model we assume there is uniformly promiscuous behavior in the population we are considering and as a simplification we consider only heterosexual encounters. The population consists of two interacting classes, males and females, and infection is passed from a member of one class to the other. It is a crisscross type of disease in which each class is the disease host for the other. In all of the models we have assumed homogeneous mixing between population subgroups.

Crisscross infection is similar in many ways to what goes on in malaria and bilharzia, for example, where two crisscross infections occur. In bilharzia it is between humans and a particular type of snail. Bilharzia, or schistosomiasis, has been endemic in Africa for a very long time. Very young male children who contract the disease start to pass blood in the urine around the age of puberty. (Bilharzia was so common that the ancient Egyptians believed that this passing of blood was considered the male equivalent of menstruation. Those boys who did not contract the disease were so unique that they were believed to have been chosen by the gods and hence should become priests! Since this perhaps implies they had some immunity they tended to live longer. Perhaps this is why so many of the mummies of older important people are of priests! There are, of course, other possible explanations.)

Since the incubation period for venereal diseases is usually quite short—in gonorrhea, for example, it is three to seven days—when compared to the infectious period, we use an extension of the simple epidemic model above. We divide the promiscuous male population into susceptibles S, infectives I, and a removed class R: The similar female groups we denote by S^*, I^*, and R^*. If we do not include any transition from the removed class to the susceptible group, the infection dynamics is schematically

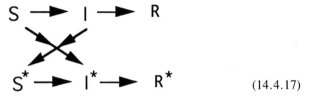

$$(14.4.17)$$

Here I^* infects S and I infects S^*.

As noted, the contraction of gonorrhea does not confer immunity and so an individual removed for treatment becomes susceptible again after recovery. In this case a better dynamics flow diagram for gonorrhea is

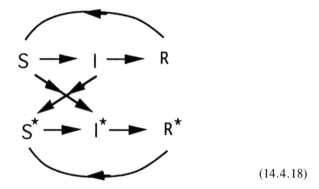

$$(14.4.18)$$

An even simpler version involving only susceptibles and infectives is

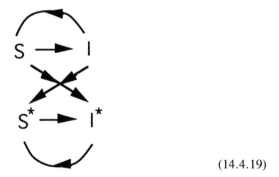

$$(14.4.19)$$

which, by way of illustration, we now analyze. It is a crisscross SI model.

We take the total number of males and females to be constant and equal to N and N^* respectively. Then, for (14.4.19)

$$S(t) + I(t) = N, \qquad S^*(t) + I^*(t) = N^*. \qquad (14.4.20)$$

We now take the rate of decrease of male susceptibles to be proportional to the male susceptibles times the infectious female population with a similar form for the female rate. We assume that once infectives have recovered they rejoin the susceptible class. A model for (14.4.19) is then (14.4.20) together with

$$\frac{dS}{dt} = -rSI^* + aI, \qquad \frac{dS^*}{dt} = -r^*S^*I + a^*I^*$$

$$\frac{dI}{dt} = rSI^* - aI, \qquad \frac{dI^*}{dt} = r^*S^*I - a^*I^* \qquad (14.4.21)$$

where r, a, I^*, and S^* are positive parameters. We are interested in the progress of the disease given initial conditions

$$S(0) = S_0, \quad I(0) = I_0, \quad S^*(0) = S_0^*, \quad I^*(0) = I_0^*. \qquad (14.4.22)$$

Although (14.4.21) is a fourth-order system, with (14.4.20) it reduces to a second-order system in either S and S^* or I and I^*. In the latter case we get

$$\frac{dI}{dt} = rI^*(N - I) - aI, \qquad \frac{dI^*}{dt} = r^*I(N^* - I^*) - a^*I^*, \qquad (14.4.23)$$

which can be analyzed in the (I, I^*) phase plane in the standard way. The steady states of (14.4.23), are $I = 0 = I^*$ and

$$I_s = \frac{NN^* - \rho\rho^*}{\rho + N^*}, \quad I_s^* = \frac{NN^* - \rho\rho^*}{\rho^* + N}, \quad \rho = \frac{a}{r}, \quad \rho^* = \frac{a^*}{r^*}. \qquad (14.4.24)$$

Thus, nonzero positive steady-state levels of the infective populations exist only if $NN^*/\rho\rho^* > 1$: this is the *threshold condition* somewhat analogous to that found before.

With the experience gained from analyzing two species interacting populations, we now expect that, if the positive steady state exists then the zero steady state is unstable. This is indeed the case. The eigenvalues λ for the linearization of Equation 14.4.23 about $I = 0 = I^*$ are given by

$$\begin{vmatrix} -a -\lambda & rN \\ r^*N^* & -a^* -\lambda \end{vmatrix} = 0$$

$$\Rightarrow 2\lambda = -(a + a^*) \pm \left[(a + a^*)^2 + 4aa^* \left(\frac{NN^*}{\rho\rho^*} - 1 \right) \right]^{1/2}.$$

So, if the threshold condition $NN^*/\rho\rho^* > 1$ holds, $\lambda_1 < 0 < \lambda_2$ and the origin is a saddle point in the (I, I^*) phase plane. If the threshold condition is not satisfied—that is, $NN^*/\rho\rho^* < 1$, then the origin is stable since both $\lambda > 0$. In this case positive I_s and I_s^* do not exist.

If I_s and I_s^* exist, meaning in the context here that they are positive, then linearizing Equation 14.4.23 about it, the eigenvalues λ satisfy

$$\begin{vmatrix} -a-rI_s^*-\lambda & rN \\ r^*N^* & -a^*-r^*I_s-\lambda \end{vmatrix} = 0;$$

that is

$$\lambda^2 + \lambda[a + a^* + rI_s^* + r^*I_s] + [a^* + rI_s^* + ar^*I_s + rr^*I_sI_s^*$$
$$+ aa^* - rr^*NN^*] = 0,$$

the solutions of which have Re $\lambda < 0$ and so the positive steady state (I_s, I_s^*) in Equation 14.4.24 is stable.

The threshold condition for a nonzero steady-state infected population is $NN^*/\rho\rho^* = (rN/a)(r^*N^*/a^*) > 1$. We can interpret each term as follows. If every male is susceptible then rN/a is the average number of males contacted by a female infective during her infectious period: a reciprocal interpretation holds for r^*N^*/a^*. The quantities rN/a and r^*N^*/a^* are the maximal male and female *contact rates* respectively.

Although parameter values for contacts during an infectious stage are somewhat unreliable from individual questionnaires, what is abundantly clear from the statistics since 1950 is that an epidemic has occurred in a large number of countries and so $NN^*/\rho\rho^* > 1$. It must be kept in mind that this model is a very simple one and principally pedagogical.

In this chapter we have tried to describe some relatively simple, but still very practical and useful, modeling techniques for the temporal dynamics of population growth and interaction. This chapter is closely based on several chapters in the book by Murray (1989) which goes into considerably more detail, describes many more modeling scenarios and gives some details of the mathematics involved.

REFERENCES

Edelstein-Keshet, L. (1988). *Mathematical models in biology.* New York: Random House.

Hassell, M. P. (1978). *The dynamics of arthropod predator-prey systems.* Princeton: Princeton University Press.

Kermack, W. O., & McKendrick, A. G. (1927; 1932, 1933). Contributions to the mathematical theory of epidemics. *Proc. Roy. Soc. A, 115,* 700–721 (1927); *138,* 55–83; *141,* 94–122.

Ludwig, D., Jones, D. D., & Holling, C. S. (1978). Qualitative analysis of insect outbreak systems: The spruce budworm and forest. *J. Animal Ecology, 47,* 315–332.

Murray, J. D. (1989). *Mathematical biology.* (2nd corrected edition, 1993) Heidelberg: Springer-Verlag.

Peitgen, H.-O, & Richter, P. H. (1986). *The beauty of fractals: Images of complex dynamical systems.* Heidelberg: Springer.

15 The Chaotic Pendulum: Model and Metaphor

Gregory L. Baker
ANC College

In interacting systems, biological properties often create cyclicities with a regulatory aspect. These systems often need to interact with other systems that can be considered as providing a "driving" input. Baker's chapter is a detailed analysis of a periodic system that is driven by a driving force with another period. His analysis shows that this simple physical configuration can reveal all of the complex possibilities of chaos.

—Editor

INTRODUCTION

During the last three decades there has been a remarkable renewal of interest in deterministic systems. This interest stems from the discovery of the surprisingly complex dynamics—*deterministic chaos*—that can arise from unstable, yet deterministic, systems. Perhaps the fascination with these new phenomena is due not only to the unexpected nature of the behavior itself, but also to the perception that chaotic dynamics is somehow behind much that we observe in the material and perhaps even mental worlds. Chaotic dynamics or some analog thereof may provide a universal mechanism for understanding the ubiquitous complexity in both forms and processes that we observe in nature. One senses that chaotic dynamics could be, in some ways, a *theory of everything*.

In this spirit, we describe the complex dynamics of the driven pendulum. We hope this discussion will stimulate comparisons of the chaotic pendulum with other systems, and we briefly suggest some comparisons between pendulum dynamics and psychological phenomena.

THE MODEL SYSTEM: A DRIVEN PENDULUM

The driven pendulum entered the canon of physical models in 1581 when Galileo observed the swaying chandeliers in the cathedral at Pisa (Robinson, 1921). Even after four centuries it continues to be the object of study (D'Humieres et al., 1982, Gwinn & Westervelt, 1985, 1986; Blackburn et al., 1989). The driven pendulum is described as a dynamical system—an equation or set of equations based upon a deterministic law.

We use Newton's deterministic law of motion—mass times acceleration equals force—to describe the driven pendulum. If θ represents the angular displacement of the pendulum from equilibrium the equation is

$$ mL \frac{d^2\theta}{dt^2} = -\gamma \frac{d\theta}{dt} - mg \sin \theta + F \cos (\omega_D t), $$

where m = mass of pendulum bob
   L = length of pendulum
   γ = strength of friction in pendulum
   g = acceleration due to gravity (9.8 m/sec^2)
   F = strength of driving force
   ω_D = angular rate of forcing
   t = time

The term on the left side is the pendulum mass times its acceleration. The forces which provide the acceleration appear on the right side of the equation. These are (1) an energy dissipative term proportional to the pendulum's velocity, $d\theta/dt$, (2) the earth's gravity, which constantly tries to restore the pendulum to verticality

473

and dictates the period of its "natural" motion, and (3) the periodic forcing that provides energy for the pendulum motion, respectively.

An approximate physical picture can be imagined by thinking of a child's swing that is pushed to maintain a periodic motion. See Figure 15.1. Usually the swing is pushed at the "natural" or *resonant* frequency of the motion, a frequency that depends, to a first approximation, on gravity and the length of the pendulum. With this rate of pushing the energy is most efficiently transferred to the swing in a way that "matches" the swing's configuration and its consequent inertial properties. As a result, resonant forcing provides a maximum amplitude of periodic oscillations. (It also gives the most comfortable ride to the child and requires the least effort from the pusher!)

In our equation we have allowed for two circumstances that differ significantly from the usual swing motion. First we have allowed for the possibility of very strong forcing. Such forcing would allow the swing to rotate completely around its pivot point. Second, the differential equation allows for the forcing to have a frequency ω_D, that differs from the resonant frequency of the pendulum. Nonresonant forcing sets up a competition between the "natural" motion imposed by gravity and the pendulum configuration, and the input of energy imposed by the forcing. For the child on the swing, vigorous forcing at a nonresonant frequency would provide a very bumpy and dangerous ride.

However, if the nonresonant forcing is very strong the natural motion will be overcome and new dynamics will result. The pendulum will be locked to the

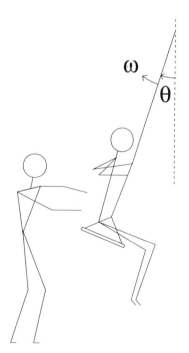

FIG. 15.1. A child being pushed on a swing as an approximate representation of the driven pendulum. (In fact, the equations require the forcing to occur periodically anywhere in the swing's motion, not just at the lowest point.)

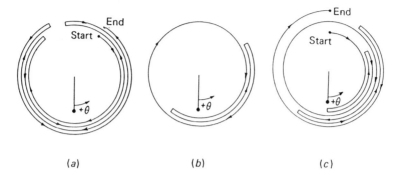

(a)   (b)   (c)

FIG. 15.2. Various periodic motions of the pendulum. The period of
the forcing is $T = 2\pi/\omega_D$. If the period of a resultant motion is nT, then
the motion is said to be period-n. In (a) the motion is period-2 and $g =$
1.07, in (b) the motion is period-1 and $g = 1.35$, and in (c) the motion is
period-2 and $g = 1.45$. In all cases $q = 2$.

forcing frequency or some subharmonic of that frequency. Though still periodic,
the motion becomes more complex as shown in Figure 15.2. With further increased forcing the motion may bifurcate again to the point where it is unstable
and nonperiodic, never repeating a trajectory—it becomes chaotic! Yet the motion is still deterministic and it is therefore termed *deterministic chaos*. While we
might think that such motions are quite uncommon, they are in fact ubiquitous in
many areas of science, and therefore our model has a strong basis in reality
(Krasner, 1990).

Chaotic phenomena are found in biology, chemistry, physics, and mathematics as well as in the applied fields of medicine and engineering. From the
fibrillation of the heart, to unstable chemical reactions, to the rings of Saturn,
chaotic behavior is everywhere. For science, it is a new realization of what has
always been manifest, that nature really is complex and marvelous.

The Geometry of Chaos

The existence of deterministic chaos is predicated upon certain conditions.
Again let us focus on our model system and rewrite the differential equation of
motion for the driven pendulum as a set of first order differential equations with
dimensionless parameters (Baker and Gollub, 1990):

$$\frac{d\omega}{dt} = \frac{\omega}{q} - \sin\theta + g\cos\varphi,$$

$$\frac{d\theta}{dt} = \omega,$$

$$\frac{d\varphi}{dt} = \omega_D.$$

In this set of autonomous first-order equations the variables are first θ, the angular displacement of the pendulum from verticality, then ω, the angular velocity of the pendulum, and finally ϕ, the phase of the forcing, which is really just proportional to time. (This latter variable is introduced in order to transform time to a variable that is periodic with the forcing motion. That is, ϕ varies from 0 to $2\pi/\omega_D$. In essence, time begins anew at the beginning of each forcing cycle.) The angle θ is also a periodic variable bounded by the values of π and $-\pi$ radians. That is, when the pendulum passes through the top of its circle θ changes from π to $-\pi$. The angular velocity is not periodic, but it is bounded in a finite region.

Accompanying the change of variables, we have also introduced three dimensionless *parameters*, g, q, and ω_D. These quantities provide a measure of the forcing strength, the damping or dissipative force, and the forcing frequency, respectively. With this parametrization, the natural frequency is equal to unity. We will find that the dynamics is rich in complexity and quite varied as the values of these parameters change.

By writing the original second-order differential equation as a set of three first-order equations we highlight a necessary condition for chaotic behavior. Chaos can only occur if there is sufficient complexity in the dynamics, and a minimum condition is that there be 3 degrees of freedom—three variables, as indicated by the triplet (θ, ω, ϕ). Hence, this system has minimal complexity for chaos. Second, this system contains *nonlinearity*, in the form of the sin θ term. Without this term no chaos is possible—the motion would always be periodic.

The presence of nonlinearity suggests one reason why chaotic dynamics is a relatively new science. Whereas linear differential equations are readily soluble, nonlinear equations are not. At the beginning of the 19th century the French mathematician Henri Poincaré developed a *qualitative* theory for nonlinear equations, but it was not until the advent of the digital computer that quantitative numerical solutions could be readily determined. In 1963 Edward Lorenz reported the first demonstration of chaotic dynamics in a simulation of a simple convective weather system (Lorenz, 1963).

Beyond nonlinearity and the minimal complexity of three variables, chaotic behavior is characterized by *sensitivity to initial conditions*. This latter condition is the result of instability. It simply means that if two identical systems have their motions initiated with slightly different initial conditions, then the states of these two systems will diverge from each other *exponentially*. Mathematically this is represented in one dimension as follows: suppose the initial difference between the two systems is represented by $x_1(0) - x_2(0) = \epsilon_0$; then at some later time t, the difference becomes

$$\epsilon(t) = \epsilon_0 e^{\lambda t},$$

where λ is a positive number called a Lyapunov exponent. Of course, this divergence happens only for relatively short times because the finite size of the dynamical "space" of the system requires that it turn back on itself fairly soon. The sensitivity to initial conditions provides "stretching" and the limited dynamical space provides a "folding" of the dynamics back upon itself. Repeated stretching and folding cause a mixing of the states in such a way that even the most minute error in the initial state will render the system unable to retrace its steps to this same initial state.

Sensitivity to initial conditions has been popularized as the "butterfly effect"—the idea being that a butterfly flapping its wings in South America could slightly perturb a developing tropical storm and change its ultimate destination significantly. Therefore, nonlinearity in meteorological equations and sensitivity to initial conditions preclude accurate long-range weather forecasting.

Much insight into chaotic dynamics is gained from various geometric representations of the dynamics. One of the simplest pictures is that of a *time series*. Figure 15.3 shows to time series for the angular velocity of the pendulum; the first time series shows a periodic variation of the pendulum velocity at the forcing frequency of ω_D. The second time series shows the angular velocity of a chaotic pendulum. While still exhibiting a strong component of the forcing frequency the motion in the latter figure is quite complex.

One standard tool for analysis of time series is *Fourier analysis*. In essence, the technique determines which frequency components are present in the time series. It does this by transforming the information contained in the time series— a representation in the time dimension—into a representation in the frequency dimension. For example, a single-frequency sinusoidal time series has only one frequency, and therefore its *Fourier spectrum* has only one point. On the other hand, chaotic dynamics contains motion with infinite number of frequencies. The dynamics never repeats itself and therefore the Fourier spectrum contains many points; it is broadbanded. Figure 15.4 illustrates the different cases roughly corresponding to the time series in Figure 15.3.

Yet Fourier analysis by itself is not an unambiguous determinant of chaotic behavior. Random systems and noisy systems can also give broadband Fourier spectra, and therefore other means are needed to further distinguish chaotic motion. We will discuss several such devices.

Dynamical systems are naturally represented in the mathematical space of their variables, known as the *phase space*. For the pendulum this phase space has three dimensions (θ, ω, ϕ), as described above, and uses periodic boundary conditions for θ and ϕ, or time. Figure 15.5 shows phase portraits corresponding to the time series of Figure 15.3. In Figure 15.5a the pendulum is executing the type of pleasing periodic motion of the child's swing. The spiral motion results from the angular displacement being a maximum when the angular velocity is a minimum, and vice versa, as time progress. The motion is repeated for each drive cycle. On the other hand, the chaotic pendulum in Figure 15.5b never repeats its motion and the phase portrait is a complex and seemingly artistic layering of many trajectories in the phase space.

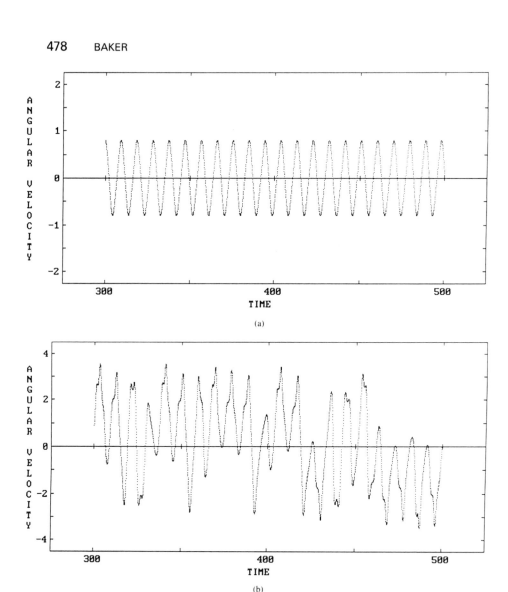

FIG. 15.3.   Time series of the angular velocity of the pendulum. In (a) the motion is periodic, and in (b) the motion is chaotic.

Despite their vastly different appearances, both structures correspond to their respective motions only after the systems have finished their initial transient motion. Both geometric figures are the sets toward which the motion is attracted. Both sets are called *attractors*. Because of its special and unusual properties the chaotic attractor is called a *strange attractor* and, as we shall discuss later, is a geometric object called a fractal.

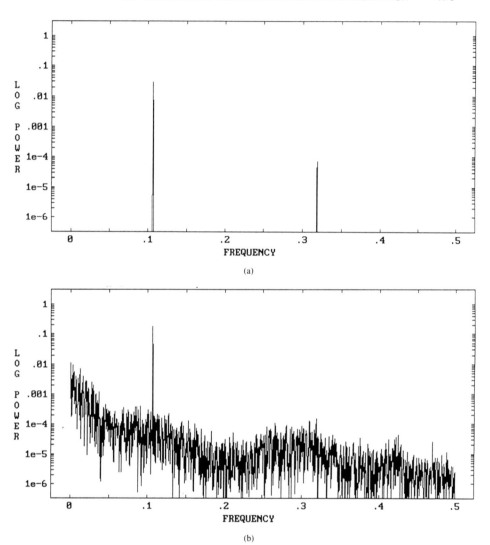

FIG. 15.4. Fourier spectra of the time series in Figure 15.3. In (a) the motion consists of a very strong component at the forcing frequency and a much smaller second harmonic component. In (b) the motion is chaotic. Aside from the strong component at the forcing frequency, there are an infinite number of unstable periodic modes. The spectrum strongly resembles "1/f" noise found in certain electronic devices.

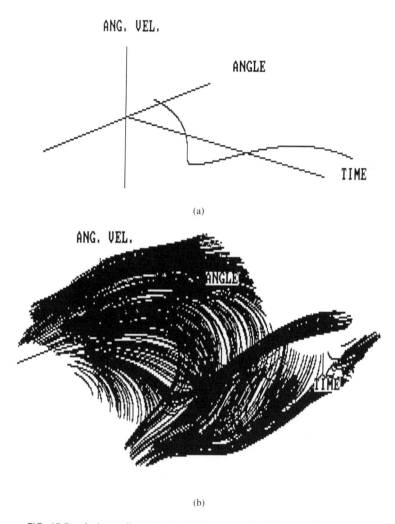

FIG. 15.5.   A three-dimensional phase portrait of the pendulum motion. The geometric configurations are *attractors* for the motion. In (a) the motion is periodic, and in (b) the motion is chaotic.

The chaotic attractor is very complex and in order to visualize the structure more clearly the attractor is often cut or sectioned across the time or ϕ axis. For example, if the sectioning is across this axis at the beginning of each forcing cycle, the appearance is as illustrated in Figure 15.6. The section now occupies a subspace of the phase space and only has (θ, ω) coordinates since ϕ or time is fixed. Of course, a section across the spiral attractor of the periodic attractor would just give a single point. (If the periodic attractor had a motion whose period was double the forcing period (period 2), then the corresponding section would have two points.) These sections are called *Poincaré sections* and they illustrate more readily the structure of the chaotic attractor. For example, if a series of sections through a single forcing period were shown in rapid succession, they would illustrate the folding and stretching of the dynamics through the forcing cycle.

Furthermore, Poincaré sections readily show the property of *self-similarity*— the property of having a similar appearance at increasing levels of magnification. Figure 15.7 shows two magnifications of pieces of the Poincaré section. Each picture shows a similar appearance of striations and more minute striations appear as the magnification increases. We shall see that self-similarity is a prominent characteristic of fractals.

We can also deduce that Poincaré sections have meaning as a different type of mathematical construct. The full attractor in its three variable space is the geometric result of a set of coupled nonlinear differential equations. On the other hand, Poincaré sections are snapshots of the dynamics taken at discrete time intervals—such as at the beginning of each forcing cycle. Such mathematical objects are called *maps* and are represented by *difference* equations, in this case

$$\theta_{n+1} = F_1(\theta_n, \omega_n), \qquad \omega_{n+1} = F_2(\theta_n, \omega_n).$$

Nonlinear difference equations may also exhibit chaotic behavior and have the advantage of being much less computationally demanding than differential equations. However, the precise form of the two-dimensional map symbolized by the Poincaré sections of the pendulum is unknown. In fact the dynamics are too

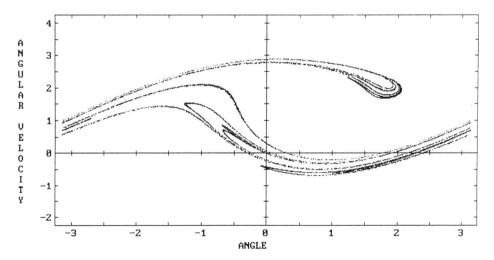

FIG. 15.6.   A Poincaré section of the three-dimensional strange attractor of chaotic motion, taken at the beginning of each forcing cycle.

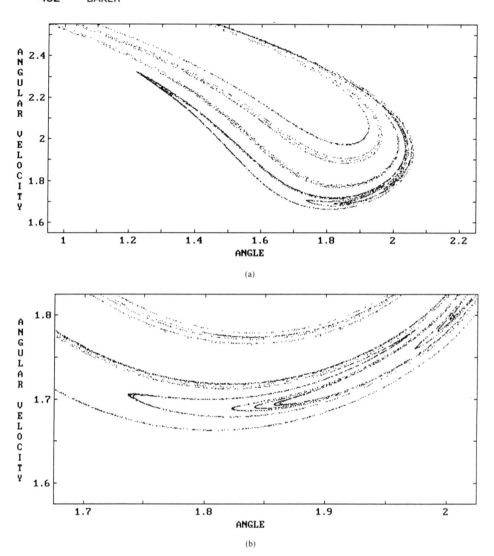

(a)

(b)

FIG. 15.7.   Two magnifications of part of the Poincaré section exhibiting the universal property of self-similarity.

complicated for complete representation by a map. Nevertheless some efforts
have been made to approximate the pendulum by the so-called dissipative circle
map (Jensen et al., 1984). Even the one-dimensional *Logistic map* (May, 1976)
has often provided a useful mathematical archetype for chaos, and, despite its
apparent mathematical dissimilarity with the pendulum, there are striking similarities in their geometric constructs. This similarity of chaotic systems is called
universality.

Global Effects

Much of our discussion has dealt with descriptions of the *local* state of the pendulum; that is, at fixed values of the parameters coordinates, (g, q, ω_D). For example, we have used one set of parameters for periodic motion and another set for chaotic motion. One can display the dynamics *globally* over some range of parameters. Typically, a dynamical variable is measured as one of the parameters is varied over a range of values. Such diagrams show the development of changes in the dynamics. Figure 15.8 shows this global approach. The forcing (g) is increased along the horizontal axis and the corresponding angular velocities—as measured from all the corresponding Poincaré sections—is plotted in the vertical direction. Where there are just a few points the motion is periodic, and where there is a scattering of points the motion is chaotic. Sometimes there are regimes where motion is periodic at the drive frequency and then as forcing increases the line splits to indicate that the period of the motion has doubled. Such splits are abrupt changes in the solutions of the differential equations and are called *bifurcations*. Period doubling may continue until the periodic orbits become unstable and chaos ensues. Period doubling represents one route to chaos. Other mechanisms exist as indicated by the varied structure of the bifurcation diagram. (See Lichtenberg and Lieberman, 1992, chap. 7, for further discussion.)

Note that the pendulum does not remain chaotic for all values of forcing beyond that of some initial chaotic state. The system also goes through regimes

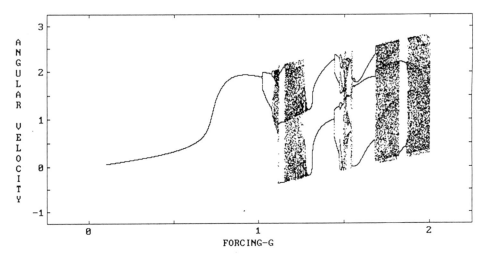

FIG. 15.8. A bifurcation diagram illustrating the various types of pendulum motion with increasing forcing, *g*. The vertical axis gives the angular velocity as found on each corresponding Poincaré section for every value of the forcing. At each line splitting the period either doubles or there are two possible motions for the pendulum.

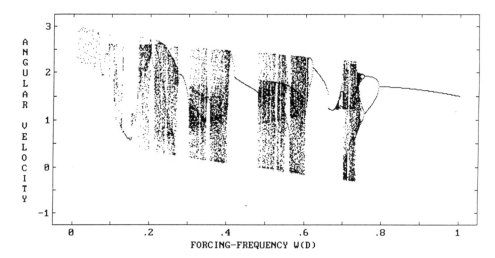

FIG. 15.9.   A bifurcation diagram illustrating the various types of pendulum motion with increasing forcing frequency, ω_D.

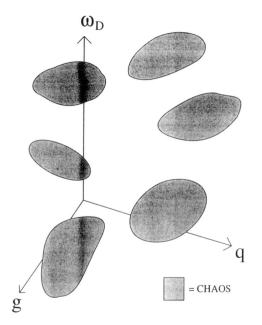

FIG. 15.10.   A schematic diagram of the bifurcation behavior in a mathematical space whose axes are the parameters (g, q, ω_D). The shaded regions represent chaotic motion. In fact, the structure would be more complex than that shown.

or *windows* of periodic motion often locking on to some multiple—like three—
of the forcing period. Other parameters can be used in bifurcation diagrams.
Figure 15.9 shows the dynamics with changing forcing frequency, ω_D. An interesting feature of this figure is the apparent locking of the pendulum to the driving
frequency when the forcing occurs nears some small ratio of the resonant frequency of the corresponding small amplitude pendulum. (We recall that the
natural frequency is unity in our parametrized form of the equations of motion.)

Finally, by combining bifurcation diagrams involving all parameter g, q, and
ω_D, one can determine regions of chaotic dynamics as sketched in Figure 15.10.

CHARACTERIZATION OF CHAOS

While pictorial representations of chaos are important quantitative measures of
chaos allow more precise description of the dynamics. Several measures are in
common use.

Dimension of the Attractor

We have seen the beautiful and complex structure of the phase portrait of the
chaotic pendulum and contrasted it with the simple spiral of the periodic pendulum. The spiral is obviously one-dimensional whereas the chaotic attractor
appears to have a higher dimension. We will show that the dimension lies
between 2 and 3—more than that of an area but less than that of a volume. This
remarkable result rests upon a definition of dimension that goes beyond conventional usage.

The concept of dimension can be defined in terms of scaling invariants; that
is, we look for properties of a geometric structure that are unchanged as the
structure is examined at increasingly higher magnifications. We will see that this
notion leads to the familiar value of dimension for lines, planes, and volumes, as
well as providing reasonable values for more complex structures.

Consider first the line of unit length as shown in Figure 15.11. We subdivide
the line repeatedly and count the number of "boxes" required to "cover" the line
at each repetition. Of course, the box size ϵ shrinks by a compensating factor at
each iteration. The tables in Figure 15.11 illustrate the process for the line,
plane, and a fractal object called the Cantor set. Focusing for the moment on the
line and plane, we see that relations between N and ϵ are expressed as equations
that are similar in form except that the exponent on the right side of each equation
is different for each configuration. This exponent provides the invariant quantity
we call dimension. The values of 1 and 2 for the line and plane are intuitively
correct.

#Boxes N	Box size ϵ	
1	1	
2	1/2	
4	1/4	
8	1/8	
–	–	
–	–	

Line

$$N = \left[\frac{1}{\epsilon}\right]^1$$

•
•
•

N	ϵ
1	1
4	1/2
16	1/4
32	1/8
–	–
–	–

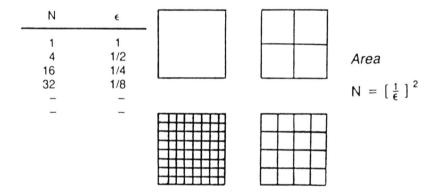

Area

$$N = \left[\frac{1}{\epsilon}\right]^2$$

N	ϵ
1	1
2	1/3
4	1/9
8	1/27
–	–
–	–

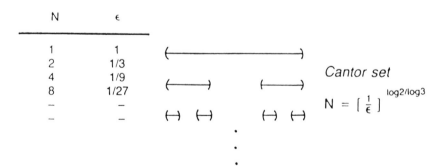

Cantor set

$$N = \left[\frac{1}{\epsilon}\right]^{\log 2/\log 3}$$

•
•
•

FIG. 15.11. Dimension as a property of scaling to smaller sizes. A line and square illustrate the process. The Cantor set is shown as the limit set of an infinite number of iterations of the process of removing the middle third.

In general, the relation between the size of the boxes and the number of boxes in the covering set is

$$N(\epsilon) = \text{constant} \cdot (1/\epsilon)^d,$$

and this equation can be applied to more complex sets such as the Cantor set shown in Figure 15.11. This set is formed by repeated operations on the points of a line. Start by removing the middle third from the line, leaving two segments. Then repeat the process on each of the pieces produced at each iteration. As the number of iterations tends to infinity the result is the Cantor set. Now, the relationship between N and ϵ yields a noninteger exponent

$$\log 2/\log 3 = 0.6309298. \ldots$$

This fractional value for dimension does have a certain plausibility in that (a) the Cantor set has an infinite number of points and therefore its dimension should be greater than the value of zero expected for a finite number of points, and (b) the Cantor set has zero length and therefore its dimension should be less than 1. Fractional dimensions are characteristic of *fractals* and chaotic attractors, found to be fractals, and are therefore called *strange attractors*.

In principle, one could apply the same box-counting technique to the set of points that constitute a Poincaré section (Figure 15.6), and determine the exponent as before. In practice this technique is computationally inefficient and most practical calculations use the technique of Grassberger and Procaccia (1983) based on calculations of a *correlation integral*. The correlation integral measures an average of the number of attractor points that are within a scaled distance R of a randomly chosen point; that is,

$$C(R) = \frac{1}{N} \sum_{i=1}^{N} \frac{1}{M} \sum_{j=1}^{M} H(|\vec{x}_i - \vec{x}_j| - R),$$

where

$$\begin{aligned} H(y) &= 1 \quad \text{for } x \geq 0, \\ &= 0 \quad \text{for } x < 0. \end{aligned}$$

For a given radius R, N data points are randomly chosen as centers for circles of radius R. Then for each circle all the other M data points are checked to see if they lie within the circle. Those points that do lie in the circle contribute to $C(R)$. The process is repeated for a spectrum of radii. As with the box-counting technique, the dimension (called the *correlation dimension*) is the exponent in the scaling relationship

$$C(r) \approx R^d.$$

The process is illustrated in Figure 15.12 for the Poincaré section. The slope of the middle, straight-line portion of the graph yields 1.35 ± 0.1 for the section

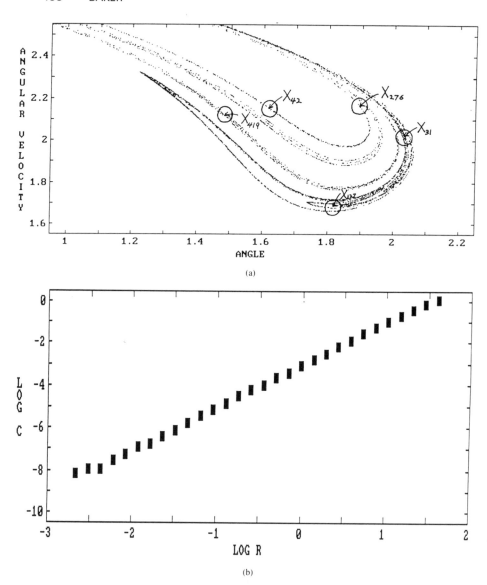

FIG. 15.12. Calculation of the correlation dimension. In (a) randomly positioned circles are drawn and the number of points within the circle are counted. In (b) the results of this counting for many circles over a range of radii are shown. The slope of the straight-line portion of the graph gives the dimension.

dimension. The method may also be extended to the full phase portrait by working with spheres in the three-dimensional phase space. But for the pendulum the extension is trivial; the third direction is simply time and it contributes one to the dimension. Therefore, for the pendulum's chaotic attractor shown in Figure 15.5b, the dimension is about 2.35 ± 0.1.

The attractor dimension changes with different sets of parameters. Of course, the difference between chaotic and periodic states are quite obvious. But within chaotic states the variations are still interesting. For example, it is found that as the energy dissipation is reduced (by increasing the parameter q) the dimensionality of the chaotic attractors seems to increase—the attractor becomes fuller and more space filling.

Lyapunov Exponents

Broadly speaking, Lyapunov exponents measure sensitivity to initial conditions. More precisely, Lyapunov exponents measure the rates of local expansion and contraction of a ball of trajectory points in phase space, as indicated in Figure 15.13a. An initial volume V_0 in three-dimensional space will evolve according to

$$V(t) = V_0 e^{(\lambda_1 + \lambda_2 + \lambda_3)t}$$

where the λ_i are the Lyapunov exponents. Dissipative systems, such as our pendulum, have attractors and this implies that volume in phase space contracts. Therefore the sum of the Lyapunov exponents must be negative. Yet sensitivity to initial conditions requires that at least one exponent is positive for the required divergence of trajectories. (Furthermore the Lyapunov exponent that measures change in the time direction is zero since time flows uniformly.) Therefore we expect that λ_1 will be positive, λ_2 will be zero, and λ_3 will be more negative than λ_1 is positive.

Lyapunov exponents may be calculated by the process suggested in Figure 15.13. A ball of trajectory points is defined around a central trajectory, with the neighboring trajectories defining the surface of the ball. As the center of the ball and its surface points evolve in time, the sphere becomes an ellipsoid, with principal axes in the directions of contraction and expansion. The average rates of expansion or contraction along the principal axes are the Lyapunov exponents. For the ith principal axis, the corresponding exponent is defined as

$$\lambda_i = \lim_{t \to \infty} \frac{1}{t} \log \left[\frac{L_i(t)}{L_i(0)} \right]$$

where $L_i(t)$ is the length of the ellipsoid along the ith principal axis at time t (Wolf et al., 1985). As indicated in Figure 15.13b, the ellipsoid grows too large as its size approaches the size of the phase space, and a new small ball of trajectories must be chosen around the central trajectory. Figure 15.14 shows the results of

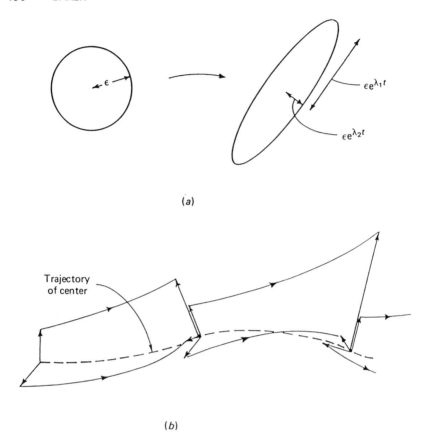

(a)

(b)

FIG. 15.13. A two-dimensional representation of the calculation of
Lyapunov exponents for a system whose differential equations are
known. In (a) a sphere of points evolves to an ellipsoid according to the
values of the Lyapunov exponents. In (b) the contracting and expanding axes are periodically renormalized. The expansion and contraction
rates are averaged along the trajectory to yield the Lyapunov exponents.

such a calculation, from which we estimate that $\lambda_1 = 0.16$, $\lambda_2 = 0$, and $\lambda_3 = -0.42$ for $q = 4$.

There are some remarkable independent connections among the dynamics of
the differential equations, the Lyapunov exponents, and dimension of the attractor. As a dissipative system the rate of contraction of phase volumes is directly
related to the differential equations. These latter may be written compactly in
vector form as

$$d\vec{x}/dt = \vec{F}(\vec{x})$$

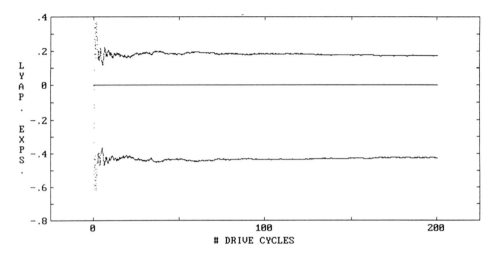

FIG. 15.14.   Calculation of Lyapunov exponents. The exponents are seen to converge numerically after many orbits of the pendulum.

where $\vec{x}$ is the vector of variables (θ, ω, ϕ) and $\vec{F}(\vec{x})$ is the set of three functions on the right side of the set of pendulum differential equations. It turns out that the rate of contraction of volumes in phase space for any dynamical system is given by

$$\frac{dV}{dt} = \int \vec{\nabla} \cdot \vec{F} \, dV$$

which is simply equal to $(-1/q)V(t)$ for the pendulum. But the previously stated definition of Lyapunov exponents implies

$$\frac{dV}{dt} = \sum_{i=1}^{3} \lambda_i V(t).$$

Therefore one has the following relationship between the dynamics and the geometry:

$$\sum_{i=1}^{3} \lambda_i = -\frac{1}{q},$$

a relationship which may be verified with the numerical results.

   Another relationship that often holds, this time between Lyapunov exponents and attractor dimension, is the so-called Kaplan-Yorke conjecture (Kaplan and Yorke, 1979). This very interesting connection can be made plausible in the following manner. We recall that dimension is the exponent in the relation

$$N(\epsilon) = \text{constant} \cdot (1/\epsilon)^d$$

in the limit as ϵ tends to zero. (In most cases, the correlation dimension is numerically very close to values obtained from this definition.) Suppose a square region of area A_0 in a two-dimensional phase space is filled with trajectory points, as in Figure 15.15. If the edges of the square are in the directions of local expansion and contraction, then the square will distort in time as shown. After a time t the area will be

$$A(t) = A_0 e^{(\lambda_1 + \lambda_2)t}$$

and the size of the squares will have shrunk to $A_0 e^{2\lambda_2 t}$. Therefore the length of each covering square will be

$$\epsilon(t) = A_0^{1/2} e^{\lambda_2 t}$$

and the number of covering squares will be

$$N(t) = \frac{A(t)}{\epsilon(t)^2} = e^{(\lambda_1 - \lambda_2)t}.$$

Combining $N(t)$ and $\epsilon(t)$ leads to a dimension

$$d = 1 - \lambda_1/\lambda_2,$$

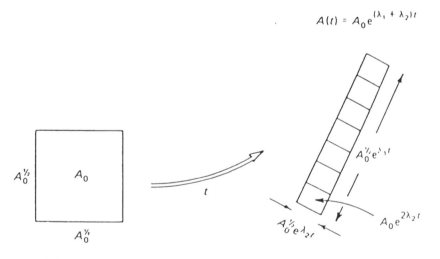

FIG. 15.15. Schematic diagram of the role of Lyapunov exponents in the stretching and shrinking of phase volumes. This illustration leads to the Kaplan-Yorke connection between Lyapunov exponents and attractor dimension.

the sought-after relation between Lyapunov exponents and dimension. This expression can be generalized for higher-dimensioned spaces as

$$d = j + \frac{\lambda_1 + \lambda_2 + \cdots + \lambda_j}{|\lambda_{j+1}|}$$

where the λ_i are ordered from largest to smallest for increasing i, and j is the index of the smallest nonnegative exponent. In our example the numerical values give

$$d = 2 + \frac{0.16 + 0}{0.42} \approx 2.4.$$

The interesting feature of both relationships is that they manifestly connect the dynamics of the pendulum with the phase-space geometry. And therefore these invariant indices give some promise of characterizing the dynamics of an unknown system whose strange attractor can, as we shall see, be reconstructed from experimental data.

There is further use for Lyapunov exponents that may be developed as follows. Positive Lyapunov exponents measure sensitivity to initial conditions and the consequent loss of information about the system's state as a result of minute errors in specifying its initial state. Therefore Lyapunov exponents may also be used to estimate the time at which the state of the system becomes unknown. Suppose the size of the attractor is L and the initial error is ϵ. Then the error grows exponentially in time until it approximates the attractor size. At this time T one finds that

$$L \approx \epsilon \cdot e^{\lambda T} \qquad \text{or} \qquad T \approx (1/\lambda) \, \text{Log} \, (L/\epsilon).$$

The time T is the point at which all information about the system has been lost and the state is completely unknown. (Arguments like this suggest a rationale for the lack of precision in long-range weather forecasting.) The positive Lyapunov exponent is therefore the rate at which information is lost and, when measured in base 2 logarithms, has units of (bits of information/unit time).

One can compare the expression for T in chaotic states with the case where the system is periodic. In this case, $\lambda = 0$ and the system is determined forever. At the other extreme, where the system is completely random, the Lyapunov exponent is effectively infinite and the system is undetermined immediately. Chaotic systems, with their short-term correlations, are clearly an intermediate case.

While this overview of the chaotic pendulum has been necessarily brief it does perhaps show the richness that is possible in the motions of an apparently simple dynamical system. It may also suggest other contexts that might reasonably be modeled by the driven pendulum. For example the pendulum archetype might be applied in the context of psychology.

PENDULUM AS A METAPHOR FOR MENTAL STATES[1]

Let us briefly suggest some comparisons between the mental state of an individual and the physical state of the pendulum. The analogies are highly speculative and intended only as stimulus for precise analysis. However the global bifurcation diagrams of Figures 15.8–15.10 are quite tantalizing. These figures illustrate the various states of the pendulum as different parameters are changed. Perhaps similar phenomena occur with mental states.

We consider a certain parallelism between the pendulum characteristics and human mental characteristics as follows. Each pendulum has its own resonant frequency as determined by its length and the local gravitational field; in our case the pendulum resonant frequency is normalized to unity. Similarly, individuals have certain psychological characteristics specific to them. These might include personality type, a certain approach to life, and so on. Continuing this parallelism we note that people are somewhat resistant to external influences; they have ego strength. For the pendulum the damping factor q provides resistance to motion. Without external forcing the pendulum motion decays. Similarly ego strength needs the leavening influence of external influences for an individual to maintain a healthy and responsive adaptiveness. Finally, the forcing term for the pendulum, g, provides energy to the pendulum, and we might consider it as analogous to external influences of other people on the individual. We note that the forcing frequency ω_D differs from the pendulum's resonant frequency just as psychological external influences do not always resonate with the individual psyche. Therefore the external forcing provides nonresonant energy, and just as the input of energy is important for the continued motion of the pendulum so also are external influences important for psychological activity and growth. The analogy is summarized in Table 15.1.

Now as to the dynamics of this parallelism. Consider first the increase in external influences in a manner similar to the increase in the forcing term as indicated in the bifurcation diagram of Figure 15.8. For small forcing the pendulum accommodates to the external influence while maintaining regular, periodic motion. As the forcing is increased, the response becomes more complex with period doubling, and so on. Eventually the pendulum is destabilized by the forcing, and chaos results. Similar behavior may occur in individuals that are under stress. People become disoriented from strong external pressures, and personality bifurcation may occur. Their lives split into several modes, and if there is too much bifurcation of identity, then instability and disorientation result, perhaps like the onset of chaos. While the foregoing language is technically imprecise, one might see something akin to multiple personality fractionation in

---

[1] I would like to acknowledge several very helpful conversations with my friend and psychologist colleague Dr. Thomas Keiser, in regard to this section. However, any errors in psychological terminology or concepts remain my responsibility.

TABLE 15.1
Possible Correspondences Between Chaos and Psychology

Pendulum Property	Psychological Property
Resonant frequency (=1)	Individual psychological profile
Damping, q	Ego strength
Forcing, g, ω_D	External influences "nonresonant" stress

Forcing (Stress)
↓
Instability
↓
Bifurcation
↓
Chaos

the initial splitting structure of the bifurcation diagram. It is possible that affective splitting in borderline states may also involve a similar mechanism.

The windows of periodicity are also suggestive. In these cases the pendulum completely locks onto the forcing frequency ω_D or a subharmonic of it over some range of the forcing parameter. One can imagine situations where an individual loses a sense of self under extreme stress and becomes locked into completely uncharacteristic behavior—for example, in brainwashing, cult entrapment (Keiser and Keiser, 1987), or various forms of identification of captives with those in control. Then, further external influences that release captives out of such a state—deprogramming—will again likely result in some disorientation and therefore destabilization. Again one enters the "chaotic" state after the highly stressed state; this might be analogous to the release from mode locking for the pendulum.

The parallels being suggested are quite speculative. Certainly the identification of a driven pendulum with the human psyche seems incredibly simplistic. Yet the chaotic phenomena exhibited by the pendulum are quite universal for unstable physical systems, and therefore if there is any connection between the psychological and physical processes these analogies may not be entirely unrealistic.

ANALYSIS OF EXPERIMENTAL CHAOTIC DATA

We have discussed the main characteristics of chaotic dynamics in the context of complete knowledge of the dynamics as provided by the equations of the driven pendulum. However, in experimental situations, knowledge of the dynamics is often sketchy or even nonexistent! Typically, some experimental quantity is measured in time and this time series $x(t)$ is the only data record. Time-series analysis is a traditional tool in many sciences and some work with chaotic time series has been done in psychology. (See, for example, the work of Redington and Reidbord, 1992.)

In this section we discuss, in an elementary fashion, some ways of characterizing the dynamics behind the such data. Current research techniques go well beyond our introduction, and the reader is referred to the review article by Abarbanel (1993) for a comprehensive overview.

Our approach will be to "manufacture" experimental data by generating time series with the pendulum equations—specifically the angular velocity as shown in Figure 15.3b. Then we treat this "experimental" time series as data of unknown origin. We demonstrate that time-series data can lead back to the same types of characterizations described earlier that are available from a full knowledge of the pendulum dynamics.

We note that traditional analysis of time series assumes that the underlying dynamics is *linear*. And therefore Fourier analysis may be used to distinguish important periodic modes from background noise. The data could then be sanitized of all but these modes, and the underlying dynamics would become evident.

Unfortunately, chaotic dynamics and noise are both broadband in the frequency domain and therefore one must look for new methods of analysis. In chaotic dynamics we would like to extract from the time series the characteristic quantities such as dimension of the attractor and Lyapunov exponents that measure sensitivity to initial conditions. We will demonstrate that this can often be done. A word of caution; we illustrate these techniques with noise-free data for which we already know the answers. In reality, noise usually adds significant complication to the process, and the algorithms are often not especially robust. One can obtain incorrect results. As we shall see, analysis of chaotic is not an automated process; it requires much insight from the scientist! Time series from complex systems, as found in psychology, are especially challenging.

Reconstruction of the Attractor

The prominent characteristics of chaotic dynamics are found on the attractor. Motion which appears complex is often the result of dynamics with only a few degrees of freedom, and therefore the essential information is contained on an attractor that is low dimensional. Takens (1981) and Mané (1981) were able to show that a time series $x(t)$ could be used to reconstruct an attractor for the motion with the same dimension and the same Lyapunov exponents as that of the original attractor produced by differential equations. These invariant parameters may then be used to check the validity of dynamical systems that are proposed as mechanisms which might underlie the experimental time series.

Let us begin with the Lorenz attractor (Lorenz, 1963) whose reconstructed attractor is similar to the attractor generated by the Lorenz's differential equations. (The reconstructed attractor for the pendulum has a different shape because of the periodic boundary conditions on θ and φ.) The Lorenz equations are a simple model of the interrelations of temperature variation and convective motion:

$$\frac{dx}{dt} = -\sigma(x + y)$$

$$\frac{dy}{dt} = -xz + rx - y,$$

$$\frac{dz}{dt} = xy - bz,$$

where σ, r, and b are constants. Solution of these equations leads to an attractor embedded in a three-dimensional space with coordinates (x, y, z) as shown in Figure 15.16a. A topologically equivalent attractor can be constructed from the time series $x(t)$ in a phase space whose points are ordered triplets called *delay coordinates* $(x(t), x(t + \tau), x(t + 2\tau))$ where the delay τ is suitably chosen—as we shall describe. The rationale—but not a proof—is that since the points in the original phase space $(x(t), y(t), z(t))$ follow a deterministic orbit, and the variables are linked deterministically by the differential equations, then consecutive points in the time series are also linked in the same deterministic way, and therefore the equivalence of the causal relationships should provide geometric structures that are also equivalent in some sense (Packard et al., 1980; Takens, 1981). Another way to understand the reconstruction is to realize that the three-dimensional dynamical information is contained in the derivatives d^2x/dt^2, dx/dt, and $x(t)$, and that these derivatives can be approximated as finite differences that involve the delay coordinates. However the delay coordinates are preferred; they do not involve a small denominator that can cause instability in the derivatives.

The space for the Lorenz attractor is reconstructed with the *delay coordinates* of $x(t)$ as shown in Figure 15.16b, and one observes the striking similarity with the previous figure. Both attractors spiral around two unstable centers and form the characteristic "butterfly" shape.

The original attractor and the reconstructed attractor are said to be topologically equivalent, which means that the structures have common geometric properties. Two such properties are important for chaotic dynamics: the attractor dimension and the spectrum of Lyapunov exponents; the latter being a characterization of the underlying dynamics. We will illustrate how both may be determined from the reconstructed attractor. The fact that this construction is derived completely from the time series suggests that this technique would seem to hold the promise of determining essential, underlying dynamics from most experimental time series.

Now let us return to the pendulum for a closer look at this process. For the pendulum, an attractor reconstructed from a time series of angular velocity, $\omega(t)$, will have a different appearance than the attractor generated by differential equa-

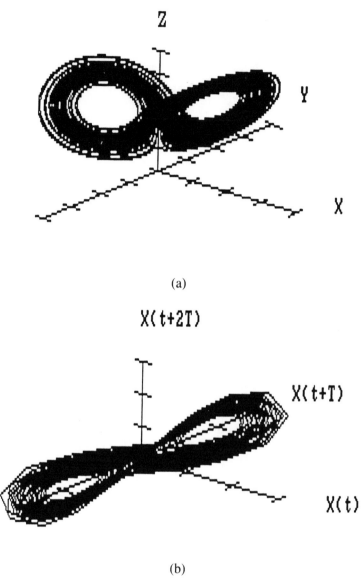

(a)

(b)

FIG. 15.16.   The Lorenz attractor. In (a) the attractor is constructed from numerical solution of the differential equations. In (b) the attractor is reconstructed from a time series x(t) using the method of delays.

tions because of the periodic boundary conditions on the θ and ϕ coordinates in the original attractor. That attractor has definite limits along these two axes as these variables are normalized back into their respective ranges.

On the other hand, the reconstructed attractor uses the time series for angular velocity which is *not* periodic, and therefore there are no abrupt boundaries on the reconstructed attractor. Figure 15.17a shows the original chaotic attractor

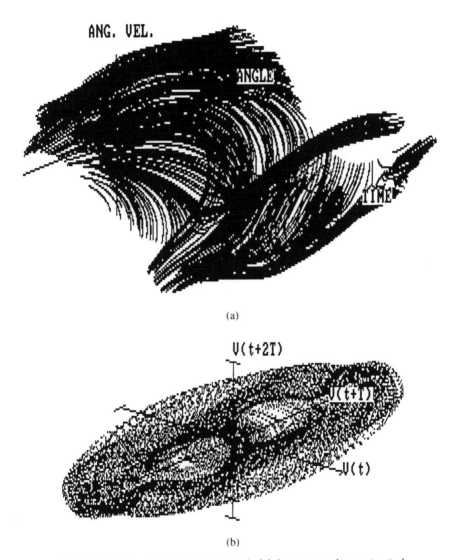

(a)

(b)

FIG. 15.17.   The Pendulum attractor. In (a) the attractor is constructed from numerical solution of the differential equations. In (b) the attractor is reconstructed from a time series $\omega(t)$ using the method of delays.

with axes (θ, ω, ϕ), and Figure 15.17b shows a reconstructed chaotic attractor with axes ($\omega(t)$, $\omega(t + \tau)$, $\omega(t + 2\tau)$) and an obviously different shape. Nevertheless the attractors in both figures are, as in the Lorenz case, topologically equivalent.

The reconstruction is not an automatic process. Some thought must be given to both the size of the delay τ and to the dimension of the space in which the reconstruction is to occur. Let us consider these two questions separately.

The Delay τ

The delay time τ is bounded on both the low and high ends. If τ is too small then $x(t)$, $x(t + \tau)$, and $x(t + 2\tau)$ do not provide enough information on the time development of the system. The points in the reconstruction will be tightly grouped around the space diagonal, and the reconstruction will be meaningless.

On the other hand, if τ is too large, then the time series values are so far apart as to be uncorrelated. Sensitivity to initial conditions and the finite size of the attractor will mean that significant folding and stretching will have occurred during τ and there is no causal relationship between the points.

Several estimation methods have been suggested (Fraser, 1989; Albano et al., 1988). If the system has some intrinsic periodicity, as does the driven pendulum, then some fraction of that period is a good estimate. Where a system periodicity is not obvious, more sophisticated techniques are needed. An often-used method is to examine the correlation of pairs of data points as a function of τ, looking for loss of correlation as the time between points grows. One evaluates the correlation function $\langle x(t) \cdot x(t + \tau)\rangle$, where $\langle\ \rangle$ symbolizes an average over time, and looks for the value of τ at the first minimum of the correlation function. Then some small fraction of that τ_{min} is used for the delay coordinates. On balance, we seek as τ that yields high correlation and contains some time development of the system. Figure 15.18 shows the correlation function for the driven pendulum. We found that τ in the range of 5 to 14 worked well. (Although the pendulum time series is treated as unknown experimental data, this delay time was of the order of $1/20$ to $1/8$ of a forcing period for the pendulum.)

Embedding Dimension and Attractor Dimension

The Lorenz attractors in Figure 15.16 are well represented in a three-dimensional space. Similarly we know that the dimension of the attractor for the driven pendulum is less than 3, and therefore it too may be embedded in a three-dimensional space. However, in reconstructing an attractor from an arbitrary time series of unknown dynamics, the dimensionalities of the attractor and, therefore, of the appropriate embedding space are completely unknown.

For nonfractal sets it is known that the correct embedding dimension d_E may be significantly greater than the attractor dimension d_A according to the relation

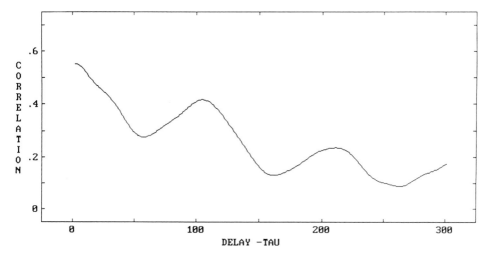

FIG. 15.18.   The correlation function for the time series $\omega(t)$. For chaotic motion the correlation between data points is fairly short term. (The exception is the strong component at the forcing frequency. For purposes of illustration, much of this component has been subtracted away from the correlation function.) For attractor reconstruction the delay is taken as a fraction of the time of the first minimum.

$$d_E \geq 2d_A + 1$$

(Takens, 1981; Mané, 1981). Figure 15.19 illustrates the cases for a simple attractor. While $d_A = 1$, the attractor must be embedded in a three-dimensional space to show its full structure. Otherwise there would be spurious crossings that imply an indeterminism in what is a deterministic system. Furthermore, at the spurious crossings there is the implication of false neighbors—a problem for accurate calculation of attractor dimension.

For experimental data whose dynamics are unknown, the attractor dimension is unknown and therefore the embedding dimension is unknown. Fortunately there is a procedure that yields both attractor and embedding dimensions simultaneously. In essence, the method consists of calculating the attractor dimension in embedding spaces of increasing dimension until the attractor dimension "saturates"—that is, until the value of the attractor dimensions stops increasing. At this point the attractor is fully "spread out" and the addition of further embedding dimensions adds nothing. (We note that if the time series represented random dynamics, then the dimension calculation would never saturate. The random points from the delay reconstruction would simply expand to fill whatever embedding space is provided. This effect suggests a complication provided by noisy chaotic data.)

$d_E = 1$

$d_E = 2$

$d_E = 3$

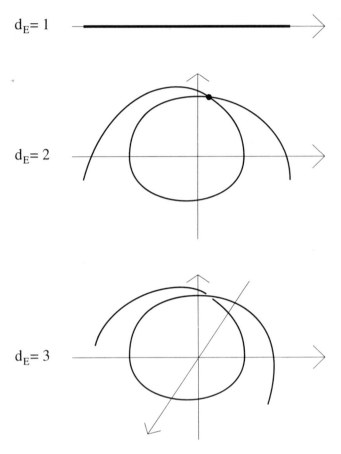

FIG. 15.19.   An illustration of the need for sufficient dimensionality in the embedding space. For this simple example spurious crossings are indicated when the spiral is embedded in one- or two-dimensional spaces.

Figure 15.20a shows the correlation integral for embedding dimension ranging from 1 to 6. Note that if the reconstructed attractor has the same dimension as found from the original attractor, $d_A = 2.35$, then an embedding dimension of 6 satisfies the Takens-Mané requirement. As in Figure 15.12b the attractor dimension is the slope of the straight-line portion of the correlation integral. Figure 15.20b shows the slopes of the correlation integrals as taken from Figure 15.20a, and the straight-line portions provide the numbers in the table below. The saturation effect is clearly demonstrated and the dimension of the reconstructed attractor is equal within error to the value calculated from the original (ω, θ, ϕ) attractor.

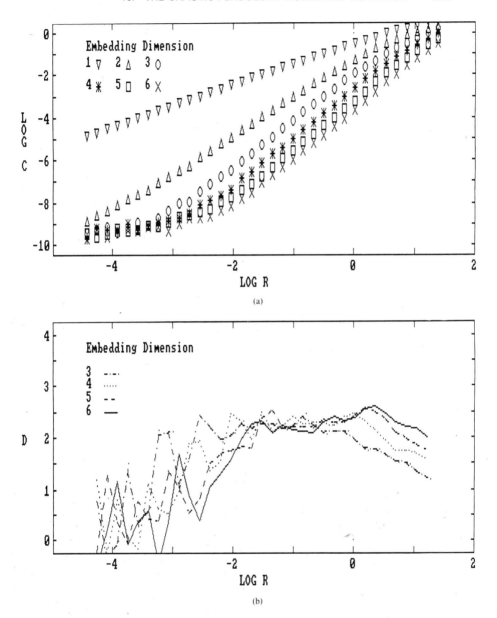

FIG. 15.20.   The calculation of dimension from a reconstructed attractor. The process parallels that used when the equations are known,
except that the embedding space for the attractor must be increased
until the dimension saturates. In (a) correlation integrals are plotted for
increasing embedding dimension. In (b) dimension is calculated as the
slopes of the correlation graphs.

d_E	d_A
1	≈ 1
2	≈ 2
3	$2.4 \pm .1$
4	$2.4 \pm .1$
5	$2.4 \pm .1$
6	$2.4 \pm .1$

Lyapunov Exponent

In theory, the Lyapunov exponent may also be calculated from the reconstructed attractor. However, if more than the largest positive exponent is sought, then the process is quite complex and beyond the scope of this introductory treatment. (See, for example Brown, Bryant, & Abarbanel, 1991.) The largest positive exponent is the primary determinate of the shaping of groups of points on the attractor. Smaller, positive exponents have less effect, while negative exponents are responsible for pulling initial transient points onto the attractor, but in the steady state their effect is sufficiently small that noise, roundoff errors, or insufficient data render accurate computation very difficult.

Nevertheless there does exist a simple method that is moderately robust for the largest positive exponent. In their paper on Lyapunov exponents, Wolf et al. (1985) provide an algorithm for calculation of the largest positive exponent from a time series. The approach is based upon establishing a fiducial trajectory of time delay coordinates and an initially neighboring trajectory that exponentially diverges from the fiducial trajectory. When the divergence becomes too large, in the sense that it approaches the size of the attractor, then a new neighbor is sought that is close on the attractor but not too close in the time series. The Lyapunov exponent is calculated by averaging the bursts of divergence of the sets of neighboring trajectories. The process is illustrated in Figure 15.21a and the results of the computation are given in Figure 15.21b. The level portion of the graph indicates an exponent of about 0.16 as expected from our earlier discussion.

NOISE, CONTROL, AND PREDICTION

Our brief and elementary description of data analysis is quite introductory. We have ignored the very important effects of noise—found in real experimental data—on the calculation of dimension and Lyapunov exponents. In general, noise produces spurious exponents and tends to expand the calculated dimensionality of the attractor. Various methods are in use to counter these problems, but they are complex. See the review by Abarbanel et al. (1993).

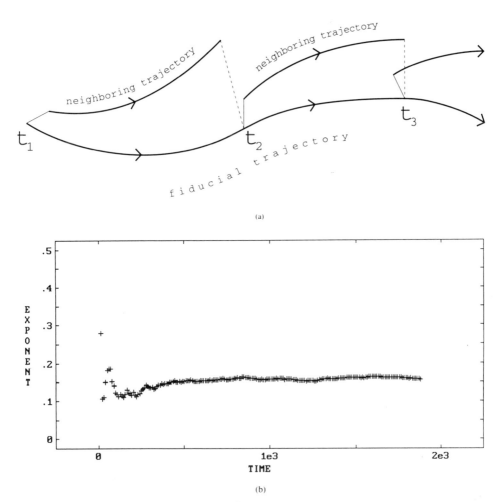

(a)

(b)

FIG. 15.21.   Calculation of the largest Lyapunov exponent from a time series, using the method of Wolf et al. (1985). In (a) two nearby points diverge at a rate governed by the largest Lyapunov exponent. Periodic renormalization occurs. In (b) the Lyapunov exponent converges to the value found when calculating its value from differential equations as in Figure 15.14.

Control and prediction of physical processes are long-standing goals of science. Chaotic dynamics is gradually making the transition from being a descriptive science to a science of prediction and control.

There is a growing interest in developing an ability to control an intrinsically chaotic system, through the application of *small* changes in the system. These continuous small changes counter the inherent instability of the myriad unstable periodic orbits that occur in the chaotic regime. The small changes maintain stability and force the system to exhibit a particular regular, nonchaotic behavior. Implications of this type of minimal control for a least-intrusive approach to mental health would seem to be very important. The control of chaos is just at its beginning but appears promising in several applications (Ditto et al., 1990).

Finally, we note the highly desirable goal of predicting the future from an experimental time series. This is a challenging problem for chaotic systems because of the lack of long-term correlations. (Hence the usual complaint about even intermediate-term weather forecasting.) Yet efforts are made to model and therefore predict chaotic systems with various mathematical functions or with neural networks. This work is in its infancy. (The reviews by Abarbanel et al., 1993, and by Casdagli et al., 1992, provide an entrée to the current literature.)

Even these brief descriptions indicate that chaotic dynamics is rapidly evolving from a quantitative, descriptive science to a potentially important means and philosophy of controlling instability.

CONCLUSION

In summary, we have provided an elementary description of chaos as illustrated with an archetypical system, the driven pendulum. We have postulated that the chaotic dynamics of this system is sufficiently universal that its behavior is suggestive of mechanisms and behaviors in several fields. Then, in contrast to the model system, we described elements of analytic methods for dealing with experimental chaotic time series, where the equations of motion are unknown. This analysis does yield invariant quantities that characterize the underlying dynamics. We hope that even this introductory treatment demonstrates that chaos is a fascinating and useful quantitative science with the potential to describe the underlying dynamics of complex systems across the spectrum of experimental sciences.

ACKNOWLEDGMENTS

Much of the material for this chapter is abstracted from the book *Chaotic Dynamics: An Introduction,* by G. L. Baker and J. P. Gollub, Cambridge University Press, 1990. Cambridge has kindly given permission to reproduce exact or modified versions of figures that appear in this chapter as Figures 15.2–15.8 and 15.11–15.15.

REFERENCES

Abarbanel, H. D. I., Brown, R., Sidorowich, J. J., & Tsimring, L. S. (1993). The analysis of observed chaotic data in physical systems. *Reviews of Modern Physics, 65,* 1331–1392.

Albano, A. M., Muench, J., Schwartz, C., Mees, A. I., & Rapp, P. E. (1988). Singular-value decomposition and the Grassberger-Procaccia algorithm. *Physical Review A, 38,* 3017–3026.

Baker, G. L., & Gollub, J. P. (1990). *Chaotic dynamics: An introduction.* New York: Cambridge University Press.

Blackburn, J. A., Vik, S., Binru, Wu, & Smith, H. J. T. (1989). Driven pendulum for studying chaos. *Review of Scientific Instruments, 60,* 422–426.

Brown, R., Bryant, P., & Abarbanel, H. D. I. (1991). Computing the Lyapunov spectrum of a dynamical system from an observed time series. *Physical Review A, 43,* 2787–2806.

Casdagli, M., Des Jardins, D., Uebank, S., Farmer, J. D., Gibson, J., Hunter, N., & Theiler, J. (1992). Nonlinear modeling of chaotic time series: Theory and applications, in J. H. Kim & J. Stringer (Eds.), *Applied Chaos* (pp. 335–380). New York: Wiley.

D'Humieres, D., Beasley, M. R., Huberman, B. A., & Libchaber, A. (1982). Chaotic states and routes to chaos in the forced pendulum. *Physical Review A, 26,* 3483–3496.

Ditto, W. L., Rauseo, S. N., & Spano, M. L. (1990). Experimental control of chaos. *Physical Review Letters, 65,* 3211–3214.

Fraser, A. M. (1989). Information and entropy in strange attractors. *IEEE Transactions on Information Theory, 35,* 245–262.

Grassberger, P., & Procaccia, I. (1983). Measuring the strangeness of strange attractors. *Physica, 9D,* 189–203.

Gwinn, E. G., & Westervelt, R. M. (1985). Intermittent chaos and low-frequency noise in the driven damped pendulum. *Physical Review Letters, 54,* 13–16.

Gwinn, E. G., & Westervelt, R. M. (1986). Fractal basin boundaries and intermittency in the driven damped pendulum. *Physical Review A, 33,* 4143–4155.

Jensen, M. H., Bak, P., & Bohl, T. (1984). Transition to chaos by interaction of resonances in dissipative systems: I. Circle maps. *Physical Review A, 30,* 1960–1969.

Kaplan, J. L., & Yorke, J. A. (1979). Chaotic behavior of multi-dimensional difference equations. In H. O. Peitgen and H. O. Walther (Eds.), *Lecture notes in mathematics: Vol. 730. Functional differential equations and the approximation of fixed points* (pp. 204–227). Berlin: Springer-Verlag.

Keiser, T. W., & Keiser, J. L. (1987). *The anatomy of illusion: Religious cults and destructive persuasion.* Springfield, IL: Charles C. Thomas.

Krasner, S. (1990). *The ubiquity of chaos.* Washington, DC: American Association for the Advancement of Science.

Lichtenberg, A. J., & Lieberman, M. A. (1992). *Regular and chaotic dynamics* (2nd ed., chap. 7). New York: Springer-Verlag.

Lorenz, E. N. (1963). Deterministic non-periodic flow. *Journal of Atmospheric Science, 20,* 130–141.

Mané, R. (1981). On the dimension of the compact invariant sets of certain nonlinear maps. In D. A. Rand & L. S. Young (Eds.), *Lecture notes in mathematics: Vol. 898. Dynamical systems and turbulence* (pp. 230–242). Berlin: Springer-Verlag.

May, R. M. (1976). Simple mathematical models with very complicated dynamics. *Nature, 26,* 459–467.

Redington, D. J., & Reidbord, S. P. (1992). Non-linear dynamics in mind-body processes. In S. Vohra, M. Spano, M. Schlesinger, L. Pecora, & W. Ditto (Eds.), *Proceedings of the 1st Experimental Chaos Conference* (pp. 203–212). Singapore: world Scientific.

Robinson, H. (1921). *The mind in the making* (p. 52). New York: Harper and Brothers.

Takens, F. (1981). Detecting strange attractors in turbulence. In D. A. Rand & L. S. Young (Eds.), *Lecture notes in mathematics: Vol. 898. Dynamical systems and turbulence* (pp. 366–381). Berlin: Springer-Verlag.

Wolf, A., Swift, J. B., Swinney, H. L., & Vastano, J. A. (1985). Determining Lyapunov exponents from a time series. *Physica, 16D,* 285–317.

Author Index

509

Subject Index